MW00563775

A SPIRITUAL REVOLUTION

A SPIRITUAL REVOLUTION

*The Impact of Reformation and
Enlightenment in Orthodox Russia*

Andrey V. Ivanov

THE UNIVERSITY OF WISCONSIN PRESS

Publication of this book was made possible, in part, by a grant from the
First Book Subvention Program of the Association for Slavic, East European,
and Eurasian Studies.

The University of Wisconsin Press
728 State Street, Suite 443
Madison, Wisconsin 53706
uwpress.wisc.edu

Gray's Inn House, 127 Clerkenwell Road
London ECIR 5DB, United Kingdom
eurospanbookstore.com

Printed in the United States of America
This book may be available in a digital edition.

Library of Congress Cataloging-in-Publication Data
Names: Ivanov, Andrey V. (Andrey Vyacheslavovich), author.
Title: A spiritual revolution : the impact of Reformation and Enlightenment
in Orthodox Russia / Andrey V. Ivanov.
Description: Madison, Wisconsin : The University of Wisconsin Press, [2020] |
Includes bibliographical references and index.
Identifiers: LCCN 2020004181 | ISBN 9780299327903 (cloth)
Subjects: LCSH: Russkaia pravoslavnaia tserkov'—History—18th century. |
Russkaia pravoslavnaia tserkov'—History—19th century. |
Enlightenment—Russia. | Russia—Church history—18th century. |
Russia—Church history—1801-1917.
Classification: LCC BR935 .I83 2020 | DDC 281.9/47009033—dc23
LC record available at https://lccn.loc.gov/2020004181

To Katia

CONTENTS

ILLUSTRATIONS

ACKNOWLEDGMENTS

Behind every book is a journey and this work is no exception. This journey— from the archives to the publication—was not a solitary one. It took the help of communities and individuals to make this book happen. I owe deep gratitude to all of them.

This work would not have been possible without generous financial and institutional support for the project I have received over the years. Most of the writing for this manuscript took place in Madison, Wisconsin, in the spring of 2018 and at Notre Dame, Indiana, in the late summer and fall of 2018. In Madison, I had the honor of holding a UW System Fellowship at the Institute for Research in the Humanities, with full access to the world-class scholarly, interlocutory, and librarian resources. In Indiana, I was a faculty fellow at the Notre Dame Institute for Advanced Study. The residential and contemplative nature of that fellowship fostered a phenomenal environment of deliberation, focus, and ardor while also giving this project much-needed interdisciplinary scrutiny. Almost a decade of travel was also invested into this project. I am thankful to the Boston College History Department, University of Wisconsin– Platteville Liberal Arts and Education Dean's Office, UW–Platteville Provost's Office, National Endowment for the Humanities, Herzog August Bibliothek, and Harvard Houghton Library Visiting Fellowship for facilitating my research stays at great libraries and archives across North America, Europe, and Russia. Among the many archivists and collections curators who facilitated my research, I am particularly thankful to Tanja Lorkovic at Yale; Fr. Manuel Nin, OSB, and Fr. Jim McCann, SJ, in Rome; Evgenii E. Rychalovskii in Moscow; and Aleksandr Sokolov in St. Petersburg.

This book would not have been possible without the great conversations that stimulated the progress of the manuscript. In Grande Prairie, AB, Reuben, and Arlene Loewen gave me much-needed counsel in sharpening the project's thematic relevance for audiences outside academia. At Notre Dame, Brad Gregory, Don Stelluto, Ulrich Lehner, Christopher Hamlin, Clare Kim, John Deak, Daniel Hinshaw, David Bentley Hart, Emily Wang, Peter Cajka, Yury Avvakumov, Laura Dassow Walls, and Fredrik Albritton Jonsson gifted me with valuable comments and critique that helped me situate the project in wider global and European contexts. In Madison, I am thankful for fruitful conversations with David McDonald, Francine Hirsch, Lynn Nyhart, Tom Broman, Max Harris, Ullrich Langer, Kirill Ospovat, Toma Longinović, Pablo Gómez, Manon van de Water, Jonathan Pollack, and Rob Cramer. In Boston, I would like to express gratitude to Franziska Seraphim, Robin Fleming, David Quigley, Virginia Reinburg, Prasannan Parthasarathi, Ben Braude, Grainne McEvoy, Julian Bourg, Lubomyr Hajda, Michael Flier, Anna Graber, and Perry So. At Yale, I am grateful to Laura Engelstein, Carlos Eire, and David Sorkin, for helping me discern the wider Russian and European intellectual contexts that this book addresses. In Wolfenbüttel, scholars from all over the world shared insightful observations and advice, particularly Michael Schippan, Jill Bepler, Elizabeth Harding, Volker Bauer, Beth Plummer, Sébastien Côté, Timothy Wengert, Margarita Korzo, Tatiana Artemyeva, Vladimir Somov, and Tricia Ross.

This book would not have been possible without great editors. I am exceedingly fortunate to have a dedicated UW Press team, who put so much of their time and effort into this project: Gwen Walker, Dennis Lloyd, Nathan MacBrien, Sheila McMahon, and Anna Muenchrath.

This book would not have been possible without guidance and mentorship. My UW–Platteville colleagues, Adam Stanley, David Krugler, Gene Tesdahl, and Melissa Gormley, encouraged and sustained my commitment to finishing the manuscript. Among the mentors in the field, I am grateful to Patrick Michelson, Nadieszda Kizenko, Alexander Martin, and Gary Marker, who read, commented, critiqued, and discussed the manuscript from its beginning to the final revisions stage. I thank Serhii Plokhii at Harvard, whose advice and many fruitful discussions helped me focus on what was important and what was not. Of all my mentors, I am most deeply indebted to Paul Bushkovitch, whose spring 2004 graduate seminar (which introduced me to the writings of St. Tikhon of Zadonsk) set me upon the path that led to this book project. His inspiration and guidance kept me on the right path ever since.

My deepest love and gratitude go to my wife, Katia, who fills my life and the lives of our children with great joy and inspiration. I dedicate this work to her.

A NOTE ON TRANSLITERATION

This manuscript adheres to the Library of Congress guidelines for the roman-ization and transliteration of words originally written in the Cyrillic alphabet. In order to follow this convention most consistently, the transliteration of personal names follows the spellings as they appear adopted in the Russian Imperial sources, not what the native appellation of that person originally was. Thus, Biron (not Bühren), Kiukhelbeker (not Küchelbecker), Prokopovich (not Prokopovych), Iavorskii (not Iavors'kyi), and so on. An exception is made for Peter Mohyla, the spelling that has become standard and is preferable to the Romanian Petru Movilă and Russian Petr Mogila. The romanization of cities excludes the soft sign (Lviv, Kazan, Tver) and follows the transliteration that generally applied to the spelling of the city in the sources current at the time. Thus, Petrograd for 1914–24, Lwów for the early modern city in the pre-1772 Polish Commonwealth; Kiev for the eighteenth-century Church Slavonic spelling of the holy city of Кіевъ or Кїевъ (as opposed to the earlier Кїовъ), and Kyiv when referring to the post-1917 capital of the independent and Soviet republic (as in the "National Library of Ukraine in Kyiv").

The manuscript follows the eighteenth- and early nineteenth-century conven-tion of preserving the first and the last names of the monastic clergy without parentheses, regardless of whether the last name was secular or ecclesiastical. Before the Synodal decree of November 18, 1846, the Russian Orthodox Church did not regulate the clergy's last and first names; by the middle of the nineteenth century, the practice of requiring clergy to have secular last names and to write those last names in parentheses after monastic tonsure became more established. The reason for that was the simple fact that prior to the nineteenth century, a last name (*familiia*, from Latin *fama* or fame) was an upper-class privilege, and most of Russia's peasants and lower clergymen were

xiv   A Note on Transliteration

known by their patronymics. Those clergy who descended from the upper classes often kept their familial last names when they became monks (e.g., Arsenii Matseevich, Stefan Iavorskii, Georgii Dashkov), while others adopted new ecclesiastical names in honor of saints or mentors upon monastic tonsure (Samuil Tsereiskii was tonsured as Feofan Prokopovich in honor of his uncle, the rector of the Mohyla Academy). Yet others exchanged their secular patronymic-based last names for new ecclesiastical ones (*famil'nye prozvishcha* as they were also known) after entering the seminary, such as Stefan Vasil'evich Timofeev, who became Serafim Glagolevskii (in honor of *Glagol*, the Word of God), or Mikhail Vasil'ev, who became Mikhail Speranskii (in honor of the virtue of hope, Latin *spes*). Therefore, the last names of eighteenth-century monastic clergy are written without parentheses in the text and in brackets in the bibliography.

For more on ecclesiastical names, see works by Vladimir Sheremet'evskii, Fedor Uspenskii, Boris Uspenskii, and Konstantin Kharlampovich in the bibliography.

A Spiritual Revolution

Introduction

Russia's Century of Reform and Enlightenment

> By the very nature of our cities, we had no such struggle as we had no
> Reformation. . . . Our Reformation remained at the stage of the peasant sect,
> because it found no leadership from the cities. Primitiveness and backwardness
> here cry to the heavens!
>
> —LEON TROTSKY, "Peculiarities of Russian Development," in
> *History of the Russian Revolution*

For many historians, the Reformation and Enlightenment undoubtedly stand
out as two of the more important episodes in the narrative of global civilization.
These three centuries of dramatic socioreligious change not only redrew Europe's
confessional and political boundaries but also led to the rise of powerful
nation-states and empires that reached beyond the continent. In short, they
made Western civilization modern. Despite their global significance, most
scholars and students of European history have so far confined their study of
these events to Western Europe and the Atlantic World. Only a few scholars
have written about their impact east of the Vistula, and even fewer have considered Russia.

In fact, almost every survey of Reformation history has so far excluded Russia
and most surveys of Russian history exclude the Reformation. The prevailing
narrative of perceived Russian backwardness and alleged underdevelopment—
epitomized in the Trotsky quote—only reinforced the view that Russia's people
never advanced far enough to grasp the intellectual debates that once shook
religious communities in the West. In short, Russia and its Orthodox Church,
always alienated from the West, were simply not influenced by the Reformation.

Just as Russia was unreformed, it also stayed unenlightened. Some scholars (like Martin Malia) perpetuated this narrative of the empire's enduring backwardness by doubting the significance of Enlightenment influence in Russia.[1]
Russia's relationship to the Enlightenment has not received enough scholarly
attention, and neither has the relationship between Orthodoxy and Enlightenment, which remains virtually uncharted territory. Elise K. Wirtschafter's

recent biography of Metropolitan Platon of Moscow (1737–1812) is an important exception to this trend. Her works challenge the narrative of eighteenth-
century backwardness by focusing on an important biographical episode in the
Russian century of light. That biography, however, is only one valuable frag-
ment in the complex mosaic of the Russian Orthodox experience of the Enlightenment. So far, a comprehensive overview of that experience—involving a broad
interaction with the *Frühaufklärung* (German early Enlightenment), Berliner
Aufklärung, the French lumières, the Austro-Bavarian Catholic Enlightenment,
and British Newtonian Physicotheology—is lacking.

This book seeks to examine the place of the Orthodox Church in the very
wide context of the European Reformation and the subsequent European
Enlightenment. It provides a comprehensive history of the cultural and intellectual revolution that took place in Orthodox Russia during the long eighteenth century (from 1700 to 1825). In the scope of existing literature, this is
the first endeavor to fully identify the impact of Western thought in the Russian church while also including Orthodoxy in a much wider European and
global movement of religious and intellectual change. By situating the Russian
church within this context, this monograph seeks to challenge the common
notion that the Orthodox Church and Western Christianity are mutually ex-
clusionary. Russian religious change, I argue, was not uniquely different from
the West, nor did religion make the West alien to Russia.

RUSSIA'S SPIRITUAL MODERNITY

This narrative uses the case of a profound reform to answer the basic question
of what and who made Russia a modern empire. The book addresses the question of "what" by focusing on religious reforms, driven by the ideas of the
Reformation and Enlightenment. Although most accounts of Russia's emerging modernity focus on the role of secular ideas, this contribution examines
the role of Orthodox Christianity. At the same time, the investigation of "the
who," or the agency of Russian modernity, will highlight the importance of
religious leaders as well as secular elites in effecting such changes. This focus on
religious reformers will allow me to highlight their role as agents of socioreligious reform who acted in concert with or independent of Russia's monarchs.

The central argument of this book is that Russia's modernizing church reform was a wide-ranging adaptation of first, the concepts developed during
the European Reformation, and later, the ideas of the religious Enlightenment. Although Russia did not and could not experience the full measure of
the Reformation and the full variety of Europe's Enlightenments, the impact
of their ideas within the church was profound, long-lasting, and even radical.
As one contemporary observer noted in 1720, Russia's reforms unleashed a

spiritual "revolution."[2] This "revolution" was no ordinary revision of the ecclesiastical statutes but a far-reaching change in the foundations of Russian Orthodox faith, culture, politics, and ideology. The whirlwind of new concepts stormed the gates of Eastern Orthodoxy throughout the eighteenth century: *sola scriptura*, *sola fide*, Pietist biblical philology, the reformulation of icon worship, heliocentrism, scientific empiricism, the rejection of serf ownership by the church, and more. The very debate of these ideas—in public and sacred spaces—was a novelty for the Muscovite milieu, and their subsequent official acceptance and development by the reformers in the Holy Synod were truly revolutionary.

Much like in Protestant Europe, this religious change was not just a cataclysmic but also a reactive event: a reformed Orthodoxy battled the Goliaths of Russia's past by supporting the Petrine and Catherinian projects of building a well-ordered and enlightened (and therefore, "modern") European empire. Much like in the Protestant West, Late Reformation ideology finally solved Russia's long-lasting anxiety over church-state relations by making the state more sacred and the church more secular.[3] Although by 1760 Protestant ideas had reformed the Orthodox Church in numerous ways, the church did not stop reforming. The period after 1762 saw the rise of an increasingly enlightened hierarchy in Petersburg, who, along with the enlightening state, embraced rationalism and scientific empiricism with the same enthusiasm as many of their peers in London, Berlin, and Leiden. The result was the eventual emergence of a more enlightened church hierarchy in pre-1825 Russia.

Defining Reformation's Impact in Russia

Situating Orthodox Russia within the larger history of the European Reformation is now possible, given the conceptual expansion that the term "reformation" has enjoyed over the last several decades. Gone are the days when "reformation" referred to the narrowly specific Gallo-Germanic Protestant event that commenced with Luther's hammering on a door in Wittenberg and ended with a mass in Paris. Most of the current literature speaks of multiple reformations that spanned several centuries and several multiconfessional spaces across Europe and the globe. The 2015 *Oxford Illustrated History of the Reformation*, for example, identifies the Catholic Reformation and the Radical Reformation in addition to the British, Lutheran, and Calvinist movements of reform. Other sources address the Unitarian Reformation, the Czech Reformation, and the Transylvanian (Romanian) Reformations. Scholars have also expanded their research to consider the global colonial dimension of parallel reformations in parts of the Atlantic World such as New England and Jamaica.[4] Along with geography, chronology expanded, too: for Peter Wallace the reformation started in 1350 and ended in 1750; Carter Lindberg also begins with the late medieval crisis (1350s) but ends in the late seventeenth century, and Ulinka Rublack's chronology is similar (1378–1649).[5]

This book accepts this broad chronology of Reformation Europe that starts with the religious upheavals of Hus and Luther, continues with the confessional consolidation of Protestant and Catholic states, and ends with the confessional renewals of Pietism, Catholic Baroque spirituality, and the early Enlightenment (*Frühaufklärung*). The Russian church (and Slavic Orthodoxy in general) was not some a remote autochthonous island, isolated from the wider series of events. It was in fact in conversation with the European ideas enveloping and permeating its western borderlands.

Since the expansion of chronological and geographical boundaries has redrawn the parameters of the Reformation(s), one can endeavor to explain what the Reformation really was by addressing the issue of its wider consequences in European history. Although daunting to classify (and no one's measurements will ever be perfect), two centuries of scholarly debate have identified at least *three* features of the Reformation that had a profound impact on early modern societies. First was the rise of charismatic leaders ("reformers"), who during the age of change and intellectual upheaval challenged the spiritual status quo ante in pursuit of new doctrinal truths. Second was the engagement of medieval and early modern Catholicism, which sought either to reform itself from within (the Catholic Reformation) or to repudiate what was without (the Protestant Reformations).[6] Third was the Reformation's *longue durée* impact on Europe's intellectual transition from a medieval civilization to an enlightened modernity (including a religious one), whether in the Weberian or the strictly chronological sense.[7]

Russia's experience in many ways paralleled developments in the early modern West. First, this experience featured a well-organized religious reform, planned by Feofan Prokopovich (1677–1736), the most audacious church reformer in the history of Imperial Russia. Feofan and his allied bishops presided over a dramatic change in Russian Orthodoxy in the 1720s and 1730s. The change affected such ecclesiastical fundamentals as doctrine (involving an adaptation of Protestant theology to a revision of official Orthodoxy) and administration (in which the Swedish synodal-consistorial system replaced the centuries-old institution of the patriarchate). But it was even more extensive than this, involving holy texts (Russia's own reformed Scripture, the Elizabethan Bible of 1751, was revised in accordance with Protestant standards) and the church's relationship to science—the church embraced Copernican heliocentrism and Cartesian rationalism, while condemning the previously accepted geocentric model of the universe, for example.

Second, Russia's church reform exhibited a very strong anti-Catholic impulse from the very beginning. Feofan and his allies argued that the Orthodox Church in Ukraine and Russia circa 1700 had lost its purity through pollution by Roman Catholic influences in such areas as doctrine, devotional literature, homiletics, and administration. The reformers then proceeded to justify their changes as a struggle against the errors of Catholic influence, real or imagined. For example, they justified the abolition of the Moscow Patriarchate as the elimination of an aberrant, Papal-style authority that contained traces of Catholic political ideology. The Holy Synod's adoption of a reworked version of Luther's catechism for popular doctrinal instruction repudiated and replaced the earlier Orthodox expression of doctrine, namely, Peter Mohyla's *Confession of Faith*, which was based on the Tridentine Catechism. Similarly, the Holy Synod prescribed Puritan measured monotone as the official mode of preaching in Russia's parishes, replacing the previously popular (but Catholic-influenced) styles of homiletic delivery.

The third aspect of Russia's religious change that parallels the larger European context concerns the issue of modernity. Simply put, religious reform also steered the empire toward what Russian monarchs and elites believed to be an improved model of organizing the socioreligious affairs of the state, a type of European modernity that the prelates and the courtiers observed in Potsdam, Dresden, Stockholm, and Copenhagen. Such reform not only "modernized" the church in aspects like administration, homiletics, and education but also paved the way for the Enlightenment's arrival in Russia. In other words, without reform, the Russian Church would have been ill-prepared to receive the religious Enlightenment.

THE HISTORICAL TERMINOLOGY
OF RUSSIA'S REFORM

While this book situates the Orthodox Church within wider European religious reform, it is important to note that both the terms "religion" and "reform" can carry a widely generic array of meanings (not exclusively religious or reformatory), which in turn could be laden with positive or negative valences depending on the context that assigns such values to a particular aspect of religion or reform. For the purpose of clarification, all references to "religion" and "reform" in this book are therefore historical, not inventive in nature. Mentions of "religion" refer to the various manifestations of European Christianity (doctrinal, political, cultural, intellectual) as experienced, understood, or imagined by Europeans themselves, including Russians. References to "reform" are also historical—reflecting the views adopted by the protagonists and antagonists of changes that rocked Petrine and Catherinian Russia. In other words, the purpose of the book's narrative is not to decide whether the changes instituted by Catherine II and her associates brought positive or negative developments to Russia but to describe how the historical actors designated these changes as "reforms" and how they contested their positive and negative values throughout the long eighteenth century.

The use of historical terminology raises the question of the historical accuracy of applying the key idea that the Reformation had an impact upon events that shaped the Russian Church. The idea of comparing radical religious changes or experiences in Russia to the Reformation in Europe is hardly unique: in the twentieth century, both Georges Florovsky and Donald Treadgold described the Petrine era as the "Russian Reformation" and the "quasi-Reformation," respectively, while Sergei Zhuk discovered a fascinating "Lost Reformation" in nineteenth-century Russia.[8] The question that needs to be addressed is whether the comparison of Russia's reforms to the Reformation was contemporaneous to the event or whether it was conjured up by the historian studying the event retrospectively. In other words, how did eighteenth-century witnesses view and interpret changes they saw around them?

This book draws on the copious records of both foreign and domestic observers who referred to Orthodox reforms by employing the language and terminology of the European Reformation from 1718 to the 1820s. Thus, Danish traveler Peder von Haven described religious change as "the Reformation of the Spiritual Order," Pietist observer Christoph Mickwitz compared it to a spiritual "revolution," Estonian pastor Anton Vierorth compared Prokopovich to Martin Luther, while Christian Martini rejoiced that the new Russian Orthodox Church had become properly a "Russian Lutheranized church [*Russisch-Lutheranisirende Kirche*]" that finally brought the Orthodox Russians into a happy community of "all other Christian comrades in faith" (that is, the Protestants).[9] This latter observation drew upon Johann Peter Kohl's 1723 book with the provocative title *Ecclesia Graeca Lutheranizans*. Not only did the label of "Lutheranization" not offend the Russian Orthodox hierarchy, but the Holy Synod played a crucial role in subsequently inviting Kohl to work for the Academy of Sciences, granting him housing and a 600-ruble salary.[10]

Roman Catholic observers and Russian Orthodox clerics, too, used the language of the European Reformation to describe what was happening in Russia. In 1728 the rector of the Vilnius Jesuit Academy, Ladislaus Dauksza, observed that Russia was experiencing "a reformation of the Greek religion that smells [*redolens*] more like a Calvinist reform than a schismatic [Orthodox] religion,"[11] while the Sacred Congregation for the Propagation of the Faith in Rome declared the new reforms to be regurgitations of "the heresies [*eresie*] of Luther and Calvin."[12] The Russian Orthodox opponents of reform used similar language. Moscow archimandrite Feofilakt Lopatinskii found "Reformation thought [*mudrovaniia reformatskaia*]" in Feofan's ideas, while other Orthodox hierarchs described reforms using similar terms (such as "rectification [*ispravlenie*]") that were also applied to the European Reformation.[13]

Thus, the comparison of Orthodox church reforms to the European Reformation is as old as the reforms themselves. Contemporaneous observers chose strong words to describe the religious change—rectification, reformation, Lutheranization, and even revolution. Using these contemporaneous terms judiciously, it is important to note that the record does not assert that the Reformation occurred in Russia but rather observes the influence of Reformation ideas in the Orthodox Church.

THE TERMINOLOGY OF RUSSIA'S ORTHODOX ENLIGHTENMENT

Among the various aspects of the European Enlightenment (such as the early Enlightenment [a transition from the late Reformation period], the high Enlightenment, and enlightened absolutism), the religious experience of the Enlightenment receives the least scholarly attention. Recent groundbreaking studies on this topic, however, point to an emerging trend. In German scholarship, the works of Johannes Wallmann and Albrecht Beutel have lucidly explained the phenomenon of Germany's "Enlightenment theology" and have described the place of this theology in the wider context of European intellectual history. David Sorkin's 2008 monograph, *The Religious Enlightenment*, uncovered the intertwined world of Jewish, Catholic, and Protestant enlightened religious cultures to English-speaking audiences for the first time.[14] Ulrich Lehner's work on the Catholic Enlightenment has carefully reconstructed the lost story of an "open-minded Catholicism that was in dialogue with the cutting-edge intellectual trends," especially among the clergy and the laity of southern Germany and Austria.[15] While these authors focused on Protestant and Catholic contexts, Elise K. Wirtschafter began the conversation about the impact of the Enlightenment on religion in Russia. This book will continue that conversation by arguing that the influence of the Enlightenment was more profound than previously thought.

Despite the geographical distance and the confessional divide, the way learned Russian Orthodox clergy experienced the Enlightenment was very similar to how clerics in Göttingen, Leiden, Oxford, or Berlin perceived the intellectual developments happening in their midst. Much like their peers in the West, Russia's reforming bishops embraced two suppositions that made their doctrinal worldview more "enlightened" than that of their predecessors. One concerned the relationship of faith and empirical knowledge: the idea that reason (including science) and belief (including dogma) did not contradict each other, and that one must reconcile the two using rational deliberation. The other concerned the utilitarian nature of religious knowledge: the idea that a religious, moral improvement of the individual would result in a general improvement of society at large, thereby turning virtues and morals into a secular and civic imperative, not just a spiritual one.

Following these two assumptions common to the strains of religious Enlightenment in Europe, Russia's bishops engaged and promoted ideas that they believed improved the conditions of their society and the teachings of their church. Such concepts as religious toleration, social contract, common good, separation of powers, social virtues, public inoculation, and enlightened autocracy came to light in Russia not in the elite, closed salons of Petersburg but through the writings or public sermons of hierarchs, which were often published by the Holy Synod for general dissemination.

The overall nature of the Russian Orthodox Enlightenment was rather eclectic: among religious enlighteners, the bishops of the Holy Synod tended to snub the writings of Austrian or Bavarian authors, preferring instead the doctrinal trends of northern German Neology, Newtonian Physicotheology, and British Latitudinarianism. Yet, among the authors of the secular Enlightenment, the bishops favored the French: they vigorously purchased the works of Jean-Jacques Rousseau, Pierre Bayle, Voltaire, and Montesquieu for their seminary libraries, even after 1789. At the same time, they unanimously condemned Deism (found in those very books). Some bishops sympathized with known advocates for the abolition of serfdom and others expressed private admiration for parliamentary constitutional monarchy, but outward support for the idea of strong enlightened autocracy remained the Synod's official line.

The church hierarchs' interaction with the Enlightenment eventually produced conservative critics and liberal supporters in the political realm. For the former, as the final chapters will illustrate, the church hierarchs were becoming "spiritual Napoleons," who used their "Jacobin theology" to turn the Synod into "Sodom and Gomorrah." For the latter, the church became an institution to dialogue with, not oppose. The enlightened clergy of Moscow and St. Petersburg found patrons, interlocutors, and supporters in the burgeoning literary scene and in the Masonic lodges, theaters, and progressive charitable societies of the time. After all, the Decembrist revolutionaries, who tried to overthrow the government of Nicholas I in 1825, did not hesitate to turn to theological arguments against "tyranny" and to include Filaret Drozdov, the metropolitan of Moscow, in the ranks of their future provisional government.

THEOLOGY, CONTESTATION, VARIETY

This book addresses three major interpretive themes that will seek to expand our understanding of the Russian Orthodox Church within its historical context. The first theme is theology, which, to paraphrase Clifford Geertz, provided Russian clergy with the modes of "seeing" the world (spiritual and temporal) as well as finding the "frameworks of meaning" within that world in ways that liturgy or praxis alone could not provide.[16] Theology motivated and compelled churchmen like Feofan Prokopovich, Stefan Iavorskii, Platon Levshin, Filaret Drozdov, and Fotii Spasskii to seek or to oppose changes within the church; theology also justified their claims to exercise authority or power over it. Much like the recent "turn to ideology" that helped reshape the study of Soviet Union (for example, the works of Igal Halfin, Jochen Hellbeck, and Stephen Kotkin), I believe that the "turn to theology" will help to highlight the significance of doctrinal concepts and spirituality in the rise of Russia as an empire in religious and ideological aspects of that development.[17]

The second theme engaged throughout the book is contestation. I argue that Russian Orthodoxy, like any organized Christian body, was not an immovable fixture with a preset frame of fundamentalist confessional standards but was subject to change, permutation, and influence from external sources. Throughout the eighteenth century, Russian and Ukrainian churchmen contested the terms, traditions, meanings, content, and practice of Orthodoxy. There was no single interpretation of what constituted true and authentic Orthodoxy; interpretive consensuses that emerged during the factional victories of the 1720s and the Enlightenment reforms of the 1760s would be contested again in the 1820s and 1830s.

A third theme of the book is variety. As discussed before, this book argues that Orthodoxy in Russia was mediated through a variety of domestic and foreign influences for most of the eighteenth and early nineteenth centuries. As such, Orthodoxy, including its doctrine, preaching, ethic, and praxis, remained a highly variegated, historically contingent confessional body that was practiced, experienced, and interpreted in a myriad of ways across the vast cultural geography of Imperial Russia. In recent times, several groundbreaking works (such as *Orthodox Russia: Belief and Practice under the Tsars*, edited by Valerie Kivelson and Robert Greene) have highlighted how this variegation existed among the wide spectrum of "folk" practitioners of Orthodoxy. My work captures variegation that appeared through contestation in the upper strata of the Orthodox clergy. These three themes—theology, contestation, and variety—will help inform the bigger picture behind the narrative of individual chapters.

A Missing Story?

If Russia had such a profound religious reform, why was so little written about it? Trotsky's famous dictum that "we had no Reformation" (just "peasant sects") mesmerized many of the twentieth-century scholars of Russia, from Alexander Klibanov to Nicholas Riasanovsky. The exception was Princeton's émigré professor Georges Florovsky, who described the eighteenth century as the age of Russia's symbiotically theological conversation with European Protestantism. Regretfully, his work on the topic remained incomplete and his access to Italian, German, and Russian archives in the 1930s was limited.[18] This book makes every effort to produce an in-depth continuation of the discussion he started.

Since Trotsky's views reflected a certain political interpretation of history, the Red Army chief is not really to blame for Russia's exclusion from the wider contexts of the Reformation and religious Enlightenment. Instead, the exclusion reflects three specific historiographical narratives that this book challenges. The first is a narrative that, with few exceptions, relegates research on Eastern Europe to the margins of the otherwise Western-centric scholarship on the Reformation. The second is the narrative of a perennial Russian Orthodox traditionalist autarchy or backwardness that overlooked historical moments of its enlightened past. The third is the problem of the institutional silence within the Russian church that viewed the eighteenth century as a sore memory, better forgotten than kept.

The exclusion of Eastern Europe from the narrative of the European Reformation is slowly on the wane. Over the last two decades, scholars such as Graeme Murdock, Sergiusz Michalski, Howard Louthan, Maria Craciun, and others moved the frontiers of Reformation research further east, making compelling arguments for revision of the view that centers its impact on Western Europe.

Russian historiography's view of Orthodox reform and Enlightenment, however, presents a more formidable challenge. During the last century, many scholars viewed the imperial Orthodox Church as an institution resistant to change. In the nineteenth century, the bishops were seemingly the bulwark of tradition and autarchy against the changes proposed by political liberals of the eras of Nicholas I and Alexander II. In the early twentieth century, they were the reactionary enemies of the revolution, a view that became the staple narrative in Soviet historiography. This scholarly view is not all wrong, but it has been challenged by Gregory Freeze (among others).[19] Furthermore, it overlooks both the historical context of the eighteenth century (when the church hierarchy was more intellectually cosmopolitan and open-minded) and the historical transition between the eighteenth century and the developments of the prerevolutionary era. In fact the unfamiliarity of this 1825 transition has become somewhat of a problem in historiography. As Luba Golburt suggested, the eighteenth century is often presented as "seemingly meaningless past" simply because it is so strongly overshadowed by the next, prerevolutionary epoch, to which it offers few direct connections.[20] Deepening our understanding of the pre-1825 period by looking at the culture of church reform will contribute to the task of making the eighteenth century more meaningful by connecting it to the *longue durée* of Russian intellectual history.

A final reason for missing the spiritual "revolution" is the fact that the story of Russia's enlightened hierarchy remained a sore topic in the institutional memory of the twentieth-century church. By 1917 the church's memory of the reform was so negative that the last chief procurator of the Holy Synod (1917–18), Anton Kartashev, derided the event as a "coup de l'eglise."[21] While a "revolution" by one standard is always a "coup" by another, negative associations remained. For many standard-bearers of Russian Orthodoxy, even today the images of clerics eating meat during Lent, wearing wigs and powder, reading Voltaire, attending theaters, and joining Masonic lodges, while allowing an icon of Martin Luther to hang inside an Orthodox cathedral, constitute an embarrassing aberration from what Orthodoxy should be, and is not worth the scholarly attention.

The Limits of the Reform

Despite the profound nature of the Western impact, its influence was not all-encompassing. The reformers did not become Protestants in the early part of the century. Rather they were philo-Protestant, that is, as a rule, they tended to display affinity to Protestant formulations or standards in aspects of theology and praxis about which the Russian Orthodox Church held no firm consensus. Similarly, many of their predecessors or opponents were philo-Catholic, influenced, by varying degrees, by Roman Catholic formulations in soteriology, anthropology, eschatology, Mariology, and church-state relations and in such notions as limbo and aerial toll houses, among others. Therefore, philo-Protestant and philo-Catholic refer to inclinations in certain aspects of theology, not Manichean divisions. There were certainly exceptions to this rule, when, for example, philo-Protestant bishops successfully challenged the consensus not only from Protestant books but also from sources acceptable to the Orthodox (like the Bible and patristic opinions). Although the use of these terms is rare, it is not unique to this study: for example, Paul Bushkovitch, Nikolaos Chrissidis, Diego Pirillo, and Miriam Burstein have used the terms "philo-Catholic," "Latinophile," and "philo-Protestant" in the context of religious histories of Russia, early modern Italy, and Victorian Anglicanism.[22]

The reformers' adaptation of Western religious ideas remained eclectic and at times contradictory. Thus, while Feofan Prokopovich adopted Protestant concepts in his reformulation of Orthodox soteriology, eschatology, or understanding of church-state relations, he remained firmly consistent with the teachings of the Eastern church in describing the economy of the Trinity. Unlike the Protestants, Prokopovich opposed the Filioque and polemicized with both Protestants and Catholics who professed this doctrine. Similarly, while Platon Levshin (in the Catherinian era) promoted a very Calvinist doctrine of Providence, he remained a fervent critic of the Filioque. Platon even argued (to Louis Dutens [1730–1812]) that Protestants were still "Papist" in this regard, lamenting that Calvin's Reformation remained incomplete if it continued to adhere to this doctrine.

Just as Russia's reformed and enlightened bishops refused to abandon the Eastern Orthodox position on the Filioque, they did not abandon Orthodoxy's liturgical culture. During the middle of the eighteenth century, the Holy Synod revised and edited the church's most sacred texts—such as the Bible and the lives of saints—to cleanse them of "superstitious" content and to make them conform to the most current standards of Pietist biblical philology and textual criticism. The textual revision did not result in radical changes of sacred rites. Liturgical structure, the vestments, and ritual space, for the most part, remained in conformity to centuries-old standards adopted by Eastern churches in late antiquity.

The impact of the Enlightenment also had its limits. Russian Orthodox bishops did not turn into Voltairian Deists nor did they join revolutionary movements en masse, even though some sympathized with such ideas as constitutionalism. Although they questioned miracles, popularized scientific concepts, or rationalized pious practices, they remained firm believers in the Trinity, the afterlife, and the supernatural. While they embraced toleration, they were more tolerant of the Protestants, Muslims, and even Old Believers than of the Catholics, Jews, and peasant sectarians.

CHRONOLOGY AND FRAMEWORK

The framework of this book is both thematic and chronological. The first half focuses on the influence of Reformation ideas during the progress of church reform in Russia from 1680 to 1740. The starting chapter presents the seventeenth-century background to eighteenth-century developments: namely, the scope and depth of the intellectual influence of Catholicism, particularly among Ukrainian hierarchs like Stefan Iavorskii, who was the effective administrative head of the Russian Church in the first years of the eighteenth century. The chapter also demonstrates the obstacles that such influence created for Peter I's attempt to reform Russian society. Chapters 2 and 3 introduce Peter's solution to these obstacles of Catholic influence—the rise of Feofan Prokopovich and his Ukrainian philo-Protestant allies. These chapters trace Feofan's studies in Rome and Germany, his embrace of numerous elements of Protestant theology, his arrival in St. Petersburg, and the formation of a party of his allied clergy.

Chapter 4 will address the factors that allowed Feofan to succeed in his struggle to refashion many aspects of Orthodoxy in the Protestant manner. Prokopovich and his allied reformist bishops constituted a tiny minority in the ranks of the clergy (most of whom were initially rather hostile toward the newcomer). Overcoming this hostile environment involved persuading the Russian elites (during the reigns of Peter I, Catherine I, Peter II, and Anna) that his Protestant-inspired change was not only the proper Orthodoxy (as opposed to the "heresies" of his opponents), but also the proper political religion for the Russian state. Without such religion, he argued, Russia would fall into the hands of the imminent "Papist tyranny." How Feofan achieved this feat is a story of political intrigues, theological debates, homiletic propaganda, brazen corruption, daring escapes, espionage, and bloody purges that in the 1730s finally cleansed the ranks of Orthodox clergy of "Papist" spies, real or imagined. Although chapters 1 through 5 depict many episodes of the key life journeys of Stefan Iavorskii and Feofan Prokopovich, they are not intended to serve as replacements for the much-needed proper biographies of these two great Ukrainian theologians. Such a task would require years of extensive exploration in Poland, Italy, Germany, and Ukraine, in addition to the Russian archives.

Chapter 5 depicts a transition from the age of reformist upheaval to the age of religious Enlightenment. It follows the immediate legacies of Feofan's reforms carried out by his disciples and appointees from the 1740s onward. These heirs of reform (the "fledglings of the Petrine nest") continued to adopt Protestant theology in the enduring revision of Russia's religious landscape. They also communicated the new doctrinal ideas to the masses through preaching Protestant-inspired theological concepts, attacking various "superstitions," and embracing the homiletical styles popular in Protestant Europe. Their interaction with the European early Enlightenment, a religious harbinger of Enlightenment centered mostly in Pietist Germany, was also very profound. Such interaction produced the new educational orientation toward Protestant universities (where Orthodox seminarians went to study) and the new hermeneutical imperative for revising Russia's seemingly outdated Slavonic Bible in accordance with the latest Pietist and enlightened standards of biblical philology.

As a transitional section, this chapter belongs to the first part of the book as much as it belongs to the second. It displays the latent Enlightenment as a logical continuation of Feofan's earlier reforms.

The second part of the book deals thematically with the arrival and impact of Enlightenment ideas in the Russian church from about 1760 to 1825. Chapter 6 narrates how the new generation of bishops—many of whom were Feofan's intellectual heirs—embraced Europe's religious and secular Enlightenment. In doing so, the episcopate became the most progressive and European-oriented social group in the Catherinian era, second only to the nobility. Chapter 7 documents how Enlightenment ideas changed Russia's pulpit preaching, or the clergy's communication of the Enlightenment to the masses, through content and style. Chapter 8 shows how these enlightened clergy took part in Russia's Alexandrine Awakening, emphasizing the tolerant ecumenical outlook of their doctrine and embracing the Protestant-influenced movement of vernacularizing the sacred texts and bringing the biblical literacy to the masses.

The flowering of Orthodox Enlightenment ends with the thunder of cannon in St. Petersburg's Senate Square in December 1825, addressed in the final chapter and the conclusion. The same Russian military men who boasted about defeating the actual Napoleon in 1814 (Aleksei Arakcheev, Nikolai Protasov, Aleksandr Shishkov) now dealt a blow to the political and "spiritual Napoleon" of Russian clerical Enlightenment and libertinism in 1825. Thus, the curtain of Russia's Orthodox Reform and Enlightenment closes with the coronation of Nicholas I and the ascendancy of the military-bureaucratic reaction in the post-1825 empire: from then on, a new story of Russia's counterreform begins.

LIMITS OF THE BOOK

While research projects may be infinite, publications are not. Books have boundaries. Choosing the boundaries of any work, a disciplinary exercise that the Germans call *Mut zu Lücken* (roughly, "the courage to leave out"), often results in difficult decisions. Not all questions that deserve an answer will receive one, not all aspects of a historical narrative that should be highlighted will be, and not all historiographical debates that need attention will be addressed. The relationship of the ideas of Protestant reform and religious Enlightenment to the parish clergy is one such issue. This work's emphasis on bishops mostly leaves out the diocesan priests, whose world Gregory Freeze described so well and whose connection to the larger theological trends of the eighteenth century merit a separate study. Equally, the relationship of the church hierarchy to millions of Orthodox parishioners needs a thorough investigation, including the process of social discipline (*Sozialdisziplinierung*) and confessionalization in the Russian context.[23] As a separate book in itself, this would be a great project, but it falls outside the scope of this work for two reasons. First, it would distract from the focus on the intellectual history of the church, and second, such a work would not fully address the arguments and themes chosen for this study, including the questions of theology and contestation.

CONTINUITY AND DISRUPTION

If the Protestant and Enlightenment impact on Orthodoxy was not sustained after 1825 to 1917, what long-term consequences or legacies, if any, did the eighteenth century have on religion and society in Russia? How does this work fit into the larger story of the synodal Orthodoxy that spanned two centuries of Russia's empire?

Russia's enlightened eighteenth century, I argue, is a narrative of disruption and continuity within the larger story of the imperial church. It is only recently that we have been able to speak about the larger story of the church in the empire as a result of the post-1988 revival of scholarship on religion, which has produced a long list of important monographs and articles exploring subjects of Russia's history that were previously ignored. Among them are the monastic revival of the late imperial period, the experience of "lived Orthodoxy," and the "meaning of Orthodoxy in modern Russian society and culture."[24] This recent wave of scholarship includes the works of Heather Coleman, Gregory Freeze, Robert Greene, Scott Kenworthy, Nadieszda Kizenko, Laurie Manchester, Patrick Michelson, Irina Paert, Barbara Skinner, Vera Shevzov, Mark Steinberg, Paul Werth, Christine Worobec, and many, many others.[25] Most of this recent research, however, focuses on the later part of the imperial period—the years 1815–1917, 1861–1917, or similar chronological boundaries. Much less progress has been achieved on the synodal Orthodoxy of the earlier period, especially before 1800.

This work pushes the chronology of imperial Orthodoxy back to its origins in the early eighteenth century. The employment of such chronology requires an elucidation of the relationship between the empire of 1700–1825 and the empire of 1825–1917, two very common periodizations in Russian history. This relationship displays evidence of both the disruption and continuity of the impact of church reforms after 1825.

The occurrence of disruption is evident from visible discontinuities of the pre- and post- 1825 eras: the church turned from embracing Protestant theology to neo-patristics, from engaging the framework of the Enlightenment to rejecting it, from espousing a utilitarian view of spiritual duties to the rebirth of asceticism, and so on. This notion of discontinuity follows Luba Golburt's understanding of the cultural re-founding of the Russian Empire after 1825, during the Pushkin era, in reaction to or in revision of what she called Russia's "first epoch," Russia's imperial era before Pushkin.

One example of disruption between the pre- and post-1825 periods was the decline and rebirth of monasticism and saintly canonizations. Since Feofan's theological reforms emphasized salvation acquired by faith, grace, and utility to society, the traditional understanding of the Eastern Orthodox monastic calling became soteriologically meaningless; in post-Petrine Russia monasticism had to acquire a new pragmatic and utilitarian ethos, such as turning monasteries into military hospitals. While it is tempting to overemphasize the state's interests in the monastic reforms, none of the changes would have been possible without the doctrinal framework established by Feofan and without the direct agency of the church reformers themselves. When it came to matters of faith, canon law, and theology of the monastic vocation, most of the reformist bishops (themselves, monks) were not passively carrying out orders.

This new theological framework with its utilitarian ethos also drove Catherinian reformers who assessed the monasterial telos to be inconsistent with the ownership of serfs and who believed that freeing the (ever-rebellious) peasants from monastic control would make nuns and monks in Russia embrace more "enlightened" occupations. The overall decline of monasticism accompanied all these changes: the number of monasteries in Russia declined from 1,153 in 1700 to 385 in 1764. The situation did not appear to have improved by 1808. After the Russian partition of Poland, the annexation of Right-Bank Ukrainian and Belarusian lands brought the overall number of monasteries in Russia up to 447, meaning that the numbers within Russia proper had declined further since 1764.[26] The disruption of 1825, however, saw growth and revival of monasticism along with neo-patristic theology: the total number of monasteries reached 667 in 1887 and 907 in 1908.[27]

The Petrine "spiritual revolution" similarly shaped a decline of sainthood. Although the sixteenth, seventeenth, and nineteenth centuries were prominent for canonizations and saintly feats of piety, the entire period from 1701 to 1801 saw only two (!) official canonizations: St. Feodosii of Tot'ma and St. Dmitrii of Rostov. In the age of light and reason, Orthodox Russia needed no saints. The disruption that the eighteenth century brought is noteworthy even in comparison to more modern times. For example, the era of Rasputin and the late Romanov neo-Muscovite Renaissance (1894–1917) was abound in the supernatural and the saintly, and that period also witnessed a total of seven canonizations in the Holy Synod. The revival of the miraculous was demonstrative of the larger process of change within the post-1825 Orthodox Church and, as works by Robert Nichols, Christine Worobec, Scott Kenworthy, Nadieszda

Kizenko, Patrick Michelson (among others) have illustrated, that process involved not only miracles but also the growth of ascetic sanctity.[28]

Although the end of the eighteenth-century epoch in 1825 serves as the temporal watershed of this book, there were also important continuities between pre- and post-1825 religious culture. The first continuity and the central argument of this book is that Protestant and Enlightenment influences played an indispensable part in Russia's religious turn to modernity. As Marc Raeff once argued, the origins of "modernity" are found not in the "revolutionary waves" of 1789–1871 Europe, but in the emergence of a new functional process of state consolidation brought about by Pietism and the Reformation. The revolutionary era reflected the "aftereffects of that process."[29]

In addition to imperial religious modernization, there are other long-term modalities that originated in the eighteenth century and persisted well into the later period. The second continuity was the emergence of an Orthodox *empire*. For the first time since the fall of Constantinople, an Eastern Orthodox monarchy had a true empire that survived until 1917. The theological origins of this "empire," however, had little to do with Constantinople or a medieval Third Rome; rather, they stemmed from Prokopovich's adaptation of the Lutheran idealization of the Holy Roman Reich. Similarly, his apology for the Russian title of emperor (imperator and kaiser) reflected the Scandinavian and German Lutheran conceptions of Pontifex Maximus and summus episcopus, notions that in the Protestant world gave the monarch a status of a final arbiter of spiritual authority within a secular realm. The religious theoretical origins of the (holy) Russian Empire were not only a novelty in Russia but also a scandal in Europe: prior to 1721, there was only one legitimate emperor in Europe (a Habsburg) and it took decades for Catholic European monarchs to recognize this title.

The most important feature of this legacy, however, was not its theory but a national reorientation of Orthodoxy as the religion for the subjects of the empire, not just the Russians. Prior to 1700, most of the Muscovite hierarchy was ethnically Russian with occasional Greeks occupying various posts in the medieval period. Throughout many decades of the eighteenth century, Russians ceased to be the dominant ethnic group in the upper ecclesiastical ranks. About two-thirds of the church hierarchy (in the so-called Great Russian dioceses outside of Ukraine) in the eighteenth century were Ukrainians and so a great part of this narrative is the story of Ukrainians reforming and modernizing the Russian church and its religious culture. However, numerous Belarusians (or "Lithuanians"), Greeks, Georgians, Serbs, and Moldavians participated too, entering the ranks of the upper clergy during this period.

This unprecedented influx of outsiders reflected a major break with the pre-1700 past but also set the trend for the future by shaping two different features of national identity that persisted until 1917 and beyond. One is that Russian Orthodoxy became Russian *imperial* Orthodoxy. Ukrainian reformers designed a church as a transnational institution not just for the Russians but for all Orthodox subjects of the empire. This was reflected from above, in the upper ranks of the hierarchy. It was also reflected from below, in bringing the empire's indigenous peoples into synodal Orthodoxy's fold through various means, including missionary activities—a subject that had already received ample attention in the existing literature on the borderlands and thus falls outside the parameters of this study.[30] A second feature is that Orthodoxy also became *Russian* imperial Orthodoxy. In building a new church for the young empire, Ukrainian reformers increasingly embraced Russian identities and Petersburg-centered religious culture, promoting the specifically Russian characteristics of this national but imperial church.

The emergence of Russia as an empire affected not only the national content of the church but also the function of the state. Throughout the nineteenth century, Russia became what Robert Crews described as the "confessional state"—a monarchy with tiered toleration of virtually all faiths of the realm, with Orthodoxy being on top.[31] The origins of this toleration go back to the eighteenth century, first to the impact of Protestantism and then to the Enlightenment described in the book. The tsar was no longer just a Muscovite potentate, reigning over the Orthodox and non-Orthodox alike, but a supra-confessional arbiter of toleration for all sacred authority.

A third continuity involved the rising tension between the powers of the state bureaucracy and the prerogatives of the church in religious affairs. The original power structure of Feofan's reforms envisioned a direct relationship between the supreme authority of the monarch and the canonical authority of the Holy Governing Synod on an equal footing with the Governing Senate. The leading bishops of that Synod enjoyed direct access to the court on the level of the members of the top aristocracy and the imperial family. However, the subsequent consolidation of state bureaucracy imposed an intermediary layer of power between the bishops and the monarchy. This tension with the bureaucracy became particularly evident in the Orthodox Church's relationship with the chief procurator. This position, rather insignificant in the earlier period, slowly evolved into a governmental department of its own that increasingly bureaucratized relations between the Synod and the court. The growing powers of chief procurators continued to be a source of tension with the church hierarchy until the abolition of that office in 1917.

A fourth continuity of the church reforms laid the foundation for a tradition of political liberalism in Imperial Russia. By 1800 enlightened church
hierarchs were among the country's most educated social groups and openly
dabbled in subjects that blurred the lines between theology, philosophy, and
political ideas. As books by Voltaire and Montesquieu entered the seminaries,
teachers and students alike engaged Enlightenment ideas, from the less sensitive
subjects like faith and reason to more sensitive ones like constitutionalism.
Enlightenment ideas also galvanized the sympathies of many of the hierarchs
toward the plight of the lower classes and even shaped some moral arguments
for the critique of serfdom. After all, the Orthodox Church was the first institution in Russia to offer the country's serfs an emancipatory experience. In general, the flourishing of Western, religiously progressive ideas certainly helped
Russia's monarchs create a more rational, ordered, and enlightened empire.
However, paradoxically, it also laid the foundation for the growth of political
freethinking within the Orthodox Church that later turned many faithful seminarians into revolutionaries, among them Anastas Mikoyan, Simon Petliura,
and Joseph Stalin.

PART I

ORTHODOX RUSSIA
REFORMED

I

Russian Orthodoxy on the Eve of the Reforms

The Ukrainian Context, 1654–1712

Luther was a vicious rogue; and Calvin, a pig's excrement.
[Liutor—liut vor, Kalvin—kal svin]

—STEFAN IAVORSKII, *Kamen' very*, 1717

THE IDES OF MARCH

On March 17, 1712, the Feast Day of St. Aleksii, Peter the Great faced a very serious challenge to his rule and his reforms. Stefan Iavorskii (1658–1722), the vicar of the Moscow Patriarchate and the administrative head of the church, denounced the tsar in none other than the Kremlin's Assumption Cathedral.[1] Stefan's scandalous sermon declared the war with Sweden to be divine punishment for the failure to keep God's commandments in "our rebellious [*miatezhnaia*] Russia."[2] He then detailed a litany of the country's sins, focusing especially on Peter's new institution of the *fiskaly* (tax inspectors). These intruding special agents of the tsar had a special place in hell reserved for them. They will "drown [*vviaznet*] in a deep pit" of the netherworld, said the bishop.[3] Stefan then made another daring denunciation, directed against anyone "who abandons his wife to take up another [Luke 16:18]"—an obvious reference to Peter's divorce and recent marriage to his mistress.[4] Finally, he declared that, in the absence of righteous leaders, it was the monarch's son, Tsarevich Aleksei, who was "our only hope."[5]

As Paul Bushkovitch has noted, the sermon was the most serious ecclesiastical critique of the monarch in Russia "since Nikon's times," that is, since the tumultuous years of the Great Schism in the mid-seventeenth century.[6] But Iavorskii's insolence was hardly news—the bishop had denounced the tsar's divorce of his Muscovite wife, Evdokiia Lopukhina, and his cohabitation with the daughter of a Baltic Lutheran pastor even before 1712. The larger problem was that Metropolitan Stefan Iavorskii was Peter's *own* appointee. Like other

Jesuit-educated Ukrainian clergymen invited to Moscow to modernize the church, Stefan owed his appointment to the tsar. Yet the beneficiary of this appointment now leaned toward the tsar's enemies. This was an indication that Peter's choice of bishops with impeccable educational credentials (from places as prestigious as Rome or Padua) was failing to provide concord in time of reformatory upheaval.

Why would Peter worry about a sermon by a bishop he could easily depose or the opinions of clergy he could have ordered hanged? First of all, as his biographers affirm, Peter was a devout believer, and as Aleksandr Lavrov has noted, his church policies were not about "secularization."[7] The tsar certainly believed (in some form or another) that his rule would perish without a divine blessing. Secondly, the church hierarchy—from village deacons all the way up to the archimandrites and the patriarch—possessed unique charismatic authority among millions of ordinary Orthodox Russians. To paraphrase Viktor Zhivov, the tentacles of the state in Russia were much shorter than the far-reaching arms of the church.[8] It was a very powerful, popular institution. Thirdly, the Romanov monarch was mindful of the historical examples of religious strife, both domestic (during the Great Schism of 1666) and foreign (the Wars of Religion), and he was in no mood to replay either experience.

In other words, the tsar could not afford a war with the church. Rather, he needed allies within the church to support the sociopolitical changes he envisioned. This was imperative, for if he had not found a suitable clergyman (or the faction of the clergy) to support his cause, he would have been a Frederick the Pious without Martin Luther, or a Henry VIII without a Thomas Cranmer. The tsar's social and political reforms would be bogged down in a quagmire of religiously inspired resistance from all levels of Russia's society.

This essential task of finding clerical allies proved to be a great challenge for several reasons. First, Peter—who was neither a theologian nor a canonist—had no clearly charted plan for church reform. His policy of improving ecclesiastical affairs by bringing the better-educated men from Ukraine to Moscow was not an innovation, it built upon the existing trend. Worst of all, this policy failed to furnish him a suitable clerical ally—at least, as of 1712. Second, inviting the Ukrainians was a double-edged sword. Certainly, the newcomers were more refined and Westernized than the traditional Muscovite clergy, having imbibed the best of the Baroque arts, Renaissance sciences, and Jesuit humanism that Italy, Poland, or Austria had to offer. But they also carried the baggage of Catholic Reformation theology and counter-Protestant polemics, reflecting the Roman Catholic influence that shaped Ukrainian Orthodoxy in crucial ways after the Union of Brest. The variety of cultural and doctrinal views that Ukrainian clergy brought with them to Moscow stimulated contestation both from within Muscovite society and from the monarch himself. Third, Peter seemed to have underestimated the relationship of this seventeenth-century Catholic context to politics, especially the "two swords" ideology that strived to demarcate the political authority of the church or spiritual monarchy from the authority of the tsar or temporal monarchy. It was not so much about "absolutism" as simply about political power, which Peter treated as a finite commodity, not to be shared with the ambitious Jesuit-educated bishops just because their theology said so. Furthermore, this theology seemed to be outright antithetical to Peter's vision of constructing the contemporary European ideal of the "well-ordered police state."⁹ And finally, Iavorskii's own ambition, inertia, and outright resistance to several elements of nascent Petrine culture only reinforced the differences between the two. The clash of the new Petrine culture with the Catholic-influenced Ukrainian context provided a very important background to the swift and successful rise of Feofan's reformists. Retrospectively speaking, there was simply no alternative to Prokopovich.

Peter's Early Church Policy Choices

Despite being (literally) the founding father of modern Russia, religious reform was not among Peter's greatest talents. It is important not to exaggerate his role in church affairs on the basis that anything happening on the ruler's watch must be the direct product of the monarch's genius. Even a quick examination of the tsar's religious policy in the 1690s and the first decade of the eighteenth century shows that he lacked a clear direction. The tsar's early dealings with the clerical estate prior to Feofan's arrival in St. Petersburg in 1716 could hardly be classed as proper reform. Of course, Peter cared about a general "amelioration [*ispravlenie*] of the priesthood [*dukhovnyi chin*],"¹⁰ but a comprehensive plan for change had never been a priority among the social, military, and political developments that took place during this period. Equally, his decrees in the first decade of the eighteenth century regarding religious affairs lacked the architecture of a reform plan that appeared in his naval or military orders. This absence of passion toward reforming the church was partially caused by the protracted military campaign that consumed so much of his time,¹¹ but there were also other, deeper issues at play. One reason was that the tsar had no theological direction for such a reform as he was not a theologian. The second was that the tsar (prior to meeting Feofan Prokopovich) had failed to find clergy either competent or enthusiastic enough to lead a substantial shake-up of the ecclesiastical order.

Peter's early decrees on religion did not seek to actively reform the church but to reflexively neutralize whatever clerical opposition confronted him. The widespread popular hostility toward his social changes (such as the adoption of "German dress," beard shaving, and legalization of the tobacco trade) also affected Russia's parish clergy as well as the monastic hierarchy. Peter's troubles with the monasteries and Patriarch Adrian (d. 1700) are well documented in the historiography.[12] Thus, when the tsar placed restrictions on the use of paper and ink in the monasteries in 1701, he was hoping to prevent political sedition that could stem from the monks' "graphomania [sochinitel'stvo]."[13] Similarly, his decision to delay the appointment of a new patriarch after Adrian's death in 1700 was an attempt to neutralize the Muscovite upper clergy's discontent (as any one of these bishops could legally be appointed to the office).

The year 1700 did not bring the formal abolition of the office as would happen in 1721.[14] When Peter installed Stefan Iavorskii, a temporary caretaker (locum tenens) or exarch for this vacant office of patriarch in 1702, he was testing a potential candidate for the throne; moreover, he was gaining the revenue in tax appropriations from the patriarchate's serf-tilled estates.[15] As Evgenii Anisimov successfully demonstrated, many of Peter's early church-related decrees had only financial motivations.[16]

If there is a discernable trend in the church affairs of Peter's reign, it would be his staffing of vacant church positions with better-educated men. And the best-educated clergymen were all in Ukraine. In the first two decades of his reign, the tsar steadily appointed clerics from the Hetmanate as the continuation of a trend already started by his predecessors. The volume of the ecclesiastics invited and the range of ranks they occupied were both unprecedented occurrences in Muscovite history. Suddenly, there were more Ukrainians in Moscow and the dioceses than ever before, and they were much more than educated visitors. Between 1699 and 1708, the tsar appointed Ukrainian candidates to half (nine out of eighteen) of the bishoprics in Russia proper, including the richest and most influential ones like Rostov, Nizhnii Novgorod, Riazan, Kolomna, and Smolensk.[17] By this time, the majority of the administrators of Moscow's influential Don, St. Savva, St. Simon, and Zaikonospasskii monasteries were Ukrainian too, and so were the archimandrites of Novgorod's St. Iurii's and Khutyn's monasteries.[18] Peter not only invited the Ukrainians to take up church positions in Moscow, but also accommodated the terms of their tenure. For example, prior to 1691, the episcopal oath in Russia contained a vow to "avoid fellowship [ne obshchatisia] with Latins, Lutherans, and Calvinists." The vow was stricken out of the oath of office; after all, many of the new bishops had received education in the Catholic colleges abroad.[19]

While this accelerated influx of the educated clergy, it brought much disappointment for the tsar. First, the newcomers' strong background in Catholic theology (specifically, the "two swords" doctrine) shaped their growing hostility toward the idea of the subordination of spiritual affairs to the will of the monarch. Second, the tsar's strategy to neutralize the traditionalist Muscovite faction within the church by promoting the Ukrainians was failing, since, by the early 1710s, the loyalties of many of these Ukrainian clerics were clearly drifting toward an accommodation with the traditionalists. During the trial of Tsarevich Aleksei (who himself embraced the Catholic-influenced "Kievan Orthodoxy"), it was a coalition of Muscovite and Ukrainian clerics who confronted the tsar.[20] Their opposition was highly theological. Influenced by Roman Catholic notions, these men invited by the tsar to Moscow increasingly used the language of the Catholic Reformation to define the new relationship of the church to Russia's state and society, language that Peter would come to despise.

THE SEVENTEENTH-CENTURY CONTEXT

How did Catholic theology find its way into the sacred books and minds of the Eastern Slavic clergy? Prior to the late seventeenth century, Russia and Ukraine had very little of what scholars today define as "theology," that is, a systematic theology (in itself a Western construct). The Muscovite church in 1600 inherited a rich corpus of Byzantine monastic and liturgical writings from its canonical ancestors of Kievan Rus', including some South Slavic patristic and hagiographic translations but not much of the Byzantine heritage of dogmatic theology, classical philosophy, or philology.[21] Florovsky called this lack of theological sophistication "Russia's ancient, enduring and centuries-long intellectual silence," while George Fedotov noted the "overwhelmingly practical and didactic character" of Old Slavonic literature.[22]

The Byzantine theological heritage was never static and remained in conversation with the West throughout the Middle Ages. Demetrios Kydones's 1364 translation of Thomas Aquinas's *Summa theologiae* and *Summa contra gentiles* into Greek was a "dramatic turning point" for the rise of scholastic theological influence in Byzantium.[23] So, during the fifteenth and sixteenth centuries, throughout the Greek-speaking Mediterranean, the Western Thomist emphasis on the systematization of "correct doctrine" slowly but decidedly replaced the traditional Byzantine Orthodox emphasis on "correct experience." Meanwhile, Western neo-Aristotelian ontology (with its quest for the positive definition of all metaphysics) began to gain followers at the expense of the Eastern apophatic (and somewhat paleo-Aristotelian) theology in which identification of metaphysical matter often encouraged negative definition (e.g., "grace is not X" as opposed to "grace is Y").[24]

As the Greeks began to accommodate themselves to some of the novel theological structures of the Latins, the sixteenth century—with its whirlwind of Protestant Reformation—brought new demands to systematize dogma in

Orthodox and Catholic Europe alike. The Catholic response to the doctrinal struggle was the 1566 Tridentine Catechism of Peter Canisius and the retrenchment of Catholic reform, known also as the Counter-Reformation.[25] The Eastern Orthodox were never indifferent to this schism in the West. Ivan the Terrible, for example, firmly rejected Protestants as pernicious rebels, while seeking a rapprochement with the Holy Roman Empire.[26] Some Orthodox in the Eastern Mediterranean, however, initially appeared to be very open to Calvinist and Lutheran theological formulations, as seen in the 1601 catechism of Metrophanes Kritopoulos (1589–1639) and the 1629 Geneva Catechism of Patriarch Cyril Loukaris. Neither of these works became official. The struggle between the philo-Catholic and philo-Protestant tendencies within the Greek hierarchy resulted in the victory of the former in 1643, when the Hellenic church accepted the Ukrainian adaptation of the Tridentine Catechism—the Peter Mohyla's *Confession of Faith*.[27]

The catechism by Peter Mohyla, the metropolitan of Kiev (1596–1647), systematized Ukrainian Orthodox dogma after a century of three-way polemical struggle between Orthodoxy, Catholicism, and various Protestant movements in the Polish-Lithuanian Commonwealth. Although many of the Orthodox polemicists—such as Zakharii Kopystenskii (d. 1626) and Stefan Zizanii (1550–1634)—attacked both Catholicism and Protestantism with impunity, Mohyla's camp chose a more nuanced approach toward Catholic doctrine.[28] By 1600 Roman and Uniate Catholicism was clearly on the rise: the decline of Polish Protestantism restored the hegemony of the Catholic Church among the Poles, while the Union of Brest of 1596 brought many Ukrainians and Belarusians into spiritual unity with Rome. Thus, Mohyla's theological system strategically embraced Catholic elements that often made the Orthodox Church appear less "heretical" in Poland and that gave it the polemical strength of having a clear and cohesive (even if borrowed) organization of concepts.

Mohyla's catechism, first published in Muscovy as *Pravoslavnoe ispovedanie* and in Ukraine as *Malyi katekhizis*, was an adaptation of Peter Canisius's *Parvus catechismus catholicorum* (A Little Catechism for Catholics) with occasional borrowings from Robert Bellarmine's *Explicatio doctrinae christianae* (The Explanation of Christian Doctrine). In this catechism and other works, Mohyla standardized Orthodox doctrine according to Canisian subdivisions and introduced clearly Catholic formulations of the cardinal virtues, the sequence of the seven mortal sins, the time of transubstantiation, the office of exorcism, and (in the Ukrainian version), purgatory.[29]

Despite the fact that some Greek and most Muscovite bishops distrusted these formulations (as "crypto-Romanism"), Mohyla's concepts defined the standard doctrine of the Ukrainian church.[30] A version of Mohyla's catechism was also approved by the 1643 Council of Jassy and it soon became the official Orthodox confession for all four Eastern patriarchates.[31] The influence of Mohyla's theology also reached to the north. After Left-Bank Ukraine became a protectorate of the Muscovite state in 1654, the Romanov court increasingly patronized Ruthenian clerics without (initially) recognizing some of their more scandalous views. Among the adherents of the latter was Lazar' Baranovich, who in the 1660s was a colleague of official court preacher Simeon Polotskii but espoused a very Catholic Mariology.[32] Another Kievan theologian who visited the court in the 1670s was Ioannikii Galiatovskii.[33] Galiatovskii preached the doctrine of limbo (*odkhlan' pekel'na*), classified aerial toll houses as a purgatorial location, and maintained devotion to the Sacred Heart, St. Teresa de Avila, and St. Margaret de Cortona.[34]

By the time Peter the Great rose to power, a certain accommodation to the Ukrainian form of Orthodoxy was underway in Russia. Patriarch Ioakim finally approved the edited version of Mohyla's catechism in 1684 and by 1698 Patriarch Adrian began to view it not only as an authoritative text, but also as a weapon against numerous "heretics," including "the Lutherans who, in their vainglory and voluptuousness, separated from the Roman church."[35] The accommodation of Ukrainian theology meant that Kievan teachers and clergy would not only increasingly visit Moscow for periods of time but would eventually settle in the Russian capital. This trend gained particular momentum around 1700, when Peter I began to actively recruit the Ukrainians to build a corps of new, more educated clergy. The most important representative of this group of recent Ukrainian arrivals was Stefan Iavorskii.

Stefan and His "Villainous Faction"

Stefan Iavorskii was born in Galicia in Western Ukraine but raised by his parents in the east, near Nezhin. Stefan (born as Simeon) studied initially in Kiev's Mohyla Academy, and then (as a Uniate convert) in the Polish Jesuit academies of Lwów (Lviv), Lublin, Poznan, and Wilno (Vilnius) before returning to Kiev in the early 1690s to teach theology and poetics.[36] Popular as a preacher as well as *poeta laureates*, Iavorskii received an invitation to come to Moscow, where in February 1700 he impressed the tsar with his funeral sermon for Generalissimus Aleksei Shein.[37]

Peter and Patriarch Adrian decided to keep the talented preacher in Moscow and then managed to force the old Avraamii (the bishop of Riazan) into retirement. The post was vacated for Iavorskii, who took it despite reservations that doing so (while the old bishop was still alive) would constitute "spiritual adultery."[38] After a quick consecration, the new bishop of Riazan settled in a house on Lubianka Square in Moscow, outside of his diocese but close to the tsar.[39] Shortly after Adrian's death, Peter made Iavorskii the locum tenens of the patriarchal throne. Aside from the office of the patriarch, this was the highest position in the Russian church at the time.[40]

Stefan was not the lone representative of the philo-Catholic Ukrainian clergy in Moscow. Between 1700 and 1712, several gifted Kievan professors joined him in the city as beneficiaries of the tsar's fast-tracked promotions. These hierarchs gathered around Stefan in what Feofan Prokopovich would later refer to as the "villainous [zlodeiskaia] faction" that threatened Russian church reform.[41] Most members of the faction, indeed, carried solid Catholic educational credentials. Iavorskii's closest ally, Feofilakt Lopatinskii (1670–1741), the bishop of Tver, studied in Jesuit schools in Polish Lwów and in Austria, moving to Moscow after 1704, where he taught Aristotelian philosophy and Thomist theology.[42] Feofan viewed him as a "weapon in the hands of Stefan"[43] and Stefan's "inspector [fiskal]," a kind of a deputy for Iavorskii in theological affairs.[44] Johann G. Vockerodt (1693–1756), who had lived in Russia since 1712 and then worked as the secretary to the Prussian ambassador, described Lopatinskii as one of the "domestic Papists [heimlichen Papisten]" among Moscow's clerical elites. The secretary highlighted the popularity of Feofilakt's philosophy course in which he "copied [copiret] word for word from the Roman teachers, quoting from [Catholic theologians] Vásquez, Suárez, Escobar, Sánchez, Oviedo, and other obscure [obscuren] scholastics."[45]

Another member of the party, Gedeon Vishnevskii (1678–1761), future bishop of Smolensk, held a doctorate from the Jesuit Collegium in Kraków. Despite his immodesty in "vainly celebrating his Jesuit doctoral beret,"[46] he found a hearty welcome in Moscow, where Stefan's colleague Feofilakt invited this "perfect theologian" to join the Slavo-Greco-Latin Academy and the philo-Catholic circle of the exarch.[47] Another important Kievan expatriate who was part of this group was Markell Rodyshevskii, the later vicar of Novgorod diocese. Supposedly "drunk with the Jesuit schools' Papist spirit," he too moved to Moscow in 1718 and eventually joined Stefan's ever-expanding circle of "Latinists [latynshchiki]" or philo-Catholic theologians.[48]

The "Latinist" party was by no means limited to the Ukrainians. At various points in time it included Anastasios, Alexander, and Sofronii Likhoudes, and Evfimii Koletti (1683–1739), an Italian Greek, educated in Padua and Venice, who was the bishop of Suzdal, and was also known as Don Liberius Coletti.[49] Last but not least were the native Muscovite hierarchs like Ignatii Smola and Georgii Dashkov, who were present in the party as a marriage of convenience against Feofan's and Peter's reforms.[50]

STEFAN'S THEOLOGY AND THE
TWO SWORDS DOCTRINE

Catholic theology was a significant influence on Iavorskii. An avid reader of Spanish, Polish, and Italian theological books, Stefan primarily based his 1697 theology course in Kiev on Bellarmine (especially his *Disputationes*) while in his other works he borrowed from Tomas Malvenda and Martinus Becanus.[51] His theological views certainly reflected his choice of books, curriculum, and education but were not alien to the cultural milieu of what Paul Bushkovitch called "Kievan Orthodoxy."[52] Among Stefan's many Catholic-influenced theological positions, three were particularly important for understanding his clash with Peter, and later, Feofan Prokopovich. One was his view of salvation (soteriology); another, his stance on the question of ecclesial authority; and third, his understanding of the end times (eschatology).

The foundation of Stefan's understanding of salvation stemmed from his high anthropology. In theology, anthropology is a view of human nature, with a high anthropological view designating humans as still capable of seeking good (despite the impact of original sin), and a low anthropological opinion arguing that humans possess no inherent capacity for good works due to the corruption of sin. In a very Tridentine manner, Iavorskii believed that human nature was only partially depraved, and that humans were able and willing to strive to do good and fulfill the law of God. Original sin, he argued, had a greater impact on the flesh than on the spirit.[53] Thus, Iavorskii fully embraced Bellarmine's understanding of *justitia inhaerens* (justification through inherited rather than imputed righteousness), which emphasized merit and good works as central to salvation. All Christians possessed inner or inherent righteousness that enabled them to commit meritorious deeds actualized through grace. One's salvation depended on personal action to utilize that grace toward good works. When the believer's personal merits were not sufficient for entering paradise after death, either the merits of the church or the purgatorial torments of the "toll-payments [*mytarstva*]" would aid one's journey in the afterlife—a very Catholic formulation.[54]

Iavorskii also professed Bellarminian views on the authority of the church. He believed that the church had two swords (*dva mecha*) or two hands (*dve rutse*)—spiritual and secular—that gave it power in religious and secular affairs. While the state also possessed secular authority, it should not be in conflict with the powers of the church since secular rulers are part of the church.[55]

The view of the parallel power structures of church and state also shaped Stefan's dedication to the patriarchate. Monarchy, according to him, was "the best and most perfect of all governments"; therefore, the church should also be a monarchy, that is, ruled by a patriarch.[56] Without the patriarch, the church "will become headless . . . and will therefore resemble a dead corpse with its head cut off."[57] The best example of such an ecclesiastical monarchy for Stefan was the Patriarchate of Constantinople, whose primacy among the Orthodox churches he compared to that of the pope in Rome and whose canonical sovereignty over Russia he would invoke when he protested the abolition of the patriarchate in 1721.[58] The opinion that the patriarchate could represent a monarchy parallel to that of the tsar was not new in Muscovite circles (it existed in the seventeenth century as well); however, by encasing it within the framework of the two-swords doctrine and the primacy of the Constantinopolitan patriarchate, he gave these ideas a new presentation.

Another important Catholic feature of Iavorskii's theological influence was his understanding of the end times spelled out in his 1703 tract titled "Znameniia prishestviia antikhristova i konchiny veka" (Signs of the coming of Antichrist and the end of the world). Iavorskii's tract (which has never been analyzed in the historiography of the Russian church) actually followed closely a Catholic source, Thomas Malvenda's *De Antichristo Libri Undecim*.[59] As such, it introduced some very novel ideas into the world of Russian eschatology.

Just like Malvenda, Iavorskii believed the coming of Antichrist to be a future event, accompanied by certain signs.[60] On the personal level, the signs were very specific: the Antichrist was supposed to be a Jew from the "tribe of Dan," the devil incarnate, born in Babylon of a virgin and of unknown familial progeny.[61] Two particular events had to precede his coming. One was the propagation of the Gospel around the globe and the other was the "desolation and fall of the Roman monarchy," by which Iavorskii and Malvenda understood the papacy.[62]

This latter idea, that "the power of Rome will disappear when the Antichrist comes," had particular ramifications for the Orthodox context in which Iavorskii wrote.[63] First, Iavorskii took Malvenda's (and generally, Catholic) position that only the Old Rome was the true Rome (that is, the center of global Christianity), noting that Constantinople, which the Orthodox viewed as the "New Rome of Constantine the Great," had been "vanquished" by the Ottomans.[64] This papal Rome, however, remained "standing in the West," and it would survive "until the coming of the Antichrist."[65] Second, this idea also presupposed that there could be no Antichrist while the Roman papacy was alive. In so arguing, Stefan situated the papacy as the sole discernible safeguard against the Antichrist: a strong providential purpose allocated to the pope by an Orthodox bishop!

Iavorskii's list of (rather erudite) adaptations of Catholic dogmatic elements certainly did not stop there. Much like Bellarmine, he declared tradition to be equivalent to scriptural revelation, believed that the church had a duty to execute even repenting heretics, and rejected heliocentrism as the "falsehood" propagated by the "new philosophers." In particular, Iavorskii denounced Copernicus, whose views "contradicted Scripture."[66]

His view of the Reformation adopted Bellarminian language. For example, he referred to Luther as the "new Goliath" who in 1517 assailed "the holy church, the Bride of Christ," that is, the Roman Catholic Church.[67] In other writings, Stefan used even more caustic language to refer to the Protestants: Luther for him was a "vicious thief," while Calvin was a "pig's excrement."[68] The Protestant attack on the Catholics was for Stefan also an attack on the Orthodox. "We know," he wrote, "how the enemy aimed his bow at the Pope and the Roman church, yet his arrows reach us too."[69]

STEFAN'S ORATORY:
THE CLIMAX OF CATHOLIC BAROQUE

In addition to being an erudite theologian, Stefan was a very talented preacher. By 1700 his sermons were making a deep and lasting impression on his listeners in Kiev and Moscow, most notably Ukraine's hetman Ivan Mazepa, Patriarch Adrian, and Peter himself.[70] Feofan Prokopovich, who reformed Russian Orthodox homiletics and eventually banned Iavorskii's Catholic-inspired preaching style, nevertheless praised his rival for his oratorical abilities. He wrote that "hardly anyone in Russia could match him in this regard" and that "his sermons moved the audience to laughter or tears, due to his body movements, his waving of hands, the change of his facial expressions."[71]

Stefan's highly theatrical and emotional preaching style was not of his own invention but rather a thorough adaptation of the Southern European Baroque style of preaching known as the *conceptus* homily, which was popular in Italy and Spain, as well as Poland and Ukraine. Like many things Baroque, this very popular form of Catholic oratory bewilders modern scholars. Yngve Brilioth, for example, called it "one of the most bizarre phenomena in the history of preaching."[72]

First of all, these sermons were often eccentrically allegorical: *conceptus* preachers focused not on expounding Scripture or doctrine (as modern preachers do), but on presenting an "architectonic organization" of emblems, strained parallels, "ingenious ruminations," and comparative images that may or may not have any relationship to the scriptural topic or the feast day on which the sermon was preached.[73] For example, the contents of Juan de Cartagena's (1563–1618) *Homiliae Catholicae* expounded the Virgin Mary's biblical virtues but also compared her to the moon, fish, lilies, birds, and cinnamon.[74] The eminent Benedetto Croce once interpreted this phenomenon as deeply rooted in the aesthetic need of the Italian and Spanish cultures of the seicento to feed "the eye as well as the other senses," with the accompanying flowering of "pageants, both sacred and profane."[75]

Second, the preaching of Baroque *conceptus* sermons was highly theatrical. The spectacle required "intense drama." For example, in Italy, the Jesuit orator Paolo Segneri (1624–1694) licked the floor while preaching, and in Poland, Tomasz Młodzianowski (Stefan Iavorskii's teacher) and Iacinth Mijakowski danced at the pulpit and dressed as cupids.[76] In Spain, Pedro de Valderrama preached Lenten sermons in a dark sanctuary while periodically animating fire torches and trumpets behind the pulpit to emphasize the horrors of hell.[77]

Conceptus preaching (often delivered at the end of the liturgy) spread around the Slavic Orthodox lands of Poland-Lithuania as early as the 1620s.[78] By the 1630s, the Mohyla Academy had adopted *conceptus* sacred rhetoric manuals as part of the required reading for Ukrainian and Belarusian clergy. Among these were the rhetoric textbooks of Cipriano Suárez (1524–93) and Cardinal Francisco de Mendoza (1508–66) as well as the homiletic compilations of Juan Osorio, Juan de Cartagena, and various Polish Jesuits.[79] By the end of the century, the domestic, Ukrainian preaching manuals and compilations predominated. Those composed by Antonii Radivilovskii (d. 1688) and Ioannikii Galiatovskii relied extensively on Catholic works.[80] From Kiev, this style of preaching traveled to Moscow, becoming particularly popular at the court after 1667 with the arrival of Simeon Polotskii (1621–80).[81] Stylistically, Polotskii followed the writings of the Polish Jesuit Szymon Starowolski (1588–1656), but he also embraced rhetorical practices popular with the court preachers in Madrid and Naples, such as those of Cristóbal de Fonseca (1550–1621) and Hortensio Paravicino (1580–1633).[82]

Of all the Ukrainian preachers of the early Petrine era, no one excelled at delivering Baroque homilies as much as Stefan Iavorskii. He was also the last great preacher to employ the *conceptus* method in Russia. This was the climax of Russia's homiletic Baroque. His own rhetoric manual taught this method to aspiring Slavic preachers, including the harmonization of physical actions with the content preached: the movement of the "muscles" with "the matter of the sermon."[83] In my comparative overview of Ukrainian preachers of this time, Iavorskii clearly stood out (in comparison even to Polotskii or Galiatovskii) in the method of "stringing" together the images that were the *least* related to the sermon's theme.[84] For example, his 1708 homily, titled "The Second Tabernacle, Created by Peter for Moses, Which Is the Maritime Fleet," described the apostle Peter's desire to build a tabernacle during the Vision of the Transfiguration, but alleged that if Peter had built such tabernacle, it would surely have been a boat.[85]

Then, the preacher presented a sequence of emblems allegorically associated with boats: Pharaoh's daughter, Moses, Noah, animals in the ark, and of course, the "Russian Noah," the tsar.[86]

A virtuoso in allegory, Stefan also mastered the art of "onomastics"—the mathematical and symbolic interpretation of biblical names and words, rooted in the adaptation of Spanish-Jewish Kabbalah. Although popular with such preachers as Nuñez Delgadillo, Juan de Cartagena, and Stefan's own teacher in Poznań, Tomasz Młodzianowski, it was controversial in both Poland and Spain.[87] Stefan's 1705 sermon "Zhatva" (The Harvest), for example, gave special mathematical meaning to the five letters in the names Maria and Jesus, while another sermon deciphered the "mystery [*taina*]" of the meaning of the name Adam.[88] The four letters of the word "Adam" meant "East [*anatole*], West [*dysis*], North [*arktos*] and South [*mesumbria*]" in Greek.[89]

Stefan's contemporaries acknowledged foreign influences in this Baroque homiletic style. Thus, Feofan Prokopovich noted that Iavorskii's inspiration and teacher, Tomasz Młodzianowski, S.J., was the "king of all obscenities [*rabularum*]" and criticized Stefan's and other Ukrainians' usage of the Spanish *sermonarios* of Juan de Cartagena and Diego Niseno. The Spaniards' rhetoric manuals were the "heaps of dung," he argued, while those who used them were "ignorant and foolish."[90] Similarly, Vockerodt noted that Stefan's "preaching" imitated the "Jesuit manner [*Jesuiter-Manier aufsetzen*], in blabbering [*herplappern*] with many gesticulations [*Gesticulationen*]."[91]

His blabbering, however, impressed audiences and attracted the attention of the elites—a recipe for success for any eighteenth-century clergyman in Russia. In fact, Peter viewed his feast-day sermons "as an indispensable part of the civil-ecclesiastical celebration . . . as were the evening fireworks."[92] The downfall of the preacher came from the content of the sermons, not their theatrical presentation. It was the result of the outbursts of veiled and often allegorical—but still very discernible—criticism of Peter's reforms that the bishop began to engage in after 1710.

THE PROBLEM OF STEFAN

Given the extent of Roman Catholic influence on Stefan Iavorskii's worldview, it is no surprise that the bishop was not without controversy from the first day he set foot in Moscow. The opposition to his views was twofold. On the one hand, he did not convince some of the members of the traditionalist, Muscovite hierarchy that he was fully Orthodox. On the other hand, he did not show enough commitment to Peter's ever-evolving social reforms to gain the tsar's full trust and to avoid friction with the reform-minded nobility.

The first problem—the Muscovite traditionalist opposition—was relatively inconsequential for Iavorskii. Although some of the clergy (like Gavriil Dometskii, Metropolitan Iov, and Bishop Afanasii of Kholmogory) were hostile toward his "Latin" views, the domestic hierarchy was not a cohesive group and some clergy were sympathetic to Stefan.[93] Their opposition was short-lived and was only bolstered somewhat in 1705 by the vilifying missive of the Jerusalem patriarch Dositheos. The letter accused many Ukrainians of being closet Catholics and then specifically requested Peter to remove the "blasphemer" Stefan for his "blasphemous" Catholic-influenced position on transubstantiation.[94] Peter, who saw few equally talented alternatives to Stefan, simply ignored the patriarch's missive.

A much bigger problem was Iavorskii's growing tension with the highest ranks of the country's nobility and most important, Peter himself. Although Stefan did have some powerful sympathizers, such as Admiral Fedor Apraksin, vice-governor of Moscow Vasilii Ershov, and Tsarevich Aleksei, he also had strained relations with a number of senators.[95] Mikhail Samarin, Tikhon Streshnev, Iakov Dolgorukii, and Ivan Musin-Pushkin were among those, who, according to (the pro-Stefan) Archimandrite Leontii Magnitskii "always hated him and sought his death."[96] Musin-Pushkin deserves special mention here due to his enormous authority as the manager of monastic landholdings. He was a nephew of the late Patriarch Ioakim (through his wife, Mavra Savelova) and an ardent reader of theology who knew Latin. Musin-Pushkin often played a decisive role in filling vacant higher clerical positions.[97] In 1708 the British ambassador to Russia referred to him as a "chief officer of state . . . in all ecclesiastical affairs."[98] Such power in the hands of a secular officer certainly did not please Stefan. He often showed hostility to him and on one occasion (in 1710) even preached a sermon against Musin-Pushkin "with so much anger that he forgot where he was present at the time."[99]

Finally, Stefan displeased not only the reformist nobility but the tsar himself. Relations with the monarch deteriorated slowly but surely, so much so that by 1717 the Prussian secretary Vockerodt noted that Peter had become "disillusioned" with Iavorskii. The bishop, he stated, "was so carried away by Papist rules about the prerogatives of the clergy [*Praerogativen der Clerisei*] and its independence [from the state]" that Stefan's views became "diametrically [*diametralement*] opposed" to those of the tsar.[100] Several of the steps in Stefan's escalating tensions with the tsar demonstrate the chronology of the conflict up to 1717.

The first step was the exarch's handling of the Grigorii Talitskii affair in 1700–1704. This Moscow dissenter declared Peter to be the Antichrist and the cutting of beards to be a violation of God's law, and spread this opinion among the Old Believers by printing leaflets from his home press.[101] Stefan's refutation came only in 1703 with the abovementioned adaptation of Tomas Malvenda's tract.

Not only was the tract unpersuasive, but its effect was opposite of what Iavorskii had intended. His 1703 essay actually strengthened the opinions of many dissenters (like Varlaam Levin) that Peter indeed was the Antichrist! Iavorskii's eschatology appeared to be easily adaptable to the dissenters' signs of the end times: they viewed Moscow as Stefan's Babylon and they conflated the vacancy of the Moscow Patriarchate with Malvenda's doctrine that the vacancy of the papal throne would precede the end times.[102] Furthermore, Stefan's attempt to defend Peter by using clumsy Kabbalistic calculations of 666 were so "badly" composed that they earned "the mockery [*ridicule*] of the whole of Europe."[103] Although, to Stefan's credit, it is hardly surprising that the Muscovite Old Believers did not grasp all the fine details of Spanish onomastic method and that the calculations were not convincing.

It is also likely that Stefan may have been half-hearted in his defense of the tsar. This is particularly seen in the aftershocks of the Talitskii affair when in 1718 the mutinous metropolitan Dosifei of Rostov (d. 1718) declared his support for some of Talitskii's ideas and endorsed Peter's estranged wife Evdokiia for the succession of power. Despite the fact that Dosifei's attacks against the tsar were political in nature, Stefan opposed his defrocking. Only a patriarch had the legal authority to defrock, he argued, a position that irritated Peter.[104]

Then, on the Feast of St. John Chrysostom, November 13, 1708—the day after Stefan anathematized Mazepa—Iavorskii composed a daring sermon. In it, he first compared Peter's *assamblei* (secular European style parties) to the iniquitous revelries of Balthasar, and then criticized the tsar's divorce of his first wife, Evdokiia Lopukhina, by forcing her "to live with the angels" (that is, to join a convent). While Evdokiia lived with the angelic nuns, Iavorskii continued, the tsar cohabitated with a "whore [*bludnitsa*]," the future empress Catherine.[105] Although the first part of that sermon remained unspoken (marked *non-dictum* in the text), the second part was *dictum*, and the manuscript circulated in Moscow in its entirety nevertheless.[106]

Then came the Ides of March of 1712, with Stefan's controversial sermon in the middle of that month expressing open sympathy for the rebellious tsarevich Aleksei as "our only hope."[107] Unlike the previous outbursts of criticism, this one was conspicuously public and was directed to an audience that included several senators, including the Senate's president Iakov Dolgorukii.[108] In a very clear way, the sermon was an offer of support (to Aleksei, against his father) and a voice of opposition to the tsar. The scandal was immediate. The sermon was seized by the senate and Peter demanded Stefan's apology, issuing a three-year ban on his preaching.[109] There was now an open conflict between the exarch and the monarch.

The 1713–18 Tveritinov heresy trial further exacerbated the tension. The controversy involved three urban professionals in Moscow and St. Petersburg who held semi-Calvinist views on the Eucharist and icon veneration. Two of them, Dmitrii Tveritinov (a physician) and Mikhail Andreev (a fiscal inspector), denied any heterodoxy before the Senate, and Peter wanted to close the case. Stefan, however, did not trust the accused and sought to move the case from the Senate in St. Petersburg to an ecclesiastical trial in Moscow.[110] Furthermore, Stefan insisted that the heretics must be burned even if they recanted— a theologically Bellarminian view.[111]

Although Moscow's vice governor, Vasilii Ershov, supported Stefan, the trial only widened the rift between the exarch and the Senate. According to the contemporary report of archimandrite Leontii Magnitskii (an ally of Stefan), most of the governing noblemen seemed prejudiced against the prosecution. Ivan Musin-Pushkin, for example, did not see heresy in their views, just "opinions."[112] Senator Mikhail Samarin was not only "filled with the same spirit as the accused" but was openly their "follower."[113] Stefan's desperation in prosecuting the case reached its climax in 1714 when he sought to condemn with anathema anyone aiding or abetting the heretics.[114] Such threats were directed at those free-thinking secular elites who sought to close the trial, but some noblemen were nonetheless sympathetic to Stefan. Mikhail Kropotkin, a lower nobleman and a friend of the vice-governor, was alarmed by the spread of Protestant ideas around him. "Wherever eyes don't see, ears hear, that the Lutheran heresy is destroying our souls," he noted in 1714.[115] Just like Iavorskii, Kropotkin saw Protestantism as the tyranny of secular elites over the church. Luther, he said, "rejected the authority of the pope and the bishops and handed it over to nobles and governors."[116] Peter, he feared, wanted to do the same.

These incidents did not exhaust the list of conflicting views between Peter and Stefan, but certainly represented some of the most crucial ones. In light of these problems, the tsar and many of the capital's elites were certainly ready to welcome a hierarch more willing to reform the church. The answer to their search came from Kiev. As early as 1709 Peter requested the governor of Kiev, Dmitrii M. Golitsyn, to look for reform-minded and loyal clergymen in the city. After some time the governor replied, "In all of Kiev, I found only one man, the prefect of the school of the Brethren Monastery, who is favorable toward us."[117] That prefect was none other than Feofan Prokopovich.

2

Escape from Rome

The Peregrinations of
Feofan Prokopovich, 1696–1704

This monk whom tsar considered as a possible ally of his reform was Feofan Prokopovich, or, properly, Feofan Prokopovich II. Although as a young man Feofan received his education in Rome, his sojourn in the Eternal City would become a catalyst for his emphatic rejection of Roman Catholic theology, much like Martin Luther's pilgrimage to the Holy See paved the way for his disillusionment with the papacy. Furthermore, Feofan's sensational escape from Rome to the German-speaking lands in 1701 was a watershed moment in his intellectual formation as a philo-Protestant reformer, resolutely opposed to Catholic influence in Muscovite and Ukrainian Orthodoxy. This event led not only to Feofan's intellectual conversion but to the introduction of a radically new variety of theology into the intellectual milieu of Ukrainian and Russian Orthodoxy, theology that would lead to bitter contestation of doctrine among the church elites of the Petrine era.

The future reformer was born in Kiev as either Eleazar or Elisei Tsereiskii, either in 1677 or 1681, into the Tsereiskii family of merchants, who may have been tied to the wax candle trade.[1] Elisei was orphaned at a young age and raised by his maternal uncle, Feofan Prokopovich I (d. 1689), the rector and prefect of the Mohyla Academy. He would later adopt his mother's last name, Prokopovich, and a different first name in honor of that uncle. Eager to pursue an academic career in the church, the young Tsereiskii-Prokopovich sought out theological learning abroad. Around 1696, he moved to Poland, became a Uniate, and took courses in the Basilian monastery school of the city of Włodzimierz (today's Volodymyr in Volhynia). The Uniate Catholic metropolitan Lev Shliub-Zalenskii (a Roman alumnus) noticed Prokopovich's erudition and within a year or so ordained him as a deacon and issued a recommendation for him to pursue further studies in Rome at the Pontifical Greek College.[2]

Figure 1. The Church of St. Athanasius, next to the Pontifical Greek College (Collegio Greco), Feofan's alma mater, on Via del Babuino in Rome. Author's photo.

The Pontifical Greek College of Rome

Founded in 1577 by Pope Gregory XIII, the Pontifical Greek College still occupies a limestone building on the quiet Via del Babuino (some three hundred meters from the Spanish Steps). The establishment of the college was part of what Zdenko Zlatar noted as a larger movement of establishing "Counter-Reformation schools," during this period, including the Collegium Germanicum (1552) and the Collegium Armenorum (1584).[3] The institution educated the Uniate believers in the Christian Eastern Mediterranean, mostly Greek-speaking areas with strong spiritual ties to Rome that stretched back to the Union of Florence-Ferrara (1447). As the official *Historia Collegii Graeci de Urbi* manuscript in the Vatican Library relates, the institution was dedicated to "safeguarding the true religious doctrines" of those "oppressed by the Turks" after the Ottoman conquest.[4] It was not envisioned for the Greeks alone, however: the College also opened its doors to the "Ruthenians," early modern term for Eastern Slavs.[5] During the seventeenth and eighteenth centuries hundreds of Ukrainian and Belarusian students enrolled there, while at least half of the Uniate metropolitans of Kiev were its alumni.[6]

What did these students learn in Rome? Despite its lofty name, the Pontifical Greek College provided only basic education in the first two hundred years of its existence. There were courses in classical languages and literature, some philosophy, and theologically, some basic catechetical instruction covering just the "initial rudiments of faith."[7] A beginner's curriculum certainly made sense, as most of the resident students of the college were Greek boys or teenagers from wealthy Uniate families from places like Corfu and Crete. In the roster of alumni, Ukrainian young men stand out as an odd exception to the multitude of eight- to sixteen-year-old Greeks, who populated the dormitories of St. Athanasius.[8]

Most of Ukrainian students were no longer in need of basic studies, having received the basics of humanist education (such as Greek and Latin languages and poetics) in such places as the Kiev-Mohyla Academy. So, their sojourn on Via del Babuino was mostly residential in nature: they stayed in the dormitories while seeking out more advanced classes around the Eternal City. After the Jesuits took over as the patron order of the college in 1622, East Slavic students gained easier access to courses taught in the Jesuit-run schools of the city, namely, the Collegium Urbanum de Propaganda Fide and the Collegium Romanum, not to mention access to their libraries.[9]

Temporary Apostasy; Or, Expedient Dissimulation

Not all students in the college came from the Uniate families. Some were proforma Catholics, who had grown up as Eastern Orthodox, converted to the

Union, and sometimes even joined the Uniate Basilian Order for the purpose of obtaining education. This temporary apostasy (for a lack of a better term) or pretense to conversion came with different degrees of sincerity and allowed an Orthodox student to embrace the Union with Rome primarily for educational gain.

Such expedient dissimulation was quietly promoted by many Orthodox hierarchs. Thus, ecumenical patriarchs Jeremias II Tranos (in office 1572–95) and Neophytos II (1602–12) openly encouraged Greek Orthodox youth to study there; the latter desired to send his nephew there.[10] In Ukraine, Peter Mohyla (1596–1647) actively encouraged temporary conversion to the Union, paying, for example, for Lazar' Baranovich's studies in Wilno and Kalisz.[11] The Kiev Academy celebrated Lazar's sojourn with the "Angelic Basilians" (his temporary joining of the Catholic Basilian order).[12] The fact that such a practice existed was neither exceptional nor confined to a particular geography. The European "art of dissimulation" had many practitioners among the Jesuit missionaries in South Asia, the Jews in Spain, and the Huguenots in France, as well as many others.[13]

So, what did the Roman hierarchy think about this temporary apostasy? Most of the available records point to their quiet toleration—if not abetment—of the practice. First, the fact that the Sacred Congregation for the Propagation of the Faith (or Propaganda Fide) began to discourage this practice starting in the early eighteenth century indicates that the phenomenon was (unofficially) previously tolerated.[14] Secondly, as Ukrainian historian Dmytro Blažejovskyj had noted, the Book of Oaths taken by the Ukrainian students enrolling in Rome's prestigious Collegium Urbanum in the eighteenth century revealed a curious fact: those students originating from the dioceses of Kiev (and likely the Hetmanate at large) were exempt from taking an oath (il giuramento) of loyalty and devotion to the Uniate rite and the Holy See.[15] It is highly likely that such an official exemption served to accommodate the conscience of the Orthodox students who temporarily converted to Catholicism.

The description of this practice of quiet toleration is also found in the 1736 *Vita* (biography) of Feofan Prokopovich written by Theophil Siegfried Bayer (1694–1738), a member of the St. Petersburg Academy of Sciences. Bayer stated that the "Jesuits" in Rome recruited the non–Roman Catholics (including Feofan) purposefully for their causes. These students, he wrote, "would be sent [*mittuntur*] to parts of the [Christian] Church and to those that they call infidels [*ad partes, vel Ecclesiae, vel quas vocant infidelium*] to promote [*promoveant*] the union between Greeks and Latins as much as possible [*ut quantum possint*]."[16]

This practice of expedient dissimulation swelled the ranks of Ukrainian Orthodox clergy with well-educated men. In fact, by the end of the seventeenth century, virtually every professor in Kiev and in Moscow's Slavo-Greco-Latin Academy as well as numerous Orthodox hierarchs in Ukraine had studied abroad. Among these people were metropolitan of Kiev Varlaam Iasinskii (1627–1707), who spent almost ten years in Austria and Poland, and his heir on the metropolitan throne, Ioasaf Krokovskii (d. 1718), who studied philosophy and theology in Rome.[17] Among the rectors of Kiev-Mohyla Academy, Gedeon Odorskii (d. 1715), Prokopii Kalachinskii (d. 1707), and the above-mentioned Baranovich studied in Poland, Lithuania, and Austria.[18] The hegumen of Tobolsk's Znamenskii Monastery and Prokopovich's older half-brother Feofan Leontovich (d. 1700), also studied in Rome as well as Paris.[19] Among the foreign-educated hierarchs who later moved to Moscow to form a philo-Catholic party were Stefan Iavorskii, educated in Lwów, Lublin, Poznań, and Wilno; the archbishop Feoflikat Lopatinskii, who studied in Jesuit schools in L'viv and in Austria; and the future bishop of Smolensk Gedeon Vishnevskii.[20] The latter studied in Rome in the 1690s, after which he traveled north to complete a doctoral degree at the Jesuit College of St. Barbara in Krakow.[21] All three became lifelong enemies of Prokopovich.

FEOFAN IN ROME

Initially, the young Ukrainian was a student without reproach. The archives of the Greek College and the Sacred Congregation for the Propagation of the Faith indicate that Samuil Tsereiskii ("Cereizcki") of "Kiev [*Chiovia*]" enrolled on November 14, 1698, with the ecclesiastical rank of deacon.[22] He did not come alone: two other Ukrainians, Innokentii Pihovskii and Germanus [*sic*] Kozachenko, arrived and enrolled at the same time.[23] While residing in the college's dormitories, Prokopovich sought advanced classes in theology and philosophy at the Collegium Urbanum de Propaganda Fide, which was just a short walk from Via del Babuino on the southern end of the Piazza di Spagna.[24] The *Registro dei nomi* of the Urbanum in fact listed Samuil and Kozachenko among its students.[25]

In Rome, Tsereiskii was a rather successful student. The records of the Greek College noted "superior progress and superior talents [*ingenii optime optimeque progressus*]" and the fact that he "publicly defended his thesis after the conclusion of the full course in philosophy with praise [*defendit publice totam philosophia cum laude*]."[26] In addition to the Collegium Urbanum, Feofan also likely took classes in the Collegium Romanum, the forerunner of today's pre-eminent Pontifical Gregorian University. Bayer's *Vita* and the 1735 record of

Prokopovich's conversations with St. Petersburg's Pietists both mention his studies in that college.[27]

FEOFAN'S DOUBTS

Although quite impressed by the education and the libraries of the Eternal City, the young Ukrainian grew increasingly disappointed. Hearing Innocent XII (d. 1700) denounce the Eastern "schismatics" left him "struck as if by a heavy bolt of lightning [*brutus fulmen*]"—a metaphor used by Feofan's German biographer Bayer that resembled Martin Luther's own lightning-strike experience.[28] This condemnation of his fellow "non-Uniate Ruthenians" did not sit well with someone who had spent most of his adolescent life as Orthodox and whose ties to the Union were fairly fresh and likely motivated by the desire to obtain an education.[29]

Studies in Rome also exposed Prokopovich to the more sinister sides of the life of the hierarchy. According to Bayer's biography, Feofan "investigated [*investigavit*] the ecclesiastic, civic and military forms of the Pontifical regime" and suffered disappointment when he "discovered the shadowy arts of the Tiberian muses" during the troubled Conclave of 1700, when the Holy See remained vacant from September 27 to November 23.[30] This was the beginning of the continent-wide War of the Spanish Succession between the Bourbons and the Habsburgs and the Conclave was bitterly divided between the pro-Austrian and pro-French factions.[31]

In addition to hearing about the intrigues, Prokopovich also witnessed the low level of spirituality in the Eternal City. "Nowhere do people doubt the truth of Christian religion more than in Italy," Feofan used to say.[32] Feofan was so "horrified" by various "religious scams [*piae fraudes*] found in Italy" that he "could not speak about it without emotion."[33] *Piae fraudes* is exactly the term that Martin Luther used to describe the "errors" of the papacy (such as the indulgences) that he also observed in Rome.[34] Among such "vanities [*bezdeliia*]," he recalled later in 1721, were the body of St. Stephen, "in Rome, at the church of St. Lawrence outside the city walls [Basilica San Lorenzo]," as well as "the nails of the Lord's Cross and the milk of the Holy Mother of God, which are plentiful throughout Italy."[35]

Books and learning, which were copious in Rome, only amplified Feofan's doubts. During his studies, he befriended an elderly Jesuit priest, who cared for the young Ukrainian with "fatherly love" and allowed him access to several "secret [*arcana*] libraries" in the city.[36] In those libraries, he discovered "unedited [*non castratos*]" volumes of classical and patristic authors, Renaissance literature (like Jacopo Sadoleto), and Protestant authors and books by condemned heretics like Aonio Paleario (1500–1570).[37] Prokopovich took to reading this literature very seriously, "studying these books day and night . . . often abstaining from meals [*saepe a cibo abstinens*], he pressed all the sap and juice from them."[38] According to a memoir by Feofan's personal acquaintance, pastor Albert Anton Vierorth of Reval, the book that made the deepest impression on Feofan's young mind was Martin Luther's *Babylonian Captivity of the Church*, found in "the library of the [Roman] mission-college." After reading this treatise, Vierorth wrote, "his former anxiety [*Unruhe*] increased and he found himself forced to flee the place."[39]

ESCAPE FROM ROME:
THE "GREAT SCANDAL"

Disillusioned with Rome, the young Prokopovich fled the Greek College, "without a single cause and with a great scandal," on October 28, 1701, as the records attest.[40] His departure must have been a surprise, since this line in his record contrasted sharply with previous references to his "superior talents."[41] In the late 1720s one of Feofan's adversaries, Markell Rodyshevskii, also noted the scandalous nature of his departure from Rome, writing in his "Biography

Figure 2. Feofan Prokopovich's alumni records at the Collegio Greco in Rome. Author's photo.

of Heretic Feofan" that the student "fled from the uproar [*ot shumu*]."[42] Roman officials later tried to explain the former student's unusual departure by questioning his mental state: the Collegio Greco's records stated that he "returned to his homeland, Kiev, and lapsed into dementia [*in dementiam abiisse*]."[43]

What exactly this "dementia" entailed is not altogether clear, but the subsequent records in Rome talk about a form of a spiritual apostasy. The 1710 report on the status of the Uniate Church submitted to the Sacred Congregation for the Propagation of the Faith speaks about Samuil Tsereiskii, "a former Basilian monk and an alumnus of our Greek College," who had become an "apostate."[44] Much later, in 1728, the congregation discussed a certain "Teofan Prokopowicz . . . schismatic and an alumnus of this city's Greek College" who was introducing "the heresies of Luther and Calvin" in Ukraine (*Ukraina*).[45] The congregation seems to have been quite dismayed that a student of such an illustrious institution would embrace "heresy."[46]

The scandal of Feofan's abrupt departure in 1701 persisted in the memory of the Roman Curia for three decades. In 1735, the congregation moved to end the toleration of temporary conversion for Orthodox students based on the memory of Prokopovich, who "vomited and cursed against the religion and the Holy See."[47] Then in 1736 the archbishop of Vienna, Sigismund von Kollonitz, brought up Feofan's "drying up of the mind" in his call for vigilance in identifying potential troublemakers among Eastern Slavic students.[48]

Return to Ukraine: A German Stopover

Feofan's exact route back to Ukraine is not fully known. Theophil Siegfried Bayer noted that Prokopovich took the difficult and perilous journey through Switzerland via Ticino and the St. Gotthard Pass, as opposed to the Brenner-Innsbruck pass that Ukrainians usually took on their way home. The reason was to avoid the hostilities raging throughout Central Europe during the War of the Spanish Succession (1701–14).[49]

Although not much is yet known about his sojourn in Germany, Feofan repeatedly spoke of his stopover in German Protestant lands en route back to Kiev.[50] In a conversation with Christian Haumann (1692–1734), a Halle Pietist and headmaster of the Lutheran school in Moscow, Prokopovich related that he traveled directly to Germany by crossing the Italian Alps.[51] Gottfried Himler (d. 1737), the rector of the cathedral school in Reval (Tallin), who met with Feofan in 1724 in St. Petersburg, also related Feofan's travels in Germany and his study of German theological works.[52]

Yet perhaps the most detailed description of Feofan's route through Germany was the account of the Swedish ambassador to Russia, Josias Cederhjelm, who was well connected to the circle of Pietists in Halle (where Feofan also kept contacts) and who met with Prokopovich personally in 1727.[53] Feofan divulged to the ambassador how, in his younger days, he became disillusioned with Rome and also was "not satisfied in his conscience regarding the faith of the Greek teachers of the church."[54] He traveled through Germany on his return trip home where "the writings of [Balthasar] Meisner [1587–1626] first opened his eyes." The young student continued reading other Wittenberg theologians, including Martin Chemnitz (1522–86) and Nicolaus Hunnius (1585–1643), as well as the Strasbourg scholars Johann Danhauer (1603–66) and Johann Schmid (d. 1671). From their books, "he took many of their theses [for his own writings] even if he did not name the authors."[55]

Feofan also developed strong connections with a number of contemporary German scholars, especially his "dearest brothers [*fratres carissimi*]" of the Pietist circle in Halle.[56] Halle was not just a physical location in Saxony but a focal point of the early Enlightenment (*Frühaufklärung*) in Europe, being part of the enlightened "Halle-Leipzig-Jena Triangle."[57] Among the Pietist scholars who regularly corresponded with Feofan were Johann Franz Buddeus, Daniel Ernst Jablonski, August Hermann Francke, Johann Peter Kohl, and Georg Bilfinger.[58] He also displayed some familiarity with Germany in his 1717 St. Petersburg sermon that praised the land as "the first queen of Europe . . . banner of other kingdoms, mother of all countries." "Whoever visits Germany," he wrote, "discovers an orderly organization of the public government, a kindness of customs, a pleasantness of mind and conversation."[59]

PROKOPOVICH IN KIEV

After his stopover in the German lands, the young monk Samuil-Elisei Tsereiskii arrived in Ukraine a new man. He quickly professed commitment to Orthodoxy, taking up the new monastic name of Feofan Prokopovich II in honor of his maternal uncle Feofan Prokopovich, formerly rector of the Mohyla Academy. Like other foreign-educated Ukrainian monks, he started teaching at the Mohyla Academy and rose through the ranks quickly. In 1705 he started teaching poetics, attaining, by 1707, the status of prefect and instructor of philosophy, and by 1708, the privilege of teaching theology, as stated in his handwritten manuscript of the course. In 1711 he became the rector of the academy.[60]

Several factors allowed Prokopovich to rise so rapidly in the academic ranks. One was the fact that he joined the staff of the academy during a shortage of educators when virtually all of most valued faculty (for example, Feofilakt Lopatinskii) had moved to Moscow.[61] Another factor was Feofan's cultivation of positive relations with the most influential people in Kiev, such as the

aggressively anti-Jesuit metropolitan Varlaam Iasinskii (d. 1707), who engaged
in written anti-Catholic polemic and corresponded with Danzig's Polish Protestant jurist and advocate Johann Ernst von der Linde (1651–1721).[62] Furthermore, Feofan enjoyed cordial relations with St. Sophia's archdeacon Ioanikii
Seniutovich, whose real-power influence often surpassed that of the metropolitans in Kiev.[63] And, above all, he made a very good impression on the
military governor of the city, Peter's trusted man, Count Dmitrii Golitsyn.[64]

A third but very important factor was the novelty of his teaching. While
teaching philosophy, Feofan criticized the hitherto prevalent curriculum based
on Thomas Aquinas, Duns Scotus, and Albertus Magnus; he also rejected the
geocentrist physics part of the philosophy course by advocating the heliocen-
trist views of Galileo Galilei, Nicolaus Copernicus, and Tycho Brahe.[65] In one
of his satirical poems addressed to the pope, he mixed his rejection of geocentrism with a virulent critique of the papal position. "God created Galileo's
stars," he wrote to the pontiff, while "your stars are made by the devil."[66]

Galileo and heliocentrism were not only novel topics but were also proscribed
in Kiev, as noted by contemporary historian of Ukrainian science Iaroslav
Matviishyn.[67] Geocentrism was official dogma not only in Kiev, but also in the
Moscow Academy where Stefan taught at the time. Thus, Feofan's views in
this matter evolved cautiously. In his 1705–6 philosophy course, he expressed
doubts about the Copernican system and embraced the system of Brahe.[68] Then
his 1711 theology course declared that Copernican theory could be proven "by
physical and mathematical evidence," and thus one must understand "the reference in the Holy Scripture [to the rotating Sun] not in the literal but in the
allegorical sense."[69] After moving to St. Petersburg in 1717, Feofan came to
embrace the Copernican system even further as he conducted astronomical
observations at Alexander Menshikov's observatory in Oranienbaum as well as
at his makeshift facility at home, set up with the approximately fourteen astronomical devices in his possession.[70] At the first-ever astronomical debate held
in Russia at the Academy of Sciences in March of 1728, Feofan sided with the
Copernicans represented by Joseph-Nicolas de L'Isle.[71]

SALVATION ACCORDING TO FEOFAN

As he rejected official Catholic geocentrism, he also rejected Catholic influences in theology. In doctrinal writings his embrace of Protestant learning was
very pronounced. While teaching in Kiev, Feofan overhauled the theology
curriculum by rejecting Thomist scholasticism and replacing it with chapters
from Lutheran and Reformed authors, like Johann Andreas Quenstdet (1617–
88), Amandus Polanus (d. 1610), Marcus Friedrich Wendelin (d. 1652), and

Martin Chemnitz, among others.[72] His chapter on the interpretation of Scripture was thoroughly borrowed (often verbatim) from preeminent Lutheran theologian Johann Gerhard's *Tractatus de legitima Scripturae Sacrae interpretatione* (see appendix, table 2).

Given the wide array of Protestant authors that inspired Feofan, his theological relationship to Protestantism was rather eclectic; he never professed allegiance to any school of Reformation thought. He was also—despite various speculations—not a Protestant, professing strictly Orthodox views on the rejection of the Filioque in the Nicene Creed and the incorruptibility of the relics found in the Kievan Caves Monastery.[73] As the next several chapters will demonstrate, Protestant theology shaped most of Feofan's doctrinal worldview, but he embraced those positions because he believed them to be truly and originally Orthodox and because he believed that Protestant formulations were cognitively effective weapons in cleansing the church from the "Papist" influence of the prior century.

The doctrine with perhaps the most Protestant influence in Feofan's theology was his new teaching on salvation, a view that embraced the primacy of Lutheran *sola fide* and rejected the absolute necessity of good works or special feats of piety. His soteriological position, based on the low-anthropological premise of total depravity,[74] argued that one could never merit salvation and that one obtained the remission of sins and justification free (*gratis*) through "justifying faith [*fides justificans*]" and by grace alone. Prokopovich called it legal justification—*justificatio forensis*—meaning that one became righteous (justified) as if in a legal Roman forum, regardless of one's good works.[75] In a typical Lutheran fashion, good works for Feofan were not the cause but the consequence of justification (*fructus justificationis*).[76] However, even then, Prokopovich distinguished between *opera in radice* (a kind of intention to do good), which was a necessary fruit of faith, and *opera in actu* (actual good works), which in themselves were not necessary.[77]

Prokopovich's soteriology directly opposed the views of his nemesis Stefan Iavorskii and the views of the Muscovite hierarchy, who stressed the necessity of good works and feats of piety (especially monastic asceticism) for gaining salvation in the afterlife. Thus, Feofan's "teaching of free justification through Christ" was the chief source of contention with the philo-Catholic hierarchs in Moscow.[78] His new formulation of salvation served as an important base from which Prokopovich built bridges to doctrinal positions in the Russian church that significantly revised previously held views on a variety of issues. Much like in Reformation Europe, the implications of *sola fide* doctrine in Russia were broad, calling into question the traditional understandings of asceticism, monasticism, fasting, icon veneration, the purpose of ceremonies, church-state relations, and more. Furthermore, his emphasis on the "perfection" of Scripture also challenged the conventional understanding of church tradition (*predanie*) as no longer doctrinally valid.[79]

FEOFAN AND THE END TIMES

Protestant theology not only influenced how Prokopovich interpreted salvation, but also how he understood eschatology, the doctrine of the End Times. Unlike Iavorskii, Feofan rejected the notion that the Antichrist would be a Jew from the tribe of Dan. He even rejected the notion that the appearance of the Antichrist would be a future event. Instead, he blended his acquired revulsion for the papacy with his affinity for Luther's early understanding of eschatology to argue that the pope was indeed the Antichrist, or, as he called him, "the Great Antichrist who Already Appeared to the World a Long Time Ago."[80] In general terms, Feofan argued that biblical characteristics of the Antichrist parallel the institution of the papacy, such as its longevity, luxury (*prelest'*), and tyrannical persecution of dissenters.[81] In specific terms, Prokopovich argued that the pope fit the profile of the "whore [*bludnitsa*]" from "the city of Great Babylon, the mother of all fornicators and debauchery."[82] Just like that "whore," the pope "has a female appearance, decorated in gold, jewels, and pearls." Similar to the prostitutes serving wine in Rome's many "secret" houses, the pope "serves wine in a golden cup under the name of [secret] mystery."[83] Although some of Feofan's details may have reflected his own experiences in Rome, this was also the way that early Protestants described the papacy, going all the way back to Luther's 1520 treatise, *The Babylonian Captivity.*[84]

Feofan's eschatological views were very important for several reasons. First, they promoted the idea that no Russian monarch could become an Antichrist. Considering Talitskii's accusations proclaiming Peter the Great to be the eschatological villain, Feofan's position that the Antichrist had already come "a long time ago" seemed a much stronger vindication of the tsar than Iavorskii's feeble defense. Secondly, Feofan did not only attack the person of the pope, but also the institutional style of ruling the church. "The name of the Antichrist denotes a kingdom or a form of government," he wrote.[85] This would become important in 1721, when Feofan (together with Peter) attacked the Russian patriarchate as a form of ecclesiastical government suspiciously resembling the papacy. Thirdly, Feofan's eschatological proclamation gave him rhetorical ammunition to dismiss any criticism of his views as essentially anti-Christian. Those disagreeing with Feofan were simply the "disciples of the Antichrist," spreading their "tales [*basni*]."[86]

The "Unbearable Yoke" of Feofan's Theology

Although his official biographer, Bayer, praised his teaching as a "new, clear, and comprehensible method through which he awakened an entire new generation to charity and humanism,"[87] Feofan's enemies at the Moscow Academy were outraged at his new teachings. In 1710 Feofilakt Lopatinskii and Stefan Iavorskii complained about the decline in the quality of Kievan schools, while Muscovite traditionalist Metropolitan Iov in 1711 noted that the schools were no longer "fully Orthodox and humble."[88] Markell Rodyshevskii, who witnessed the transformation in Kiev and later allied himself with Iavorskii's party in Moscow, accused Prokopovich of spreading heterodoxy. He stated, "[Prokopovich] began to teach his heresy back in Kiev, not only orally but also in the written form in accordance with the Calvinist, Lutheran, and other heresies. Today, many of his disciples and others have his heretical books in Kiev and many people are captivated by his heretical teachings."[89]

Feofan's Latin-language theology courses certainly raised a few eyebrows among the educated clergy in Moscow and Kiev, but few outside the walls of the elite academies could read Latin. Feofan's bold reformist worldview, however, did not stay within those walls. In 1712 he vernacularized his attack on the "Papist" view of salvation by good works through his militant Russian language treatise *Ob neudobenosimom zakonnom ige* (The unbearable yoke of law). The essay's success is attributed to Feofan's powerful "patron" in Moscow, Count Ivan Musin-Pushkin, a lay afficionado of theology and an enemy of Iavorskii.[90] Written for a lay audience, the manuscript circulated in Moscow under the titles of *Igo gospodne blago* (The yoke of the Lord is good) and as *Izveshcheniie* (The declaration).[91] The work presented a very Protestant teaching on law, grace, justification, and salvation. Weighing in on the subject of the centuries-old Christian theological question of the merits of law and grace for human salvation (also known as the Law and Gospel debate), he adopted a more Protestant view that humans are too depraved to be able to gain salvation by fulfilling the law through good works or following ceremonial, divine, or moral precepts, and that the law in itself constituted an "unbearable yoke."[92] Salvation and justification, the treatise argued, were available through faith only, a "light yoke."[93] As Feofan explained, "the light yoke of Christ is not the law of God, as some think. It is the grace of God that forgives sin, not the oppressive torture [*istiazatel'stvo*] of being sinless."[94] The emotional ease that such a yoke produced allowed Orthodox believers to live with their "shortcomings and sins, since those shortcomings are forgiven by Christ."[95] It would also help them stop "being burdened by law" and abandon the elusive "search to be sinless."[96]

On the superficial level, this work was the first instance of an Orthodox adaptation of the Protestant hermeneutical principles of "Law and the Gospel," explained in the 1577 *Formula of Concord* (article 5), a staple of Reformed and Lutheran theology alike.[97] Yet, on a deeper level, the work offered relief to a hypothetical layperson burdened by the requirements of church regulations, even if it lacked clarity on the amount of freedom that grace provided to such a person.

This lack of clarity and possible license for libertinism made the treatise an easy target of Iavorskii's wrath. In a show of theological force, Iavorskii quoted the fifth, sixth, and ninth canons of the Council of Trent against Feofan to argue that God's grace did not free believers from the law, but further obliged them to follow it.[98] He also attacked the superficiality of the work's social ethics that lightened Muscovite believers' obligations. This treatise, he argued, was written by "the enemies of God's law who are lazy or unwilling to follow the Lord's commandments . . . and who want to circumvent [*izviniaiutsia ot*] them due to their laziness or melancholy [*ounynie*]."[99] Thus, Feofan's theology simply appealed to the slackers within Russian society, who lacked proper devotional discipline.

Iavorskii's views had allies in the Moscow Academy. The Likhoudes brothers came out with a critical evaluation of Prokopovich's work as "appearing to contain heretical theses [*theses esse hereticas*]."[100] Finally, Feofilakt Lopatinskii composed an even more detailed analysis of Prokopovich's points, titled similarly *Igo gospodne blago* (The yoke of the Lord is good). This work concluded that Feofan "introduced Reformation ideas [*mudrovaniia onaia reformatskaia*] into the Russian world, ideas that were hitherto unheard of in the Orthodox Church."[101]

Feofan would respond to the refutation later in 1716, accusing Lopatinskii of being "the enemy of God's grace" and of using "sophistic empty words" (code for Catholic scholasticism) instead of the sound doctrine. The debate rested there: neither author could define what constituted the originally Orthodox teaching of justification outside the Protestant or Catholic formulations of this concept. Instead, both focused on excluding the other based on the foreign influence of their argument. Feofan excluded Iavorskii's and Lopatinskii's view as heterodox, because it appeared to be influenced by Catholicism and the Tridentine formulations.[102] Similarly, Lopatinskii accused Prokopovich of simply promoting "Reformation ideas," without going into detail as to what the non-Tridentine or genuinely Orthodox definitions of justification were.

CONCLUSION

While this debate raged between 1713 and 1716 in Moscow, Feofan was still in Ukraine, using his pen to respond to his critics. Yet his notoriety was growing and with it, calls for the rector's promotion in the church ranks. Peter I and

Prince Menshikov became very interested in Feofan's future. Both in fact already knew Feofan in some way. In 1706 Prokopovich delivered a homily during the tsar's visit to Kiev, and again, in 1709, when he preached his famous sermon about the Battle of Poltava. The latter sermon made enough of an impression on the tsar that he soon had it committed to print and circulated in Moscow and St. Petersburg. Feofan also preached in the army chapel during Peter's 1711 Balkan campaign.[103] The tsar's 1711 visit to Ukraine also coincided with Feofan's promotion to the rector of Kiev-Mohyla Academy and the head of the Brotherhood Epiphany Monastery. According to Vockerodt, the tsar's acquaintance with Feofan was fortuitous for Peter as he "encountered the exact [*praecise*] same attitudes in him as he [the tsar] wanted to promote in his empire."[104]

Favorable relations with Prince A. D. Menshikov also played a crucial role in Feofan's promotion. Feofan delivered an oration on December 5, 1709, when Menshikov was in Kiev, listing the prince's military exploits and comparing him to his namesake Prince Aleksandr Nevskii.[105] Shortly afterward, Menshikov pressed the idea of inviting the rector to St. Petersburg further.[106] The prince's lobbying for Feofan intensified with Iavorskii's fall from grace in March of 1712.[107]

Yet, despite such lobbying, it was only in 1716 that Feofan received an official invitation and arrived in St. Petersburg. What can explain such a long waiting period for a monarch who did not tarry with many of his reforms? Vockerodt explained the hesitation as stemming from the truly radical nature of Feofan's views. The tsar did not want to cause an "uproar [*Aufsehen*]" and he viewed a possible church reform a "precarious project [*delicates Werk*]."[108] T. S. Bayer noted a similar reason for Peter's hesitation to bring Prokopovich to the capital—the opposition of Iavorskii and the Muscovite clergy was a serious obstacle.[109] Priorities of the war campaign may have played a role as well: Peter was still in the "full flame of the Swedish war" and in the cauldron of dealing with his son Aleksei's rebellion, and had little time to pay attention to the church.[110] Whatever the cause, this hesitation also underlined Peter's lack of specific commitment to urgent church reform.

The tsar's eventual disillusionment with Iavorskii, however, ended any further doubts he may have had about calling up the controversial rector from Kiev. In 1715–16, Feofan received an invitation to come to the capital. Although Peter and the reformist elites had no more doubts in their minds, there were still clouds hanging over Feofan's future. The rector of the Kiev Academy would arrive in St. Petersburg to face an uphill battle against Moscow's entrenched ecclesiastical elites, both domestic and Ukrainian.

3

A Russian Luther

Feofan in St. Petersburg,
1716–1725

Everyone is theologizing here, even those who barely know what the Holy
Scripture is, loudly proclaiming the teachings of the apostles, the dogmas of
the Fathers. Drunken soldiers, unworthy clerks, merchants and craftsmen, day
laborers and lackeys, also, women—all are theologians. And our little Latins
[i.e., philo-Catholic Ukrainians] think highly of themselves, claiming to have
swallowed an ocean of wisdom. Everyone dogmatizes, all theologizing,
deciding, formulating, opining.

—FEOFAN PROKOPOVICH on daily life in St. Petersburg, 1716

But as Martin Luther could overcome his obstacles, by God's help, so he
[Feofan] hoped that little by little, the Lord's Hour [of renewal] would come
upon [*Herrn Stunde schlagen werde*] the Eastern Church.

—ALBERT ANTON VIERORTH, Baltic Pietist leader, 1721

Feofan Prokopovich, the main protagonist and architect of the Russian church
reform, arrived in St. Petersburg in October 1716. He came at the personal request of Peter I and Prince Aleksandr Menshikov, who planned to nominate
him to the bishopric of Pskov. Feofan had quite an unpleasant journey. Bad
roads between Moscow and St. Petersburg made him sick on account of frequent and long bridges over the marshes, and the six-hour rough ride across
"that brutal lake" Ladoga made him seasick.[1] He was very happy to make it to
shore unharmed.

Stormy weather on the water was followed by some theological tempests
on the ground. Both Moscow and St. Petersburg were teeming with doctrinal
controversies. Memories of the Tveritinov controversy, the Talitskii trial, and
Iavorskii's confrontation with the tsar were still fresh but also relevant. In a letter
to his Ukrainian Cossack friend, patron, and former student Iakov Markevich,
Feofan noted that almost everyone he met in Moscow was "theologizing,

Figure 3. Archbishop Feofan Prokopovich (1681–1736). Engraving from *Tractatus de Processione Spiritus Sancti* (Gothae, 1774). Courtesy of Bayerische Staatsbibliothek, Munich. Dogm. 804, Frontisp. 1 (Portr.), urn:nbn:de:bvb:12-bsb10399193-3.

deciding, [and] formulating"; including "clerks, merchants and craftsmen, day laborers and lackeys, also, women." "All are now obsessed with theology!" he exclaimed.[2] According to this same letter, the involvement of Feofan's philo-Catholic archnemeses had only added heat to the boiling cauldron of religious debates that involved Old Believers, Nikonites, smaller heretical groups, and the beard-shaving modernizers. Prokopovich, however, did not arrive to put out the old flames but to add new fire. This Ukrainian "Martin Luther" was determined to live up to the reputation of "heretical" reformer he earned during his time in the Mohyla Academy.

In 1716 Feofan was one of the very few church functionaries who professed the view that the Russian Orthodox Church was not only heading in the wrong direction theologically but also needed major doctrinal reform. This view was shared by Peter the Great. In Prokopovich's opinion, both the medieval Russian model of practical (rather than dogmatic) spirituality and the Catholic-inspired model of theology that was popular in Ukraine failed to produce true orthodoxy. One was superstition; the other, simply put, "Papist heresy."[3] For Feofan, reforming Orthodoxy therefore first and foremost involved reforming theology. This chapter underscores the significance of theology (and its contestation in St. Petersburg and Moscow) in the course of church reform and in the ideological rise of the Russian Empire. Feofan's plan for redirecting the Russian church toward the correct teaching was inspired by the theology of the Protestant Reformation. Yet, despite their foreign influence, Prokopovich viewed his reformist ideas to be the "Orthodox opinion," the "correct and fundamental doctrine," fit for his image of a true church. He rejected his opponents' doctrinal views as both "heresy" and the "tradition of old wives' fairytales [*predaniia bab'ikh basen*]."[4] Simultaneously, this vision of reform fit very well within the kind of religious change that Peter the Great would support in molding Russia into a modern and European empire. While the tsar lacked a clear agenda for doctrinal change, Feofan (and his allies) ultimately provided the theological vocabulary, ideological framework, spiritual inspiration, practical direction, and dedicated leadership necessary to carry out such a reform through theological works and legal documents. The works that had the greatest impact on reforming the church were the 1720 Catechism of 1720 (which reformed rudimentary doctrinal instruction), the *Spiritual Regulation* of 1721 (which reformed the organizational and canonical constitution of the church), the *Historical Investigation* of 1721 (which reformed the spiritual status of the monarchy), and the *Declaration on Monasticism* of 1724 (which reformed monasticism). Feofan wrote these works while facing determined opposition from those who viewed his theology, preaching, and lifestyle as highly disruptive.

CHRISTMAS IN PETERSBURG

Despite cold and inclement weather in Petersburg, Feofan received a very warm welcome. While Peter was away in Mecklenburg, Prince Menshikov (along with several powerful senators) invited him to begin regular preaching and catechetical teaching among the capital's aristocracy. In his 1716 letter to Markevich, he highlighted this latter function as a unique privilege: he was "the only one who is catechizing here [in St. Petersburg]."[5]

Prokopovich's teaching in the new capital was very doctrinal in nature, highlighting many of the controversial theological positions he had already developed in Kiev. One of the best examples of this was his 1716 Christmas Day sermon, delivered in Menshikov's house church. In it, Prokopovich repeated many of the same talking points articulated in his essay *The Unbearable Yoke* concerning human depravity, sin, and salvation. In antinomian fashion, he challenged a view (popular in the church at the time) that Old Testament laws had been replaced with Christ's commandments or "laws" and that fulfilling those new laws led to salvation. Instead he argued that no human being could possibly fulfill any of God's laws because of humanity's "depraved condition after the Fall."[6]

In classical Protestant fashion, Prokopovich painted a very grim picture of "desperate human depravity [*okaianstvo*]," stating that man by nature is "cold to the love of God and neighbor, blind to divine contemplation, dark, mad, unresponsive to truth and holiness, and dead."[7] Feofan contrasted the depth of human depravity with the simplicity and availability of salvation. Christians, who were as depraved as anyone else, found their salvation through "justification that is forgiveness and remission of sins."[8] This simply entailed faith, a belief in Christ's redemptive work. "Sin and curses were upon us, but now we are justified and blessed," exclaimed Feofan.[9]

To an audience that must have been used to hearing about the necessity of fasts and acts of piety, Feofan emphasized the idea that abstract justification released the Orthodox believer from the search for spiritual perfection. Feofan encouraged the believer to embrace his or her own imperfections and to live by the grace that "covers our shortcomings and spiritual poverty."[10] In other words, the Russian Orthodox faithful should become less concerned about their sins here on Earth and look forward to achieving perfection in the afterlife. "Those who are justified and dwell in Christ," he wrote, "do not follow God's law flawlessly because St. John [the apostle] called it a 'deception' to say that 'I have no sin.' For even the holy faithful of God . . . still expect the complete removal of the sting of death—that is sin—only upon reaching Heaven."[11]

The Christmas sermon became an instant hit among the capital's elites. Feofan observed that his message "was accepted with such enthusiasm and general acclaim that various persons openly praised it in various ways and I was greatly humbled that they all desired to print it out immediately."[12] Among the admirers was Prince Menshikov himself, Admiral Fedor Apraksin, Senator Ivan Musin-Pushkin, the "first among senators" Iakov Dolgorukii, General Grigorii Chernyshev, and Tikhon Streshnev. In addition to the senators, the archbishop of Novgorod, Feodosii Ianovskii, was also among those who now "loved and deeply respected him."[13]

The Installation Controversy

Feofan's bold theological statements may have pleased the Petersburg aristocrats, but it seemed reckless given his notoriety within Muscovite church circles. As early as August 1716, the tsar made clear his intention to grant Feofan a bishopric. While Feofan was overjoyed by the prospect, he was cognizant of the fact that getting the church hierarchy's approval for such a post would involve concealing his true theological inclinations, something that he was not ready to do. "I envy the bishop's mitres, copes, candleholders . . . as well as some fat large fish," he wrote to Markevich, "I love a bishop's duties and would love to become a bishop, but only as long as it did not entail becoming a stage actor, too."[14]

In fact, it took Feofan over a year of conflict with Moscow's hierarchs to become a bishop in 1718. The newcomer's preaching clearly revealed that he showed no caution in propagating his ideas. During the fall, winter, and spring of 1717–18, the clerical opposition was determined to derail plans for his installation. Feofilakt, two of the Likhoudes brothers (at the Moscow Academy), and Stefan Iavorskii penned scathing attacks on Prokopovich and his "Calvinist heresy" to discredit him and to "prevent the depraved Feofan from attaining a bishop's status."[15] To make sure that his knowledge of Feofan's heresy was accurate, Iavorskii ordered a manuscript copy of Prokopovich's theology course from Kiev for examination. Stefan's hand crisscrossed the manuscript with thirty-nine different notations ranging from charges of "Calvinism" to suspicions of "Pelagian heresy."[16]

In his reports to the Secret Chancellery between February and April 1718, Stefan warned the tsar of Prokopovich's "heresies" in a detailed seventeen-point protest. Among the more prominent items were Prokopovich's view of total depravity (that "man has no internal righteousness from God"), the centrality of grace (that "man cannot earn the grace of God and eternal glory by good deeds"), sin (that Christians who sin still remain forgiven), and antinomianism (that "no one can completely fulfill the law of God, even if one was very righteous").[17]

None of these items were news for Peter or Menshikov—Feofan preached them all in the open—but the monarch needed a formal reply from the accused before proceeding with the investiture.

Feofan's response absolved Peter of the prospect of appointing a heterodox bishop. Prokopovich asserted the authentic dogmatic orthodoxy of his views. His refutation, titled "Response to the Report of Metropolitan Stefan Accusing Me of Heretical Teaching," first highlighted Stefan's alleged misunderstanding of his theology and grammatical errors.[18] Then, secondly, it accused Stefan of hypocrisy, pointing to Iavorskii's publications on the "Latinist opinion on transubstantiation" in Chernigov containing his "countless erroneous views [that were] opposed to Orthodoxy."[19] If Stefan allowed the proliferation of Roman Catholic theological opinions but not Protestant ones, he argued, then his opposition to Feofan had nothing to do with his "zeal" for the Orthodox faith but rather his "grudge" and "extreme jealousy" toward the candidate as well as his prejudice in favor of the "Latins."[20]

Third, Feofan defended his opinions as being fully Orthodox.[21] "Our teaching is Orthodox," he wrote, "and whatever is opposed to it is heresy."[22] His "independent scholarly opinion" was Orthodox by virtue of being based solely "on the foundation of primary sources" (such as the Bible). His opponents, however, based their opinions on what the "swamp of teaching fools [i.e., Catholic scholastics]" had taught. These teachings, Feofan argued further, were so erroneous that they had "nauseated the enlightened world," that is, the European countries that rejected Catholic scholasticism.[23] In addition, Feofan would later argue that by attacking his "enlightened" views, the philo-Catholic clergy attacked the famous Kiev Academy, whose rector, teacher, and "representative" he was. "The entire reputation of the school would be affected if his [the rector's] reputation suffers," he noted.[24] This latter point had an important implication—if Feofan was no longer Orthodox, then Kiev (the best theological school in the East Slavic lands) was heterodox by extension as well.

The controversy ended in defeat and humiliation for Iavorskii and his philo-Catholic party. Prokopovich submitted his reply to Peter on May 31, 1718, the day before his officially scheduled installation. Given the fact that the tsar likely had little time to investigate the doctrinal particulars of the Iavorskii-Prokopovich debate, it seemed that the defense was just a necessary formality for Peter.[25] The installation went forward on Pentecost; Prokopovich was invested as the bishop of Pskov and Narva and received the "special distinction" of wearing the *Sakkos* mantle, which was usually reserved for the metropolitans and patriarchs.[26]

Shortly after the festivities, Stefan sensed that this was an uphill (if not futile) battle and withdrew his protest. In the Secret Chancellery, he recanted his opinions about Feofan, stating that he had not personally read Feofan's writings but relied on reviews sent to him by his assistants, Feofilakt and Gedeon. This was clearly a lie, given his personal notations on the aforementioned theological manuscript. In June 1718, Musin-Pushkin called for a reconciliation session and Stefan "humbly asked for forgiveness" from Feofan in the presence of the senator and the "most eminent archimandrite," Feodosii Ianovskii.[27] The reconciliation was sealed by an exchange of kisses and Feofan now became a legitimate bishop with ecclesial recognition, his "service to Jerusalem [i.e., St. Petersburg] pleasing to the saints."[28]

THE "WICKED ASSEMBLY" OF FEOFAN PROKOPOVICH

By the middle of the summer of 1718, Feofan had successfully resolved the controversies surrounding his episcopal installation. His winning streaks amplified whatever trust he had already gained among the court elites and the monarch himself. From 1718 on, he would become "something approaching the State Secretary of Religious Affairs" under Peter I.[29] However, Feofan was not alone in eliciting controversy or in steering the reformist spirit within the Orthodox Church. He had important allies. Between 1718 and 1725, some lower clergy, bishops, and archimandrites chose to side with Prokopovich in supporting the direction of his reform and embracing his doctrinal vision of Russia's new Orthodoxy.

Some of them were partial backers, dissatisfied with Stefan Iavorskii or seeking to align with Feofan for opportunistic reasons. They included Muscovite bishops of noble origins, such as Aleksei Titov (who installed Feofan in 1718) and Aaron Eropkin, and a hierarch of Greek origin, Afanasii Kondoidi.[30] Others, however, were principled supporters, members of the core faction that coalesced around Feofan's theological vision. Markell Rodyshevskii (d. 1742), one of Prokopovich's former students, who turned against his teacher in 1726, identified the nucleus of the reformist "heretical" faction in a report to the Secret Chancellery. They were "Feodosii the Most Lawless, Feofan the Heresiarch, Gavriil the Jew, [and] Krolik the Villain." According to the report, Feofan and his allies as well as "others like them" were "the wicked assembly [*zlochestivoe sborishche*]" that threatened Russia's true Orthodoxy.[31]

The first member of this "wicked assembly," Feodosii Ianovskii, was a crucial early supporter. His theological proclivities were already obvious in 1714 when he took Tveritinov's side against Stefan Iavorskii in the heresy trial.[32] The "Most Lawless Feodosii" held this titular distinction (from Markell) for a reason. His antinomian tendencies shaped his very liberal understanding of Orthodoxy: he frequently stripped icons of decorations, skipped fasts, and exempted members of the military from Lent.[33] Tsarevich Aleksei (Peter's son) once noted that "my father loves him because he introduces Lutheran customs and permits everything."³⁴

Among Prokopovich's most learned associates was Gavriil Buzhinskii, known by Markell as "Gavriil the Jew." (There is no basis to suppose he had any Jewish background; Markell's label may be a reference to Gavriil's knowledge of some biblical Hebrew, or the fact that he hailed, like Prokopovich, from a merchant family.) Originally from the Eastern Ukrainian town of Izium, he studied in Kiev during Feofan's prefecture there, moved to Moscow in 1707, and in 1719 the tsar invited him to settle in St. Petersburg.³⁵ Being close to the court, Buzhinskii pursued a career typical of the reformist hierarchs. Administratively, he first served as the chief hieromonk of the navy (i.e., the chief monastic priest of the navy) and then as the "director and protector" of the ecclesiastical printing presses, which made him the de facto chief censor for religious books. In the spiritual ranks, Gavriil also held the abbacy of Russia's most important monastery—Moscow's Trinity-Sergius—and later, the bishopric of Riazan, all while residing in St. Petersburg.³⁶ Buzhinskii maintained relationships not only with other reformist Orthodox clergy but also with foreign Protestants. In Petersburg, he befriended Danish traveler Peder von Haven, Baron Heinrich van Huyssen (a tutor to Tsarevich Aleksei), and British chaplain Thomas Consett.³⁷ Huyssen would become a valuable friend as he supplied Feofan (and other reformist clergy like Lavrentii Gorka) with books from Germany and Holland.³⁸

Gavriil distinguished himself at the court of Peter I as an erudite translator. Although he eschewed translating works of Catholic authors (who "exalt their Popes" and "praise the Roman gang and its infamous head," he claimed), he was fond of literature popular in the Protestant lands.³⁹ Among his translations was Erasmus's *Colloquies*, which Mikhail Kropotkin claimed "prepared the road to Martin Luther" for the children of the St. Petersburg elites.⁴⁰ In 1718 he translated Samuel Pufendorf's *Introductio ad historiam Europae* with its large tractate on the papacy, and in 1724, Wilhelm Stratemann's *Theatrum Historicum*.⁴¹ The Russian version of this work preserved the language that praised "the divinely inspired Martin Luther," who "attacked the entire Papistry [*papezhstvo*], opening the doors of Christian freedom and true piety," as well as assertions that the pope was indeed the Antichrist.⁴² The "protector" of the printing presses also edited liturgical books. In June 1723, he successfully petitioned the Synod to remove the special appendix, the *Izvestie uchitel'noe* (Instructional announcement) from the 1723 edition of the liturgical manual, the *Sluzhebnik*. This appendix, first appearing in the Russian *Sluzhebnik* editions of 1699 and 1717, contained the Catholic-inspired and "somewhat dubious [*sumnitel'nye*]" eucharistic formulas of Peter Mohyla.⁴³

The third member of Feofan's "wicked assembly" was Feofil Krolik, known as Feofan's "favorite disciple."[44] Feofil was fluent in German and moved permanently to the capital in 1722 after a long sojourn in Prague.[45] First an assessor and then an adviser at the Holy Synod, Feofil actively assisted Prokopovich in drafting church reforms and translating German authors alongside Buzhinskii.[46] In particular, Feofil drafted the instructions on monasticism, which became a crucial addition to the *Spiritual Regulation* after 1724.[47]

THE "CHEERFUL" LIFESTYLES OF
FEOFAN AND HIS ALLIES

For Feofan and his allied reformers, appealing to the hearts and minds of the Petrine elites also involved building social relationships that centered on court life and St. Petersburg. Thus, church reform in St. Petersburg also involved cheer. The social world of the reform and reformers was in fact an "associative" culture that intertwined with the rambunctious court culture of the last decade of the Petrine era. The lives of Feofan's "wicked assembly" were part and parcel of that newly emerging "anti-sober" social order described by Igor Fedyukhin, Robert Collis, and Erik Zitser.[48] The highly jovial lifestyle of these bishops greatly diverged from the social culture of their predecessors, even the philo-Catholic Ukrainian clerics. As Tsar Peter I himself noted: "Stefan lives like a monk, but Feofan like a bishop; his place is cheerful and not boring."[49]

One important aspect of that "cheerful" lifestyle was entertainment. Feofan, Feodosii, Gavriil, Feofil, and other reformist clergy spent time at parties (sometimes called *assamblei* in imitation of the secular gatherings) that featured music, drinking, and chess-playing sessions at the Synod or clerical residences.[50] Whether there was any dancing at these *assamblei* is an open question, but future bishop Varlaam Skamnitskii (1696–1761), Feofan's protégé and teacher in his St. Petersburg orphanage, "enjoyed dancing and danced eagerly and well."[51] There were a particularly large number of assemblies held in Moscow in 1724, following the coronation of Catherine I, with parties at Feodosii Ianovskii's residence, Voskresenskii Monastery, and other monasteries of the old capital.[52]

Feofan's bishop's residence on the city's Apothecary Island was replete with musical bands, among several other forms of entertainment, a flotilla of pleasure boats, yachts, and barges, as well as marvelously designed gardens, planned by the imperial palace landscaper Ludwig Günther Tater.[53] However, he also served good beer, brewed by his estate manager Gerasim in Novgorod. The beer was likened to Moses's manna and declared a "true miracle," the subject of poems and accolades in Moscow, St. Petersburg, and Novgorod.[54]

In addition to drinking with Russian elites, Feofan, Feodosii, and other reformist bishops also socialized with foreigners, mostly Protestants. The diary

of Holstein nobleman Friedrich Wilhelm Bergholz, who accompanied Duke
Charles-Frederick (of Holstein-Gottorp, 1700–1739) to Russia, vividly described
his multiple interactions with Feodosii, Feofan, and Gavriil at various monastic and city residences in 1722 and 1723.[55] These social events involved "elaborate cannon fire," "the best wines," and becoming "strongly inebriated [*scharf
getrunken*]."[56] Some of these parties were quite disorderly. British Huguenot
traveler Aubry de la Montraye described the revelry that took place at St. Aleksandr Nevskii Monastery in July 1727. Cheer was high on the agenda and some
dozen very well-educated and Latin-speaking monks (together with Feofan and
Archimandrite Petr Smelich, "a good divine and able Mathematician") com-
peted with each other in drinking the oversized cups of wine ("large Bum-
pers"), fist-fought with Menshikov's servants and each other, and then brought
the "broil" to their great library. There, the visitor found monks "boxing one
now another with their Books and being boxed in return."[57]

The jovial lifestyle of the reformist clergy was fertile ground for criticism.
Thus, Markell Rodyshevskii accused the reformers of going to concerts and
dance parties, attending comedies, playing cards, blessing other monks' cohabitation with the nuns, and drinking "expensive alcohol," among other
things. Feodosii and Feofan apparently smashed and tore away expensive jewels and precious metals from the decorative frames of icons so that they could
raise money to buy more alcohol.[58] Furthermore, Feofan's behavior was setting a bad example for the monastic clergy in the capitals. "The entire monastic estate have fallen into such audacity [*bezstrashie*] and spiritual weakness,"
he wrote, "that many of them are always drunk and always eat meat [during
Lent]."[59]

Markell's accusation of constant Lenten meat-eating was in fact seconded
in a later, April 1730 Secret Chancellery report by the Novgorodian nobleman
Ivan Nosov. Based on his allegedly eyewitness observation of the lifestyles of
the reformist bishops, he recalled the following:

> Feofan surpassed Feodosii in many crimes. During his office as the bishop of
> Pskov, he looted monasteries and holy churches for his sacrilegious gluttony
> [*bogomerskogo lakomstva*] and used the income of his diocese for luxuries not fit
> for the monastic calling. . . . For example, Feofan stripped the gold and silver off
> the icons' frames and then shipped them to Riga to exchange for just a few
> bottles of foreign alcohol [*zamorskikh pitei*]. . . . Archbishop Feofan is a rabid
> iconoclast and a church thief; he also eats meat during Lent and all other fasts,
> and in fact, Feofan's violation of fasts is so great that in his meat-eating Feofan
> even surpassed his ally [*soobshnika*] the bishop of Riazan [Gavriil Buzhinskii]
> who eats meat habitually [*obychenno*] all the time.[60]

THE CATECHISM CONTROVERSY OF 1720

The cheerful social environment of church reform was undoubtedly disruptive, however, the greatest disruption for the Russian church was theological. Feofan not only preached his Protestant-inspired doctrine in public, he also sought to establish new formulations as canonically binding expressions of official Orthodoxy in Russia. The root of virtually all Feofan Prokopovich's reforms was theology. So, between 1718 and 1725, Prokopovich wrote, edited, prepared, and published theological works that left a lasting impact on the Russian church until 1917.

The new catechism, *Pervoe uchenie otrokom* ([*sic*], also known as *The Primer*), was the earliest of these works. It combined pedagogical instruction with doctrinal edification by combining an elementary grammar manual with a catechism. Although the catechism had the goal of educating children, it also achieved a particular reformist aim for Feofan—the replacement of the previous Catholic formulations taught in Mohyla's catechism and the spread of Protestant-inspired ideas (that the catechism officially validated as new doctrinal truth). To achieve both goals, Feofan penned his rejection of Mohyla and then patterned the new catechism after Martin Luther's similar work.

By its very design, *The Primer* was doctrinally and structurally very different from the (Tridentine-influenced) Orthodox confession of Peter Mohyla, the gold standard of Orthodox doctrine at the time. Prokopovich clearly intended his work to be an alternative to Mohyla's catechism. For example, in 1721 he judged the Orthodox confession to be "unfit for all edification, especially for the simple folk."[61] Furthermore, he considered it to be outdated. The book contained "high theological mysteries," he argued, "and they articulate matters that happened to be fashionable then, according to the custom of the nation and the circumstances of the time."[62]

The catechism was first printed in June 1720 at the St. Aleksandr Nevskii Monastery.[63] In content and structure, the primer drew upon the existing Lutheran pedagogical instructional manuals of the time. Among the works that influenced Feofan's catechism (and which could be found in Feofan's library), Margarita Korzo identified the *Kleine Catechismus-Fragen* (Braunschweig, 1639) and the *Katechismus Schule* (Hannover, 1635) of Superintendent Justus Gesenius (1601–73), but there were others—the *Epitome Catecheticorum praeceptorum* (Ulm, 1642)—for example. All these works were patterned after the Martin Luther's *Small Catechism*.[64]

As my textual analysis has shown, the catechism also replicated and condensed the patterns of Martin Luther's *Large Catechism*.[65] Just as in Luther's work, Feofan subdivided parental authority into three kinds: natural fathers, spiritual fathers, and governing fathers (such as the ruler).[66] The formulations of one's spiritual duties, questions of salvation, definitions of idolatry, and the omission of celibacy (from the seventh—or the Lutheran sixth—commandment) were also similar. In the discussion of idolatry, Feofan prohibited the sacred worship of icons (known theologically as *latreia*) but allowed "ordinary esteem, such as embracing and kissing," as well as commemoration.[67] The catechism also addressed situations specific to the Russian context: it condemned the preference for "images decorated by gold rather than plain ones," and condemned those who "would not pray without the use of icons."[68]

Reactions to Prokopovich's new catechism came soon after its publication. The Prussian ambassador in St. Petersburg, Gustav von Mardefeld, wrote in an August 11, 1721, report to King Frederick William I that Prokopovich's catechism was "thoroughly composed in a Lutheran manner."[69] A year earlier, the Moldavian (and now Russian) prince Dmitrii Kantemir (1673–1723), a member of the tsar's service nobility, had spotted what he saw as deviations from acceptable Orthodox dogma and wrote a scathing critique of *The Primer's* theology almost as soon as it came off the presses. His 1720 manuscript, *Loca obscura in Catechisi* [Dubious sections in the Catechism], contained detailed objections to the Protestant nature of the catechism with passages cited in Russian and objections in Latin.[70]

In his critique, Kantemir identified Prokopovich's low anthropology as influenced by Calvin, which was "in direct contradiction to the dogma of the Orthodox Church about the creation of man in the image of God."[71] He further accused Prokopovich of elevating the centrality of Scripture at the expense of "the tradition of the Orthodox Church, the dogmas of the holy Fathers."[72] Kantemir's notations displayed not only a good level of theological erudition but also knowledge of Calvin's commentaries unusual for an Orthodox layman.

Kantemir also disliked the catechism's position on icons, arguing that *latreia* of images was not a sin but a believer's obligation as explained in the Mohyla catechism and the writings of Pope Hadrian.[73] He attacked *The Primer's* denial of the superiority of venerating some icons above others by pointing to the "extraordinary miracles" that some, but not all, icons could produce.[74] In the end, the prince deemed this work to be inferior to the "Ruthenian Catechism" of Mohyla and proclaimed Prokopovich an unworthy author to write such a dogmatic work, being an "impious, blasphemous . . . pagan [*ethnicus*] and Pharisee, separated from the Church of God."[75]

Feofan's stern response did not take long. In his 1721 letter, he responded that Kantemir's review had "two mistakes: grammatical and theological."[76] Grammatically, the prince misconstrued the meaning of *latreia*; theologically, he was guilty of "heresy" by encouraging idolatry instead of icon-veneration.

Feofan filled his tirade against Kantemir with rhetorical questions: "Those who disagree with us would like to venerate icons through sacred worship [*sluzhenie*]. What new things do I hear? How then should we worship these icons? . . . How can we ascribe such worship to created matter? Are we going to equate created things with God?"[77]

The significance of *Pervoe uchenie* can hardly be underestimated. As an educational-theological manual, the work became the most widely printed piece of catechetical literature in eighteenth-century Russia, spreading deep into provincial Russia and circulating in all dioceses and parishes. As Margarita Korzo has noted, *Pervoe uchenie* "remained the fundamental school catechism of the Russian Empire for the entire eighteenth century."[78] The work appeared in at least sixteen printed editions between 1720 and 1798.[79] The frequency of publication suggests the indispensable nature of the new doctrinal manual for the empire's parishes, comparable to high-demand liturgical books like the *Trebnik*, also published sixteen times during the same time period.[80] In fact, the Holy Synod treated this catechism as an indispensable part of parish life. For example, in 1722 *Pervoe uchenie* became the official textbook of all diocesan schools.[81] The children studying in these so-called bishopric schools and arithmetic schools were required to memorize portions of it by heart.[82] In 1723 *Pervoe uchenie* replaced the readings from St. Ephrem the Syrian and the seventeenth-century *Sobornik* as mandatory Lent reading in churches.[83] Nevertheless, the reformers' success in popularizing the use of the new catechism was somewhat gradual: as late as 1756, the Synod had to warn the dioceses against other doctrinal instruction manuals, reiterating the significance of *Pervoe uchenie* as Russia's "officially permitted catechism."[84]

Pervoe uchenie was not only widely distributed in Russia but circulated in translations abroad. There were Serbian (1744), German (1723), and Romanian (1726) translations of the work, as well as two editions of Jenkin Philipps's English translation (*The Russian Catechism*, 1723 and 1725) and two 1845 English translations (*The Doctrine of the Russian Church*).[85] It also inspired other catechetical literature in Russia and Ukraine. Archimandrite Ioil' Bykovskii, who taught theology according to Feofan's method in Chernigov and Iaroslavl in 1760s and 1770s, also composed a similar primer, *Bukvar' ili nachal'noe uchenie* (Chernigov, 1765) following the patterns of Prokopovich's work.[86] Then, Metropolitan Platon Levshin's 1765 and 1775 children's catechisms were also based on Feofan's, as Margarita Korzo has shown.[87]

Although the dissemination of the catechism throughout Russia is documented, its reception among the laity will require further study. From the history of Viatka diocese, for example, we know that its reformed bishop Varlaam Skamnitskii made it a requirement for local clergy to memorize Prokopovich's catechism. Failure to do so was punishable by "fine and defrocking" and the bishop's use of force to enlighten the populace with reformed doctrine was unprecedented.[88] In Tambov and Voronezh regions, however, the widespread use of Feofan's official catechism produced the unintended consequence of stirring up peasant rejection of the official church dogma. As Aleksandr L'vov has shown, in the 1760s the peasants of Tambov and Voronezh regions interpreted *Pervoe uchenie* too literally by rejecting icons, veneration of saints, fasts, and many church ceremonies, alarming the bishops who saw church attendance and veneration plunge as a result.[89] According to L'vov, Nikolai Vysotskii, and P. Ryndziunskii, this "Tambov Schism [*tambovskii raskol*]" very much contributed to the origins of the Molokan, Dukhobor, and Subbotniki sects in peasant Russia.[90]

"Coup de l'Eglise": The *Spiritual Regulation*

The archbishop's most important and lasting contribution to church reform was the *Spiritual Regulation* or *Dukhovnyi reglament*, which redefined the administrative and canonical structure of the church and created its highest administrative organ, the Holy Governing Synod.[91] The document gave Tsar Peter a clear theological sanction to abolish the patriarchate. It gave Feofan a legal charter (or *constitutiones*) to alter the new administrative structure of the church in accordance with the Lutheran synodal-consistorial model and its principle of the episcopal privilege of the territorial lord (*Landesherrschaft*). This structure was durable, lasting until the end of the empire in 1917. In practical terms, it also gave Prokopovich wide-ranging powers to take over the church hierarchy, to bypass his higher-ranking opponents (he was merely the bishop of Pskov at the time), and to take the church in the direction of Protestant-inspired reform. His changes were so profound and abrupt that Anton Kartashev (the last chief procurator of the Holy Synod during 1917–18) called them a "*coup de l'église* [sic]."[92]

The "coup" took more than two years of preparation to materialize. Tsar Peter had no plan to reorganize the church in the early part of the century. His idea to establish an "ecclesiastical college" emerged only after "conversations with Feofan," according to Pavel Verkhovskoi.[93] The original (but vague) idea for the establishment of the collegiate organ of church administration was undoubtedly Peter's, as he wrote to Stefan Iavorskii in 1718 that "a Spiritual College" should replace the patriarchate.[94] Here, the tsar suggested a church institution along the lines of the other colleges (like the College of Commerce), which were established in 1715 and were subordinated to the Senate.[95]

Peter's initiative did not relegate Prokopovich to the status of a ghost writer. Although Feofan was most certainly actively sympathetic to Peter's impulses to reform the church, it was theology, not the monarch's dictate, that shaped his arguments. Thus, the *Spiritual Regulation* was not just an administrative document but also a theologically sophisticated treatise. The main theological arguments of the *Regulation* fully reflected Feofan's views on the patriarchate, superstition, and monasticism, all of which were formed before he set foot in St. Petersburg in 1716. They were not dictated by the monarch. As noted by Prussian diplomat Vockerodt, Feofan and Peter's convergence was a rare coincidence of the meeting of the minds, not subordination of one to the other.[96]

Prokopovich probably began writing the *Spiritual Regulation* in 1719. In 1720 his team of writers and editors (which included Feofil Krolik and Afanasii Kondoidi) went through critical revisions of the work.[97] One major obstacle was Feofan's disagreement with the tsar about the legal status of the new institution. Although the tsar wanted the establishment of a mere "Ecclesiastical College" (that would be one of many other colleges or ministries, subordinated to the Senate), Feofan insisted on the establishment of a Synod with a legal authority equal to the Senate. His insistence on the special political authority of the Synod (vis-à-vis the Senate) likely reflected his desire to secure the church's independence from the nobility or the state bureaucracy while subordinating the church to the monarch directly. As later chapters will illustrate, this special authority had long-term consequences: it allowed Feofan to survive the reaction of 1727–30, but it also laid the foundation for the post-1825 conflict between the Holy Synod and the state bureaucracy that remained until the end of the empire in 1917.

Feofan's first draft version of the *Regulation* alternated between several names for the new institution, including "Collegium," "Synedrion," "Synod," and "Holy Council."[98] In his May 10, 1720, letter to Iakov Markevich, Feofan referred to this new document as a *constitutiones* (a charter) and a *reglamentum*.[99] In the same letter, he also demonstrated the interchangeability of institutional terms by referring to the proposed body simultaneously as "Collegium," "Synodus," and "Consistorium Ecclesiasticum generale."[100] The latter title was particularly intriguing, since the only country in the world that had a supreme ecclesiastical council by that name was Sweden. The general contours of the Swedish Consistorium Ecclesiasticum generale [General Ecclesiastical Consistory] under the reign of Gustavus Adolphus very much resembled the kind of institution envisioned by Feofan in his regulation.[101] The document was ready in February 1721, and the tsar summoned the bishops to the capital to sign the new constitution of the church.

The signing of Russia's church regulation ended two years of fruitful work and the debate about the name of the new institution. Peter the Great's "Spiritual College" lasted only one day, the very first day of the bishops' meeting to sign the *Regulation* on February 14, 1721. Prokopovich requested that the tsar name the institution the "Holy Governing Synod," putting it on an equal footing with the Senate, while Peter wanted to continue the use of "the college."[102] After some discussion, Feofan persuaded the tsar, who, according to Verkhovskoi, "changed his views to a new opinion." Thus, the college was substituted for the Synod on February 16. The institution received an autonomous juridical status vis-à-vis the Senate and the colleges, giving the leading bishops a status like those of senators in the Russian Empire.[103]

The blueprint for the *Spiritual Regulation* undoubtedly came from the Protestant West, where *Kirchenordnungen* ("church ordinances," also known as *Kirchenregimenten*) proliferated during the late Reformation period. Among the best examples of such ordinances were the *Casimiriana*, written by the eminent Lutheran theologian Johann Gerhard (1582–1637) for Johann Casimir of Saxony in 1626, and the *Agenda, oder Kirchenordnung . . . Kirchenregiment* adopted in Hesse in 1574. But there were many, many more, written in virtually every Protestant state.[104] All these ordinances were similar in substance: they started with the monarch's introduction that explained the importance of having a well-regulated church, then outlined the duties of higher and lower clergy; in describing those duties, they devoted special attention to the visitation of bishops to the countryside, the proliferation of high-quality preaching, the promotion of education in diocesan schools, and spiritual *disciplin* in general.[105] They even contained instructions on what days the clergy should pronounce particular prayers, vespers, or collects. They also had formulae of confession and absolution, and exhortations against sins.[106] In other words, the *Kirchenordnungen* lived up to their titles: they ordered, standardized, and regulated the duties of the church hierarchy from the top down, from the bishops (superintendents) to the deacons and schoolmasters.

Russia already had a regulated rhythm of liturgical life thanks to its well-developed corpus of missals such as the *Trebnik*. Feofan did not seek to rewrite the liturgical cycle to which Russians were accustomed, and, in fact, his reforms pursued very few liturgical changes. However, in the absence of the patriarch, the administrative duties of the clergy required redefinition and recalibration. Feofan sought to establish a clear chain of authority from the Synod all the way down to the bishops and lower clergy in diocesan life. Similarly, Russia's church-run education system as well as church-administered homiletics needed regulation and reform.

To pursue these changes, Feofan turned to the existing Protestant examples. The *Spiritual Regulation* of 1721 was very similar to *Kirchenordnungen* like the *Casimiriana* in language, content, and intentions. Just like the Protestant ordinances, the *Regulation* begins with an introduction by the ruler (Peter I) outlining the need for orderly concord and reform in religious affairs. In comparison, the *Casimiriana* contains an introduction "written" by Johann Casimir of Saxony, while the Hessian *Agenda* contains a foreword by Wilhelm of Hesse.[107] The next part of the *Regulation* focuses on the duties of the "bishops," including their "general" obligations (such as observing the law and caring for the spiritual edification of the laity) and their "particular" ones.[108] The "particular" duties were especially numerous, such as convening of the local "church councils," examination of miracles for fraud, determining ecclesiastical punishments, watching over religious observances in the countryside to prevent superstition, and so on.[109] This all resembled the outlines of the duties of the Lutheran "superintendents" in Saxony, who also had to watch out for superstition, convene consistorial councils, and examine and punish the clergy.[110]

The *Regulation*, just like the *Kirchenordnungen*, reserved a special place for the practice of visitation (*poseshchenie*). The Russian ordinance's instructions for episcopal visitations are detailed. Bishops must visit their dioceses in the summer, convene meetings with the village or town's clergy together, preach at such meetings, and request that this bishop's visitation sermon circulate in other churches as well. Bishops must examine all members of the church hierarchy in their diocese and submit annual reports on visitations to the Holy Synod in St. Petersburg.[111] All these rules resemble the *Casimiriana*, in which Lutheran visitation must also take place in the summer ("yearly, before Michaelmas") and superintendents must inspect and examine their clergy and preach to them upon arrival (teaching them the "concepts" of homiletics).[112]

Just like the *Casimiriana*, the *Regulation* paid special attention to preachers, outlining in detail the manner in which they must preach and the topics that they must avoid in their sermons.[113] The *Regulation* also contained a special section on schools (*doma uchilishchnye*), defining their curriculum in great detail, as well as the reading assignments for diocesan lay students (such as Pufendorf), the structure and content of the libraries, and the various duties of teachers, students, and administrators. Similarly, the *Casimiriana*'s lengthy "Leges und Ordnung Gymnasii" outline the regulations that governed diocesan schools in Coburg, Gotha, and throughout the realm.[114] Specific duties of the lower clergy (such as deacons, sacristans, and priests) occupy a special role in both German and Russian church ordinances as well.[115]

The *Spiritual Regulation* was published at least eleven times between 1721 and 1794, making it (along with Feofan's catechism) one of the most important religious publications in the country.[116] The significance of the ordinance is already very well described in the literature, but its central tenet—the abolition of the long-established Orthodox office of the patriarch—needs further discussion. The political motivations for this act are clear: the abolition served Peter's goals of establishing a better-regulated state, in which religion played a crucial role in the new social order. However, the act also served Prokopovich's theological objectives: namely, the cleansing of Orthodoxy from any vestiges of "Papism" in its administration, and the reform of that church in accordance with Feofan's ideals of doctrinally correct ecclesiastical government. To serve these objectives, Feofan offered two major dogmatic premises for abolishing the patriarchate: the denunciation of the Catholic "two swords" doctrine and the endorsement of a collegial church administration as a more Orthodox (and theologically pure) model.

The first premise for the abolition of the patriarchate rested on the fear that the mere existence of such an office might lead to a Catholic-inspired usurpation of the monarch's power. As early as 1718, Feofan preached against Iavorskii's idea of the "two swords" or "two hands" doctrine, stating that if the church had any political autonomy it would create "an alternate state" inside Russia.[117] His view of church-state relations proclaimed that "priesthood is a different duty, and a different estate among the people, but it is not a different government."[118] Since he considered the church to be another estate within the government, he rejected the idea of ecclesial monarchy, whether in the form of a pope or a patriarch. In fact, Prokopovich frequently conflated the two, seeing papal "immoderate lordship" in the institution of patriarchate.[119] In an argument with an imaginary opponent (a follower of Iavorskii, whom he called "a bugler"), he stated that

> our bugler proclaims that both tsar and patriarch are the chief highest potentates and is telling the people that the patriarch should not meddle in the tsar's secular affairs, just like the tsar should not meddle in the patriarch's spiritual ones. So, one power does not depend on the other and one is not subject to the other. He also says that it is sinful for the tsar to judge the patriarch, and that the patriarch is not subject to the tsar. The logic of his words is not difficult to unmask since the Papists speak this way about the Pope.[120]

Feofan's conflation of the offices of pope and the patriarch is very interesting, because the Catholic doctrine of "two swords" was not the same as the old Muscovite or Byzantine tradition of separating the kingdom (tsarstvol imperium) from the priesthood (sviashchenstvol sacerdotum). Whether Feofan knew the difference between medieval Orthodox and Roman Catholic approaches to church-state relations is not clear, but the Spiritual Regulation did state that the "simple people" would not understand the difference between the offices of the tsar and the patriarch. Even worse, they might conclude that the latter was a "Second Autocrat" and "that the spiritual estate [a hint at Byzantine *sacerdotum*?] is a second and a better state."[121]

Regardless of whether Feofan understood the differences between Catholic and Byzantine concepts of sacred authority, he conflated Muscovite tradition with papal examples nevertheless, almost to the point of equating the two. For the reformer, the threat of "Papism" hid behind the veneer of the patriarchate, and only the abolition of the office could uproot any attempts to establish the menacing "duality of power," whereby patriarchs (like popes) could exclude monarchs from curating the spiritual realm.[122] In fact, the *Spiritual Regulation* argued further that the presence of the patriarch was destructive to strong autocracy (a type of monarchy he advocated for Russia), because it would seek to imitate papal authority: "The Pope prevailed in his power by destroying the Roman state completely, taking a great part of it for himself, and by plundering other states multiple times, almost to their complete ruin. Let us be mindful of similar attempts that befell us too [hint at Nikon]. Such evil has no place in the conciliar spiritual government."[123]

It is no surprise then that Feofan considered the conciliar form of church administration to be superior to one-man rule. This was his second premise for abolishing the patriarchate. The premise was based on both utilitarian and historical arguments. From the pragmatic standpoint, he argued, "the truth is better determined by a council rather than a sole person." There was much less room for personal bias and the collegial government carried out affairs more efficiently in cases of individuals' illness or absence.[124]

The historical argument invoked past biblical and ancient Christian examples of administration. Here, Prokopovich did not appeal to Protestantism, but rather presented the biblical examples of the past synodal systems. The innovation was in fact a restoration. It was not, he stated, "some new and unknown [matter] as some wicked-minded and foolish people will claim."[125] "Spiritual conciliar government" was in fact very ancient, as exemplified in the "Synedrion of the Old Testament Church in Jerusalem."[126] However, this form of administration was also sanctified by the church's centuries-long tradition of holding "holy councils." His chronological boundary for the church's historical orthodoxy and the correct status of church-state relations was, however, limited to the first five centuries CE, following the Protestant formula of *Consensus quinquesaecularis*. According to this formula, the *Spiritual Regulation* officially designated "500 CE to 1400 CE" as "the time of darkness."[127] During this time, Feofan argued, bishops often invoked the authority of councils and did not inflate the powers of their office. "None of the bishops were arrogant before the year 400 CE," he stated. "They began to be so afterward, especially the bishops of Rome and Constantinople."[128] Feofan's stated goal in the *Spiritual Regulation* was to return to late antiquity's ideal of humble bishops, obedient to the decisions of the councils and the will of Christian emperors. This highlighted Feofan's well-known idealization of ancient Christianity, and his promotion (like the leaders of the Reformation) of "a return to the first church [*reductio ad ecclesiam primam*]."[129]

The *Regulation* did not only affect the fate of the country's highest bishop (the patriarch) but also reorganized Russia's episcopal office in some crucial ways. Prokopovich wanted to mold a new church hierarchy by reserving the vacant bishoprics for the well-educated candidates. So, the *Regulation* made it impossible for all except seminarians to become monks before the age of thirty.[130] (Canonically, Orthodox bishops had come from the monastic clergy.) Since Feofan's educational reforms would advance a seminary curriculum based on Protestant theological textbooks, the young seminarians nurtured in the era of Petrine reforms would provide Russia with a very different church hierarchy than what Muscovy had before.

Furthermore, this restriction of early monastic tonsure to seminary students had another goal—limiting the influence of the monasteries on the hierarchy. Seminary students (even those becoming monks) were not ascetics and were increasingly exempted from monastic-ascetic probationary experience (*poslushanie*) to concentrate on their studies. In the past, those wishing to become monks or those who were monks but wished to ascend the ecclesiastical ladder needed to spend a certain amount of time inside the monastery walls on ascetic probation of sorts. Now, seminary students remained focused on their studies after tonsure, and climbed the ladder of church promotion through further education, teaching, or administrative service, not monastic experience.

Russian church historian Petr Znamenskii would later call these newly minted and well-educated bishops "emancipated monks."[131] Not only were they "emancipated" from ascetic experience, but the *Regulation* mandated that after 1721 the best educated and most qualified bishops would be exempted from living in their dioceses and be given high administrative positions in St. Petersburg, while handing the administration of their dioceses over to the vicariate, with sporadic administrative visits.[132] This rule ensured that church culture would remain in the close proximity to court culture, while the church administration was physically proximate to the politics of the Winter Palace (or Peterhof). The new synodal administration meant that Russian Orthodoxy was ruled not by the personal agency of a patriarch but by a collective body, geographically centered in St. Petersburg.

PONTIFEX MAXIMUS: A SACRED MONARCHY

Prokopovich used theology not only to alter church doctrine and administration, but also to change the projection of the Orthodox monarch's political power. His instrument of reform was another theological essay, the *Rozysk istoricheskii* (Historical investigation) of 1721. Like his other doctrinal innovations, the key concepts of the essay also reflected the influence of late Reformation theology. Similar to the jurists of the *ius Reformandi* in Europe, Feofan viewed monarchy as a sacred institution, sanctified by Providence to oversee and direct the ecclesiastical affairs of the realm. Pontifex Maximus, an ancient and Christian Roman ruler who combined in himself the offices of the emperor and the high priest, served as the ideal for such an institution. Just like the Holy Synod replaced the "Papist" institution of patriarchate in spiritual matters, so the Pontifex, in this case the monarch, would replace the person of the patriarch as supreme canonical authority. In other words, without the presence of the patriarch, the Russian church still needed a formal, even if symbolic, head.

Feofan's political ideology as it relates to the power of the monarchy is a well-studied subject, while the notion that his ideology promoted "enlightened absolutism" has its supporters and detractors.[133] The related subject of the tsar's religious authority, however, has received far less attention in the scholarly world. The bishop's theory that the tsar possessed final and supreme authority in church affairs (as "Pontifex Maximus," "the bishop of bishops," or "Summus Pontifex," in Feofan's words), however, was not new in early modern Europe.

This theory developed during the late Reformation period (1555–1685), when German princely states experienced not only confessional but also political consolidations. The debate as to how much authority a secular ruler should have went back to the early years of the Reformation, when Martin Luther designated local princes as "emergency bishops." These "bishops" filled vacant clerical positions and supervised church affairs in the absence of formal bishops, who had fled their posts during the Protestant upheaval.[134] In addition to allowing the princes to administer church affairs temporarily, Martin Luther and Philip Melanchthon viewed them as "custodians" of the moral law in their realm, caring for the spiritual and ethical improvement of believers.[135]

The idea that a secular ruler could be the final arbiter of sacred and secular authority in the territorial realm originated not with Luther but with theologians of the later, post-Augsburg period, when the principle of *cuius regio, eius religio* consolidated Protestantism within clearly defined territorial boundaries. The late sixteenth and the early seventeenth centuries saw the emergence of growing criticism by Lutheran clerics of the abuses of princely "emergency" powers in Germany as well as the Puritans' often blatant contempt for royal authority in England. This, in turn, prompted a reaction and a more concerted effort to define the spiritual powers of a Protestant secular ruler.[136] The seventeenth-century movement of Protestant jurisprudence in the Holy Roman Empire (Reichspublizistik) embodied this endeavor to turn against Lutheran and Puritan critics of secular authority. It endowed the prince with the final authority to legally oversee religious reform in their realm (*ius Reformandi*), becoming the realm's supreme bishop (*summus episcopus*).[137] Among the famous jurists of this movement were the architects of Danish "absolutism" Henning Arnisaeus (1575–1636) and Dietrich (Theodor) Reinkingk (1590–1664), as well as theologians like Joachim Stephanus (1577–1623) and Johann Gerhard.[138]

So, to sacralize the office of the monarch, the Protestant jurists bestowed upon it the ecclesiastical title of the highest bishop, including *summus episcopus* and pontifex maximus. According to Reinkingk and Stephanus, the title of pontifex maximus belonged to the emperor and not the pope. In Roman times, they argued, pagan emperors were the supreme priests of Rome's civil religion, yet this special status as pontifex maximus continued after Constantine the Great converted to Christianity, with one caveat: emperors were now in charge of regulating the Christian religion, not the pagan cult.[139] The emperor became the supreme priest of the church (*summus Ecclesiae Pontifex*).[140] Johann Gerhard's argument, that such authority made the monarch a chief bishop of the church holding the office of *summus episcopus* or *Summepiskopat*, was very similar to Reinkingk's idea of pontifex maximus.[141] The powers of a Christian pontifex, however, were limited only to the temporal sphere of church life: he could not preside over the sacraments, ordain deacons, nor take the place of the clergy in the spiritual care of believers. There was still a difference between a "political kingdom [*regnum Politicum*]" and the "kingdom of Christ." While the ruler belonged to both kingdoms as a Christian person, his responsibilities and "calling" were different from those who possessed purely religious duties.[142]

The Protestant jurists' intellectual impetus for giving the princes custodial powers over the church also came from their reaction to Niccolò Machiavelli.[143] Thus, Reinkingk's *Biblische Policey* (1651), dedicated to the king of Denmark-Norway, argued against Machiavellian political ethics by elevating the example of a godly ruler who rules by "ordained authority [*Obrigkeit*]" and "supervision [*policey*]" over religious affairs, bringing blessings to his nation, including "godliness [*Gottseligkeit*]," love, the calming of passions, splendor, peace, education, "unity [*Bündniss*]," and "orderly home management," among many others.[144]

Unfortunately for Reinkingk, the Protestants lived in the world where a German Holy Roman Emperor should ideally have become the *summus episcopus*;

but in reality, the emperor (being a Catholic) rejected the title. Therefore, the title was extended to the local prince or king. Stephanus, who coined the phrase *cuius regio, eius religio*, argued that the authority of pontifex belonged to the princes due to their privilege of territorial jurisdiction.[145] (It was only in 1871 that Lutherans got their true *summus episcopus*, when Wilhelm II assumed the imperial mantle of Germany.)

Unlike Lutheran polities in late Reformation Germany, the eighteenth-century Russian church had no such obstacles. In this one way, Feofan's work exceeded and intuitively completed the *Reichspublizistik* project when the Synod and the Senate crowned their own emperor in 1721 and when Prokopovich invoked the sacred title that Protestants used to covet for the Holy Roman kaiser.

Feofan's essay expounded upon the reformed status of the Russian monarch: emperors are "sacred, sanctified, and divine."[146] Similar to Protestant jurists in Europe, Feofan defended the "episcopal authority [*vlast' arkhiereskaia*]" of the ruler, invoking the titles of "Summus Pontifex," "bishop," and "bishop of bishops."[147] Like Joachim Stephanus, Feofan argued that the title originally belonged to the pagan Roman emperors, who transferred it to Christian emperors after the time of Constantine.[148] Similar to the jurists of *Reichspublizistik*, Feofan also presented the territorial (*Landesherrliches*) argument of the ruler's episcopal authority as "a lord in his dominion."[149] Like Machiavelli's Protestant critics, Feofan emphasizes the providential benevolence of the monarch's rule or *Policey*; for example, tsar is the "physician of his ailing fatherland [and] architect of the common good [*obshego dobra*]."[150] Finally, in parallel to Reinkingk and others, Prokopovich differentiated between the spiritual and political realm of the pontifex's authority. While pagan emperors could lead ritual acts of worship, Christian ones could not. "For the power of the Pontifex was solely political [*politicheskaia*], separated from the sacramental rite [*sviashchenodeistviia*]," he wrote.[151] The Russian pontifex was a benevolent overseer, manager, and symbolic sacred leader of the church here on earth, but not an ordained priest within the heavenly body of Christ (even if he was a member of that body as a Christian).

The earthly sacredness of the tsar's power was justified not only by legal arguments but also by empirical observation. In the natural world, Feofan argued in his later manuscript on the nature of the Antichrist, *Pokazanie*, there were few miracles, because the powers of the monarch limited the need for them. What rulers could achieve by mustering the combined force of their power was truly miraculous. Any other miracles were either supernatural, or more likely, forged by the clergy who envied the majesty of the sovereign's power. Prokopovich explains:

> When a secular ruler [*mirskoi vladetel'*] seeks greater power or wealth, he does this through force. He sees no need to make up signs and wonders. This is found plainly in the history of the expansion of kingdoms and the convention of the world. Only the clerical estate resorts to the hypocrisy of displaying self-righteousness and of making up visions and miracles for ungodly profit, because they do not possess the power of force [given to the ruler]. . . . Such clergy arrogate for themselves [*promyshliaet*] not only some wealth and honor but also the power of dominion [*vlastitel'skuiu silu*].[152]

Thus, endowed by God with the force of the sword, the tsar had the power to expand his domain or enrich it by means available only and solely to the anointed ruler. The clergy's invocation of supernatural miracles was the usurpation of the natural miracle given to the ruler by Providence. It was driven by their desire to assume the powers of the ruler, powers that did not belong to them in the natural order of things. There was hardly anything more sacred for Feofan than secular authority.

More Soldiers, Fewer Monks: Monastic Reform

The *Spiritual Regulation* did not exhaust the scope of reforms introduced by Feofan and his allies. The reforms also involved reformulation of the Russian Orthodox Synod's positions on asceticism, monasticism, and the spiritual duties of the Orthodox believer. This was best articulated in Feofan's 1724 *Declaration on Monasticism* but also appeared in other works as well. The basis of Feofan's reforms was the new theology that emphasized remission of sins and justification through faith and grace, thus rejecting the importance of self-denial (especially monastic asceticism) as "truly an evil and godless view."[153] But if feats of piety and monastic asceticism had no salvific value, what did?

To answer this question, Feofan introduced the concept of the necessity of the fulfillment of one's civic duties and social utility as the key virtues of a good Christian. Much like the Protestants, Feofan placed all offices and estates on an equal footing: a monk was no different in his vocation from a navy officer and enjoyed no special dispensation with regard to salvation. Indeed, a "path to salvation" no longer entailed feats of piety or special status but solemn faith followed by the fulfillment of one's civic duties and commitment to what Luther referred to as one's vocation (*Beruf*).[154]

Fulfillment of one's secular calling trumped any feat of piety for Feofan. "Whoever wants to walk on the path of salvation ought to act according to his vocation," the archbishop stated.[155] To illustrate how one's devotion to secular duty should look in real life, Feofan related two parables. One was the parable of a praying judge who spent too much time praying in church and not enough working in court, fulfilling his duties. "The victims are awaiting the court trial and cannot get one," asked Feofan, "and for what reason? The judge is praying to God in church. Oh, how sinful is his prayer!"[156] Prokopovich was perhaps the first Orthodox hierarch in Russian history to state that praying could in fact be a sin.

The second was the parable of a fasting judge. While Feofan did not oppose fasting, he argued that fasting should only be practiced in accordance with one's "vocation or status [zvaniia ili sostoianiia]," so that certain people should not fast at all, lest they fall into sin.[157] The reason for that was the fact that "a hungry man is angrier and more sadistic [svirepee] than a satiated one."[158] Therefore, fasting could affect the work performance of that overly pious judge. "If a judge, especially of choleric or melancholic type [prirody], is hungry—then, can we expect justice or levelheaded case inquiry from him?" he asked.[159]

Feofan's critical and utilitarian approach to asceticism formed the basis for the legal restrictions on monasticism in Russia. On January 31, 1724, the Holy Synod and Tsar Peter promulgated a declaration (ob'iavlenie) that reformulated the role of monasticism in Russia, infusing it with a new utilitarian ethos.[160] This document essentially answered the dilemma of what the Russian government should do with all its numerous holy monasteries and convents now that monasticism was another form of secular vocation and monastic piety had no special salvific value.

The foundational premise of the 1724 Declaration was the monks' allegedly hitherto unremedied idleness and abuse of piety. Contemporary monks were "hypocritically pious [khanzhi]" "idlers [bezdel'niki]" and "parasites [tuneiadtsy]," who embraced an "intolerable heresy" of believing that they should "live off other people's labor." Fending off potential counter-arguments, the document asked, "And to those that argue that the monks pray [as their job], well then, everyone prays . . . what benefit [pribyl'] does this bring to society?" To remedy the monks' "laziness [lenost']" Prokopovich encouraged them to carry out their vocation (or spiritual calling) in pursuing useful work in the arts, sciences, or physical labor. "All people must labor in accordance to their calling," he stated, adding that carrying out one's vocation was superior "not only to taking up contemporary monasticism, but even very ancient monasticism."[161]

More importantly, the archbishop cautioned against the proliferation of monasteries in the country. An abundance of monasteries can destroy the country's economy and undermine its security. To prove this point, Feofan brought up the example of Byzantine decline, in which the proliferation of monasteries supposedly ushered in the fall of Constantinople:

As the history of Constantinople tells us, there were three hundred monasteries on a barely thirty-verst stretch of land between the Black Sea and Constantinople. There were others in other places, and all of them enjoyed large incomes. As a result of this negligence [*neusmotrenie*], the Greeks met with catastrophe when they could find less than 6,000 soldiers to defend besieged Constantinople against the Turks.[162]

The moral of this story was clear: Russia needed more soldiers and fewer monks. However, while Feofan favored fewer monastics, he did not envision abolishing the institution. Although deeming some monastic rules "burdensome," he believed that the institution was necessary for practical reasons.[163] Among such practical reasons was the fact that all bishops were appointed from the cadres of the learned monastic clergy. Another reason was the fact that some elite monasteries were important centers of theological education. Furthermore, monasteries also had utilitarian value. As well-organized (and in many cases, well-endowed) institutions, they could help fulfill the new Orthodox ethical imperative to benefit the state and society.

Thus, from the 1720s on, and as late as the 1760s, the reformist Synod restricted access to monastic tonsure to very few categories of people (such as retired soldiers) in order to prevent those "who are fit for military service" from becoming monks.[164] For the young adults, tonsure came only through special dispensations from the Synod. To discourage tonsuring without synodal decrees, provincial bishops periodically inspected monastery grounds. Thus, in 1735, Nizhnii Novgorod's Archbishop Pitirim (Feofan's ally) returned 293 monks and 224 nuns in his diocese to secular status. In Feofan's Novgorod diocese, 411 monastics were defrocked that same year.[165] In Moscow, the crackdown reduced the number of monks from 647 to 338 in the city's ten most important monasteries.[166]

While the number of monks and nuns declined, the institutional incomes (often derived from ownership of large lands and many serfs) did not, allowing the Synod to fill the vacant cells in the monasteries with non-monastics. Monasteries and convents were increasingly repurposed to serve wider social and military needs: as retirement homes for soldiers, officers, and their widows; as hospitals; as prisons and detention centers for the secret police; as supply bases for the army; and as centers of public education and enterprise (like craft-making).[167] The monastery's land-derived incomes funded these new operations inside the monastery walls. In monasteries that served as hospitals, the ratio of monks to patients was as high as one to three; the monasteries that housed retired military personnel were required to feed and house them at ratios of one monk to one soldier and one monk to one and a half

officers (in terms of space and available provisions).[168] One can only imagine the
new reality of such repopulation: the halls and cells once filled with monks and
nuns, exercising their devotions, were now also crowded with retired soldiers
or invalids, requiring round-the-clock care. To prevent the monks from shirk-
ing their civic responsibilities, the Synod instituted a new passport system that
banned even short absences without special papers. Much like the military
confined to their bases, the monks were now confined within the walls of their
monasteries.[169]

There were important exceptions to these regulations. Among the excepted
were the elite monasteries (like the ones in St. Petersburg and Moscow), which
became intellectual centers of Protestant-inspired theological learning that
supplied the Holy Synod with festive celebrations, enlightened hierarchs, and
"emancipated monks."[170] The decrees also did not affect the Ukrainian dioceses
that provided Russia with so many learned clerical cadres. Prokopovich argued
that the laws applied to the dioceses of the "Russian Empire," but excluded
Ukraine from the jurisdiction of that empire.[171] As a result, the number of
monks in Kiev remained stable or even increased up until 1756. In 1749, some
court officials grumbled in the Synod that "even seventeen-year-olds could
become monks" in Ukraine.[172] These exemptions served to sustain the flourishing of the Kievan tradition of learned monasticism (exemplified by such
erudite monks as Feofan himself) and ensured that Ukrainians staffed most of
the bishoprics and synodal positions in Russia for several decades to come.[173]

Overall, the reforms' social imperative that the monastic calling have utilitarian value led to the decline of monasteries. From 1724 to 1739, the number of
monks and nuns in Russia declined from 25,207 to 14,282. By 1762, there were
a total of 12,392 monastics in Russia (7,659 monks and 4,733 nuns). In 1700
there were 924 male monasteries and 229 convents, by 1764, there were 318 and
67 respectively, or 385 total.[174] The decline of monasticism would not be halted
until the middle of the nineteenth century as a result of the reaction to many
aspects of Feofan's reforms, a subject that will be addressed in the epilogue.

THE OPPOSITION OF 1721

These theological treatises provoked reactions from the party opposed to Feofan.
His 1720 catechism received a critical appraisal almost from the start, as seen
in Dmitrii Kantemir's manuscript. But the preparation of the *Spiritual Regulation* also stirred tempers among Feofan's opponents. In March 1721, shortly
after the inauguration of the new Synod, Prokopovich survived his first assassination attempt. The plot involved the vicar-abbot of the Aleksandr Nevskii
Monastery in St. Petersburg, Varlaam Golenkovskii, as well as two hierodeacons
of the same monastery, Meletii and Pavel. Their discontent with the reforms

motivated them to attempt the murder of Feofan and Feodosii so that "their cause would not prevail further."[175] Luckily for Feofan, Feodosii Ianovskii staffed the monastery with the best clerical inspectors or "commissioners [*komissary*]," who were loyal particularly to him. Among such loyal monks were Hierodeacon Pafnutii and Father Gerasim—the latter oversaw the monks' auricular confessions, through which he learned about the plot. Although Golenkovskii's guilt remained unproven, he lost his position at the monastery and the lower clergy involved in the case were imprisoned or demoted.[176] This would not be the only death threat against Feofan.

Although some members of the clergy appeared desperate to stop the reforms, most influential opponents preferred to use less radical means of opposing Feofan, namely written polemics. The most important objection to the founding document of the Holy Synod, the *Spiritual Regulation*, came from the former exarch of the church and now member of the Synod, Stefan Iavorskii. According to one account, he opposed the *Regulation* from its inception, "resisted it strongly," and even "avoided signing it for a while."[177] However, his official and written protest against the institution of the collegial system of church governance came in June 9, 1721, when he submitted his *Apologia or Verbal Defense of the Candid Invocation and Prayerful Remembrance of the Holy Orthodox Patriarchs in Churches*.[178]

The *Apologia* did not challenge the abolition of the Moscow Patriarchate but argued that the "Holy Governing Synod" must still invoke the name of the Patriarch of Constantinople.[179] Stefan questioned the autocephalous authority of the Russian, Serbian, Bulgarian, and other national churches as "the vice of lust for power [*vlastoliubie*]" and called for the restoration of the prerogatives of the Ecumenical Patriarchate.[180] "Nothing prevents the Russian Synod from showing a loving, filial subordination to the Patriarch of Constantinople, according to the ancient tradition," he wrote.[181] His belief in placing Russia under the transnational Constantinopolitan patriarch was not altogether strange given that patriarch's tutelage over the Kievan metropolitan throne until 1685. Yet it cut directly against the Russian canonical tradition, by which Moscow had had its own patriarchs since 1589.[182] Revising the liturgical litany of mentioning the patriarchs in the way that would emphasize Constantinople's preeminence would then make the Synod more canonical, since, he argued, without acknowledging the authority of the pan-Orthodox patriarch, the Synod would resemble "headless assemblies, heretics, and schismatics for whom there is no need for patriarchs, metropolitans, archbishops, or any other shepherds."[183]

Despite this strongly worded protest, the balance of power was not on Iavorskii's side. The Patriarch of Constantinople never came to support this view, nor did jurisdiction of Constantinople apply or extend to Moscow.[184] Furthermore,

Feofan never held a high view of the Eastern patriarchs to begin with, calling them "vagabond beggars" and arguing "that we should not rely on them in the matters of faith, for whoever offers the most bribes, becomes a patriarch among them."[185] When further pressed to explain his position, Prokopovich maintained that the corruption of the Eastern patriarchs was "well known around the world" and that, by the way, "some Patriarchs were heretics, too."[186]

Feofan's opinions likely shaped his brazen attitude toward Constantinople in February 1721, when he drafted the Russian church's request for the Ecumenical Patriarch's recognition of the Holy Synod. The document essentially lectured Jeremias III on the virtues of collegial government and the perils of ecclesiastical monarchy. This draft displeased Peter so much that the tsar scrapped it altogether and composed (or ordered someone else to compose) another letter, a much more unpretentious appeal, deferring to Jeremias as the "chief Archpriest [*arkhipastyr'*]" of the Orthodox world.[187] The patriarchs of Constantinople and Jerusalem sent their approvals to Peter in 1723.

What happened to Iavorskii and his idea to embrace stronger hierarchical ties to Constantinople? During the swift pace of reforms in 1721, his *Apologia* was ignored, and then rejected as a "villainous and rebellious composition with much falsehood against the Synod."[188] Consequently, Stefan was barred from spreading or publishing this work.[189] Such disregard for the president of the Synod was a clear sign that Stefan (who rarely attended Synod meetings)— was a "mere decoration" whom Feodosii and Feofan treated like a "stubborn capricious child."[190] As James Cracraft aptly put it, by the time he died in November 1722, "Iavorskii, at least, regarded himself as a failure."[191]

RUSSIAN ORTHODOX REFORM:
THE PROTESTANT VIEWS

Feofan obviously had plenty of critics and supporters among the secular and ecclesiastical elites, whose denunciations and backing would continue to play an important role in the debates of 1725–30 that will be addressed in the next chapter. However, Prokopovich also had admirers among Protestant clergymen and diplomats, both the ones living abroad and those resident in the Russian Empire. How did the European Protestants view Feofan's reforms? Their contemporaneous assessments of the religious change in Russia underlined its comparatively radical nature. However, at the same time, they noted the cautious pace of reforms and their avoidance of the extremes that produced many of the calamities of the sixteenth century in Europe.

One interesting account comes from an Estonian Pietist observer, Albert Anton Vierorth, who visited Feofan in July and August of 1721 at his residence and in the company of Russian Army general Ludwig Nicolaus von Hallart

and his wife, Baroness Magdalene Elisabeth von Hallart.[192] Vierorth noted
Feofan's observation of the "miserable [*elend*]" state of the church in need of
reform, where "the real worship of God was supplanted by innumerable superstitious [*abergläubische*] ceremonies."[193] To change this sad reality in Russia,
Feofan and the tsar sought to learn from the experience of "the Protestant
Church" toward whom both were "well disposed." The bishop's determination
and the many hurdles that he needed to overcome to succeed in his reforms
elicited Vierorth's comparison to the struggles of early Protestant leaders. "But
as Martin Luther by God's help could overcome his obstacles," Vierorth observed, "so he hoped that little by little, the Lord's Hour [of renewal] would
come upon the Eastern Church."[194]

An even bolder comparison of the church reform to the European Reformation was found in the anonymous 1725 *Curieuse Nachricht*, likely of Saxon
provenance. According to this treatise, Russia's religious reform was "fashioned
[*eingerichtet*] in accordance with Evangelical-Lutheran foundations [*Grund-
saetzen*]."[195] Prior to reform, the author argued, patriarchs in Russia behaved "as
Roman Popes in Italy" and the country had "many monasteries, fashioned in a
Roman Catholic way, where monks studied so little that they could only read
in Russian."[196] Realizing that "sciences will not flourish without a true religion
[*ohne wahre Religion*]," Peter looked to the examples of "Holland, England, and
Germany" to promote reform within his church.[197] The Lutheran character
of the changes that ensued was very obvious. The author compared Russian
church reform to Luther's:

> Traveling among the Protestants only increased the tsar's resolve. In Luther's
> times, the greater acceptance and growth of sciences opened people's eyes to
> learn something truthful and to shun the darkness of ignorance, greatly fostering
> the blessed Reformation. Similarly, in Russia, the tsar's Imperial Majesty opened
> their eyes to the worldly sciences and stately wisdom, to promote true religion.
> And here, we will not err in stating that His Imperial Majesty made his religion
> identical [*gleichförmig*] to the Evangelical-Lutheran religion.[198]

There were more references to Russia's reform that compared it to the
Reformation. Thus in 1736, the Danish observer Peder von Haven referred to
the church reforms as "a reformation of the spiritual order."[199] Professor Christian Martini in 1731 also used the framework of the European Reformation to
proclaim the new Orthodoxy created by Feofan and Peter as a "*Russisch-
Lutheranisirende Kirche*"—which stemmed from "changing [*sich geändert*]" the
"church organization [*Kirchen-Staat*]" and the "improvement of learning [*Ver-
besserung der Lehren*]."[200]

Martini's conclusions echoed the 1723 observations of Johann Peter Kohl, whose aforementioned book employed the provocative title *Ecclesia Graeca Lutheranizans* (Lutheranization of the Greek Church). Not only did this assertion of "Lutheranization" not offend Prokopovich, but the Holy Synod played a crucial role in inviting Kohl to the Academy of Sciences two years later, granting him an apartment and a six-hundred-ruble salary.[201] Later English accounts in the eighteenth century echoed German terminology: John Bancks in his 1740 biography of Peter the Great used the term "Reformation" to describe the church reform, while John Glen King's *Rites and Ceremonies of the Greek Church in Russia* contained a lengthy description titled a "history of the Russian church and its reformation."[202]

Another interesting assessment came from a later period. The 1745 dissertation of Jakob Wilhelm Feuerlein (1689–1766), a Göttingen professor and former student of Feofan's old friend Buddeus, compared Russia's "recent" theology with the "old [*veterum*]" Muscovite set of beliefs and declared the new Orthodoxy to be a "holy modern [*hodierna*] doctrine" that emulated the "fundamentals of true religion" found in the Protestant West.[203] He argued that much like the Protestants, the Russian church embraced the doctrine of revelation through "sacred Scripture only [*solam Scripturam sacram*]."[204] He praised the reforms even further, arguing that "today's Russian religion is clearly explained, established, and led by the Holy Scripture, and is restored by the example of the ancient and pure church. If we ever compare this religion with other general flowerings of religion today, we will easily recognize it to be directly alien to the dogmatic character of the Romanists or the Reformed, but truly more closely approaching our Evangelical-Lutheran religion."[205]

Although some foreign observers highlighted the wide-ranging parallels between Russia's "holy modern doctrine" and the Protestant Reformation, others remained very cognizant of the manifest differences. In general, the pace of change was much slower in Russia than in Reformation Germany, and Feofan, unlike Luther, favored more cautious methods of transformation than an urgent rupture with the status quo. As Vierorth had observed, Prokopovich retained "sensibility . . . to the imperfections [*Gebrechen*] of the Church to which he belonged, [and] he submitted to all its ceremonies and regulations so that he might not tempt the weak and the ignorant [*Unwissende*]."[206]

Feofan's diplomatic sensibility to the ancient corpus of Russian liturgical and ceremonial traditions appears also in the account of Swedish geographer Philip von Strahlenberg. The Swede met Feofan personally and visited the same Pietist circles as Vierorth and General Hallart in 1722–23.[207] According to him, Feofan tolerated many ceremonial elements of Russian Orthodox faith, such as the special services for the dead, the opulent clerical vestments, the incense

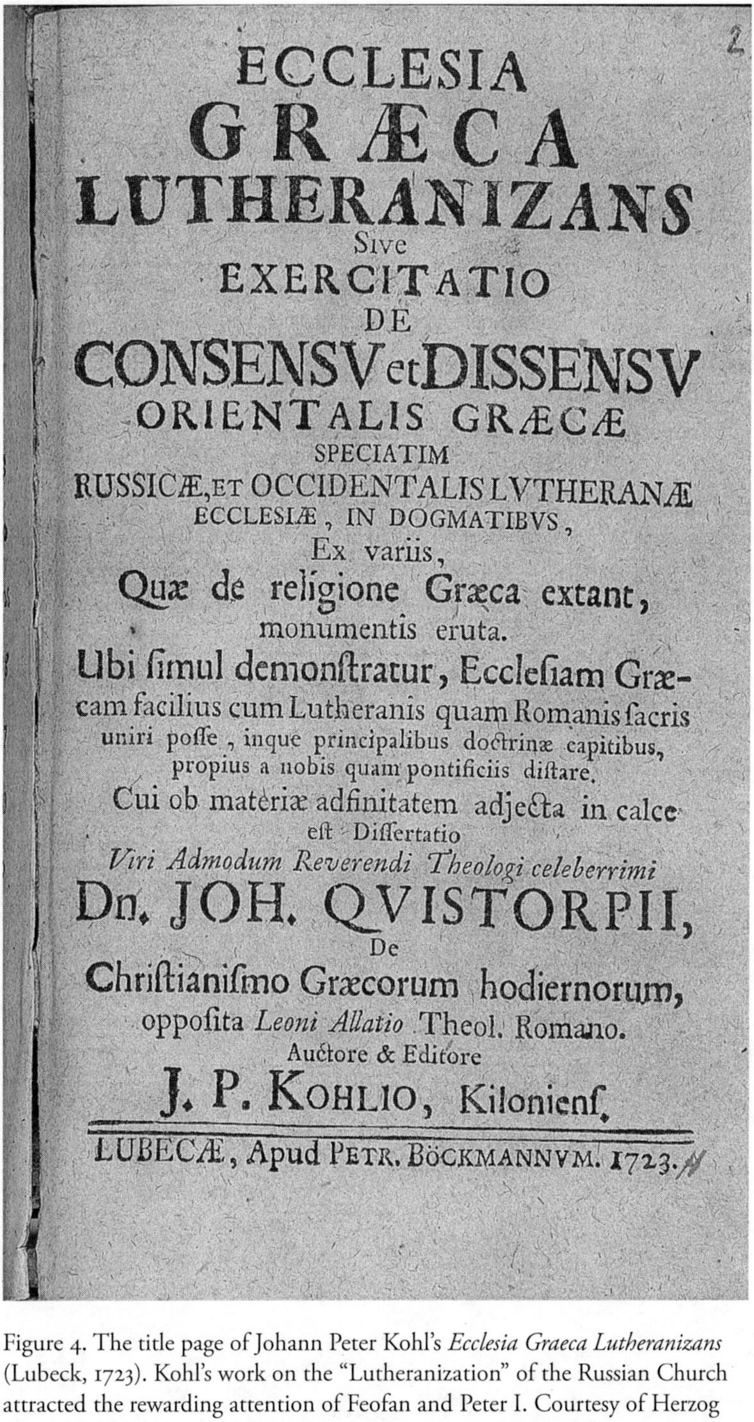

ECCLESIA
GRÆCA
LUTHERANIZANS
Sive
EXERCITATIO
DE
CONSENSV et DISSENSV
ORIENTALIS GRÆCÆ
SPECIATIM
RUSSICÆ, ET OCCIDENTALIS LVTHERANÆ
ECCLESIÆ, IN DOGMATIBVS,
Ex variis,

Quæ de religione Græca extant,
monumentis eruta.

Ubi fimul demonftratur, Ecclefiam Græ-
cam facilius cum Lutheranis quam Romanis facris
uniri poffe, inque principalibus doctrinæ capitibus,
propius a nobis quam pontificiis diftare.

Cui ob matériæ adfinitatem adjecta in calce
eft Differtatio
Viri Admodum Reverendi Theologi celeberrimi

Dn. JOH. QVISTORPII,
De
Chriftianifmo Græcorum hodiernorum,
oppofita *Leoni Allatio* Theol. Romano.
Auctore & Editore

J. P. KOHLIO, Kilonienf.

LUBECÆ, Apud PETR. BÖCKMANNVM. 1723.

Figure 4. The title page of Johann Peter Kohl's *Ecclesia Graeca Lutheranizans*
(Lubeck, 1723). Kohl's work on the "Lutheranization" of the Russian Church
attracted the rewarding attention of Feofan and Peter I. Courtesy of Herzog
August Bibliothek, Wolfenbüttel. Signatur: M: QuN 460.1 (2).

burning before images, and the long, repetitive liturgies. At the same time, in private he wished that "instead of these [ceremonies], it would be much better to serve God with the singing of psalms, praying, and reading the Word of God and instructing the people with pious sermons."[208] The slow-paced nature of the reform was highlighted also in the recollections of Prussian ambassadorial secretary Vockerodt. The diplomat noted that it took the tsar and Prokopovich over a decade to bring reform to fruition due to the fact of "the war with Sweden being in full swing [*in voller Flamme*]" and therefore it was "not the right time to begin such a sensitive [*delicates*] work of reform." "Peter did not want to stir up controversy," Vockerodt concluded.[209]

CONCLUSION

While "sensitive" to the liturgical and ceremonial aspects of Russian religious culture, Feofan's *coup de l'église* was highly radical and disruptive doctrinally, ideologically, administratively, and canonically. From the purely dogmatic standpoint, the content of the new Orthodox teaching was undeniably Protestant-inspired in virtually all major points of systematic theology, save for the Filioque. Yet most of the ceremonial and liturgical life of the church retained its original Byzantine frame, inherited in 988. In a similar fashion, such ancient church institutions as monasticism retained their form, but the substance of the monastic telos was now infused with a utilitarian (and in many ways, Protestant-inspired) ethos. Meanwhile, the old Russian-Byzantine Caesarean conception of the monarch as a protector of Orthodoxy was preserved in form, but infused with new meaning influenced by European political theology. Reforms sacralized the proclamation/kerygma of the monarchical state as the guardian of the common good, while every Christian's salvation now depended on the fulfillment of duties toward that state! Protestant in substance but Orthodox in form, Feofan's "coup de l'église" made a deep-lasting impact on Russian society. The state became more sacred, while the church (and its purpose in society) far more secular than before.

4

A Struggle for Orthodoxy

Saving Russia from "Papist Tyranny," 1725–1736

Away, Away,
The sorrowful night!
What darkness befell us,
And what horror!
Till Anna the Sun had risen.

—FEOFAN PROKOPOVICH, "Poem on the Occasion of
Anna's Coronation," 1730

THE "SORROWFUL NIGHT"
OF FEOFAN PROKOPOVICH

Peter I, Feofan's greatest patron, died on January 28, 1725. According to the official sources, the tsar died from acute inflammation of the kidneys and urinary tract, having struggled with worsening urinary ailments in the preceding year.[1] The night before his death, January 27, 1725, Feofan, Gavriil, Feofil, and Feofilakt joined some senators and family members at the tsar's bed, to pray and express empathy.

According to the official account, Peter listened attentively to Feofan's teaching on justification during his last days.[2] As his death appeared imminent, Feofan instructed the emperor to place his trust for gaining eternal life into "the justification of sinners by grace through Christ." Hearing these words, the tsar raised his hands and replied, "This alone quenches my thirst, this alone soothes me!"[3] This dramatic bedside experience led the Swedish ambassador to erroneously conclude that Peter died as a Lutheran, an opinion that circulated among other Protestant divines.[4] However, it also reflected the extent to which the emperor personally came to profess Feofan's (rather novel) theological formulations, with their emphasis on justification through grace and faith.[5] Innovation did not stop at the deathbed: Feofan's famous funeral oration imitated the Prussian Lutheran *Abdankungsreden* (burial homilies), while the funeral ceremony of March 1725 (in which the bishops played no small role) introduced many elements of the "Brandenburg protocol" of 1688 and 1713.[6]

Peter's death inaugurated a period of factional struggle, described, in Feofan's own words, as a "sorrowful night" filled with "horror."[7] During this era of palace coups spanning the reigns of Catherine I (1725–27) and Peter II (1728–30), the fate of church reform hung in the balance between Prokopovich's supporters (the so-called *Feofanisty*) and the members of the patriarchate restorationist party.[8] The two ecclesiastical factions thrust themselves into the shifting alliances of the new political-oligarchical entity, the Supreme Privy Council, dominated first by Menshikov and later by the Dolgorukii and Golitsyn family clans. Meanwhile, enthusiasm for the changes of the Petrine era waned among the secular and ecclesiastical elites, the political fortunes of the reformist camp in the church declined, and the court abandoned St. Petersburg, returning the capital to Moscow for the period 1728–30.

How Feofan survived this challenging period will constitute the chief focus of this chapter. Although confronting a formidable opposition, Prokopovich emerged victorious, not simply because of his theological and polemical talents but also due to his careful statesmanship. During these years Feofan was not only a bishop but also a politician. He, and the ecclesiastical elites in general, played a much more engaged role during this period of "palace coups" than has so far been emphasized in the recent historiography on this turbulent period.[9] Therefore, while theology played a crucial role in shaping Feofan's reforms and worldview, political power played a crucial role in helping him and his allies during the reform's contestation.

In 1725, Feofan inherited one fundamental disadvantage that did not allow him to sustain the pace of reform after Peter's death. This was the composition of the Holy Synod. Prokopovich sought to exclude the philo-Catholic hierarchs from synodal membership, or perhaps even purge them altogether (which he ended up achieving during the purges of 1730–36). Peter, however, promoted both Iavorskii and Lopatinskii to their positions of power in the Synod, ostensibly out of "respect" for their spiritual standing.[10] Ultimately, this meant that Feofan's struggle against the philo-Catholic faction was not necessarily Peter's battle also. Hints of the bishop's disappointment with the tsar's "respect" for Feofan's enemies surfaced during the installation of the Synod on February 14, 1721, when Prokopovich, in the opening speech, hurled insults at the "vulgar ignoramuses" and "mad men" who rejected Feofan's "correct and fundamental doctrine" and whose theological views threatened "this institution as the most precious attribute of your [Peter's] eternal legacy."[11] Although the tsar's patronage thwarted any resistance to reform during the first four years of the Synod's existence, the tsar's refusal to staff the hierarchy with Feofan's men alone meant that the opposition outlived the tsar.

Peter's death bolstered the forces of the opposition. Feofan's enemies, old and new (such as bishops Feofilakt Lopatinskii and Georgii Dashkov), built powerful alliances with the members of the Supreme Privy Council to advance the idea of restoring the patriarchate. Their cause ultimately failed for several reasons. First, the mercurial and occasionally chaotic court politics under Catherine I and Peter II helped Feofan maneuver between the quickly waning and rising alliances, allowing him to place his bets on the winning sides. Then, the patriarchate restorationists miscalculated both the political fortunes of the Golitsyn and Dolgorukii oligarchical clans and the strength of the newly consolidated Petrine elites who remained steady in their support for the new Russia. Finally, Feofan's somewhat hysterical anti-Catholic polemics presented the oligarchs and those who sympathized with the patriarchate as seditious; these polemics played no small role in his final triumph. As Prokopovich himself summarized it later, the struggle against the enemies of the Petrine reforms saved Orthodox Russia from the impending doom of "Papist tyranny." The result of Feofan's victory was the systematic purge of clerics who were suspected of "Papist" sympathies or political sedition in 1730–36. The purges altered the composition of the Russian hierarchy and staffed key positions with Feofan's appointees and allies, who shared the theological worldview of their patron and teacher.

CATHERINE I AND THE INTRIGUES OF MENSHIKOV

Peter, as Reinhard Wittram correctly noted, died "without designating a successor to the throne."[12] One of the leading candidates for the throne was Catherine, the wife of the late tsar. An outsider to Russia and the Romanov dynasty, her obscure origins and her meteoric rise from a humble orphan to an empress in her own right were the source of speculation, legends, and even theatrical plays (such as the "Mädchen von Marienburg") in the eighteenth century.[13]

Peter crowned Catherine empress of Russia in 1724, although he also berated her for her affair with Willi Mons. Nevertheless, she enjoyed support from Prokopovich as well as many members of St. Petersburg's new elite, including Prince Menshikov.[14] Feofan ended up playing a particularly important role in arguing the case for Catherine. According to the record of cabinet discussions immediately following the monarch's death, Prokopovich argued "with emotional eloquence" that the 1724 coronation designated Catherine as the heir and that the senators and synodal members' 1722 oath to obey the tsar's wishes in matters of succession obligated them to support her.[15]

When the objection arose that coronation alone did not necessarily imply a designation, Feofan recalled an instance in which Peter disclosed his intention ("opening up his heart") to designate his wife as his successor in a private meeting with "four government ministers and two synodal members."[16] Then, the archbishop asked the cabinet ministers (Menshikov among them) and Archbishop Feodosii to testify to the veracity of this conversation. After these testimonies turned persuasive, Prokopovich proclaimed Catherine's right to the throne, not through "an election [*elektsiia*]" but through a "declaration [*deklaratsiia*]."[17]

While Prokopovich emerged as one of Catherine's proverbial queenmakers and thus a savior of Menshikov's dominant position at the court, he did not reap many benefits from it. In the first months, relations remained cordial: Menshikov, for example, supported Feofan's promotion to the archbishopric of Novgorod in June 1725.[18] Yet, as the summer of 1725 progressed, the two eventually parted ways. This was not Feofan's problem alone: the prince's inordinate powers worried many of the members of the 1725 pro-Catherine coalition, among them General Anton Devier and counts Petr Tolstoi and Aleksander Naryshkin.[19]

What put Prokopovich directly at odds with the prince was the bishop's support for the so-called Holstinian party, a connection that has not received enough scholarly analysis. The party was headed by Karl Friedrich, duke of Holstein (1700–1739), who married Peter's and Catherine's daughter Anna Petrovna in May 1725.[20] Although the ruler of a German duchy greatly reduced by territorial losses to neighboring Denmark in the Great Northern War, his male-line offspring provided the Russian throne with a succession of tsars until the downfall of the Romanov dynasty in 1917.

Catherine I elevated the couple to a high position of favor as her "first care [*premier soin*]," announcing the new Order of St. Alexander Nevsky on the day of Karl-Friedrich's marriage on May 21, 1725, and then bestowing the order on the members of his Holstinian court entourage.[21] In contrast, Alexander Menshikov was not granted the order of his patron saint until August 30, and he likely took affront to that very fact.[22] When Catherine established the Supreme Privy Council (a consultative organ patterned after the *Geheimen Räten* of the various German states of the Holy Roman Empire) in February 1726, Karl Friedrich was one of its key members, alongside Prince Menshikov.[23] It seems clear that the empress was balancing Holstinians against Menshikov's influence at court.[24]

Feofan supported the Holstinians. He officiated the marriage of Karl Friedrich and Anna Petrovna in St. Petersburg (in Russian and Latin), arranging to have the local Lutheran pastor Remarius bless the ceremony (Karl Friedrich remained Lutheran).[25] Their relations grew even warmer after 1725, when Feofan supported the idea of the couple's regency on the Russian throne should Catherine die and Anna become pregnant. When Catherine I died and Anna

Petrovna did indeed become pregnant that summer, Menshikov, alarmed, banished the couple to Kiel in July 1727. Prokopovich objected to the expulsion.[26]

Menshikov's animus against the archbishop may have been motivated by the latter's place in court politics, but the conflict extended into church affairs. After the summer decrees of 1725, Menshikov began curtailing Feofan's powers in the Synod by elevating Feofilakt Lopatinskii to the bishopric of Tver and to the status of second in command of the Synod (after Feofan).[27] The same decrees also appointed the bishop of Rostov, Georgii Dashkov, as the third-highest-ranking member of the Synod, replacing Feofan's ally and Kievan friend Rafail Zaborovskii (who was retired to Pskov).[28] A scion of the old boyar Dashkov clan, this man "hated Ukrainians" (but paradoxically, not his ally, Lopatinskii) and had a very conspicuous pretention to the patriarchal throne.[29] By late spring 1727, Menshikov had also orchestrated the accession of traditionalist hierarchs Ignatii Smola of Suzdal and Lev Iurlov of Vornonezh to the Synod. In July 1727, the Privy Council gave Ignatii Smola, Georgii Dashkov, and Feofilakt Lopatinskii the power to oversee the religious instruction of the young tsar Peter II, which was carried out by Prokopovich.[30] After 1727 the Lopatinskii-Smola-Dashkov triumvirate significantly weakened Feofan's influence in the church.[31]

THE FATES OF FEOFAN'S ALLIES

Just as Feofan's relations with Menshikov deteriorated, his alliance with Feodosii Ianovskii ended. The cause was Ianovskii's increasing arrogance: among many of his misbehaviors were demands to sit in on Admiralty meetings and to have the right-of-way in St. Petersburg's traffic; he also showed up at Catherine's palace unannounced, waking her from her afternoon naps.[32] Against Feofan's teaching, Feodosii started arguing for the restoration of clerical powers, railing against "state tyranny [tiranstvo]."[33] According to Gustav von Mardefeld, the rumor on the street was that Feodosii sought to "turn himself into [aufzuwerfen] a patriarch."[34]

The Secret Chancellery initiated a case against Ianovskii. However, as the Chancellery collected sworn testimonies from synodal members, two distinct groups of accusations against Ianovskii emerged. One favorable to Feofan, another, not. The first group of testimonies came from Feofan and his allies, Gavriil Buzhinskii, Feofil Krolik, and Petr Smelich (the priest of SS. Peter and Paul Cathedral), but also Tsar Peter's former batman, Vasilii Pospelov. Their accounts accused Feodosii of deviating from the correct view of church-state relations in his arguments for "clerical freedom, satisfaction, and preeminence" and his claims that Peter's death was divine punishment for "intrusion into ecclesiastical affairs."[35]

The second group of testimonies, submitted by Prokopovich's rivals, Feofilakt and Sil'vestr Kholmskii (of Kazan), contained a different set of accusations. While agreeing with many of the points of the first group of accusations in the Secret Chancellery's report, their report primarily aimed at Feodosii's reform-ist actions during Peter's reign. They highlighted his zeal in stamping out "idolatrously possessed superstition," his comparison of icon veneration to idol worship, and his claim that Muslim conquest of the Greek lands was a divine punishment for the Eastern churches' "idolatry."[36] Feodosii was report-edly guilty of further crimes: desecrating icons, playing chess, allowing "*assam-blei* [dance parties] and music" at his residency, taking "German baths," and even removing the church bells near his residence so that he could sleep in late during the morning hours.[37]

Such charges against Feodosii were dangerous for Feofan and his allies, who were similarly zealous in their struggle against "superstition" and whose life-style was far from ascetic. Feofan persevered, thanks to a robust defense by Petr Tolstoi, the head of the Secret Chancellery, who argued that the campaign against superstitious icon-veneration took place under "the emperor's express order."[38] Thus, the Synod indicted Feodosii only on charges of offensive be-havior and an erroneous view of the church-state relations. He was exiled to Nikolo-Korelskii Monastery near the subarctic coast of the White Sea.

With Feodosii exiled, Feofan's remaining allies from Peter's days experi-enced their own tribulations. Feofil Krolik lost his synodal membership in 1726 and the Privy Council instructed him to leave the country in May 1727 for Austria but gave no instructions on when or how to travel abroad. Since no clarification on the details of his banishment came through, he stayed in Mos-cow, losing his abbacy and residency of the Chudov Monastery and resorting to living in Novospasskii Monastery as a simple monk.[39] Gavriil Buzhinskii encountered a similar situation, although less harsh. After being elevated to the bishopric of Riazan in October 1726, Buzhinskii was instructed to leave Petersburg for his diocese the following January.[40] Following Peter II's acces-sion to the throne (in 1727), the Privy Council banned Gavriil's liturgical canon dedicated to St. Aleksandr Nevskii and ordered him to reinstate the old (pre-reform) menology canon to the saint.[41] Furthermore, the Synod assem-bled a number of cases for corruption and doctrinal deviation, piling up some fifty-five files against Buzhinskii by 1730.[42]

THE FORTY-SEVEN COUNTS OF HERESY

In 1726 Feofan faced a fresh round of accusations from his former student and vicar Markell Rodyshevskii. The catalyst for the conflict was Markell's report of the looming "deadly riot" against the "iconoclasts and enemies of the Church [presumably, Feofan included]" planned by the soldiers of the Preobrazhenskii and Semenovskii regiments. Although Markell urged Prokopovich to panic and "hide in the islands somewhere," the archbishop was not convinced that the guard regiments were planning a palace coup against him. Suspecting that it was "melancholic" Markell who was actually planning mischief against the reformer, Feofan used the Secret Chancellery to arrest the monk on July 2 for further investigation. Outraged by the arrest, Markell produced a long report accusing the reformers (Feofan and his "comrades, Feofil Krulik [sic], Gavriil of Riazan, [Lavrentii] Gorka, and others") of spreading "heretical roguery" in Russia.[43]

The report contained no less than forty-seven counts of heresy, mostly of Protestant origin. Among them were the notions that a "Christian is justified by faith only," that "there is only one Mediator [between God and man], the Lord Christ" (not the saints), and that "only faith can save us, not good deeds."[44] In addition, the "heresiarch" denied fasts as mandatory, was guilty of "multiple insults against the miracle-working St. Nicholas," and doubted the story of the Dormition of the Mother of God.[45] Interestingly, Markell was intelligent enough to know that Lutherans did not completely oppose the veneration of images and his description of Feofan's position on that issue was appropriately nuanced. Prokopovich "did not hold icons in the appropriate honor, but venerated them like the Lutherans," he stated.[46] As a way to remedy Feofan's heresy, Markell suggested the same treatment that Muscovite clergy recommended in the Tveritinov trial: death by burning at the stake, to "send him [Feofan] to his father, Satan"![47]

None of these accusations were new, as most of the church and court elites had a very good grasp of the Protestant influence in Prokopovich's teachings. What was new was the timing of the report. The end of 1726 was a challenging time for Feofan, as his secular and ecclesiastical enemies (such as Menshikov and Archbishop Georgii) were becoming more and more powerful. Despite that, Feofan managed to keep Rodyshevskii in jail while responding to the charges point by point.[48] In a recognizable pattern, Feofan attacked Markell's theological and educational credentials: not only did the monk have Catholic sympathies, but the doctrinal content of his preaching was so bad that Peter I had banned it as "mad and blasphemous." As a former teacher, Feofan also pointed out that his knowledge of Latin (and therefore theology) was weak.[49] Based on these factors, he argued, trusting Markell's assessment of his doctrine was akin to trusting a "blind man to analyze paints and colors."[50]

Feofan's second (and predictable) response to the accusations was to deny any theological deviation, presenting his views as fully Orthodox. First, he used the

Bible to prove that his theological positions were Orthodox, without denying that they appeared in Protestantism as well. "[My] teaching on justification was firmly grounded in Holy Scripture and especially, the epistles of Apostle Paul," he stated. Anyone denying it must be a "blasphemer." Second, while accepting that "the saints prayed for us," he argued, based on the Bible again, that Christ was the only mediator between God and man. Whoever denied that "insulted the Apostle [Paul]."[51]

Regarding fasting, Feofan employed a utilitarian argument, highlighting the fact that the Orthodox Church issued a "dispensation" to forego fasting for several categories of people during the Great Northern War. Only "a garbage-head [*pomoinoi golovy chelovek*]" like Rodyshevskii could ignore the usefulness of that decision, he argued. At the same time, the "insult" against St. Nicholas, Feofan explained, was directed not at the saint but at the two liturgical hymns to St. Nicholas whose origins were dubious. Thus, it was Markell and not Feofan who was the real heretic, for he dared to "label Orthodox teaching as heresy, and is now cursed by anathema."[52]

As a further confirmation of his orthodoxy, Feofan referred to the political support for his doctrine. For example, he recalled how he expounded his doctrine of justification in 1716 to "His Eminence the Prince [Menshikov] and His Eminence Admiral [Apraksin]," and how "no one saw heresy in my teaching." Furthermore, he recalled how he had instructed the tsar to put his faith in this doctrine of justification on his deathbed, and how "all those present observed it with emotion." By implication, anyone denying his teaching on justification would have to admit that the tsar died a heretic. "What Markell calls heresy, [Peter] accepted with kissing on his deathbed," he stated.[53]

Despite the refutation, Feofan did not fully clear his name. The new head of the Secret Chancellery, Ivan Romodanovskii, submitted the matter to Catherine I in December 1726. The empress did not concur with the charge of heresy but issued a stern warning to Feofan that "the archbishop should produce no more deviations against the Holy Church, which were described by the archimandrite. Instead, he [Feofan] ought to live a pure and temptation-free life like all the Great-Russian [that is, non-Ukrainian] Orthodox bishops do, so that he does not produce changes in the church service or church ordinances and so he does not act differently from the Great Russian bishops. If he becomes guilty of deviation from the Holy Church by someone else's accusation again, no more mercy will be shown to him by Her Imperial Majesty."[54]

The warning was particularly ominous for Prokopovich. The empress's call to conform with the "Great-Russian hierarchs" meant deferring to the pro-patriarchate party of Dashkov, Iurlov, and Smola. It also reflected an earlier 1726 synodal report by aspiring patriarch Georgii Dashkov, who condemned the "educated and sophisticated [*politichnye*] persons" (that is, reformist Ukrainian clergy) who spent their time in pleasures, "parties [*vecherinki*]," and "decorating their carriages."[55]

Silenced by the reprimand and weakened by the accusations of heresy, Feofan spent the last months of Catherine's reign and the first months of 1727 in utter despair. "My state of affairs was so dire that I thought everything was over," wrote Feofan in 1728, reflecting on the previous year.[56] Increasingly ostracized from synodal politics and excluded from court life, he planned an escape. According to Swedish ambassador Josias Cederhjelm, it was during that time that Feofan and Feofil Krolik asked him about asylum in Sweden. Feofan approached the ambassador "*sub fide silentii* [under the promise of silence]" and related to him that he was "under suspicion for his thoughts in affairs of religion" and that Menshikov was maneuvering against him.[57] Fortunately for the archbishop, however, the fall of Menshikov and the brief power struggle that took place after it brought Prokopovich a temporary respite. The patriarchate restorationists (like Dashkov and Lopatinskii) would have to wait until 1728 to launch a renewed attack on Prokopovich's "Lutheran heresies" and reforms.

The Viennese Candidate: Peter II

Feofan's affairs worsened after the death of Catherine on May 6, 1727. As her death approached, Menshikov assembled chief senators, court members, and various Romanov family relatives (including Elizabeth and the Holstinians) to decide the succession. Feofan was excluded from that event, although Georgii Dashkov had a seat at the meeting.[58] The outcome of the negotiations was the production of the so-called Testament of Catherine I, rumored to have been signed by Elizabeth since the negotiations continued into the final hours of Catherine's death.[59]

The sixteen-point "Testament" was a feat of external and internal diplomacy that prevented a war in the Baltic over the question of Russian succession—an idea not well developed in the literature. The diplomacy involved three rather belligerent German claimants to the Russian throne, who inherited their claims as the consequence of Peter's *Heiratspolitik* (marriage diplomacy). One claimant was the House of Holstein-Gottorp with their yet unborn son of Karl Friedrich and Anna Petrovna (the future emperor Peter III). Peter's other daughter (and future empress) Elizabeth Petrovna was also tentatively an ally of Holstein, as she soon expected to marry Karl's cousin, the prince-bishop of Lübeck, Karl August. Another claimant was the House of Mecklenburg-Schwerin, through Peter's sister Catherine Ioannovna, who married Karl-Leopold of Mecklenburg and gave birth to Anna Karlovna, also known as Grand Princess Anna Leopoldovna

(1718–46, born Elisabeth Christine of Mecklenburg-Schwerin). And the third rival was the duke of Wolfenbüttel, Rudolf Ludwig, whose daughter married Tsarevich Aleksei in 1711 and whose grandson was Russian tsar Peter II Alekseevich, who had powerful relatives in Vienna, such as his aunt, Holy Roman Empress Elisabeth Christine.[60] None of these rivalries affected Feofan directly, although they may have highlighted the new cultural reality that the future of the House of Romanov in Russia was partially in the hands of the German "heretics."

Although the Viennese candidate (Peter II) inherited the throne, the "Testament" granted several concessions to the Holstinians and nothing to Mecklenburg. Anna Petrovna (and her descendants via Karl Friedrich) had the right to inherit should young Peter remain childless. The next in line of succession was Elizabeth and "her descendants" through the prince-bishop of Lübeck— again, to the satisfaction of the Holstinians. Yet the "Testament" also pacified Menshikov's interests, as the last section appended an obligation for Peter II to marry Menshikov's daughter Maria.[61]

Luckily for Feofan, this last item in the "Testament" was so unpopular with many Russian elites (including Petr Tolstoi, Andrei Ostermann, and the prince's own brother-in-law General Anton Manuel Devier) and with the courts of Wolfenbüttel and Gottorp that it led to Menshikov's banishment from politics.[62]

Prokopovich greeted the news with joy. "This large giant," he wrote, "was abandoned by Fortune, which made him so drunk with success that he fell down with a great racket."[63] The fall of Menshikov with the ensuing power struggle between the relatives of Vasilii L. Dolgorukii and those of Dmitrii Golitsyn gave Feofan a temporary respite from political disfavor at the Supreme Privy Council and even eased access to the court of Peter II. Thus he drafted Peter's coronation manifesto in October 1727 and greeted the teenaged tsar personally in January 1728.[64]

THE PATRIARCHATE RESTORATIONIST MOVEMENT

A short break, however, did not stop the continuing decline of Feofan's influence. A sign of this decline was the relocation of the court to Moscow in January 1728, a symbolic move away from Feofan's former center of influence in Petersburg. Field Marshal Mikhail Golitsyn, however, rejoiced about the relocation. "Petersburg is a part of the body infected with gangrene [*gangräniten Glied*]," he declared. "If one does not cut it off, the whole body will suffer."[65] Moving the capital was just the first step in healing Russia from the "gangrene" of reform.

The emptying of the northern capital must have been difficult for Feofan to see. The synodal buildings were vacated and churches lost the attention they had received from the synodal preachers as well as from the court nobility and the imperial family. Prokopovich left Bishop Pitirim of Nizhnii Novgorod (1665–1738), a strong ally of reform, to preach to those remaining in the city and to take care of the vacant synodal property.[66] Along with the Synod, he also left behind his fine residences and his boats. He was not even sure if he would ever see his home again—the Privy Council began reviewing his properties for expropriation in the summer of 1728.[67] Nevertheless, with some hope, he asked his Kievan friend, Rafail Zaborovskii, to take good care of his Aptekarskii Island estate.[68]

The move to Moscow accompanied the rise of Feofan's Moscow-centered enemies, who launched fresh theological attacks at the archbishop and rallied for the restoration of the patriarchate. In December 1727, Markell produced new discoveries of Prokopovich's "Lutheran and Calvinist teachings," launching a campaign, encouraged by Lopatinskii and Dashkov, to oust Feofan from the Synod.[69] The archbishop spent part of 1728 on the defensive, battling the charges of heresy all over again.

What saved Feofan this time was Rodyshevskii's own inanity, tied, perhaps, to one of his bouts of "melancholy." Markell was at the Aleksandr Nevskii Monastery when the court left St. Petersburg. Desiring to relocate to Moscow to see "Her Highness Empress Evdokiia Fedorovna" (Peter I's first wife, the grandmother of Peter II and a perceived martyr of Petrine excesses), he escaped his monastic cell.[70] A hasty pursuit followed, during which Feofan's Ukrainian "servants" Taras and Verbitskii hunted Rodyshevskii down at the residence of General Korchmin and dragged him out by his hair before bringing him to the Secret Chancellery as a monastic escapee without papers. According to Markell's recollection, the number of "Feofan's servants" was ten and they not only beat him but also tried to strangle him.[71] Markell's imprisonment, however, did not last long—by 1729, the Supreme Privy Council had released him and settled him in Moscow's prestigious Simonov Monastery, where he continued to pen his opposition to reform.[72]

Feofan's most important challenge, however, was neither Markell nor theological accusations but a growing momentum to restore the patriarchate.[73] The core of the Muscovite clerical elites still had not fully reconciled themselves to the idea of the Holy Synod. As early as 1726, barely a year into the Synod's existence, Georgii Dashkov criticized its bureaucratic inefficiency when compared to the old patriarch's office. He advocated "reducing the number [*poubavit'*] of the Synod, for the Synod is a vainglorious gathering [*sobranie suetnoe*], bringing no good [*pol'zy*] to the religious or secular estate, but a great loss [*ubytok*] for the Treasury."[74] Along with the reduction of the size of the Synod, he also advocated restoring "patriarchate" levies for monastic landholdings (which were lower than the new synodal ones) and staffing the new Synod with hierarchs of Russian nationality only.[75] The report called for the weakening of the institution of the Synod, setting the stage for a stronger alternative, the patriarchate.

The notion of restoration needed more than just theological or fiscal justification. The idea needed a body, that is, a concrete person who could rally the restorationists to their cause. By the time the court moved to Moscow in January 1728, there were two potential aspirants to the post, both allies in the Synod. One was Feofilakt Lopatinskii, supported by D. M. Golitsyn and the lower clergy circles of Tver hegumen Iosif Reshilov. He did not appear to be a strong candidate, however. His Ukrainian origins, his love for Western music (with string orchestras), and his lack of robust enthusiasm for the position were just some of the reasons.[76]

A stronger and more willing candidate, however, was the Muscovite hierarch Georgii Dashkov of Rostov. Although originally Menshikov's man in the Synod, Dashkov enjoyed strong support from the Dolgorukii clan after the fall of the prince. Dashkov showed not only a spiritual but also material interest in maintaining his influence at court: according to several accounts, he bribed officials and noblemen with his well-bred Rostov horses, depleting the bishop's stables.[77]

Movement toward restoring the patriarchate began as early as August 1727. It was then that Aleksandr Menshikov ordered some of the former Synod members to return the property of the diseased Patriarch Adrian to the patriarchal chest, including jewelry, crosses, cassocks, and various ceremonial garments. He also prohibited taking any items away from the chest.[78] This was a clear insinuation that patriarchal property would soon be needed for its proper use.[79]

With the return of patriarchal ornamental items came the political weakening of synodal powers, particularly as they affected Feofan. Significant decisions, including higher clerical appointments and liturgical changes, were decided in the Supreme Privy Council, where Feofan's clerical enemies (such as Dashkov) often participated in discussion. The council, for example, appointed Ignatii Smola to supervise the capital's clergy in the summer of 1727, replacing Afanasii Kondoidi (Feofan's ally), and banned the 1724 special liturgy of St. Aleksandr Nevskii (composed by Buzhinskii), stopping its commemoration on August 30 of each year.[80]

The final stage of restoring the patriarchate was approaching in early 1728 when Dashkov brought the idea to the Privy Council. Actively engaged in the internal squabbles between the Golitsyn and Dolgorukii clans, the council did not treat this matter with urgency.[81] Yet the danger was so imminent that Prokopovich noted to Kantemir that Dashkov, through bribery of the clergy and political influence at court, was dangerously close to attaining the office "of the Pope [*Pontificis*]."[82] The reference to the pontificate was not accidental: patriarchate restorationism, for Feofan, was associated with papal "plots" (real and imagined). Prokopovich recalled that

> after the death of Peter, Iavorskii's supporters rose from the dead: Feofilakt Lopatinskii, bishop of Tver, Georgii Dashkov, also Bishop Aleksei Titov of Kolomna. They entered the Synod with the help of superstitious slaves, unfaithful to Peter and the Fatherland, and destroyed the seeds of all the good that were planted in the Synod. Pleasing their whims, they worked to install a Papist tyranny. One of them, Dashkov, the good shepherd of his flock of horses, was so close to becoming a Patriarch that no doubt remained that he would soon become one.[83]

Despite the imminence of the event, the restoration of the "Papist tyranny" did not materialize and the institution of the Synod appeared somewhat safe, at least for the time being. Feofan's vision of church reform survived, but his survival through the difficult years of the "dark night" were the result of not only the council's procrastination on the issue, but also Prokopovich's own, sometimes clever, strategies of survival.

STRATEGIES OF SURVIVAL

While in Moscow, Feofan adopted several strategies of survival in the hostile court environment. First, he became very vigilant financially. He broke with tradition and refused to take gifts from visiting Ukrainian clergymen in case it might be viewed as "simony."[84] This fact alone caused him some loss of income.[85] On New Year's Day 1728, Feofan made a resolution to record all incoming and outgoing mail at his residence. "The record book," as he called it, helped him maintain full transparency in case of a criminal or ecclesiastical investigation.[86] He kept this record book for two years until December 1729.

The second important survival strategy was maintaining proximity to the influential Andrei Ostermann (1687–1747). Baron Ostermann was Feofan's ally (albeit inconspicuously so) and as a member of the Privy Council was in a position to intervene and prevent Feofan's ouster from the Synod.[87] A Lutheran and a graduate of the University of Jena, Ostermann was a man of many political talents. His knowledge of foreign languages and diplomatic skill propelled his career in the 1720s from a translator to the vice president of the Foreign Affairs College under Peter I. He played a crucial role in the enthronement of Catherine and then maneuvered wisely between various parties: first, he supported Menshikov, then helped mastermind his downfall; he then supported the Dolgorukii and Golitsyn clans at the height of their power, only to turn against them later.[88]

During the four years of the Privy Council's existence he remained a member of this exclusive oligarchical institution, not because of his pedigree but because of his indispensable diplomatic skills. Ostermann was essential to the conduct of the Privy Council's foreign affairs, maintaining correspondence with the court of Peter II's grandparents in Wolfenbüttel, whose connections extended to Peter II's aunt in Vienna and to the family of Peter I's niece Catherine Ioannovna of Mecklenburg.[89] Petrine marriage politics of the 1710s–20s implanted the Romanovs among the various German monarchies in Europe and staying in contact with them (all legitimate claimants to the throne, to varying degrees) was of paramount importance for the council. Ostermann also maintained the council's ties to Anna's Courland court, to the Holstein court in Gottorp ("our Holstinian duchy"), and to The Hague and Spain.[90]

The Privy Council also entrusted Ostermann with the education of the young emperor, Peter II. Ostermann hired Prokopovich in 1728 to become the instructor of religion for the thirteen-year-old tsar—a favor that ensured the archbishop's proximity to the court in a way that did not include interaction with the Privy Council. The curriculum, which included the 1720 catechism, patterned after Luther's, was organized well enough that it received praise from abroad.[91] While steering clear of politics, Prokopovich also occupied himself with various ceremonial pursuits. He composed verses in honor of the tsar and his family, such as the tsar's sister Natalia Alekseevna, and even designed emblems for her birthday fireworks.[92] When Prince Aleksei Dolgorukii decided to engage his daughter, Ekaterina, to Peter II on November 30, 1729, in order to expand oligarchical influence over the monarch, Feofan conducted a grandiose ceremony.[93]

Feofan's third strategy, and probably the most important one, was to stay silent. During this difficult time, Feofan almost entirely retired from theology and stopped preaching doctrinally.[94] "I remained silent due to my great tribulation [bedstvie] and long suffering from tyranny," Feofan wrote to his friend Iakov Markevich in 1728, adding that he had to—remain "in the kingdom of silence" to avoid the "jaws of the earthly Tartarus."[95]

THE ROCK OF FAITH

Thus he maintained silence when Stefan Iavorskii's Kamen' very (The rock of faith) was first published by the Synod in 1728. By that time, Feofan had not only lost his influence at the synodal press (with censorship in hands of his enemies) but was on the defensive for the works he had previously published.[96] For example, the Privy Council banned his Pravda voli monarshei [The right of the monarch's will], an essay that defined Petrine succession law, on the basis that Feofan's implicit rejection of Tsarevich Aleksei's right of succession in the essay made Peter II appear less legitimate.[97]

Iavorskii wrote the *Rock of Faith* around 1714 (in the midst of the Tveritinov trial), but Musin-Pushkin prohibited its publication due to its "inappropriate" language and "affront" to the Protestants.[98] The exarch's attempts to publish it in Chernigov in 1717 through Archbishop Antonii were not successful either. Apparently the "great sovereign" himself intervened and Antonii refused to print it without revisions.[99] The situation could not have been more different in 1728. Between 1728 and 1730, the book enjoyed three editions and widespread popularity among the devotees of the Iavorskii party.

The publication of *Kamen' very* unleashed the late Stefan's incendiary polemic against Protestants in print, attacking the long-dead but still dangerous "new Goliath, Martin Luther."[100] It also advocated burning heretics (including Lutherans) alive, at the stake. Just like Iavorskii's other theological works this book adopted much of its rhetoric from Jesuit sources, especially Bellarmine and Martinus Becanus.[101]

In *Kamen' very*'s 1728 introduction, Feofilakt Lopatinskii stated giddily that "everyone, from little children to adults, loves this book very much, reading it day and night."[102] The book served as a kind of a manifesto that rallied the anti-Protestant party during this period; even more, it aimed to shake the very foundations of the new theology.[103] For example, in its attack against the view that "salvation is by grace not works," *Kamen' very* equated Protestant *sola fide* soteriology with libertinism: "Who would not be inclined to commit a crime, if he knew firmly that one shall be saved by faith only?"[104]

THE INTELLECTUAL OFFENSIVE

Although unable to defend his position against the *Rock of Faith* publicly, Feofan enjoyed the support of anonymous polemicists as well as his domestic and foreign allies. In the case of the latter, Feofan's connections to Lutheran theologians in Saxony and Prussia played no small role in launching the German intellectual offensive against the *Rock of Faith*. Although the exact details or inner workings of this offensive will require a separate study (based on Saxon and Prussian archives), what is known is that it featured the release of several printed treatises in defense of Feofan and against Iavorskii.

By far the most important refutation of Iavorskii's work was 1729's *Epistola apologetica* written by Feofan's trusted friend, Jena professor Johann Franz Buddeus (1667–1729).[105] Apart from being the most authoritative Lutheran theologian in Europe at that time, Buddeus also appeared to be Peter's favorite Lutheran theologian.[106] To underscore the high esteem in which the Russian bishops were supposed to hold this Jena professor, British diplomat Claudius Rondeau stated, "Peter the first [sic] did not think fit to permit his clergy to refute Buddeus."[107]

Buddeus and Prokopovich maintained regular correspondence before and after the emperor's death, but their letters from 1729 showed particular solidarity in maintaining Lutheran and Orthodox churches "free from the Papal yoke."[108] It is with this task in mind that Buddeus set forth to defend both Lutheran and Russian churches from "Papist" attacks and wrote an epistle in Feofan's defense, based on the description of Iavorskii's work supplied to him by a (supposedly anonymous) archbishop.[109] Buddeus's acquaintance with *Kamen' very* was actually thorough and the theologian's 137-page treatise confronted in great detail all of its major points, such as the authority of Scripture, the character of Martin Luther, fasts, images, the Church Fathers, and the teaching of justification.

To assuage Orthodox sensibilities, Buddeus assured his (possibly Orthodox) readers that Lutherans were not some licentious monsters, but accepted fasts (voluntary not "hypocritical" ones), that they "tolerate and retain images" as memorial testaments to the saints, and that they esteemed good works as "necessary fruits and evidence [*documenta*] of [one's] faith" but not as bases of justification.[110] He also stated that the Lutherans—contrary to "Iavorskii's errors"—accepted the authority of the Church Fathers of the first four centuries CE, a position directly espoused by the *Spiritual Regulation*.[111] Thus, Buddeus, much like Prokopovich before him, drew on the authority of the Bible, and even the Fathers, to present Lutheran opinion as Orthodox.

Other critical reviews of Iavorskii's publication included the works of Johann B. Mencken and Johann Theodor Jablonski. Mencken's review appeared in the May 1729 issue of Leipzig's *Acta eruditorum*, one of the top scientific journals of the time, which was well respected in the Russian Academy of Sciences.[112] The reviewer doubted the originality of the work, arguing that it copied arguments from "Bellarmine, Becanus, and other Roman and Polish authors."[113] Then the review lamented that Russia under Peter II appeared to be going backward in its reforms by banning the works of Pufendorf and Stratemann but allowing the "Papist" work of "this foolish author" to proliferate.[114] Similar arguments followed in Johann Theodor Jablonski's review from 1730, titled *Genius Stephani Jaworscii* (The mind of Stefan Iavorskii), which argued that Stefan's "alien mind" was consumed by Catholic theology and was threatening to Russia.[115] The arguments of the Halle philosopher Georg Bernhard Bilfinger (1693–1750) and the famous Helmstedt author Johann Lorenz Mosheim followed Jablonski's publication with very similar negative reviews of *Kamen' very*.[116]

While these foreigners emphasized Iavorskii's "foolishness," they extolled Feofan Prokopovich's virtues. For Buddeus, he was "the most learned man [*vir doctissime*]" in the Russian church.[117] For academician Kohl, he was "a man . . . who overflows with admiration and abundance in his erudition, genius [*ingenii*], and charity [*humanitatis*]."[118]

Support for Feofan came not only from abroad but also domestically, from the circle of the so-called learned company (*uchenaia druzhina*), which included historian Vasilii Tatishchev and poet Antiokh Kantemir (the son of Dmitrii Kantemir). The latter criticized the enemies of church reform through satire. Kantemir's 1729 poem, "Against the Critics of Learning," lampooned a certain bishop ("Egor Daskov"), who "sits idly with a rosary and complains."[119] The indolent bishop grumbled that "people now read the Bible" and they reject "the right of the church to possess secular authority."[120] The satire contrasted this "horse thief" (Dashkov was a horse collector) and "goats' shepherd" with Prokopovich, the "wonderful high priest," "true shepherd," and "defender of his church," who cared for his flock.[121]

Support for Feofan went beyond the circle of the "learned company" and included many quiet sympathizers in the nobility.[122] Some of these noblemen respected not only his academic credentials but also his doctrinal views. As Petersburg academician Christian-Friedrich Gross observed in 1729, there were "many" (among the nobility) who "support the principles of the most reverend bishop Prokopovich, acknowledging the need for a Luther-style reformation."[123] These supporters of Feofan's "reformation" among the larger circles of Petrine era-nobility would emerge as key backers of the archbishop's cause in the crisis of 1730.

THE SUCCESSION CRISIS OF 1730

The months of January and February 1730 were an emotional rollercoaster for Feofan Prokopovich. Peter II died on January 30, childless and unmarried. Succession negotiations ensued in the Supreme Privy Council, meeting at the late tsar's palace. Prokopovich was called to attend negotiations alongside three other Synodal hierarchs, although his opinion had little worth in the meeting where the Golitsyn and Dolgorukii clans called all the shots.[124] According to the "Testament" of 1727, the Holstinian family of Anna Petrovna or Peter's other daughter Elizabeth Petrovna should have inherited the throne. But Anna Petrovna was dead, her son Peter III was just barely a toddler, and unmarried Elizabeth found few supporters in the council.

Among the several candidates to the throne, the oligarchs decided to choose the weakest one politically, Peter the Great's niece Anna Ioannovna, who was currently living in Mittau as the widow duchess of Courland.[125] Anna was no longer married—her husband Friedrich Wilhelm of Courland drank himself to death during their wedding feast in 1711. The influence that her lover Johann Ernst von Biron (Bühren) had at her court led to a perception of weakness, and Vasilii L. Dolgorukii, according to Shcherbatov, fancied replacing Biron in his role.[126] The political intention of inviting her to the throne, however, was to limit the powers of the autocracy by asking the new empress to sign a set of conditions before assuming the throne. These "conditions [*konditsii*]" required the empress to defer to the eight-member oligarchical Supreme Privy Council, which would have a de facto veto power over the monarch.[127]

This was not good news for Feofan, Baron Ostermann, and others who feared the unlimited power of the council and its intentions to backpedal on the Petrine reforms. "There is no light seen from anywhere—only storms," wrote Prokopovich sentimentally at the end of January 1730. "There is no hope. Oh, how sorrowful is my fate!"[128] For Prokopovich, restricting autocracy was equivalent to establishing the kind of "civil hell" that he saw in Poland and opening the door for all kinds of problems. In his view, "oligarchy" was nothing but a form of "tyranny."[129]

Luckily for Feofan, there was a large party of some 390 gentry and upper nobility gathered in Moscow who opposed the oligarchy of the Dolgorukii and Golitsyn clans, and thus were against attaching conditions to the monarchy. Among the nobility were also the cautious Ostermann, the Cherkasskii family, the Saltykov family, the Trubetskoi family, learned company members Kantemir and Tatishchev, and numerous officers in the guards' regiments.[130] Anna Ioannovna knew about the existence of the opposing party at the time that she met the Privy Council's representatives in Mittau at the end of January.

According to Burkhard Christoph von Minikh (Münnich), Count Reinhold von Löwenwolde and Baron Ostermann sent a separate secret representative to Courland to inform the future empress of the council's plans.[131] Feofan played a crucial role in this exchange of information by drafting a "petition from all estates [*vsekh grazhdan*]" requesting Anna to renege on the Privy Council's conditions.[132] According to another account, Feofan slipped a secret note in a clock presented to Anna, informing her of the opposition's plans.[133]

This was a dangerous gamble for Feofan, since Anna, by that time, had already formally agreed to the Privy Council's demands and there was no guarantee that she would change her mind. Furthermore, the council controlled all the roads in and out of Moscow, sharply reducing opportunities for the guard regiments stationed outside the city to intervene and limiting the arrival of more lower gentry. When Anna entered Moscow on February 12, the representatives of the estates swore the oath of loyalty to the empress and the council.

Feofan Prokopovich, in opposition, delivered a speech first in the Synod and then in the gathering of the estates, calling on the people (*narod*) to forego swearing any oaths against their conscience. His oration was interrupted by Dmitrii Golitsyn and the council "refused [*otrekl*]" to allow him to continue.[134]

The opposition, however, remained firm in their plans. On February 25, some 390 people gathered at the imperial palace. There, Counts Aleksei Cherkasskii (representing supporters in the Senate) and Grigorii Iusupov (representing the Military College) petitioned the empress to restore the autocracy, based on the appeals drafted earlier by Prokopovich and Kantemir. Anna's sister, Catherine Ioannovna Duchess of Mecklenburg, supported the petition.[135]

The plot worked: the empress tore up the conditions, scheduled a new oath for March 1, and then abolished the Supreme Privy Council. It was replaced with the newly empowered Senate on March 4. Feofan then crowned her as empress on April 25 in Moscow's Dormition Cathedral. The cabinet became the new consultative body at court, with Aleksei Cherkasskii, Gavriil Golovkin, and Andrei Ostermann as its top members.[136] To celebrate, Feofan distributed his estate-brewed beer to guests at his Moscow residence in Vladykino.[137] The beer was so popular with the empress's cabinet minister Artemii Volynskii (1689–1740) and the family of Volynskii's archrival, Biron, that both later petitioned the archbishop to send them more of his "excellent beer."[138] Feofan would later reflect upon this time period as the end of the "sorrowful night," banished by Anna, "the Sun."[139]

Saving the Orthodox Church from "Papist Tyranny"

The 1730 coup was not only a political but also very much a religious event, by which Feofan returned the Russian church to its path of reform.[140] The oligarchs and the patriarchate restorationists compromised themselves through various connections to Catholic diplomats and agents and appeared eager to explore a new level of relationship between Russia and the Holy See. During the succession crisis of 1730, Feofan exploited these connections to paint his opponents as spies who plotted to "install Papist tyranny" in Russia through their attempt to restore the patriarchate and by conspiring with foreign Catholic agents.[141]

The convergence of three situations in 1729–31 led Feofan to believe that Orthodoxy was threatened with a turn toward Rome. First was the movement to restore the office of the patriarch. The second was the emergence of conspicuous Catholic and philo-Catholic support for the restoration, and third was the emerging prospect of an Orthodox-Catholic Union in Russia, which now seemed more realistic than ever before. Each one of these situations emerged separately for their own different reasons, but in Feofan's mind they were all interconnected.

The possibility of bringing Russia into union with Rome was one that Feofan had already encountered before it was raised again during the period of 1728 to 1731. In 1717–18, Jansenist theologian Laurent François Boursier (1679–1749) along with thirteen other scholars of the Sorbonne addressed Peter I (during the tsar's visit to Paris) with a formal written proposal to unite Roman Catholic and Russian Orthodox communions on the basis of establishing national patriarchates (including one for France) and limiting papal prerogatives.[142] The proposal seemed doomed from the start. The initiative came from Paris, not Rome; the Curia did not assent to it; and Moscow's resident Jesuits criticized it as a sign of French "national spirit . . . hostile to the Pope."[143] Prokopovich shredded it to pieces in his official reply in 1718, arguing that such a decision must be undertaken by the global Orthodox community, not just the Russian church.[144]

In 1728 the Sorbonne produced another proposal, through Boursier's close associate Jacques Jubé (1674–1745), an ultra-Gallican priest who proposed establishing "the Gallican patriarchate" and uniting this newly reformed Roman Catholic Church with the Orthodox one.[145] In 1727 Jubé accompanied Irina Dolgorukova (1700–1751), a Russian noblewoman who had converted to Catholicism, on her return to Russia. Irina's personal life exemplified the growing entente between the powerful Dolgorukii and Golitsyn clans: as the daughter of Count Petr Golitsyn (1660–1722), she was the wife of the diplomat Count Sergei Dolgorukii. After she returned to Russia, she and her husband's relatives occupied important positions of power in the Privy Council.[146]

Boursier, the author of the 1718 proposal, placed much hope in Jubé's unique access to Russia's preeminent families, but unlike in 1718, his strategy no longer involved petitioning the tsar (Peter II) for the union. Instead, in his 1728 instructions to Jubé, Boursier called for using the influence of the preeminent families to orchestrate an internal coup within the Russian church. Such a coup would involve supporting philo-Catholic Russian clergy and promoting the idea of restoring the patriarchate while removing the "grand obstacles" to the union—Feofan as well as other bishops who "favored the Lutherans."[147] Following his 1728 arrival in Russia, Jubé began to carry out the plan. He cultivated contacts with Feofilakt Lopatinskii, Evfimii Koletti, and Sil'vestr Kholmskii, and even met with the infamous Markell Rodyshevskii, encouraging him to attack Feofan. All these hierarchs, in his opinion, sought the restoration of the patriarchate, but they were also, surprisingly, "very favorable" to the union.[148] The problem for Jubé, however, was that his mission never received official approval in either higher ecclesiastical or diplomatic circles in Rome or Paris.

His main backer, Boursier, was purged from the Sorbonne in 1729 along with other ultra-Gallican doctors.[149]

Although the second Sorbonne proposal also appeared doomed, Jubé stayed in Russia as another, better-formulated, and more realistic proposal emerged in the circle of Spanish ambassador Duke de Liria and his Dominican father-confessor Bernardo Ribera. Jacques Jubé ended up assisting the Spanish embassy with this 1729–30 plan.

Who was the Spanish ambassador to Moscow? Jacobo Francisco Fitz James Stuart de Berwick y Liria y Xérica (1696–1738) was a man of many connections, having served the new (Bourbon) Spanish crown in Parma and Naples after the new dynasty successfully reconquered Sicily.[150] Yet his familial background as the illegitimate grandson of the deposed James II of England defined him as a Jacobite opponent of the House of Hanover, devoting his life to the overthrow of that British dynasty. His embassy in Moscow sought the support of the Supreme Privy Council for a treaty of alliance between Russia and Spain, with a specific provision for Russia's support of the Stuart cause, including, but not limited to, diplomatic and even military aid.[151] Unlike Jubé, de Liria and his religious adviser Father Ribera were not self-employed amateurs but came with full diplomatic support for their mission from the crown and from the Holy See. Their plan for church union had the ecclesiastical sanction of the anti-Jansenist cardinal Cornelio Bentivoglio, the Spanish plenipotentiary in Rome. Furthermore, Ribera's title as a "preacher [*concionador*] and Apostolic Missionary" was not academic but strictly ecclesiastical.[152] Also, unlike Jubé, de Liria's party enjoyed a number of formal connections to Moscow's elites: the duke became the recipient of the Orders of St. Andrew and St. Aleksandr Nevskii, and Ribera co-officiated an Orthodox liturgy in Moscow's Novospasskii Monastery.[153]

De Liria's seven-point plan for the unification of churches (written on April 29, 1729) contained specific strategies for approaching the Russian church. These included such actions as bribing the nobility, exerting Austrian diplomatic pressure upon Peter II (whose grandmother's sister was the Holy Roman Empress), and even finding a Catholic princess for Peter II to marry.[154] The plan included full support for the restoration of the patriarchate, since, de Liria argued, only a patriarch could sanction a church union.[155]

Although the plan did not identify a candidate for patriarch, de Liria verbally expressed preference for someone close to the Dolgorukiis (especially those who were close to the Catholic converts in the Golitsyn family), in particular the junior and (still) unmarried Ivan Alekseevich Dolgorukii (1708–39). Once the Russian church had appointed such a patriarch, de Liria argued, the Holy See would appoint Ribera as the plenipotentiary to Moscow with a bishop's title.[156] Only a formally invested bishop could conduct union negotiations with

Russia, de Liria believed, and only a patriarch could, formally and legitimately, bring Russia into the Uniate fold.

The note recognized that this was a difficult task, dependent especially on the success of the Dolgorukii and Golitsyn clans in Russia's politics and on the success of the patriarchate restorationists in the Synod. Among the major steps in executing the plan was Prokopovich's removal. For the ambassador Feofan was a major thorn in his side, "a man with a great proclivity toward Lutheranism, a bold and educated enemy of the Catholic religion."[157]

How much did the Russians know about the plan? As the Spanish ambassador drafted his plan in April 1729, Ribera shared it with Jubé. According to Jubé's diary, some of the Dolgorukiis knew the details of the plan. Jubé reportedly joined the duke de Liria and Irina Petrovna Dolgorukaia and her brothers in meeting secretly in a private house outside Moscow in late 1729 to discuss the proposal and to consider suitable candidates to fill the patriarchal throne.[158] Whether the synodal hierarchs of the time knew about it remains an open question, but it was in Feofan's obvious interest to portray his enemies as colluding with Catholic agents, even if there was only association or collaboration. Among the hierarchs, Feofilakt Lopatinskii and Markell Rodyshevskii certainly socialized with de Liria, and their social interactions with Roman Catholics also involved discussions about the prospects of the union between the papacy and the Russian church. The patriarchate restorationists' interactions with Ribera and de Liria's circle were not just social in nature; they also involved official functions as well as co-officiated liturgical service in Moscow.[159]

De Liria's plans collapsed in 1730–31 after the downfall of the Dolgorukii faction. The pretext for de Liria's subsequent expulsion from Russia was the scandal Feofan raised over Bernardo Ribera's book, which circulated in manuscript in 1730 and was printed in Vienna in 1731. The book, *Responsum antapologeticum*, was a defense of *Kamen' very* and the patriarchate restorationists, with direct attacks against Buddeus and indirect attacks against Feofan.[160] Thus it was not only Prokopovich who enjoyed the support of intellectuals— in an interesting twist of fate the philo-Catholic Feofilakt now had a Roman Catholic polemicist to support him. In this way, the ongoing struggle between Iavorskii's opponents and proponents resembled Roman Catholic-Lutheran theological debate in Europe.

Prokopovich in his review of Ribera's book was gravely incensed that the "little Dominican liar-monk Ribera" dared to write against "the famous theologian Buddeus."[161] However, he presented the book as political sedition, which would lead to both external war and internal "civil war and discord."[162] For domestic purposes, the book was dangerous since it argued that the Russian nation was "inclined [*blagosklonnyi*] toward the Roman faith," that "her Majesty [Anna]" was favorable to the idea of union with Rome, and that Ribera was "an Apostle to Russia, in whom Russia put the hope of its eternal salvation."[163] He also "insulted" all Protestants serving in the Russian court, army, and navy, as well as those Protestants who were relatives of the empress.[164]

Diplomatically, the work was dangerous, since the author (who was the confessor of Duke Stuart de Liria) praised the "pretender James as James III, the true English king," and criticized King George II as "a tyrant." Since Ribera dedicated his book to Empress Anna and since Ribera openly "rattled [*garkal*]" his sermons in Moscow denouncing King George, any official recognition this book might receive in Russia would be a "spark for igniting a war between the Russian Empire and the English Crown."[165] After all, he noted, the "accusations against King George" circulated "not in some private groups [*v privatnykh uglakh*]," but "in the presence of the highest ministers"—and England knew about it.[166] Furthermore, the book risked ruining Russian-Austrian relations: in his criticism of Protestants, Ribera "vomited" against "the entire German nation," including "His [Holy] Imperial Majesty."[167]

Feofan's presentation of Ribera's book as seditious followed an earlier investigation into de Liria's religiously threatening activities. According to the testimony of a Greek Uniate visitor in Moscow (who presented himself as Count General Kantakouzenes), the Spanish ambassador received a papal letter "about compelling [*o preklonenii*] Russia into the union," which he sought to present to the Synod (including Feofan) and to the empress after the success of the oligarchs in 1730.[168] Since Kantakouzenes did not wish to cooperate with the ambassador to carry out the instructions of the papal letter, he turned himself into the Secret Chancellery to relate the information and to receive "protection from the attacks of the Spanish duke's retinue."[169]

Feofan's display of Ribera and de Liria as a threat to Russia's security *and* to the integrity of the Orthodox Church proved to be very successful. According to the report of British ambassador Claudius Rondeau, the Russian court was "much displeased with the duke of Liria" for permitting the publication of Ribera's "most scandalous reflections."[170] Russia stopped all official diplomatic contact with Spain in 1730 (it was restored only in 1760), while fathers Bernardo Ribera and Jacques Jubé were promptly expelled from Russia.

HUNTING FOR "PAPAL SPIES"

The thwarting of de Liria's plan surely validated Feofan's lifelong obsession with the "great threat" that the "thrice-cursed Papists" posed to Orthodoxy.[171] In this regard, the triumph of 1730 was just part of his endeavor to rid Russia

of Catholic "spies" and seditious agents. From 1721 to 1727, for example, Prokopovich mobilized the Secret Chancellery to successfully monitor the activities
of Catholic visitors to Russia and even Catholic residents in Russia.

Thus, on August 18, 1721, synodal assessor Afanasii Kondoidi intercepted
two Italian letters addressed to some anonymous Franciscan fathers living in
St. Petersburg. The first, undated letter was from the secretary of Propaganda
Fide in Rome, Pierluigi Carafa (1677–1755), while the second one was from
the papal nuncio in Warsaw.[172] According to Kondoidi, the letters "ordered
the Franciscan priests to spread the Roman faith in Russia," and noted that the
fathers had already engaged in such propaganda by inviting the Orthodox to
the private home masses and sermons held at the homes of famous foreigners.[173] Among such foreigners were the sculptors Carlo Bartolomeo Rastrelli
(1675–1744) and Antonio Tarsia (1662–1739) as well as the admiralty officer of
Dalmatian origin, Matvei (Mateja) Izmaevich (1680–1735).[174]

Although the assessor worried about clandestine proselytism, he was also concerned that Franciscan missionaries—who were admitted to Russia under the
pretext of traveling to China—did not actually travel east, but stayed in Reval,
Riga, Russian-occupied Abo, and St. Petersburg. These were all naval bases,
and Kondoidi feared that sedition was underway.[175] He stated, "Without a
single doubt, I believe that these Franciscans are Papal spies and the Papal
designs can be so inhumane, evil, and blasphemous that sometimes they plot
to murder emperors through the help of such hypocrite monks [*zakonniki*].
We see this in history, in 1589 when the Dominican Jacques Clément [Iakov
Klement] treacherously murdered Henry the Third, the King of France."[176]

The report raised the alarm about a possible assassination plot. So the Synod
decided to consider all Catholics serving in the navy to be under suspicion and
requested the College of Foreign Affairs and the War College to provide lists
of the naval officers of "Roman confession" and to investigate their loyalty
to Russia. The colleges provided the information promptly on September 2
and the Synod reviewed the officers' loyalty oath records and took no further
action.[177]

A much more scandalous case transpired in April 1725 when General Pavel
Iaguzhinskii arrested several Capuchins in the naval city of Reval and sent them
to the Secret Chancellery. The arrests took place after a riot in which Catholic
sailors assaulted a local bystander, Freytag von Loringhoven (from "the respected
knightly family"), who refused to take off his hat during a Catholic funeral
ceremony. Loringhoven died from the assault, prompting Reval's noble families to petition Catherine I to ban all Catholic processions in the city.[178]

One of the arrested Capuchins was Father Chrysologus, who received a de-
portation order in 1724 but did not leave Russia, instead hiding out in Reval.

Interrogated by Afanasii Kondoidi and Prokopovich, Chrysologus revealed that his mission had received the sanction of both the Sacred Congregation for the Propagation of the Faith and Peter II's aunt, Holy Roman Empress Elisabeth Christine. The Capuchin's task was supposedly to "pray for her nephew," to meet him, and then to "find ways to carry out the duties for which we were sent here."[179] This last statement was ominous enough to warrant the suspicion that Chrysologus actually tried to convert Peter II to Catholicism.[180] The suspicion was confirmed by Feofan's interrogation of another Capuchin, Apolinarius. Apolinarius's baggage turned up two letters, one from the pope and another one from Rome's Sacred Congregation thanking the monk for "converting many Russians of the Greek confession to the Roman faith."[181] Further examination revealed the names of the people he tried to convert, such as staff members of the military, the College of Commerce, and the College of Foreign Affairs.[182] After interrogation, the Secret Chancellery decided that both Capuchins were in Russia for "political purposes" and promptly sent them to Riga under military convoy and then deported them at the end of July 1725.[183]

Feofan's fight against the Catholic threat to Orthodoxy, however, was not only about hunting down foreign spies but also about identifying their domestic collaborators. In this case, Feofan's allies turned to circumstantial evidence or to their own imaginations to make the allegations. Thus, after the patriarchate restorationists published Iavorskii's *Kamen' very*, Prokopovich (with Ostermann's express approval) promoted the circulation of the anonymous *Molotok na Kamen' Very* [Hammer against the Rock of Faith].[184] The handwritten pamphlet defended church reforms and many elements of Protestant theology as congruent with Orthodoxy, such as the acceptance of fasting.[185] However, it also attacked the opponents of the reform indirectly, by assailing their revered teacher, Stefan, as a Catholic agent. The pamphlet presented Iavorskii as a Uniate-born member of the Society of Jesus, who led a "two-faced" life, concealing his true identity, which allowed him to be presentable and acceptable to the Orthodox tsar.[186] According to the pamphlet, Stefan came very close to disclosing his true identity in 1721, when Peter I asked him to sign the *Spiritual Regulation*, a signature he hesitated to pen, since giving such approval allegedly required "Papal permission" first.[187] Such permission was allegedly promptly obtained, allowing Iavorskii to remain undercover.

Feofan was not the only person who made insinuations of Iavorskii's Roman loyalties. His friend and correspondent in Jena, Buddeus, while responding to the *Kamen' very* and the patriarchate restorationist debate of 1729–30, stated that Iavorskii and his supporters "worshipped the Romanists," seeking to bring Russians "to bend their necks to their [Romanist] yoke."[188] Such charges obviously suggested that Stefan's students and allies worked for the benefit of the

Holy See. Mencken's assessment was milder; he stated that Iavorskii was dangerously silent on the issue of Roman Catholic influence, implying ignorance or complicity in opening the "doors" of the Russian church to Rome.[189] A much later 1736 account by Gustav Georg Zeltner continued to criticize Iavorskii's Jesuit connections, his education ("imbibed from the shadows of Bellarmine"), and Roman Catholic efforts, including those of Ribera, to actively recruit Russian Orthodox believers to their cause.[190]

If Iavorskii was indeed a papal infiltrator operating in Russia, he must have been the highest-ranking such emissary in the history of East Slavic Orthodoxy. Although such insinuations did not have much support in the church outside of Prokopovich's immediate circle, for Feofan the implications of (real or imagined) Catholic spy activity were serious and far-reaching. If papal influence and Catholic theological ideas had penetrated so deeply into the circles of the church hierarchy and even the nobility, it was the reformers' duty to purge the church of the elements alien to the spirit of the reform. Purge was a task that Prokopovich did not pursue in 1721–25 due to Peter's lack of support for such a radical action and it was a task he was unable to carry out in 1725–30, due to his loss of political influence. The triumph of 1730 and the downfall of his political enemies, however, untied Feofan's hands, enabling him to "cleanse" the church rank-and-file of the enemies of the newly reformed synodal Orthodoxy.

The Purges

Feofan Prokopovich reaped many benefits from his status as queenmaker (again) during the drama of Anna's accession to the throne. In the ecclesiastical administration, he became the unchallenged head of the Synod, giving him full powers to replace enemies with allies in key positions of power. In politics, he became the right hand of Andrei Ostermann, who led the most powerful faction at court, which gave him essentially unrestricted access to the resources of the Secret Chancellery, the army, and the police. Prokopovich needed these resources as he endeavored to get rid of his opponents. The great purges of the 1730s that followed were not only about cleansing the hierarchy of papal spies or papist threats; they were also about securing Feofan's legacy so that his program of reforming Orthodoxy would endure in the church after his death.

The first steps in the purges were purely administrative in nature and consisted of dismissing Dashkov, Smola, and Lopatinskii from the Synod in July and August 1730. Reportedly, the dismissal came as a rude awakening—one morning, Feofilakt showed up in the synodal building only to find himself turned away at the door, due to not being on the list of members "drawn up by the Archbishop of Novgorod [Feofan]."[191] The complete ban on Iavroskii's *Kamen' very* followed shortly thereafter.[192] In November 1730, Dashkov was further demoted in rank and exiled to a monastery in Vologda. The newly promoted replacements in the Synod were either Prokopovich's allies (like Pitirim of Nizhnii Novgorod) or were less influential hierarchs who posed no challenge to him.[193] For example, he appointed Georgian bishop Iosif Khvabulov as his vicar: Khvabulov spoke no Russian but was a better candidate for Feofan than the more independent and less amenable Aaron Eropkin.[194] He then moved to improve the lot of his ally Gavriil by halting the investigation of all synodal cases against him and by nominating him to the bishopric of Rostov, a post that he ultimately could not fill due to his death in 1731.[195] Furthermore, Buzhinskii's liturgical canon to St. Aleksandr Nevskii was restored in August 1730, while the old Menology was abolished again.[196]

Markell Rodyshevskii, as a more dangerous member of the party, received a harsher treatment at this early stage of the purge. In 1730–31 Markell joined a circle of patriarchate restorationists who gathered at the Moscow residence of Anna's father-confessor Varlaam Vysotskii. Many hoped that Varlaam's influence at court might persuade Anna to turn against Prokopovich. They were deeply disappointed: in 1731, the father-confessor betrayed them to the Secret Chancellery. Rodyshevskii was arrested together with his associate Mikhail Avramov in 1731 and in February 1732 they were exiled north to the Kirill-Belozersk and Iversk monasteries respectively.[197] The arguments used to condemn him included Markell's dissent against the *Spiritual Regulation* (a legal document) and his "insult against European Christians," an offense directed against those of the Lutheran nobility who intermarried with Romanovs and who held positions of power in the Senate and at court.[198]

The next step in the purges involved a series of protracted criminal investigations, summary arrests, and gruesome torture cases, with the extraction of confessions as well as exile and executions. The pretext for this next step was the discovery of some "seditious letters" (also known as "false letters [*podmetnye pis'ma*]") against "Her Majesty" Empress Anna. The full text of the letters was not available to nineteenth-century historians like Chistovich; they are a rather recent archival discovery.[199] Written around 1731, they circulated in Moscow as well as St. Petersburg, making their way to the "great hall of the court."[200]

The letters, addressed to Anna, contained a very daring critique of both the new political culture and the Petrine church reforms. In relation to the new culture, the authors criticized the adoption of the title of "emperor" by Anna's "uncle [Peter I]" arguing that, unlike the term "tsar," the title of emperor was absent from Orthodox liturgy and the Bible, and that Peter's premature death was God's punishment for this. Peter's titular innovation was not his only sin:

the letters lamented that the tsar "fell in love [*uliubil*] the Lutheran faith," lived with a "fornicating wife," and replaced the office of the patriarch with that of the Synod.[201]

The establishment of the Synod and the introduction of the title of emperor drove "poor Russia" to "weeping . . . having no patriarch and no tsar." The state of affairs was particularly grave at court, where the Russian nobility married Lutherans, where the empress herself blessed the engagement of the "heretic" Count Löwenweld to Princess Varvara Cherkasskaia, and where "Senators turned against the fasts," while "the Germans wielded control over the Orthodox" and the former cowherds (*khodili za korovami*), like the "secretive Biron," as stablemaster, now possessed unchecked powers. The letters questioned the tsarina's awareness of Russia's decline ("Do your Germans report this to Your Majesty?") as well as her legitimacy ("[the empress] is anointed to rule, but improperly, by the heretical hands [of Feofan]"), while at the same time criticizing her relationship with Biron, without whom she did not spend "a single minute." The author went so far as to compare Anna to Jezebel and Evdokiia and to call on the true faithful to take up the "crown of martyrdom" like Theodore the Studite, Stephan the New, and Theophilaktos the Confessor, who resisted Byzantine iconoclasm.[202]

The letters also attacked Feofan and his disciples, the "Feofanists [*feofanisty*]." In these letters, Prokopovich was "a well-known heretic," "an Origenist with an insatiable belly," and, according to the "testimony" of the bishop of Vilnius, Feofan's former Roman classmate, even a "beloved [*kokhanyi*]" friend of the pope who studied in Rome to convert Russia to "heresy." Using his immense authority (" having the power of the patriarch over Russia's clergy") Feofan, "along with his Feofanists," led many to "fall away [*uklonilisia*] into that faith." In fact, the tract stated that "the greater part of the Synklitos [i.e., the Synod] have already accepted the German faith." While many Ukrainians accepted it voluntarily, "the Orthodox, that is the bishops of Russian nationality, were simply forced to follow these doctrines under the threat of exile, banishment, and even death."[203]

The Feofanists turned the church into the prophet Jeremiah's "desolate wilderness." They replaced the ten commandments with their own ten "innovations [*noviny*]," which featured the summary dispensation of fasts, the promotion of marriages between young monks and nuns, restrictions on monastic tonsure, prohibitions on the painting of wooden icons in the countryside (only canvas fabric paintings were allowed), the proliferation of "amusements in imitation of Jesuits and Benedictines," limitations on the promotion of bishops to Ukrainians only, and promotion of bell music, "akin to organs," in churches. Other "commandments" and "Synodal rules" were simpler: "whoever does not smoke tobacco is a schismatic Old Believer [*raskolshchik*], whoever fasts is also a schismatic, whoever . . . does not wear German dress is not worthy of priesthood."[204]

Having lost all doctrinal and canonical purity, the author concluded, Feofanists turned the Orthodox into Uniate Protestants: "Finally, they resolved to unite with the Germans in a religious Union [*uneia*], declaring their heresies to be not very distant from our faith. They said it so that the Orthodox would not dare to disagree with or debate the heretics."[205] Such a fearless attack against the court and essentially the entirety of the Petrine reforms demanded a swift and resolute response. With the full assistance of the head of the Secret Chancellery, General Andrei Ushakov, Feofan set up a commission to investigate anyone even remotely connected to those letters. The commission included Baron Ostermann, as well as Feofan's clerical allies such as the "fearsome" Pitirim (bishop of Nizhnii Novgorod), Leonid (archbishop of Sarsk and Podonsk [d. 1743]), Ilarion Rogalevskii (the archimandrite of Novospasskii Monastery), Aaron ([1688–1738], archimandrite and future archbishop of Arkhangelsk), and later Amvrosii Iushkevich.[206]

Feofan's team of investigators had extensive powers that included summary arrests with interrogations in the synodal jail (at the St. Aleksandr Nevskii Monastery), Feofan's home, and the chambers of the Secret Chancellery. The examination of witnesses was complex and included interrogation in separate chambers as well as cross-examination in the presence of other witnesses, with liberal use of corporal distress.[207] Feofan Prokopovich sometimes gave detailed suggestions on how to extract truthful confessions, such as "watching the change on his [the witness's] face," noting when the witness "turned his face to the window," threatening the witness with the "shedding of blood [*krovoprolitie*]," or "torture."[208] Overall, the team went beyond the original scope of the investigation into the scandalous letters, netting hundreds of cases of trials against clerical enemies of reform (real or perceived) in the final years of Feofan's lifetime (from 1730 to 1736). Of these cases, six involved bishops who were completely defrocked, that is, returned to secular status, by 1735— a rare punishment for a hierarch in the Orthodox Church.[209]

The starting point for the investigation into the letters was closely connected to Feofan's struggle against "Papist tyranny" in the coup of 1730. Ostermann suspected that the pamphlets originated from the clerical circles connected to "the duke of Liria's chaplain," father Ribera.[210] Prokopovich seconded Ostermann's opinion in arguing for the existence of a conspiracy instigated by foreign "Papists" and their domestic sympathizers. "It appears that some foreign faction [*faktsiia*] has forged an alliance [*soglasie*] with our domestic enemies," he stated.[211] Feofan pointed out that Ribera used to host a circle of ten "fools" and "Latinists" who were either "subversives [*plevoseiateli*] secretly sent from the Papal side" or "in a secret agreement with the Papists [*papezhnikami*]."[212] The circle of "fools," however, was not just a leaderless gathering that lacked a chief conspirator. Among them, wrote Feofan, "there was one man with whom he had union and agreement [*soiuz i zgovor*], as now [in 1733] has become known."[213]

This "one man" was obviously Lopatinskii, Feofan's chief theological antagonist at the time. He was originally retired to his diocese of Tver in 1730, where he reportedly remained "in fear, day and night."[214] Prokopovich based his suspicions of Feofilakt's ties to Ribera on many grounds, including Feofilakt's offer to translate the Catholic monk's work as well as the friar's "inordinate praise" for Feofilakt.[215] Lopatinskii was arrested twice, in 1732, when he was briefly interviewed about his connections to Ribera, and then in 1735, when he experienced the full force of the Secret Chancellery's investigative fervor.[216] His closest associates from Tver diocese were also arrested, forced to testify against him, and later lost their freedom. Among them were Hegumen Iosif Reshilov and Archimandrite Ioasaf Maevskii (imprisoned in St. Petersburg), Alimpii Davydov (sent to Siberia), and Antonii (last name unknown) of the St. Savva of Storozhi Monastery (an archimandrite who lost his position in 1734). Reshilov and Maevskii, caught during an escape attempt near the border with Poland, proved to be particularly important witnesses for the investigation.[217] Their testimonies helped produce a litany of charges against Feofilakt. He was accused of commissioning the odious 1732 "pasquil" against Anna's court, written by his "team and faction," of criticizing the *Spiritual Regulation*, of accusing Feofan of being a Lutheran, of seeking the restoration of the patriarchate, of criticizing the Lutheran relatives of Empress Anna, and even of sympathizing with the Uniates during his sojourn in Poland as a young man.[218] The case dragged on after Feofan's death in 1736, with Pitirim continuing to interrogate Lopatinskii, who was defrocked and eventually sent to Vyborg in December 1738.[219]

Feofilakt's associates also suffered during the same time period. In November 1731, Feofan convinced the empress of the dangers that the would-be-patriarch Georgii Dashkov posed to the monarchy and exiled him to a Vologda monastery on the pretext of the financial mismanagement of his Rostov diocese. In 1735 Dashkov appeared at the Secret Chancellery again and was sentenced one last time to the Far Eastern fort of Nerchinsk, where he died in 1739.[220]

Ignatii Smola was first defrocked for his association with Dashkov, but later, in 1732, arrested and locked up in Arkhangelsk. While there, he engaged in the "most heinous crime" of insulting the empress. Apparently, in one of his inebriated conversations in Arkhangelsk, Ignatii complained (rhetorically) that "they took away my rank unjustly—how does she, a woman, have the right to judge a bishop?"[221] This was clearly an insult against Anna Ioannovna.

In addition to Georgii, Ignatii, and Feofilakt, less powerful hierarchs also came under the axe of Prokopovich's campaign to purify the church of the "Papist spirit" using political or theological charges, either before or after 1732. Some of them were associates or members of the patriarchate restorationist party.[222] Among the defrocked was also Voronezh bishop Lev Iurlov (1678–1755), who in 1730 had refused to remember Empress Anna in his public prayers, praying instead for "our tsaritsa and Grand Duchess Evdokiia Fedorovna," the mother of the executed tsarevich Aleksei and the ex-wife of Peter I.[223] The bishop lost not only his episcopal rank but his tonsure as well: no longer a monk, the Synod sent Lev in the winter of 1730–31 as a prisoner to the Kresty Monastery near the Arctic White Sea.[224]

Similarly, the new Synod removed Sil'vestr Kholmskii from his bishopric in Kazan in 1732, despite the bishop's friendly relations with the empress's powerful chamberlain, Ernst Biron. Feofan suspected Kholmskii from the start, as he had associated himself with Jubé and thus with the "Papists." The synodal charges that defrocked him were serious: Kholmskii disagreed with the "canonical legitimacy of the Synod," continued to invoke the Eastern patriarchs during the liturgy, and complained about women's rule in Russia.[225] Another of Jubé's associates and a former confessor of tsarevich Aleksei, Evfimii Koletti, suffered a similar tragic fate: the 1732 investigation, led by Stefan Kalinovskii, concluded that Evfimii was a bribed agent of the Spanish ambassador.[226] He was then imprisoned in the SS. Peter and Paul fortress where he died in 1738 or 1739, "punished with death for his grave crimes."[227]

The purges affected not only the hierarchy of the church but also the lower clergy, especially those deemed implicated in a wider case. This was seen in the case of Sil'vestr Kholmskii of Kazan, arrested in 1732 for refusing to honor the Synod in the liturgy. What followed was "the total thrashing [*razgrom*] of the clergy," as Feofan sent the new bishop of Kazan, Ilarion Rogalevskii, to carry out a public punishment campaign that included whipping and threats of dismissal. Ilarion's task was to discourage, as vividly as possible, any further sympathies for the former bishop's support for the patriarchate. His punishments affected a wide range of clergy—"hiermonks, protopriests, priests, deacons of Kazan and Sviazhsk and the neighboring villages."[228] Ilarion also dismissed the archimandrites of the area's most important monasteries, sending Archimandrite Pitirim to "labor" in Siberia; Iakov to Ustiug in the north; Ioakim, also to Siberia; and sentencing Evfimii of the Zilantovskii Monastery to the northern edges of Perm.[229]

Kazan was hardly the only place where the reformist purge trickled down to the lower ranks. The reputation of Feofanist bishops during the 1730s was so frightening that when the Synod appointed Lavrentii Gorka to the bishopric of Viatka, the locals exclaimed that "a hierarch from Ukraine [*arkhierei iz khokhlov*] came to rid Viatka of her priests [*obezpopit'*]!"[230] Gorka (who also happened to be Feofan's cousin) indeed had a fearsome record, possessing not only "spiritual gifts," but "physical [*telesnye*]" ones also.[231] He was known for his "hand-to-hand combat [*rukopashnaia rasprava*]" with the clergy in Moscow and was reprimanded for cracking the skull of his Tatar servant in a drunken stupor while celebrating Anna's coronation, and for doing the same to his inferiors on other occasions.[232] This latter offence prompted an investigation by General Andrei Ushakov, but the intervention of his patron and cousin, Prokopovich, softened the punishment to Lavrentii's demotion from Riazan to Viatka in 1733.[233]

It was not unusual for the lower clergy to be subjected to investigations of political disloyalty. In 1733 the priests and a deacon of St. Petersburg's Holy Transfiguration Church, as well as a priest in Kaluga, were found guilty of not serving the coronation commemoration liturgy and were sent into exile and "monastery labor."[234] In 1734 the priests of Starodub and Chernigov dioceses were arrested and punished for ignoring state holidays in their liturgies. Those who refused to serve liturgies for Anna's birthday were similarly deemed politically disloyal: this offence led to the downfall or punishment of priests in Riga, Riazan, and Pskov in 1734.[235] Suspicions of political disloyalty even reached China—in 1732 Beijing's hieromonk Ioasaf was arrested and sent to St. Petersburg for interrogation for not serving a funeral liturgy for Anna's sister, Tsarevna Praskovia Ioannovna.[236]

There were notable exceptions in the crackdown on the anti-reform hierarchs. Aleksei Titov's (1672–1750) friendship with Anna's father-confessor Varlaam helped him remain in the ranks even after 1733, when Anna appointed him to the newly vacant bishopric of Riazan.[237] Despite attaining such a high post, he remained subject to Secret Chancellery investigations. In 1735 Anna and the Synod sent him a "reprimand [*vygovor*]" for spreading rumors of Feofan's sickness. Among the punishments, the Synod prohibited him from wearing the archbishop's mantle for a year while forcing him to "oral repentance [*samoustnoe pokaianie*]" in public, "after the liturgy, in the gathering of many ecclesiastical and secular persons."[238] But while Aleksei escaped defrocking or exile, his own father-confessor Archimandrite Aleksandr Korchemkin was arrested in 1733, interrogated by the Secret Chancellery, and finally decapitated on February 5, 1735.[239]

CONCLUSION

The clerical purges of 1730–36 helped fulfill Feofan's vision of reorganizing the church hierarchy and securing their loyalty to the reform. His inability to complete this task earlier, in the last years of Peter's reign, meant that his road to securing the reformist majority within the Synod would become arduous, especially during the period of his "sad night" of 1727–30. It was also a road that after 1730 included the use of less gracious *Blut und Eisen* (blood and iron) to bring the Russian church to a more enlightened era. As the next chapters will illustrate, the achievements of Petrine era shaped religious policies during the reigns of Elizabeth and Catherine II (1741–96) in many crucial ways. The most important feature of those religious policies was an obvious continuity of the reformist course first set by Feofan Prokopovich: a course that was continued by his disciples and the enlightened "eaglets of the Petrine nest."

PART II

ORTHODOX RUSSIA ENLIGHTENED

5

"The Fledglings of the Petrine Nest"

Early Enlightenment and the Continuities of Reform, 1736–1765

Feofan Prokopovich died on September 8, 1736, at 4:24 p.m.[1] Surrounded by his synodal allies Pitirim and Stefan Kalinovskii, his last act was to dictate a will, bequeathing his estate to his orphanage.[2] The Synod then organized a rather grandiose stately funeral for its deceased leader: the procession included grenadiers, state ministers, military officers, and clergy, and traveled around the center of St. Petersburg before the body was transferred to its final resting place in Novgorod.[3]

Although he died in 1736, the influence of his reforms lasted throughout the rest of the eighteenth century. The Elizabethan period (1741–62) was the era of the "fledglings of the Petrine nest" (to borrow a phrase from Pushkin's *Poltava*), the generation of secular elites whose intellectual formation took place during Peter's reign and who continued the legacies of the Petrine revolution in arts, culture, literature, education, politics, and the military, among other areas of change. The endurance of Petrine religious reform paralleled continuities in secular culture: Feofan Prokopovich, too, had his numerous "fledglings," who carried on his legacy.

As this chapter will illustrate, the new generation of bishops during Elizabeth's reign were, for the most part, the disciples, allies, appointees, or intellectual heirs of Feofan Prokopovich. Like their former teacher, they embraced theological, philological, homiletical, and educational features of reformed Orthodoxy though their continued interaction with the (mostly) Protestant intellectual world of the early Enlightenment, or *Frühaufklärung*, as it is known in German historiography. An early phase of the Enlightenment, this was a mostly continental European (and especially German) movement that accepted human reason as a source of religious knowledge alongside revelation. It also cautiously emphasized toleration (especially for freethinkers, Jews, and Anabaptists), while deemphasizing sectarian differences (especially between Calvinists and Lutherans) and promoting literary criticism and the study of sacred texts, including the Bible. In philosophy, this movement shaped the early stages of the Scientific Revolution through the ideas of René Descartes, Christian Wolff, Pierre Bayle, and Gottfried Leibniz, among others.[4] In theology, however, it was intertwined with Pietism. Among the early enlightened theologians were scholars from Göttingen and the "Jena-Halle-Leipzig Triangle" such as Johann F. Buddeus, Johann Georg Walch (1693–1775), Christian Thomasius (1655–1728), Johann Lorenz Mosheim (1693–1755), Siegmund Jakob Baumgarten (1706–57), and the famous biblical philologists Johann Heinrich Michaelis (1668–1738) and his great nephew Johann David Michaelis (1717–91).[5] The early Enlightenment was not an alien context for elite Russian clergymen: many of these scholars were already familiar to Feofan and his peers. Their engagement with this context underscores the growing variety of Russian Orthodox theological interaction with the Protestant West.

The lasting legacy of Feofan's reforms included numerous continuities, five of which will be discussed in detail in this chapter. The first important continuity was the domination of the ecclesiastical institutional ranks by the allies, students, and colleagues of the reformer, as well as their derivative appointees. The second continuity was theological. Feofan's doctrinal direction, which encouraged the adaptation of Protestant (including Pietist) theology for Orthodox use, continued to shape the learning trends and theological curricula in Russia well beyond his death. His doctrinal writings also informed and inspired theologians from the 1730s to the 1760s. By the time of Catherine II's and Alexander I's reigns, Feofan was not just a legendary churchman, celebrated in the memory of Petrine Russia, but also the venerable founder of the new direction of Russian theological education.

A third important legacy of reform was the educational escape from Rome—the abandonment of the previous trend of sending the brightest Ukrainian and Russian seminarians to Italy or Poland for advanced study. The universities of the Protestant West replaced Roman Catholic schools—a trend that continued into the Catherinian era. The schools of the early Enlightenment "Triangle" (Jena, Halle, and Leipzig) as well as the esteemed university towns of Königsberg, Göttingen, and Oxford became notable destinations for young Orthodox seminarians.

The reform of the Slavonic Bible is closely related to this educational reorientation and is a fourth continuity of the reforms. In west-central Europe, Reformations often led to revisions or translations of Christianity's most sacred text; Prokopovich's church reforms embraced a similar impulse to revise the Bible. Although the archbishop originally formulated the need for the revision, the Synod lacked the educated personnel to initiate this project. Only after enough Orthodox students of Pietist biblical philology returned to Russia with the necessary linguistic training was it possible to complete the revision and publication of Russia's new reformed Bible.

The fifth important area of continuity was preaching. For Feofan and his allies, reforming Russia's pulpits was one of the chief imperatives of Petrine religious change, because sacred oratory was among the most important instruments for communicating new ideas and doctrine to the laity. Feofan's preaching manuals and instructions sought to regulate homiletic style and content in accordance to the preaching models found in the Protestant West. His successors thoroughly adopted the new preaching style and followed Feofan's example in the doctrinal content of their homilies, thus ending the popularity of the philo-Catholic *conceptus*-style preaching that was widespread in Ukraine at the turn of the century.

EMPRESS ANNA, REGENT ANNA, AND EMPRESS ELIZABETH

The stability of Elizabeth's reign was preceded by the calamities of Empress Anna's later years and the regency of Anna Leopol'dovna. The 1736–39 campaign to recruit sons of the clergy for the military was one of the darkest episodes in the history of the Russian church in the eighteenth century, leaving many parishes without ordained ministers and clerical families without heirs. The sheer destructiveness of this campaign against the non-monastic clergy seems absurd, given the small number of soldiers the church could actually provide. The rationale for it has befuddled past historians and remains largely unexplained in the historiography. Lacking a clear explanation, I speculate that Feofan's departure in 1736, which left the Synod without a strong leader and intercessor at court, played no small role in it. Empress Anna's general inattention to church affairs and the rise of the increasingly unchecked powers of her cabinet and its capricious policies, often associated with the so-called German factions (Minikh, Biron, and Ostermann), are likely part of the explanation as well.[6]

The onset of the Russo-Turkish War in 1736 served as the formal pretext for the recruitment drive. A September 28, 1736, decree obligated the Synod and the dioceses to supply army recruits from among the sons of lower clergy.[7] Although the Synod sent some 6,000 recruits (from among the "uneducated" clergy), requests for more came in 1737–38. The church struggled to find enough recruits and these campaigns (known as *razbory*) were replete with abuses, overzealous operations by the military authorities, retribution against the clergy, and even illegality, with some boys as young as ten sent to war.[8]

The Synod lodged futile complaints in the Senate against the policies of Anna's Cabinet, the executive and consultative organ that replaced the Privy Council. They noted, for example, that in June 1737, Suzdal diocese had 13 churches that lacked priests, 73 were without deacons, and 139 without sub-deacons, while 5 churches had no clerical staff whatsoever. By September, the number of priestless churches had increased to 65.[9] By the end of that year, Arkhangelsk, for example, lacked sixty priests, and Nizhnii Novgorod diocese, which had experienced the "disaster" of losing 1,384 young men of the clerical estate in 1736, was short of 165 priests and 187 deacons.[10] In March 1739, the Synod submitted a comprehensive protest, outlining the bitter fruits of the *razbory*: by then, in all dioceses excluding Ukraine, a total of 1,264 churches lacked priests, while 706 were "empty."[11] The Moscow Synodal Chancellery even refused to satisfy the army command, stating that there were no children left to be drafted.[12]

As the war was winding down in 1739–40, the Synod sent more (futile) requests to stop further recruitment.[13] By then, however, the Synod was critically understaffed, a shadow of the vigorous institution that Prokopovich had created. In early October 1740, it had only two bishops (Amvrosii Iushkevich and Stefan Kalinovskii) and one priest (Petr Grigor'ev) in its ranks.[14] The emptying of the Synod must have been as distressful as the emptying of the diocesan churches. Amvrosii and Stefan were left to hope for a miracle.

The miracle came on October 17, 1739, when Empress Anna died and then, three weeks later, the palace guards, led by Generalissimus Minikh, arrested her lover, Biron, and exiled him to Siberia.[15] The late empress's niece, Duchess Anna Leopol'dovna of Mecklenburg (proclaimed grand duchess in Russia), together with her husband, Anton-Ulrich of Braunschweig, became regents for their baby son, Emperor Ivan VI Antonovich.

The regents had a very special relationship with Archbishop Amvrosii Iushkevich. Just a year earlier he had married them. His elaborate wedding sermon praised the pedigrees of both bride and groom ("the glory of Europe"): the groom, Anton-Ulrich of the House of Braunschweig-Wolfenbüttel, had familial connections to the Holy Roman emperors, while his "pious [*pravovernaia*]" bride, Anna of Mecklenburg-Schwerin, descended from the Romanovs as well as Prince Pribislaw of Mecklenburg (d. 1178), "who radiated his faith in Christ" to the pagan Pomeranian Slavs.[16] In 1740 Amvrosii supported the duchess's claims against Biron, gaining, in return, not only her personal trust but also virtually unrestricted access to the palace.[17] In meetings with the court elites, he also advocated for expanding her political powers beyond that of a regent and supported the right of her future daughters (not just sons) to succession to the throne.[18] In other words, should the baby emperor Ivan die, Amvrosii supported the continuous reign of the Braunschweig couple with their issue: a position opposite to Catherine I's 1727 "Testament," which gave Elizabeth and the Holstinians rights to the throne.

The Synod reaped the fruits of Amvrosii's relationship with Regent Anna almost immediately. Her November 18, 1740, manifesto ended all *razbory* and returned the drafted children of the clergy to their parents and their parishes. The dark period was over.[19] While the release of military recruits likely helped the church fill many of the vacancies in the parish, this act alone was not enough. A few months later, on February 14, 1741, the Grand Duchess announced a general amnesty for various categories of "state officials," including the clergy, on April 28, 1741.[20] This clemency ranged widely, affecting a colorful collection of cases: priests who were imprisoned for abusing village serfs, corrupt priests caught taking bribes, violent (*buinyi*) clerics of all ranks, subdeacons who bootlegged moonshine, clergy living "immoral lives," drunkards, and even those guilty of murder. In no way did the amnesty clear their "culpability [*viny*]." It was clemency only, but the Synod exercised discretion to allow many to return to their ministry, thus filling even more vacant posts.[21]

Among the pardoned "guilty" clergy were also many of the bishops exiled during Feofan's purges of 1730–36, such as Feofilakt Lopatinskii and Georgii Dashkov. The Holy Synod's official documents show some unease at the realization that, on the one hand, the administrators of the amnesty (including Varlaam Skamnitskii, Stefan Kalinovskii, and Amvrosii Iushkevich) were all Feofan's appointees and therefore participated in persecuting his opponents; and on the other, that the purged bishops were now of no threat to them. As the condition for amnesty, the Synod restored their nominal titles without restoring their power in the bishoprics. So, Feofilakt Lopatinskii was released from prison at the end of November 1740, then pardoned in 1741; from there, he went to the Biziukov village monastery on the eastern fringe of the Smolensk region, dying shortly afterward in May 1741.[22] Synodal clemency for Lopatinskii did not include the rehabilitation of his theology, particularly his *Igo Gospodne Blago*, which polemicized against Prokopovich (as described in chapter 2). The Synod refused to publish it even later, despite the 1749 request by Empress Elizabeth and her morganatic husband, Aleksei Razumovskii (who kept Feofilakt's manuscript reverently in a "lacquered box").[23]

In the continuing wave of pardons, Ignatii Smola was released in October 1741 as a simple monk (albeit with a generous pension) and died in December of that year, while Georgii Dashkov was amnestied posthumously, having died in 1739.[24] Varlaam Vonatovich (d. 1751), likewise, did not return to his Kiev archbishopric. The Synod removed him from the capital to the Tikhvin Monastery, where they failed to arrange proper care for this former adversary of Feofan. The Synod allocated him a salary from the charity fund earmarked for the Middle Eastern Orthodox churches—not from the regular budget. Since these funds were not regularly available, Varlaam ended up borrowing money from local merchants to make ends meet.[25] Overall, the ecclesiastical amnesty of 1741 achieved the goal of enabling Feofan's appointees to pardon many of his former theological enemies, therefore correcting many of the excesses of the reformists' purge of the church ranks in the early 1730s. At the same time, the pardons ensured that the opponents of Feofan did not return to power within the church and the existing reformist status quo was not upset.

The enthronement of Elizabeth during the December 1741 "revolution" continued this spirit of reconciliation and clemency.[26] The first recipient of it was Amvrosii Iushkevich himself, who had earlier opposed Elizabeth's right to the throne. After the coup, Elizabeth was predisposed against him and planned to issue a "strong reprimand [scharfen Vorweis]," which seemed reasonable given the coup supporters' commitment to the 1727 "Testament" that gave the rights of succession to Elizabeth Petrovna and her nephew, Grand Duke Peter Fedorovich of Holstein.[27] The archbishop, however, fell to the empress's knees and pleaded for forgiveness with tears (Thränen).[28] Elizabeth showed mercy (his rank was preserved), while the Synod authorized a wave of church services across the country to celebrate her ascent to the throne and to emphasize her legitimacy.[29] In addition, the Synod busied itself with removing any prayers or liturgical material mentioning Ivan VI from the parishes.[30]

After forgiving Amvrosii, the empress continued Regent Anna's policy of the country-wide amnesty. Between 1742 and 1743, clemency was issued for clergy implicated in political crimes (slovo i delo) as well as "various offences [raznye viny]."[31] In a show of a wider reconciliation with the church, Elizabeth went on a piety offensive in the 1740s, attending churches, visiting monasteries, fasting, inviting preachers to court to deliver sermons, and even making a pilgrimage to Kiev.[32]

Yet, despite the display of devotion, Elizabethan piety and culture—as Bushkovitch and Solov'ev have noted—was not a return to the old Muscovite ways.[33] The empress emphasized her ascent to power as the triumphal restoration of her father's policies, a "return to the regulations of Peter the Great."[34] While she liked going to monasteries, she enjoyed "ballets, masquerades, and comedies" just as much. Her trip to Kiev was as entertaining as it was devotional: in addition to the Holy Caves, the empress attended Cossack jousting matches and was greeted by ceremonial processions of Roman gods, Greek heroes, and Pegasi.[35]

Most importantly, her religious policies remained firm in following the letter and spirit of Petrine church reform. She reaffirmed the social-disciplinary provisions of the *Spiritual Regulation* and rejected any speculation about restoring the patriarchate.[36] She also restored the office of the chief procurator, which effectively lapsed from 1731 to 1742, when Anna did not bother to appoint one.[37] In the spirit of the reforms, however, Peter's daughter promoted the episcopal candidates who were (mostly Ukrainian) "fledglings" of Feofan's reforms and loyal adherents of Russia's new religious culture. It is during her reign that those five continuities of Prokopovich's reforms bore their fruits.

THE FIRST CONTINUITY: FEOFAN'S DISCIPLES

The first continuity was institutional, resulting from the struggle for reform between 1721 and 1740, during which the composition of the church hierarchy changed in favor of the "Feofanists." While, as mentioned earlier, the Synod pardoned some of the remaining followers of Stefan Iavorskii and patriarchate restorationism, their influence in church affairs remained marginal. The great influential bishops and metropolitans of the Elizabethan (1741–61) and Catherinian (1762–96) eras were not the students of Feofilakt or Stefan but the hierarchs who traced their nominations directly to Feofan or to his closest associates.

Throughout the 1730s, Prokopovich affirmatively promoted and appointed many colleagues, students, and clergymen with philo-Protestant views to positions of power in the church and the Synod. One might start this list with Bishop Luka Konashevich (d. 1758), for example, a member of Feofan's social circle at his St. Petersburg Karpovka estate, who distinguished himself in 1719 as the chief hieromonk of the navy. Feofan originally promoted this Mohyla Academy graduate to teach at the Imperial Cadet Corps in 1732, and he also taught religion in Feofan's orphanage school alongside Theophil Siegfried Bayer. Prokopovich was quite impressed by him and composed verses in Luka's praise.[38] As bishop of Kazan (1738–58), Konashevich would promote clergymen who distinguished themselves in their parish service through preaching, teaching, or missionary work to Synodal positions. Among Konashevich's appointees were the influential future bishops Dmitrii Sechenov (1709–67), Veniamin Putsek-Grigorovich (1706–82), and Gedeon Krinovskii (1726–63).

Among Konashevich's colleagues was Varlaam Skamnitskii (1696–1761), who also taught in Feofan's orphanage school while Luka was in St. Petersburg. Educated at the Mohyla Academy and recommended to Prokopovich by his friend Rafail Zaborovskii, Varlaam played an important role in the case of the final defrocking and defamation of Feofilakt Lopatinskii in 1739. In 1740 he became a full member of the Synod (as archimandrite of Chudov Monastery) and in 1743 the bishop of Viatka. Although strict to the lower clergy, he, like

Prokopovich, lived jovially with the local elites, exhibiting a "proclivity to extensive feasting." As a true confessor of the new religious culture, he staged theatrical productions at the local seminary and even "danced eagerly and well."[39]

Other bishops may not have been good dancers, but they played a more direct role in the purges of the 1730s and benefited from doing so. One was Ilarion Rogalevskii (d. 1738), a "man of Prokopovich's school and party" and Feofan's former theology student. He led the criminal case against Sil'vestr Kholmskii and benefited from it directly by taking Kholmskii's position in Kazan. While in Kazan he broke ground for the diocesan school and staffed it with Feofan's former Kievan students; this school would be further developed by Konashevich.[40] Another was Stefan Kalinovskii (a future presiding member of the Synod), who took an active role in the 1732 case, denouncing Evfimii Koletti as a "Spanish spy." He was later rewarded (in 1735) with the prestigious abbacy of the St. Aleksandr Nevskii Monastery.[41]

Another very important ally of the reform, who took part both in the purges and in the promotion of new personnel, was Rafail Zaborovskii (1676–1747), an old friend of Feofan's, described in previous chapters. He replaced the purged Varlaam Vonatovich in 1731 as the archbishop (later, the metropolitan) of Kiev and All Ukraine.[42] Zaborovskii owed his first major promotion to Gavriil Buzhinskii who appointed him as the chief hieromonk of the Russian navy and as assessor of the Holy Synod in St. Petersburg in 1723. Feofan's patronage helped him secure subsequent appointments to the bishoprics of Pskov in 1725 and Kiev in 1731.[43] While in Kiev, Zaborovskii embraced opposition to Catholic influence zealously by purging the local liturgical books of "Roman influences" while improving education and the clergy's relationship with Ukraine's hetman Danylo Apostol (1654–1734).[44] Zaborovskii's improvement of education came at a moment when the Kiev Academy was in such decline in the late 1720s that the Holy Synod feared it might become "empty" with "students eager to desert it by going to study abroad."[45] Zaborovskii played a key role in the patronage and promotion of such important Ukrainian bishops of the Elizabethan and Catherinian eras as Halle-educated Simon Todorskii (more on him later) and Georgii Konisskii (1717–95). Among Rafail's other important beneficiaries was Amvrosii Iushkevich. This alumnus of the Kiev Academy distinguished himself in opposing the Uniates in Vilnius in 1732, and, with Rafail's recommendation, arrived in St. Petersburg in 1734, becoming a member of the Synod under Feofan and the bishop of Vologda in 1736.[46]

Thus the ranks of the church hierarchy swelled with higher clergy affiliated with Feofan and his party, mostly Ukrainians, but also some Russians (such as Pitirim of Nizhnii Novgorod).[47] By the 1740s and 1750s, the majority of the members of the Synod owed their presence in the institution to Feofan and his promotions. For example, of the eight members of the 1749 Synod, only one, Platon Malinovskii of Moscow, could trace any connections to the Lopatin-skii and Iavorskii party. (Although even Platon was an avid reader of Protes-tant literature, including Johann Arndt, John Pearson, and Johann Heinrich Michaelis.[48]) Among other members of the Synod, the presiding member (Stefan Kalinovskii) was Feofan's former colleague, three were his former stu-dents and junior colleagues, two were Todorskii's students, and the rest owed their promotions to Kalinovskii.[49] The picture changed even more in 1759, when none of the members of the six-person Synod could be traced to the philo-Catholic party of the late 1720s.[50]

Feofan's influence in the promotion of church elites went beyond the walls of the Synod and its most elite bishoprics. By 1750 the leadership of many of the dioceses of the Russian Empire was dominated by clergy with connections to Feofan's promotions. Thus, in 1750, the bishop of Kolomna was Gavriil Kremenetskii, a student of Simon Todorskii, from whom he gained mastery of Greek and Hebrew philology. Feofan appointed him to teach at St. Aleksandr Nevskii Seminary in 1736; he later become the prefect of that seminary and then gained successive titles as the archimandrite of Novospasskii Monastery, the bishop of Kolomna, and finally the metropolitan of St. Petersburg. Accord-ing to Titlinov, he was a somewhat liberal monk, who allowed fourth and sub-sequent remarriages, sought to simplify the access to divorce, and wanted to relax the limits on blood relations in marriage.[51]

At the same time, some 400 kilometers north, in Kostroma, the bishop was Sil'vestr Kuliabka (1701–61), a follower of Feofan's oratory.[52] When the Synod invited Kuliabka to preach at Anna's court, it opened the door for his subse-quent promotion to the bishopric in Kostroma (in 1745) and then St. Petersburg (in 1750).[53] Even many of the dioceses on the periphery of the empire had bish-ops connected to Prokopovich in 1750. Sil'vestr Glovatskii, originally a student of the Mohyla Academy during Feofan's rectorship, was bishop of Tobolsk; Ilarion Rogalevskii had called him up to the seminary in Kazan together with another of Prokopovich's "followers," Veniamin Putsek-Grigorovich. After Ilar-ion's death in 1738, Glovatskii helped carry his torch in the Kazan circle of reformers led by Konashevich.[54] The bishop of Chernigov, Amvrosii Dub-nevich, was also an intellectual follower of Feofan and a protégé of Rafail Zaborovskii.[55]

The Insolence of Matseevich

Although most of the elite hierarchs of the Elizabethan era were Feofan's appointees or his disciples, or otherwise intellectual heirs of his reform, Arsenii Matseevich (1697–1772), metropolitan of Rostov, did not fit that profile. Born

in Polish Volhynia to a family with a Polish noble (*szlachta*) background, Matseevich received most of his education in a strictly Roman Catholic setting,
studying first at Waręż Piarist school as a child and later in the Lwów Jesuit
Academy.[56] Although he advanced quickly through the ranks of upper clergy
(due to his service in the navy, Cadet Corps, and Siberia), he was much closer
to the ideals of the late Stefan Iavorskii than to any of his contemporaries.[57]

Thus, his writings and ecclesiastical activism looked back to the views of
Iavorskii and the patriarchate restorationists of the 1720s. For example, he
attacked (the late) Feofan Prokopovich and derided the church reformers as
"devious [*zlokovarnye*] people, who with their intrigues confused and deceived
the innocent soul of the most pious and most gentle monarch, Peter the
Great."[58] Similarly, in attacking the *Spiritual Regulation*, he blamed Feofan for
authoring a text "surely of Protestant spirit if not worse."[59] At the same time,
he vigorously called for the restoration of the patriarchate and the inviolability
of church property (in relation to state policy) in his April 1742 treatise titled
O blagochinii tserkovnom (On the proper order in the church).[60] He called on the
Orthodox Church to "vomit out the Protestant spirit" and "restore the former
Patriarchal throne in Moscow in accordance with the holy rules."[61] Doing so,
he believed, would rebuke the Protestants who thought that the Orthodox
Church "approves their evil faith" by establishing a similar administrative
model for its church, the Synod.[62] Much like Iavorskii, Arsenii based all of his
arguments on his Catholic-inspired conception of the "two powers" doctrine,
whereby the patriarchs and bishops oversaw the spiritual realm of society
while the tsars oversaw the temporal.[63]

It is not difficult to imagine that such theological ruminations did more
than echo Iavorskii's protestations. They also placed the metropolitan of Rostov in a series of direct confrontations with Empress Elizabeth and the Synod.
His enemies in the Synod were numerous, among them Stefan Kalinovskii,
Palladii of Riazan, and, most importantly, the future bishop of Novgorod,
Dmitrii Sechenov.[64] Thus, between 1742 and 1760, the Synod censured Arsenii
seven times for his "episodes of extreme insolence [*prederzosti*]" by issuing
official reprimands (*vygovory*).[65] One of the reprimands came from the empress
herself, who stated that the bishop was insulting her father.[66]

Arsenii's relationship with the court continued to deteriorate: in 1745 he
opposed the wedding between the future Catherine II and Peter III on the
basis of their blood relation (as second cousins).[67] His opposition irritated
Elizabeth, who was eager to marry her nephew off and who noticed that other
hierarchs were agreeable to the marriage. How exactly the Synod consented to
the ceremony is not yet known, but the report of Prussian ambassador Mardefeld shows that he bribed one "archbishop" (likely Amvrosii Iushkevich) with

1,000 rubles to clear the obstacle. (This report was confirmed by French ambassador Jacques-Joachim, Marquis de la Chétardie.[68]) Having no support for his opposition to the marriage, Arsenii returned in 1745 to Rostov, where he boycotted Synod meetings and received more official "reprimands."[69] The intensity of Arsenii's conflict with the court abated when he left the capital. Amvrosii Iushkevich, who was hesitant to support him on many "general ecclesiastical issues," seems to have protected him, while the rather conciliatory attitude of the empress to the clergy in general meant that he was not dismissed, at least not at that time.[70] (Catherine II would be less conciliatory, as the next chapter will illustrate.)

The Second Continuity:
The Educational Curriculum

With the exception of Matseevich, most of the church hierarchs of this period continued Prokopovich's legacy. One of the areas where this legacy was most pronounced was theological education in Russia's seminaries. Feofan's Kievan courses, taught between 1704 and 1716, introduced future Russian and Ukrainian clergy to the new Protestant-based curricula in theology and philosophy, challenging the dominance of Jesuit-Aristotelian scholasticism. The best way to track the new trends in the Orthodox curriculum of that period is to study the content of theological courses in Russian and Ukrainian seminaries after Feofan.

Thus, in Ukraine, the incorporation of new Protestant material as well as Feofan's textbooks was a feature in the curriculum of Feofan's junior colleague Iosif Volchanskii (d. 1745), who developed theology courses for the Kiev Academy and Chernigov seminary.[71] Mikhail Kozachinskii's 1741–43 theological lectures in Kiev introduced students to textual interpretation methods developed by Swiss Protestant biblical commentator Sébastian Castellion.[72] Later course textbooks by Georgii Konisskii (his theology manuscript of 1751–55), Manassii Maksimovich (who taught theology in 1755–58), David Nashchinskii (his 1758–59 curriculum), and Samuil Mislavskii (his 1759–63 curriculum) showed the pronounced influence of Prokopovich and Protestantism more generally.[73] On May 1, 1764, the new metropolitan of Kiev, Arsenii Mogilianskii, finally banned any theological curricula that deviated from Feofan's course, making Prokopovich's text the academy's theological canon. His academy-wide "Instruction" banned professors from compiling their own courses (*vnov ne sochiniat'*) and bound them to follow Prokopovich's curriculum in its entirety. Subsequent publications of Feofan's courses in 1773 (as well as a second edition in 1782 and a third edition in 1791) made this work a printed (rather than handwritten) textbook and the task of teaching his theology much easier overall.[74]

Together with theology, philosophy courses also underwent significant changes in Ukraine in the replacement of Jesuit-Aristotelian and scholastic content with curricula more popular in Protestant Europe. Thus, Stefan Kalinovskii's 1729–30 course rejected Aristotelian categories, criticized Duns Scotus, and introduced the ideas of Descartes.[75] He set the trend for the subsequent teaching of Cartesian philosophy in Kiev in the 1730s and 1740s.[76] Stefan's lectures on logic also borrowed from Philip Melanchthon's standard sixteenth-century Lutheran textbook on the subject, *Dialecticae Libri Quator* (Four Books on the Dialectics), while his philosophy manuscripts cited Feofan's beloved theologian, Buddeus.[77]

After 1752 Kiev's philosophy courses increasingly began to adopt the rationalist Wolffianism that was in vogue in early Enlightenment Europe. Wolff, whom Halle first expelled (in 1721) and then begged to return (in 1740), did not appeal to Prokopovich, who preferred Leibniz.[78] By the 1750s, however, Feofan's followers (and the University of Halle) had changed their attitude about this philosophical school. The prefect of Kiev Mohyla Academy (and future metropolitan) Samuil Mislavskii, for example, corresponded with Wolffian professor Friedrich Christian Baumeister personally, and upon the philosopher's advice sent one of his students, Ivan Khmel'nitskii, to study Wolffianism in Halle, Leipzig, and Königsberg. Mislavskii's attraction to Baumeister's works made his book "required and commonly accepted" in Kiev by the mid-1750s.[79] From then on, Baumeister's textbook remained not only part of the Mohyla Academy's curriculum but spread north as well: it was "popular" in Moscow and this philosophy course was reprinted there in 1777.[80]

The grounds for adopting Wolffian philosophy in Kiev (in lieu of Descartes) were theological. In his 1755 letter to Kievan metropolitan Timofei Shcherbatskii, rector of the Mohyla Academy David Nashchinskii tried to convince the reluctant hierarch to end the teaching of Edmond Pourchot's Cartesian system (taught by the metropolitan's brother Georgii in the 1740s). Nashchinskii's arguments were theological. While he agreed that Pourchot was better than "the old Jesuit books," the Wolffian philosophy of Johann Heinrich Winkler and Friedrich Christian Baumeister allowed students to learn the basics of theology better. "Wolffian philosophy," he wrote "utilizes all same terms and definitions for both philosophy and theology and contains in itself natural theology that provides light for revealed doctrine."[81] Georgii Konisskii, the archbishop of Mogilev, seconded Nashchinskii's opinion in à letter to the metropolitan that same year. For him, too, Pourchot was clearly inferior to Baumeister since the former followed Calvin in ascribing to God *causa peccati*, the cause of sin occasioned by God's predestination of Adam's fall. Still, for

Georgii, both were preferable to the old philosophy, or "garbage [*smettia*] of Jesuit Aristotelian commentators."[82]

Purging the curriculum of Jesuit "garbage" continued the reform of Orthodox education along the lines originally envisioned by Prokopovich, but this change extended well beyond the walls of the Mohyla Academy. Much like in Kiev, the Moscow Slavo-Greco-Latin Academy continued to hold on to the Jesuit-inspired curriculum in theology and philosophy for much of the 1720s and 1730s, especially when Feofilakt Lopatinskii and Kirill Florinskii taught there.[83] After 1740, however, teachers at the Moscow Academy began incorporating elements of Prokopovich's theology together with the Lutheran systems of David Hollatz, Johann Quenstedt, and Johann Gerhard. Smirnov called this pattern "a mix of [Lutheran] scholasticism with a better elucidation of theology as seen in Feofan's method."[84] At the same time, the philosophy courses in the late 1740s and early 1750s exhibited a switch from Aristotle to Bacon and Descartes, and then to the rationalist method of Leibniz and Wolff.[85] By 1762 the Moscow Academy theology course taught by Gavriil Petrov (the future Catherinian metropolitan of Novgorod) followed Feofan's theological curriculum more "literally" than previous courses, which still contained elements of Catholic scholasticism.[86]

Prokopovich's legacy also influenced the curriculum at Moscow's other theological school—the Holy Trinity Seminary at the Trinity-Sergius Monastery. The course of Afanasii Vol'khovskii (the school's first theology professor), titled "Systema theologiae coepta anno 1751," was largely structured on Feofan's Kievan lectures. "In structure and delivery of content," stated Smirnov, "Afanasii's curricular system is almost a copy of the theological lessons of Feofan Prokopovich."[87] Afanasii's courses also invoked the authority of two Protestant theologians, the Braunschweig Lutheran divine Georg Callixt (d. 1656) and Basel's Calvinist theologian Lukas Gernler (d. 1675), who was one of the signers of the Helvetic Confession.[88]

Prokopovich's legacy in education also spread to the provinces. The manuscripts of theological courses in the Novgorod seminary from the 1740s and 1750s show a clear pattern of departure from scholasticism and the adoption of Feofan's curriculum.[89] In Viatka, Feofan's cousin Lavrentii Gorka (1672–1737) founded a seminary in 1735, teaching the locals the arts of rhetoric and poetics in accordance with Feofan's curriculum in these subjects, as well as rudimentary theology courses that were influenced by the "Protestant authors."[90] What kinds of Protestant authors influenced this bishop's courses in Viatka can be seen from his seminary library, which featured Luther's catechism as well as books by Johann Gerhard, Samuel Bochart, Johannes Bustorf, Christopher

Pfaff, and Johann Buddeus.[91] How the local Viatichi (Viatka inhabitants) responded to the new bishop and his teachings is not clear, but the local chronicle insinuated that it was an uphill battle. Gorka, according to this account, was "a great man of learning," who sought to "correct disorder [*bezchinie*] and vice . . . to create educated [*prosveshchennykh*] servants of the church, who are able to comprehend the depth of Christianity's ideals."[92]

The Third Continuity: International Education

Another major continuity of Feofan's reforms appeared in the direction of Orthodox seminarians' international education. Feofan's opening to the Protestant West charted Orthodoxy's own escape from Rome, which manifested itself as a disengagement from the widely tolerated practice of sending students to the Catholic West. This trend can be seen, for example, in the decrease in Eastern Slavic enrollments in Rome (such as the Collegio Greco) and in Polish Jesuit schools in the late 1730s.[93] In fact, after 1721 a new trend emerged whereby newly emerging domestic seminaries as well as Protestant universities abroad increasingly attracted young Orthodox men.[94]

For Prokopovich and his reformist colleagues, it was Germany, and particularly Pietist Halle, that was most deserving of receiving young Ukrainian seminarians for further study. His contacts with Pietist circles were extensive and included correspondence with Buddeus and August Hermann Francke and personal relationships with Pietist ministers in Russia such as Wilhelm Tolle, Gottfried Himler, and Heinrich G. Nazzius in St. Petersburg; Justus S. Scharschmid in Moscow; and Philipp Michaelis in Arkhangelsk.[95] The circle also extended to Russian noblemen who had studied in Halle (like the sons of Admiral Apraksin, Fedor Golovin, and Aleksandr Golovkin) as well as German scientists in St. Petersburg who were friends with Feofan and Francke (like Theophil Siegfried Bayer and Johann Albrecht von Korf).[96] A very important connection for Feofan was Albert Anton Vierorth, Halle alumnus, cathedral pastor at Reval, and "the head of Baltic Pietism."[97] Prokopovich was quite eager to emphasize the fraternal spirit of his interconfessional friendship with Vierorth. "We acknowledge [*erkennen*] you as our brother in Christ," he told Vierorth, "and ask that you would consider us as such also."[98]

Prokopovich's cordial contacts with Pietism served as a catalyst for preparing the brightest seminarians for academic study in Halle. The first candidate for such study was Simon Todorskii (1700–1754). The scion of a Cossack family from Zolotonosha, he started his studies in Kiev during Feofan's rectorship there in 1717. Then in 1727 the archbishop brought his former student to St. Petersburg to learn German.[99] During the next two years, Simon not only learned German (after residence with "a Baltic German family") but also traveled to nearby Reval, where he met that same "brother in Christ" Reverend Vierorth to prepare for further studies in Germany.[100]

Carrying a recommendation from Vierorth, the young Ukrainian arrived in Halle in June 1729, taking up ancient languages, biblical philology, and Pietist theology under the direction of Johann Heinrich Michaelis, Gotthilf August Francke, and Johann Callenberg.[101] Feofan, who received updates from Germany on Simon's progress, was pleased to hear that he also attended theology courses in Jena in 1736, where the intellectual legacy of Johann Franz Buddeus continued to shape the university's Pietist-inspired curriculum.[102]

In addition to his studies, Todorskii began to amass a large library while in Germany. Some of the books were gifted to him by Professor J. H. Michaelis and Gotthilf August Francke; some he purchased. The collection was large enough that he hired special transport to help move the large wooden crates on his trip across Central Europe and the Balkans in 1736–37.[103] Upon his death, the library contained more than eight hundred volumes, featuring not only biblical philological material but also numerous classics of Lutheran theology. Martin Luther, Philip Melanchton, Joachim Lange, Johann Franz Buddeus, Johann Heinrich Michaelis, Christian Crusius, and Christian Thomasius were all part of his collection.[104] Although Todorskii's library was by far the largest among his contemporaries, the kind of literature it contained was not altogether unique.

While in Germany, Todorskii also endeavored to make Pietist ideas accessible to the entire literate public in Russia. With financial help from Feofan Prokopovich, Rafail Zaborovskii, and Empress Anna, he translated and published the works of Johann Arndt (including his famous *True Christianity*), August Hermann Francke, and J. A. Freilinghausen.[105] Todorskii viewed these translations, but particularly Arndt's, as important spiritual and devotional aids, beneficial not only for Protestants but for the souls of Orthodox believers as well. Thus his introduction to the Slavonic edition of *True Christianity* stated that "many of those who care for the salvation of their souls read these [Arndt's] books with great diligence."[106]

Simon finished his studies in 1736, taking the next two years to travel around Central Europe and the Balkans. He returned to Kiev in 1738 with a zeal of a reformer: he was about to confront "idolatry and unrighteousness" within his Orthodox Church and was preparing, in the words of Petersburg pastor Nazzius, "to win the youth in Kiev to the knowledge of the Word of God."[107] While in Kiev (1738 to 1742), he built a new, Halle-inspired curriculum for the study of biblical languages, Hebrew and Greek in particular.[108] His doctrinal teaching emphasized such concepts as total depravity and justification by faith while condemning those opposed to this doctrine as "polluted by the Jesuit spirit" and as adherents of the "Papist [teaching] on the forgiveness of sins."[109]

ЧТИРИ КНИГИ
ѡ
ИСТИННОМЪ
ХРИСТІАНСТВѢ

Содержащіи

ВЪ СЕБѢ ꙋЧЕНІЕ ѡ СПАСИТЕЛНОМЪ ПО-
каѧнїи, сердечномъ жалѣнїи и болѣзнованїи ради грѣ-
ховъ; ѡ истиннои вѣрѣ, ѡ сватомъ житїи и
пребыванїи истиннихъ неложнихъ
христіанъ:

ТАКОЖДЕ ѡ СЕМЪ, КАКѡ ИСТИН-
ныи христіанинъ имать побѣдити грѣхъ, смерть, діа-
вола мїръ и всакое бѣдствіе, вѣрою, молитвою,
терпѣнїемъ, божіимъ словомъ и небес-
нимъ ꙋтѣшенїемъ,

ВСЕЖЕ СІЕ ВЪ ХРИСТѢ ЇНСꙊСѢ.

Сложеннїи
чрезъ

ЇѠАННА АРНДА

Бывшаго Епископа церквеи въ княженїи
Линебꙋргскомъ,

ЗЪ НѢМЕЦКАГѡ ІАЗЫКА НАРꙊСКЫИ
переведеннїи и напечатаннїи.

ВЪ ГАЛѢ ѤАѰЛЕ. ГОДꙊ.

Figure 5. A page from Johann Arndt's *Wahres Christentum* (*True Christianity*) (1605–10), translated by Prokopovich's Halle-educated disciple Simon Todorskii (1700–1754). Courtesy of Beinecke Rare Book and Manuscript Library, Yale University.

His fame in Kiev and Germany earned him an invitation to St. Petersburg, where he preached in 1742–43 in the presence of Empress Elizabeth. She was quite satisfied with Prokopovich's disciple, appointing him as the confessor and instructor to the empress's nephew, the future Peter III, and to his wife, Sophia-Frederica of Anhalt-Zerbst (or colloquially, Fike). Many years later, Fike would become known worldwide as Catherine the Great.[110] Simon's Pietist education, his ability to speak German, and his sensitivity to Lutheran theology were very helpful in converting the daughter of a pious Lutheran nobleman to Orthodoxy. So impressed was Catherine's mother (Johanna Elisabeth, duchess of Anhalt-Zerbst) with this teacher that she noted how the instructor "showed preference to the Lutheran confession [*preferablement appliqué a la lutherienne*]."[111] In one of his doctrinal lessons, Father Simon reportedly compared the Orthodox "confession of faith" (probably, Feofan's *Pervoe uchenie*) with the catechism of Martin Luther to show that both contain the "same fundamental teachings."[112] In a letter to her father, Fike stated that her religious instruction led her to see "almost no difference between Lutheranism and Orthodoxy."[113]

Todorskii's swift rise in the ranks accompanied his success in converting Catherine II. On March 31, 1744, the Synod appointed him as the bishop of Kostroma.[114] A year later, Simon became the bishop of Pskov, an ecclesiastical position that then ranked third in Russia, after Novgorod and Moscow.[115] As was the case with other court bishops, the rank secured his status but did not require him to attend to the business of his diocese.[116]

Simon Todorskii's stellar rise and his successful education proved to be an example to emulate for other graduates of the Mohyla Academy. Throughout the 1730s, Archbishop Rafail invested shrewdly in the school's growth, so much so that it acquired the name of the Kievo-Mohylan-Zaborovian Academy. In his desire to promote the study of Protestant biblical philology and to turn Ukrainian theological education away from Roman influence, the archbishop sponsored other Ukrainians to study in Halle in addition to Todorskii.[117]

Two such Kievan alumni who received Rafail's support were Varlaam Liashchevskii (1702–74) and David Nashchinskii (1721–93). Liashchevskii went to Halle in 1737 and studied Greek and Hebrew philology under Johann Heinrich Michaelis. He was later one of the main teachers of biblical languages in Kiev and then in Moscow, where he became rector of the Slavo-Greco-Latin Academy in 1753.[118] His most important contribution to Russian theological education was his 1744 Greek grammar book, *Grecheskaia grammatika*, which saw several Latin and Russian editions in the eighteenth century.[119] Liashchevskii based his textbook partly on the work of Jacob Weller (1604–64), whose *Grammatica graeca nova* (1636) provided reference points for Varlaam on issues of

Greek dialect and syntax.[120] Liashchevskii's books reflected the influence of Pietist theology and philology, and his doctrinal teaching displayed this influence alongside a very negative assessment of Roman Catholic doctrines. Like a true follower of Feofan, he proclaimed the doctrine of grace and justification in 1740s Kiev; he also condemned "Papists and Uniates" as "heretics" and presented the pope as the Antichrist.[121]

David Nashchinskii likewise studied in Halle and in Königsberg in the late 1730s. He returned to Kiev in 1747, starting his career there as a teacher of biblical languages and German. In addition to languages, Nashchinskii taught philosophy, mostly based on Wolffian rationalism. He also translated at least one Pietist devotional work into Russian. The work was Carl Heinrich von Bogatzky's 1718 *Golden Treasury for the Children of God*, known in Russian as *Zlatoi kleinod detei Bozhiikh* (1762).[122]

This educational turn—away from Roman Catholic theological learning—was hardly limited to the most elite or most erudite alumni of the Mohyla Academy. After 1730 the spectrum of students going to early Enlightenment Germany broadened. In 1733 Vasilii Shcherbatskii, a Russian embassy priest stationed in Potsdam, took classes in Halle and joined the circle of Pietist professor Heinrich Milde (1676–1739).[123] A number of Kievan alumni studied in Kiel in the 1740s and 1750s, which was a natural choice due to the dynastic union of Holstein with the House of the Romanovs. Among the students were Hieromonk Iov Charnutskii (future priest of Holy Trinity Cathedral), Vasyl Khanenko, Stefan Mashkovich, Mykyta Maiboroda, Grigorii Timchenko, Ivan Advenin (of Moscow's Spasskii Cathedral), and "hieromonk Venedikt," who later served in the bishopric of Novgorod.[124]

In addition to Kiel and Halle, Breslau attracted a number of Ukrainian students in the 1740s and 1750s, due to the special relationship between the city's book merchants, who supplied theology textbooks and printed volumes of Prokopovich's works, and the Kiev Academy, who purchased them.[125] Königsberg and Leipzig were other important destinations where students from ecclesiastical and Cossack elite ranks pursued their studies.[126] Among the less frequented destinations were Lutheran gymnasia, such as the one in Pressburg (where Bishop Irinei Fal'kovskii studied) and Gdansk (where Kharkov alumnus Pavel Mariamskii took classes).[127]

While studying abroad, students soaked up the social pleasures of Germany as well as theological learning. Muscovite priest Advenin was reported to be "dragging himself around [*taskaias'*] coffeehouses and other dangerous places day and night" in Kiel, while Vasyl Khanenko "exerted himself [*uprazhnialsia*] in card playing and bowling."[128] The archimandrite of Ukraine's Nezhin Monastery, Modest, ran away with a married woman while studying in Breslau; it took the Synod five years to track him down.[129] As East Slavic Orthodoxy discovered new sources of learning in Protestant Europe, Russian and Ukrainian seminarians were experiencing this Europe in their own special ways.

GÖTTINGEN AND BEYOND

Protestant universities remained popular among Orthodox seminarians even after the Elizabethan era. In 1765 Catherine II and Foreign Minister Nikita Panin proposed to send ten students to Oxford and Cambridge to study "the higher sciences . . . not excluding theology" with the goal of this education "to serve the Holy Church with most desired benefit."[130] The Synod, in general, and metropolitans Gavriil Petrov and Dmitrii Sechenov, in particular, submitted a counterproposal. Instead of ten, the Synod assembled sixteen of the best seminarians and instead of Oxford and Cambridge, it decided to send them (in three groups) to Oxford, Leiden, and Göttingen.[131]

Choosing the two continental institutions may have been a money-driven decision, as the cost of living in Britain was notoriously high. Likewise, the logistics of funding were much easier to handle due to the well-established supply networks between the Mohyla Academy and Germany along the Kiev-Brody-Breslau-Halle route.[132] Yet it likely also reflected a concern about the quality of education. While the Oxford of the 1760s was known as "a place of torpor and stagnation," Göttingen and Leiden, by contrast, had very dynamic theological faculties.[133] In the 1760s and 1770s, Leiden's theology department included the notable Jan Jacob Schultens (1716–88), a "theologien éclairé," whose exposition emphasized the principle that "rational argumentation and not faith is the final arbiter of Christian belief and dogma."[134] Also, due to the popularity of natural law and jurisprudence during the Catherinian era, many members of the Synod certainly found Leiden (revered as the College of Grotius or Collegium Grotianum) intellectually attractive. Among its professors of the 1760s and 1770s were Frederik Willem Pestel (1724–1805), the author of the United Provinces Constitution, and the "Leiden literati": Meinardus Tydeman (1741–1825), the eighteenth-century editor of Grotius, and Willem Bilderdijk (1756–1831), a theologian of natural law.[135]

Göttingen University was also an important center of the religious Enlightenment. Founded in 1737 by Georg-August of Hanover (King George II of England), the university owed its existence to the British Crown but followed much of Halle's curriculum, while allowing its faculty to be "free to teach subjects as they saw fit."[136] Promotion of toleration and the Lutheran "middle way" was the intellectual foundation of the university and was shared by many of its faculty.[137] One such professor was Chancellor Johann Lorenz von Mosheim, a former Helmstedt preacher and moderate Pietist theologian who wrote a treatise in defense of Prokopovich in 1731. Another was Johann David Michaelis (grandnephew of Halle's Johann Heinrich Michaelis), a Semitic linguist and philologist who laid the foundations for the modern exegetical method in Hebrew.[138]

The first group of Orthodox seminarians that departed St. Petersburg for Oxford in November 1765 consisted of only six people: four students (from Moscow, Tver, and St. Petersburg), one inspector, and one secretary.[139] Another student, Andrei Samborskii, a Kievan graduate, left for England separately in 1765. Although he arrived with a group of agronomy students, he ended up studying theology as well.[140]

At the time of their departure, they received Panin's instruction to take up "various sciences" as well as "non-general [i.e., specialized] theology"; he urged them especially "to attend sermons, paying careful attention to the purity of their language and the preacher's style of delivery."[141] Panin also requested that students not only learn the style of the sermons but discern the difference in doctrine because "learning them would only further help students gain necessary pastoral expertise on the differences of doctrines among Christian confessions."[142] For the most part, the seminarians studied well, taking courses in mathematics, foreign languages, biblical languages, English, jurisprudence, theology, dialectics, and church history.[143] In addition to academics, the students were exposed to Oxford's social life. Aleksei Levshinov, brother of Moscow's metropolitan, for example, spent eight times more money on gloves and chocolates than he did on books. Two students (Prokhor Suvorov and Vasilii Nikitin) joined the "gown"-centered Freemasonic Lodge of Alfred, acceding to the ranks of master masons and, in Suvorov's case, even to the office of junior warden.[144]

While six people went to England, five students were sent to the Netherlands, where they also demonstrated success in sciences, theology, and languages. Lodewijk C. Valckenaer (1715–85) commended them for their accomplishments in biblical studies and Greek philology, while Jan J. Schultens applauded their diligence in Oriental languages. Others noted achievements in physics, logic, philosophy, and natural law.[145]

The Göttingen group was smaller than the previous two, and included three seminarians (two from Moscow and one from Novgorod), accompanied by the Synodal inspector, future bishop Damaskin Semenov-Rudnev.[146] Their accomplishments were much better documented, as the Göttingen professors took reporting the Russians' academic progress to St. Petersburg more seriously. Thus, the reports of Gottfried Less praised the efforts of Damaskin, who learned both moral and dogmatic theology from him with "untiring dedication," demonstrating "true Christian piety." In his report to St. Petersburg, Professor Otto David H. Beckmann commended the students as the "most honorable Russian men," while professors J. P. Murray, Johann Christoph Gatterer, J. N. Liering, and the famous J. D. Michaelis all gave accolades to the group.[147]

The fortunes of the seminarians who completed their study abroad varied, but most of them ended up serving the church in some capacity. Upon their return to St. Petersburg in 1773, the students faced a special commission in the main hall of the Aleksandr Nevskii Monastery that examined their knowledge of church history, Protestant theology, sciences, and languages (particularly French, German, Latin, Greek, and Hebrew). After successful examinations, graduates were certified as seminary instructors, and most took up teaching: five in Moscow, two in Novgorod, and one in St. Petersburg.[148]

Among those who did not become seminary professors, one joined the Russian diplomatic corps and three joined the ranks of the clergy.[149] Thus, Damaskin Semenov-Rudnev became the bishop of Sevsk and later of Nizhnii Novgorod.[150] Aleksei Levshin (or Levshinov) became the preacher at Moscow's Annunciation Cathedral and then a protopriest at the prestigious Spasskii Cathedral. He was a famous city preacher who translated English sermons into Russian and preached them in Moscow using the English style of delivery.[151] Another former student in England, Andrei Samborski, married an Englishwoman, Elizabeth Fielding, and then worked as a parish priest in London's Russian embassy for the next fifteen years.[152] After returning to St. Petersburg from his "enlightened Britain," he was "well received by the hierarchs, and some secular officials," and promoted to the rank of protopriest at St. Sophia Cathedral on the imperial estate of Tsarskoe Selo.[153] He then served as a father-confessor to Grand Duke Paul (from 1782) and as a tutor to future emperor Alexander I (from 1784), influencing the latter's religious "worldview" in the promotion of the Holy Alliance as well as the mystical piety (referred to as "Quaker" piety).[154]

THE FOURTH CONTINUITY: REFORMING THE BIBLE

No church reform in Reformation Europe was complete without its own revision or translation of the Bible, as was the case with *Lutherbibel*, Agricola's Finnish Scriptures, or the Tridentine Clementine Bible revision of 1561–98.[155] Russia's religious change was hardly an exception in this regard: the same impulses and the similar philological approaches that shaped the scriptural projects in Europe inspired the Orthodox church reformers. The Halle alumni of the 1730s, in fact, proved to be particularly useful in the decades-long project of revising Russia's Slavonic Bible.

The project originated in 1712, when Peter tasked Feofilakt Lopatinskii to revise the 1663 Muscovite Bible, which was "almost literally" a version of the

1581 Ostrog Bible.[156] In 1724 the tsar transferred the project from Feofilakt's team to a new commission led by Prokopovich. The archbishop was a vociferous critic of the 1581 Ostrog Bible: he decried its "Arian" influences (due to the ties of the sixteenth-century Volhynian Ostrog Orthodox nobles to the circle of Szymon Budny and other anti-Trinitarians). He also noted the translation's "discrepancies" when compared with the Greek original as well as numerous archaisms ("outdated and incomprehensible [*neudoborazumennye*] language") that were no longer universally intelligible by the clergy at the time.[157]

When Feofan took over the project in 1724, he emphasized the need to consult the Septuagint, the Hebrew manuscripts, and the rarer Greek translations of the Old Testament by Aquila of Sinope (ca. 130 CE), Theodotion (ca. 150 CE), and Symmachus the Ebionite (ca. 180 CE), available in printed form from Protestant Europe.[158] The original plans for the project were ambitious: Feofan anticipated completion sometime in 1725, with printing to be carried out in Holland, possibly with the option of issuing a parallel Dutch-Slavonic Bible.[159] The project, however, moved rather slowly: Peter's death ground the revision to a halt and only in May 1735 did Feofan petition Anna to restart the translation due to "the extreme need for the [revised] Bible."[160] Due to the lack of enough people with the academic knowledge of Greek, however, Feofan paused the project in April 1736 and his successors were not able to overcome this challenge. Stefan Kalinovskii complained in 1739–40 that there was a dearth of competent translators from Hebrew and Greek.[161]

The arrival of Todorskii and the ascent of Empress Elizabeth injected new vigor and expertise into the project: Elizabeth considered it her mission to finish the task started by her father. Simon's return to Ukraine from Halle led to the birth of Greek, Hebrew, and Aramaic philology in Kiev, and his "Hebraic studies school" at the academy maintained its focus on ancient languages until the beginning of the nineteenth century.[162] Arriving in St. Petersburg, Todorskii not only brought his own Pietist-educated philological expertise to the project but also summoned Halle alumnus Liashchevskii in 1747, along with his students from the Mohyla Academy.

Infused with new experts, the synodal committee made significant progress on the revision. Thus, Todorskii played a crucial role by correcting and checking the Septuagint verses against the Hebrew original.[163] Liashchevskii made an important contribution by checking the New Testament and Septuagint against other published translations. In his revision, he relied on the Western published editions of Greek texts published by some of the best-known Protestant biblical philologists of the time. According to Feodosii Eleonskii, among the works used, the most important were the eighteenth-century editions as well as the philological and grammatical guides of Dutch critic Lambertus Bos (1670–1717) from the University of Franeker, Leipzig's Christian Reineccius (1688–1752), and the Swiss Hebrew philologist Johann Jakob Breitinger (1701–74).[164] The committee also finished correcting the "ambiguities [*sumnitel'stva*]" in the texts translated by Lopatinskii using the Vulgate in 1712; the translators reaffirmed Feofan's insistence on relying on the Greek texts.[165]

The project to revise the Bible was completed in 1751. The first edition of the work was printed in four volumes and reflected the editors' Protestant-influenced tastes not only in philology but also in aesthetics. The Bible featured over four hundred illustrations engraved by Christopher Weigel (1654–1725), Caspar Luyken (1672–1708), and Jan Luyken (1649–1712). The choice of these Protestants' sacred art was deliberate: finding no illustrators in Moscow capable of properly depicting historical images (such as "Old Testament clothing"), the Holy Synod turned to the Academy of Sciences, who eagerly supplied "four illustrated Old and New Testaments in Dutch and French."[166] The Academy also commissioned St. Petersburg artist Johann-Elias Grimmel (1703–59), who painted for the court and for the city's Lutheran churches, to provide other illustrations and train Moscow's seminarians in the art of engraving for the Synod's printing press.[167]

Among the engravings likely provided by the Grimmel school was the cover page with sacred symbolic and geographic images such as Moscow's Kremlin and St. Petersburg's Neva Embankment, similar to many early modern European Bibles.[168] Finally, the book featured an aesthetic dedication to the monarch (in parallel to Western examples): a painting that shows Peter I and Catherine I in heaven, handing over an unfinished manuscript to their daughter Empress Elizabeth for the completion of the task they started (see figure 6).[169] This metaphor undoubtedly sought to reinforce the empress's self-image as the sustainer of the Petrine legacy while giving the "eaglets" of the tsar's reforms (who carried out the project) the mantle of both imperial and divine sanction. The cover pages of the new work ended with the introduction, in which the main editor Varlaam Liashchevskii lamented the "shortcomings" and "inaccuracies [*sumnitel'stva*]" of the old Bible while extolling the virtues of the project, which had been carried out over the span of several reigns by a new generation of scholars who had "completed their theological education" and received the necessary linguistic training to lead this endeavor to its final success.[170] Liashchevskii's exuberance about the accomplishment of the task and the education that helped him complete it reiterated the original ethos of Feofan's reform: Protestant learning brought improvement, not demise, to the Russian church.

Figure 6. The second title page of Russia's reformed Bible, Bibliia, sirech knigi sviashennago pisaniia Vetkhago i NovagoZaveta (Moscow, 1751). The image shows Empress Elizabeth receiving the divine sanction for Bible revision from Peter the Great and Catherine I, her parents, highlighting the continuity of reform. Courtesy of Boston Public Library.

The Fifth Continuity:
The Homiletical Change

Just as Prokopovich's reforms influenced how the church revised the written divine word, they also impacted the ways in which the clergy delivered the spoken word. Homiletics, often ignored in the literature, had undergone a radical change during the era of reform. As mentioned in the first chapter, seventeenth-century preaching in Ukraine, and increasingly at the court in Moscow, reflected the influence of the highly theatrical and somewhat convoluted Catholic Baroque style of homiletics (known as *conceptismo*), popular in Poland and Spain.

Feofan's reforms put an end to the proliferation of this Baroque homiletic style by promoting the highly didactic and doctrinal preaching that was popular with Protestants and northern humanists. His 1706 rhetorical manual thoroughly adopted the key elements of Protestant sermon composition in the structural use of rhetorical genus, exordium, the preacher's thema, as well as homiletical purpose. The manual emphasized preaching as a method of doctrinal instruction and moral edification, devoid of affected performance.[171] The sources for this rhetoric manual underscored a radical departure from the existing convention: instead of Polish or Spanish *sermonarios*, Prokopovich relied on the works of Erasmus, Johann Gerhard, Melchior Iunius (1545–1604), Iustus Lipsius (a northern humanist, 1547–1606), Gerardus Johannes Vossius (1577–1649), Lucas Osiander, Martin Chemnitz, and Melchior Zeidler.[172]

Feofan's fondness for this rhetorical style informed and influenced the Holy Synod's official legislation aimed at reforming the pulpit in Orthodox Russia. For example, the *Spiritual Regulation* of 1721 contained official rules (*reguly*) for Russia's preachers that required all of a sermon's primary sources to be biblical, that allowed the use of patristic sources (especially St. John Chrysostom) as secondary, and that warned against the use of miracle stories, "superstitions," and "fables" (*basni*) in public preaching.[173] The *Spiritual Regulation* also restricted motion and emotion, so characteristic of Stefan Iavorskii's preaching style. "It is not necessary to wave the arms about, to stand sideways, to jump, to laugh, nor is it necessary to weep," argued the *Regulation*.[174] Feofan ordered Russia's preachers to speak "with a humble self-deprecation," appear somber, and stay put in the pulpit.[175] Such instructions were not only part of the *Spiritual Regulation*—in the special 1726 synodal instruction, *Veshchi i dela* (Tasks and matters), for the "doctrinal teachers who preach to the Christian people," the reformers not only reinforced the 1721 rules but also recommended that preachers use "proofs of natural reason [*estestvenymi dokazatel'stvami*]" in their public discourse.[176]

Controlling emotion may seem strange given the eighteenth-century context of the growing popularity of theater, banquets, and court festivities. Yet this restraint was part of the custom of the Protestant court and parish preaching of the day. For example, as the court chaplain in Dresden and Berlin, Philipp Jakob Spener, preached in somberness and "serene tranquility," the archbishop of Canterbury, John Tillotson (1630–94), spoke with "dull sobriety" and "unadventurous reasonableness."[177] Even Jonathan Edwards's fire-and-brimstone "Sinners in the Hands of an Angry God" was delivered in a "measured monotone."[178] A sermon—in the view of the Protestants, and of Feofan—was not supposed to be entertaining but edifying and grave.[179]

Feofan's rhetorical rules not only instructed priests how to preach but also provided examples counter to good preaching. In his Kievan rhetorical manual, Prokopovich attacked the Baroque Catholic preaching embraced by Iavorskii, including the "unstable and scattered style" of the sermons' structure as well as the reliance on obscure "fables," onomastics, and speculations.[180] Feofan carried his offensive against Catholic-inspired preaching into the *Spiritual Regulation*, which condemned the elements of Iavorskii's preaching style: excessive crying, laughing, "proud movement of the hips," and the proclivity for "swinging as if he is in a boat, rowing the oars" while in the pulpit.[181] There was also an explicit restriction on sources. "Do not read the light-minded preachers, especially the Polish ones," Feofan warned.[182]

Feofan preached what he taught. His Kievan sermons, delivered between 1704 and 1714, were mostly short expository homilies, articulating doctrinal topics (like God's love) or condemning false doctrines (like purgatory).[183] His preaching in St. Petersburg (as described in previous chapters) was also highly doctrinal. His sermons from 1717 to 1720 explained such Protestant-inspired doctrines as vocation, total depravity, and salvation by faith.[184] They also promoted living "under grace, not under the law," while attacking those filled with "viper's vermin, the Papist spirit," who preached their Catholic-influenced doctrine of "pharisaic justification."[185]

THE SERMONS OF FEOFAN'S SUCCESSORS

Feofan's homiletic reform had a profound impact among the preachers of the Elizabethan era. The sermons of Sil'vestr Kuliabka, Simon Todorskii, and the lesser-known preacher Vladimir Kalligraf are among the many good examples of the systematic adoption of Protestant preaching norms. As mentioned earlier in this chapter, Sil'vestr Kuliabka's adoption of Feofan's rhetorical manual in his own homiletic pedagogy placed him in the ranks of the "fledglings" of the Petrine educational reforms. But he followed these reforms in his preaching, too.

Thus he followed Prokopovich's homiletic norms very closely in sermon composition, style, and expository content.[186] He opposed the "light-mindedness" of the older Baroque preachers by stating that a "sermon with no edification [*nazidanie*] is just flattery."[187] Much like Feofan, he valued "strict moral composure and prudence" while standing in the pulpit.[188] Overall, his preaching "contained not a single trace [*sled*] of acquaintance with the contemporary Polish sermon."[189] The expository and didactic content of his oratory can be seen in his emphasis on explicating the doctrines of human depravity, antinomianism, grace, and salvation in the homilies delivered between 1732 and 1750. Like Feofan, Sil'vestr also condemned those who put their trust in formal observances to gain salvation. "It is better not to know God at all, than to limit His knowledge and worship for 'external ceremonies' alone," he said.[190]

Simon Todorskii's sermons likewise continued the trend set by Feofan in the 1710s. Upon his return to Kiev, the Halle alumnus became a popular preacher. "Kievans flocked eagerly [*s zhadnost'iu*] to listen to him," noted one of his biographers.[191] He also made an impression at court. Catherine's mother (Johanna Elisabeth, duchess of Anhalt-Zerbst), for example, found his sermons "beautiful and touching" and noted that they caused people to burst into tears.[192] Such popularity, however, was based not on expressive technique but on content: in Kiev, the "people's great respect" for him stemmed from the highly expository nature of his sermons, delivered mostly in the form of pedagogical "grand instructions [*instruktsii*]."[193]

Many of his "grand instructions" from 1741 and 1742 centered on a variety of Protestant-influenced theological issues: redemption, justification, original sin, the nature of grace ("justification that justifies all of us believers by His grace alone"), and total depravity.[194] In the Pietist fashion, he warned against those who disregarded the "fruits of their justification," while at the same time asserting that faith and justification always come first: "without being first justified by Jesus Christ, no good deed can be good by itself."[195] Like Feofan, Simon also attacked the opponents of the Protestant-inspired doctrine of justification. In one sermon, he harangued those who were concerned "about fasts, about abstinence, about monastic living" but ignored the fact that they "need to be justified by faith in Jesus Christ."[196] In another polemic, he attacked those who were "polluted by the Jesuit spirit," which for him meant rejection of his doctrine and acceptance of ideas like the "Papist forgiveness of sins in our church."[197]

The Protestant and Pietist imprint manifested itself not only in the theology of his sermons but also the structure. His highly expository court sermon delivered on February 10, 1743—the birthday of Grand Duke Peter Fedorovich—

contained a rather unusual structural element: the insertion of a prayer following the homily's exordium. This was a feature uncommon to Russian preachers
before Todorskii but very widespread in Pietist sermons. For example, it was
normal for August Hermann Francke to insert a prayer (*Gebet*) after the exordium and introduction (*Vortrag*) but before the exposition (*Abhandlung*) of
the main text—exactly the pattern manifested in Todorskii's homily.[198]

Although both Todorskii and Kuliabka were renowned court preachers,
lesser-known homilies during this period also displayed the influence of Feofan's
reforms. One of these lesser-known preachers was Vladimir Kalligraf (d. 1760),
a Mohyla Academy alumnus and friend of Metropolitan Timofei Shcherbatskii; he moved to Moscow in 1754 to become the prefect and preacher of its
academy.[199] His claim to fame in ecclesiastical circles of the time came from his
sermons deriding the superstitious features of Muscovite icon veneration. For
example, in his May 21, 1757, public homily in Moscow, Kalligraf warned that
those who "put all their hope in the saints of God, their icons, and the Mother
of God, creating various superstitions" will merit "eternal damnation."[200] To
make his point very clear to the parishioners, he exclaimed,

> You can bring, if you will, a thousand candles or a hundred *poods* of incense
> for St. Nicholas, St. George, or other saints of God. But if you have no love for
> God and your neighbor, your offering makes you their enemy. Decorate all you
> want the icon of God's Mother; shout all you can, "Hail Mary, full of grace!" But
> if you ignore that very grace, you depart from the Lord in your sins.[201]

This sermon was popular, circulating in handwritten manuscript (*khodila po
rukam*) throughout Moscow, Iaroslavl, and Rostov.[202] It also reached St. Petersburg and the Holy Synod. In Rostov, Arsenii Matseevich also heard about it
and complained to the Synod that the Kievan preacher spread "Lutheranism,
Calvinism, and Judaism."[203] The Synod appeared split about Matseevich's
complaint: two hierarchs wanted Kalligraf to suspend his regular preaching
but continue his prefecture in Moscow; others, however, recommended no
action. Unlike Matseevich, they simply found "no contradiction [*protivnost*]
to the Orthodox faith" in the sermon.[204] Finding no heresy, they gave Kalligraf
mild citation and he continued preaching.[205] His growing fame as a preacher
earned him an invitation to preach at Elizabeth's court and in the capital in
1758, where he stayed between January and July, after which he was given the
title of seminary rector. Given the career trajectories of many tonsured intellectuals of his day, were it not for his illness and early death in 1760, Kalligraf
would clearly have been on his way to becoming a bishop.[206]

CONCLUSION

By 1761 the impact of Prokopovich's reforms produced a doctrinally and structurally different form of Orthodoxy than had existed in Russia before 1700. This change produced a new generation of bishops, scholars, and hierarchs who followed the new direction in theology, public preaching, and education set by Feofan. They also continued to spread the influence of Pietism (and the associated ideas of the *Frühaufklärung*) in the Orthodox Church between 1721 and 1761. The lasting legacy of the continuity of the reforms had significant implications for the subsequent developments in Russian religious thought that appeared in the second half of the eighteenth century, after 1762. The networks of intellectual exchange that the Catherinian Russian Church inherited from the era of Petrine reforms became conduits for the arrival of the European movement so pivotal to the rise of global modernity: the Enlightenment.

6

Enlightening the Church

Faith and Culture in the Age of Reason, 1762–1801

The Church Fathers are not our teachers in physics.

—EVGENII BOLKHOVITINOV, the metropolitan of Kiev

Empress Elizabeth died on Christmas Day 1761, piously reciting the prayers specially written for her by Father-Confessor Dubianskii.[1] Her death and the enthronement of Peter III thrust the Russian court into a months-long factional struggle between the supporters of the emperor and those of his wife, Catherine, resulting in another palace coup that brought the latter to power.[2]

Unlike during previous palace coups, the Holy Synod remained an island of tranquility. The official sermons from this period (unlike the imperial manifestos) give the impression that the entire change of regime was smooth and uneventful. Thus the January–February 1762 sermons by the presiding member of the Synod, Dmitrii Sechenov of Novgorod, praised Peter III as a "pillar and foundation of Christ's Church" and continued praising his piety as late as June, when the Semenovskii and Preobrazhenskii Guards were already preparing his overthrow.[3] By the way, Dmitrii's brother, Ivan Andreevich Sechenov (1719–83; grandfather of the famous physiologist Ivan Sechenov) was a corporal in the Preobrazhenskii Guards at the time.

The bishop's service to Peter was not viewed as a demonstration of factional loyalty and was no impediment to the rise of his career under the new monarch—in September, the very same Dmitrii crowned and anointed Catherine, praising her in his New Year's sermon as "the most glorious Empress."[4] In a similar fashion, Gavriil Petrov, the rector of the Moscow Academy and the bishop of Tver, also proclaimed Peter as a "zealot of Christian piety," only to extol Catherine's "God-like soul" shortly thereafter.[5]

For Catherine, Gavriil and Dmitrii represented a new generation of bishops in harmony with court culture, whose service to the court was no longer partial to any particular faction and whose enlightened outlook reflected the kind of sophistication due to European influence that Prokopovich sought to

promote among the clerical elites. The empress was pleased to have highly erudite clerics at her court: in her November 17, 1765, letter to Voltaire, she praised
Dmitrii as a defender of toleration and an opponent of the largely Catholic
doctrine of "two powers [*deux puissances*]."[6] Gavriil's "enlightened" views also
made an impression on her. In dedicating her 1768 translation of Jean-François
Marmontel's novel *Bélisaire* (1767)—a work banned by the Sorbonne—to the
bishop, she praised him not only for his "virtue" but also his "humility, moderation," and "enlightened piety." The bishop not only cherished this dedication but also "boasted about it."[7]

Thus the "revolution" of 1762 represents a watershed moment in the intellectual history of the Russian church as the new generation of Western-educated
religious reformers discovered the new world of the European Enlightenment.
Although the advent of the Enlightenment in Russia has been the subject of
some studies, articles, and monographs, very little literature exists on its impact
among the church hierarchy. As this chapter will demonstrate, a variety of
Enlightenment theology and ideas shaped the church's intellectual development
in relationship to similar currents in the West. This relationship was complex
and eclectic, conditioned as it was by the two different European Enlightenment contexts engaged by the bishops: the secular and the religious. The secular context brought the bishops (as some of the most educated men among
Catherinian elites) into direct conversation with the French and English philosophical and literary works that circulated widely among the literate public
of that time. To testify to the proliferation of such ideas in Russia it suffices to
mention that, for example, between 1760 and 1792 some fifty of Voltaire's works
were translated and published in Russia.[8] The bishops were not only aware of
this context but were actively engaged in it.

The second and more important context for this study was the influence of
the European religious Enlightenment in Russia. The bishops of the Catherinian era readily explored, translated, adopted, critiqued, and embraced British Latitudinarians, the authors of Newtonian physicotheology, the Berliner
Aufklärung and Neology, and religious rationalism and Deism. The most important intellectual feature of the Orthodox Enlightenment was its eclecticism:
new ideas often shared space with the older influences of Lutheran orthodoxy in
Russian theology; the popularity of the French philosophes accompanied the
rise of interest in Huguenot theologians; while in the bishops' minds, Voltaire
contended with the anti-Deist polemics of Grotius.

The European Religious Enlightenment

The setting of the European religious Enlightenment represents the most important context for understanding intellectual developments in the Russian

church during the Catherinian era. The religious current within the European Enlightenment was by no means organized or uniform; however, the general tendencies embraced by the enlightened clergy of Europe included such novel concepts as the denial of revelation without reason, confessional toleration, the incorporation of natural law and scientific empiricism into theology, and moderation in avoiding the extremes of both dogmatism and Deism. The new ideas often produced similar results (such as greater emphases on toleration and empirical reason) in different confessional settings, turning many Calvinists to Latitudinarianism and "enlightened orthodoxy," many Lutherans to Neology, and many Jews to Haskalah.[9] Intellectual historians of Europe such as David Sorkin and Ulrich Lehner identified this movement as "the religious Enlightenment," which evolved out of narrower, older German studies of *Aufklärungstheologie* (Enlightenment theology), a concept that was limited to an examination of doctrinal changes in the eighteenth century.[10]

Eighteenth-century Catholic bishops and theologians also engaged in freethinking that promoted toleration of Protestants and Jews and in rationalist textual criticism of the Bible, doubted the necessity of clerical celibacy (as detrimental to population growth), and supported the ideas of regalism in matters of royal privilege in the ownership of ecclesiastical estates.[11]

In late seventeenth- and eighteenth-century Britain, clerical opposition to both Deism and Puritan dogmatic orthodoxy produced the Latitudinarian movement, which rejected the priority of revelation over reason. For example, the Latitudinarians allegorized the biblical miracles without denying the existence of wonders as such.[12] Due to their intellectual temperance as well as occasional ties to the philosophy of John Locke and the Scottish Moderatists, Latitudinarians such as John Tillotson (1630–94) were often equated with Moderatism.[13]

In addition to their views on revelation, the Latitudinarians also embraced an empirical "faith in the new science," especially Newtonian physicotheology. The God of the Moderatists was a rational architect, "a Newtonian hero who designed the world as a system of benevolence."[14] Although the concept of physicotheology was coined by John Ray (1627–1705) in his *Three Physico-Theological Discourses* (1692), it was his disciple William Derham (1657–1735) who popularized it through the Oxford Boyle Lecture and influenced the writings of such famous anti-Deists as Richard Bentley and Samuel Clarke.[15] Physicotheology not only portrayed faith as harmonious with reason but also emphasized scientific evidence for Christian belief, showing "the Providence of God" in creation.[16] It essentially cemented an alliance of science and religion in Britain that was largely unopposed until Darwin's *On the Origin of*

Species.[17] The spread of this philosophical school was hardly limited to Great Britain: according to Albrecht Beutel, some thousand book titles in eighteenth-century Western Europe included physicotheology in their title.[18]

In Germany, the representatives of religious Enlightenment also sought to reconcile reason with revelation and science with faith. Two broad intellectual movements or phrases from the German religious Enlightenment were influential in eighteenth-century Russia: Wolffianism and Neology.[19] The first phase included the movements that Albrecht Beutel loosely defined as "transitional theology" and "theological Wolffianism."[20] The chief representatives of this phase were theologians whose work (as discussed in previous chapters) was connected with Halle Pietism in various ways, such as Johann Franz Buddeus, Johann Lorenz von Mosheim, Christoph Pfaff, Georg Bernhard Bilfinger, Wolff's own disciple Siegmund Jakob Baumgarten, and others. For Beutel, Pietism served as "the forerunner, the road breaker and the primer of the Enlightenment," while Sorkin noted that many of the Wolffianists and Neologists came out of the Pietist circles and Pietist centers of Göttingen and Halle.[21] Many of these "transitional" theologians had points of contact with physico-theologians in England; much like their English colleagues, they upheld the idea of "the harmony between reason and revelation."[22] For Baumgarten, for example, the exercise of theology involved the logical "demonstration method," with mathematical objectivity and the use of rationally ordered systems of inquiry that balanced "revelation" with "reasonableness and empiricism [*Erweisslichkeit*]."[23]

The second phase of the religious Enlightenment in Germany was Neology. Although it greatly overlapped with the previous phase, for the sake of chronology Beutel dated its arrival at 1740: the beginning of Frederick the Great's reign and the "triumphal return" of Christian Wolff to teach at Halle.[24] While Neologists embraced the Wolffian incorporation of revelation and reason, they departed from Wolff by emphasizing the importance of individual morality and the "compatibility of reason and feeling."[25] Their emphasis on individual piety became a major point of attraction for the Lutheran and Reformed laity and sparked the flowering of popular preaching (which will be discussed in the next chapter).[26] One of the most notable features of Neology was its moralistic (and rational) approach to textual criticism, scriptural hermeneutics, and exegesis.[27] Neologians generally considered Scripture to be infallible in moral truth and dogma but not necessarily in matters of science, geographic information, or historical chronology. Thus they separated the Bible as a "historically developed collection" from the Bible as a moral "guide for the truthfully lived life."[28]

Liberal Monks and Gentlemen Bishops:
The General Outline of the Church Hierarchy

Who were these new bishops of the Catherinian era? Before describing their theological views and administrative reforms, a sketch of some very general features of this generation will establish their cultural and biographical context. The new generation of Russian bishops was young, many of them ascending to bishop's status in their thirties: Gavriil Petrov and Platon Levshin were only thirty-three years old when invested with their titles; Feofilakt Rusanov, thirty-four; Gedeon Krinovskii was thirty-five; Anastasii Bratanovskii and Arsenii Vereshchagin, thirty-six; and St. Tikhon Sokolov, thirty-seven.[29] Their young ages defied both the stereotype of the episcopate as a senior post reserved for experienced administrators and the traditional Orthodox expectation of having long-term monastic and ascetic experience before assuming such rank.

Monastic tonsure was often a pathway for an already distinguished scholar or church official to elevate his status within the hierarchy. Thus, Evgenii Bolkhovitinov, a gifted theology professor from the Voronezh seminary, was a monk for barely three years before becoming a bishop with Synod membership in St. Petersburg. Damaskin Semenov-Rudnev, who distinguished himself as a synodal inspector of Russian clerical students in Göttingen, became an archimandrite (abbot) after less than three years as a monk, and bishop within seven years.[30] These positions were often titular, since their real jobs did not necessarily involve managing a monastery or a diocese but tending to the affairs of the court and national church in St. Petersburg. Bearing an ecclesiastical title was important for status and promotion: This was the case in 1788, when Moisei Gumilevskii, the chief hieromonk of Grigorii Potemkin's Moldavian Army, received the abbacy of Ekaterinoslav's Spaso-Nikolaevskii Monastery. Like many of Potemkin's other projects, the monastery never actually existed, but its phantom title helped Moisei secure a bishopric three years later.[31]

Despite holding high office and status in the capital, most Russian bishops during the second half of the eighteenth century came from lower social ranks. Only a few bishops, like Dmitrii Sechenov and Georgii Konisskii, were scions of the landed gentry, while many others came from the background of rural or urban clergy.[32] Two influential bishops—Simon Lagov and Innokentii Nechaev—were born serfs.[33] The humble or lower-class origins of some, however, did not prevent them from enjoying upper-class culture or a lifestyle commensurate with their rank. Many bishops fit well into the Enlightenment culture regnant at court and in Russian high society. Thus, Moscow Archbishop Platon Levshin, whom Petr Znamenskii once called a "liberal monk," frequented the theater at the Imperial Hermitage.[34] Evgenii Bolkhovitinov, the future metropolitan of Kiev, never missed a performance in Voronezh; for him, theater was a mark of belonging to the higher society of local nobles and merchants.[35]

Personal appearance was also an important mark of adhering to high culture. Bishop Gedeon Krinovskii of Pskov—the "lively, emancipated monk"—wore hair powder and wigs, braided his beard, put on the stockings and diamond-decorated shoes of the latest European fashion and had a walk-in closet of silk cassocks.[36] The fine taste for clothes was shared by other bishops. The 1771 listing of property made at the death of Amvrosii Zertis-Kamenskii of Moscow, for example, described hundreds of shirts, velvet and silk cassocks, furs, as well as women's dresses.[37] Much like Krinovskii, Andrei Samborskii, the protopriest of the official St. Sophia Cathedral at the court estate of Tsarskoe Selo, also wore hair powder. Yet unlike Krinovskii, this Ukrainian priest (who was Alexander I's tutor) shaved his beard altogether, following the customs he learned from a long sojourn in London.[38] Feofilakt Rusanov of Riazan also enjoyed Western clothing and customarily walked around the Neva Embankment with a parasol. One noblewoman who followed his preaching once publicly commended him, saying, "Ah! Your High Eminence, why did you become a monk? You would have made such a great worldly gentleman [*svetskii kavaler*]."[39]

Enlightenment-era fashions spread not only among the elite bishops but also into theological seminaries in the countryside. Seminarians with powdered wigs appear in the Iaroslavl seminary portraits commissioned by Archbishop Arsenii Vereshchagin, for example (see figure 7). Wigs were not the only fashionable attributes of high culture. From 1742, Trinity-Sergius seminary professors (many of them higher clergy) wore épée dueling swords, "in accordance with the example of other countries."[40] In the 1790s, bishops embraced the fashion of accepting membership in military cavalier orders, and wore the medals of the Imperial Orders of St. Andrew, St. Anna, St. Aleksandr Nevskii, and St. Vladimir, among others.[41]

Changing fashions even affected monastic clothing. In 1825 Maksim Nevzorov, a lay critic of Protestant influence in the Russian church, complained to St. Petersburg metropolitan Serafim about how monks in the city "dressed well" and "made their hair appear curvy."[42] He then added that just as some people go to the trendy Kuznetsky Most street in Moscow to watch "stylish [*razriazhenykh*] French madams and mademoiselles," so others visit the "monastery [*lavra*]" in order to "look at [*smotret'*] the stylish [*razriazhenykh*] monks."[43] In the convents, nuns and novices dressed immodestly, too: they "contended in fashions [with each other]," ignoring the old Russian *klobuk* (a type of monastic headwear) in favor of "thin long silk trenches," "laced broad collars with

Figure 7. Seminary life during Orthodox Enlightenment. Archbishop Arsenii
Vereshchagin along with teachers, staff, and students of the Iaroslavl Seminary,
ca. 1780. Note the wigs and the "French" attire of the student candidates for
ordination as parish priests. From A. A. Titov, "Poslednii rostovskii arkhiepiskop
Arsenii," Istoricheskii Vestnik 23, no. 2 (1886): 392–96. Courtesy of Widener Library,
Harvard University.

velvet," "black capots [hooded cloaks] with fashionable bras," as well as "narrow
sleeves and decorated breast patterns."[44] In early nineteenth century, an anonymous poet from the circle of Count Petr Shalikov (1768–1852) seconded such
remarks but with attention to the priest's wives and daughters, who wore cro-
chet laces, corsets, and salons instead of traditional fur coats, and danced
"cadrille" and drank with Frenchmen and Germans, while being attracted
more to "white tie or uniform" than to the ordination candidates.[45] Such fashions attracted government attention: Alexander I's August 1825 decree mandated the Holy Synod to devise a dress code (o blagoprilichnom odeianii) for
the clergy.[46]

Clothing was only one of the fashions that Catherinian bishops embraced—
another, more important trend was the use of the French language. Communication in French was one of the hallmarks of Russian elite culture (depicted
so well in Tolstoy's War and Peace), and the popularity of the language extended
to church elites. French appeared in Ukrainian and Russian seminaries fairly
early on, suggesting that the ecclesiastical learning of the language took place
concurrently with secular elites. The language was introduced in the Kharkov

Collegium as early as 1736 and Kiev's Mohyla Academy in 1739–46.[47] From the 1750s to the 1780s, permanent curricular teaching of French spread to Moscow and St. Petersburg and beyond, including Nizhnii Novgorod, Riazan, Pskov, Tver, Kazan, Smolensk, and Voronezh. By the 1790s, seminarians (mostly future priests) in Penza, Tula, Chernigov, Poltava, Ekaterinoslav, Arkhangelsk, Kaluga, Orel, and other provincial cities were learning French as part of their curriculum.[48]

How the clergy used this language is well attested in biographical sources. Archbishop Arsenii Vereshchagin's diary shows how Iaroslavl's clergy read the Gospel passages in French (and German) during the divine liturgy, while the seminarians recited poems in various languages (including French) during the holiday celebrations.[49] When Nikolai Karamzin visited Trinity-Sergius Monastery in 1802, he was pleasantly surprised to see the enlightened monks fluently conversing with each other in French and mixing Russian and French phrases in teaching colloquies in the classrooms. Their fluency in the language, he argued, helped the monks maintain "decorum [*blagorodstvo*]" and respect from the "educated secular public, who eagerly invited them to join their circles."[50] When Evgenii Bolkhovitinov began teaching French at the Voronezh seminary in January 1789, the language was already a subject there. He also communicated with students as well as the bishop of Voronezh in that tongue and the popularity of the language (and literature) in the seminary did not diminish even after the 1790s ban on "revolutionary" authors in the Russian Empire.[51] The "gentleman" bishop Feofilakt Rusanov was also well known for his promotion of modern languages among the seminarians. His 1800 instruction to the young archdeacon Filaret Drozdov was that "with ancient languages alone, you will not go too far; therefore, you must study new languages, especially French, so that through them you can become acquainted with the newest ideas."[52]

Another important aspect of the general profile of the Russian hierarchy during the Catherinian era was its emerging ethnic diversity. During the first two-thirds of the eighteenth century, Ukrainians dominated the ranks of the ecclesiastical elites, reflecting the Petrine policy of appointing the best-educated candidates described in chapter 1. For example, in the period from 1725 to 1741, 51.5 percent of all upper ecclesiastical appointments in the strictly Russian (so-called Great Russian) dioceses went to Ukrainians. For the 1741–62 period, 76 percent of appointments went to Ukrainians.[53] Between 1754 and 1757, not a single Russian was nominated to an episcopal see, while five Ukrainians and one Georgian were.[54] Ukrainian influence was prevalent even among the court clergy: Catherine II recalled that she first recited her declaration of conversion to the Orthodox faith in Ukrainian because her catechist and confessor was Simon Todorskii.[55]

After 1762 the number of well-educated ethnic Russian candidates increased, decreasing the need to appoint Ukrainians. Dmitrii Sechenov particularly stressed the importance of promoting "Great Russian seminary students" to the position of archimandrite and to upper clerical appointments to support the "development of education [*prosveshchenie*] and the promotion of piety" among the Russians.[56] As a result, the Catherinian period saw the appointment of thirty-six new hierarchs who were Russian and twenty-one who were Ukrainian.[57]

However, the increase of Russians in the hierarchy was also accompanied by the diversification of the ethnic composition of the church, especially in the newly formed dioceses of the Black Sea region, partitioned Poland-Lithuania, and the Caucasus. By 1796 the ranks of the Russian imperial church had recorded twenty-six hierarchs who were Belarusian or Lithuanian, six Greeks, three Serbs, four Moldavians, and three Georgians (who received appointments outside Georgia).[58] Many of these Greeks, like bishops Evgenii Voulgaris (1715–1806) and Nikiforos Theotikis (1731–1800), were representatives of the "Neo-Hellenic Enlightenment," who advanced toleration and scientific rationalism and were conversant with the writings of Voltaire and Locke, among others. Unlike the previous generation of Greeks, they gained their education not only in Venetian Catholic universities but also Halle and Leipzig.[59] These foreign-born bishops also fostered Russia's empire-building, which included the integration of ethnically diverse new subjects (including many Bulgarians, Greeks, Moldovans, and Gagauz) living or settled on the territories recently conquered from the Ottoman Empire.[60]

SERFDOM AND EMANCIPATION

One of the most important material realities of life among the new "enlightened" hierarchy of Catherinian Russia was the fact that this church no longer owned souls. The "emancipated monks" of the Catherinian era were freed not only from the burdens of ascetic life but also from the cares of serf management and the perils of serf rebellions. The reforms of 1764 emancipated the ecclesiastical peasants from their servitude to the church, requiring them only to pay taxes to the state that would in turn fund the church (with varying degrees of generosity) through budgeted operations. The gentlemen bishops no longer had to chase the villagers to obtain their pay. The ecclesiastical land reform gave them stability through regularized state pay that was deemed "orderly" and "enlightened." In the long run, however, the reform also made the church more attuned to the plight of the countryside, since the church was no longer a serf-owning institution.

Before the reforms, the church was Russia's second-largest serf owner, hold-ing 991,761 men or almost 14 percent of the peasantry in the empire (exclud-ing Ukraine). Sixty-nine percent of the monasteries and 36 percent of the convents in the country owned peasants, and monasteries were far more likely than private landowners to possess large estates of over one hundred souls each.[61] The largest monastery, Trinity-Sergius, for example, owned 106,000 men, many more than the Sheremetevs (Russia's wealthiest landowners), who held 44,561 in 1767.[62]

Although the church owned many serfs, it was not very efficient in collect-ing income from them, especially when the state requested additional funds during war, pestilence, or other exigencies. While much of the literature on the topic has focused on the issue of state "usurpation" of church land owner-ship, initially the secularization of church-owned serfs did not originate in a debate over the titular ownership of church lands, but over the actual man-agement of land incomes.[63] In 1701 Peter I restored a state agency called the Monastery Prikaz to collect much-needed state taxes for the war while also allocating money and material goods to the church according to specific quo-tas. The debate was not about who owned the serfs but who collected the taxes from them, and in the case of the Great Northern War, the state was a more efficient collector. Between 1725 and 1744, the management of income from church land was transferred back and forth between the Synod and the (more efficient) state agency, the College of Economy, with Elizabeth fully restoring the ecclesiastical management of income in 1744.[64]

Why was the Russian Orthodox Church so inefficient in collecting taxes? One part of the explanation is that decades of switching jurisdictions of income management had made it a weaker tax collector institutionally. Another factor to consider is the abuses inherent in all forms of servitude and the reaction that such abuses elicited from the oppressed. Just like secular serf owners, church administrators confronted a reality of sustained peasant resistance.

The main point of contention between the church and its peasants was cor-vée labor, known as *barshchina*. While some monasteries only required peas-ants to pay an annual tax (in kind or in currency, called *obrok*), most required them to carry out corvée labor duties (such as harvesting the monastery fields). Some monasteries even assigned labor duties in addition to *obrok*.[65]

The abuses associated with *barshchina* were numerous: archimandrites or monastery supervisors could be partial, based on the bribes they received, to which peasants were forced to work or were drafted into the military. Tor-ture and abuses were common: such monasteries as Novospasskii and Savvin-Storozhevskii Monastery would beat and torture their peasants to extract bribes and forced labor. With the permission of their protopriest, the priests of Murom Cathedral also beat their peasants routinely, demanded hefty bribes for permission to marry, and even raped peasant women for weeks at a time. Appealing to higher powers was often useless as the Holy Synod was exempt from the authority of the secular judiciary. Peasants (and the village priests who supported them) sent protests to Moscow or St. Petersburg that were ignored or resulted in the arrest and torture of the plaintiffs.[66]

With no legal recourse for their grievances, peasants picked up their pitchforks. Their insurgencies made tax collection a very challenging task for the Russian church. Thus the 1748 uprising of 11,000 peasants in Viatka disrupted tax collection until 1751, when the Senate sent dragoons to quell the revolt.[67] In the 1750s, peasants rebelled all over the country, demanding the end of ecclesiastical *barshchina* and its replacement with *obrok*.[68] In 1752 the serfs of Novgorod region's Khutyn Monastery rose up, followed by the peasants of Murom Cathedral, who raided the priests' grain stores, fish ponds, and even the wine cellars. In 1760 Savvin-Storozhevskii Monastery was besieged by three hundred peasants demanding an end to bribes and excessive labor: seventy-nine of the rebels were arrested, twelve died. One of the most successful insurgencies was the 1753–57 uprising of the Novospasskii Monastery peasants in Riazan diocese. There, the peasant leader Mirzin successfully organized the insurgents into armed units that set up checkpoints in the villages belonging to the monastery. Peasant women (and men) took up cudgels, stones, and sticks, demanding the end of *barshchina*. Only cannon fire, grenades, and the capture of Mirzin along with the sustained rape and pillage of the villages ended the revolt in 1757.[69]

The spectacle of besieged monasteries launching grenades at defiant peasants was not a sight that the elite "gentlemen bishops" of the Holy Synod in St. Petersburg wanted to behold.[70] An even less pleasant sight was the disruption of harvests, the burning of fields, and the impossibility of collecting taxes, badly needed in the time of the Seven Years' War. To resolve this issue, the Synod held a joint conference with the Senate in October 1757. The conference decided that the nature of the monasteries' serf-management duties was incompatible with their spiritual vocation. According to the meeting's protocol, the monks were "uselessly burdened with the duty of collecting the funds for themselves and conserving the remaining funds [for the state]."[71] The very nature of the monks' ascetic vocation precluded them from being efficient in managing the "worldly cares" of tax collection, and for this reason, the conference recommended the restoration of secular control over the management of ecclesiastical lands.[72]

The 1757 recommendations were fully acted upon by Peter III, whose 1762 manifesto restored the College of Economy, abolished *barshchina*, monetized the peasant tax, and put the state in charge of funding the church.[73] Peter's decrees hid behind the legitimacy of the "piety and reverence" of Elizabeth, who had already approved this reform.[74] Furthermore, he declared that the 1757 resolutions of the Synod and the Senate interpreted the spiritual vocation of the monks based on "the correct dogmas of faith and truthful foundations of our Orthodox Eastern Church."[75]

Catherine's ascent to power and her temporary suspension of her murdered husband's decrees in July 1762 created much confusion and controversy. In church-owned villages the return to ecclesiastical ownership seemed like betrayal, fueling rural legends of Catherine's husband as a "peasant tsar," who had escaped and was hiding among the people. To calm the countryside, the Senate and the Synod joint conference reconvened in November 1762, organized by state adviser Grigorii Teplov (1717–79), a graduate of Feofan's orphanage school who was rumored to be Prokopovich's illegitimate child.[76] But it was too late. As Catherine wrote to Voltaire, some 100,000 church peasants took up arms in the winter of 1762–63, although 150,000 is probably a more accurate number.[77] Field Marshal Petr Saltykov reported that the army was stretched for resources and soldiers to quell "daily" revolts throughout the empire.[78]

The largest of the revolts was a peasant insurgency known as the Dubinshchina (The cudgel revolt). It took place in the southern Urals, where the monks of Dalmatov Monastery and the nuns of Vvedenskii Convent confronted rebellious serfs who refused to send provisions, brew beer for the monastics, tend to their horses, and perform other labor duties.[79] The rebels, armed with bats or cudgels (*dubiny*) as well as other makeshift weapons, set up checkpoints and besieged the monasteries.[80] The rebellion ended in early May 1764, after the Azov Dragoon Regiment (based in Orenburg) put down the insurgency and pillaged the area, while monks tortured arrested rebels in monastery prisons.[81]

Despite the pressure from below, Catherine II and her court officials vacillated on the issue of church ownership of serfs.[82] The state needed the full agreement of the church leadership to free the serfs, and the Holy Synod did not hold a unanimous opinion. According to Igor Smolitsch and Isabel de Madariaga, the Synod was divided between the recently promoted Russian bishops and some Ukrainian hierarchs, who held serf ownership to be an inviolable and inalienable privilege (similar to the privileges of the Polish nobility). The "Great Russians, led by Dmitry Sechenov," wrote Madariaga, "accepted without difficulty the idea of giving up the burden of administering agricultural estates and becoming paid servants of the state on the same footing as the army or the bureaucracy."[83] In reality, the situation was likely more complicated than that, since Archimandrite Feofan Leontovich (an opponent of the reform) described most of the Ukrainians in the Synod as "neutralists [*neutralisty*]."[84]

In the end, the only Synod member who became an outspoken opponent of the "secularization" of the church peasants was the controversial bishop of Rostov, Arsenii Matseevich, whose insolence (described in the previous chapter) irritated the Synod in the 1740s and 1750s. Theologically a philo-Catholic, Matseevich based his opposition on the "two powers" doctrine of church and state, arguing also that church's special serf-owning privileges were guaranteed by the Golden Horde and by Mosaic Law.[85] In 1763 he threatened to anathematize anyone involved in the project and called on the Holy Synod to imitate the French clergy, which "defended its rights against the French kings at the councils."[86] Otherwise, he warned, Russia would disintegrate "into a schismatic, Lutheran, Calvinist, or atheist state."[87]

Arsenii's philo-Catholic theologizing provided the right kind of fuel for his enemy, the metropolitan of Novgorod, Dmitrii Sechenov, who, as Catherine II noted to Voltaire, was "neither an oppressor nor a fanatic and completely rejects the two powers thesis."[88] Dmitrii's rejection of the Catholic two swords doctrine gave him and his Synod allies (the bishops of Tver and Riazan) formal grounds upon which to oppose Arsenii. In his own theological opinions, Dmitrii did not mince words in describing the supremacy of only one political authority, Catherine, who for him was the "true vicar of the true God and the true Protector of the true Piety."[89] In fact, the Synod's official arrest of Arsenii in March 1763 was grounded on charges of "pernicious Latin principles, contrary to the Orthodox faith."[90] Sechenov's "enlightened" opinions certainly influenced Catherine's final decision by giving her assurance of the Synod's support; they also swayed the hesitating neutral Synod members to accept his views.[91]

The result of the Holy Synod's deliberation with the Senate was Catherine's February Manifesto of 1764. Unlike previous examples of secular land management, this decree permanently freed the serfs from ecclesiastical control. The empress's voluminous decree addressed, among other issues, the enlightened, orderly, and virtuous features of the reform. The manifesto contrasted the current "disorder [*besporiadok*]" in estate management against the need for "order." It also contrasted "the burdensome management . . . the worries [*khlopoty*] and difficulties" of current ecclesiastical serf-ownership against the "God-pleasing work" that clerics—freed from their tax-collecting burdens—could be doing "to enlighten the simple folk with sermons and by their life examples."[92] It also mentioned the need to find a solution that would be "naturally suitable [*skhodstvenno*] and convenient for the peasants," a recognition of their persistent discontent.[93]

With such rhetoric the manifesto established the Spiritual College of Economy. This new state body (managed by secular and ecclesiastical representatives) streamlined the income distribution in the church by creating set salary structures and budgetary controls as well as monetizing church revenue, which for centuries had relied on the taxes and labor in kind (*natura*) provided by its serfs.[94] In terms of acreage, the church appeared to have lost a lot: about 8,557,688 desiatin of land (roughly the size of Indiana) with some 1,069,711 male serfs.[95] While monasteries were the biggest institutional losers within the church, some bishoprics also lost a large number of "souls." Arsenii Matseevich's Rostov bishopric, as the largest owner, lost some 55,000 peasants; by comparison, the bishopric of Riazan only had 3,000 souls to lose, and Nizhnii Novgorod, 4,000.[96]

Peasants, not the state, appeared to be the biggest winners in this reform. Although many members of the gentry (including Mikhail Shcherbatov) opposed the emancipation of the church peasants or demanded that the peasants be transferred to the nobility, Catherine II resisted these calls.[97] Peasants received their own special legal category as *ekonomicheskie* or economic peasants (managed by the College of Economy), which they maintained until 1838.[98] Their level of freedom was unprecedented for the time and was akin to partial emancipation. Thus, unlike in the emancipation of 1861, the economic peasants kept most of the fields formerly belonging to their landlords and in case they needed more, they could rent additional land.[99] In 1788 the economic peasants received the right to purchase and own the gentry's serfs. As Radishchev attested, they often used this right to buy replacements for military conscription, although this practice was illegal.[100] Most importantly, however, the economic peasants were protected from transfer into private ownership; this principle was broken by Paul I but restored by Alexander I.[101] While some of them fared worse than others, peasants in central and southern Russia appeared to have become wealthier after the reform.[102] Ironically, some of the bishops benefited, too. The Viatka bishopric, plagued by uprisings, finally entered "a state of flourishing [*tsvetushchee sostoianie*]" under Varfolomei Liubarskii (bishop 1758–72), who utilized streamlined state tax collections from presumably happier, freer peasants to build new churches and improve the seminary.[103] Similar improvements occurred in the Solovki Monastery after its serfs were freed in 1764.[104]

Although it had lost much land, the church emerged as a long-term moral winner in this reform.[105] It is true that the freeing of ecclesiastical serfs appeared to be a form of pragmatic emancipation, a response to the intensity of peasant resistance and to the inability to stem it. Yet the pragmatic decision also appeared as enlightened and the idea of order was intertwined with virtue. Sechenov's enlightened relief of the Synod's "burden" received praise from Catherine and Voltaire in the short term; and in the long term, it allowed the church to become more concerned about the improvement of village life and to develop even bolder views on agrarian servitude.

Thus, the metropolitan of Novgorod, Gavriil, defied local gentry in the diocese to establish and promote village schools, spreading literacy among the serfs.[106] One of the most ambitious endeavors to improve the plight of the peasants was the synodal decree of 1808 that opened up "bishops' pharmacies" in the dioceses to bring rudimentary medical care to places as far away as Tobolsk. To staff the pharmacies, the Synod promoted medical education for seminarians, including the establishment of a special medical-surgical academy for them.[107] The church also exercised higher moral ground in defending manorial serfs against their lords in such matters as protecting them against forced marriages arranged by the aristocrats and observing Sundays and other holy days of rest. The Synod even encouraged rural clerics to report on the gentry who forced corvée work on such days.[108]

The hierarchs also became more opinionated with regard to serfdom. Platon's reputation as a "liberal monk" manifested itself in his criticism of serfdom. While Platon often supported and protected many abolitionist liberals of his time, like Nikolai Novikov and the activities of his Rosicrucian lodge, he criticized the plight of privately owned serfs himself.[109] He compared their treatment to "murder" and maintained that peasants ought to have the right to sue oppressive landowners in court.[110] He also defended the separate status and freedoms of the College of Economy's peasants and opposed the nobility's desires to appropriate them.[111]

ENLIGHTENED THEOLOGY AND EDUCATION IN RUSSIA

Freed from the cares of tax-collecting and from the terrors of the rebellious peasantry, many Russian bishops pursued the life of the mind. In their intellectual and pedagogical pursuits, they were engaging the ideas of European religious Enlightenment—however, while the impact of the new Protestant and Enlightenment literature on the church hierarchy was substantial, it was eclectic. Russian bishops read, used, and assigned a colorful array of books, although newer Enlightenment-era works were quite numerous. Several categories of books, however, can be identified. One smaller category included the traditional Lutheran and Calvinist authors of the sixteenth and seventeenth centuries, such as Salomon Gesner, Johann Osiander, Johann Andreas Quenstedt, and Sébastian Castellion—many of whom had been popular in Russia since the 1730s. A second, larger category included authors generally associated with late seventeenth- and eighteenth-century English Moderatism or Latitudinarianism and German Enlightenment theology. Among such authors were not only Buddeus and Mosheim, who were already familiar to Russian seminarians, but also new authors such as William Derham (1657–1735), William Whiston (1667–1752), John Tillotson (1630–94), and Johann Joachim Spalding

(1714–1804). There were also a few Catholic (mostly French) authors, such as Jean Baptiste Massillon (1663–1742) and Antoine Augustin Calmet (1672–1757). The latter was an enlightened French prelate and friend of Voltaire who was popular in England, Germany, and France.[112]

Throughout the Catherinian era, the bishops' eclectic embrace of the religious Enlightenment was evident in what they read and what they assigned to seminarians. Thus the metropolitan of Novgorod and St. Petersburg, Gavriil Petrov (1730–1801), became involved in improving the curriculum of the St. Aleksandr Nevskii Lavra seminary in St. Petersburg in 1788—one of the top centers of learning for Russia's clergy. Using his personal funds, Gavriil purchased the works of the Wolffian *Aufklärer* Johann Heinrich Winkler (1703–70) for the seminary's philosophy class, Gabriel François Lejay (1657–1734) for homiletics, and François Turretini's (1623–87) *Institutes of Elenctic Theology* (1685) for dogmatic theology. This latter work served as a special "study supplement" to Prokopovich's 1782 theology textbook in the seminaries.[113] Despite its seventeenth-century origins, Turretini's *Institutes* was far from outdated: it was highly popular in Calvinist seminaries of the time and was the standard theology textbook at Princeton until the late nineteenth century. Jonathan Edwards in fact considered Turretini his favorite theologian.[114]

In such seminary subjects as moral theology and exegesis, Gavriil assigned the more enlightened authors such as Buddeus, Calmet, and Johann Ernst Schubert (1717–74), alongside the traditionalist Johann Osiander (1622–97).[115] Another new subject, hermeneutics (*germenevtika*), was taught via a compendium from Johann Jakob Rambach (1693–1735) and Daniel Albert Wyttenbach (1746–1820), both of whom had connections to Halle and Lutheran theological Wolffianism.[116] Homiletics courses featured the ever-popular Buddeus as well as the work of Romanus Teller (1703–50), a professor of theology at Leipzig and confessor to Johann Sebastian Bach.[117]

At the same time, the seminary courses explored a wide variety of European works, among them writers as diverse as Cesare Beccaria (1738–94), Alexander Gottlieb Baumgarten (1714–62), Johann Georg Sulzer (1720–79), François René de Chateaubriand (1768–1848), Georges-Louis Leclerc, comte de Buffon (1707–88), and Jean le Rond d'Alembert (1717–83).[118] The seminary's canon law classes interpreted the Greek Nomocanon almost exclusively in accordance with eighteenth-century Anglican scholarship on ecclesiastical jurisprudence. In addition to the popular *Synodicon* of William Beveridge (1637–1709), students read the *Antiquities of the Christian Church* by Joseph Bingham (d. 1722) and *Scriptorum ecclesiasticorum historia* by the Puritan theologian William Cave (1637–1713).[119] The use of Anglican canonical material was not limited to St. Petersburg. In the Moscow Academy, Platon Levshin also assigned William

Beveridge as the most appropriate aid for the study of the Orthodox Nomo-canon (*Kormchaia kniga*).[120]

The bishops' effort to spread Protestant and Enlightenment theology to Russian seminaries was particularly evident in Moscow. Its newer Trinity-Sergius Monastery Seminary, located on the city's outskirts, benefited from being attached to Russia's most important monastery. Also, Elizabeth's gener-ous book-buying grants enabled the seminary to amass one of the largest col-lections of Protestant theology in Russia between 1744 and 1762. During this time, the library collected a total of 2,655 books, intended for "the study of the dogmas of the Greek Orthodox faith," including some costly volumes of Protestant-published editions of the patristic compendia, biblical commentar-ies, and doctrinal works.[121]

After 1784, the Trinity-Sergius Monastery's Seminary curriculum was increas-ingly influenced by new European theology under the rectorship of Mefodii Smirnov (the archbishop of Pskov). Mefodii's choice of books for the curricu-lum, however, was eclectic. He not only relied on Protestant authors already popular in other Russian seminaries, such as David Hollatz, Joachim Justus Breithaupt, and Joseph Bingham, but he was also interested in newer literature that used scientific reason in theological discussion.[122] He thus introduced his Trinity-Sergius students to William Whiston—an anti-Trinitarian freethink-ing Cambridge divine, who nevertheless defended the biblical account. Whis-ton's account of the flood in Genesis (in his *Nova telluris theoria*)—assigned by Mefodii—introduced a scientific apology for the scriptural event that won acco-lades from Isaac Newton and John Locke.[123]

In addition to Whiston, Smirnov also urged his students to read the work of a famous English Enlightenment author who was one of the advocates of Newtonian theology: William Derham (1657–1735). His famous work, *Physico-Theology*, which invoked scientific reason and Copernican cosmology in ana-lyzing the creation and God's attributes, was quite popular in the Protestant and English-speaking world.[124] The book was also popular in Russia: it was read not only by the Trinity-Sergius Seminary students in Latin but by the general public in its 1784 Russian translation.[125]

Mefodii's own writings demonstrated his extensive use of Protestant and con-temporary theological material in scholarship. His 1793 *Rassuzhdenie o Paskhe Iudeiskoi i Khristianskoi* (Treatise on the Jewish and Christian Passover) dis-cussed the theological and historical grounds for the Christian celebration of Easter in lieu of Passover. The author based his arguments on the writings of William Beveridge and Pierre Gaultruche.[126] His 1792 commentary on the Epis-tle to the Romans cited the works of Erasmus, Johann Georg Walch (d. 1775), and Feofan Prokopovich, even though its title claimed that the work was exclusively "based upon the writings of the Holy Fathers."[127]

The curriculum offered at the Moscow Slavo-Greco-Latin Academy by the Göttingen-educated Damaskin Semenov-Rudnev was very much in line with the intellectual tastes of Mefodii Smirnov at Trinity-Sergius Monastery seminary and Gavriil Petrov in St. Petersburg. To enhance the library's collections in contemporary theology, Damaskin ordered a number of books from Germany between 1783 and 1787, among them the works of religious enlighteners John Tillotson, A. F. W. Sack (1703–86), and Johann Joachim Spalding; however, the works of his former Göttingen teacher, Gottfried Less, featured prominently.[128] Damaskin followed his Göttingen preferences in teaching philosophy and church history. His philosophy classes assigned the works of largely Wolffian authors, such as Georg B. Bilfinger, Israel G. Canz (d. 1753), Johann H. Winkler, Johann J. Brucker (1696–1770), and Wolff himself.[129] He was particularly fond of the Göttingen professor of natural law, Samuel Christian Hollmann (1696–1787), whom he not only assigned in the seminary but also cited in his sermons.[130]

The spread of Enlightenment theology was hardly confined to the capitals. Evgenii Bolkhovitinov (the future metropolitan of Kiev) taught theology in Tula in the 1780s using the works of the eighteenth-century German and English theologians Mosheim, Bingham, and Lange.[131] When he began teaching in Voronezh in 1792, he likewise used Johann Lorenz von Mosheim's system to teach dogmatic theology and Johann J. Rambach and Joachim Lange to teach hermeneutics. Following the Pietist ideas of Rambach and Lange, Evgenii emphasized not only the literal and grammatical but also the mystical meanings of Scripture.[132] His use of Mosheim was not limited to theology: he also assigned the chancellor's *Institutiones historiae ecclesiasticae* for his church history course in order to share his conception of sacred history as divided into pre- and post-Reformation periods.[133]

Like other bishops of his era, Bolkhovitinov did not limit his scholarly pursuits to the seminary curriculum. The bishop's library exhibited a wide-ranging interest in Protestant and Enlightenment-era theology with a marked preference for Calvinist and Lutheran authors. Authors with the largest number of volumes in his library were Gerardus J. Vossius, Ralph Cudworth (1617–88), Samuel Werenfels (1657–1740), Christian Stock (1672–1733), Wyttenbach, Schubert, Pfaff, Buddeus, and Thomas Hobbes (1588–1679).[134] It is notable that Bolkhovitinov also owned eighty-six copies of William Ames's (1576–1633) *Conscience with the Power and Cases Thereof* (1630), a systematic ethical manual, dubbed by Keith L. Sprunger "a wholesome guide to godliness."[135] Ames was a charismatic

English Puritan preacher and a strict nonconformist theologian, who founded Reformed casuistry and codified Puritan applied ethics.[136] Both his *De conscientia* and his other work, *The Marrow of Theology* (*Medulla theologiae*, 1623), became influential in English North America and served as early textbooks for Harvard and Yale.[137]

Evgenii's own works were representative of the burgeoning interest in the literature of the religious and secular Enlightenments in Russia. Evgenii's 1790 essay "O trudnostiakh estestvennogo bogopoznaniia" (On the challenges of the natural knowledge of God) engaged the works of Christian Gottfried Hoffmann, Christian Wolff, Jean-Jacques Rousseau, Gerardus Vossius, Buddeus, and Abbot Pierre-Joseph Thoulier d'Olivet.[138] His edited work, *Razsuzhdenie o neobkhodimosti grecheskogo iazyka dlia bogoslovii* (Treatise on the necessity of Greek for theology), published in Moscow in 1793 and Voronezh in 1800, relied on a wide variety of Protestant and Enlightenment-era authors such as Salomon Gesner, Henri Estienne (translator of Calvin's catechism), Jean-Bénigne Bossuet, Nicolas-Charles-Joseph Trublet (d. 1770), and Voltaire.[139]

The Catherinian era witnessed not only the wider adoption of Protestant and Enlightenment-era theology but also the proliferation of that theology in popular print and translation. The establishment of free printing presses in 1783 and the wider growth of urban culture and literacy from the 1760s to the 1790s served as major catalysts for the growth of the ever-expanding print market during this period.[140] To make Enlightenment and Protestant literature available to the wider audience of the literate public, Russia's educated clergy engaged actively in publishing and translation. One of the bishops well known for his translation of Western literature into the Russian language was Feofilakt Rusanov (d. 1821), the bishop of Kaluga and Riazan. Rusanov was a "gentleman [*dzhetel'men*] among the bishops," fluent in French and secular culture, whom contemporaries often called the "Russian Brienne," after the liberal pro-republican archbishop of revolutionary France, Etienne-Charles de Brienne.[141]

Rusanov's tastes tended toward the literature of Brienne's era. Among the works he translated were Soame Jenyns's *A View of Internal Evidence of the Christian Religion* (1776), *Considérations sur divers points de la morale chrétienne* by César-Guillaume de la Luzerne (1738–1821), and *Mélanges de littérature et de philosophie* (1801) by Friedrich Ancillon. Ancillon's work was very sympathetic to the ideas of Rousseau.[142] Like Rusanov, other bishops took part in translating French, German, and English literature spanning both religious-apologetic and theological genres. Anastasii Bratanovskii (1761–1806), the archbishop of Astrakhan, translated a number of Enlightenment-era works for the lay and clerical audience in Russia. One was the work of an English Jewish convert preacher,

Paul Isaiah (Eliazar Bar-Isajah), titled *A Vindication of the Christians Messiah* (London, 1654) and published in Russian in 1801 and 1851. Another was a work by Jean Henri Samuel Formey (1711–97, Huguenot theologian and *Encyclopédie* collaborator), titled *Essai sur le Perfection* (1751).[143]

The list of Russia's clerics who engaged Enlightenment authors cannot be exhausted here. In general, however, their interaction with Western theology signaled an enlightened, non-sectarian approach to the study of theology and literature. Unlike Feofan Prokopovich, who viewed Protestant thought as a means to purify Orthodox dogma from its Catholic influences, eighteenth-century bishops began to view theology as a science that could tolerate or accept varying views, innovation, and change. The bishops valued the new theological learning that emanated from London or Göttingen not for its ingenuity but for its academic prestige and scientific merits.

Mefodii Smirnov, for example, thought that systematic theology was a scientific method of studying and classifying doctrine, with rules of that scientific method shared and accepted by all Christian theologians, regardless of denomination. By following the systematic method, he argued, theologians could apply "mathematical order" to theology and then "determine empirically [*opytom*], whether it would be possible to abolish or reduce the quarrels in theology that are alien to the liberal mathematical sciences."[144] The idea of viewing theology as a science with its own mathematical systematic method was also echoed in the writings of Petr Alekseev (d. 1801), the protopriest of the Moscow Archangel Cathedral and close confidante of Catherine's father-confessor Ivan Pamfilov. Alekseev viewed theology as part of the universal human inquiry alongside other sciences that was subject to the same empirical methods and rules as those sciences.[145] His expanded Russian edition of Grotius's *Truth of Christian Religion*, titled *Istinnoe blagochestie* (True piety), openly compared theology to science and specifically to mathematics.[146] He stated, "The Mathematicians argue whether a square can be found inside a circle, but they do not debate the fact that dividing a number by two would make its two parts equal. The same is seen in medicine and other sciences. Therefore, different opinions among Christians do not prevent them from agreeing on the most important doctrines, especially in those commandments that bestow special honor upon the practice of Christian piety."[147]

The precision of core mathematical principles was, essentially, a model for agreement on the main Christian doctrines within the "science" of systematic enlightened theology. Such a focus on core agreements in doctrine highlighted an ecumenical strain in the otherwise eclectic interest of Russian bishops in Western theology. In this regard, Russia's church elites were intellectual kinfolk of the German or English Protestant divines they read and translated, fully engaged in the theological context of the eighteenth-century religious Enlightenment.

Secular Enlightenment and Its Limits

The Enlightenment literature that Russian bishops learned and taught was not exclusively religious. Between 1762 and 1801, the bishops embraced many aspects of the rationalist Enlightenment with its regard for empiricism and the use of scientific reason. The bishops not only read this literature but used it in their scholarship and teaching. Their embrace of the secular Enlightenment also had its limits, as they eschewed viewpoints they deemed radical, such as Deism.

Thus, Feofilakt Rusanov was fascinated with the newest strains of European philosophical thought. His seminary curricula assigned the works of Christoph Meiners (1747–1810) as well as such famous French authors such as Jean le Rond d'Alembert, Jean-Baptiste Racine (1639–99), and Charles-Louis Secondat, baron de Montesquieu (1689–1755) as required readings for the seminarians.[148] In order to give the future clergy a "multifaceted [*mnogoobraznoe*] education," he also taught some of Immanuel Kant's ideas.[149] He seemed to regard highly the use of reason and empiricism in the Orthodox Church, criticizing those who operated without them.[150] This was well documented in a letter to a former classmate, Mikhail M. Speranskii. "We no longer live in a world, where it suffices to say: 'examine not, but simply believe,'" he stated. "They [Deists] will begin to examine against our will, and then our fearful silence will elevate their triumph and will reduce the number of believers." Clerical apologetics needed both reason and empiricism, he believed.[151]

The trend of reading the newest secular Enlightenment literature also reached beyond St. Petersburg. In the 1760s and 1770s, Metropolitan Platon purchased volumes of Voltaire, Charles Bonnet, and Montesquieu (*De l'esprit des lois*), among other authors, for the library and seminary of Russia's holiest monastery, Trinity-Sergius, outside Moscow.[152] When teaching at the Voronezh seminary, Evgenii Bolkhovitinov promoted the acquisition of the works of French enlighteners for the library. Despite the 1794–97 ban on "revolutionary" authors, Evgenii still managed to obtain several volumes of Voltaire's works for the seminary library, along with the French *Encyclopédie* and the dictionary of Huguenot Deist philosopher and freethinker Pierre Bayle (1647–1706). This may not have been illegal due to the impossibility of enforcing secular censorship laws on the church.[153] This purchase clearly revealed what Evgenii thought was appropriate reading for provincial seminary students, and he himself was an avid reader of seventeenth- and eighteenth-century French literature. His library featured a wide-ranging collection, among which

Enlightenment-era volumes predominated: Voltaire, Rousseau, Montesquieu, Molière, François Fénélon, Pierre Corneille (1606–84), Jean-François Marmontel, Michel de Montaigne (1533–92), and Gabriel Bonnot de Mably (1709–85), among others.[154] At the same time, Evgenii also engaged in translating and interpreting Enlightenment-era literature for Russian readers. His *Razsuzhedenie* relied on the work of Voltaire and others.[155] His 1788 European literature review essay, "Parnasskaia istoriia" (Parnassus story), extolled the virtues of French literature, including Racine, Pierre de Ronsard, François de Malherbe, and Pierre Corneille, while it "heaped praises on Voltaire."[156] Between 1785 and 1792, he translated numerous French authors, among them François Fénélon, Louis Coquelet, Laugier de Tassy, and Honoré Gabriel Riqueti, comte de Mirabeau.[157]

Evgenii's literary interests may have also influenced his rationalist conception of the relationship between science and religion. For example, he rejected the cosmology of St. John of Damascus in favor of modern astronomy by stating that "the Church Fathers are not our teachers in physics."[158] Equally, he did not believe that natural phenomena, such as earthquakes, had supernatural causes. In 1802, when a major Eastern European earthquake rattled St. Petersburg and destroyed houses in Moscow, Evgenii warned against jumping to any extra-natural conclusions.[159] He stated: "This all happened in Russia in the past and as a natural occurrence, it cannot therefore cause any fear. We need to wait for the news about eruptions of volcanic fire somewhere. All other prophecies are superfluous. Before this we had numerous floods from the sea."[160]

Many other clergymen of the era also held favorable views toward rationalist thought and Western philosophy. Amvrosii Serebrennikov, prefect of the Moscow Academy from 1778 and the future bishop of Ekaterinoslav, translated both John Milton's *Paradise Lost* and Alexander Pope's *Essay on Man* in 1780.[161] Iaroslavl's archimandrite Ioil' Bykovskii was an avid reader of contemporary literature: his 1787 compilation of literary and liturgical texts, *Istinna ili Vypiska o Istinne*, contained copious extracts from Diderot, Jean-Francois Marmontel, Catherine-Joseph de Propiac, Alexander Pope, and Voltaire, which, by the way, appeared alongside passages from St. John Chrysostom and the Minaion.[162] Vasilii Protopopov, a cathedral priest from Kolomna, was an enthusiastic reader of Rousseau. "I love Jean-Jacques," he stated, "not as an antagonist of religion, but as an emotional writer, who can touch the soul and speak to the heart." Such views hardly alienated the priest from his supervising bishops. Amvrosii Podobedov, then vicar of Moscow diocese, remarked that "it is so pleasing to us that the Holy Church has such teachers [as Protopopov], filled with the spirit of piety and eloquence."[163] Ivan Kandorskii, another priest from Moscow, was the author of *Nauka o dushe* (The science of the soul), which admired the "glorious Englishman John Locke" with respect to his views on the human soul. He analyzed Locke's views in comparison to the ideas of Wolff and Descartes.[164]

Voltaire was popular in the works of another Catherinian bishop, Evgenii Voulgaris, the archbishop of Kherson and Kremenchug and one of the intellectuals behind Catherine's neo-Hellenic project. While studying in Halle, Göttingen, and Leipzig, Voulgaris translated Voltaire's *Memnon* and his essay on Poland's religious intolerance into Greek (*Peri tōn Dichonoiōn tōn en tais ekklēsiais tēs poloniais*, Leipzig, 1768). He also utilized Voltaire's ideas to write essays on logic (*Hē logikē ek palaiōnte kai neōterōn syneranistheisa*, Leipzig, 1766) and toleration (*Schediasma peri anexithrēskeias*, Leipzig, 1767).[165] His 1804 *Treatise on Euthanasia* (printed in St. Petersburg) made him one of the chief proponents and discussants of the concept of "good death" (euthanasia) in Europe at the time.[166]

The clergy's embrace of the new philosophy, however, was limited. While they sympathized with numerous rationalist and empiricist features of the secular Enlightenment, their agreement with Voltaire, Rousseau, or Locke ended where the religious skepticism so prominent in many such works began. Just as the bishops read and used authors of the French or English Enlightenment, they also composed works against their Deism, atheism, or skepticism. Thus, Vasilii Levshin (son of Aleksei Levshin) wrote a refutation of Voltaire's poem on the Lisbon earthquake in 1788. Bishop Irinei Klement'evskii edited a treatise against "unbelievers and free-thinkers" in 1792, while Anastasii Bratanovskii wrote against "impiety and unbelief" in philosophy.[167] Archbishop Amvrosii Zertis-Kamenskii composed his 1765 treatise against atheists and agnostics, which built upon Grotius's arguments for revealed and natural religion.[168] Evgenii Bolkhovitinov, too, wrote against Deism in 1793, when he translated *Erreurs de Voltaire* by Abbot Claude Nonnotte (1711–93) into Russian (with several omissions of anti-Protestant content).[169] Thus, while Russian clerical elites found various features of secular literature engaging, Deism constituted one of the red lines that formed the limits of the Orthodox Enlightenment.

PLATON LEVSHIN: THE "LIBERAL MONK"

Catherine the Great once asked Joseph II to name his favorite sightseeing attraction from his 1780 visit to Moscow. Without hesitation, the Austrian emperor replied, "Metropolitan Platon."[170] Of all the bishops of the Catherinian era, Platon Levshin, the metropolitan of Moscow, stood out among his peers with respect to his level of learning and dedication to the cause of reform and enlightenment within the Russian church. While Joseph II called him a sight worth seeing, Count Iakov Shakhovskoi upon first meeting him in 1763 called him "not a man, but an anomaly," who had "gained such a level of enlightenment" that he was truly outstanding among his peers.[171]

Platon Levshin clearly exemplified and embodied the image of an enlightened and Western-looking prelate, an archetype of what Znamenskii once called "the liberal monk" (see figure 8).[172] Platon's theology demonstrated a major preoccupation with English and French Protestant sources and concepts. At the same time, his intellectual worldview embodied both the church's acceptance of the European religious Enlightenment and the limited embrace of rationalism. Much like other bishops of his period, and perhaps even more so, Platon was an admirer of Protestant theology, a patron of contemporary philosophical thought, and a gentleman-bishop in manners and demeanor.

Platon Levshin's origins were humble. Born as Petr Grigor'evich Danilov in the village of Chashnikovo outside Moscow, the future prelate hailed from the family of a poor deacon.[173] His father was shrewd enough to enroll his son in Moscow's Slavo-Greco-Latin Theological Academy, foreseeing that clergy with education fared better than those without. Petr turned out to be a very good student, succeeding in Latin, mathematics, theology, and even in learning Greek as an autodidact. It is in the seminary that Petr (together with his brother, Aleksei) acquired his ecclesiastical last name of Levshin or Lëvshin, likely derivative of the Russian word for lion.[174] His enthusiasm for education overshadowed his poverty. According to his autobiography, the future metropolitan walked to academy classes barefoot, putting on his only pair of shoes when entering the building.[175]

His career was both meteoric and remarkable. The young seminary student became a monk and then the deputy abbot of Trinity-Sergius Monastery at the age of twenty-four. Catherine (and Count Shakhovskoi) met Platon in Moscow when he was twenty-six and appointed him to be the official tutor and religion instructor to Catherine's only son and successor, Grand Duke Paul Petrovich. His appointment came after Courtmaster Nikita Panin successfully tested the young monk to determine that he was not "superstitious." At age twenty-nine he earned the title of archimandrite of Trinity-Sergius, being ordained in Peterhof in 1766. The following year, he became a member of the Synod; at age thirty-three, the archbishop of Tver, and at thirty-eight of Moscow.[176]

Much of his rise had to do with well-placed connections. Platon met the famous preacher Gedeon Krinovskii early in his studies in Moscow, and the latter liked him, taught him to preach, and promised him "promotion [promotsiia]."[177] During Platon's summer vacations, Krinovskii invited the young student to St. Petersburg, where he spent evenings chatting with Count Ivan Ivanovich Shuvalov and Aleksei G. Razumovskii (the widowed morganatic

Figure 8. Metropolitan Platon Levshin (1737–1812) as an Enlightenment allegory. Commissioned by Prince Aleksander Beloselskii, engraving by Christian Friedrich Uhlemann, ca. 1795. From Dmitrii Rovinskii, *Podrovbnyi slovar' russkikh gravirovannykh portretov,* vol. 3 (St. Petersburg, 1888). Courtesy of Indiana University Library.

husband of Empress Elizabeth). His love of company helped him enjoy St. Petersburg life after his appointment as Grand Duke Paul's tutor. Following lessons, Platon often visited with such elite audiences as Ivan Betskoi (the president of the Academy of Arts), Ivan Shuvalov (the de facto minister of education), General-Field Marshal Zakhar Chernyshev (the de facto minister of war), playwright Aleksandr Sumarokov, and Director of Court Theater Ivan Elagin, spending long evenings in drink and conversation.[178] As he remarked in his autobiography, Platon "always possessed a special desire to talk."[179]

During the first part of his career, Platon liked the court and the court liked him. He even compared his life in St. Petersburg elite society to life in the monastery, arguing that just as monks strive to please the abbot so courtiers endeavor to gain the empress's favor.[180] During those years he managed to make a good impression on Catherine as a result of his "enlightened" lessons with Paul and his sermons that made Catherine cry, laugh, or, on a few occasions, even kneel down in agony. Some at the court were also impressed by his manners. In 1787 Prince Charles de Ligne followed the archbishop into the garden, where the latter conversed with Princess Varvara Golitsyna, Potemkin's niece. The princess "asked for his blessing, and he clipped a rose and gave it to her." This proved to the French visitor that Platon was not only "divine" (as others had told him) but also "human."[181]

Curiously enough, Platon often attributed his own popularity to his facial features. His autobiography, written in the third person as was customary, stated that as a baby he was admired by "all" in the village for his "affectionate, beautiful, and pleasant [*milovidnyi*] face."[182] This infantile beauty would later translate into handsomeness as a young adult: the metropolitan noted that in 1759 his "young and attractive face" as well as "pleasant and clear voice" positively affected his popularity in church services and preaching in Moscow.[183]

Vanity was a peculiar feature of the metropolitan. Platon liked silk robes, good food, Flemish paintings, and items that highlighted his unique connection to the imperial family. Such things included portraits of Catherine, Paul, Alexander, and Constantine, as well as their letters to Platon, which he kept framed on the walls of his house.[184] He also had a penchant for ecclesiastical ornaments: during the period when he was still an archbishop, he was envious of other hierarchs like Gavriil Petrov and Samuil Mislavskii who wore the beautiful metropolitan mitres he had yet to earn. He was particularly resentful of Catherine's confessor, priest Ivan Pamfilov, who also wore a mitre and bore the nickname "*popa mitratus* [priest with a mitre]." Platon's day of fame came on his birthday in 1787 when Catherine (with Pamfilov) personally visited Moscow and bestowed a beautiful mitre with a diamond cross on him in a surprise ceremony at the Dormition Cathedral.[185] Platon was extremely pleased, although

Catherine joked in a letter to Potemkin that this mitre made him look like "the Peacock of Kremenchug." (Incidentally, the metropolitan of Moscow also bred peacocks at the monastery.)[186] Several years later, in 1795, the Peacock of Kremenchug added another diamond mitre to his collection, and in 1797 the cavalier medals of the Orders of St. Andrew and St. Anna.[187]

Yet what made the bishop so influential in the Russian church and at the court were not his refined manners or nice face but his love of education, or "enlightenment." In 1763 Catherine asked him why he chose monastic life. "Out of a special love for education [*prosveshchenie*]," replied Platon, adding that it was much harder to "foster one's education" when burdened by "wife, children, and various worldly cares."[188] The fact that a desire for education or "enlightenment" (and not for ascetic living) was the reason for his choice of career greatly pleased Catherine.[189] Throughout his career, this devotion to education played a pivotal role in his promotions, such as at Tver, where the townsfolk praised him for "dedicating his life to our enlightenment and the public good" by improving seminary education for clergy and burghers alike.[190]

Vain, smart, popular, sentimental, and vindictive—these were just some of the features of the hierarch's character that habitually elicited contradictory reactions to his behavior from the people at court. Count Fedor Golovkin, who knew the inner workings of high society in Catherinian Russia quite well, summed up Platon's contradictions in his memoirs. The count painted a very colorful picture of the hierarch.

> When serving at court, he [Platon] acquired a tendency, or perhaps a habit of getting into intrigues. He was friendly and kind to the simple folk, who adored him, but was very condescending and harsh toward the court nobility—he always made them attend to his needs. He was also constantly more or less an inconvenience to his lord [Paul I]. His enemies called him a charlatan of the altar and a Calvinist deep in his heart. Yet he never served a liturgy that did not make people cry and his sermons always circulated later in popular quotations. After preaching, he always retired into the tranquility of his office, where he read Voltaire, Helvétius, and Rousseau and then discussed them with others with a full grasp of the subject.[191]

Platon's love for education and the authors of the Enlightenment manifested itself in his theological tastes, which differed little from other bishops of his generation, or from numerous English and German divines. Much like them, the metropolitan of Moscow followed Quenstedt, Hollatz, and Prokopovich in teaching systematic theology, while reading numerous French and English preachers, including Saurin, Fénélon, Massillon, and Tillotson.[192]

Platon Levshin's most seminal contribution to Orthodox theology, however, was his catechism, *Pravoslavnoe uchenie*. This work's great importance lies not only in the fact that it was—initially—used in instructing the young members of the imperial family in the Orthodox faith but also because it represented the standard Orthodox expression of doctrine for decades to come. His theological system remained in use in Russia's seminaries until the early nineteenth century.[193]

In structure and theological content, his catechism appears to have striking similarities to the Larger Westminster Catechism, a standard of Reformed doctrine composed in Edinburgh and at Westminster in 1648.[194] It also represented the rise of interest in Calvinist and Huguenot theology in the clerical circles at the time. This fact has never been acknowledged in the literature. The similarities between the British and the Russian works are not only structural but also theological, and include such topics as the attributes of God, the questions of ecclesiology, the "offices" of Christ, and even sacramental definitions. Platon also shared the Calvinist doctrine of Providence—his catechism (just like the Westminster document) highlighted two major features (or as they are called, branches) of God's Providence—the "preserving," and the "governing" of creation.[195] (See this book's appendix for further comparison.)

Pravoslavnoe uchenie was well received abroad and soon translated into English (Edinburgh), Latin (St. Petersburg), Greek (Vienna), German (Riga and Leipzig), Armenian, French, and Dutch.[196] In his review of the German and Russian editions, Riga's literary critic, H. L. Christian Bacmeister, remarked that according to Platon's theology, "this [Orthodox] Church deviates less from the Lutherans, and departs even more from the Papists [*Paebstlichen*]."[197] Such a statement was hardly extraordinary. During the Catherinian era, it was common for German Lutherans to remark that Russian church doctrine was closer to Protestantism than Catholicism.[198] The reviewer further highlighted the Lutheran agreement with Platon's concept (*Begriff*) of the sacraments, sanctification, and veneration of images but did not overlook the catechism's differences in teaching on the procession of the Holy Spirit and apostolic exclusivity.[199] He also praised Platon for relegating fasts to the function of being "merely a means to tame the passions and bind the lusts."[200] Such a positive reception from a well-known Baltic Lutheran reviewer reflected the metropolitan's popularity in the Protestant world. It is worth noting that Platon was entrusted with converting Paul I's wife, Wilhelmina of Hesse-Darmstadt, to Orthodoxy. Her mother (Caroline of Zweibrücken) required a pledge that the Russian church would assure her daughter's salvation in the same manner as the Lutheran one did.[201]

Platon's doctrinally Westernized views also manifested themselves in his opinions on church tradition and church history. Much like Prokopovich before him, he was skeptical of the extra-scriptural authority of the Fathers: for him, their writings contained "much that had been written with bias or ignorant lack of enlightenment," including "fables, legends, and mistakes."[202] Similarly, he pointed out mistakes in the Nomocanon (*Kormchaia*), or book of canon law (with its copy of the Donation of Constantine "a blatant falsehood"), and doubted the veracity of stories like St. Andrew's visit to Kiev.[203] He criticized the lack of "simplicity and purity" and the "immoderate monasticism" in the medieval Russian church while condemning the avarice of the Greek Kievan metropolitans.[204] His views on Kievan and Muscovite Christianity were not unique at the time: Bishop Damaskin was critical of many aspects of the medieval and pre-Petrine Orthodoxy in his church history lectures.[205]

PLATON AND TOLERATION

As a liberal monk, Platon exemplified not only the kind of an "enlightened" Orthodoxy that emerged in Catherinian era but also a more tolerant one as well. Over the last decades of the eighteenth century, the Russian church developed tolerant attitudes toward a whole range of Protestants, sectarians, and Old Believers. These attitudes would come to change not only the confessional but also the demographic landscape of the empire's new lands in the east and south. The development of this toleration is a subject not very well studied, and even less discussed is the theological impetus for it, which lies in a new conceptual ecclesiology that allowed for a more ecumenical vision of the church.

Platon Levshin's tolerant attitudes included the high level of respect he held for many Protestants that lived or passed through Russia in late eighteenth century. One of his best friends in the nobility was a Russian Protestant, Count Fedor Golovkin, who returned to Moscow to marry Natal'ia Izmailova in 1790 with Platon's express permission. Platon noted that during Paul's coronation in 1796, when he was out of favor at court, Golovkin was the only one on "whom I could rely for support."[206] Among other friends in Moscow was the local Lutheran pastor Benjamin Heidecke; he taught Trinity-Sergius seminarians organ lessons, helping Platon stage theatrical plays and organ, string, and chamber music concerts.[207] In his interactions with foreign Protestants, Platon developed a habit of delivering parts of the divine liturgy in French and German, especially in the Easter service when there were foreigners in the crowd. At one point, he even interrupted a service to greet English travelers with "*pax vobiscum*," as Clarke described it, "to the astonishment of the crowd."[208]

Platon also defended Protestants from the attacks of the less tolerant Orthodox clergy. In 1769 the protopriest of the Archangel Cathedral, Petr Alekseev, submitted his catechism, *The Orthodox Confession of Faith*, for review by Moscow's Synodal Bureau, where Platon and his brother Aleksandr Levshinov held significant influence. Although Alekseev's theological views were rather enlightened (as discussed above), his catechism, the Bureau reported, contained "slander [*ponoshenie*]" of Protestants along with some "common idioms [*poslovitsy*] inappropriate for theological matters."[209] The catechism did not contain any references to Protestant heresy per se; what constituted "slander" was the assertion that "Lutherans and Calvinists do not have a true priesthood, because they cannot prove that they have an unbroken Apostolic succession for their bishops." The Bureau instead defended Protestant ordination by stating that it contained "a shadow of true consecration."[210]

Among the examples of "inappropriate" language that Platon had found in this catechism were Alekseev's description of how a person of low status in Protestant countries ("some farmer [*fermer*] or even a house servant [*lakei*]") could become a barely educated pastor, a "foolish custodian" for a "foolish gathering."[211] Given the fact that even some of the bishops of the Catherinian era were former serfs, such snobbery seemed clearly inappropriate for a catechetical instruction for the masses. So, even though this work had the blessing of the influential senator Vasilii Adadurov (1702–88), the Holy Synod issued a full-scale "reprimand [*repremand*]" against the author and prohibited the publication.[212] The protopriest was warned not to utter such remarks in his catechism lessons at Moscow University.[213]

Platon Levshin's relationship with Protestants also included correspondence with the Huguenot theologian Louis Dutens (1730–1812), who sought various clarifications on points of Orthodox doctrine that appeared to him to be irrational, such as prayers for the dead. The bishop's tone was conciliatory: he praised Protestants for overthrowing the "Papal yoke and all of the aberrations of the Roman bishops" and reassured them that their baptism, as the baptism of "all who believe in the Trinity," was valid.[214] Then he rationalized the prayers for the dead as an act of "Christian love" for a deceased family member, not a supplication to "alter the judgment of God."[215] Confession was necessary "for no reason other than the easing of one's conscience," while icons were "honorific" images that served as "an encouragement [*pobuzhdenie*] to piety."[216] In a similar tone, Platon declared that the changing of substance in the Orthodox Eucharist was not "substantial [*estestvennoe*]" but "mysterious [*tainstvennoe*]."[217] Given theological affinities between Protestant and Orthodox viewpoints, Platon argued, the only major issue that prevented closer ties between the two churches was the Filioque. Despite the rejection of Papal "mistakes," he argued, the "reformed [*reformaty*] with full conscience accepted this Papal error in the Holy Creed."[218] Thus, the communion between the two churches could only occur when the Protestants had fulfilled the goals of their Reformation and eliminated this final "Papal error" and stumbling block to reconciliation.

Platon's open-minded approach toward Protestants was not a passing fashion but a reflection of his (and other enlightened bishops') ecclesiology, which increasingly downplayed confessional divides in Christianity. Just like his sacramental view, his definition of the church is simple and Calvinistically concise: "a gathering of people who believe in Jesus Christ."[219] It was not an uncommon definition; the author of the standard Orthodox theology book in the later eighteenth century, Irinei Fal'kovskii, defined the church in a similar manner. He stated that the "church is a group [*coetus*] of true believers, who have faith in Christ based on the Word of God."[220] Similar ideas appeared in the writings of Platon's disciple Filaret Drozdov, who did not consider Protestants to be heretics and who believed any Orthodox ecumenical council to be invalid without the voice of the Western church, broadly defined.[221]

The growth of toleration in the Catherinian era also affected the status of the Old Believers, the Russian dissenters who left the official Orthodox Church in the dramatic schism of 1666. Among the main points of the contention were the preservation of old rituals (such as the two-fingered sign of the cross) that the Muscovite hierarchy abandoned in favor of more recent Greek and Ukrainian practices.[222] Enlightenment ideas along with the impact of Prokopovich's reforms, however, placed a greater emphasis on dogma than on ritual, on intellectual concepts rather than outward ceremonies. Thus, the Holy Synod eventually came to see the Old Believers' insistence on keeping their own formal observances as trivial; what became far more important was their recognition of the imperial sovereign (after all, some of them believed Peter I to be the Antichrist) as well as their acceptance of the reformed hierarchical and doctrinal architecture. In his 1766 work, *Uveshchanie*, Platon argued that Old Believers and Orthodox "agree in faith and disagree only in trifles." It is better, he argued, "to change church traditions [*obychai*] than the love and unity within the Church."[223]

Based on this new understanding, the Holy Synod and Catherine II gradually abolished the persecution of Old Believers in a series of decrees in 1762, 1763, and 1764 and even issued privileges to those who were willing to settle Russia's frontier lands in the Volga and southern Ukraine.[224] The basis of this toleration was the redefinition of heresy along the lines expressed by Platon: the person practicing different rituals was no longer a heretic as long as one was not inimical to the official church.[225] The first rapprochement between officials and groups of Old Believers took place between 1781 and 1783, when representatives of the Starodub Old Believers met with Potemkin and church officials: metropolitans Gavriil Petrov, Innokentii Nechaev, and Platon Levshin. The result of this negotiation was that Old Believers were given permission to operate their own churches, as long as they recognized the authority of the Holy Synod and prayed for the empress.[226]

This compromise led to the process of "unification [*soedinenie*]" and "union in doctrine [or faith, *edinoverie*]" between the parishes who practiced old rituals and the administrative structure of the Synod. In the 1780s, thousands of Old Believers received legalization and pursued new church construction throughout the Starodub area and other parts of Ukraine (especially in the south, where Potemkin needed settlers).[227] Similar developments took place in the Urals.[228] The process of legalization entered a new phase when in 1799–1800, Moscow's Old Believer elite (some sixty-nine merchant families) negotiated the agreement with Platon Levshin that became the legal basis for the recognition and operation of *edinoverie* in the empire until 1906. The Moscow Points, as they have become known, negotiated certain privileges for the Old Believers (such as permission for the laity to wear beards and for Old Believer priests to confess to Old Believer priests only). There were also some serious compromises: Old Believer parishes were subordinated to the regular dioceses and recognized the authority of the Synod.[229]

Russian bishops' views on toleration extended not only to Orthodox sectarians but to Protestant ones, too. When the Moravian Brethren of Herrnhut requested settlement in Russia in 1768 to escape maltreatment in the Austrian Empire, Catherine turned to her open-minded bishop, Dmitrii Sechenov. Sechenov, together with another "enlightened" bishop, Gavriil Petrov, decided to allow the settlement of the Hernhutter German sectarians in the Volga region. The sect, they argued, had a "resemblance to the early Christian church . . . a prototypical apostolic church," and the Synod's president was "glad [*shchastie imeiu*]" to learn about their imminent arrival in Russia.[230] Thus, the Moravian sectarians, who were not afforded full toleration by the Josephinist enlighteners in Austria, moved to the Volga region.[231] The Moravians even developed professional relations with the Russian church; their pastors Johann Wiegand and Johann Pauli, for example, taught in Kharkov's seminary.[232] Their arrival was followed by the settlement of thousands of others, including Mennonites, Hutterites, and radical Pietists who permanently changed the physical, demographic, and spiritual landscape of the Russian Empire.[233]

One curious instance of toleration in Catherinian Russia involved the question of sacred images. In 1774 the Holy Synod discovered that the parishioners of the Transfiguration Cathedral venerated the "Swedish icon" of Martin Luther at the iconostasis "as if he were some saint."[234] How long this practice had been going on was not known, but the provenance of the icon likely stemmed from the 1704 Russian capture of Narva from the Swedes. One of the priests of the cathedral, Ivan Vasil'ev, defended the sanctity of the icon; another, Evfimii Obraskov, demanded its removal. The St. Petersburg diocesan authorities eventually decided to compromise by keeping the icon in the church but away from the iconostasis—it was "honorably removed one level up from it."[235] This respect for images was often reciprocated by the Lutherans: in 1774 in Mogilev, a Lutheran church placed the portrait of local Orthodox bishop Georgii Konisskii next to the image of Luther inside the church's walls.[236]

PLATON'S POLITICS

Platon also engaged with Enlightenment political theories. Of the various European philosophical ideas, the metropolitan most approved of the theory of the social contract. Much like Rousseau, Hobbes, and others, Platon argued that the nature of the state rested upon the "social contract [*obshchestvennyi dogovor*]," which required citizens "to commit their peace and security to the government of others."[237] In his early sermons, he tied the importance of such a "contract of common life" to elevating the "common good" over the "love toward oneself" and even accorded a special role to the church in securing this "sacred union" between the people and their government.[238]

Platon's belief in the possibility of idealized, harmonious government were later accompanied by more realistic critical appraisals of the state of the government in Russia. In his "enlightened" conversations with Venezuelan revolutionary Francisco de Miranda (1750–1816), held over tea and orgeat in 1786–87 in Moscow, the bishop disclosed his candid views of Catherine's court politics. "Her ministers," he said, "are trying to deceive her, but she fools them all."[239] While this comment reflected his elite experience of living at court, "my friend the archbishop," noted Miranda, cared about the state of the lower classes. "He is distressed by despotism in his country," Miranda wrote, especially the treatment of the serfs.[240]

What Miranda found interesting was Platon's views on religious toleration, which tied the freedom of faith to the necessity of political liberty. "Toleration must be absolute," said the archbishop. "One cannot allow the criticism of religious beliefs [*dogmaty*] without also allowing the criticism of political decrees."[241] This understanding of toleration was hardly unique at the time. For the Voltaire-translating bishop Evgenii Voulgaris, toleration had three parts: religious or church toleration, political or state toleration, and toleration of the individual or personal liberties.[242]

For Platon, the idea of state "toleration" was not only a concept but a familiar battle. As recent works about the Moscow censorship conflicts in the 1780s and the 1790s illustrate, Platon was often at odds with state censorship offices. The metropolitan tried to preserve the ecclesiastical freedom of printing whatever the bishop deemed necessary and opposed the mixed censorship boards that included state representatives introduced in the late 1790s.[243] This sense of disillusionment with the repressive elements of government policies matured throughout the 1790s, so much so that when Cambridge scholar Edward Clarke visited Platon, the metropolitan appeared somewhat envious of British freedoms. One time, walking in the monastery garden, Platon looked around to make sure that no monks around him understood French. After that, he following conversation unfolded.

> PLATON: Some of your divines write beautifully, but with inconceivable freedom. It was once discussed in an English sermon, "Whether a people had power to dethrone their King?"
>
> CLARK: Your Grace may say more, we once had a prelate, who, preaching before his Sovereign, felt himself at liberty to discuss his conduct to his face.
>
> PLATON: I wish we had such a fellow here! We would send him to enjoy the full liberty of preaching in the free air of Siberia.[244]

By the time Reginald Heber, the lord bishop of Calcutta (1783–1826), visited Platon in 1805, the metropolitan appeared to have become even more despondent in his assessment of Russia's state of affairs and more open in his appraisal of Enlightenment liberties. He complained to Heber about "the power of an emperor in Russia," stating that "it would be much better . . . had we a constitution like that in England."[245]

While "the liberality of his sentiments pleased us highly," wrote Heber, they also alarmed him, as they appeared to weaken the Russian people's resolve to fight Napoleon, the United Kingdom's enemy. According to the metropolitan, "the clergy throughout Russia are inimical to their government," while Napoleon was "rather popular among them." Platon "contemplated his [Bonaparte's] success as an inevitable and not very alarming prospect," and he even "refused to draw up a form of prayer for the success of the Russian arms." "He does not wish particularly well to us [the British] in our war with France," concluded Heber.[246]

Platon's political views were alarming not only to the British allies but also to the more traditional Russians, who, as the last chapter will illustrate, were worried about the freethinking clerics. Such alarm was certainly an exaggeration, since most of the bishops remained dedicated monarchists. In 1812, for example, only Varlaam Shishatskii (1750–1820), archbishop of Mogilev, welcomed Napoleon with the majority of his clergy also swearing an oath of loyalty to Bonaparte.[247] Platon himself died during Napoleon's invasion of Moscow and appears to have "blessed" the Russian troops on his deathbed. Yet despite this final act, Platon's political views remain "an obstacle to canonization" of the bishop as a new saint in contemporary Russia.[248]

CONCLUSION

In terms of its theology, education, and devotional literature, the Russian Orthodox Church of 1801 was very different from that of 1701. When Feofan Prokopovich came to St. Petersburg in 1718, he found most elite members of the church hierarchy consumed by the desire to persecute and burn those city dwellers who dabbled in Protestant heresies. When Filaret Drozdov, the future metropolitan of Moscow, arrived in St. Petersburg in 1809, he found the members of the Synod piously reading the "miracles of Swedenborg," speaking French, and dashing to palaces to attend "balls and masquerades."[249] In 1701 the Russian church was a centuries-old institution confronting a sea of social, cultural, and intellectual change; in 1801 it was an institution acting as a vehicle of change, Westernization, and reform in Russian society.

By 1801 the impact of Protestant theology and the Enlightenment appeared to have altered the ways in which the church hierarchy defined Orthodox beliefs, doctrinal learning, and devotion. As the next chapter will demonstrate, the influence of the West was hardly limited to the impact of its theology. The Enlightenment also reshaped the art of sacred rhetoric in Russia.

7

Light from the Pulpit

Preaching Reason to
Russia's Masses, 1754–1801

Russia entered the Enlightenment not only by engaging the new trends in theology or philosophy but also by adopting new homiletical content. The sacred oratory of 1754–1801 did not deviate much stylistically from the regulations that Prokopovich set; other requirements for preachers, found in the *Spiritual Regulation*, continued to apply. What made the sermons of this period different was the new content. Unlike the homilies of the previous generation of Protestant-influenced bishops, the new sermons focused on topics popularized in the preaching of the European religious Enlightenment of the era.

The impact of religious and secular Enlightenment on homiletics in Russia has never been studied, although Elise Wirtschafter's extensive examination of Platon Levshin's preaching laid the groundwork for further inquiry into the subject.[1] As this chapter demonstrates, the sermons of the Orthodox Enlightenment followed eighteenth-century French and northern European Catholic and Protestant homiletic trends, known as neoclassicism or rationalism, very closely, reflecting the continuing impact of Western ideas on Orthodox elites. Much like in the West, the content of the Russian homilies tended to emphasize the grand and ethical attributes of doctrine (love, mercy, Providence) as opposed to its polemical or systematic elements (as was the case in the period of Prokopovich). At the same time, the sermons engaged the subject of reason broadly (when rationality was affirmed and celebrated) and particularly (insofar as reason applied to daily life, ethics, and piety).

THE NEOCLASSICAL SERMON: AN INTRODUCTION
Although the Russian pulpit began to adopt this new preaching style after 1754 (the first year of Gedeon Krinovskii's preaching at court), neoclassicism had existed in France and Protestant Europe since the end of the seventeenth

century. The term originated from French preachers' desire to emulate the classical oratory of the fourth-century Antiochian and Cappadocian fathers.[2] Historians, however, viewed it as the continuation of the Erasmian northern humanist tradition, influenced by the Calvinist and Jansenist imitation of Chrysostom.[3] The French branch of this school crossed the Huguenot-Catholic divide and included such preachers as Jacques Saurin (the court preacher to the House of Orange in The Hague), Jean-Frederic Ostervald (in Neuchatel, 1663–1747), and prominent Catholic bishops like Jean-Baptiste Massillon (1663–1742), and François Fénélon.

In Great Britain, neoclassicism, known also as Moderatism, was associated theologically with Latitudinarians. Much like Latitudinarians, Moderatist preachers avoided both what they viewed as the excesses of the secular Enlightenment (e.g., Deism) and radical Puritanism.[4] Such court divines as Latitudinarian archbishop John Tillotson—a nephew-in-law of Oliver Cromwell—and Robert South (1634–1716) generally identified with this trend. The Moderatists developed strong connections to the French homiletical tradition due to the presence of a Huguenot refugee community in London.[5]

In northern Germany and Denmark-Norway, a similar homiletical movement emerged, known as rationalism or "the Mediating school." Theologically, it moderated between some of the near-ascetic elements of Pietism and the radical skepticism of the Enlightenment.[6] Such divines as Johann Lorenz von Mosheim (a Wolfenbüttel preacher before he became Göttingen chancellor), Johann J. Spalding, his brother-in-law A. F. W. Sack, and Leipzig preacher Georg J. Zollikofer (1730–88) belonged to this school.[7]

Despite their wide geographical spread, these clergymen shared a common approach to the relationship between faith and reason in their preaching. First, their sermons avoided the high level of polemical dogmatism of the Reformation era. Second, they featured a much greater emphasis on the ethical attributes of God and humanity (love, mercy, grace, greatness, edification) than economical ones (justification, hypostatic union).[8] Third, the concept of Providence (especially the providential utility of reason) formed one of the favorite ethical points of reference, particularly for the French and English preachers.[9] Then also, moralization was deliberately very general; preachers from Tillotson to Louis Bourdaloue maintained a certain "court etiquette" in addressing general points of morality without condemning the courtiers' sins directly.[10] It was not uncommon for the nobility or the monarch to cry profusely during such sermons and then continue with their sinful business as usual.[11]

At the same time, the most distinct characteristic of the contents of the neoclassical or Moderatist sermon was the preaching of reason. First of all, this concern involved a broad polemic against radical rationalists, Deists, atheists, naturalists, and Unitarians (still marginal intellectual movements emerging in eighteenth-century England, Germany, and France).[12] Secondly, it involved a consistent affirmation that it was reasonable, rational, and useful (for the public and for each individual) to profess the basic tenets of Christian faith, that "it was more prudent to believe the Gospel, in a modified sort of way, than not."[13]

This "reasonableness" and utilitarian character are reflected in the titles given to sermons at the time. Jean-Baptiste Massillon, for example, liked to rationalize the practice of faith in topics such as "The Respect Which the Great Ought to Have for Religion," "The Truth of Religion," and "The Evidence of the Law of God."[14] Jacques Saurin championed a similar cause in "The Advantages of Piety," "The Necessity of Progressive Religion," and the "Fatal Consequences of a Bad Education."[15] Georg Zollikofer preached on utility and the rationality of faith in "The Value of Intellectual Pleasures," "The Value of Religion in General," and "Of the Detriment and Danger of Too Frequent Dissipation and Diversion."[16] Comparing these titles with those of the Pietist sermons of Philipp Jakob Spener (e.g., "Constant Prayer," "Patience in Suffering," and "Self-Denial") demonstrates that religious Enlightenment was a different era indeed.[17]

THE ARRIVAL OF NEOCLASSICISM AND MODERATISM IN RUSSIA

Neoclassical homiletics spread first among Russia's court preachers as a fashion connected to the inclination to imitate Enlightenment religious culture in general. By the middle of the eighteenth century, not only the religious but also secular elites of St. Petersburg had become conversant with this Western preaching culture. Thus, if in the 1720s Russian bishops were flattered if secular writers compared them to Cicero or Chrysostom, by 1760 they were also compared to the modern British or French preachers. As early as 1750, playwright Aleksandr Sumarokov was likening the late Feofan Prokopovich to "Mosheim and Bourdaloue, men of greatest eminence."[18] Later, he would call Gedeon Krinovskii a "Russian [Esprit] Fléchier" and Platon Levshin "a Russian Bourdaloue."[19]

In a similar fashion, Synod members Amvrosii Podobedov and Damaskin Semenov-Rudnev compared the sermons of Metropolitan Platon to his Western counterparts, "the English Tillotson and the French Massillon, the two most eminent preachers of their time," whom Platon resembled "by the plainness and beauty of his prose."[20] Amvrosii and Damaskin did not use only French and English sermons as a point of reference in their praise of Platon. They also alluded to the Prussian Enlightenment pulpit, showing that the "the way he expressed his thoughts" was similar to "Spalding and Sack, the two now eminent [slavnymi] moral teachers in the German land."[21] Russian playwright Denis Fonvizin also shared this sense of catching up to the West when commenting on the current state of Russian homiletics. As he wrote in 1788, "At least our churchly eloquence shows that Russians are not worse than any other nations. Our most reverent Metropolitans, Gavriil, Samuil, and Platon, are our Tillotsons and Bourdaloues."[22]

Russian bishops not only compared their colleagues to the famous Western divines but also enjoyed reading these "most eminent preachers of their time."[23] Metropolitan of St. Petersburg Gavriil Petrov (1730–1801) was quite fond of Protestant and Enlightenment authors. The sermons he personally read from the pulpit contained his translations and adaptations of Mosheim, Saurin, Gesner, and Bourdaloue.[24] In Moscow, Platon Levshin did not simply read Massillon, Tillotson, and Saurin; he "read and reread them [chital i perechityval]."[25] He furthermore advised his students at the seminary of Trinity-Sergius to read such preachers, and for that purpose he provided the library with the homiletic compendia of Jacques Saurin, Esprit Fléchier, Georg Joachim Zollikofer, Johann Lorenz von Mosheim, and Christoph Christian Sturm (1740–86).[26] The trend of assigning Western homiletic authors was widespread elsewhere: Kharkov Collegium's readings, for example, included Fléchier, Mosheim, and Saurin.[27] In Voronezh, Evgenii Bolkhovitinov made compilations from Johann Jakob Rambach and Nicolas Trublet to be used for the seminarians' study of sacred rhetoric.[28]

The proliferation of Western neoclassical sermons in Russia, however, was not meant for the consumption of educated elites alone. The Synod desired to make the modern court sermons and the Western sermons available in the provincial dioceses and town centers. In 1772 metropolitans Platon Levshin and Gavriil Petrov decided that the Russian countryside was in need of "the development of the sense of moral duty, the awareness of social obligation, and the uprooting of superstition and hypocrisy."[29] The best way to address that need would be to spread enlightened European preaching.

To reach that goal, Gavriil and Platon, together with Holy Synod's editorial team, translated and prepared a printed compilation of selected sermons, titled *Sobranie raznykh pouchenii na vse voskresnye i prazdnichnye dni* (Collection of various homilies delivered on Sundays and Feast Days [St. Petersburg, 1775, and Moscow, 1776]). In terms of Russian authors, the compilation featured eight homilies by the main editor, Gavriil; thirty-seven by the coeditor, Platon; and nineteen by Gedeon Krinovskii.[30] There were also nine sermons by Ilias Miniates (1669–1714), considered to be one of the early preachers of the Greek Enlightenment and one of the late representatives of Greek humanism.[31] Among Western authors, only one Roman Catholic sermon—Bourdaloue's "La foi victorieuse du monde"—made it into the collection. The Protestant homilies were more plentiful: the compilation featured five sermons by the

French Huguenot Jacques Saurin and five sermons by Lorenz Mosheim.[32] The homilies of the Göttingen chancellor may have been particularly appealing due to the Russian Orthodox educational connection to that university described in chapter 5; his high reputation as one of the best preachers in Europe of the time probably played a role too.[33] Among the selection of Orthodox and Protestant sermons there was also a category of mixed or adapted sermons, written by Russian authors "with very significant borrowing [*s vesma znachitel'nymi zaimstvovaniiami*] from Chrysostom, Meniates, Saurin, and Gesner."[34]

The collection's editors highlighted the urgency of public reading of these sermons in parishes, stating that the Synod "strongly decreed that those sermons should be read in all churches, all without exception."[35] The fact that the Synod wanted to expose the average person in the provinces to the sermons of Mosheim, Saurin, or Bourdaloue meant that the bishops did not see the homiletic value of Western Enlightenment preaching as limited to elites. In fact, in the 1780s and 1790s, the Synod continued authorizing its printing press to publish not only the sermons of domestic court preachers like Platon but also Protestant authors like Saurin and Zollikofer.[36]

THE FREQUENCY OF PREACHING

The extent of the dissemination and the popular reception of Russian Enlightenment homilies is not well known and deserves a separate study. In general, Paul Bushkovitch's observation about the seventeenth century's sermons, that "what was heard at court in 1670 was read in the provinces by 1690," also remained true for the 1760s and the 1770s.[37] This is evident in the abovementioned 1775 compilation: consisting largely of court-delivered sermons, it was now meant to edify the countryside as well as reach the lower classes through publications to be read by the provincial priests after the liturgy.

Some of the mechanisms of sermon proliferation and reception can be gleaned from the biographical accounts of the era. Reginald Heber stated in 1804 that Russian clergy "do not preach regularly except in Cathedral Churches," noting that elsewhere, "the sermons are always read."[38] This suggests that the luxury of hearing original sermons was limited to the provincial centers and that priests in the more remote parishes would read sermons written by someone else, such as those published by the Synod. This view is partially corroborated by the proliferation of printed sermons in the provincial centers during this period and the bishops' travels to deliver sermons in the periphery. One example was Antonii Zybelin (1730–97), the archbishop of Kazan, who preached in his diocesan center as well as in Simbirsk and Nizhnii Novgorod.[39] Another was the archbishop of Riazan, Simon Lagov, who traveled beyond the cathedral city to Pereiaslavl and Kostroma.[40]

Outside St. Petersburg, Moscow had the richest preaching scene for the lower classes. Platon Levshin inspired people of all ranks to hear his oratory: the multitudes gathering for his homilies required police crowd control, while merchants from Siberia flocked to his sermons when visiting Moscow and spread his fame around the country.[41] According to Fedor Golovkin's memoirs, "people adored [*obozhal*] him but those who were his enemies called him a showman of the altar." Platon's "preached sermons always circulated later in popular quotations."[42] Platon was not the only show in town. The priests of the Archangel and Annunciation Cathedrals preached regularly in the 1770s in accordance with a prearranged schedule.[43] The Assumption Cathedral (which also had a very busy preaching schedule) was home to the metropolitan's Oxford-educated brother Aleksei Levshin, who attracted visitors to hear his novel style of delivery. As the Platon noted in his conversation with Clarke: "The English taught him to declaim in their way: he used to preach his fine flourishing sermons to us Russians. Very fine sermons! But they were all translated from English."[44] Other preachers of the Assumption Cathedral were less popular. The archimandrite of Simonov Monastery, Amvrosii, was relieved of his preaching duties in 1774, due to his "unusual screaming and strange movements" and reading a "badly composed" sermon that lasted over an hour, which bored the audience and led listeners to leave the cathedral before the homily ended. Bishops Samuil of Krutitsy and Gennadii of Suzdal had to interrupt the preacher to end the homily; the archimandrite was later barred from the pulpit permanently.[45]

While the homiletic scene was vibrant in Moscow, the quality and frequency of preaching differed from place to place. The diary of Arsenii Vereshchagin (the archbishop of Iaroslavl and Rostov) contains detailed information about preaching in his diocese between 1786 and 1791. According to the diary, local clergy or seminary students from advanced classes delivered homilies every Sunday at most of Iaroslavl's churches. While seminarians tended to compose their own sermons, local priests would often read the printed homilies of known ecclesiastical authors (such as Platon Levshin). The archbishop did not speak in the cathedral often (preferring others to take turn at preaching), although he almost always preached during visits to rural parishes.[46]

The situation in Tula region was different from Iaroslavl. Andrei Bolotov's memoir from 1790 describes the protopriest Filipp, who served in the small town of Bogoroditsk, Tula region. Filipp, the diary noted, earned his highest clerical title because he was "more educated than his predecessor and was an outstanding [*izriadnyi*] preacher."[47] The nearby village of Ivanovskoe did not have a preacher as good as Filipp, but the archbishop of Tula, Afanasii, visited the village in 1794 and delivered a short discourse.[48] The memoir of

Dmitrii Rostislavov (son of a provincial priest) shows that preaching was important in the town of Kasimov, Riazan region; however, sermons were not delivered every Sunday and the only man educated enough to compose them from scratch was the protopriest Polikarp Kistrovskii, the headmaster of the local school.[49]

PREACHING REASON: THE UTILITY OF GODLINESS

The content of Russia's enlightened sermons reflected their engagement of wider European trends. In this regard, the sermons of the late Elizabethan and early Catherinian eras displayed numerous similarities to Western neoclassical homilies. One example was the preacher's focus on rationality and the utility of faith. Just like the European preachers, Russian bishops believed that Christianity and virtuous living were in harmony with reason and that, in turn, made them useful for society and the individual alike.

One of the earliest heralds of reason from the pulpit was Gedeon Krinovskii, the bishop of Pskov, court preacher since 1753.[50] As a non-Ukrainian, he was one of the first in Petersburg to preach without the "Ukrainian [*khokhliatskii*] accent."[51] Gedeon was also one of the first to rely extensively on the homilies of Elias Meniates and the French Reformed authors.[52] Because he had to compose sermons frequently and speedily, Krinovskii often copied entire portions of foreign sermons into his own.[53]

This "emancipated monk," who owned a walk-in wardrobe the size of a bedroom and wore a wig, hair powder, stockings, diamond-decorated shoes, and locks in his beard, was a celebrity at Elizabeth's court.[54] According to Ivan Snegirev, Gedeon had "the gift of eloquence and a fortunate composure" that made a strong impression on his audience.[55] Platon Levshin noted his skill and popularity. "Gedeon had a special gift of eloquence," he wrote. "He pronounced his words so pleasingly and kindly that all the listeners were beside themselves in suspense, fearing that he would stop talking."[56]

His sermons often argued for the utility of Christian faith. For example, his 1755 "Sermon about the Samaritan Woman" noted humankind's "desire to seek a life of happiness," and advocated faith and virtue as the true sources of human satisfaction.[57] His January 2, 1754, sermon, "Longevity and Any Blessing Given to Man by God for a Life of Virtue," strongly emphasized the utility of virtuous living for the achievement of longevity. Virtue rather than "fate [*fortuna*]" was the main source of an extended lifespan.[58] "If one wants to live long and happily, which is also what God wants, then one needs to always endeavor to do good," he stated.[59] To buttress the idea that "all happiness and longevity follow from a virtuous life," Krinovskii used the examples of Noah, Jonah, Solomon, and others for whom God had extended longevity.[60]

Krinovskii's career ended with his death in October 1763. That same month, Platon Levshin, the Holy Trinity Seminary rector, became the official court preacher and religious preceptor to the heir, the future tsar, Grand Duke Paul Petrovich.[61] Platon was already a popular preacher in Moscow at the time, with strong connections to Gedeon, who was Holy Trinity's archimandrite. He made Platon his "favorite [*liubimets*]," invited him frequently to St. Petersburg for vacation (especially between 1759 and 1763), introduced him to powerful court noblemen like Ivan Shuvalov and Aleksei Razumovskii, and let the young man take lessons in "the art of pronunciation" from Gedeon.[62] Although he was already known at court from visits, Platon's real chance to become a court preacher came in 1763 when Catherine visited Moscow.

On May 19, 1763, Catherine made a pilgrimage to the Trinity-Sergius Monastery and toured its seminary. Platon, the rector, arranged for a stately welcome: rose petals covered the empress's path to the monastery and the seminary students, wearing white robes and holding palm branches, greeted her at the roadside, with the traditional bread and salt reception afterward.[63] Then Platon delivered a sermon, "On the Utility of Godliness." This speech fed into Catherine's vision for reform and Enlightenment. Godliness, he said, benefited "national matters [*obshchenarodnye dela*]" since it promoted "diligence in agriculture, fairness in commerce, and ease in lending credit." In contrast, ungodliness was detrimental as it made one "lazy in plowing . . . deceitful in trade . . . stingy in lending to another."[64]

The sermon impressed the empress: she gave the rector some money and velvet cloth for his robes and then invited him to a dinner with Nikita Panin as well as bishops Gedeon Krinovskii and Dmitrii Sechenov. In Moscow, Panin tested the rector about "whether he was superstitious" and determined that he was not.[65] Two months later, in July 1763, the twenty-five-year-old rector officially received an invitation (from Panin) to preach at court and instruct the nine-year-old heir Grand Duke Paul. Neither Panin nor Catherine were ever disappointed in their choice. Platon (who would become the metropolitan of Moscow within a decade) remained a full-time court preacher until 1780 and then an occasional one until his death in 1812.

His sermons and manner of speaking made a lasting impression at court, as attested by several eyewitness accounts. The English envoy, Lord Cathcart, who observed Platon's sermon during the ground-breaking for the third St. Isaac's Cathedral in 1768, noted that "Father Plato . . . by his gesture and the sound of his voice seemed to be as he is reckoned here, a man of consummate eloquence."[66] Eyewitness I. F. Timkovskii recalled in his memoirs that Platon preached by "inspiring and moving the emotions of the audience." He was also prone to sudden changes of speech.[67] Semen Poroshin (an instructor to Grand Duke Paul Petrovich) also noted the emotional effect of Platon's sermons but was less impressed with their content. "It is better to hear his sermons than to read them," he said.[68] While Poroshin did not find Platon's sermons particularly remarkable, they made Catherine cry on at least two recorded occasions—June 29, 1765, and July 22, 1775. On the latter date, Field Marshal Rumiantsev cried as well.[69] Catherine was perhaps more impressed with Platon's "wonderful rhetorical gift" than anyone else at court.[70] "Father Platon makes us do what he wills," she exclaimed, "if he wants us to cry—we cry, if he wants us to rejoice—we rejoice!"[71]

Platon also was particularly vocal about the rationality of faith during the sermons of Lent, when Catherine II and the court elite tended to be more pious than usual. Platon endeavored to make the demands of faith seem reasonable and profitable considering recent scientific and philosophical advancements. During his sermon for the second week of Lent in 1764, Platon made a scientific case for fasting. While godliness and fasting were salubrious, the preacher observed, sin and passion caused sickness. "Whoever gives oneself to passions, suffers from much illness," he said. "For daily experience shows us how many people suffer from drunkenness, how many various diseases come from fornication, how many paroxysms from unconstrained rage, and weakness from idleness."[72] Fasting, however, had the opposite effect on one's body. Citing the current science, he compared the church's fasting to a medically prescribed diet, arguing that

> doctors recommend a *diet* [*dieta*], that is, abstention from food, as one of the main methods for preventing sickness. No one debates this when doctors prescribe it. Yet many scorn it when the Church prescribes it. They believe doctors but not the Church on the very same matter. For when the Church prescribes fasts, it has in mind objectives that are very similar or identical to those that doctors have in prescribing a diet. But if there is any difference, it is the fact that doctors seek the end of illness while the Church seeks the calming of one's passions. Yet, if the passions are the causes of sickness, then the treatment of sickness ought to begin with the treatment of one's passions.[73]

Thus, medicine and religion, reason and godliness were mutually inclusive when it came to promoting a healthy lifestyle. "Reason triumphs when we do not give in to the passions," argued Platon.[74] This view resonated well with his opinions on natural corporeal needs. He did not view the "carnal inclinations [*plotskie sklonnosti*]" as being evil in themselves; in fact, they were "sinless and harmless" as long as "guided by reason [*razum*]." Fasting constituted an example of the triumph of utilitarian reason over the passions that were destructive and harmful to one's health.[75]

The Lenten sermons also took philosophical turns in redefining true piety. His "Sermon in the Third Week of Lent" of 1767 argued that many listeners wrongly believed that self-denial contradicted the natural law ("the laws of the Creator") that guide humans to seek pleasure or nutrition. They wrongly thought of self-denial as "isolation in the mountains," for example, or just needlessly "burdening oneself." True self-denial, the preacher argued, consisted in being faithful to one's civic obligations and rejecting the "inclinations" that are "contrary to truth, contrary to conscience, and contrary to our own true happiness." While ipso facto this implied that the pursuit of happiness was therefore true self-denial, the preacher did not elaborate further the limits of rejecting obstacles to happiness.[76]

"Father Plato" also combined reason and science with theological speculation to make a strong case for vaccination. This was the central message of his November 22, 1768, sermon, delivered on the day when Catherine and her son Paul Petrovich inoculated themselves against smallpox.[77] This joyous medical occasion at the court induced the preacher to declare November 22 as the day that light triumphed against ignorance. "From this occasion we ought to begin a completely new era," he stated. The triumph of reason, for Platon, was also the triumph of conscience, since the two were one and the same. He explained, "The cause of all miseries of the body and soul is the failure to follow the law of reason and the rule of conscience correctly—this is the indubitable truth, worthy of our humble knowledge. Therefore, there is no illness that does not originate from the corruption of natural law."[78] Reason and rationality fit Platon's conception of true faith perfectly, since reason, he argued, originated from God. Ignorance, conversely, was God's punishment for those who disregarded divine guiding light.[79] Thus, in equating the work of science with the gifts God bestowed on humanity, Platon thanked God's Providence for the "good deed" of vaccination.[80] Much like Protestant preachers in Europe at the time, Platon connected the idea of Providence in his sermons with reason and with the polemic against Deism.[81]

THE PERILS OF SUPERSTITION: AMVROSII PODOBEDOV

Enlightened preachers of the Catherinian era did not only speak about the utility of faith and the rationality of godliness; they also rallied their audiences against superstition. One of the most famous homilies against superstition preached in early Imperial Russia was the 1771 public sermon delivered by hieromonk Amvrosii Podobedov right after the outbreak of the Moscow

Plague Riots. The riots, which raged in the summer of that year, pitted the Muscovite mob—who sought access to churches and icons during the outbreak of the disease—against the archbishop of Moscow, Amvrosii Zertis-Kamenskii, who enacted a quarantine and banned all close veneration of icons (such as kissing), while the plague remained active. He also called on the crowds—who congregated around the Mother of God icon in hopes of a cure—to disperse. In response, the mob murdered him and mutilated his body on September 16, 1771, inside Don Monastery.[82]

The army, headed by Catherine's paramour General Grigorii Orlov, brutally suppressed the riots.[83] Even so, given the Muscovites' attachment to the practice of icon-kissing, the October 1771 sermon was daring. Preaching to the public, Amvrosii condemned the murder of his namesake, Amvrosii Zertis-Kamenskii, and derided the superstitious attachment to the icons in his sermon appropriately titled "On the Negative Effects of Superstition." To build the case for his message, the preacher first defined superstition: "Superstition consists in the adherence to things external, viewing these external things as somehow special for holiness and salvation. The superstitious, when they have a need, abandon God, faith, and law, running toward the sacred places of veneration."[84]

For Podobedov, the Muscovites were guilty of the sin of superstition in two ways. First, they chose to seek supernatural healing when medical quarantine was prescribed to them and second, they practiced idolatry. To highlight the gravity of their first transgression, Amvrosii showed how God favored medical treatment over miraculous cures. The preacher's conception of "enlightenment" dictated that reason and science were fully part of God's plan for human healing. He said, "The superstitious seek healing through a miracle. Yet these poor souls do not realize that God vehemently rejects those prayers that seek healing when we can get deliverance from the means given to us by reason. Why should God perform a miracle where harm can be remedied through the natural order?"[85]

The second sin of superstition was idolatry. Just as the "holy Apostles" were murdered by the people's "mad attachment to pagan idols," so was the archbishop martyred "by this cursed superstition"—attachment to the practice of icon-kissing.[86] Furthermore, he argued that while the Mother of God icon was not an idol in itself, murder for its sake made them idolaters and the icon, an idol! He stated, "Their hearts were attached to the external sacred things by the power of superstition and they sought salvation in these things. Filled with rage, persecution, and threats, they sought his life, a life that was useful to society, and finally, oh horror!, they sacrificed him to their idol, which controlled their hearts and poured out their evil and hateful poison upon him."[87]

This sermon catapulted the hieromonk to fame. Grigorii Orlov judged it to be "extremely audacious," and even called it a "heroic act of civic courage [*podvig grazhdanskogo muzhestva*]." Following the public sermon, he arranged for Amvrosii's physical protection, since the hieromonk needed it.[88] Furthermore, he sent the homily to Catherine, who ordered the Senate to print it immediately in both St. Petersburg and Moscow.[89] It was also promptly translated into German and French, with copies sent out to various Russian embassies abroad.[90] Perhaps the empress and her government wanted to show foreigners that despite riots, there were clergy in Russia who had the courage to die for or promote reform and Enlightenment in the face of threats.

More importantly, Orlov's patronage ensured Amvrosii's swift promotions: within a year he rose from hieromonk to prefect and then rector of the Moscow Slavo-Greco-Latin Academy. In June 1775, he introduced him to the empress personally, by inviting Amvrosii to deliver a sermon on the Kuchuk-Kainarji Peace Treaty. The 1775 sermon made the correct impression: after it, Catherine would move to make him a bishop with the privilege of synodal membership.[91] Later, he would become the president of the Synod, from 1799 to 1808.

The June 1775 sermon (titled "That Godliness Makes the State Truly Happy") marked the birthday of Grand Duchess Nataliia (Paul's first wife); Catherine and Paul Petrovich were in the audience.[92] Interestingly enough, the tone of Amvrosii's first appearance before the empress resembled that of Platon's very first homily in her presence, which may not have been accidental. Like Levshin, the rector advocated the utility of virtuous living and the rationality of Christian faith. "That nation is truly happy," he said, "that fulfills its obligations toward its rulers and its neighbors, being guided by godliness."[93] Love of neighbor and moral concern for the common good of society were the two pillars upon which society functions: the godly cared for "the common good," he stated, while "the wicked can never be trustworthy, diligent, or fervent in anything."[94]

Furthermore, godliness "preserved the innocence of hearts and the purity of morals," which in turn "guided us to the love of mankind and agreement with our neighbors." This very fact, however, made the godly not only the most trustworthy but also the most patriotic subjects of the empire. For Amvrosii, they were "the true sons of our Fatherland, diligent and fervent perpetrators of our vocations, faithful subjects to the governing authority."[95]

This homily greatly pleased Catherine. She awarded the preacher a diamond cross and declared him a candidate for any vacant bishopric.[96] Three years later, Amvrosii used his connections to Count Grigorii Orlov, Grigorii Potemkin (the new paramour), and especially Moscow's "famously handsome gentleman," Police Chief Nikolai Arkharov, to get Catherine to give him the post he wanted: the bishopric of Sevsk and the vicariate of Moscow.[97] Amvrosii was consecrated on July 1778 in the presence of the empress, who gave him "a rich episcopal sacristy, a diamond-covered vestment, and three thousand rubles."[98]

CONCLUSION

The examination of the sermons of Gedeon Krinovskii, Platon Levshin, and Amvrosii Podobedov has demonstrated how much the culture of the religious Enlightenment penetrated not only their theology but also their art of sacred oratory. The content of their sermons fully confirms the fact, underlined in the third chapter, that Russia's religious elites of the later eighteenth century were fully conversant in the culture and worldviews of their European peers. Much like numerous theologians in Western Europe, the Russian bishops sought to reconcile reason and science with faith and piety. They also sought to present the utility of the Christian religion in a rational, well-ordered society without weakening the dogmas that underlined the religion's theological foundations. While their preaching certainly fulfilled a very particular function at the court of Catherine the Great, the proliferation of their printed and manuscript homiletic works was intended to impact all reading audiences in the empire.

8

Spiritual Napoleons

Awakened Bishops and the Bureaucratic Reaction, 1801–1824

Where is the Church?

—ADMIRAL SHISHKOV

18(12) +12+12=1836

    —ARCHIMANDRITE FOTII, calculation of the revolutionary
apocalypse

Around the year 1800, many Europeans were questioning the ideas and the consequences of the Enlightenment. As Napoleonic war clouds shrouded the continent, many people turned away from the empirical reason of the lumières and toward the inward light of the senses, toward sublime essences and mystical spiritualities. Although intellectual apostasies from the Enlightenment emerged in many guises, including romanticism, nationalism, transcendentalism, and conservatism, in the Protestant world, the religious movement that questioned the Enlightenment the most was the Awakening. (I use the term as exclusive of most American Great Awakenings but inclusive of the Second Great Awakening, the Réveil, and Erweckungsbewegung.) Shaking up people's souls and minds from Glasgow to Philadelphia and from Berlin to Cape Town, the Awakening was neither alien nor indifferent to those in St. Petersburg and Moscow. Just as in the West, the mystical literature, introspective secret societies, and awakened pieties spread in the East as well. As Leo Tolstoy's prototypical conversion of Pierre Bezukhov in *War and Peace* demonstrated so well, many Russians, shaken by the visions of Austerlitz and Borodino, were trading their previous enlightened decadence for the life of contemplation, mysticism, and social responsibility.

Russian Orthodox receptivity to the Protestant Awakening ultimately shaped the debates about the direction of church reform and Enlightenment during the first two decades of the nineteenth century. The fact that such a reception was possible was hardly surprising: if Prokopovich and Peter I opened the front gates of the church to Western influence, the reign of Alexander I witnessed the dismantling of the fence altogether, with European religious ideas flowing freely across the continent. Yet these ideas produced two diametrically opposed responses within the church and secular hierarchy of the time. Many of the "gentlemen" bishops of the Catherinian generation welcomed the arrival of the new Protestant literature and spiritual trends with fascination. Paradoxically, however, they did not reject all of the Enlightenment ideas that they had cherished for most of their adult lives, true to their spirit of ecumenical eclecticism and intellectual cosmopolitanism. They were joined by many acolytes in the church and by many secular elites, including, for a time, the chief procurator of the Synod (Aleksandr Golitsyn) and the tsar.

Other clergymen, however, rejected the Protestant Awakening, and turned not only against the religious Enlightenment but also against its associated cultures thriving among the church elites, including material extravagance, freethinking, intellectual eclecticism, and theological heterogeneity, connected to the century-long Russian Orthodox interaction with the West. These clergymen were joined by secular intellectuals who had already established themselves as critics of the Enlightenment, like Admiral A. S. Shishkov. For many of these secular and clerical critics of the Awakening, Russia's entire century of church reform was a deviation from true Orthodoxy, the ideals of which were found in returning to the golden age of early medieval Byzantine spirituality, in rejecting most foreign influence, and in embracing the proto-Slavophile concept of Russia's exclusive path of historical development. The opposition coalesced in the spring of 1824, successfully executing a coup that checked the influence of the awakened and Westernized hierarchy and charted a new course of action that would eventually put many aspects of Protestant and Enlightenment influence in the Russian church into retreat. Many of these elites were "romantic conservatives" (to borrow Alexander Martin's description), who voiced opposition to religious reforms based on their desire to cleanse the Russian church of foreign influence. For some of them, like Shishkov, this turn against Western religious influence was an extension of the broader view that Russian language and culture (including religion) should be free of foreign influence and must instead conform to their ideals of the Russian national essence.[1]

The result of the coalescence of these two opposite theological camps was bitter contestation over the variety of doctrinal orthodoxies of the Enlightenment, the Awakening, and the Bible Society movement (and by extension, over the entire question of Protestant influence); a contestation the likes of which had not been seen in Russia since the 1720s. As in the 1720s, the contestation acquired also a political dimension, although this time the fear of a papal take-over of Russia gave way to a much more tangible threat. Thus, the timing of the opposition's rise in Russia (after 1812) was also important: shrouded in the liberation myth of defeating the physical Napoleon and the Western military invasion, they argued for the ousting of the spiritual Napoleon as well, that is, the Western invasion of the souls and minds of the Russian people. The church was a key institution in this battle, yet Shishkov's rhetorical question, "where is the Church?," implied that the church had lost its way and its authenticity; it needed to be freed from what the opponents of religious Enlightenment and the Awakening deemed were foreign, heterodox, and even revolutionary rela-tionships with the Protestant West. Archimandrite Fotii's revelatory calcula-tions reinforced the urgency of the opposition's task to execute a coup: if the influence of the Enlightenment and Awakening continued unabated, the rev-olutionary apocalypse was guaranteed to subsume Russia by 1836.

The Awakening in the Protestant World

The catalyst for the reaction against reform was the Awakening, a religious movement that by 1820 had managed to captivate millions of souls around Europe and North America. German historians employ the term *Erweckungs-bewegung* (the Awakening movement), but it was known under different names elsewhere, including in Russia as a movement of religious mysticism.[2] The movement indeed had the characteristics of mysticism insofar as it guided its followers toward the renewal of the soul, contemplative practices, millenari-anism, ecstatic experiences, and to memberships in the widely proliferating secret societies. Yet it was also very outward and dynamic, with its charis-matic mass revivals, ambitious social agenda (including abolitionism), promo-tion of scientific discovery, and the chiliastic geopolitics of the Holy Alliance. The Awakening was a fissiparous gathering of diverse forces and experiences that valued the individualistic search for truth while emphasizing that such individual spiritual experiences served a wider rational purpose. One common-ality of the Awakening was that, with some exceptions, such as France and Bavaria, it was primarily a Protestant phenomenon.[3] Another commonality was that the awakeners tended to react against the Enlightenment, as scholarly consensus argues.[4] However, a minority of scholars have assessed the Awaken-ing as harmonious with many of the ideas and goals of the Enlightenment, as seen in the promotion of science, industry, confessional toleration, and the con-struction of rationally planned urban spaces such as Philadelphia and Korntal.[5]

In continental Europe, the Awakening saw a modest resurgence of interest in medieval esoteric spirituality, and a major revival of Pietism, reborn as late

Pietism or Neupietismus. In Southern Germany, the followers of "neo-Pietism" or late Pietism formed vigorous devotional communities led by charismatic and chiliastic preachers such as Johann Albrecht Bengel (1687–1752), Philipp Matthäus Hahn (1739–90), Michael Hahn (1758–1819), and Friedrich Christoph Oetinger (1702–82).[6] The growth of new piety also spread to France, where the preachers of the Réveil, such as Adolphe Monod (1802–56) and Frédéric Monod (1794–1863) awakened the populace through preaching and French-language publications of the Paris Bible Society (founded in 1818).[7] In Geneva in 1813, the Russian-born Pietist Baroness Juliana von Krüdener (1764–1824) took to the streets, preaching penance and direct revelation.[8]

Revival preaching in Europe had plenty of kindred souls across both the Channel and the Atlantic: John Wesley (1703–91), Jonathan Edwards (1703–58), and Charles Finney (1792–1875), among many others, emerged as the generals of the Awakenings. As on the continent, the spiritual renewal was closely intertwined with the popularization of the printed Word, as seen in the rise of the British and Foreign Bible Society (1804) and the Religious Tract Society (1799).[9]

While on the continent some revivalists strived to remain within the boundaries of "confessional Lutheranism," others ventured beyond the boundaries of doctrinal orthodoxy in pursuit of new spiritual revelations.[10] Thus, in the late eighteenth century, Emmanuel Swedenborg explored the three layers of heaven, traveled to Mars and other planets (where he found intelligent life!), and received new revelation, a Third Testament.[11] Catholic mystic Karl von Eckhartshausen (1752–1803) used spiritual ecstasy and special herbs to induce apparitions, then used mirrors and optical instruments to study them.[12] In North America and Germany, radical late Pietists and even less radical ones embraced new revelations of chastity that led some of them to contract platonic spiritual marriage (*geistliche Ehe*) between believers and others to form celibate late Pietist "monasteries" and "cloisters."[13]

Chiliasm, greatly inflamed by the turbulence of the French Revolution and Napoleon, was an important feature of this movement. Among the late Pietists, millenarianism predated the revolution—Bengel and Oetinger, for example. They calculated 1836 as the year of Second Coming of Christ, the relocation of the church to Palestine, the collapse of the papacy, and the fulfillment of the medieval prophecy of Joachim de Fiore (d. 1202) about the coming millennium of Christ's kingdom on earth.[14] Johann Heinrich Jung-Stilling (1740–1817)—one of the main figures in the German Awakening, who served as a spiritual advisor to the duke of Baden—eagerly adopted the dating of 1836: the doom and gloom of the revolution and Napoleonic Wars reinforced the relevance of the Pietist chiliastic calculations for him.[15] As the revolutionaries marched from the West, Jung-Stilling's sentimental *Heimweh* (1794) promised mystical salvation from the East.[16]

The Awakening also manifested itself in the dynamism of social progress and what Nathan Hatch called the "democratization" of the public sphere.[17] The awakeners often embraced abolitionism and advocacy for the improvement of the working class (as seen in the Quaker Lancaster School movement in England).[18] Wesleyanism promoted the growth of Christian utopian socialism and the British labor movement.[19] In Germany, awakeners inspired the rise of a "national spirit," a term originally coined by Oetinger, which was further developed in the writings of Georg Wilhelm Friedrich Hegel and Friedrich Wilhelm Joseph Schelling.[20] Romanticism and mysticism had many connections to each other and to the progression of German nationalism: Johann Gottfried Herder was under the influence of German mystics (such as Jakob Boehme and Franz Xaver von Baader) and esoteric spirituality in general; he was also a classmate of both Johann Wolfgang von Goethe and Jung-Stilling.[21]

THE AWAKENING IN RUSSIA

The influence of the Awakening on Russian secular elites has received thorough attention in Imperial Russian historiography and in a more recent monograph by Alexander Martin. This chapter will complement what we already know about the Awakening among the laity with a further analysis of the role of church elites. Much like Western Europe, Russia too experienced a dynamic spiritual movement that emphasized mystical renewal and revival, promoted biblical literacy, and saw a growth of secret societies. One of the reasons why Orthodox Russians were open to the Awakening was because of the eighteenth-century experience of engaging Western religious ideas. Another reason was the non-sectarian nature of the movement, which, as Martin noted, manifested itself "as a spiritual attitude rather than a formal church, [because] it was compatible with a membership in the Orthodox Church and required no formal conversion."[22]

The mysticism of the Russian Awakening had both foreign connections and domestic followers. For example, in 1819 and 1820, Ignaz Lindl and Johannes Gossner—former priests from Bavaria who preached what Chistovich described as "Mystical Protestantism"—arrived in St. Petersburg, sometimes attracting thousands of Petersburgers on the weekdays as well as Sundays.[23] Various members of high society were often in attendance, including Dmitrii Runich, Mikhail Magnitskii, and nobleman Karl A. Lieven, the high officials of the Ministry of Education. Vasilii Popov (one of the directors of the Ministry of Education and former tutor of Pushkin) translated Lindl's and Gossner's sermons into Russian.[24]

In addition to foreign preachers, domestic awakeners also spread spiritual renewal in the capital. Thus, Ekaterina Tatarinova, a friend of Empress Elizabeth Alekseevna (Alexander's wife) held revivalist conventicles at her residence in the imperial St. Michael's Castle (the former residence of Tsar Paul I), where in 1817 she founded "the Brotherhood of Christ."[25] The Brotherhood combined prayer meetings with what one eyewitness called "hypnotic trance and ecstasy," which were attended by such high-level guests as Aleksandr Golitsyn, Chamberlain Rodion Koshelev, General Evgenii Golovin, Elizabeth Alekseevna, and Vasilii Popov. The tsar also attended one of the meetings.[26] Eyewitness Filip Vigel' (1786–1856) described "supreme priestess" Tatarinova as chairing the meetings, where "women began to whirl, while men sang, beating themselves on the knees . . . in a stupor; in ecstasy both began to imagine things around them."[27] Although such behavior was similar to the ecstatic prayer meetings (known as *radeniia*) of the Russian Khlysty sect, Vigel' called them "a type of Quakers, who are known in England as Shakers," which is not surprising given some objective similarities between the two and the Orthodox Church's historical association of the Khlysty with the Quakers.[28]

One of the most ardent devotees of the Awakening was Aleksandr N. Golitsyn, a childhood friend and chamberlain of the tsar who came to occupy several of the most important positions at court, including the chief procurator of the Holy Synod. Golitsyn's spirituality involved regular Bible reading (often guided by Courtmaster Koshelev) as well as more esoteric practices such as self-flagellation and sleeping on a wooden bench.[29] The high point of his spiritual journey was 1812, when Golitsyn built a chapel inside his Petersburg home. On October 1, 1812, Archimandrite Filaret Drozdov (the future canonized metropolitan of Moscow) consecrated it and began preaching there. Golitsyn marked (in Pietist phraseology) this date as "the day of his spiritual rebirth."[30]

Golitsyn's conversion and the events of 1812 also influenced Alexander I. "The fire of Moscow enlightened my soul," he recalled. Encouraged by Golitsyn and Koshelev, Alexander began reading the Bible every day.[31] He read the Bible in French, not Slavonic, using the version of imprisoned Jansenist Louis-Isaac Lemaistre de Sacy (1613–84), which was widely published in Protestant Europe.[32] The exact date of his embrace of new spirituality is disputed, but it is generally accepted that the surrender of Moscow in the late autumn of 1812 induced the emperor's mode of pensive reflection and chiliastic cogitation, aided by prayers with Golitsyn and Filaret.[33]

Following his spiritual rebirth, Alexander would eventually speak the coded language of the Pietist and the awakened. He "devoured" the Bible, recalling how he relied on "the Inward Teacher [the Holy Spirit]" to "understand what I read therein." He also obtained an assurance of salvation through having "the peace of God." He proclaimed, "I believe that my sins are pardoned."[34] He also met Jung-Stilling in Baden in 1814; the mystic saw in him the fulfillment of his own prophecies of salvation from the East and viewed "Russia as the last land of hope."[35] The tsar not only met but also "married" him. In July 1814, with "tears of joy," he entered a "mystical marriage [*mariage mystique*]" with Jung-Stilling and Roxandre Stourdza, also known as "*lien d'amour et de charité*," a version of the Pietist practice of *Geistliche Ehe* (spiritual marriage), popular at the time.[36]

His foreign policy reflected his spirituality as he saw awakened religion not only as a personal spiritual path but also a basis for the new post-Napoleonic Christian order in Europe. In his correspondence with European monarchs, he employed the phraseology of awakened ecumenism, referring to his addressees as "my brother" or "Your Christian Majesty." His alliance agreements with Baden (1813), Denmark (1814), and Austria (1814) invoked the formulae of Christian unity and "the Holy Trinity."[37] Likewise, the final version of the Holy Alliance signed by Alexander also invoked the name of "the very Holy and indivisible Trinity," with Trinity underlined by hand in the original document.[38]

SECRET SOCIETIES AND THE RUSSIAN CHURCH

How did the enlightened Orthodox hierarchy respond to the growing upsurge of this new spirituality? While the Awakening had its critics among the clergy, many bishops, archimandrites, and priests freely interacted with this Western-influenced religiosity in three important areas: secret societies (in which some clergy participated), the growth of mysticism and mystical theology (to which many of the clergy contributed, including Filaret), and the activities of the Bible Society (which many of the clergy supported).[39]

The phenomenon of clerical involvement with secret societies was not new to post-Napoleonic Russia. In Catherinian Moscow, church hierarchs often valued the philanthropic and ethical appeal of Freemasonry, insofar as they saw its members to be committed to the public good. One of the early clerical supporters of these societies was Metropolitan Platon, who associated with Nikolai I. Novikov of Moscow's Rosicrucian-rite Masonic lodge. In Platon's correct assessment, the circle's members were not secular Deists but harmless mystics who were otherwise faithfully Orthodox in their creedal allegiance.[40]

Nikolai Novikov, Ivan Lopukhin, and other elite members of the lodge founded the Society of Learned Fellows (Druzheskoe uchenoe obshchestvo) in 1779 with the approval of Metropolitan Platon and the Moscow Synodal Bureau, which, in fact, preceded official permission from St. Petersburg.[41] This group engaged in public charity, purchased books for provincial theological students, and even sponsored those Moscow seminarians wishing to take university classes (including many of Platon's pupils). Many of those students became clergy and continued to work with Novikov's circle. The society also printed the works of the clergymen of Platon's circle such as Simon Lagov, Arsenii Vereshchagin, Amvrosii Serebrennikov, Ieronim of Vladimir, Apollos Baibakov, Antonii Znamenskii, and finally, of Platon himself.[42] Platon's cooperation with the lodge members in enabling the work of the Learned Fellows was so dynamic that bishop of Calcutta Reginald Heber (d. 1826) mistakenly claimed that the metropolitan formed "at Moscow a society called the Christian free-masons, on a very wide and extended plan, by which all sects of Christians were allowed to become members."[43]

Such collaboration also had its strong critics. While some priests in Moscow called the Freemasons' cooperation with the church "enlightenment," others viewed it as "perversion" spread by "false prophets."[44] Petr Alekseev, Moscow's influential protopriest and a close friend of Catherine's father-confessor Ivan Panfilov, denounced the metropolitan in his letters to St. Petersburg in 1785.[45] In Alekseev's opinion, Platon was a "patron and secret enabler of the Moscow freethinkers" who used Novikov's printing press to bring "temptation to weak minds."[46] Platon allowed some sixty or so Moscow seminarians to study under Novikov's sponsorship, leading to some dangerous outcomes, as these clergymen "spread the teaching of the Martinists [Rosicrucians] across Russia."[47]

The subsequent downfall and arrest of Novikov (who along with Radishchev became too radical and revolutionary for the government) damaged Platon's hitherto warm relations with the court. By 1785 Catherine began to conflate Martinism with French libertinism and to encourage Petr Alekseev's surveillance of the metropolitan.[48] Her December 23, 1785, decree ordered searches and investigations of Masonic activities in Moscow that implicated the bishop.[49] Platon, however, refused to capitulate and spoke in Novikov's defense. In his appraisal of the rebel intellectual, the bishop stated, "I must declare in accordance to my calling and my conscience, that I wish and pray to All-Merciful God that not only in my flock, but in the entire world, there were more Christians like Novikov."[50]

It was not only Metropolitan Platon (and his acolytes) who seemed supportive of the Rosicrucian lodges' commitment to charity and education. In the later, Alexandrine era, numerous clergy in the capitals be-came involved with the secret societies. In St. Petersburg, Aleksandr Labzin's lodge, the Dying Sphinx (1800–22), attracted the future leading member of the Synod, Filaret Drozdov, who was listed as no. 36 in the lodge's membership roll.[51] How often Filaret attended the lodge's meetings, if at all, is any-one's guess. Although Filaret's enemy Archimandrite Fotii clearly exaggerated the scope of secret societies' influence in the church, he claimed that the entire Holy Synod of "honored [*chtit*]" Labzin's conventicle.[52] As membership rolls attest, there were others who belonged to the same lodge as Filaret at some point during its existence: Hieromonk Feofil Finikov of the First Cadet Corps, Father Aleksei Speranskii of the Pokrov Church and Father Iov Korotskii of the Navy Corps.[53]

Other prominent Freemasons included Metropolitan Mikhail Desnitskii, Synod member Father V. I. Kutnevich (1787–1865), archimandrite and rector of the Moscow Slavo-Greco-Latin Academy Germogen Speranskii (1778–1845), and Archimandrite Feoktist Orlovskii (d. 1829).[54] Father Fedor Golubinskii (1797–1854), future professor at the Moscow Academy, joined Moscow's Rosicrucians together with his son D. F. Golubinskii.[55] Another well-known Muscovite Mason was Father Semen Sokolov, who was also associated with the Moscow Academy. Poet Nikolai Sushkov, one of Sokolov's parishioners, called his priest a "mystic and Martinist," while Metropolitan Filaret recommended him as an "enlightened and morally upright" priest.[56] Although clerical involvement in secret societies may come as a surprise to some readers, Rosicrucian lodges in Russia tended to have a distinctly pious quality. As Nikolai Sushkov explained, this lodge at the time was a "society of true Christians, who spread enlightenment, promoted good morals and sacrificed what they had for the good of their neighbor."[57] At times the clergy's role in the lodges accentuated that quality and the public purpose of the organization. For example, Feoktist Orlovskii's position in the Neptune Lodge in 1817 was described as "trustee [*popechitel'*] for the poor."[58]

THE CHURCH, THE AWAKENING, AND MYSTICISM

As previous chapters have demonstrated, Pietism was no stranger to Russia, with Feofan Prokopovich cultivating strong connections to Halle in the early part of the century. The spiritual writings of Johann Arndt and Jakob Spener were widespread in Russian and Ukrainian seminaries, the homes of the nobility, monasteries, and episcopal libraries throughout the eighteenth century.[59] For example, there were four separate editions of the Russian translation of Johann Arndt's *True Christianity*, published in 1735, 1784, 1790, and 1800.[60] Two of them came directly off the presses of the associates of Lopukhin and Novikov.[61]

The works of another Pietist favorite, Johann Gerhard, also circulated widely in Moscow and were connected to the Metropolitan Platon's circle. Johann Gerhard's 1606 *Meditationes sacrae* was translated and published in Moscow several times between 1783 and 1800.[62] One of these was the 1795 translation by Moscow Academy's Iakov Romanovskii, published as *Glas trubnyi* (The voice of the trumpet), with a dedication to Bishop Serapion, Platon's vicar-bishop.[63] Another translation of the same work but under a different title, *Myslennyi vertograd* (The Orchard of Contemplation), was dedicated to Amvrosii Podobedov

(Platon's well-known disciple and at the time bishop of Krutitsy), and contained the translator's introduction attesting to the doctrinal and devotional benefit of the work.[64] "Having examined this work in accordance to the Holy Fathers," the introduction stated, "we judged it to be the wellspring of the most precious treasures, which every pious Christian can use for his salvation."[65]

Platon Levshin's circle of Moscow clergymen also spread non-Pietist mystical literature. Thus, Ivan Mikhailov Kandorskii translated a mystical work of "the glorious [James] Hervey"—an Anglican—titled *Meditations and Contemplations* (1747), which Kandorskii dedicated to Metropolitan Platon, "the Great Christian Philosopher."[66] James Hervey (1717–58) was the bishop of Oxford; he developed a well-recognized talent for meditating on natural and man-made objects, such as monuments or flower gardens.[67] In addition to rendering Hervey's spiritual reflections in Russian, Kandorskii also translated his theological view of redemption as an imputation of Christ's righteousness to believers.[68]

Mystical literature enjoyed popularity among some clergy in the early nineteenth century as well. Metropolitans Amvrosii and Platon recommended Labzin's *Messenger of Zion* (including the English Quaker literature published in it), while the St. Petersburg Theological Academy subscribed to it.[69] The latter's seminarians found Jung-Stilling and Eckartshausen in the school's library and read them freely.[70]

In Moscow, Father Fedor Golubinskii became fascinated with the ideas of German Catholic theosophist Franz Baader and medieval mystic Thomas à Kempis, and then began to study the mystical aspects of the Talmud.[71] Father Semen Sokolov, who in the words of his parishioner Sushkov was "a deeply spiritual mystic," studied Jakob Boehme, Louis Claude de Saint-Martin, and the Quaker George Fox.[72] Another Muscovite cleric, Archimandrite Germogen Speranskii, was (like many elite clergy of the time) fluent in French; he used this knowledge to read mystical literature. He experienced a mystical conversion in 1812 and then again in 1818: he preached and awaited the chiliastic "heavenly Jerusalem" in Moscow, nearly starved himself to death by fasting, and temporarily lost his voice in singing and "religious exaltation."[73]

Pietism and Western mysticism also affected the contemplative and introspective religious journeys of Russia's monastics. The best early example of Protestant devotional influence on Russia's "monastic revival" (a term coined by Igor Smolitsch) was St. Tikhon of Zadonsk (1724–83), whose piety inspired Dostoevsky to create the character of Father Zosima in *Brothers Karamazov*.[74] Although he was seen as a quintessentially Russian *starets* (elder), Tikhon's writings on piety and devotion were anything but purely quintessentially Russian. His most popular works, *On True Christianity* (*O istinnom khristianstve*) and *The Spiritual Treasure* (*Dukhovnoe sokrovishche*), borrowed heavily from

Johann Arndt's opus *On True Christianity*. He also employed the Pietist theological language of total depravity, the narrow way, justification, and especially,
the regeneration (rebirth or *Wiedergeburt*) that resonated with the enlightened
monastic calling.[75] At the same time, Tikhon's other treatise, *The Occasion and
Spiritual Meditation Thereupon* (*Sluchai i dukhovnoe ot nego razmyshlenie*), borrowed from and imitated the contemplative works of Joseph Hall, the bishop
of Exeter (1574–1656), who developed the art of meditating on external objects.[76]

The Pietist influence on St. Tikhon was an important contributor to the revival of Russian monastic spirituality, but he was by no means the only example.
At the end of the eighteenth century, the monks and nuns of the Kirillo-
Beloozero Monastery in the Vologda region received inspiration from various
examples of Western devotional literature. Their library collection featured the
works of Arndt, Gerhardt, Adolf Hoffman, and John Bunyan.[77] (John Bunyan's
works were popular in Russia—editions of his *Pilgrim's Progress* appeared in
1782 and 1787.[78]) The meditations of Joseph Hall also found their way to the
library of the Vologda monastics, specifically the 1784 Russian translation of
Hall's *The Way of Enoch, or, A Treatise on Walking with God*.[79] The monastery's
library contained a complete version of this work, including the controversial
introduction that, according to the 1787 decree, was supposed to be "torn
[*vyrvano*]" from the book.[80] Western mystical influence was not limited to
Protestantism—in the late eighteenth century, the works of the Athonite mystics Makarios Notaras and Nikodemos the Hagiorite made an impact on East
Slavic monasticism. Makarios and Nikodemos composed works on frequent
communion and spiritual warfare influenced by such notable Catholics as St.
Ignatius of Loyola, Lorenzo Scupoli, Paolo Segneri, and Miguel de Molinos.[81]
Notaras's compilation of medieval Byzantine meditative texts, the *Philokalia of
the Holy Neptic Fathers* (Venice, 1782), became by far the most popular Athonite
work at the time, and was translated in 1793 and popularized in Russia by Paisii
Velichkovskii (1722–94).[82]

THE AWAKENING THEOLOGY OF
METROPOLITAN FILARET

The key ecclesiastical leader during the period of the Awakening's influence in
Russia was St. Filaret, then Metropolitan Filaret Drozdov (see figure 9). Hailing from humble origins in Kolomna, Filaret excelled in his theological studies
under Platon Levshin, receiving the latter's patronage as well as the support of
Amvrosii Podobedov in the important early stages of his career as the archimandrite and rector of St. Petersburg Theological Academy (from 1811 and
1812, respectively), and then as bishop of Revel (1817), Tver (1819), and Moscow (1821). He was deeply involved in the Awakening in Russia: as the person

Figure 9. Metropolitan Filaret Drozdov of Moscow, early nineteenth century. From Nikolai Shil'der, *Imperator Aleksandr Pervyi, ego zhizn' i tsarstvovanie*, vol. 4 (St. Petersburg, 1898). Courtesy of Widener Library, Harvard University.

who "converted" Golitsyn to the right path, as a one-time member of Labzin's secret society, and as one of the leaders of the Bible Society.

Filaret's mysticism was reflection both of the fashion of the day (in the early years, he read Eckartshausen and Swedenborg, both popular with many members of the Holy Synod) and of the development of his own mystical theology, which appeared in his sermons.[83] His October 1, 1812, homily delivered on the opening of Golitsyn's house church noted the beauty of the chief procurator's chapel but emphasized the greater importance of the "invisible temple" and the "inner temple" that must be consecrated in the hearts of the renewed. In his Christmas 1812 sermon, he explained the importance of experiencing a spiritual "rebirth [*vozrozhdenie*]."[84] The Pietist keyword of rebirth (*Wiedergeburt*) and renewal are notable in this sermon; however, there were also mystical references. The preacher spoke of the invisible "mystical gates" of the soul and the cleansing of the "inner body" by the Spirit (as opposed to the external body that is cleansed by water), and he reflected on accepting revelation from esoteric non-Orthodox sources (a reference to Jung-Stilling?) that come from "enlightened spirits who, similar to transparent objects, receive and transmit light but do not feel that light themselves."[85] Filaret also spoke of the "inner Kingdom," the "inner church," and "the mystery of your own personal Bethlehem," seeing mystical meanings in familiar biblical story lines.[86]

His close relationship with Golitsyn and with the culture of the Awakening in the capital had strong critics. Fotii said the following about Filaret:

> He was the chief culprit of all disruption during the days of Prince Golitsyn. He was a friend and ally of Koshelev and Labzin, as well as of all overt and covert enemies of the faith and church. No one could stop his audacity, for he was well-connected to the powers that be . . . Filaret's influence extended to all in positions of authority, nobility and others followed his will. . . . Wherever I attempted to destroy a conventicle of wickedness [*sborishche zlochestiia*], I found Filaret there.[87]

As was the fashion during the Awakening, Filaret's views were also very ecumenical. In his 1815 work, *Conversations between a Doubter and a Believer about the Orthodoxy of the Greco-Russian Church*, Filaret addressed the question of the exclusivity of the Eastern Orthodox Church in relation to other confessions and to Roman Catholicism in particular.[88] In this work, Filaret argued that anyone believing in the Nicene Creed, the Trinity, and the Incarnation was a Christian and a member of the mystical Church, "since all Christian Churches accept the Eastern Creed as the truth."[89] In a very ecumenical fashion, Filaret referred to "Churches [*Tserkvi*]," not "the Church" (with the capital *Ts*), and inserted the following conversation on the specific issue of difference between the Roman and Eastern communions:[90]

> DOUBTER: According to this criterion, both the Eastern and Western Church are from God.
>
> BELIEVER: Yes, because both confess Jesus Christ, incarnate, and have the same common spirit in this, that is from God.

DOUBTER: But aren't the two churches in disagreement with each other?

BELIEVER: Yes, they are, because each of them has its own special [*osobennyi*] spirit or special relationship to God's Spirit.

DOUBTER: Well, I need to examine this relationship. Which Church's spirit is more faithful to the Spirit of God?

BELIEVER: Then examine where you stand. . . . There, where the spirit of two great Churches meets the Spirit of God. Have you reached the altitude [*vysota*] to stand there and discern it?[91]

Filaret's sublime thoughts on the inclusivity and compatibility of Christian confessions were not limited to Catholicism. According to his close friend, Nikolai Sushkov, Filaret held the view that "everyone baptized in the name of Holy Trinity is a Christian, no matter what denomination," until the last days of his life.[92] In one of the conversations Sushkov witnessed, Filaret discussed his opinion on Protestants with a local priest:

This priest called Protestantism a heresy. "Who told you that it is a heresy?" asked Filaret. "Well, then, it is not a heresy," said the priest. "Who told you, that it is not a heresy?" responded the Metropolitan, "only an Ecumenical Council can resolve the question whether Protestantism is a heresy or not."[93]

Given Filaret's published assertions that to be ecumenical a council must include the Western Christianity and that only seven Ecumenical Councils had been truly Orthodox, it was clear that the question of Protestant hetero-doxy was not going to be resolved soon. Meanwhile, Christians must discern the fact that the "body of Christ" has "internal" and "external components [*sostav*]" and that the external Orthodox Church is only a visible part of the body that spans the entirety of "the invisible Church."[94]

In addition to his ecumenical views, Filaret's political ideas were also a sub-ject of controversy. Unlike Platon Levshin, whose thoughts about the advan-tages of constitutional government were recorded (and discussed in chapter 7), Filaret did not talk politics with his interlocutors. Although Imperial Russian and Soviet historiography tended to view him as a conservative monarchist, many observers at the time called him a "theological Jacobin" and compared him to Giuseppe Mazzini's revolutionary Carbonari.[95] He was probably a cau-tious political liberal in his early years who matured later into a conservative monarchist. One interesting feature of his early relationship with liberalism was his involvement in the Quaker Lancaster Schools movement in Russia. These elementary schools, opened in 1819 with the aid of British specialists, used a new pedagogical method of accelerated learning using tables and charts for easier comprehension and memorization of various subjects. Until the 1827 imperial closure of all the Lancaster schools, some 213 schools opened all over Russia.[96]

Filaret's contribution to this movement was the composition of a scriptural reading table that adapted the Quaker methodology of popular Bible study.[97] The Quaker connection, however, was not the reason why the Lancaster School movement became controversial. Rather, the controversy involved the political ramifications of spreading literacy among ordinary peasants and soldiers. There were Lancaster Schools not only in the elite Palace Guard Corps and Pavlovskii Regiment in St. Petersburg but also in the more ordinary artillery and infantry regiments located in Kishinev, Gomel, and Smolensk. The teachers of these schools included intellectuals of the day such as Nikolai I. Grech; Vasilii N. Karazin, the founder of Kharkov University; and Decembrist Nikolai N. Raevskii.[98] In addition to literacy, soldiers studied such terms as "equality [ravenstvo]," konstitutsiia, freedom from serfdom, and in the case of one school, the soldiers even read George Washington and Mirabeau. The 1820 Semenovskii and Preobrazhenskii Regiments Mutiny, which proclaimed liberation from serfdom and the "sovereign tyrant," had various connections to the curricula of these schools.[99]

Although Filaret did not teach the soldiers about constitutions, his work in the schools movement elicited respect from some of the members of the Decembrist Revolt. G. S. Baten'kov, for example, sought to include him in the revolutionary Provisional Government as he considered him to be "a very respected and honorable man."[100] The liberals' respect for Filaret was also confirmed in the memoirs of Russian socialist revolutionary Aleksandr Herzen. He wrote (in reference to the early years of Nicholas's reign) that "Filaret knew how to cleverly humiliate the temporal powers; his sermons showed that undefined Christian socialism seen in [Jean-Baptiste] Lacordaire and other progressive Catholics. From his episcopal pulpit, Filaret preached that the law should never allow one man to become an instrument of another, that only exchange of services between men is permitted. He used to say this in a country where half of the population were slaves."[101]

As an example of his (relatively) progressive preaching, Herzen recalled Filaret's work in the convicts' transit center on Sparrow Hills in Moscow, where he preached repentance and spiritual renewal to those who were about to be sent to Siberia. In commenting on the story of the crucified Christ and the thief on the cross, he comforted them with the idea that "a new life" awaited them in heaven, while "the greater criminals," found among the officials who condemned them, would surely be doomed to eternal damnation.[102] Much like among the Quakers or the Wesleyans in the West, the message of religious Awakening also had strong social implications for Filaret.

THE BIBLE SOCIETY MOVEMENT:
THE RUSSIAN CONTEXT

The dramatic thirteen years of the existence of the Russian Bible Society (1813–26) were the high point of the Awakening's influence in Russia. The appraisal of this society's contribution to the church was and still is a much-discussed subject. Numerous studies and monographs have traced the rise and fall of Russian Bible Society, although few of them have been as exhaustive as those by Aleksandr Pypin and Ilarion Chistovich, and in the English-language scholarship by Stephen Batalden. This section of the chapter will not retrace the roads already traveled but will highlight the context of the origins the Russian Bible Society that remain underexplored in the existing works. As Batalden had clearly elucidated, four factors were essential in the formation of this new institution. One was the emergence of the new religious culture of the Awakening; another, "Russian Orthodox support for the new piety"; followed by court patronage; and fourth, the participation and influence of British Bible Society missionaries in Russia.[103]

One additional aspect of the origins of the society merits special consideration: the context of the historical development of Orthodox biblical philology, exegesis, and hermeneutics. The Bible Society movement, having arrived on the shores of St. Petersburg in the early nineteenth century, was not alien to the Russian church's theological culture, which for decades had emphasized the need for the revision and new translation of biblical texts, the need for the philological and critical-textual study of the Scriptures, and an understanding that the vernacularization of the sacred text would benefit the laity. Nor was this culture out of touch with decades of early Enlightenment and Enlightenment influence in the Russian church's efforts to revise and translate the Holy Writ, especially during the reign of Empress Elizabeth.

The idea that the Bible needed both revision and vernacular translation was hardly new to the reformed Orthodox Church. In the 1730s, Feofan Prokopovich had advocated the revision of the seventeenth-century Slavonic Bible in accordance with the standards of Protestant philology, yet he also regarded the language of the Bible as in need of vernacularization.[104] His August 1736 instruction stated that "the old grammar of the Slavonic language is very coarse [gruboe] . . . the words of the language have become archaic, the Hellenisms found in it are contrary to the nature of Slavic languages."[105]

As chapter 4 demonstrated, the revision of the Elizabethan Bible by Halle-educated bishops reflected the hierarchy's concern for textual improvement of the Holy Writ—primarily through revising and retranslating the text from the original Greek, Hebrew, and Aramaic but also through grammatical corrections in the Slavonic. The high regard for Protestant exegetical studies was hardly limited to Elizabeth's reign. When Bishop Damaskin and his Orthodox seminarians studied in Göttingen in 1765–72, they paid special attention to the famous philologist J. D. Michaelis.[106] Michaelis, in turn, praised their diligence in studying the Book of Isaiah and St. Paul's Epistle to the Romans as well as in "numerous biblical literature courses," in Michaelis's words.[107] The seminarians of the Catherinian era were quite enthusiastic about new scholarly approaches to learning about the Bible as "literature." When Filaret was a seminarian in Moscow, around 1800, his study of biblical texts was guided by the Pietist hermeneutics of Johann Jacob Rambach and the Dutch Reformed historicist exegetics of Campegius Vitringa—as chapter 6 has illustrated, Protestant philologists such as these were popular in other Orthodox seminaries as well.[108]

The Russian Orthodox Church not only adopted the Protestant model of biblical textual research but also promoted a similar hermeneutical vernacularization of Scripture that eventually paved the way for the popularity of the Bible Society. Catherinian hierarchs had embraced the idea of making Holy Scripture accessible to the laity long before the Bible Society movement took hold. Thus, in the 1770s and 1780s, Platon Levshin established daily Bible readings in the Moscow parishes and the seminary. Vernacular explication of texts was a regular feature of these readings and attracted many of the lower classes, even though as Maksim Mikhailov has noted, Church Slavonic was hardly a foreign tongue for Muscovites.[109] Platon's colleagues and disciples continued to promote the vernacularization of scriptural readings. Like Platon, the metropolitan of Novgorod and St. Petersburg, Gavriil, also established ecclesiastical schools throughout the diocese with an emphasis on the teaching and study of the Bible to the laity.[110] In 1786 Afanasii, the rector of Moscow Academy, began public readings of the Old Testament, dispensing with Slavonic text altogether and using his own original translations from the Hebrew and the Septuagint. While the rector initiated the public readings, the seminarians in Moscow were instructed to interpret the Bible and explain the unclear passages to the public "naturally, in the [modern Russian] language."[111]

To do so, the clergy did not need to know Hebrew or have much seminary education; they could rely on any of the handbooks for interpreting Scripture that began to proliferate in the late eighteenth century. As Barbara Skinner has rightly noted, the "scriptural 'Reformation'" in Russia was a product of the ever-growing activity of the printing press that kept fueling an appetite for reading among the devout.[112] One popular work was Amvrosii Podobedov's adaptation of the works of Wittenberg theologian Karl Gottlob Hoffmann (1703–70), titled *A Brief Guide to the Reading of the Old and New Testaments*.

Platon Levshin adopted the *Guide* in his public instruction; it then became a handbook, reprinted numerous times in Moscow and Kiev, and used by the priests to explain Scripture to the laity.[113] Archbishop Feoktist Mochul'skii authored similar works, such as his 1799 *Attempt at a Hermeneutic Explanation* or his 1809 *Abridged Rules for the Reading of Holy Scripture*.[114] Metropolitan Mikhail Desnitskii followed the same spirit when he published his *Explanation of the Fiftieth Psalm* in 1798.[115] So did Archbishop Mefodii Smirnov (1761–1815), whose translation of the Epistle to Romans was printed in 1794 and later formed part of the official synodal Russian Bible.[116] Thus, some two decades before the establishment of the Bible Society, the church was already promoting and valuing the translation and explication of biblical texts in the vernacular.[117]

In fact, the vernacular approach to the Bible became an important hallmark of Eastern Orthodoxy. When in 1812, Tsarina Elizabeth Alekseevna requested the Synod's opinion on the difference between the Orthodox and Catholic churches, three bishops, Mefodii Smirnov, Feofilakt Rusanov, and Filaret Drozdov, offered their responses.[118] Amid the litany of the usual political and creedal statements about the Filioque and the powers of the pope were also the opinions of Filaret and Feofilakt stating that believers' reading and interpretation of the Bible in their mother tongue constituted one of the chief differences between the two churches. Furthermore, Feofilakt's opinions (labeled by Golitsyn as Protestant) went even further. The bishop argued that the Bible was "the only pure and satisfactory basis for knowledge of the faith" and that the Latin Vulgate and Catholic policy discouraged lay Bible reading, thereby impeding laypeople's salvation. The Orthodox Church, by contrast, affirmed the right of any nation to have the Holy Writ available in their language.[119]

Hermeneutical vernacularization was in many ways a continuation of the Enlightenment. First, it was part of the much broader movement to expand the social base upon which the culture rested (that is, beyond the elites), as seen in the Catherinian and Alexandrine reforms and the reconstruction of physical space highlighted in Alexander Martin's *Enlightened Metropolis*.[120] Second, as Rafaella Faggionato noted, the laicization of the Scriptures allowed the "society of the enlightened" few to promote the "society of the Enlightenment" among the many.[121] In this regard, she notes, the ideals of the Bible Society were "linked with the ideas of the Enlightenment and, above all, with ideas of tolerance and the equal dignity of the individual. Their members considered that confessional and cultural distinctions among people should be eliminated."[122] In other words, reading culture, including the culture of scriptural reading and interpretation, was no longer reserved for the domain of the elites, but the Bible was to benefit the public at large.

THE RUSSIAN BIBLE SOCIETY

The establishment of the Bible Society certainly reflected the growing vernacularization of biblical studies as well as the long-term Enlightenment impulse toward better education and the laicization of sacred learning. However, the immediate impetus for the establishment of the Russian Bible Society, as Stephen Batalden had noted, came from the arrival of the spiritual Awakening and the British biblical awakeners in Russia. Established in 1813, the Russian Society had direct ties to the British and Foreign Bible Society that had already been operating in the Baltic provinces of Russia for several years before that.[123] The Russian Society replicated not only the structure of the British one but also its ecumenical outlook. Headed by Golitsyn as well as Synod members like Amvrosii Podobedov and Filaret Drozdov, it also included Lutheran, Anglican, and Presbyterian pastors, notably the Scottish missionaries John Paterson and Robert Pinkerton, who represented the British and Foreign Bible Society. The society distributed Bibles and New Testaments to Russia's various non-Christian nationalities. However, it also undertook the project of translating the New Testament into the contemporary literary language, promoting the vernacular reading of the book in towns and villages.[124]

The arrival of cylindrical stereotype printing technology, imported from Britain, opened up new opportunities for mass production.[125] From 1821 to 1823 the society's press in St. Petersburg made 150,000 Russian and Slavonic-Russian diglot copies of the New Testament. This was larger than the print run of any Slavonic Bible from 1672 to 1820 in Russia.[126] Meanwhile, the Psalter "became the single most popular volume published by the society," exceeding the New Testament's print run.[127] The sky was the limit: as one archbishop told Pinkerton in 1816, the Synod planned to publish "not thousands but millions of copies."[128] Indeed, from 1813 to 1825, the total print run of all Bibles in twenty-six languages approached one million.[129]

The Holy Synod took an active part in promoting the society as well as opening chapters and offices of the Russian Bible Society all over the empire. The capitals as well as the smaller cities of Novocherkassk, Feodosiia, Iaroslavl, Voronezh, and Tula (among others) had such offices.[130] The wide distribution of the Bibles sparked mass spiritual interest in the reading of the vernacular Scripture. In 1816 Moscow's metropolitan Avgustin Vinogradskii spoke of "the spiritual hunger of our fellow countrymen for the word of God" and noted that local people were very eager to obtain a copy of the new edition, no matter the cost or the wait.[131] The same year, the rector of Tver seminary, Archimandrite Samuil, also rejoiced (in a somewhat chiliastic tone) over "the astonishing dissemination of the word of God as the glorious prelude of the approaching day of the Lord."[132] In Voronezh, the "zealous" local bishop noted "the eagerness with which many of the peasants search for the word of God" and the fact that many of them possessed and read the Bibles, and gave an example of a local convert for whom "it pleased God to open his eyes solely by reading the Bible."[133] Whether peasant or noble, the public were eager to spend money on the Bible as attested by the astounding commercial success of the society's operation. During its existence from 1813 to 1826, sales revenues from the Bibles approached 5.5 million rubles, which was impressive given the fact that the total annual Russian state revenue was in the vicinity of 100 million.[134]

The Bible Society movement also spurred the growth of enlightened philanthropy. The national and local functionaries of the Bible Society such as Golitsyn, Filaret Drozdov, Aleksandr Turgenev (historian and official at the Ministry of Education), and P. P. Pomian-Pesarovius (philanthropist and the editor of the Russian war veterans' newspaper) patronized the opening of charitable trusts for the greater improvement of society. Among them were the synodal initiative to subsidize free Bibles for the poor, the Prisons Trust, the Women's Charitable Society, and the Free Society of Lovers of Russian Literature that aided poor writers. Russia's veterans received financial help through the vice president of the Bible Society, while Golitsyn promoted the Quaker Lancaster Schools of mutual learning among the lower classes.[135]

The movement also bridged the divides among confessions. In the late 1810s, Robert Pinkerton and other agents of the British and Foreign Bible Society traveled around the country, finding cooperation and collaboration from Orthodox and non-Orthodox alike. The bishops of Tver, Tula, and Moldavia actively cooperated with the British and Foreign Bible Society.[136] Old Believers and Molokans participated and opened their own chapters of the Bible Society. Some of the Old Believers approvingly mistook British stereotype printing as *staro*-type or "old style" printing.[137] Even some Crimean Tatar Muslims took part in selling and supporting the society financially, with many Tatars requesting the New Testament in their own language. Out of the two hundred subscribers of the Crimean Bible Society, seventy-three were Muslim.[138] The involvement of non-Russians was hardly surprising—as an imperial institution representing a multiethnic state, the Orthodox Church instrumentalized the Bible Society in its efforts to "awaken" the non-Christian peoples of the empire to the Orthodox faith. Thus, the Kazan branch of the Russian Bible Society involved local priests Andrei Al'binskii and Andrei Okhotin in translating and publishing biblical literature in the Mordovian, Mari, and Chuvash languages of the Volga River in 1819–20.[139] In 1821 Tver priests Matfei Zolotinskii and Grigorii Vvedenskii translated the Gospel of Matthew into Karelian, using the French Bibles and biblical commentaries of Reformed theologians Théodore Beza and Sébastien Castellion.[140] The treasurer of the Russian Bible Society,

Iakov Shmidt (1779–1849), translated the New Testament into Mongolian.[141] At the same time, the Bible Society printed Scripture in a dozen other languages of the empire, including Lithuanian, Latvian, Finnish, German, Greek, Estonian, Moldavian, Armenian, Polish, and Farsi.

The synodal members of the society, particularly Metropolitan Filaret and Mikhail Desnitskii, saw the movement as an opportunity for greater Christian renewal and awakening. In their introduction to the first Russian-language New Testament, the bishops praised the new translation as "a lamp shining in a dark place," and hoped that this Word would revitalize those who were "dejected, hungry, thirsty, and spiritually dead." They also rejoiced that "now the door of the Gospel is more open than ever before."[142] The jubilant attitude of the awakened clergy was echoed in Filaret's 1822 speech at the Bible Society, where he rejoiced to see "the word of God is now read" among the laity and, especially, "in prisons, where convicts . . . begin to read the word of God and to recognize their Saviour."[143]

SODOM AND GOMORRAH:
THE SECULAR CRITICS OF THE AWAKENING

While many laypeople enthusiastically embraced the Scripture-buying spree, others became disillusioned with the growth of spirituality inspired by the Protestant Awakening in Russia just as they had become skeptical about the Russian Orthodox hierarchy's decades-long engagement with European Enlightenment. In fact, nineteenth-century conservatism—both in Europe and Russia—was born out of "a rejection of the Enlightenment rationalism and materialism that culminated in the French Revolution," as Alexander Martin noted.[144] Yet, while many Russian conservatives rejected the Enlightenment as a catalyst for revolution, they similarly condemned the ideas of the Awakening as potentially egalitarian, seditious, and revolutionary.

These conservative critics included such noblemen as Aleksei Arakcheev (1769–1834), Sergei Uvarov (1786–1855), Sergei A. Shikhmatov (1783–1837), A. S. Shishkov (1754–1841), and Nikolai Protasov (also Pratasov, 1798–1855). They were not a unified group by any measure, but they shared a common concern about the influence of the Bible Society movement. Their opposition to the religious status quo in Russia can best be summarized in three features: a disapproval of the spirituality of the Awakening (which they saw as manifested in Golitsyn and Filaret); an opposition to the vernacularization of holy texts that it promoted; and a general dissatisfaction with the results of Petrine and Catherinian church reforms (a less coherent concern). In their common concerns, the secular opponents of reform found allies in the church—particularly, the very motivated Archimandrite Fotii (an ally of Arakcheev and Shishkov) and an ally of convenience who had been promoted by Arakcheev—Metropolitan Serafim—whose role will be discussed separately.[145]

Their opposition had different foundations. Thus, Sergei Uvarov—a sentimental liberal-turned-conservative, who always carried a letter from Goethe in his pocket—based his opposition on dissatisfaction with Catherinian Enlightenment and the "conditions of the minds" it produced in Russia. Among the "conditions" that he criticized were the popularity of Montesquieu, the early 1820s St. Petersburg seminarian debates on the merits of Prussian writer Friedrich Ancillon's rejection of constitutionalism, and "the absurdities [bredni] of Jung-Stilling," who was also popular in the seminaries.[146] "A safe [bezopasnoe] Enlightenment is like fire that doesn't burn," he concluded in disillusionment.[147]

Sergei A. Shikhmatov, "a devoutly Orthodox young naval officer," believed that the Catherinian Enlightenment was not the only erroneous turn in Russia's path of development but that the deviation had started at the time of Feofan Prokopovich and the Petrine reforms.[148] His 1824 essay, "On the Conspiracies of the Enemies of Russia," stated that "the foundation of Russia's might [mogushchestvo] is . . . its Orthodox faith and unbounded obedience to the sovereign."[149] This foundation, he wrote, first came under attack during the reforms of Peter I, when foreign influence led to the rise of "the party of the heterodox, with heretical aberrations." Although Shikhmatov does not identify the members of this "heterodox" party, the fact that he is insinuating Prokopovich can be gleaned from his positive depiction of the most ardent opponents of the party—Feofilakt Lopatinskii ("who wrote a book against Lutherans and Calvinists") and Stefan Iavorskii, author of Kamen' very, "written . . . in defense of Orthodoxy."[150] Continuing to lament the victory of Petrine reforms over the old piety, Shikhmatov recounts the enlightened ideas of Catherine II, the rise of Masonry, and the fashionable nature of education in Germany ("the poison of German freethinking"), culminating in "the utmost deception from hell"—the Russian Bible Society.[151] The key to the society's plan "to destroy Russia's Orthodox faith" was vernacularization of Scripture, "the free reading and interpretation of the Bible," which Shikhmatov connected to the birth of the Reformation in Europe and the subsequent "projected reformation [predpolagaemaia reformatsiia] in this [Russian] Empire" with the "overthrow of the Orthodox faith."[152] Quoting one of the Bible Society leaders (real or imagined), he highlighted how lay Bible reading would lead to the "confusion [smiatenie]" of the Reformation: "Vernacularization [obnarodovanie] and distribution of the Holy Scripture in the Roman church led to the well-known reformation [preobrazovanie] and gave us Protestantism."[153]

Perhaps one of the most outspoken critics of the religious Awakening in St. Petersburg was Admiral Shishkov. Like other conservatives of his day, he evolved from being an "Enlightened moralist to [a] romantic nationalist" over the course of several decades.[154] Although he opposed foreign influence in Russia (like Shikhmatov and Nikolai Turgenev), his opposition was primarily rooted in the linguistic and philological critique of the laicization of Russian religious culture promoted by the awakeners.[155] Shishkov's linguistic theory declared Church Slavonic to be "sacred," "divine," and "the ancestor of all modern languages."[156] He abhorred "our dependence on the French" and called for the replacement of foreign words with new (but "native") Slavonic terminology.[157]

As a defender of Church Slavonic as Russia's truly native language (as opposed to the Western-influenced vernacular), Shishkov was against the vernacularization of Scripture long before the Bible Society movement started, so in his polemics he attacked the movement's clerical supporters. When Filaret Drozdov's catechism came out in 1823 with its translations of the major liturgical prayers and the Decalogue from Slavonic into the vernacular, Shishkov was outraged. In a letter to Arakcheev, he accused Filaret of "trading the language of the church for the language of the theater." He also noted grammatical incongruities in the bishop's translation of the Nicene Creed: the statement "I believe in one God," "*vo edinogo Boga*" (in one single God), appeared as "*v odnogo Boga*," which could be misconstrued as "in some God."[158] This was only one of the numerous times he criticized Filaret. In 1824 the admiral accused the prelate of "breeding schism" when Moscow's branch of the Russian Bible Society (under Filaret's control) enthusiastically delivered new scriptural translations to the Old Believers, who eagerly embraced the translation as written, they claimed, "in their natural language" and as uncorrupted by the 1666 Nikonian schism.[159]

The admiral's condemnation of the "new thought [*novomyslie*]" of ecclesiastical elites extended not only to individuals but to the entire Orthodox Church.[160] In his view, the hierarchs were treading dangerously close to the borders of heterodoxy. As a lay theologian, Shishkov struggled with the question of "whether, according to the doctrine of our Holy Church, the Orthodox can join or assist the Bible Societies?" Having studied the apostolic rules, the councils, and the writings of the Church Fathers, Shishkov concluded that they could not, stating that "even bishops" deserved excommunication if they did so.[161] Furthermore, "anyone who becomes a self-appointed interpreter of the Bible," he wrote, "shall be expelled [*ottorgnetsia*] from the communion of the Church."[162] The admiral's line of attack was filled with rhetorical questions. In his 1823–24 essay on the Bible Society, he asked: "Having received proof of the heretical purpose of the Bible Society, or, having at least partially understood it, how can the clergy, and especially the bishops, participate in the meetings of the Society with a clear conscience and without creating temptation for the people?"[163] Shishkov's critical questions for the Orthodox bishops did not end there. In an 1824 letter to Alexander I, he launched another rhetorical salvo, asking the tsar,

> Isn't it strange, I dare say, isn't it comical, that in our Bible societies, our own metropolitans and bishops sit together with Lutherans, Catholics, Calvinists, Quakers, i.e., with all the heterodox [*inovertsami*]? This is contrary to the Apostolic rules. Where is the reverence, where is the respect for God's service, where is the Church? They gather in houses where walls are adorned with paintings of pagan gods or passionate images of lovers. They sit in these meetings like in a theater, without any prayers or Gospel readings, with no reverence, and they consider these meetings to be a service to the Church! . . . Isn't this Sodom and Gomorrah?[164]

Shishkov's rhetorical question, "Where is the Church?," obviously presupposed an answer that the "Church" was nowhere to be found. At least not the kind of "Church" that the admiral had hoped to find in his proto-Slavophile search for an idealized ecclesial body. Yet his search for pure and authentic Orthodoxy was not a cry in the wilderness. Fortuitously, he found allies in the church hierarchy who had become critical of Filaret, the Enlightenment, and the Awakening. One of them was a former reader of Voltaire, Evgenii Bolkhovitinov. In his December 1824 letter to Bolkhovitinov, Shishkov called on his ally to come from Kiev and to join him "in the common and very difficult work" of cleaning up "the desolation and abomination [*merzost' i zapustenie*] in the holy place [i.e., the Synod]."[165]

THE CLERICAL OPPOSITION

Invited by Arakcheev and Shishkov, Bolkhovitinov arrived in February 1825 and joined the circle of clerical opposition.[166] In the decade leading up to the successful "coup" against Filaret in 1824, members of the opposition included such clerics as Archimandrite Innokentii, Metropolitan Serafim, Archimandrite Fotii, and Metropolitan Evgenii. They did not share identical opinions on everything; however, they tended to agree with Shishkov more than Filaret agreed with Shishkov. The same trifecta of displeasure with vernacularization, the mystical Awakening, and reformed Orthodoxy that drove Shishkov's criticism had also affected their worldviews.

Among the earliest and most vocal critics of the Awakening was Archimandrite Innokentii Smirnov (1783–1819), rector of St. Petersburg Theological Academy from 1813 to 1819. In his sermons and writings, he railed against the growth of Awakening spirituality in Russia, calling it a plot to "unite the

Lutheran and the Eastern Greco-Russian Church . . . under the guise of puri-
fied religion and a born-again Church."[167] He especially singled out the "impious writings" of Jung-Stilling, Jakob Boehme, and Labzin's *Messenger of Zion*
as dangerous, seeing in them "the old heresy of Origen the Evil-Minded"
rather than a new false teaching. He called on believers to abjure "the fables of
Stilling the Deceitful, Eckartshausen the Mad, Thomas à Kempis the Seducer."
Instead, he proposed that the Russian laity read "St. Efrem, St. John of Damascus, St. Cyril, John Climacos . . . and Maximus the Confessor" and practice
the constant prayer of Marcus Eremita, a fifth-century ascetic.[168] In his call
to reject Protestant authors in favor of early Christian ascetics and Church
Fathers, Innokentii was perhaps one of the earliest representatives of the so-
called neo-patristic turn in the Russian Orthodox Church, to which scholars
attribute the fundamental reshaping of theology in Russia in the 1825 to 1917
period.[169]

Innokentii Smirnov died in 1819; however, his restless disciple—Archimandrite Fotii Spasskii (1792–1838)—became one of the leading figures in the clerical opposition to reform. Hailing originally from the Novgorod region, Fotii
(born Petr) had the privilege of being selected to study at St. Petersburg Theological Academy in 1814 during Innokentii's rectorship there.[170] The capital city
and the academy shocked the pious seminarian. "The Church Fathers were
not available in the Academy's library," he wrote, "while all recommended
commentaries on the Bible were German."[171] Like Innokentii, he was fond of
medieval patristics and ascetic elders (*startsy*); in fact, he found a nickname
assigned to him, "the young elder [*iunyi starets*]," to be a high compliment.[172]

The intellectual cosmopolitanism of Fotii's fellow students disgusted him:
they read Jung-Stilling and Eckartshausen, and (ostensibly with Filaret's permission) attended the theater and ate meat during Lent.[173] "None of the students of the Theological Academy kept the fasts," he wrote. "The monastic
hierarchs in the Academy ate meat without any disguise."[174] Fotii particularly
disliked the current clerical fashion of theater attendance, calling the institution a "pagan temple [*kapishche*]" and expressing horror at the sight of such "a
temple of Satan near the holy dwellings of the Kremlin."[175] He was also dismayed over the heterogeneity of theological opinions in the seminary—"there
were doctrinal differences among students, as if they belonged to different
confessions," he recalled.[176]

Fotii was also a mystic who did not shy away from direct revelation. During
his lifetime, he experienced countless dramatic visions and met angels and
demons in the flesh and in spirit. Sometimes he chased these demons all over
St. Petersburg; sometimes the demons chased him.[177] Periodically he indulged
in extreme fasting without food or water. On other occasions, he fasted with

an herbal infusion of linden flowers. He rejected black tea as "pagan idolatrous communion" yet for some reason enjoyed drinking coffee at the St. Aleksandr Nevskii Monastery.[178] (Filaret, however, drank plenty of tea, regularly.[179])

His theological struggles pitted him against the Bible Society, with its various "freethinkers, children of the Antichrist."[180] In his doctrinal vision, he rejected all Lutheran influence, emphasized the preeminence of the holy Fathers, and (in contrast to Filaret) considered only the "Holy Eastern Church" to be Christian.[181] His opinions clearly echoed Innokentii's, but they also appear to have embraced many elements of pre-Prokopovich Muscovite piety that likely seemed rather esoteric to many Petersburgers of the time.

In his struggles, he maneuvered carefully against Filaret. Although he often showered the bishop with compliments, he condemned his many sins, such as leading the Bible translation project and the "heretical" edition of the New Testament, supposedly exiling Innokentii to Penza, and "adoring" Golitsyn's friends and mystics at the court like Rodion Koshelev.[182] Like Shishkov, he disapproved of Filaret's 1823 catechism, calling it "sewer water," and advocated the return of Peter Mohyla's Tridentine-inspired catechism, the doctrinal staple of pre-Petrine Ukrainian Orthodoxy.[183]

Fotii attracted supporters in high society, particularly among noblewomen, with whom he shared his letters and visions, including countesses Praskoviia Tolstaia, Dariia Derzhavina, Sofiia Meshcherskaia, and Anna A. Orlova-Chesmenskaia (see figure 10). Orlova-Chesmenskaia's sponsorship of Fotii's ministry gave the monk financial security, something that many peers of his social background lacked.[184] Aleksandr Pushkin once poked fun at their relationship, writing insultingly that she "gave her sinful flesh to Archimandrite Photius."[185] Fotii also attracted the attention of Shishkov, who supported the young monk. Most importantly, he developed a close rapport with Arakcheev. He visited Arakcheev's Gruzino estate in the fall of 1821, from which point their amicable relationship grew. Due to Gruzino's proximity to Fotii's Derevianitsa Monastery, he nicknamed his patron "the Neighbor."[186] After the murder of Arakcheev's mistress Anastasia Minkina, the archimandrite comforted his patron, said the burial liturgy, and declared her a "great martyress [*velikomuchenitsa*]."[187] Like everything else in Fotii's life, his closeness to "the Neighbor" stemmed not only from shared interests but also from direct revelation: once an angelic vision showed him Arakcheev aiding the defeat of the enemies of the Church.[188]

Clerical opposition to the Awakening would have lacked organizational logistics without Serafim Glagolevskii, who became the metropolitan of St. Petersburg in 1821. Fotii's revelations and ecstatic preaching in Kazan Cathedral were simply not enough to launch a concerted attack on Golitsyn and the

Figure 10. Archimandrite Fotii and his spiritual devotee, Countess Anna Orlova-Chesmenskaia. Engraving by I. I. Khelmitskii, early nineteenth century. From A. Slezhinskii, "ArkhimandritFotii i grafinia A. Orlova-Chesmenskaia," *Russkaia Starina* 100 (1899). Courtesy of Widener Library, Harvard University.

Bible Society; the opposition needed the support of the Holy Synod. Serafim, who quickly became the president of the Synod, was more conservative than many other clerics of the Catherinian era but was hardly the most fervent member of the opposition to Filaret. A board member of the Bible Society, he sometimes agreed with Filaret and disagreed with Shishkov.[189]

What brought him into Fotii's fold was his "great discord" with Golitsyn and his disdain for "heresiarch Koshelev," an awakener with influence at court.[190] The metropolitan opposed the inordinate influence over church affairs that Golitsyn, the minister of Education and Spiritual Affairs, and secular courtiers exercised. While not initially opposed to vernacularization, he wanted more synodal control over the Bible Society than Golitsyn permitted. In turning against Golitsyn's "Egyptian yoke" over the Synod, Serafim also turned against the minister's alliances. By 1824 Serafim had "raised his sword against the insolent heretics" by urging Alexander I to dismantle the Bible Society and to fire Golitsyn. He also worked to send Filaret away from St. Petersburg to Moscow and to exclude the allies of the Russian Bible Society, bishops Iona and Dmitrii, from the Synod altogether.[191]

Evgenii Bolkhovitinov, the metropolitan of Kiev, was another important member of the clerical opposition. Fotii greeted his arrival in early 1825 "from godly Kiev to the city of St. Peter [*grad Sv. Petra*] for God's work" as a "miracle" and compared the bishop to "our St. Nicholas, a new St. George."[192] Evgenii's association with Fotii's party is somewhat puzzling; after all, Bolkhovitinov was one of those enlightened hierarchs who in chapter 6 promoted Voltaire in the seminaries, among other authors. By 1824 it appears that he had radically changed his views and turned against vernacularization and even Filaret's vernacular catechism.[193] Furthermore, he became increasingly critical of foreign influence in Orthodox theology. "Our students have a long tradition of learning from foreign theologians, not domestic ones," he stated in 1825. Among the theologians that he sought to revive in the seminaries were Mohyla, Stefan Iavorskii, and St. Dmitrii Tuptalo. In other words, he too seemed to be calling for the return to pre-Prokopovich Ukrainian Orthodoxy, emphasizing that seminaries ought to teach "the veneration of saints, the fasts, the cross, and the relics."[194]

THE REVOLT OF 1824:
DEFEATING THE "SPIRITUAL NAPOLEON"

The forces of the secular and ecclesiastical opposition coalesced in what Filaret referred to as the "revolt [*vosstanie*]" of 1824.[195] According to Fotii, the close circle involved included Arakcheev, Shishkov, Count Platon Shirinskii-Shikhmatov, Palace Guards' commander General Fedor Uvarov, and Chief of Police Ivan Gladkov.[196] The high point of the coup was Golitsyn's dismissal from the Ministry of Education and Religious Affairs in May 1824.

The formal pretext for Golitsyn's dismissal was his involvement in the so-called Gossner Affair. The Munich awakener Johannes Evangelista Gossner (1773–1858) arrived in St. Petersburg in 1820, seeking to continue his spiritual work in a new setting. In Russia, his preaching engaged in spontaneous revelation and chiliasm, emphasizing the imminent end of the world. He drew large crowds—allegedly as large as 40,000—and gained popularity at court, especially with Golitsyn.[197] In Russia, the translation of Gossner's *Herz des Menschen, ein Tempel Gottes* sustained many editions from 1819 to 1853 and was a standard work of the genre of awakened literature, emphasizing inner spirituality and the importance of inviting Christ into one's own heart.[198] Yet in 1823 he commissioned a translation of his rather controversial commentary on the Gospel of Matthew, previously published in Nuremberg as *Geist des Lebens und der Lehre Jesu Christi im Neuen Testamente*. This Gospel of Matthew commentary passed Golitsyn's censorship and work on its editing and publication was underway, in some secrecy, at Nikolai Grech's printing press by February 1824.[199]

The work had piqued Shishkov's and Fotii's interest and they were able to obtain some (but not all) pages of the work through the undercover operations of Police Chief Gladkov. They were appalled by the contents of the Gospel of Matthew commentary. In it, Gossner allowed himself unimaginable liberties, including attacks on the established Christian churches (arguing that no church could claim to have the exclusive possession of true dogma); a reference that the Savior came to save people not only from spiritual but also from political bondage; a statement that Jesus's criticism of Pharisees was also applicable to contemporary clergy; and a suspicious comment on King Herod that reminded readers that most kings in the Bible were evil kings (*tsars*, in Russian) and in fact, most rulers in the world "were evil people [*byli liudi zlye*]."[200]

In short, for critics like Shishkov, the commentary seemed to present Jesus as a nineteenth-century revolutionary heretic. Because it was a Gospel commentary, the opposition feared that Golitsyn might publish it alongside the Russian text of the Russian Bible Society New Testament, which would take the commentary to every corner of Russia. They had to act fast to stop its publication. In the early spring of 1824, Shishkov, Fotii, and Serafim related their suspicions to the tsar directly, supported by Arakcheev. The written version of Fotii's visions (related to the tsar as direct divine revelation) were particularly colorful: in his April 12, 1824, letter, Fotii related a March 30 visit by an angel in which the "mystery [*taina*]" of Gossner's book was revealed to him. According to the revelation, Gossner was connected to the Carbonari revolutionary societies in Europe and Gossner's book contained the "codeword [*parol'*]" to start a revolution in Russia in four years.[201] Furthermore, Fotii discovered that Gossner's designs for a "secret revolution in the church and the government" were confirmed in his sermons.[202] In addition to the extravagance of Fotii's visions, metropolitan of St. Petersburg Serafim's official complaints prompted the convention of the Committee of Ministers on April 22, 1824. At the meeting, the copy of the Gospel of Matthew commentary was presented and St. Petersburg's military governor, Mikhail Miloradovich (supported by Shishkov), spoke in defense of Serafim's warnings. The resolution of the Committee prompted the imperial decrees of April 25, 1824, sending Gossner into exile and starting a full investigation of all other individuals implicated in the affair.[203]

The chronological trajectory of the coup after April 25 was as follows. On May 15, the tsar dismissed Golitsyn from his posts as chief procurator of the Holy Synod and minister of education. Count Admiral Shishkov became the new education minister. Then followed the suspension of Russian Bible Society translation activity and the ban on Filaret's catechisms, which ironically drove up the demand for it among Moscow's booksellers.[204] Then came the event that strengthened the opposition to vernacularization in the Holy Synod:

Evgenii Bolkhovitinov's arrival in St. Petersburg in February 1825. By the time the Decembrist rebels entered Senate Square in 1825, many of the reforms of the Russian Awakening—and even the Enlightenment—were in full retreat.

Why did the coup of the secular and clerical opponents of Western influence enjoy such swift success, given the extent of the influence of eighteenth-century reforms in the hierarchy? There is no one best answer to explain this rapid success of the coup plotters, but several factors need to be highlighted. One was the change in the tsar's mentality. The meeting of the Holy Alliance powers at the congresses of Troppau (1820) and Laibach (1821) to address the upswing of revolutionary movements in Europe made the tsar anxious about larger forces behind the movements. Meanwhile, Klemens von Metternich promoted the idea that the Awakening was one such seditious force, and the Austrians' resolve was further strengthened by Leo XII's papal bull of May 3, 1824, condemning the Bible Societies.[205] By 1824 it appears that Alexander I had come to the conclusion that "the only alternatives were reaction or revolution."[206] The former would entail a policy of suppressing the Russian Bible Society (which Alexander hesitated to do), but allowing the latter would likely doom the Romanov dynasty. Although Alexander hesitated and vacillated, it appears that the tsar found himself agreeing more with Arakcheev than with Golitsyn by 1824.

Another important factor in the success of the 1824 coup is not widely discussed in the historiography. It is the generational shift in the church hierarchy, or, rather, the natural attrition of Catherinian enlightened bishops who played a key role in the first decade of Alexander's reign but whose absence in the last decade of that reign made Filaret's party more vulnerable. As Evgenii Liut'ko noted in his study, some 32 percent of the hierarchs (bishops and archimandrites) of the Alexandrine era came from Platon Levshin's circle of seminarians, even though that circle in general accounted for less than 2 percent of the total number of seminarians in Russia.[207]

Many of these enlightened hierarchs (and even some disciples of Platon) began to die. Gavriil Petrov died in 1801. Anastasii Bratanovskii died in 1808. Platon Levshin died in 1812. Amvrosii Podobedov in 1818. Irinei Klement'evskii in 1818. Mikhail Desnitskii in 1821. Feofilakt Rusanov, the "gentleman bishop," died in 1821.[208] Although these bishops were intellectual champions of the religious Enlightenment in Russia, they did not get involved in the most bitter church debates about the Bible Society movement. The newer generation of hierarchs, however, emerged already polarized between those who supported and those who opposed the Russian Bible Society in a display of disunity and polemics not seen since the Prokopovich era. In this context, the shake-up of the Synod in 1823–24 was strategically important for the later success of the coup. Arakcheev and Shishkov persuaded the tsar to remove the pro–Bible Society hierarchs, dismissing bishops Iona and Dmitrii and sending Filaret away to Moscow.[209]

A third factor was the ability of the opposition to connect Western influences in the Russian church to the revolutionary threat to the monarchy. According to Shishkov, the awakeners' (and Gossner's) chiliastic preachers emboldened those liberals in Russia who interpreted the coming apocalyptic societal break-down as a convenient catalyst for revolutionary action.[210] The emotional insta-bility of awakeners like Gossner also made them potential assassins or terrorists. "Did not the same state of mind," wrote Shishkov, "convince the mad [Fran-çois] Ravaillac to murder Henry IV or sway Sand to carry out the assassination of von Kotzebue"?[211] The latter was a reference to the 1819 assassination of conservative August von Kotzebue by radicalized German student Karl Sand, which led to Metternich's adoption of the Carslbad Decrees.[212] Shishkov also presented the activities of the Bible Society and Filaret to the tsar as equally politically seditious. The Russian Bible Society inserted "calls to universal in-surrection" in the Bibles it sent out, he claimed, and the Saratov branch of the society "spread heresy and mutiny [*buistvo*] among the simple folk."[213] The Bible Society and Filaret's catechism were "the two strongest instruments of revolutionary conspiracy," wrote the admiral.[214]

Shishkov was not the only source of such warnings at Alexander's court. Many noblemen close to the tsar's circles voiced similar apprehensions. Mag-nitskii, for example, accused the Bible Society of promoting "*tolerans*" in how the Russian vernacular translation of 1 Corinthians 7:21 (on slaves obtaining freedom) addressed serfdom.[215] Shikhmatov also equated Protestant influence with radicalism, stating that "all our Protestant churches were born out of polit-ical struggles and rebellions [*smiatenii*]."[216]

The accusations that the Bible Society movement influenced the movement for the abolition of serfdom were not without merit. Thus, the clergy of the Iaroslavl branch of the Bible Society corresponded with individual landlords in the 1820s, petitioning them to free their serfs.[217] In Ostrogozhsk (Voronezh region), the local Bible Society convinced Count Nikolai Sheremet'ev to free one serf—Aleksandr Nikitenko (1804–77)—who would become a famous pro-fessor of St. Petersburg University.[218] An anonymous letter sent to Nicholas I in 1826 argued that among the causes of political "liberalism" among the young officers and students of Tsarskoe Selo Lyceum in the 1820s were the "ideas of free, individualistic [*proizvol'nogo*] interpretation of Scripture," as promoted by the Russian Bible Society.[219] Even Grand Duke Constantine Pavlovich in his letter to Count P. M. Volkonskii connected the "freethinking" in the regiments (in the wake of the mutiny of 1820) to the influence of the Bible Society.[220]

FOTII'S VISIONS

A fourth reason for the coup's success that is not emphasized in the historiography was the effectiveness of the psychological impression of Fotii's visions. What is so fascinating about Fotii is not the fact that he rejected the Awakening but that he used a standard tool of the awakeners—direct revelation—to bolster his arguments. Many chiliastic Pietists of the day were fond of directly accessing the divine, and Gossner, too, advocated for closer communication with the angels.[221] While many Western awakeners used direct revelation to bypass any scriptural dogmatic norms that contradicted them, Fotii used it to bypass the oversight of the Synod or higher authorities opposed to him. This is exactly what Rasputin would do, and Alexander Martin's comparison of Fotii to Rasputin is quite on point.[222] Fotii possessed the unique advantage of appealing directly to the court as his supernatural visions needed no prior approval from the authorities standing between him and the monarch. If Fotii's visions came from God and were intended directly for the tsar, no Holy Synod official was going to stop God from communicating with the tsar through a visionary ascetic.

Fotii did not support his claims with revelation alone; he also used mathematical calculations. In August 1824, as the government investigation to uncover Russians connected with Gossner was ongoing, he sent two epistles to Alexander. One was titled "The Revelation of the Conspiracy of the Number of Apocalyptic Beast 666 and England's Influence on Russia"; the other, "The Revolution in Russia, Prepared for 1826 by Secret Societies and English Methodists under the Pretext of Christ's Millennial Kingdom."[223] As the titles suggest, Fotii accused England of plotting a revolution in Russia by sending English missionaries (who were in fact Scottish) to bring "poison through the channel of the Bible Society."[224] The roots of the "English plot," he argued, went back to 1666, when the "bloodsucker" Oliver Cromwell started a rebellion to bring the millennial kingdom to earth. The plotters then decided to bring their revolution to completion in 1836. He argued that "1836" comes from multiplying six times three (equaling eighteen) and adding it to six times six (equaling thirty-six).[225]

To make his calculations ring true for the tsar, Fotii also multiplied the prophetic number twelve by the sacred number three. Thus, twelve years after the start of the new millennium, Napoleon invaded Russia (=1812); twelve years after that, the Bible Society and awakener Gossner began plotting the revolution in Russia (=1824); and, twelve years further on, the revolution with its "spiritual Napoleon" would destroy Russia (=1836).[226] To stem the tide of the revolution, he urged the tsar to ban the source of English influence in Russia—the Bible

Society—thus nipping the revolution in the bud. "Just as you defeated the visible Napoleon," he exclaimed, "let us now defeat the spiritual Napoleon."[227]

Fotii's warnings about the revolutionary nature of the Russian Bible Society and Gossner's disciples in Russia certainly made an impression on the tsar, but Alexander was less convinced that the revolution had English connections. Although he hesitated to close the Bible Society, its translation activities and public outreach were curtailed. Furthermore, the tsar allowed the unimaginable: thousands of copies of the recently translated Scriptures were committed to a bonfire of Bible-burning in early 1825, set up inside the ovens of the St. Aleksandr Nevskii brick factory.[228]

CONCLUSION

Several months later, on December 14, 1825, another revolutionary bonfire lit up St. Petersburg. Between November 19 and December 13, 1825, members of the Northern Secret Society struck in the capital with the hope of establishing a constitutional government. They were taking advantage of the chaotic interregnum and a perception (described in State-Secretary Vasilii Marchenko's memoirs) that Nicholas was a usurper, "taking the throne away from [his] brother [Grand Duke Constantine]."[229] Some two thousand soldiers and officers of the Moscow, Grenadier, and Naval Guards Regiments entered Senate Square, some shouting slogans in support of Grand Duke Constantine, a "constitution," or both. Whether or not they understood the term *konstitutsiia* is the subject of debate; however, the context of their lessons in the Lancaster School Movement suggests that perhaps many of them did. The show of force disturbed Nicholas I, who decided to try the force of moral persuasion first. Since Filaret was still "exiled" to Moscow, the new tsar turned to Serafim. According to Marchenko's account, "Nicholas obliged [*vytreboval*] him to depart from the Palace and go to the Square," but the "shouts and threats of the rebels" chased the bishop back to the safety of the Winter Palace."[230] Eventually reinforcements consisting of artillery brigades and the Finland, Pavlovskii, and Cavalier Guards regiments (among others) arrived and cannon fire put the revolt to an end.[231]

The Decembrists, who fascinated Russian revolutionaries for a century after 1825, were not rabid atheists. Their religious views were hardly uniform, but they offer a unique window into what direction the Orthodox Church could have taken should the revolt have been successful. Gavriil Baten'kov and Nikita Muraviev advocated the continuation of the existence of the state church, while Pestel's constitution designated the Orthodox Church as "a branch of the government, its most honorable branch."[232] Nikita and Sergei Muraviev's theological visions incorporated the language of the Enlightenment constitutional heritage in emphasizing "human rights given by God" and arguing that God cursed tyranny or "evil authority."[233]

Whatever the religious views of the participants, the December artillery charge effectively ended any hopes for a more liberal form of government. Yet it also ended any hypothetical possibility of rolling back the religious reaction that started in 1824. The new tsar, Nicholas I, was clearly not fond of the Awakening or the reformed Orthodox theology of the eighteenth century. By personal decree, he closed the Bible Society on April 12, 1826. The Orthodox counterreform had begun.

Conclusion

Protasov's Apocalypse, 1836

What? The seminarians study philosophy? This iniquitous, atheistic, and rebellious discipline [*nauka*]?!

—NICHOLAS I

As the year 1836 approached, many chiliasts across Europe—south German Pietists, Dutch numerologists, and Molokan Russian peasants, among others—expected the world to end that year, in fulfillment of Johann Albrecht Bengel's and Johann Heinrich Jung-Stilling's prophecies.[1] Aleksandr Golitsyn spent 1836 as postmaster general, in deteriorating health. His personal letters from 1834 disclosed his expectation of the "second coming of the Lord" with the upcoming fulfillment of chiliastic prophecies.[2] Meanwhile his archnemesis Fotii rested on his laurels as slayer of the "spiritual Napoleon" and archimandrite of Iur'ev Monastery. There on the banks of the Volkhov River, Fotii wrestled more demons: the "disorderly" and "unholy" undergarments of the local monks. Although he grounded his opposition to such undergarments theologically in the fact that underwear contradicted the "angelic" nature of the monastic physical body, his stance likely also reflected his resentment against the fashions and bodily indulgences of the time. So he forced his subordinates to wear full-length mantles with nothing underneath. He passed away in February 1838.[3]

Although the world did not come to an end in 1836, something very important happened during that year that closed the curtain on the story of the long eighteenth century's Orthodox reform and Enlightenment. On February 24, 1836, Lieutenant General Count Nikolai Protasov (also Pratasov, 1798–1855) became the new chief procurator. His tenancy of the office spanned almost twenty years, the longest ever in Russian history up to that date.[4] Protasov's career epitomized the high tide of the reaction against the Bible Society movement and the intellectual cosmopolitanism of church elites; the reaction started in the 1820s and resonated throughout the first half of the century. The logical culmination of this change was Protasov's endeavor to adapt religion to the conditions of the changed society of the Nikolaevan era. Doing so entailed not only elevating the powers of the chief procurator even more than under Golitsyn but also exercising greater direct bureaucratic and administrative control over the church and its theology. The chief procurator's control came with an unprecedented militaristic zeal that was really part of the context of the 1830s, when the military became the regime's model for reconceptualizing the social system as a whole. Theologically, however, Protasov's changes involved contestation against the preceding century's variety of Protestant- and Enlightenment-influenced theologies that went back to the Petrine reforms. As one contemporary British observer noted, Protasov's counterreforms were nothing but "a reaction against the school of Theophanes Procopovich [sic]."[5]

Protasov's "Reaction"

Who was Lieutenant General Protasov? Educated by the Jesuits in his early years, Protasov showed some sympathy toward certain Roman Catholic doctrinal formulations but also shared similarities with A. S. Shishkov.[6] Like Shishkov, he was an admirer of Mohyla's catechism, a theological compendium of doctrine on the Tridentine model that was embraced by the Orthodox hierarchy in the seventeenth century but largely ignored by the Russian church after the Petrine reforms.[7] Much like Shishkov, perhaps even more so, he sought to purge Orthodoxy of eighteenth-century elements that he believed to be in conflict with his vision of the true church.

Protasov began his time in the office by staging what some clergy called "raids [nashestviia]" on St. Petersburg Theological Academy and even the provincial seminaries.[8] During these unannounced inspections, the chief procurator attacked the seminarians for their "masquerade" of fashions, lack of discipline, and their utter ignorance of Mohyla's philo-Catholic theology.[9] He was surprised to discover that seminarians studied contemporary philosophy.[10] His concern was seconded by Nicholas I, who was distraught that future priests studied "this iniquitous, atheistic, and rebellious discipline!"[11] He also opposed theological disputations between seminarians—an old Kievan practice popularized in the eighteenth century by Feofan and Platon. Such meetings, he argued, promoted the politically deviant skill of exchanging opinions.[12] "In the West, the theological principle of free investigation of dogma led to the political principle," Protasov wrote.[13] Protasov also chided the seminaries for teaching arithmetic and trigonometry instead of more practical subjects like "note singing" and agronomy. As Gregory Freeze has noted, while many of Protasov's reforms were utilitarian, they clearly sought to stifle the church's intellectual life, which was dismissed as "vanity [fanfaronstvo]."[14]

Protasov also "raided" the Synod, where, according to biographer Rostislavov, he "rattled his saber [*sableiu*]" at the bishops' meetings.[15] During one such visit to the Synod, he declared: "Your theology is arrogant [*vysprenna*]. Your sermons are too haughty. We do not understand you. You lack the language of the people. You are estranged from the character of the church [*tserkovnost*]."[16]

Protasov's accusation that the bishops were estranged from "the character of the church" resonated well with Shishkov's earlier question, "Where is the Church?" Much like Shishkov, the chief procurator had a specific plan to recover the church's authenticity by contesting and reacting against Petrine and Catherinian Orthodox theology. As Protasov himself disclosed in a conversation with Reverend William Palmer in 1840, "we too have had a Calvinistic or Protestant spirit among us which Platon started . . . but this has all been corrected and now there is an orthodox reaction."[17] The chief secretary of the Holy Synod, Andrei Muraviev (1806–74), seconded his superior by stating that the ecclesiastical "leaning toward Protestantism . . . is past and there is everywhere a reaction."[18] While a few "liberalized" clergy remained in the capitals, Protasov believed that the "interior" of Russia remained faithful to "ancient Greek orthodoxy" and the resurrection of these "ancient" traditions on the official level would deal a blow to ecclesiastical "liberalism."[19]

Protasov's "reaction" against what "[Metropolitan] Platon started" and the restoration (or, rather, reinvention) of this "ancient" Orthodoxy that the chief procurator envisioned involved a mixture of expanded emphasis on late antiquity's Church Fathers and seventeenth-century Kievan theology, and the imitation of Roman Catholic examples. His adoption of Mohyla's catechism was motivated by his desire to adopt a "symbolic book" to match *Confessio fidei Tridentinae* (Tridentine Creed) and other symbolic books.[20] His educational reforms of 1837–40 mandated the use of Peter Mohyla's catechism (which the seminarians were to "read without ceasing") and "the historical teachings of the Holy Fathers" for dogmatic theology.[21] His November 1842 report to the monarch advocated active measures against the spreading of "heresy" in Russian seminaries and emphasized that the origins of this "heresy" were introduced by Feofan Prokopovich.[22] Finally, to make good on his promise to stamp out any remaining ecclesiastical liberalism, he banned the teaching of Western (and all other) philosophy.[23]

But the chief procurator was not the only bureaucrat who contested eighteenth-century reformed Orthodoxy: his assistant, Privy Councillor Konstantin Serbinovich (1797–1874), a graduate of Polotsk Jesuit Collegium, played a crucial role in forcing Filaret to revise his "Lutheran" catechism "in accordance with the strict requirements of the ancient Orthodoxy," which included the introduction of the Catholic teaching on the Nine Beatitudes and the equivalency of church tradition with revelation.[24] To demonstrate its commitment to ending eighteenth-century Protestant influence, the Synod also reprinted Iavorskii's *Kamen' very* for the first time since 1728.[25] This was the work that adopted the anti-Protestant arguments of Martinus Becanus and Robert Bellarmine, while reducing Calvin and Luther to "pig's excrement."[26] Some one hundred years after Stefan Iavorskii's death, the polemics of the 1720s were now back in vogue.

Protasov's so-called orthodox reaction was sustained by his newly promoted hierarchs who shared his opposition to enlightened Orthodoxy. One of Protasov's men was Bishop Afanasii Drozdov (1800–1876), the rector of St. Petersburg Theological Academy after 1841. Afanasii "claimed that all Russian theologians before him [Afanasii] were un-orthodox [*ne pravoslavny*]."[27] His doctrinal inventions and educational policies were just as bold. He called for the "canonization" of the Septuagint, the banning of Hebrew biblical philology, and the acknowledgment of the "inadequacy" of the Bible for "doctrinal truths." In his enthusiastic promotion of Greek and Roman patristics, he declared the Fathers' writings to be "the oral Word of God," equated with the Gospel, "the written Word of God."[28] Afanasii was not alone in his espousal of the new theological direction. His disciple was Makarii Bulgakov (1816–82), a "theologian bureaucrat" (in Florovsky's characterization) who was promoted by Protasov and dabbled in the philo-Catholic Ukrainian theology of the early Petrine era. Not surprisingly, his doctrinal works received official promotion during the subsequent over-procuratorship of the reactionary Konstantin Pobedonostev under Tsar Alexander III.[29]

How did Metropolitan Filaret and his allied clergy react to the changing theological culture around him? Many of the seminary professors and Synod members appeared bewildered with the newfound affection for Mohyla's text, viewing the catechism as outdated, "strange," promoted by the Jesuits, and in unnecessary competition with Filaret's more modern work.[30] Filaret viewed Protasov's policies as "a return to the times of [Catholic] scholasticism" and stated that any decisions that reflected the opinions of the 1672 Jerusalem Council (which affirmed Mohylan theology and condemned lay Bible reading) carried a "Catholic *stain*."[31] He complained about the return of the ancient "persecutions of the Church," while contesting Serbinovich's accusations that he was a "steadfast [*upornyi*] Lutheran."[32]

Filaret was really both the last representative of the eighteenth-century reformed hierarchy and the transitional hierarch entering the new, post-1825 religious culture. This explains many of the contradictions in his life and thought. As the representative of the eighteenth-century Westernized religious milieu, he was wary of the popularity of Mohyla and medieval Byzantine

devotional texts like the *Philokalia*.[33] He continued to promote vernacularization of sacred texts, opposing Serafim and Evgenii on that count, and speaking
against General Nikolai Demidov's prohibition against the cadets reading the
Bible in the military schools.[34] He used eighteenth-century philo-Protestant jar-
gon to condemn his opponents for behaving "in a Papist manner [*papisticheski*]"
and for sanctioning "the domination of Papism [*papizm*]" in the Russian
church.[35] Yet, as someone who transitioned to the new post-1825 era, Filaret
complied with state orders.[36] In his acceptance of the new state of affairs, he
cherished his special position at the court as Nicholas's personally valued (but
not necessarily like-minded) metropolitan, who remained an authoritative
churchman throughout Nicholas's reign. Then also, Filaret acknowledged that
the turn against Enlightenment theology and Awakening spirituality (as well
as Protestant influence in the Church) had long been underway even before
1824 and standing in its way would require combat on barricades he was not
willing to climb. As he later expressed to Golitsyn, he did not want to force a
"schism in the Church" by defending his positions.[37]

QUO VADIS, ECCLESIA? CONTINUITY AND DISRUPTION OF CHURCH REFORM

Between 1700 and 1836, no other institution of the Russian Empire experienced changes as radical as those affecting the church. During this period,
Russia's Orthodox Church experienced the profound influence of Protestant
and Enlightenment ideas that altered its doctrine, canonical administrative
structure, political theology, education, spirituality, and homiletics, among
other things. The bishops who built this reformed and enlightened intellectual
world of Russian Orthodoxy were not pawns of the monarchs' whims but
motivated agents who used state support to improve their church using the
blueprints and formulas they discovered in the West.

The fact that Western influence permeated several spheres of Orthodox doctrine underscores the importance of theology in understanding Russian church
history. Yet, at the same time, since such formulas were far from homoge-
neous, the story of Russian Orthodoxy in the eighteenth century is thematically crisscrossed by a great variety of Western doctrinal influences (including
Tridentine Catholicism, Pietism, religious Enlightenment, and Protestant
Awakening) as well as a variety of opinions within the church as to what constituted true orthodoxy. This variety inevitably led to contestation, the doctrinal struggle that continued to emerge at key junctures of the period from Peter
I to Nicholas I. It is only after 1825 (but before the tumultuous Great Reforms)
that contestation in many areas of systematic theology (such as soteriology or
bibliology) gave way to an emerging neo-patristic consensus that Orthodoxy

should return to its Byzantine roots and ideals, as those ideals were imagined in the nineteenth century.

In the spectrum of wider European religious history, the Russian Orthodox experience was hardly unique: the Reformations (Protestant and Catholic), the Enlightenments (secular and religious), and the Awakening(s) or *Erweckungsbewegung* played their crucial roles in the formation of modern states and societies across the continent and the Atlantic world. But in comparison to other bodies of Eastern Christendom, the Russian Orthodox experience was rather unique. Although many Eastern ecclesiastical communities experienced contact with Reformation and Enlightenment ideas during the early modern period, in Russia such ideas were instrumental in ushering in religious reform of revolutionary magnitude and in forming the spiritual foundations of the empire.

The spiritual "revolution" that began in 1700, however, came to a halt with Protasov's "reaction." Nevertheless, the new intellectual life of Orthodoxy after this time period cannot simply be reduced to the rise of the church hierarchy as guardians of autarchy and reaction. It involved new directions, such as the considerable revival of monasticism, the resurrection of medieval ascetic practices, the rejection of empiricism and rationalism, the rise of miracles and canonizations, the appearance of active saintly ascetics from the heights of the court to the far reaches of the countryside, the expansion of connections with the Orthodox Middle East, the proliferation of neo-patristic theology, and the doctrinal development of Orthodox Tradition (*predanie*). These became the dominant but hardly the sole directions in the complex story of nineteenth-century Orthodoxy.

None of these features of Orthodox religious experience (familiar to anyone studying the church circa 1900) reflected continuity with the eighteenth century, although one could certainly make some sort of a connection to the much earlier, pre-1700 period. In this way, 1700–1825 represented a major disruption (if not an outright anomaly) in Russia's church history. Orthodox reform and Enlightenment had no parentage in Russia's medieval past and had only a few heirs in the country's post-1825 future. As Luba Golburt noted in *First Epoch*, the eighteenth century in Russian history appeared as a "seemingly meaningless past" because many intellectuals of the Pushkin era turned against it as they "overcame the eighteenth century's key political and cultural paradigms" and imagined the authentic Russian national ethos to be rooted in the pre-1700 period.[38] In this way, the post-1825 reaction to Petrine and Catherinian religious culture represented a refounding of the Russian Empire and with it, the refounding of a new Orthodoxy set against the disruptive anomaly of the imperial "first epoch" of 1700–1825.

Despite its highly disruptive nature in the timeline of Orthodox history, Russia's religious reform and Enlightenment had its few inheritors in the array of legacies that persisted in religious culture until 1917. Apart from the fact that Orthodox reform and the Enlightenment played an indispensable part in Russia's turn to Western modernity, there are three more long-term continuities that originated in the eighteenth century and persisted well into the contemporary era.

One major legacy was the presence of an ongoing tension between the episcopate and the state bureaucracy, the chief procurator's office in particular. During the eighteenth century, the office often had little actual power and was even vacant under Prokopovich for some time. Meanwhile, the enlightened bishops enjoyed varying degrees of control over their own affairs as well as access not only to the court but also to the court's politics. There were no intermediary institutional barriers standing between the upper episcopate and the court. Protasov suppressed this eighteenth-century privilege of the Synod's access to the monarch, ostensibly to "direct [*dirizhirovat*]" the affairs of the church as if it was his personal chancellery.[39] "Pratasoff is our Patriarch," said one Petersburg priest in 1840.[40] He was a "serf-master over the bishops," said another in Muraviev's report.[41]

The amplification of procuratorial powers was not the original design of Prokopovich's reform. Nor was the idea of the church turning into "the handmaiden [*sluzhanka*] of the state" easily accepted among the hierarchy.[42] The eighteenth-century context and the bureaucratic reaction to it after 1825 set in motion a long-term tension between the Synod and state bureaucracy, with the latter increasingly controlling the former's access to the court. Yet wasn't such tension already latent due to the Petrine subordination of the church to the monarchy? Hardly so; as Feofan Prokopovich placed the Holy Synod under the authority of pontifex maximus (the holy emperor), he specifically rejected its subordination to the Senate and, by extension, the bureaucracy. There was a difference between the church deferring to the authority of the sacred monarch (what Feofan had done) and acceding to the capricious sway of secular bureaucracy, which is what Nicholas I allowed to happen after 1825.[43] This tension continued well until 1917 and as Freeze has demonstrated, far from being the "handmaiden" of Protasov or Pobedonostsev, the Russian clergy found new ways to resist the bureaucratization of the sacred sphere and even emphasize new divergences between state and ecclesiastical interests.[44]

Another lasting continuity of reform was the construction of the imperial Orthodox Church in Russia. For the first time since the Byzantine Empire, an Orthodox monarch with an Orthodox hierarchy governed a transcontinental empire. This empire, however, was not the resurrection of some medieval

Third Rome but a theoretical adaptation of the late Reformation's Holy Roman ideals of pontifex maximus and *summus episcopus* to the reality of constructing a well-ordered modern state (as demonstrated in chapter 3). The Western origins of Prokopovich's empire-building enterprise endowed the new church with a certain ecumenical outlook that manifested itself not only in theological openness to Western ideas but later in other areas as well, like interconfessional dialogue or an acceptance of pan-Christian political pretensions (the Holy Alliance being one example).

The most important legacy of this empire-building, however, was the emergence of the Orthodox Church as both a Russian and an imperial ecclesial body. The original builders of the Petrine and Elizabethan spiritual empire were mostly Ukrainian, at some point (roughly between 1740 and 1762) constituting 76 percent of all hierarchical appointments. However, these Ukrainians built a church that was culturally and administratively centered on St. Petersburg. They were consciously or subconsciously building an imperial institution, which came with its own sets of contradictions. Thus, on the one hand, this imperial institution became open to reflecting its growing ethnic diversity, with Ukrainians, Greeks, Moldavians, Georgians, and others joining the ranks of the upper clergy, serving an increasingly diverse laity of Belarusians, Yakuts, Mordovians, and Ossetians (among many others). Yet, on the other hand, over the course of the eighteenth and nineteenth centuries, the church became more and more culturally Russified, with ethnic Russians increasingly dominating key ecclesiastical positions. For example, in 1901, among the sixty-four dioceses (eparchies) of the church across Europe, Asia, and North America, only a dozen or so had Ukrainian and Belarusian bishops. Among the more than seventy representatives of the monastic clergy at the 1917–18 Church Council, only seven were Ukrainian, with one Estonian, one Pole, one Serb, and one Moldavian present. This difference between the international (or rather, interethnic) form of the Russian Orthodox Church and its nationally Russian content still contributes to the lingering tensions in the Orthodox spaces of the post-Soviet world today.

Another lasting continuity of the reforms, and particularly the pre-1825 Orthodox Enlightenment, was the existence of clerical liberalism that persisted despite the growth of reaction and autocratic conservatism after 1825. Although the adoption of Western religious ideas helped Russia's monarchs create a more rational, ordered, and enlightened empire, it also, paradoxically, laid the foundation for the growth of political freethinking within the Orthodox Church. Despite Protasov's "orthodox reaction," the seminarians in Moscow (under Filaret's protection) continued to read enlightened and mystical literature, to enjoy "personal and academic freedom," and even to hold disputations on topics like "whether there is any relevance in belonging to a confession or, whether any religion can lead to salvation."[45] Meanwhile, Metropolitan Filaret occasionally voiced his opposition to the new order, sometimes even criticizing the tsar, who was once "enraged [*vzbeshennyi*]" by the prelate's sermon blaming the 1831 Moscow cholera outbreak on the monarch's inaction. Still, he remained a loyal member of the hierarchy, which prompted Herzen once to recall that Filaret was "an oppositional hierarch. . . . The purpose of his opposition was something I could never understand."[46]

As far as the clergy overall is concerned, the phenomenon of seminarians reading Voltaire in the eighteenth century likely had a comparative continuity in the reading of the radical *Church-Social Messenger* by seminarians during the Great Reforms. As Freeze has meticulously documented, late imperial "clerical liberalism" adopted "quasi-Protestant attitudes" that included a critique of the post-1825 neo-patristic trend of "a blind, ritualistic Byzantinism," yet criticism of the ecclesiastical status quo resonated well beyond theology.[47] As Laurie Manchester had shown, the institutional endurance of the unique and independent seminary culture that originated in the eighteenth century created an environment in which many sons of the clergy (the *popovichi*) could imbibe radical ideas, meet radical teachers, read forbidden literature, and engage in clandestine activities during the late nineteenth century.[48] It should be no surprise then, that as Stephen Kotkin noted, the activist culture of the Tiflis seminary (where young Stalin studied) was so radical that, by 1898, the Caucasus governorate authorities decided to close the institution, which they did in 1907.[49]

Although this radicalizing trend was not mainstream and most seminarians did not join revolutionary movements, it had broader ramifications. One "apotheosis" of this movement was the rise of Renovationism in 1905 and the appearance of the "red priests" of the Living Church in the 1920s. Another outcome was the rise of a new intelligentsia who grew up in what Il'ia Kravtsov described as the cultural milieu of "ecclesiastical anticlericalism."[50] Among such intellectuals were Sergei Bulgakov, Apolinarii L'vov, Nikolai Durnovo, Vasilii Kliuchevskii, Veniamin Fedchenkov, Nikolai Zernov, Agapit Vishnevskii, and others.[51] Yet another outcome was the broader contribution that such clerical "liberalism" made to turning some of the lower clergy and the lower classes from being "uneducated to miseducated" (in Freeze's observation) and that prepared Russia for the revolution rather than causing it (in Manchester's assessment).[52] Thus, in the long term, the spiritual revolution of 1700–1825 not only turned Russia to Western modernity but also helped ready Russian society for the liberal and illiberal revolutions that accompanied such a turn.

APPENDIX

Table I. Structural Parallels between Platon's *Pravoslavnoe uchenie* and the Larger Westminster Catechism

Pravoslavnoe uchenie (1765)	The Larger Westminster Catechism (1648)
Paragraphs	*Questions*
PART I	
1: Man's self-knowledge, "Where does human self-knowledge begin?"	1: Self-realization, "What is the chief and highest end of man?"
2–3: Proofs of the existence of God	2: Proofs of the existence of God
4–5: On the nature of God	3–5: On Scripture
6–7: God's act of creation	6–14: On the nature of God and the Trinity
8–9: God's Providence, including Providence toward man	
	15–17: God's act of creation
10–12: On worshipping God	18–20: God's Providence toward creation, toward man and the angels
13: Eternal life	
14–18: Human corruption and depravity	20–29: Human fall and depravity
	30–36: Covenant of grace
PART II	37–45: Incarnation of Christ (including offices of Christ)
1–3: Revelation and Scripture	
4–7: On Church	46–54: The life, death, suffering, and resurrection of Jesus Christ
8: Nicene Creed	
9: On faith (including justifying faith)	55: Intercession of Jesus Christ
10: Holy Trinity	56: Last Days and Last Judgment

11: Angels

12–13: God's Providence

14: Blessed end of the believer

15–17: Adam's transgression and original sin

18: Human depravity and the inability of man to save himself

19–20: Incarnation of Christ (including offices of Christ)

21–25: The life, death, suffering, and resurrection of Jesus Christ

26–27: Descent of the Holy Spirit and apostolic calling

28–29: On the nature of the church

30–39: On sacraments

40: On tradition and rituals

41–42: On the resurrection of the dead, the Last Judgment, and the Last Days.

Part III

1–4: On Law

5–14: Explanation of each of the Ten Commandments

15–16: On prayer and explanation of Lord's Prayer

57–60: Partakers of Christ's redemption

61–65: Nature of the church and members of the church

66: Union of the elect

67–69: Effectual calling and communion of grace

70–71: Justification

72–73: Faith and justifying faith

74–78: Adoption and sanctification

79–81: Perseverance of the saints (assurance of salvation of the elect)

82–90: Death, Last Judgment, and communion in glory

91–98: On moral law

99–149: On the Ten Commandments and explanation of each commandment

150–53: Transgressions and different types of sins

154: Christ's visible mediation

155–60: Preaching of the Word of God

161–77: On Sacraments

178–196: On prayer and explanation of the Lord's Prayer

Table II. Examples of thematic similarities in content between Platon Levshin's
Pravoslavnoe uchenie and the Larger Westminster Catechism

Pravoslavnoe Uchenie	*Larger Westminster Catechism*
The Three Offices of Christ: King, Priest, Prophet	

On the mystery of the Incarnation of Christ. From the very Incarnation of the Son of God he worthily assumed the most august title of Christ or Messiah. Both of these mean the same thing, that is, the anointed one. In the Old Testament, the Kings, Priests, and Prophets were the ones anointed. This anointing signified election by God. Secondly through the anointing—as a visible sign—spiritual authority was given to the anointed in order to fulfill the office worthily. By assuming flesh, the Son of God assumed all these offices and became, all in one: our *King [tsar]* governing the church by his almighty power and defending it from the enemies, Luke 1:32; then the Priest who satisfied God by the sacrifice of his death, Hebrews 5:6; and also the Prophet who showed us the will of God, Acts 3:22. To these offices the Son of God was anointed not by a simple oil but by the Holy Spirit as He testified in Luke 4:18. (*PU*, 2, paragraph 20; emphasis added)

Q. 42. *Why was our Mediator called Christ? A.* Our Mediator was called Christ, because he was anointed with the Holy Ghost above measure, and so set apart, and fully furnished with all authority and ability, to execute the offices of prophet, priest, and king of his church, in the estate both of his humiliation and exaltation. John 3:34, John 6:27, Acts 3:21–22, Hebrews 5:5–7, Psalm 2:6. Q. 43. *How doth Christ execute the office of a prophet? A.* Christ executeth the office of a prophet, in his revealing to the church in all ages, by his Spirit and Word, in divers ways of administration, the whole will of God, in all things concerning their edification and salvation. John 1:18, John 15:15, 1 Peter 1:10–12, Hebrews 1:1–2, Acts 20:23. Q. 44. *How doth Christ execute the office of a priest? A.* Christ executeth the office of a priest, in his once offering himself a sacrifice without spot to God, to be reconciliation for the sins of his people; and in making continual intercession for them. Hebrews 9:14, Hebrews 9:28, Hebrews 2:17, Hebrews 7:25. Q. 45. *How doth Christ execute the office of a king? A.* Christ executeth the office of a king, in calling out of the world a people to himself, and giving them officers, laws, and censures, by which he visibly governs them; in bestowing saving grace upon his elect, rewarding their obedience, and correcting them for their sins, preserving and supporting them under all their temptations and sufferings, restraining and overcoming all their enemies, and powerfully ordering all things for his own glory, and their good; and also in taking vengeance on the rest, who know not God, and obey not the gospel. Acts 15:14–16, Psalm 110:3. Thy people shall be willing in the day of thy power, in the beauties. Ephesians 4:11–12, Isaiah 33:22, Matthew 18:17–18, Acts 5:31, Revelation 22:12, Revelation 3:19, Isaiah 63:9, 1 Corinthians 15:25, Romans 14:10–11, Romans 8:28, 2 Thessalonians 1:8–9. (*LWC* Qs 41–46)

The Incarnation of Christ: Human Nature, Human Feeling, and Fulfillment of the Law

It was necessary for the Son of God to become man, because (1) God the Father in the task of our redemption needed a Mediator [*Khodatai*] and a guarantor [*sporuchnik*] for us who appeared to be a mere human sinner, such was an image He assumed. This would not have been possible if he had not assumed human nature/humanity [*chelovechestvo*]. (2) So that he can be seen by us and show us the will of our Heavenly Father. This is why He is the Savior. (3) In order to fulfill the law completely, not only to cover our disobedience to the law, but also to give us an example of his most holy life to follow. This would not be possible without assuming an image of man. (4) So that by dying, his death might satisfy the justice of God to deliver us from our deserved punishment and give us eternal life. These are the most important reasons for the Incarnation of the Son of God. 2 Cor. 5:21, John 15:15, Gal. 4:4, Hebr. 2:14. (*PU*, 2, par. 20)

Why was it requisite that the Mediator should be man? A. It was requisite that the Mediator should be man, that he might advance our nature, perform obedience to the law, suffer and make intercession for us in our nature, have a fellow-feeling of our infirmities; that we might receive the adoption of sons, and have comfort and access with boldness unto the throne of grace. Heb. 2:16, Gal 4:4, Heb. 2:14, Gal. 4:5, Heb. 4:16. (*LWC*, Q. 39)

Branches of Providence

On the Providence of God: God did not abandon the world He created, but provides for it, by (a) preserving [*sokhraniaia*] the existence and actions of all things, and (b) governs [*upravliaet*] all creation most wisely toward their superior purposes [*kontsy*]. (*PU*, 2, par. 8)

What are God's works of providence? A. God's works of providence are his most holy, wise, and powerful preserving and governing all his creatures; ordering them, and all their actions, to his own glory. (*LWC*, Q. 18)

Sacrament: A Sensible Sign for Invisible Grace

In his church, Jesus Christ established sacraments or holy rituals [*obriady*] in which under the sensible signs [*chuvstvuemye vidy*] a believer is given the unseen grace of God. (*PU*, 2, par. 30)

What is a sacrament? A. A sacrament is an holy ordinance instituted by Christ in his church, to signify, seal, and exhibit unto those that are within the covenant of grace . . . *What are the parts of a sacrament? A.* The parts of the sacrament are two; the one an outward and sensible sign, used according to Christ's own appointment; the other an inward and spiritual grace thereby signified. (*LWC*, Qs. 162–63)

NOTES

INTRODUCTION

1. Malia, *Russia under Western Eyes*, 39–59; for a concise survey of the impact of German, English, and French Enlightenment thought in Russia, see Raeff, "The Enlightenment in Russia."

2. Christoph F. Mickwitz, "Auszug aus Brief von Christoph Friedrich Mickwitz an [Unbekannt]. 15.01.1720," AFSt/HA, C 491:27, s. 27a.

3. The sacredness of this "state" (monarchy, not bureaucracy, in a proper early modern sense) was both personal and charismatic (as highlighted in Erik Zitser's work) as well as societal and kerygmatic, as highlighted in my discussion of the new public presentation of the monarchy as "sacred" guardian of the common good. See Zitser, *Transfigured Kingdom*.

4. Marshall, *Oxford Illustrated History of the Reformation*, 115–86. For an overview of the Catholic Reformation, see Olin, *The Catholic Reformation*. For a discussion of Europe's diverse reformations mentioned in this introduction, see the compendia of articles in Louthan and Murdoch, *A Companion to the Reformation*; and Pettegree, *The Reformation World*. See also Tracy, *Europe's Reformations*, 297–310. On the inclusion and exclusion of various reformations in scholarly debates, see McGrath, *Reformation Thought*, 5–6. Among the examples of works on trans-Atlantic reformations are Pestana, *Protestant Empire*; and Manning, "Reformation."

5. See Lindberg, *European Reformations*; Rublack, *Reformation Europe*; and Wallace, *The Long European Reformation*.

6. The first two defining events of the Reformation are widely but not universally accepted. For an example of the definition of Reformation that includes both the emergence of movements of religious change and those movements' interaction with Catholicism, see Hillerbrand, "Reformation," 7656; and McGrath, *Reformation Thought*, 2–6. For a discussion of the debates surrounding the definition of the Reformation, see Lexutt, *Die Reformation*.

7. Quoted in Dixon, *Contesting the Reformation*, 181. Among the more recent works that argue for the Reformation's role in the transition to modernity are Gregory,

An Unintended Reformation; and Parker and Bentley, *Between the Middle Ages and Modernity*.

8. Florovskii, *Puti russkogo bogosloviia*, 84; Treadgold, *The West in Russia and China*, 1:84–115; Zhuk, *Russia's Lost Reformation*.

9. Haven, *Reise in Russland*, 22; Vierorth, "Lebenslauf," 118; Martini, *Nachricht aus Russland*, 45–46.

10. Pekarskii, *Istoriia Imperatorskoi akademii nauk*, 1:77–79.

11. Dauksza's report (in Latin) is printed in *Akty i dokumenty*, 2:132.

12. *Acta SCPF*, 3:241.

13. Feofilakt [Lopatinskii], "Igo gospodne blago i bremia ego legko," OR RGB, f. 196, op. 3, rukopis' 173, ll. 3, 5; Gavriil Buzhinskii, Feofan's ally, used terms like "rectification," "establishment," "change," and "transformation" when describing the reformations in Germany, Scotland, and other parts of Europe. See, for example, his preface and translation of Pufendorf's *Vvedenie v gistoriiu evropeiskuiu*, 7, 141, 154, 330.

14. Wallmann, *Kirchengeschichte Deutschlands*, 154–55. See numerous references throughout Beutel, *Aufklärung in Deutschland*; and Sorkin, *The Religious Enlightenment*.

15. See Lehner, *The Catholic Enlightenment*; and Lehner, *Enlightened Monks*.

16. Geertz, *Interpretation of Cultures*, 119.

17. See Halfin, *From Darkness to Light*; Hellbeck, *Revolution on My Mind*; and Kotkin, *Magnetic Mountain*. For a recent discussion of the turn to theology, see Silano, "'In the Language of the Patriarch.'"

18. Florovskii, *Puti russkogo bogosloviia*, 86–98.

19. Freeze, "Subversive Piety," 309–12.

20. Golburt, *The First Epoch*, 4.

21. Kartashev, *Ocherki*, 2:349.

22. Bushkovitch, *Peter the Great*; Burstein, *Victorian Reformations*; Chrissidis, *An Academy at the Court of the Tsars*; Pirillo, *The Refugee-Diplomat*.

23. For an overview of the "confessionalization thesis" in English, see Hsia, *Social Discipline in the Reformation*; and the collection of essays (including by Heinz Schilling) in Headley, *Confessionalization in Europe*.

24. Worobec, "Lived Orthodoxy in Imperial Russia," 341; Freeze, "Recent Scholarship on Russian Orthodoxy: A Critique," 270; Werth, "Lived Orthodoxy and Confessional Diversity," 849.

25. See, for example, Worobec, "Lived Orthodoxy in Imperial Russia" and "The Long Road to Kiev"; Werth, "Lived Orthodoxy and Confessional Diversity" and "Miraculous Healings"; Steinberg, "Workers on the Cross"; Shevzov, *Russian Orthodoxy on the Eve of the Revolution*; Skinner, *The Western Front of the Eastern Church*; Paert, *Spiritual Elders*; Michelson, *Beyond the Monastery Walls*; Manchester, *Holy Fathers, Secular Sons*; Kizenko, *A Prodigal Saint*; Kenworthy, *The Heart of Russia*; Greene, *Bodies Like Bright Stars*; Freeze, *The Parish Clergy in Nineteenth-Century Russia*; and Coleman, "Tales of Violence" and *Russian Baptists and Spiritual Revolution*. See also Greene and Kivelson, *Orthodox Russia: Belief and Practice under the Tsars*; and Michelson and Kornblatt, *Thinking Orthodox in Modern Russia: Culture, History, Context*.

26. Zverinskii, *Monastyri*, ix–xi.

27. Ibid.; Denisov, *Pravoslavnye monastyri Rossiiskoi Imperii*, ix–x. For the overview of the revival of monasticism after 1825, see Kenworthy, *The Heart of Russia*.

28. Nichols, "Orthodox Spirituality in Imperial Russia"; Worobec, "The Long Road to Kiev" and "Miraculous Healings"; Michelson, *Beyond the Monastery Walls*; Kenworthy, *The Heart of Russia*; Kizenko, *A Prodigal Saint*.

29. Raeff, "The Well-Ordered Police State," 1222.

30. See, for example, Geraci and Khodarkovsky, *Of Religion and Empire*.

31. Crews, "Empire and the Confessional State," 50–83.

CHAPTER 1. RUSSIAN ORTHODOXY ON THE EVE OF THE REFORMS

1. The Senate copy of the text is found in "Pis'ma kasaiushchiesia do Sv. Prav. Sinoda ot 1712 . . . ," RGADA, f. 9, otd. 1, d. 31, ll. 3–18. For more on the sermon, see Ustrialov, *Istoriia tsarstvovaniia*, 6:30–32.

2. "Pis'ma kasaiushchiesia do Sv. Prav. Sinoda ot 1712 . . . ," RGADA, f. 9, otd. 1, d. 31, l. 7 ob.

3. Ibid., ll. 11 ob.–12.

4. Ibid., l. 15 ob. Peter married Catherine (the future Catherine I) on February 19, 1712.

5. Ibid., l. 18.

6. Bushkovitch, *Peter the Great*, 340.

7. Lavrov, *Koldovstvo i religiia v Rossii*, 344. See Paul Bushkovitch's discussion of Peter's church attendance in "The Clergy at the Russian Court," 105–28.

8. Zhivov, *Iz tserkovnoi istorii*, 50.

9. Raeff, "The Well-Ordered Police State," 1222–35.

10. Anisimov, *Vremia petrovskikh reform*, 330–31.

11. On the war's diversion from Peter's reform efforts, see Hughes, *Russia in the Age of Peter*, 337–38.

12. See, for example, Bushkovitch, *Peter the Great*, 199–201; Hughes, *Russia in the Age of Peter*, 333–34.

13. Anisimov, *Vremia petrovskikh reform*, 342.

14. Cracraft, *Church Reform*, 119. Cracraft also notes that Peter was considering appointing a patriarch in 1718. Ibid.

15. The term "exarch" appears in the 1737 memoir of Johann Gotthilf Vockerodt, *Russland unter Peter dem Grossen*, 15. "Exarch" and "exarchat" also appear in Haigold's discussion of church reform in *Beylagen zum neuveränderten Russland*, 1:17–20. The term "locum tenens" is used in Bushkovitch, *Peter the Great*, 436; for a discussion of the canonical status of the vacancy, see Zhivov, *Iz tserkovnoi istorii*, 44–49.

16. Anisimov, *Vremia petrovskikh reform*, 344–46. See also Hughes, *Russia in the Age of Peter*, 335–38.

17. Kharlampovich, *Malorossiiskoe vliianie*, 507–38. The following eparchies were staffed by bishops from the Hetmanate: Rostov, Riazan, Tobolsk, Kolomna, Arkhangelsk, Belgorod, Smolensk, Nizhnii Novgorod, Kholmogory.

18. Ibid., 575–85.

19. Zhivov, *Razyskaniia*, 306–8.

20. Bushkovitch, *Peter the Great*, 424.

21. Thomson, *The Reception of Byzantine Culture*.

22. Ibid., 355; Thomson identified only the works of three fathers "known to have existed in their entirety in Russia at this time": Cyril of Jerusalem's *Catecheses*, St. Athanasius's *Contra Arianos*, and Pope Leo I's *Tomus*. Ibid., 110–11.

23. Yannaras, *Orthodoxy and the West*, 45; Karl Christian Felmy also points out that Western influences upon Orthodoxy can be traced to earlier times, for example, the 1274 Council of Lyons, after which the Eastern church formally accepted the number of ecclesiastical sacraments or "mysteries" as seven in line with the Western custom. Felmy, *Die Orthodoxe Theologie*, 170.

24. Yannaras, *Orthodoxy and the West*, 45–58; for a discussion of the differences between Byzantine and Western Aristotelianisms, see pages 52–56.

25. See, for example, O'Malley, *Trent and All That*.

26. See Ivanov, "Reformation and the Muscovite Czar," 1109–29.

27. Ibid., 77–81. For an excellent overview of catechetical formation in Eastern Slavic churches, see Korzo, *Ukrainskaia i belorusskaia katekhicheskaia traditsiia*.

28. Filaret [Gumilevskii], *Obzor russkoi dukhovnoi literatury*, 1:177, 179; Frick, *Meletij Smotryc'kyj*; and Niess, *Kirche in Russland*. For a discussion of the Orthodox use of Protestant ideas in their polemics with Catholics, and the borrowing of Catholic formulae in their polemics with the Protestants, see Oparina's *Ivan Nasedka i polemicheskoe bogoslovie*. While many of the church hierarchs in Russia and Ukraine pursued a heated anti-Protestant polemic, many Ukrainian noblemen closely cooperated with Polish and Lithuanian Protestant nobles in the common defense of religious freedom. See Kempa, *Wobec kontrreformacji*.

29. Compare Mohyla's *Pravoslavnoe ispovedanie* with Canisius's *Petri Canisii Societatis Jesu theologi*. For a full scholarly comparison of Mohyla's appropriations, see Malvy and Viller, *La Confession Orthodoxe*. For the seventeenth-century reception of the catechism as a borrowing from Catholicism, see Cherviakovskii, "Vvedenie v bogoslovie Feofana Prokopovicha," 15; and Skuminowicz, *Przyczyny porzuczenia dysunii*. Felmy has shown that Mohyla's understanding of the Eucharistic transubstantiation was purely Roman Catholic, but that Meletios Syrigos's Greek translation of his Confessio altered the text and added the Orthodox teaching on epiclesis. Felmy, *Die Deutung der Göttlichen Liturgie*, 129–31.

30. For positive and negative reactions to Mohyla, see Kharlampovich, *Malorossiiskoe vliianie*, 117–33; Florovskii, *Puti russkogo bogosloviia*, 52.

31. Yannaras, *Orthodoxy and the West*, 82.

32. Rolland, "'Nieskoro' prawi 'munsztuk do tych trąb otrzymacie'," 205–16.

33. Kharlampovich, *Malorossiiskoe vliianie*, 421–22, 426–27; Shliapkin, "O polemike," 210–52.

34. Chepiha, "Kliuch Rozuminnia Ioanykiia Galiatovs'kogo," in Ioanikii [Galiatovskii], *Kliuch Rozuminnia*, edited by Ivan Chepiha (Kyiv, 1985), 5–34. For stories of St. Theresa, apparitions at Compostela, and so on, see ibid., 5–34; Ioanikii, *Kliuch Rozuminia*, 264–65. See also Bida, *Ioanikii Galiatovs'kyi*.

35. Mohyla, *Pravoslavnoe Ispovedanie* (1763), ll. 4–4 ob. On Adrian and Ioakim and Mohyla's catechism, see Hauptmann, *Die Katechismen der Russisch-orthodoxen Kirche*, 21.

36. According to Ternovskii, young Stefan apparently wanted to study in Paris. Ternovskii, "Stefan Iavorskii," 50–52. He finished the Poznań and Wilno Jesuit academies in 1689 with a *Magister artium liberalium et philosophiae magister et consummate theologiae*. Ibid., 56.

37. Morozov, *Feofan Prokopovich kak pisatel'*, 57–62, 61–65.

38. Vvedenskii, "K biografii mitropolita Stefana Iavorskogo," 892–99. The full text of Iavorskii's refusal is in "Pis'mo [. . .] Stefana Iavorskogo," RGADA, f. 153, op. 1, d. 1700.

39. Runkevich, *Uchrezhdenie i pervonachal'noe ustroistvo*, 1:84.

40. For example, monastic and patriarchal landholdings had been managed by the Monastery Prikaz since 1701. Ternovskii, "Stefan Iavorskii," 254–55.

41. "Delo Feofana Prokopovicha," 81.

42. Moroshkin, "Feofilakt Lopatinskii," 3–6; Florovskii, *Puti russkogo bogosloviia*, 99.

43. Moroshkin, "Feofilakt Lopatinskii," 7.

44. Feofan [Prokopovich], "Pis'mo k professoram Kievskoi Akademii [from June 1718]," in "Pis'ma," *TKDA* 1 (1865): 153.

45. Vockerodt, *Russland unter Peter dem Grossen*, 16. He is referring to Spanish theologians Gabriel Vásquez, SJ (1549–1604), Antonio Escobar y Mendoza (1589–1669), Tomás Sánchez, SJ (1550–1610), Francisco de Oviedo, SJ (1602–52), and the celebrated rhetorician Cipriano Suárez, SJ (1524–93). For an in-depth discussion of the popularity of Spanish Baroque homiletics and theology in Ukraine and Belarus, see Ivanov, *Reforming Orthodoxy*, 266–74.

46. Chistovich, *Feofan Prokopovich i ego vremia*, 33. Feofan [Prokopovich], *Filosofs'ki tvory*, 3:197. Feofan claimed that Gedeon was "expelled" from the academy, according to his June 1718 letter to Kiev professors printed in Feofan [Prokopovich], "Pis'ma," *TKDA* 1 (1865): 152–53.

47. Chistovich, *Feofan Prokopovich i ego vremia*, 33.

48. "Delo Feofana Prokopovicha," 2, 24, 69.

49. Ibid., 2. For the most well-researched available study of the Likhoudes brothers in Moscow, see Chrissidis, *An Academy at the Court of the Tsars*. Chistovich claims that Liberius Coletti called himself *don* in his writings. He decorated the house church of his patron, Musin-Pushkin, in a Catholic manner, with statues. Chistovich, *Feofan Prokopovich i ego vremia*, 424–25. See also Ramazanova, "Ekzempliary sochinenii patriarkha Khrisanfa Notara," 180–81.

50. Ternovskii, "Stefan Iavorskii," 40.

51. Numerous parallels can be found between Iavorskii's *Tractatus theologiae controversiae traditus in Collegio Kijovomohilaeano* (OR RGB, f. 173, op. 1, rukopis' no. 278) and Bellarmine's *Disputationes de Controversiis Christianae fidei*, 4 vols. (Paris, 1613). Iavorskii's borrowings from Bellarmine have also been described by Morev in his *"Kamen' very"*; Maslov, *Biblioteka Stefana Iavorskogo*, 8–39.

52. Bushkovitch, *Peter the Great*, 424.

53. Samarin, *Stefan Iavorskii i Feofan Prokopovich* (1880), 42–44. Iavorskii's views that human will was not completely corrupted are similar to the theological stance of Luis Molina (1535–1600).

54. As Samarin pointed out, Stefan based his doctrine of toll houses on same justifications as the doctrine of purgatory by tying the notion of "toll-payment" to the sacrament of penance. Samarin failed to note, however, that such views were generally considered Orthodox in Kiev, as seen in Galiatovskii's case (n35). Samarin, *Stefan Iavorskii i Feofan Prokopovich* (1880), 50–51.

55. Ibid., 241.

56. Iavorskii, "Apologiia ili slovesnaia oborona," 261; the original is stored in OPI GIM, Uvar. no. 1728 (378) (588), ll. 1–14. "Just like all levels of civic government are under authority of the Sovereign as members to a head, so does the same wisdom of authority apply to the spiritual world," he argued. Ibid., 255.

57. Zhivov, *Iz tserkovnoi istorii*, 109.

58. Ibid., 257.

59. Stefan [Iavorskii], "Znameniia prishestviia antikhristova"; Malvenda, *De Antichristo*; the comparison of the two works is mine.

60. For this reason, Malvenda and Iavorskii referred to the previous "Antichrists"— Simon Magus, Nero, Diocletian, Julian, and Mohammed, as being the "precursors of the Antichrist." Compare Stefan [Iavorskii], "Znameniia prishestviia antikhristova," 40–41; and Malvenda, *De Antichristo*, 11–20, 62–71.

61. Malvenda, *De Antichristo*, 56, 66–68; Stefan [Iavorskii], "Znameniia prishestviia antikhristova," 41, 90–95; for Iavorskii's similar views on the incarnation of Satan, see page 102.

62. Compare Stefan [Iavorskii]'s "Znameniia prishestviia antikhristova," 54–57, with Malvenda, *De Antichristo*, 180.

63. Stefan [Iavorskii], "Znameniia prishestviia antikhristova," 56.

64. Ibid., 57.

65. Ibid.

66. Samarin, *Stefan Iavorskii i Feofan Prokopovich* (1880): 35–37; Ternovskii, "Stefan Iavorskii," 55–56; Morozov, *Feofan Prokopovich kak pisatel'*, 80; see also Jabłonowski, *Akademia Kijowsko-Mohylańska*, 187.

67. Iavorskii, *Kamen' very*, 4 ob.

68. This epigraph is found on the cover of the earliest known manuscript copy (scribe's reproduction) of Stefan's original *Kamen' very*. "Zaglavnyi list na sochinenie Stefana Iavorskogo," RGADA, f. 18, op. 1, d. 10, l. 1. 1.

69. Ibid. In another instance he referred to Luther as "a worm, filled with infernal poison, hideous heresiarch." Morozov, *Feofan Prokopovich kak pisatel'*, 141–42.

70. Ternovskii, "Stefan Iavorskii," 59–67, 237–38; James Cracraft, *Church Reform*, 163.

71. Quoted in Tal'berg, *Istoriia russkoi tserkvi*, 393.

72. Brilioth, *A Brief History of Preaching*, 144. Frederick McGinness dismissed the importance of content in Baroque oratory, stating that "what the preacher said mattered little as long as he filled his sermons with resounding Ciceronic periods and mythological allusions" (McGinness "Preaching Ideals and Practice," 112–13). For a very detailed description of the origins of the Southern European Baroque preaching style, see Ivanov, "Reforming Orthodoxy," 266–70.

73. Vengco, *Juan de Cartagena*, 299–300; Matseevich, "Polskii propovednik Foma Mlodzianovskii," *TKDA* 4 (1870): 143. This homiletic school advocated the use of exaggerated antitheses, metaphors, and florid wordplay, and had much in common with Luis de Gongora's *cultismo* movement in seventeenth-century Spain. For more on *conceptismo* and sermons in Spain, see Fitzmaurice-Kelly, *History of Spanish Literature*, 299–305.

74. Vengco, *Juan de Cartagena*, 180–85. At the same time, he viewed the six days of creation in Genesis as proof of Mary's Immaculate Conception (her sinless birth), based on the speculation that the creation of the sea (*mare-Maria*), moon, and fish all symbolized the Virgin. Ibid., 179–80, 283. A similar trend in Spain can be observed in the sermons of St. Tomás de Villanova (ibid., 165–67).

75. Croce, *Storia dell'età Barocca*, 489; Mario Praz identified this trend as an all-encompassing cultural movement that utilized images and emblems in various spheres of life as "simple allegorical designs . . . destined to teach an intuitive form of a moral truth." *Studies in Seventeenth-Century Imagery*, 1:14–15.

76. Norman, "The Social History of Preaching," 161–62; Petrov, "Vyderzhki iz rukopisnoi retoriki," 618–20; Markovskii, *Antonii Radivilovskii*, 16.

77. One's ability "to draw tears" was considered a special "talent" for most preachers. H. Smith, *Preaching in the Spanish Golden Age*, 65–68.

78. "One preacher enters the pulpit with [Juan] Osorio, another with [Walenty] Fabricius, and another with [Petr] Skarga," wrote Meletii Smotritskii (1577–1633), who criticized his contemporaries for reading from collections of Spanish and Polish sermons at the end of the liturgy. Pekarskii, "Predstaviteli Kievskoi uchenosti," 572.

79. Petrov, "Iz istorii gomiletiki," 86, 91–93; Polish *postyly* of the *conceptus* type were also well accepted, especially those of Petr Skarga, Szymon Starowolski, and Tomasz Młodzianowski. The latter's popularity reached its peak toward the end of the seventeenth century with the rectorship of Stefan Iavorskii, as the Kiev-Mohyla Academy rhetoric courses in 1698 employed Młodzianowski's homilies as models. Ibid., 105.

80. Radivilovskii's collection of sermons, titled *Ogorodok Marii Bogoroditsy* (The Garden of Mary the Mother of God), was patterned after Meffreth's *Hortulus Reginae* (A Little Garden of the Queen). Markovskii, *Antonii Radivilovskii*, 65, 82–86. Similarly, his other compilation of sermons, *Venets Khristov*, bore the influence of the Polish *conceptus* (*koncepty*) homilies of Szymon Starowolski's *Wieniec . . . kazania*. Ibid., 13. Among the authors Antonii used were Peter Canisius (1521–97), Pietro Galatino (1460–1540), Simone Maioli (1520–97), Diego de Estella (1524–78), and Cornelius á Lapide (1567–1637). Markovskii, *Antonii Radivilovskii*, 17–20. There were also plenty of medieval sources, like Hugo de St. Victor (d. 1141), Anselm of Canterbury, or Albertus Magnus. Ibid. Galiatovskii's *Kliuch Razumeniia* (The Key to Understanding) employed the rhetorical techniques of the *conceptista* Spanish Jesuit Baltasar Gracian y Morales (1601–58) as well as the Bavarian Jesuit Jeremias Drexellius (1591–1638). Tarasov, *Rama o obraz*, 44.

81. Between 1660 and 1675, the most notable Ukrainian preachers, including Ignatii Evlevich, Ioann Shmatkovskii, Lazar' Baranovich, and Epifanii Slavinetskii, as well as Galiatovskii and Radivilovskii, delivered *conceptus*-style homilies at court.

Kharlampovich, *Malorossiiskoe vliianie*, 421–22, 426–27. On Epifanii Slavinetskii, see Bushkovitch, *Religion and Society*, 152–54.

82. For a deeper and fuller analysis of Polotskii's homiletics and the Spanish influence on them, see Ivanov, "Reforming Orthodoxy," 273–74, especially the footnotes.

83. Stefan [Iavorskii], *Ritoricheskaia ruka*, 103–4.

84. Ivanov, "Reforming Orthodoxy," 274–80; Petrov, "Iz istorii gomiletiki," 107–8. On the art of "stringing" the images of the sermon, see Vengco, *Juan de Cartagena*, 277; Ternovskii, "Stefan Iavorskii," 68.

85. Stefan [Iavorskii], "Slova," *TKDA* 10 (1875):117–18.

86. Ibid., 117–26.

87. This was something that became popular in Christianity in medieval Catalonia, during the time of Raymond Lull (1232–1315), but before Lull it was "an exclusively Jewish phenomenon." Yates, *Art of Memory*, 189–90; H. Smith, *Preaching in the Spanish Golden Age*, 44–45. This phenomenon, curiously enough, did not spread to Italy, so it appears to have been limited to Spain, Ukraine, and Poland. Vengco, *Juan de Cartagena*, 283, 284; Młodzianowski also used onomastics in his preaching; Stefan likely borrowed this practice from his teacher. Matseevich, "Pol'skii propovednik Foma Mlodzianovskii," *TKDA* 9 (1870): 510, 524–26.

88. Stefan [Iavorskii]'s *Zhatva torzhestvennaia* sermon is printed in his "Slova," *TKDA* 10 (1875): 120–21.

89. Ibid., 137–38.

90. Lachmann, *Feofan Prokopovic*, 48; Samarin, *Stefan Iavorskii i Feofan Prokopovich kak propovedniki*, 394–95; Petrov, "Iz istorii gomiletiki," 108; Zhivov, *Iz tserkovnoi istorii*, 56.

91. Vockerodt, *Russland unter Peter dem Grossen*, 11.

92. Ternovskii, "Ocherki iz istorii," 309.

93. See Chistovich, *Novogorodskii Mitropolit Iov*, 80–85.

94. The full text of the missive is in Kapterev, *Snosheniia Ierusalimskogo Patriarkha Dosifeiia*, pril. 11.

95. Tikhonravov, "Moskovskie vol'nodumtsy," 240–41, 245–46, 250; see also Bushkovitch, *Peter the Great*, 424.

96. Tikhonravov, "Moskovskie vol'nodumtsy," 202, 243–47; Magnitskii, *Zapiska Leontiia Magnitskogo*, 12.

97. Savelov, *Savelkovy i Savelovy*, 38–39; pril. 14–16, 21; see also Ustrialov, *Istoriia tsarstvovaniia*, 4:553–54. For the example of the Kholmogory diocese, see Runkevich, *Uchrezhdenie i pervonachal'noe ustroistvo*, 75–76. Musin-Pushkin was one of the students of the Likhoudes brothers in the Slavo-Greco-Latin Academy in Moscow and was one of the members of the educated elite who knew Latin. Chrissidis, "Creating the New Educated Elite," 276; and Bushkovitch, *Peter the Great*, 435–37.

98. Cracraft, *Church Reform*, 138.

99. Tikhonravov, "Moskovskie vol'nodumtsy," 182. Musin-Pushkin in turn appointed a chancellery official to spy on Stefan. Runkevich, *Uchrezhdenie i pervonachal'noe ustroistvo*, 74–75.

100. Vockerodt, *Russland unter Peter dem Grossen*, 11.

101. Ibid., 10; Tikhonravov, "Moskovskie vol'nodumtsy," 179–80; "Akty otnosia-shchiesia k istorii raskola," 44–45.

102. Tikhonravov, "Moskovskie vol'nodumtsy," 179–80; Ternovskii, "Stefan Iavor-skii," 261–62; especially Solov'ev, *Istoriia Rossii*, 9:499. In fact, Stefan once referred to Moscow as "Babylon" himself. Ternovskii, "Ocherki iz istorii," 310.

103. Vockerodt, *Russland unter Peter dem Grossen*, 10.

104. Chistovich, "Neizdannye propovedi Stefana Iavorskogo," 830–32.

105. Ternovskii, "Ocherki iz istorii," 312.

106. Ibid.

107. Bushkovitch, *Peter the Great*, 340; Cracraft, *Church Reform*, 138.

108. Magnitskii, *Zapiska Leontii Magnitskogo*, 12.

109. Panchenko, *Russkaia istoriia i kul'tura*, 333.

110. Tikhonravov, "Moskovskie vol'nodumtsy," 247–49.

111. Magnitskii, *Zapiska Leontii Magnitskogo*, 14, 47; Bilfinger, *Stephanii Javorskii*.

112. Magnitskii, *Zapiska Leontii Magnitskogo*, 10; Tikhonravov, "Moskovskie vol'nodumtsy," 194.

113. Magnitskii, *Zapiska Leontii Magnitskogo*, 13–14, 47. He noted furthermore that the president of the Senate, Iakov Dolgorukii, was "very disposed against the hierarch [Stefan]." Ibid., 13–15.

114. Magnitskii, *Zapiska Leontii Magnitskogo*, 17–18.

115. Pokrovskii, "Bor'ba s protestantskimi ideiami," 226.

116. Ibid., 231. He also grasped the details of Lutheran political theology rather well to understand the implications of these new ideas for church-state relations in Russia. Ibid., 227–31.

117. Tikhonravov, "Moskovskie vol'nodumtsy," 155; Stupperich, "Feofan Prokop-ovič und seine akademische Wirksamkeit," 81.

CHAPTER 2. ESCAPE FROM ROME

1. His family apparently had no ownership of land in the countryside and no family connections to the landholding classes, a rarity among the Ukrainian hierarchs at that time. Nichyk, *Feofan Prokopovich*, 10. One of the available eighteenth-century biographies of his life is the 1736 "Vita Theophanis Procopovitsch," written by acade-mician Theophil (also known as Gottlieb) Siegfried Bayer. Bayer's relationship with Feofan is mentioned in his letters to Halle and other universities in Germany, for example, "Brief von Theophil Siegfried Bayer. 02.10.1732," in AFSt Film ALMW/DHM 9/19:5, and "Materialen zur Orientalistik, Geographie, Altertumskunde und Numismatik," fols. 31r–35v, Cod. Guelf. 115.1 Extravagantes, HA HAB. Another offi-cial biography ("Vita Auctoris") was written in 1767 by the Göttingen-educated bishop Damaskin Semenov-Rudnev and published in Feofan's *Tractatus*. There is also the 1731 polemical biography written by Markell Rodyshevskii, "Zhitie Novgorodskogo arkhi-episkopa, eretika Feofana Prokopovicha," in "Delo Feofana Prokopovicha," 1–9.

2. Nichyk, *Feofan Prokopovich*, 12; Runkevich, *Uchrezhdenie i pervonachal'noe ustroistvo*, 1:99; Markell, "Zhitie . . . eretika Feofana," in "Delo Feofana Prokopovicha," 1; Avtukhovich, "Prokopovich," 488–96.

3. Zlatar, *Our Kingdom Come*, 226.

4. "Historia Collegii Graeci de Urbi," t. 10, fols. 10–11, Cod. Vat. Lat. 5527, BAV.

5. Ibid., fols. 38–38v.

6. Ibid.; Blažejovskyi, "Ukrainian and Bielorussian Students at the Pontifical Greek College," 143; Tamborra, "Il Collegio greco."

7. "Historia Collegii Graeci de Urbi," fol. 40v.

8. "Catalogus alumnorum qui erant in collegio Graecorum de Urbe" (henceforth, "Catalogus alumnorum"), t. 14, fols. 3–47, APCG. See also Netzhammer, *Das griechische Kolleg*, 19–21.

9. Netzhammer, *Das griechische Kolleg*, 19–21, 44–45; Blažejovskyi, "Ukrainian and Bielorussian Students in the Pontificio Collegio Urbano," 202–3; for the Jesuit takeover of the Greek College, see Blažejovskyi, "Ukrainian and Bielorussian Students at the Pontifical Greek College," 144–45.

10. Frazee, *Catholics and Sultans*, 69–72, 82; Binnis, *An Introduction*, 80.

11. Matushek, *Propovidi Lazaria Baranovycha*, 17–19.

12. Ibid., 19.

13. Eliav-Feldon and Herzig, *Dissimulation and Deceit*; Frick, *Meletij Smotryc'kyi*, 4, 173–75; Ivanova and Viise, "Dissimulation and Memory."

14. For an in-depth discussion, see Ivanov, "Escape from Rome."

15. Blažejovskyj writes that there were no students from the Kiev region in the college's book of oaths, "Ukrainian and Bielorussian Students in the Pontificio Collegio Urbano," 203; this is despite the fact that the college required the oath to be administered within seven months of enrollment. See, *Regole da osservarsi dal rettore*, 5–6.

16. Bayer, "Vita Theophanis Procopovitsch," 252.

17. Titov, Russkaia pravoslavnaia tserkov', 2:307–8; Jabłonowski, *Akademia Kijowsko-Mohylańska*, 192.

18. Briukhovets'kyi and Khyzhniak, *Kyevo-Mohylians'ka akademiia*, 245–46, 402–3.

19. Askochenskii, *Kiev*, 251, 382; Jabłonowski, *Akademia Kijowsko-Mohylańska*, 193. Leontovich was a nephew of Feofan Prokopovich I.

20. Ternovskii, "Stefan Iavorskii," 50–56; Moroshkin, "Feofilakt Lopatinskii," 3–6; Florovskii, *Puti russkogo bogosloviia*, 99.

21. The fact of his Roman education is recorded in the deliberations of the Sacred Congregation for the Propagation of the Faith in Rome in 1735 and in the 1736 letter to that congregation from the archbishop of Vienna, Sigismund von Kollonitz. Both letters are printed in *Acta SCPF* (1954) 3:279–84; Chistovich, *Feofan Prokopovich i ego vremia*, 33; Prokopovich, *Filosof'ski tvory*, 3:197. See also Treadgold, *The West in Russia and China*, 1:61.

22. "Catalogus alumnorum," 14:45.

23. Ibid., 14:44. They stayed until 1702, whereas Feofan left in 1701.

24. Ibid.

25. *Acta SCPF*, 2:147.

26. "Catalogus alumnorum," 14:45. It is likely that his study of philosophy in Rome included physics, mathematics, and geometry—all subjects part of the regular philosophy curriculum at the time and subjects he extensively wrote on in Ukraine, as seen in volumes 2 and 3 of his *Filosof'ski tvory*.

27. Bayer, "Vita Theophanis Procopovitsch," 253. This fact is also corroborated by the 1735 account of Moravian Brethren minister David Nitschmann, quoted in Teigeler, *Die Herrnhuter in Russland*, 538, also 133–35, 538.

28. Bayer, "Vita Theophanis Procopovitsch," 253.

29. Ibid., 253, 252.

30. Ibid., 254.

31. Pirie, *The Triple Crown*, 223–31.

32. Bayer, "Vita Theophanis Procopovitsch," 254.

33. Vockerodt, *Russland unter Peter dem Grossen*, 12.

34. Luther, "Assertio 1520," in *LW* 7:125.

35. *DR*, 15.

36. Bayer, "Vita Theophanis Procopovitsch," 253.

37. Ibid.; Winter, *Frühaufklärung*, 330–32.

38. Bayer, "Vita Theophanis Procopovitsch," 253.

39. Vierorth, "Lebenslauf," 116. Prokopovich's trip to Rome is also confirmed by Prussian embassy secretary Vockerodt in *Russland unter Peter dem Grossen*, 12, and by the Swedish ambassador to Russia, Josias Cederhjelm. See Krupnyts'kyi "Teofan Prokopovich i shvedy," 296–98. August Hermann Francke also discussed the presence of Protestant works in Roman libraries in "Bericht von August Hermann Francke über Gespräche während einer Einladung bei Kronprinz Friedrich in Preussen. 30.03.1725," in AFSt/HA 179:38b.

40. "Fugit Collegio 28 Octobris 1701 sine ulla causa et cum scandalo omnium nec usquam repertus fuit," in "Catalogus alumnorum," 14:45–46.

41. His departure seems to have shocked the rector, given an earlier entry in the "Catalogus alumnorum" stating that Prokopovich was an exceptional student. Ibid.

42. Markell, "Zhitie . . . eretika Feofana Prokopovicha," 1.

43. Ibid.

44. "De Statu Ecclesiae Unitae," report presented in Congregatio Generali 8 Apr 1710, printed in *Acta SCPF* 2:284.

45. "Schisma de Graeci e dale eresie di Lutero, e di Calvino, principia in oggi a respirare sotto la condotta di Teofane Prokopowicz . . . Scismatico, gia Alunno del Collegio Greco di questa Città." *Acta SCPF*, 3:241. This report was presented by Petro Koss, a "noble Ruthenian from Ukraine," to the General Congregation on January 12, 1728.

46. Ibid.

47. "A relation by R. P. D. Philippi de Montibus to the Congregation for the Propagation of Faith, 28 March, 1735," in *Acta SCPF*, 3:279–80 (No. 1104).

48. In 1736 the archbishop of Vienna, Sigismund von Kollonitz, in his letter to the congregation, brought up Feofan as an example in arguing that "drying up of the mind" and "retiring into idleness" could cause Ukrainian students in Rome to leave the Catholic faith. His letter to the congregation in Rome is printed in *Acta SCPF*, 3:283–84.

49. Bayer, "Vita Theophanis Procopovitsch," 254.

50. It is my intent to complete a thorough study based on the existing archival collections in Halle, Berlin, Wernigerode, and Wolfenbüttel (among other locations) to learn more about this period of Feofan's life.

51. Christian Haumann, "Brief von Christian Haumann an [Ernst Salomon Cyprian]. 08.09.1720," AFSt/HA 174:150 ss. 3–4. On the biography of Haumann, see Winter, *Halle als Ausgangspunkt*, 175; Wotschke, "Pietismus in Moskau"; and a reference in *Acta historico-ecclesiastica*, 9:655.

52. Gottfried Himler, "Brief von Gottfried Himler an Gotthilf August Francke. 19.04.1727," AFSt Film Stab/F 29/31:1. For more on Himler, see Freyer, *Programmata latino-germanica*, 707.

53. The Franckesche Stiftungen Archives in Halle preserved much of Cederhjelm's correspondence with the Pietist center, such as AFSt Film Stab/F 29/46:7 ("Brief von Josias Cederhielm an August Hermann Francke. 07.04.1725"); AFSt Film Stab/F 29/46:6 ("Brief von Josias Cederhielm an August Hermann Francke. 05.05.1725"). A discussion of Pietist ministers' meetings with Cederhjelm is in AFSt/HA 179:38b ("Bericht von August Hermann Francke über Gespräche während einer Einladung bei Kronprinz Friedrich in Preußen. 30.03.1725").

54. Krupnyts'kyi, "Teofan Prokopovich i shvedy," 297.

55. Ibid., 297, 300. These authors were strictly orthodox Lutheran.

56. "Viri admodum reverenti, fratres carissimi" (Very reverend Masters, dearest brothers!) is how Feofan addressed the scholars at Halle in this March 1720 letter. Francke inserted the letter into the middle of another correspondence, titled "Brief von [August Hermann] Francke an Henry Newman. 1721," AFSt Stab/F 30/35:22 Mikrofilm-Nr.: 20, fol. 1085. Regular correspondence between Feofan and Halle Pietists is also mentioned in "Brief von Peter Müller an August Hermann Francke. 18.12.1719," AFSt Stab/F 28/23:13 Mikrofilm-Nr.: 19, 941–942, and in Vierorth, "Lebenslauf," 115–18.

57. The connection of the Halle-Leipzig-Jena "middle German" university triangle with the Enlightenment is well established in the literature. See, for example, Kasper, *Das Reichsstift Quedlinburg*, 214; Rudolph, *Christian Wolff*, 61; Czok and Hoyer, *Leipzig und Sachsen*, 78. For the relationship of Pietism to German Enlightenment, see Beutel, *Kirchengeschichte*, 92–103.

58. His relations with Buddeus are well described in the following chapters. See his other letters in Feofan [Prokopovich], *Filosofs'ki tvory*, 3:214–15, 228–29, 262–63, and his letters to Francke, 301–5. For correspondence with Daniel Ernst Jabłonski, the head of the Berlin Academy of Sciences, see Chistovich, *Feofan Prokopovich i ego vremia*, 368.

59. Feofan [Prokopovich], "Rech', kotoroiu Ego tsarskoe velichestvo Petr Pervyi po vozvrashchenii svoem . . . ," in *Slova i rechi*, 1:190–91.

60. Chistovich, *Feofan Prokopovich i ego vremia*, 14–15; Feofan Prokopovych, "Kurs dogmaticheskogo bogosloviia, chitannyi Feofanom Prokopovichem v Kievo-Mogilianskoi akademii v 1708–1710 gg.," *OR RGB*, f. 173, op. 1, rukopis' 245.

61. Thanks to the tsar's generosity, Moscow's Slavo-Greco-Latin Academy actively recruited Kiev's best teachers. Kharlampovich, *Malorossiiskoe vliianie*, 405–15.

62. Iasinskii, for example, expelled both Jesuits and Uniates from Kiev. Askochenskii, *Kiev*, 2:6. On Varlaam's promotion of Feofan, see Evgenii [Bolkhovitinov], *Slovar' istoricheskii*, 325. Feofan also enjoyed good relations with the next metropolitan, Ioasaf Krokovskii. Askochenskii, *Kiev*, 2:10–19. Good relations between the rector and the metropolitan were not common, as the academy often took sides with the city burghers in

their numerous disputes with ecclesiastical authorities and property owners—during much of the 1720s, for example. Kryzhanovskii, "Feofan Prokopovich i Varlaam Vanatovich," 282–91; Titov, *Russkaia pravoslavnaia tserkov'*, 442–43 and 453.

63. Kryzhanovskii, "Feofan Prokopovich i Varlaam Vanatovich," 282–91, Chistovich, *Feofan Prokopovich i ego vremia*, 21; Bushkovitch, *Peter the Great*, 339.

64. Chistovich, *Feofan Prokopovich i ego vremia*, 21.

65. A thorough description of Feofan's philosophy course manuscripts is found in Stratii, *Opisanie kursov filosofii i retoriki*, 208–22.

66. Feofan [Prokopovich], "Pro paps'kyi vyrok Galileevi," in *Filosof'ski tvory*, 3:348; For a more thorough discussion of Ukrainian and Russian Orthodox attitudes toward heliocentrism, including Feofan's opinions, see Obolevitch, "Galileo in the Russian Orthodox Context," 788–808.

67. Matviishyn [Matwiiszyn], "Idee Kopernika na Ukrainie," 657–76.

68. Matviishyn [Matwiiszyn], "Feofan Prokopovych i Astronomiia," 569–78.

69. Damaskin [Semenov-Rudnev], "Vita Auctoris," 667; Pypin, *Istoriia russkoi literatury*, 3:20.

70. Matviishyn [Matwiiszyn], "Feofan Prokopovych i Astronomiia," 557–60.

71. Nevskaia, "Pervyi disput," 124–30.

72. Cherviakovskii, "Vvedenie v bogoslovie," 52; Chistovich, *Feofan Prokopovich i ego vremia*, 14; Samarin, *Stefan Iavorskii*, 44; Koch, *Die russische Orthodoxie*.

73. See Feofan [Prokopovich], *O iskhozhdenii Sviatogo Dukha* (Moscow, 1773) and "*Apologia* sacrarum reliquarium patrum nostrorum," in *Miscellanea Sacra*, 75–83.

74. This also included the depravity of the will—*corruptio voluntatis*—meaning that all humans lacked a desire to do good works. Given this fact, the Old Testament law was never intended to be fulfilled (since humans did not have the will to fulfill it) and always remained a "dead letter." Samarin, *Stefan Iavorskii*, 111–14. Samarin here used Prokopovich's treatise *De corruptione voluntatis* in *Christianae Orthodoxae Theologiae*, vol. 2. In 1744 David Nashchinskii published several chapters of Feofan's manuscript theology course in the *Miscellanea sacra* collection. Russian translations of Feofan's theological treatises abound. See, for example, *Chetyre sochineniia* or *Nachal'nye traktaty bogoslovskikh lektsii*. According to Kowalyk, Prokopovich's belief in the complete corruption of the human will attacked Peter Mohyla's position that "in animam hominis invisibilem gratiam inferri [the human soul carries invisible grace within it]." Kowalyk, *Ecclesiologia Theophanis Prokopovycz*, 14.

75. Good works, therefore, played no role in one's justification since they by nature and definition were "imperfect." Samarin, *Stefan Iavorskii*, 142. Prokopovich believed justification to be more than just a remission of sins, indeed, the "forensic proclamation of becoming pure." Kowalyk, *Ecclesiologia Theophanis Prokopovycz*, 15.

76. Samarin, *Stefan Iavorskii*, 133–38; Samarin's synopsis is based on Feofan's treatise *De justificatione*, written as a part of his Kievan theology course and printed in volume 2 of the Leipzig edition of Feofan's *Christianae Orthodoxae Theologiae*, 504–44. On the Lutheran teaching of *justificatio forensis*, see McGrath, *Reformation Thought*, 120–21.

77. Samarin, *Stefan Iavorskii*, 139.

78. Feofan [Prokopovich], "Pis'ma," *TKDA* 1 (1865): 147, 149.

79. Feofan [Prokopovich], *Christianae Orthodoxae Theologiae*, chs. 8 and 9; Feofan [Prokopovich]'s chapter "De Sacra Scripturae legitima interpretatione," in *Christianae Orthodoxae Theologiae*, 1:198–205.

80. Feofan [Prokopovich], *Pokazanie prorechennogo prezhde v slovesakh Bozhiikh i davno uzhe iavivshegosia v mire Velikogo Antikhrista*, OR RGB, f. 556, r. 8, ll. 1–67. Prokopovich's work appears in several manuscript copies including the National Library of Karelia (NB RK inv. No. 36551 R) and the Moscow Vifaniia Seminary collection, OR RGB, f. 556, r. 9.

81. Ibid., ll. 21–43 ob.

82. Ibid., l. 33 ob.

83. Ibid., l. 33 ob.

84. Luther, *Babylonian Captivity*. The Book of Revelation in Luther Bibles in the sixteenth century typically depicted the pope as effeminate and as a prostitute decorated in gold and jewels.

85. Feofan [Prokopovich], *Pokazanie prorechennogo prezhde*, ll. 18–18 ob.

86. Ibid., l. 30 ob.

87. Bayer, "Vita Theophanis Procopovitsch," 255; Damaskin [Semenov-Rudnev] noted similarly that his teachings "brought forth light among the Russians [*studiorum genere apud Russos exoriretur lux*]" and that his "listeners avidly inhaled [his teachings] into their pipes." Chistovich, *Feofan Prokopovich i ego vremia*, 17.

88. Chistovich, *Novogorodskii Mitropolit Iov*, 74.

89. Rodyshevskii, "Zhitie . . . eretika Feofana," 2.

90. The treatise was dedicated to Musin-Pushkin. Feofan [Prokopovich], *Ob neudobenosimom ige*, 1–3; Prokopovich's 1712 letter to I. A. Musin-Pushkin is printed in *Filosof'ski tvory*, 3:289–90. The treatise circulated in manuscript form as seen from the Russian State Library manuscript collections in ORG RGB, f. 173, op. 1, r. 165.

91. *Izveshchenie glagolemykh ot Stefana Iavorskogo*, OR RGB, f. 194, op. 1, rukopis' 21; Anton Grigor'ev, "Sochinenie metropolita riazanskogo," *Vestnik PSTGU: Bogoslovie* 38 (2011): 101–14. Grigor'ev later printed the GIM (State Historical Museum–Moscow) manuscript copy of *Izveshchenie* in "Sochinenie metropolita riazanskogo, *Izveshchenie glagolemykh ot Stefana Iavorskogo" Vestnik PTSGU: Bogoslovie* 39 (2012): 87–113.

92. Feofan [Prokopovich], *Ob neudobenosimom ige*, 6, 154–55. Feofan's rejection of justification by law can be seen ibid., 93. On justification in general, see ibid., 169–70.

93. He advocated full forgiveness for the believer: "not only of original sin, but personal sins as well, not only the sins before conversion but the sins that occur after conversion." Ibid., 89. He furthermore stated that only faith is necessary for salvation, faith in "both mind and heart." Ibid. 117–18. Feofan believed that one would have to become used to living in "struggle with sin" for one's entire lifetime. Ibid., 202.

94. Ibid., 154.

95. Ibid., 158.

96. Ibid., 159–61.

97. Wengert, *Law and Gospel*; Elert, *Law and Gospel*.

98. Grigor'ev, "Sochinenie metropolita riazanskogo," 114.

99. *Izveshchenie glagolemykh*, OR RGB, f. 194, op. 1, rukopis' 21, l. 7 ob.

100. Chistovich, *Reshilovskoe delo*, 46.

101. Feofilakt [Lopatinskii], "Igo gospodne blago i bremia ego legko," OR RGB, f. 196, op. 3, rukopis' 173, ll. 3, 5–11; the tract apparently began circulating during the Tveritinov trial in 1713–15. Moroshkin, "Feofilakt Lopatinskii," 687–88.

102. Feofan [Prokopovich], *O neudobenosimom ige*, 214–16. The "paradoxical" nature of this polemic is highlighted in Korzo, "O protestantskikh vliianiiakh," 8.

103. Pekarskii, *Nauka i literatura*, 1:485; Peter I, *Pokhodnyi zhurnal*, 107–8.

104. Vockerodt, *Russland unter Peter dem Grossen*, 12. For Feofan's promotions, see Chistovich, *Feofan Prokopovich*, 14–17.

105. Prokopovich, "Slovo Pokhval'noe v chest' slavnykh del . . . Gospodina Aleksandra Danilovicha Menshikova," in his *Slova i Rechi*, 1:53–73.

106. Morozov, *Feofan Prokopovich kak pisatel'*, 122–24; Runkevich, *Arkhierei petrovskoi epokhi*, 79–81.

107. Chistovich, *Feofan Prokopovich i ego vremia*, 61–64; Cracraft, *Church Reform*, 138.

108. Vockerodt, *Russland unter Peter dem Grossen*, 12.

109. Bayer, "Vita Theophanis Procopovitsch," 255–56.

110. Vockerodt, *Russland unter Peter dem Grossen*, 12.

CHAPTER 3. A RUSSIAN LUTHER

1. Feofan [Prokopovich], "Pis'ma," 149.

2. Ibid., 146, 148.

3. Feofan [Prokopovich], "Pis'mo k arkhiereiu chernigovskomu," in "Pis'ma," *TKDA* 2 (1865): 309.

4. Feofan [Prokopovich], "Pis'mo k professoram Kievskoi Akademii," in "Pis'ma," *TKDA* 1 (1865): 155; Feofan [Prokopovich], "Slovo pri nachatii Sviateishego Pravitel'stvuiushchego Sinoda," in *Slova i rechi*, 2:66–67.

5. Feofan [Prokopovich], "Pis'mo k professoram Kievskoi Akademii," 150.

6. Feofan [Prokopovich], "Slovo v den' Rozhdestva Gospoda nashego Iisusa Khrista, dekabria 25 dnia 1716 goda," in *Slova i rechi*, 1:126.

7. Ibid., 128–29.

8. Ibid., 133.

9. Ibid., 134.

10. Ibid., 138.

11. Ibid., 137–38.

12. Feofan [Prokopovich], *Filosofs'ki tvory*, 3:209; it was, in fact, printed on July 25, 1717.

13. Ibid.; Menshikov, *Povsednevnye zapiski*, 95.

14. Feofan [Prokopovich], "Pis'ma," 142.

15. Ibid., 155; Chistovich, *Feofan Prokopovich i ego vremia*, 38, 41–42.

16. The marginal notations are still on the manuscript, "Kurs dogmaticheskogo bogosloviia, chitannyi Feofanom Prokopovichem v Kievo-Mogilianskoi akademii v 1708–1710 gg.," OR RGB, f. 173, op. 1, rukopis' 245, notations on ll. 238–40, 240 ob.–242 ob. (accusations of Calvinism), l. 244 ob. (accusations of Pelagianism), l. 249

(accusations of heresy in general). Stefan's signature of ownership is on l. 250 of the manuscript.

17. Stefan [Iavorskii], "Poslanie Stefana Iavorskogo," 6–7. Stefan submitted a seventeen-point protest that was given to Bishop Aleksei Titov of Krutitsy, who was on his way to St. Petersburg (as Stefan's vicar) to ordain Feofan. Izvekov, "Odin iz maloizvestnykh literaturnykh protivnikov," 7. NB: In theology, antinomianism generally denotes a view that emphasizes the importance of grace over law, and in some cases rejects the applicability of Old Testament law for Christian believers. Feofan's earlier description of the "unbearable yoke" of the law was deemed to be antinomian by his Muscovite critics (see previous chapter).

18. The response was written in Russian with a Latin subtext. RGIA, f. 796, op. 6, d. 153, ll. 25–26 ob.; Chistovich, *Feofan Prokopovich i ego vremia*, 41–42.

19. Morozov, *Feofan Prokopovich kak pisatel'*, 191.

20. Ibid., 191–92; Feofan [Prokopovich], "Pis'ma," 153; Tikhonravov, "Moskovskie vol'nodumtsy," 417.

21. Feofan, "Pis'ma," 155.

22. Ibid.

23. Ibid., 158.

24. Ibid., 157.

25. It was obvious that the tsar conducted no "investigation of the matter," as Shevelov noted. Shevelov, *Two Orthodox Ukrainian Churchmen*, 60. For the account of the appointment controversy, see also Philipps, *The Russian Catechism*, 48.

26. Evgenii [Bolkhovitinov], *Slovar' istoricheskii*, 326; Haven, *Reise in Russland*, 22–23. The installation was conducted by Aleksei Titov, the metropolitan of Moscow-Krutitsy. Chistovich, *Feofan Prokopovich i ego vremia*, 40.

27. Feofan [Prokopovich], "Pis'ma," 157. Feofilakt and Gedeon also asked for forgiveness, claiming that "they did not read all of Feofan's theology." Their statement is in RGIA, f. 796, op. 6, d. 153, ll. 6–6 ob.

28. Feofan [Prokopovich], "Pis'mo k professoram Kievskoi Akademii," in "Pis'ma," *TKDA* (1865): 158.

29. Morozov, *Feofan Prokopovich kak pisatel'*.

30. See Runkevich, *Arkhierei petrovskoi epokhi*, 43–48 (on Titov), and 94–95 (on Aaron); see also Moroshkin, "Feodosii Ianovskii," 279.

31. Pekarskii, *Istoriia Imperatorskoi akademii nauk*, 1:236; Izvekov, "Odin iz maloizvestnykh literaturnykh protivnikov," 65.

32. Ianovskii heard their confessions and administered communion to them, and was accused of being "corrupted by the same heresy for a long time." Magnitskii, *Zapiska Leontiia Magnitskogo*, 13–14.

33. Moroshkin, "Feodosii Ianovskii," 31–32. See also Bartenev, "Podlinnoe delo," 168–207. Feodosii Ianovskii also corresponded with Protestant clergy such as the Livonian general superintendent Heinrich Brüningck (1675–1736); allegedly he minimized the differences between Lutheranism and Orthodoxy and called the superintendent "brother." Vierorth, "Lebenslauf," 111.

34. Moroshkin, "Feodosii Ianovskii," 31.

35. Runkevich, *Uchrezhdenie i pervonachal'noe ustroistvo*, 210.

36. Evgenii [Bolkhovitinov], *Slovar' istoricheskii*, 57–58. He left the capital in 1727–28 as a result of the reaction against Feofan's party that will be discussed later in this chapter.

37. Letter of H. Huyssen from September 12, 1728, in Consett, *The Present State*, xix. Gavriil Buzhinskii was also a friend of Huyssen and of Consett. See Consett's and Gavriil's letters, ibid., 367–69; for more on Huyssen, see Paul Bushkovitch, *Peter the Great*, 231, 339–40.

38. Buevskii, "Epizody iz zhizni," 286.

39. Gavriil [Buzhinskii], "Predislovie, presvetleishii i nepobedimyi avtokrator i imperator," in his translation of Pufendorf, *Vvedenie v gistoriiu evropeiskuiu*, 8.

40. Pokrovskii, "Bor'ba s protestantskimi ideiami," 227–28; Erasmus, *Razgovory druzheskiia*.

41. "Gavriil Buzhinskii," *RBS*, 4:31; Evgenii [Bolkhovitinov], *Slovar' istoricheskii*, 57–59; see also Gavriil [Buzhinskii], "Predislovie," 7.

42. Strateman, *Featron ili pozor istoricheskii*, 380–81, 398; Evgenii [Bolkhovitinov], *Slovar' istoricheskii*, 57–59.

43. Gavriil's explanatory notes for removing Mohyla's theological formulations are stored in RGIA, f. 796, op. 4, d. 336, this particular reference in ll. 1–4 ob.

44. He also maintained a regular correspondence with the Swedish ambassador Josias Cederhjelm. Krupnyts'kyi, "Teofan Prokopovych i shvedy," 298.

45. He lived in Prague from 1716 to 1722 and translated Buddeus's works. Akimov, "Feofil Krolik."

46. "Po sinodal'nomu opredeleniiu o bytii monakhu Feofilu Kroliku v sv. Sinod asssessorom," *ODDS* 2 (1722): no. 204.

47. Akimov, "Feofil Krolik"; Moroshkin, "Feodosii Ianovskii," 274.

48. Fedyukhin et al., "Drinking Diplomacy."

49. Maikov, *Razskazy Nartova*, 73–74.

50. Bogoslovskii, *Issledovaniia*, 26–27.

51. Leskov, "Sviatitel'skie teni," 60–61.

52. Buevskii, "Epizody iz zhizni," 275–76.

53. Golikov, *Deianiia Petra Velikogo*, 15:212–21; Feofan [Prokopovich], "Pis'ma," 289; May 6, 1720, letter to Admiral Apraksin in RGADA, f. 18, op. 1, d. 41, l. 1; Pyliaev, *Zabytoe proshloe*, 241; Haven, *Reise in Russland*, 19–23.

54. Feofan [Prokopovich], "Blagodarenie ot sluzhitelei domovykh za solod novovymyshlennyi domovomu ekonomu Gerasimu," in his *Sochineniia*, 222–23; Chistovich, *Feofan Prokopovich i ego vremia*, 641.

55. Bergholz, "Tagebuch. III. Theil," 212 and 349.

56. Ibid., 506; Bergholz, "Tagebuch. II. Theil," 349–50.

57. Motraye, *Voyages*, 275, 277–78.

58. "Delo Feofana Prokopovicha," 3–4.

59. Ibid.

60. "O dvorianine Ivane Nosove obviniavshem Feofana Prokopovicha v eretichestve," RGADA, f. 7, op. 1, d. 262, ll. 1–2, 4–4 ob.

61. *DR*, 17.

62. Ibid.

63. The original printed edition of the catechism is stored in Halle as *Pervoe ouchenie otrokom* (St. Petersburg, 1720), showing the date (June 23) and the place (St. Aleksandr Nevskii Monastery) of printing. AFSt/178 A2 27.1, Bl. 1–55. I thank Margarita Korzo for the discovery of this first edition in Halle.

64. Korzo, "Sintez kul'turnykh," 103–4.

65. See the in-depth discussion in the table of appendix 1, in Ivanov, "Reforming Orthodoxy," 408–13.

66. *PUO*, 21–22; and Luther, *Luther's Large Catechism*, pars. 109, 129, 130–69.

67. *PUO*, 13–15.

68. Ibid.

69. "Durchgehend auf gut Lutherisch abgefasset." Mardefeld wrote that Prokopovich's teaching on justification and the "careful prohibition of superstitions and worship of the saints" made it more Lutheran. Letter quoted in Hauptmann, *Katechismen der Russisch-orthodoxe Kirche*, 24.

70. Kantemir, "Loca Obscura in Catechisi quae ab Anonyme Authore Slaveno idiomate edita," OR RGB, f. 173, op. 1, rukopis' 277.

71. Ibid., ll. 2–4. "Fide Orthodoxi hominis nati fuissent boni," he argued, denying depravity among Orthodox believers. Ibid., l. 4.

72. Ibid., ll. 53–55.

73. Ibid., ll. 78–80.

74. Kantemir attacked the idea that one cannot distinguish one icon from another and must venerate them all equally by showing there were some icons that possessed a higher value, being capable of "extraordinary miracles." Ibid., ll. 60–61.

75. Ibid., ll. 78–80; see also ll. 78, 115; "blasphemus . . . publicanus, phariseus, ab Ecclesia Dei separatus et ethnicus est." Ibid., l. 64.

76. Feofan's 1721 letter to Anastasii Kondoidi, in *Filosof'ski tvory*, 3:279.

77. Ibid., 278.

78. Korzo, "Katekheticheskie sochineniia," 273; see also Korzo, *Ukrainskaia i belorusskaia katekheticheskaia traditsiia*, 539–44.

79. Apart from the first 1720 edition, there are also at least fifteen in the Russian State Library catalog, for the years 1721, 1722, 1723, 1724, 1744, 1759, 1762 (two editions), 1768, 1771, 1782, 1786, 1794, and 1798, all published by the Synod.

80. The eighteenth-century editions of the *Trebnik* are 1725, 1747, 1754, 1755, 1758, 1761, 1763, 1773, 1779, 1782 (two editions), 1785, 1794, 1796, and 1798.

81. *PSZ* 6, 4021; Verkhovskoi, *Uchrezhdenie Dukhovnoi Kollegii*, 1:393.

82. *PSZ* 6, 4021; Frumenkova, "Tsifirnye i arkhiereiskie shkoly," 136–39.

83. *PSZ* 4172.

84. *PSP* 4 (1756): no. 1513.

85. For Serbian, see Feofan [Prokopovich], *Pervoe uchenie otrokom* (Grábóc, Diocese of Buda, 1744); Philipps, *The Russian Catechism* (London, 1723) (Philipps's translation had a second edition in 1725); Blackmore, *The Doctrine of the Russian Church*; Korzo, "Sintez kul'turnykh," 105.

86. Moiseeva, "Ioil' (Bykovskii)," 302–3.

87. Korzo, "Sintez kul'turnykh," 105.

88. Alekseev, "Varlaam," 600–601. See chapter 5 for more on the bishop of Viatka and his methods of spiritual discipline.

89. L'vov, "Pervoe uchenie otrokom."

90. Ryndziunskii, "Antitserkovnoe dvizhenie"; and Vysotskii, "Novye materialy," 66–86, 235–61.

91. Most Russian historians of the nineteenth and twentieth centuries (including Chistovich and Verkhovskoi) ascribed this work exclusively to Feofan. However, it is entirely possible that this was a work of collaboration between Prokopovich and a team of his allies (such as Gavriil Bushinskii and Feofil Krolik), with Feofan serving as the supervisor and the final editor of the project.

92. Kartashev, *Ocherki*, 2:349.

93. Ibid., 2:156.

94. Verkhovskoi, *Uchrezhdenie Dukhovnoi Kollegii*, 2:155.

95. Ibid.

96. Vockerodt, *Russland unter Peter dem Grossen*, 12.

97. See Feofan's original rough drafts and corrections in Verkhovskoi, *Uchrezhdenie Dukhovnoi Kollegii*, 2:26–105.

98. This can be seen in the rough draft of the *Spiritual Regulation* published by Verkhovskoi in his *Uchrezhdenie Dukhovnoi Kollegii*, 2:26–28. When Peter read the first draft of the text, he crossed out the latter title and ordered it removed from the text. Ibid., 2:26.

99. Feofan [Prokopovich], "Pis'ma," 287–90.

100. Ibid.

101. Verkhovskoi, *Uchrezhdenie Dukhovnoi Kollegii*, 1:260–61.

102. *PSP* 1 (1721): no. 3; see also *PSZ* 3749.

103. *PSP* 1 (1721): no. 3; Verkhovskoi, *Uchrezhdeniie Dukhovnoi Kollegii*, 1:500. Just like the title of the Synod, the name of its new legal document, *Dukhovnyi Reglament*, was authored by Feofan. In its draft form, the work bore the name *Description and Discussion of the Spiritual College* [*Dukhovnago Kollegium opisanie i rassuzhdenie*] and the first officially corrected draft of February 1720 did not carry the title *Spiritual Regulation* (ibid., 2:27, 1:156–57, 1:171). The official title of *Reglament* only appeared around the time the Synod opened in February 1721 (Verkhovskoi, *Uchrezhdenie Dukhovnoi Kollegii*, 1:172).

104. The *Casimiriana* was printed officially as *Ordnung Wie es in des Durchleuchtige[n] Hochgebornen Fürsten und Herrn Johann Casimiri Herzogen zu Sachsen*; on the origins of the *Kirchenregiment*, see Estes, *Peace, Order*, 48–53.

105. See, for example, Gerhard, [*Casimiriana*], 275.

106. Ibid., 287–96.

107. Compare *DR*, 1–16, which contains the monarch's introduction with an exhortation to bring order to religion, with Gerhard, [*Casimiriana*], which contains a similar introduction ["Vorrede,"] by Johann Casimir in fols. a–n: containing an introduction with a call to orderliness in religion and "observance." Similar language is also found in Wilhelm of Hessen's introduction to Hessen's regulation, titled *Agenda, das ist*.

108. *DR*, 19–20.

109. Ibid., 20–33; These duties did not apply to the elite bishops, like Prokopovich, who lived in St. Petersburg, serving the court or the Synod. The regular duties in such cases would be carried out by their vicars.

110. Gerhard, [*Casimiriana*], 127–56.

111. *DR*, 30–34.

112. Gerhard, [*Casimiriana*], 237–243, 247–250.

113. *DR*, 49–52, compare with Gerhard, [*Casimiriana*], 157–63.

114. *DR*, 34–48, compare with Gerhard, [*Casimiriana*], 337–70.

115. *DR*, 71–88; Gerhard, [*Casimiriana*], 209–35, 262–306.

116. The eighteenth-century editions of the *Spiritual Regulation* are 1721, 1722, 1723 (two editions), 1738, 1749, 1761, 1765, 1776, 1779, and 1794.

117. This is a quote from his April 6, 1718, sermon, "O Slave i Chesti Tsarskoi [On the honor and power of the tsar]," in Feofan [Prokopovich], *Izbrannye sochineniia*, 88.

118. Ibid.

119. Verkhovskoi, *Uchrezhdenie Dukhovnoi Kollegii*, 2:155.

120. Ibid., 2:138.

121. *DR*, 10.

122. Verkhovskoi, *Uchrezhdeniie Dukhovnoi Kollegii*, 367–68.

123. *DR*, 11.

124. *DR*, 6–8.

125. Feofan [Prokopovich,] "Pis'mo k Iakovu Markevichu," in "Pis'ma," *TKDA* 2 (1865): 292.

126. *DR*, 7–10.

127. For the description of the Protestant formula, see Florovsky, *Bible, Church, Tradition*, 111; *DR*, 35–36.

128. *DR*, 34–35.

129. Winter, *Ketzerschicksale*, 241.

130. *DR*, 87–96; on nuns, see p. 97.

131. Znamenskii, "Chteniia iz istorii russkoi tserkvi," 2:113.

132. Some bishops (like Gedeon Krinovskii) never even saw their diocese. Solov'ev, *Istoriia Rossii*, 9:486.

133. Gurvich, *"Pravda voli monarshei"*; Bushkovitch, "Political Ideology," 1–19. For a deeper discussion of absolutism in eighteenth-century Russia, see LeDonne's *Absolutism and Ruling Class* and Whittaker's *Russian Monarchy*. See also Ospovat, "Kazn' avtora."

134. *LW*, 8:396, 53:255, 5:256, 3:255–257; Gritsch, *A History of Lutheranism*, 24; Spitz, "Luther's Ecclesiology," 113–14.

135. Witte, *Law and Protestantism*, 125–31.

136. Friedeburg, *Luther's Legacy*, 100–101; Estes in *Peace, Order*, 48, states that Luther's original "church order proposed in the *Reformatio* had virtually nothing in common with the *landesherrliches Kirchenregiment* that would come to characterize German Lutheranism."

137. Kolb, *Lutheran Ecclesiastical Culture*, 80–81.

138. The Danish king served as an example for these theorists. Friedeburg, *Luther's Legacy*, 192; on Gerhard, 195.

139. Reinkingk, *Tractatus*, 122–26, 401–2, 1112–17; Joachim Stephanus, *Institutiones iuris canonici*, 2–6.

140. Reinkingk, *Tractatus*, 124.

141. Honecker, *Cura religionis*, 74, 106, 149.

142. Reinkingk, *Tractatus*, 1039–40; see also the limits of princely authority in Drummond, *German Protestantism since Luther*, 241, and in Lehner, *The Oxford Handbook*, 250.

143. Friedeburg, *Luther's Legacy*, 4–5, 24–25, 36, 87.

144. Reinkingk, *Biblische Policey*, 15, 23, 42–43, 51–56, 160–78, 189, 672, 833–34.

145. Friedeburg, *Luther's Legacy*, 143–44; Stephanus, *Institutiones iuris canonici*, 51–53.

146. Feofan [Prokopovich], *Rozysk istoricheskii*, 37.

147. Ibid., 2–4, 22–23.

148. Ibid., 10–16.

149. Ibid., 22–24; Friedeburg, *Luther's Legacy*, 200–205.

150. Feofan [Prokopovich], *Rozysk istoricheskii*, 24.

151. Ibid., 16.

152. "Pokazanie," OR RGB, f. 556, d. 9, l. 80 ob.

153. Feofan [Prokopovich], *Sochineniia*, 96.

154. Ibid., 96; Luther, *Martin Luther*, 407–10.

155. Feofan [Prokopovich], *Sochineniia*, 96.

156. Ibid., 97–98.

157. This parable is printed in Tatishchev, *Izbrannye proizvedeniia*, 51–132; it is based on Tatishchev's conversations with Feofan. See Ibid., 145.

158. Ibid., 65.

159. Ibid.

160. "Ob'iavlenie kogda i kakoi radi viny nachalsia chin monasheskii," *PSZ* 4450 (1724).

161. Ibid.

162. Ibid.

163. Feofan's manuscript, "Otiagotitel'nye obriady rimskoi i grecheskoi tserkvi," stored in the National Library of Ukraine, NBU ruk. 367/221 P. His other manuscript, "Zamechaniia o monakhakh," questioned the necessity of monastic celibacy for Eastern Orthodox bishops: RGADA, f. 18, op. 1, d. 81. His hesitation to uproot monasticism and many traditional ceremonies will be discussed further in this chapter.

164. Titlinov, *Pravitel'stvo imperatritsy Anny Ioannovny*, 283–84; PSP, 4:v.

165. Ibid., 287.

166. Ibid., 286.

167. These purposes are spelled out in the Synodal policies in *PSZ* under regulation numbers *PSZ* 5034 (1727), *PSZ* 5688 (1731), *PSZ* 6803 (1735), *PSZ* 7610 and 7611 (1738), *PSZ* 7793 (1739), *PSZ* 7761 (1739); for subsequent reaffirmations of these policies, see *PSZ* 9172 (1745), *PSZ* 10684 (1757), *PSZ* 11690 (1762).

168. Titlinov, *Pravitel'stvo imperatritsy Anny Ioannovny*, 283–84; PSZ 5688 (1731).

169. Titlinov, *Pravitel'stvo imperatritsy Anny Ioannovny*, 277–79.

170. Znamenskii, "Chteniia iz istorii russkoi tserkvi," 106, 113.

171. Titlinov, *Pravitel'stvo imperatritsy Anny Ioannovny*, 280, 293–94.

172. *PSP*, 4:v.; Iaremenko, *Kyivs'ke chernetstvo*, 211–25.

173. Kharlampovich, *Malorossiiskoe vliianie*, 460–91; after many complaints from the Russian clergy, Empress Elizabeth proposed that the Holy Synod recruit more Russians in 1754, although between 1754 and 1760, the Synod chose only one Russian to fill a vacant bishopric post. Ibid., 489; RGIA, f. 796, op. 35, d. 211, ll. 1–1 ob., 5–59.

174. Smolitsch, *Russkoe monashestvo*, n. 1044; Vodarskii, "Tserkovnye organizatsii," 79–95; Zverinskii, *Monastyri*, 1:xi.

175. Moroshkin, "Feodosii Ianovskii," 281. "Po donosu Pafnutiia . . . na Varlaama Golekovskogo," RGIA, f. 796, op. 1, d. 187, ll. 1–5.

176. "Po donosu Pafnutiia . . . na Varlaama Golekovskogo," RGIA, f. 796, op. 1, d. 187, ll. 1–5; Moroshkin, "Feodosii Ivanovskii," 282–83. The use of the term "commissars" for Feofan's and Feodosii's agents operating among the clergy is found in the report "Mnenie o dukhovnoi kollegii," RGADA, f. 9, otd. 2, op. knig. 93, ll. 614–17.

177. Quoted in Arsenii Matseevich's "Vozrazhenie na paskvil' liuteranskii," OR RGB, f. 173, op. 1, rukopis' 127, l. 10 ob.

178. Zhivov, *Iz tserkovnoi istorii*, 72–73.

179. Ibid., 73; 110–12.

180. Iavorskii, "Apologiia," 248.

181. Iavorskii, "Apologiia," 257.

182. Despite what many historians have believed, Stefan did not wholeheartedly advocate the restoration of the Muscovite patriarchate, he preferred to institute Russia's subordination to Constantinople. See Zhivov, *Iz tserkovnoi istorii*, 109–12.

183. Ibid., 255.

184. Consett, *The Present State*, 17.

185. "Delo Feofana Prokopovicha," 48.

186. Ibid., 32, 38.

187. Verkhovskoi, *Uchrezhdenie Dukhovnoi Kollegii*, 1:672–82.

188. Zhivov, *Iz tserkovnoi istorii*, 74.

189. Zhivov, *Iz tserkovnoi istorii*, 74.

190. Runkevich, *Uchrezhdenie i pervonachal'noe ustroistvo*, 167–74. Despite being a formal president of the new body, Stefan attended the Synod only twenty times in 1721, whereas the council's regular schedule had meetings several times a week throughout the year (after 1724, on Mondays, Wednesdays, and Fridays). Ibid., 351–53.

191. Cracraft, *Church Reform*, 163; Runkevich, *Uchrezhdenie i pervonachal'noe ustroistvo*, 173.

192. By 1722, Hallart was one of the five generals of the Russian army and was well connected to Petersburg's Pietist circles. Bushkovitch, *Peter the Great*, 430; and Teigeler, *Die Herrnhuter in Russland*, 140–41.

193. Vierorth, "Lebenslauf," 114.

194. Vierorth, "Lebenslauf," 118.

195. Peter I, *Curieuse Nachricht*, 1.

196. Ibid., 2.

197. Ibid., 4.

198. Ibid., 4–5.

199. Haven, *Reise in Russland*, 22.

200. Martini, *Nachricht aus Russland*, 45, 60.

201. Pekarskii, *Istoriia Imperatorskoi akademii nauk*, 1:77–79.

202. Bancks, *The Life of Peter the Great*, 347–48; King, *Rites and Ceremonies*, 433–68.

203. Feuerlein, *Dissertatio historico-ecclesiastica*, 30–31, 43–44. He also emphasized the importance of Prokopovich's catechism and the *Spiritual Regulation* for church reform. Ibid., 22–23, 37.

204. Ibid., 30–31.

205. Ibid., 69–70. He also stated that the "Russians, if judged under the articles of faith, would come closer to the Lutherans than the Papists." Ibid., 70.

206. Vierorth, "Lebenslauf," 114.

207. Ibid.; Strahlenberg, *An Historico-geographical Description*, 286–87.

208. Ibid., 287.

209. Vockerodt, *Russland unter Peter dem Grossen*, 12.

CHAPTER 4. A STRUGGLE FOR ORTHODOXY

1. Feofan [Prokopovich], *Kratkaia povest'*, 1–6; *Kratkaia povest'* was first printed in 1725, then translated into Latin and German in 1726 (Reval and Hamburg editions). Wittram, *Peter I*, 2:500–501.

2. Feofan [Prokopovich], *Kratkaia povest'*, 3–4; Feuerlein, *Dissertatio historico-ecclesiastica*, 51.

3. Feofan [Prokopovich], *Kratkaia povest'*, 13; Martini, *Nachricht aus Russland*, 88–91. Two of Feofan's allies were present at the deathbed—Feofil Krolik and Gavriil Buzhinskii, who administered the eucharist. Feofan [Prokopovich], *Kratkaia povest'*, 12–15. According to Feofan, this was the same philo-Protestant doctrine of justification that he taught to Petersburg elites in 1718–21. "Delo Feofana Prokopovicha," 19.

4. Krupnyts'kyi, "Teofan Prokopovych i shvedy," 297. Feuerlein mentions this circulating rumor that Peter died as a Lutheran but is skeptical about it. Feuerlein, *Dissertatio historico-ecclesiastica*, 51–52.

5. Feofan [Prokopovich], *Kratkaia povest'*, 14.

6. Feofan [Prokopovich], "Slovo na pogrebenie Petra Velikogo," in *Sochineniia*, 126–28; Prokop'ev, "Pogrebenie Petra Velikogo," 47–67.

7. Feofan [Prokopovich], "Proch', ustupai proch', pechal'naia noch'!," in *Sochineniia*, 218.

8. Among the more active members of this party were Evfimii Koletti, Feofilakt Lopatinskii, Markell Rodyshevskii, Sil'vestr Kholmskii, Georgii Dashkov, Lev Iurlov, and Ignatii Smola. The patriarchate restorationist party included both the Russian hierarchs opposed to many of the Petrine reforms and Ukrainian philo-Catholic clerics who had earlier coalesced around Iavorskii.

9. See, for example, Kurukin, *Epokha "dvorskikh bur',"* 72–75, 85, 96–142, 172–74, 193; Petrukhintsev, *Tsarstvovanie Anny Ioannovny*, 37–65; Longworth, *The Three Empresses*. Lorenz Erren's recent Habilitationsschrift devotes more attention to the religious dimensions of the politics of the palace coup in "Der Russische Hof," 43–103, 205–12.

10. Feofan [Prokopovich], "Tsarskomu velichestvu na rassmotrenie osob, kotorye do dukhovnoi kollegii godiatsia," in *Filosof'ski tvory*, 3:282–83; Zhivov, *Iz tserkovnoi istorii*, 42–45; Maikov, *Razskazy Nartova*, 70–71. At the same time, Peter refused to promote Feofan's close ally Gavriil Buzhinskii to the status of bishop.

11. Feofan [Prokopovich], "Pri nachatii Sviateishego Pravitel'stvuiushchego Sinoda," in *Slova i rechi*, 2:66–67, 70.

12. Wittram, *Peter I*, 2:501.

13. See, for example, Kratter, *Das Mädchen von Marienburg*. According to one account, she was the illegitimate offspring of a Swedish nobleman (*Edelmann*) from the famed aristocratic family of von Rosens and a serf woman from a village near Dorpat. She was orphaned at an early age and raised by the Livonian Lutheran super-intendent (*praepositus*) Glück, who was a talented linguist of Latvian and "Slavonic" and was therefore able to homeschool her respectably. Her polished manners as well as "a certain *Je ne sai quoi* [sic] in her physiognomy" caused her first to attract the Russian officers passing by Livonia, and then, the tsar himself. Catherine I, *Die Gewisse Nachricht*, 1–4; Motraye, *Voyages*, 195–98.

14. Campredon, "Diplomaticheskaia perepiska," 427–38. For the nuances of Feofan-Catherine relationship, see Marker, *Imperial Saint*, 199–202.

15. Bassevitz, "Zapiski grafa Bassevicha," 628–32; Feofan [Prokopovich], *Kratkaia povest'*, 15–16.

16. Feofan [Prokopovich], *Kratkaia povest'*, 16–17.

17. Ibid., 17. Behind the veneer of Feofan's speeches and tearful testimonies stood an entire itinerary of actions, bribes, and the strategic movement of the palace guards that tipped the balance of power in favor of the empress. Kurukin, *Epokha "dvorskikh bur',"* 72–96.

18. Motraye, *Voyages*, 214–15, 277.

19. *Steigen und Fall*, 55–67; Campredon, "Doneseniia . . . za 1725," 11.

20. Wittram, *Peter I*, 2:414, 446, 450, 457–62.

21. Campredon, "Diplomaticheskaia perepiska," 432; Motraye, *Voyages*, 72–73; Durov, *Ordena rossiiskoi imperii*, 31–35.

22. Durov, *Ordena rossiiskoi imperii*, 31–35.

23. "Geheimer Rat," 461–62.

24. Shubinskii, "Graf Osterman," 460; see also Campredon, "Doneseniia [. . .] za 1725," 355, 505.

25. Petrov, *Istoriia Sankt-Peterburga*, 228, 232–33, 245.

26. Feofan [Prokopovich], "Pis'mo k gerzogu Gol'shtinskomu," in "Pis'ma," 597–99.

27. Synodal decrees in RGIA, f. 796, op. 6, d. 204, ll. 1–3, ll. 9–10 ob.

28. Ibid., ll. 2 ob.–3, 6–6 ob. Catherine signed new appointments in June and July 1725, and they were initially announced in St. Petersburg's Trinity Cathedral.

29. Morozov, *Feofan Prokopovich kak pisatel'*, 324.

30. *PVTS*, 57.

31. Petrov, *Istoriia Sankt-Peterburga*, 244.

32. Bartenev, "Podlinnoe delo," 171, 181–86; Martini, *Nachricht aus Russland*, 48.

33. Bartenev, "Podlinnoe delo," 183–85.

34. Mardefeld, "Diplomaticheskie dokumenty," 284.

35. Ibid., 168–73, 181.

36. Ibid., 173–76.

37. "German baths" may be a reference to German bathtubs (*Wanne*), not wide-spread in Russia at the time. It could also have been an early eighteenth-century slang word for lewd or rambunctious bathing. Chistovich, *Feofan Prokopovich i ego vremia*, 704–8.

38. Motraye, *Voyages*, 276.

39. *RBS*, 25:473–75.

40. *RBS*, 4:29.

41. Evgenii [Bolkhovitinov], *Slovar' istoricheskii*, 58.

42. *RBS*, 4:29–30.

43. "Delo Feofana Prokopovicha," 40–41, 39, 40, 4, also 44.

44. Ibid., 45.

45. Ibid., 45–49.

46. Ibid., 45. In the 1720s, a Huguenot eyewitness, de la Motraye, observed that the Lutheran churches in places like East Prussia and Eastern Pomerania rivaled the Catholic ones in their profusion of ornate sacred imagery. *Voyages*, 104–5.

47. "Delo Feofana Prokopovicha," 9, 11.

48. Chistovich, *Feofan Prokopovich i ego vremia*, 204–5.

49. "Delo Feofana Prokopovicha," 24, 37–38. For Peter's comment, see p. 19.

50. Ibid., 33.

51. Ibid., 19, 21–22.

52. Ibid., 21–22, 24, 22.

53. Ibid., 19.

54. Ibid., 51. Markell launched another round of accusations in 1727 when he wrote a wide-ranging report against the heresies of Feofan's catechism and the heresies in Gavriil's translation of Wilhelm Stratemann's *Theatrum Historicum*. Pekarskii, *Istoriia Imperatorskoi akademii nauk*, 1:496–97.

55. Georgii [Dashkov], "Mnenie o dukhovnoi kollegii," RGADA, f. 9, otd. 2, op. kn. 93, ll. 615–16.

56. Feofan [Prokopovich], in "Pis'ma," *TKDA* 2 (1865): 600.

57. Krupnyts'kyi, "Teofan Prokopovych i shvedy," 397–98. The Swedish original of the ambassador's pro memoria is in Hjärne, "Ett svenskt vittnesbörd," 1–34. Feofan's relations with Cederhjelm are well documented in the synodal archive but not studied in the literature. In his December 8, 1725, report, for example, the archbishop arranged for his visit to Moscow in order to see its "churchly and other curiosities [*kurioznye tserkovnye i drugie veshchi*]." RGIA, f. 796, op. 6, d. 375, ll. 1, 2–2 ob.

58. Solov'ev, *Istoriia Rossii*, 19:97.

59. Heinrich Christian Stryck, *Bericht*, HA HAB, Cod. Guelf. 30.3 Extrav., f. 37–38r; Kirchner, "Death of Catherine I," 254–61.

60. Campredon, "Doneseniia [. . .] za 1725," 231–34, 463; "Testament Katharinas I," HA HAB, Cod. Guelf. 30.3 Extrav., 41–42r. Copies of the "Testament" are not very numerous, although one was stored in Kiel and delivered to Aleksei Bestuzhev-Riumin in 1741 to support Elizabeth's claims. Bil'basov, *Istoriia Ekateriny Vtoroi*, 1:74. Another one, quoted here (also likely of Holstinian origin), is from Wolfenbüttel.

61. "Testament Katharinas I," f. 41r–42r; Campredon, "Doneseniia [. . .] za 1725," 584–85.

62. Stryck, *Bericht*, 38r–39r; Shubinskii, "Graf Osterman," 463.

63. Prokopovich, "Pis'mo k gerzogu Golshtinskomu," in Pis'ma, *TKDA* 2 (1865): 598.

64. Morozov, *Feofan Prokopovich kak pisatel'*, 332. The children who lived at the orphanage in his Karpovka residence in St. Petersburg were mostly from the city of Novgorod. *PVTS*, 67; Zdravomyslov, *Ierarkhi novgorodskoi eparkhii*, 63–64. See his letter to Francke during this period in Feofan [Prokopovich], *Filosof'ski tvory*, 3:262.

65. Mardefeld, "Diplomaticheskie dokumenty," 365.

66. Petrov, *Istoriia Sankt-Peterburga*, 252. On Pitirim's close ties with Prokopovich, see Morokhin, *Arkhiepiskop Nizhegorodskii i Alatyrskii Pitirim*, 154–55. Like Feofan, Pitirim came from a merchant family. Ibid., 1–4.

67. In the summer of 1728, he had to plead with the Supreme Privy Council to overturn its decision to expropriate Feofan's Novgorod bishop's manor (*podvor'e*) in St. Petersburg. See his September 3 petition to Golovkin, Vasilii L. Dolgorukii, D. M. Golitsyn, and Andrei Osterman in Feofan [Prokopovich], "Pis'ma," 3:555–56.

68. Ibid., 559.

69. Full text in Chistovich, *Feofan Prokopovoch i ego vremia*, 229–40.

70. Ibid., 239–40.

71. Ibid., 242–43.

72. Solov'ev, *Istoriia Rossii*, 19:187.

73. Chistovich, *Feofan Prokopovich i ego vremia*, 223–26.

74. "Mnenie o dukhovnoi kollegii," RGADA, f. 9, otd. 2, op. kn. 93, ll. 616 ob.–617.

75. Ibid.

76. Pokrovskii, "Feoflikat Loptinskii," 693–96. For the description of Golitsyn's involvement, see Kartashev, *Ocherki*, 2:411–12.

77. Morozov, *Feofan Prokopovich kak pisatel'*, 229–30.

78. Chistovich, *Feofan Prokopovich i ego vremia*, 224.

79. Ibid., 225; also see prilozhenie no. 7 in Chistovich.

80. Ibid., 223, 225, also prilozhenie no. 7. The liturgy was restored in 1731.

81. Alekseev, "Rasskaz Petra Velikogo," 706.

82. Chistovich, *Feofan Prokopovich i ego vremia*, 609–12.

83. Matseevich, "Vozrazhenie na paskvil' liuteranskii, Molotok na Kamen' very," OR RGB, f. 173, op.1, ruk. 127, ll. 14–14 ob.

84. In his 1726 letter, for example, Feofan asked Chernihov bishop Irodion Zhurakovskii to stop his usual practice of sending him gifts. Feofan [Prokopovich], "Pis'ma," *TKDA* 2 (1865): 301.

85. In early 1730 Feofan wrote that the move to Moscow caused him a sizeable debt, 1,300 rubles. Feofan [Prokopovich], "Pis'ma," *TKDA* 2 (1865): 266.

86. Feofan [Prokopovich], "Pis'ma," *TKDA* 3 (1865): 538. The record book was called "Kniga zapisnaia iskhodiashchim za podpis. Preosv. Feofana . . . s 1 ianvaria 1728 po 16 dekabria 1729."

87. Morozov, *Feofan Prokopovich kak pisatel'*, 330–35. On Osterman's Lutheran faith, see Petrukhintsev, *Tsarstvovanie Anny Ioannovny*, 43.

88. Hempel, *Merckwürdiges Leben*, 191–238, 299–316.

89. His letters to Peter II's parents, Rudolf Ludwig and Christiana Louisa, with references to wider family relations (including Mecklenburg) are found in "Correspondenz des fürstlich braunschweig-blankenburgischen Hofes" in NLA-W 1 Alt. 6. Nr. 224, f. 37–53r, 78, 134r; 1 Alt. 6. Nr. 789, 64–65. The diary of Anton-Ulrich, the husband of Anna Leopol'dovna of Mecklenburg, provides some interesting insights on the relations between the Russian court, Ostermann, and the duchy in "Tagebuch der Reise Herzog Anton Ulrichs II. Von Braunschweig nach St. Petersburg 1732/33," HA HAB, *Cod. Guelf. 161.1 Extrav.* Ostermann's role in the Supreme Privy Council's foreign connections and his relations with Feofan during this period need further study. Most Russian historiography on the subject has been incomplete as it does not engage the copious German archival collections on the matter.

90. *Pis'ma russkikh gosudarei*, 4:235–58; Hempel, *Merckwürdiges Leben*, 297–99.

91. Morozov, *Feofan Prokopovich kak pisatel'*, 330–33; Shubinskii, "Graf Osterman," 464; "Erziehungsinstruktion Ostermanns für Peter II," folia 1–55v, G. W. Leibniz Landesbibliothek Hannover, Handschriftenabteil.

92. Morozov, *Feofan Prokopovich kak pisatel'*, 332–35.

93. *PVTS*, 111.

94. Morozov, *Feofan Prokopovich kak pisatel'*, 336.

95. Prokopovich, "K odnomu iz russkikh arkhiereev," in "Pis'ma," *TKDA* 2 (1865): 600–601.

96. Chistovich, *Feofan Prokopovich i ego vremia*, 407; Zeltner, *Breviarium Controversiarium*, 25.

97. Solov'ev, *Istoriia Rossii*, 19:129.

98. "Pis'mo Grafa Ivana Alekseevicha Musina-Pushkina k Stefanu," *ODDS* 1 (1721): pril. no. 3.

99. Morev, "Kamen' Very," 289.

100. Stefan [Iavorskii], *Kamen' very*, ll. 4 ob.–5 ob.

101. See Morev's *"Kamen' very"* for a very detailed description of the work and its Catholic sources.

102. Ibid., vi.

103. Ibid.

104. Stefan [Iavorskii], *Kamen' very*, ll. 925–26.

105. Feofan's further extensive collaboration with Buddeus will be discussed in chapter 5.

106. "He was considered the most universally accomplished German theologian of his time." "Buddeus" in Schaff, *The New Schaff-Herzog Encyclopedia*, 2:291.

107. Claudius Rondeau, October 14, 1732, letter to Lord Harrington, in Rondeau, "Doneseniia i drugie bumagi," 524.

108. Stupperich, "Feofan Prokopovič und Buddeus," 349–50.

109. Buddeus, *Epistola Apologetica*.

110. Ibid., 35–39, 49, 109.

111. Ibid., 129.

112. Mencken, "Stephanii Iavorscii," 226–29; Pekarskii, *Istoriia Imperatorskoi akademii nauk*, 1:78.

113. Mencken, "Stephanii Iavorscii," 226.

114. Ibid., 226–27.

115. Jablonski, *Genius Stephani Jaworscii*, 13. He was a brother of Daniel Ernst Jablonski, president of the Berlin Academy of Sciences and a correspondent of Feofan's. Chistovich, *Feofan Prokopovich i ego vremia*, 368.

116. Bilfinger, *Stephani Javorskii*, also denied the originality of the content in Stefan's work ("excerpsit Javorskius argumenta sua ex Bellarmino") and attacked his view on the necessity of capital punishment for heretics. Ibid., 4, 11–32. See also Mosheim, *De poenis haereticorum*.

117. Buddeus, *Epistola Apologetica*, 2–4.

118. Kohl, *Introductio in historiam*, 26.

119. Kantemir, *Satiry*, 3.

120. Ibid., 4.

121. Chistovich, *Feofan Prokopovich i ego vremia*, 609–12.

122. Feofan [Prokopovich], "K avtoru satiry," in *Sochineniia*, 217.

123. Pekarskii, *Istoriia Imperatorskoi akademii nauk*, 1:216.

124. Feofan [Prokopovich], "Zateika," 187–88; Hempel, *Merckwürdiges Leben*, 304–5.

125. Kurukin, *"Epokha dvorskikh bur',"* 171; Korsakov, *Votsarenie imperatritsy Anny*, 100–101.

126. Shcherbatov, *O povrezhdenii nravov v Rossii*, 48.

127. The conditions remained secret until their publication on February 2, 1730, in the Kremlin. *PVTS*, 117–20. Some foreign ambassadors interpreted this event as an attempt to set up a "republic" or a limited monarchy akin to Poland or England. Kurukin, *"Epokha dvorskikh bur',"* 176–83.

128. Feofan [Prokopovich], "Plachet pastushok v dolgom nenast'i," in *Sochineniia*, 216.

129. Morozov, *Feofan Prokopovich kak pisatel'*, 354.

130. Schmidt-Phiseldek, *Materialien*, 20–24; Shcherbatov, "O povrezhdenii nravov v Rossii," 49–50; Petrukhintsev, *Tsarstvovanie Anny Ioannovy*, 43.

131. Petrukhintsev, *Tsarstvovanie Anny Ioannovy*, 43–44.

132. Shcherbatov, "O povrezhdenii nravov v Rossii," 50.

133. Liria, "Zapiski," 180–81.

134. Feofan [Prokopovich], "Zateika," 189–90, 210–14; Liria, "Zapiski," 83–95; Korsakov, *Votsarenie imperatritsy Anny*, 147–49, 297–98.

135. Korsakov, *Votsarenie imperatritsy Anny*, 297–98; Schmidt-Phiseldek, *Materialen*, 21–25, 398–400; Hempel, *Merckwürdiges Leben*, 312. For the historiography of this event, see Kurukin, *"Epokha dvorskikh bur',"* 164–70.

136. *PVTS*, 123–24; Chistovich, *Feofan Prokopovich i ego vremia*, 296.

137. Pekarskii, *Istoriia Imperatorskoi akademii nauk*, 1:216. For Biron's letter and opinion, see Chistovich, *Feofan Prokopovich i ego vremia*, 641–43.

138. Chistovich, *Feofan Prokopovich i ego vremia*, 641–45.

139. Feofan [Prokopovich], "Proch', ustupai, proch'," in *Sochineniia*, 218.

140. Feofan [Prokopovich], "Zateika," 196. The religious dimension of the events of 1730 remains unstudied even in the latest well-researched narratives of the event

such as the abovementioned works by Kurukin and Petrukhintsev. While this section reconstructs an overview of the religious politics of 1730 from some of the Russian, German, French, and Spanish sources, a more thorough study is necessary.

141. Arsenii, *Vozrazhenie na. . . . Molotok na Kamen' very*, ll. 14–14 ob.

142. Morozov, *Feofan Prokopovich kak pisatel'*, 208–9. For the full text of the points, see "Beylage des Projects," in Weber, *Das veränderte Russland*, 433–43; Avgustin [Nikitin], "Rossiia i Sorbonna," 56–57; see also Pierling, *La Sorbonne et la Russie*, 20–65.

143. Avgustin [Nikitin], "Rossiia i Sorbonna," 59.

144. Morozov, *Feofan Prokopovich kak pisatel'*, 210–11. The main arguments of Prokopovich's reply were printed in Latin by Feofan's intellectual patron Buddeus in his 1719 work *Ecclesia Romana cum Ruthenica Irreconciliabilis*.

145. Mervaud, "Introduction," 2–5, 29; he was known for conducting the Mass in both Latin and in French. Ibid., 29. On his idea of "le patriarcat gallican," see Pierling, *La Sorbonne et la Russie*, 330–32.

146. Mervaud, "Introduction," 29. See also Kurukin, *"Epokha dvorskikh bur',"* 144–53.

147. Mervaud, "Introduction," 31. Jubé also proposed initiating French-Russian negotiations to be held in Paris. Ibid., 30–31.

148. Ibid., 36; Pekarskii, *Nauka i literatura*, 1:42–43.

149. Mervaud, "Introduction," 23, 38.

150. Paz y Melia, *Conquista de Nápoles*.

151. As stated in King Philip's ambassadorial missive in *CODOIN*, 93:87–88. See also Weber, *Das veränderte Russland*, 169.

152. Mervaud, "Introduction," 43; Zeltner, *Breviarium Controversarium*, 25. On Cornelio Bentivoglio, see Mazzuchelli, *Gli scrittori d'Italia*, 2:867–82.

153. Pekarskii, *Nauka i literatura*, 1:42–43.

154. *CODOIN*, 93:445–49.

155. Mervaud, "Introduction," 43–44; *CODOIN*, 93:447–49.

156. *CODOIN*, 93:447–49; Chistovich, *Reshilovskoe delo*, 8.

157. *CODOIN*, 93:447. De Liria wanted to remove him from the Synod and replace him with someone more amenable. "There are those [bishops]," he wrote, "who showed sympathy toward Catholicism, although some are suspected of being outright Catholics." *CODOIN*, 93:448.

158. Mervaud, "Introduction," 44; Jubé also wanted Iakov Dolgorukii to be patriarch.

159. *CODOIN*, 93:87–88, 445–49; Mervaud, "Introduction," 2–5, 29–44; Pekarskii, *Nauka i literatura*, 1:42–43.

160. Ribera, *Responsum ant-apologeticum*.

161. Feofan's review ("Otzyv") of Ribera's book is printed in Chistovich, *Reshilovskoe delo*, prilozhenie, 17–31.

162. Ibid., 17.

163. Ibid., 21–23, 28.

164. Ibid.

165. Ibid., 25–27.

166. Ibid., 27. Prokopovich defended the House of Hanover again in 1734 when he refused to pursue relations with some non-juring Anglican bishops due to their support for the "illegitimate" Stuart dynasty. "Iz poslaniia Kantemira, poslannika russkogo v Londone Feofanu," RGB, f. 528, Sobranie Viazemskikh, d. 3.

167. Chistovich, *Reshilovskoe delo*, 25.

168. "Pokazanie neizvestnogo o diuke de-Liriia," RGADA, f. 18, op. 1, d. 64, ll. 1–2.

169. Ibid., 1–1 ob.

170. Rondeau, "Doneseniia i drugie bumagi," 524.

171. See his correspondence with Chancellor Golovkin about this threat in Ukraine and Belarus: Feofan [Prokopovich], "Pis'ma," *TKDA* 3 (1865): 604–7.

172. RGIA, f. 796, op. 1, d. 453, l. 1. The synodal file has the description and translation of these Italian letters, but no original, ll. 6–18.

173. Ibid., ll. 1 ob.–2.

174. Kondoidi was afraid that Catholic proselytism in Russia would begin to attract Russians to the Uniate faith, as happened in "Armenia, Persia, India, the Archipelago, Crete, etc." Ibid., ll. 2–2 ob.

175. Ibid., l. 3.

176. Ibid., ll. 3–3 ob.

177. Ibid., ll. 32–42.

178. "O kaputsinakh . . . vziatykh po podozreniiu chto oni poslany v Rossiiu po politicheskim tseliam," RGADA, f. 7, op. 1, d. 204, ll. 1–2 ob.; for the description of the riot, see Esipov, *Liudi starogo veka*, 219–221.

179. The exact quote is "vsiacheski sotvorim to na chto my obiazany." RGADA, f. 7, op. 1, d. 204, ll. 25–25 ob.; also 27–28.

180. Ibid., 10, 17–18, 23–25, 28.

181. Ibid., ll. 29–38, Esipov, *Liudi starogo veka*, 231–33.

182. Esipov, *Liudi starogo veka*, 232. Count Savva Raguzinskii (1669–1738) was one of them.

183. Ibid., ll. 70–76.

184. Arsenii Matseevich's "Vozrazhenie na pashkvil' liuteranskii," in OR RGB, f. 173, op. 1, rukopis' 127, contains a refutation of *Molotok* but also its text. The earliest known copy is from 1732. Chistovich in *Reshilovskoe delo*, page 2, states that the pasquil circulated in public shortly after the publication of *Kamen' very*, so around 1729 to 1730.

185. The full text is in Arsenii Matseevich's "Vozrazhenie na pashkvil' liuteranskii" in OR RGB, f. 173, op. 1, rukopis' 127. For the passages in support of the Protestants, see ll. 46–53.

186. Ibid., ll. 1 ob.–2 ob., 9–10.

187. Ibid., ll. 10–10 ob.

188. Buddeus, *Epistola Apologetica*, 4.

189. Mencken, "Stephanii Iavorscii," 228–29.

190. Zeltner, *Breviarum Controversiarum*, 24–28.

191. Chistovich, *Reshilovskoe delo*, 4.

192. Kartashev, *Ocherki*, 2:414–15.

193. For the full list of Synod members, see the introduction in *ODDS* 11 (1731): 1–4.

194. Zdravomyslov, *Ierarkhi novgorodskoi eparkhii*, 65–68. He spoke no Russian at all. Ibid., 74.

195. He died from poor health in April 1731. "Gavriil Buzhinskii," *RBS*, 4:29–30.

196. Chistovich, *Feofan Prokopovich i ego vremia*, 223.

197. Krashennikova, "Podmetnoe pis'mo 1732 goda," 88–89.

198. "Delo Feofana Prokopovicha," 70.

199. The St. Petersburg text of the letter was accidentally discovered by Hermitage scholar Sergei Androsov in *Zhivopisets Ivan Nikitin*, 123. Details of his discovery are described by Krashennikova, "Podmetnoe pis'mo 1732 goda," 1–2. The full text can be found in "Izvestnoe podmetnoe pis'mo," RGIA, f. 468, op. 39, d. 17, ll. 19–25. The author found similar letters that had circulated in Moscow, such as "Podlozhnoe pis'mo," RGADA, f. 18, op. 1, d. 80, ll. 1–2.

200. Rondeau, "Doneseniia i drugie bumagi," 524.

201. "Izvestnoe podmetnoe pis'mo," RGIA, f. 468, op. 39, d. 17, ll. 21–22, 24.

202. Ibid., ll. 20–24 ob.

203. Ibid., ll. 20–25.

204. Ibid., ll. 21 ob.

205. Ibid.

206. Rondeau, "Doneseniia i drugie bumagi," 526; Chistovich, *Reshilovskoe delo*, 53–57; Chistovich, *Feofan Prokopovich i ego vremia*, 431. On Pitirim's role in the Secret Chancellery and his "fearsome" reputation, see Morokhin, *Arkhiepiskop Nizhegorodskii i Alatyrskii Pitirim*, 185–86, 190–92.

207. Izmozik, *Zhandarmy Rossii*, 119, 154–56.

208. Chistovich, *Reshilovskoe delo*, 41.

209. Zakrzhevskii, "Arkhiereiskaia vlast'," 107.

210. Rondeau, "Doneseniia i drugie bumagi," 525.

211. Chistovich, *Feofan Prokopovich i ego vremia*, 428.

212. Chistovich, *Reshilovskoe delo*, prilozhenie, 18–19.

213. Ibid., 19.

214. Pokrovskii, "Feofilakt Lopatinskii," 698.

215. Chistovich, *Reshilovskoe delo*, prilozhenie, 22; Ribera, *Responsum antapologeticum*, 27.

216. Pokrovskii, "Feofilakt Lopatinskii," 698–700.

217. Chistovich, *Reshilovskoe delo*, 19, 31–36.

218. Ibid., 29–32, 56–62.

219. Ibid., 62; Makarii, "Ivlechenie iz sledstvennogo dela o Tverskom Arkhiepiskope," 59.

220. Chistovich, *Feofan Prokopovich i ego vremia*, 289–91; Titlinov, *Pravitel'stvo imperatritsy Anny Ioannovny*, 119–24.

221. Kartashev, *Ocherki*, 2:403.

222. See note 8.

223. Titlinov, *Pravitel'stvo imperatritsy Anny Ioannovny*, 90.

224. Ibid., 100–102.

225. Morokhin, *Arkhiepiskop Nizhegorodskii i Alatyrskii Pitirim*, 182; Titlinov, *Pravitel'stvo imperatritsy Anny Ioannovny*, 109–21.

226. Chistovich, *Feofan Prokopovich i ego vremia*, 431–32.

227. Bushkovitch, *Peter the Great*, 396n27; RGIA, f. 796, op. 20, d. 94, ll. 2–28.

228. Buevskii, "Aleksei Titov," 395.

229. Ibid.

230. Leskov, "Sviatitel'skie teni," 59.

231. Vozdvizhenskii, *Istoricheskoe obozrenie Riazanskoi ierarkhii*, 241; for his relationship to Prokopovich, see Buevskii, "Epizody iz zhizni," *Pamiatnaia knizhka Viatskoi gubernii za 1899 god* (1898), 265 and 268.

232. Leskov, "Sviatitel'skie teni," 58; Buevskii, "Epizody iz zhizni," *Pamiatnaia knizhka Viatskoi gubernii za 1902 god* (1901), 51–52.

233. Buevskii, "Epizody iz zhizni," *Pamiatnaia knizhka Viatskoi gubernii za 1902 god* (1901), 52.

234. Titlinov, *Pravitel'stvo imperatritsy Anny Ioannovny*, 191–95.

235. Ibid.

236. Ibid., 316–17.

237. Vereshchagin, "*Sviatitel'skie teni* gospodina Leskova," 340–347; Vozdvizhenskii, *Istoricheskoe obozrenie Riazanskoi ierarkhii*, 242–43.

238. Vozdvizhenskii, *Istoricheskoe obozrenie Riazanskoi ierarkhii*, 243–46, Vereshchagin, "*Sviatitel'skie teni* gospodina Leskova," 348.

239. Buevskii, "Aleksei Titov," 58–62, 68–95.

CHAPTER 5. "THE FLEDGLINGS OF THE PETRINE NEST"

1. Chistovich, *Feofan Prokopovich i ego vremia*, 646.

2. Ibid., 646–65. Reports of Kalinovskii and Pitirim are in RGIA, f. 796, op. 17, d. 318, ll. 1–2, "O smerti pervenstvuiushchego Sinodal'nogo chlena preosv. Feofana."

3. *KFZh* entry for September 12, 1736; also, "Opisanie byvshei v St. Peterburge tseremonii pri prestavlenii Sv. Prav. Sinoda vitse-prezidenta velikogo gospodina preosviashchennogo Feofana," *ODDS* 16 (1736): pril. 22.

4. Israel, *Radical Enlightenment*; Mainberger, *Die französische Gelehrtenrepublik*.

5. See chapter 2 for discussion of the triangle. Bödeker, *Strukturen der deutschen Frühaufklärung*; Lehmann, *Die Transformation des Kirchenbegriffs*; Vollhardt, *Christian Thomasius*.

6. Titlinov, among others, struggled to find an explanation for this destructive government policy against the church and the Holy Synod. In his explanation, he exonerated Biron and put all the blame on overly zealous Ostermann and his allies. Titlinov, *Pravitel'stvo imperatritsy Anny Ioannovny*, 12–20, 209–50. For other explanations in historiography, see Kurukin, *Epokha "dvorskikh bur'"*; Longworth, *The Three Empresses*; and Petrukhintsev, *Tsarstvovanie Anny Ioannovny*. For a new approach, see Fedyukhin, "The 'German' Reign," 363–84.

7. Titlinov, *Pravitel'stvo imperatritsy Anny Ioannovny*, 208–17.

8. Ibid., 235–38, 241–43, 247–48.

9. Ibid., 232–36.

10. Ibid., 245–48; Morokhin, *Arkhiepiskop Nizhegorodskii i Alatyrskii Pitirim*, 217.

11. Titlinov, *Pravitel'stvo imperatritsy Anny Ioannovny*, 269.

12. Ibid., 250–51.

13. Ibid., 257–66.

14. "Predislovie," *ODDS* 20 (1740): iv.

15. Ibid., iii–iv; Solov'ev, *Istoriia Rossii*, 21:27–42.

16. Amvrosii [Iushkevich], "Slovo Amvrosiia."

17. Hempel, *Merckwürdiges Leben*, 553–56, 560–61; Solov'ev, *Istoriia Rossii*, 21: 56–58.

18. Ibid.

19. "Manifest," in *ODDS* 20 (1740): no. 537.

20. Amnesty announcement in *ODDS* (1749): no. 198, p. 183.

21. Ibid., the list of the clergy is on 183–96.

22. Ibid.; *ODDS* 20 (1740): no. 535, p. 530; no. 571, p. 618.

23. *ODDS* 29 (1749): no. 26, pp. 71–74. In contrast, later the Synod decided the opposite—to publish Prokopovich's essay "The Unbearable Yoke" as "very useful and essentially necessary [*vesma poleznoe i neobkhodimo nuzhnoe*]." Ibid., 74.

24. "Predislovie," *ODDS* 20 (1740): vi; "Ignatii (Smola)," *RBS* 8:51–52; Iosif Reshilov and Ioasaf Maevskii met a similar fate, being sent to Kiev's monasteries. Their case is in *ODDS* 21 (1741): no. 3, pp. 3–6.

25. The monastery's report on Varlaam is in *ODDS* 20 (1740): no. 535, pp. 528–33.

26. Hempel, *Merckwürdiges Leben*, 599; for the British use of this term, see Bil'basov, *Istoriia Ekateriny Vtoroi*, 1:30.

27. Hempel, *Merckwürdiges Leben*, 600–601; Solov'ev, *Istoriia Rossii*, 21:157–60.

28. Hempel, *Merckwürdiges Leben*, 601.

29. Ibid., 601–2.

30. Soldatov, *Arsenii Matseevich*, 58.

31. Reports and amnesty announcements in *ODDS* 21 (1741): no. 82, pp. 74–78; no. 108, pp. 107–11; no. 637, pp. 460–64. The amnesty was also extended to various state officials: Solov'ev, *Istoriia Rossii*, 21, 246–48.

32. Solov'ev, *Istoriia Rossii*, 21:195, 337–38; Bushkovitch, "The Clergy at the Russian Court," 116–18; Bil'basov, *Istoriia Ekateriny Vtoroi*, 1:143–44. Even Markell Rodyshevskii was invited to deliver a Christmas sermon in the palace in 1741, as seen in his *Slovo na den' rozhdestva*. One of the most interesting "amnesties" of this early Elizabethan period was the lifting of the prohibition on selling Iavorskii's *Kamen' very*. The impetus for this decision seems to have been more practical than ideological. In Kiev, Archbishop Rafail needed to remove some one thousand unbound, rotting volumes of this book that were "locked up" in the space in the Caves Monastery that he wanted for the expansion of the library. By receiving Synodal permission to sell whatever remained of the books, he could profit financially from clearing the much-needed room. A similar fate awaited all nineteen boxes of this book that were locked inside the SS. Peter and Paul Fortress: despite the fact that the books "rotted away [*sgnivshye*]," the Synod ordered sales rather than disposal to gain revenue. *ODDS* 21 (1741): no. 282, pp. 227–28. Synodal republication of the book only took place once—in August 1749—and seems to have had a financial objective ("*dlia razmnozheniia kapitala*").

ODDS 29 (1749): no. 417, p. 548. However, there were no subsequent publications of this work until 1841.

33. Solov'ev, *Istoriia Rossii*, 21:177; Bushkovitch, "The Clergy at the Russian Court," 118–19.

34. Solov'ev, *Istoriia Rossii*, 21:177.

35. Bil'basov, *Istoriia Ekateriny Vtoroi*, 1:143–44, 146.

36. Solov'ev, *Istoriia Rossii*, 21:184–85; Soldatov, *Arsenii Matseevich*, 60–61. For very thorough overviews of Elizabeth's reforms aimed at restoring the Petrine heritage in the 1740s and 1750s, see Anisimov, *Rossiia v seredine XVIII veka*; and Liechtenhan, *La Russie entre en Europe*.

37. "Predislovie," *ODDS* 21 (1741): iii–iv. Nikita Krechetnikov was appointed in 1740 but never accepted the position. "Predislovie," *ODDS* 23 (1743): iv. Feofan Prokopovich likely considered the office to be rather trivial (due to his ability to communicate directly with Ostermann or the empress), and second, tolerated few checks on his power in church affairs. Elizabeth appointed Iakov Shakhovskoi as the chief procurator.

38. Chistovich, *Feofan Prokopovich i ego vremia*, 631–33; for poems and contemporary commentary, see Feofan [Prokopovich], *Sochineniia*, 221, 487–89.

39. Leskov, "Sviatitel'skie teni," 60–61.

40. Znamenskii, *Dukhovnye shkoly*, 158; Liubarskii, *Sbornik Drevnostei Kazanskoi eparkhii*, 89; Makarii [Miroliubov], *Istoriia nizhegorodskoi ierarkhii*, 127–28.

41. Chistovich, *Feofan Prokopovich i ego vremia*, 432; Stefan was one of the three people present at Prokopovich's deathbed in 1736 and was a witness to his deathbed will. Ibid., 646, 650.

42. Morokhin, *Arkhiepiskop Nizhegorodskii i Alatyrskii Pitirim*, 174.

43. Khyzhniak, "Zaborovs'kyi, Rafaiil," 213–14.

44. Ibid.; Feofan Prokopovich's 1736 letter to Rafail Zaborovskii is in *Filosofs'ki tvory*, 3:273–77; Domanitskii, "Dva Ukaza Rafaila Zaborovskogo," 307–9.

45. Shchukin, "Simon (Todorskii)," February 1898, 57.

46. "K biografii preosv: Amvrosiia Iushkevicha," 389–94.

47. Vysotskii, "Feofan Prokopovich," 263–65; Morokhin, *Arkhiepiskop Nizhegorodskii i Alatyrskii Pitirim*, 182–88.

48. "Opis' uchenennaia 16 sentiabria 1754 goda ... ostavshim posle pokoinogo preosviashchennogo Platona arkhiepiskopa Moskovskogo," *ODDS* 34 (1754): pril. 19.

49. Thus in 1749 the Synod was composed of Platon Malinovskii (Moscow), Stefan Kalinovskii (Novgorod), Simon Todorskii (Pskov), and Ilarion Grigorovich (Krutitsy). Grigorovich was a former student of Feofan at the Mohyla Academy. "Ilarion Grigorovich," *RBS* 8:82–83; also, Platon Petrunkevich (bishop of Vladimir), a student of Feofan's and fluent in German, was promoted by his teacher to the Cadet Corps. "Platon (Petrunkevich)," *RBS* 14:56–57.

50. The following bishops were members of the Synod in 1759: Dmitrii Sechenov (Novgorod), Sil'vestr Kuliabka (St. Petersburg), Veniamin Putsek-Grigorovich (Pskov), Palladii Iur'ev (Riazan), Gedeon Krinovskii (archimandrite of Trinity-Sergius Lavra).

51. Titlinov, *Gavriil Petrov*, 244–45; for more on him, see Askochenskii, *Kiev*, 2:297–315.

52. Zalesskii, "Sil'vestr Kuliabka," 66–82; see more on Kuliabka in the last section of this chapter.

53. Zalesskii, "Sil'vestr Kuliabka," 205–26; Evgenii [Bolkhovitinov], *Slovar' istori-cheskii*, 283–84.

54. Makarii [Miroliubov], *Istoriia nizhegorodskoi ierarkhii*, 127–29.

55. Lytvynov, *Ideii rann'oho prosvitnytstva*, 24, 57, 84–86, 90–92; in another Ukrai-nian diocese, Belgorod, the bishop was Ioasaf Gorlenko, a grandson of Danylo Apostol and a protégé of Rafail Zaborovskii. Zhevakhov, *Sviatitel' Ioasaf Gorlenko*, 2:171–76.

56. Ikonnikov, "Arsenii Matseevich," 1–2.

57. Ibid., 3. Arsenii served in the navy (until 1738), the Cadet Corps in St. Peters-burg, and as the metropolitan of Tobolsk and Siberia between 1741 and 1742 before being promoted to the wealthy and influential Rostov bishopric. Ibid., 3–9.

58. Popov, *Arsenii Matseevich*, appendix, 19.

59. Ibid., appendix, 20.

60. Ibid., appendix, 17–18; Soldatov, *Arsenii Matseevich*, 53.

61. Popov, *Arsenii Matseevich*, 91–92.

62. Popov, *Arsenii Matseevich*, 118, and appendix, 24–25.

63. Ibid., appendix, 16–18.

64. Ikonnikov, "Arsenii Matseevich," 14; Popov, *Arsenii Matseevich*, 362.

65. These reprimands were given for a range of issues from refusing to house war invalids in his monasteries to refusing to swear an oath to Elizabeth as "the highest arbiter of the Holy Synod" and are documented in *PSP* 1 (1742): no. 112; *PSP* 1 (1743): nos. 342, 378, 434, 469; *PSP* 4 (1756): no. 1524; and *PSP* 4 (1760): no. 1668. The Synod also rejected his 1742 attack on the canonicity of the Synod. Popov, *Arsenii Matseevich*, 93.

66. *PSP* 1 (1743): no. 434.

67. Soldatov, *Arsenii Matseevich*, 62.

68. Mardefeld allegedly offered a thousand rubles, to be tripled (*tripler la dose*) if the archbishop could theologically formulate an opinion that the marriage was not con-trary to the "canons of the Greek church." Bil'basov, *Istoriia Ekateriny Vtoroi*, 1:62–64.

69. Soldatov, *Arsenii Matseevich*, 62–63.

70. Ibid., 60–61.

71. Filaret [Gumilevskii], *Obzor russkoi dukhovnoi literatury*, 2:314–15.

72. Ibid., 298–99.

73. Sutorius, "Bogoslovie v Kievo-Mogilianskoi Akademii," 133–65.

74. Ibid., 183.

75. Stratii, *Opisanie kursov filosofii i retoriki*, 275; also see, Kashuba, *Pamiatniki eticheskoi mysli*.

76. Stratii, "Hryhorii Shcherbats'kyi i Kartezianstvo," 152–74; Nichyk, "Filosofiia v Kyevomohylians'kii akademii," 88–90, 308–15.

77. Nichyk, "Filosofiia v Kyevomohylians'kii akademii," 88–90.

78. Lytvynov, *Ideii rann'oho prosvitnytstva*, 136. Wolffian philosophy is a term ascribed to the German philosophical system developed by Christian Wolff (1679–1754), which emphasized empirical reason as the basis of human knowledge. In matters of doctrine, Wolffianism highlighted the rationality and self-evidence of Christian

dogmas in nature. Wolffians adopted a rationalist "natural theology" in which they rejected revelation that could not be brought into harmony with empirical reason.

79. *ADKA*, 2:221–23; Nichyk, *Kyevo-Mohylians'ka akademiia*, 101.

80. Lytvynov, Ideii rann'oho prosvitnytstva, 25; Shpet, *Ocherki razvitiia russkoi filosofii*, 50–51, 56–57.

81. *ADKA*, 2:176.

82. Ibid., 179–80.

83. Smirnov, *Istoriia Moskovskoi dukhovnoi akademii*, 117–18, 130–51; Vostokov, *Opisanie russkikh i slovenskikh rukopisei*, no. 317.

84. Smirnov, *Istoriia Moskovskoi dukhovnoi akademii*, 153.

85. Such as those by Ivan Kozlovich and Vladimir Kalligraf. Both were Kievans teaching in Moscow. Ibid., 169–70.

86. Ibid., 156.

87. Smirnov, *Istoriia Troitskoi Lavrskoi seminarii*, 36–37; for a full comparison of the theology of Feofan and Afanasii, see ibid., 37–40; also Filaret [Gumilevskii], *Obzor russkoi dukhovnoi literatury*, 2:352.

88. Schaff, *Theological Propaedeutic*, 391.

89. Petrov, *Opisanie rukopisei*, no. 95.

90. Buevskii, "Epizody iz zhizni," 263–66.

91. Ibid., 267.

92. Leskov, "Sviatitel'skie teni," 58–59.

93. APCG, "Catalogus alumnorum," 14:10–20, shows a large number of students from dioceses with a significant Orthodox population for the period of 1630–1700, including Kiev, Podolia, Minsk, and Polotsk, while the period 1731–91 identifies only students from Podolia (seven of them), one from Kam'ianets-Podol'skii and one from Kiev. The entries in Evgenii [Bolkhovitinov], *Slovar' istoricheskii*, show the steep decline of Ukrainian seminarians seeking education in Polish or other Catholic schools in the eighteenth centuries, such as the entries on pages 71, 121, 158, 184–222, 258, 285, 290–91.

94. Valeriia Nichyk and Zoia Khyzhniak show that most Ukrainian students who sought education in Germany did so in the last two-thirds of the eighteenth century. Khyzhniak, "Kyevo-Mohylians'ka akademiia"; see also Nichyk, *Kyevo-Mohylians'ka akademiia*.

95. Fundaminski, "The Communications Network," 120, 122; Vierorth, "Lebenslauf," 112–14; "Brief von Gottfried Himler an Gotthilf August Francke. 19.04.1727," AFSt Stab/F 29/31:1, Mikrofilm-Nr.: 20, 623–24. Feofan's correspondence with Halle Pietists is also discussed in the records of the Frankesche Stiftungen archives in Halle, such as "Brief von Hermann Schröder an Joachim Lange. 1729," AFSt/H A 188a: 324; "Brief von Albert Anton Vierorth an Gotthilf August Francke. 29.01.1730," AFSt/H C 380:26; "Brief von Theophil Siegfried Bayer. 02.10.1732," AFSt/ DHM 9/19:5.

96. Fundaminski, "The Communications Network," 122–30. Bayer's connections to Halle were substantial; according to Otto Teigeler, he was "*the* man Francke trusted [die *Vertrauensperson Franckes in Russland*]." Teigeler, *Die Herrnhuter in Russland*, 136.

97. Winter, *Ketzerschicksale*, 247; Vierorth, "Lebenslauf," 118–19.

98. Vierorth, "Lebenslauf," 113.

99. Shchukin, "Simon (Todorskii)," April 1898, 74; Winter, *Ketzerschicksale*, 245–46.

100. Winter, *Ketzerschicksale*, 247; Vierorth, "Lebenslauf," 113.

101. Winter, *Ketzerschicksale*, 247–48.

102. Nichyk, *Symon Todors'kyi i hebraistyka*, 34; Evgenii [Bolkhovitinov], *Slovar' istoricheskii*, 290–91; Winter, *Ketzerschicksale*, 246–47.

103. Winter notes that the weight of all his books was "2.5 Zentner," which could be 125 or 250 kg, depending on whether the centner he has in mind is metric or the old German hundredweight. Winter, *Ketzerschicksale*, 249.

104. Nichyk, *Symon Todors'kyi i hebraistyka*, 28; the full list is in "Opis' . . . preosv. Simona," RGIA, f. 796, op. 35, d. 424, ll. 1–115. Curiously enough, the list of books contained works like *Ecclesia Graeca Lutheranizans* and the Koran.

105. Arndt, *Chtiri knigi o istinnom khristianstve*; Shishkin, "Simon Todorskii."

106. Simon [Todorskii], "Predoslovie [*sic*]," in Arndt, *Chtiri knigi o istinnom khristianstve*, 2.

107. Winter, *Ketzerschicksale*, 248–49.

108. Khyzhniak, "Zaborovs'kyi, Rafaiil," 213–14.

109. Todorskii, "Ieromonakh Simon Todorskii," 1513–18.

110. *PSP* 1 (1742): no. 102.

111. Johanna-Elisabeth, "Izvestiia," 29.

112. Bil'basov, *Istoriia Ekateriny Vtoroi*, 1:122. "External ceremonies, however, are very different from ours," she noted.

113. Ibid., 126.

114. *PSP* 2 (1744): no. 335.

115. See introduction in *ODDS* 28 (1748): iii–vi. The rankings for Russia excluded Ukraine.

116. Kislova, "Propoved' Simona Todorskogo," 113.

117. Khyzhniak, "Zaborovs'kyi, Rafaiil," 213–14.

118. Khyzhniak, "Liashchevs'kyi, Varlaam," 338.

119. Varlaam [Liashchevskii], *Grecheskaia grammatika*, predislovie.

120. Ibid., 427; especially on syntax and dialects (411–87), compare with Weller, "De vocalium mutatione," in his *Grammatica graeca nova*, 3–25.

121. Shchegolev, "Primechanie ot Izdatelia," 380–81, 458, 463–64. He preached at Kiev's St. Sophia Cathedral with his benefactor, Rafail Zaborovskii, present.

122. Khyzhniak, "Nashchyns'kyi, Danylo," 386–87. On Bogatzky, see Bautz, "Carl Heinrich von Bogatzky."

123. Dziuba, "Ukraiintsi v evropeis'kykh mistakh," 61.

124. Ibid., 56–57, 61.

125. Ibid., 61–62.

126. Los'kyi, "Ukraiintsi na studiiakh," 105–7.

127. Dziuba, "Ukraiintsi v evropeis'kikh mistakh," 58; Evgenii [Bolkhovitinov], *Slovar' istoricheskii*, 121; on Pressburg Gymnasium, see Craig, *History of the Protestant Church*, 198–99.

128. Dziuba, "Ukraiintsi v evropeis'kikh mistakh," 56–57.

129. Ibid., 61.

130. Gorozhanskii, *Damaskin Semenov-Rudnev*, 28; Aleksandrenko, "Iz zhizni russkikh studentov," 1, 2; Aleksandrenko, *Russkie diplomaticheskie agenty*, 2:107.

131. Gorozhanskii, *Damaskin Semenov-Rudnev*, 23–39. Some Russian clergymen volunteered to go abroad; others were recommended by the Synod. Aleksadrenko, "Proekt bogoslovskogo fakul'teta," 304.

132. Dziuba, "Ukraiintsi v evropeis'kikh mistakh," 61–62.

133. Cross, "Russian Students," 93.

134. Eijnatten, *Liberty and Concord*, 91–94.

135. Ibid., 256–59; Blom, "Grotius and Socinianism," 123.

136. Gorozhanskii, *Damaskin Semenov-Rudnev*, 47–55.

137. Sorkin, *The Religious Enlightenment*, 159.

138. Michaelis's theory (still relevant in today's seminaries) was that when a Hebrew word's meaning is obscure the answer must lie in other Oriental languages. Gorozhanskii, *Damaskin Semenov-Rudnev*, 75.

139. Cross, "Russian Students," 92.

140. Barsov, "Samborskii, Andrei," *RBS* 18:147, 152.

141. Aleksandrenko, *Russkie diplomaticheskie agenty*, 2:106.

142. Ibid., 108.

143. Aleksandrenko, "Proekt bogoslovskogo fakul'teta," 307–9.

144. Ibid. Aleksandrenko, "Iz zhizni russkikh studentov," 7; Cross, "Russian Students," 101–3.

145. Aleksandrenko, "Proekt bogoslovskogo fakul'teta," 308.

146. Gorozhanskii, *Damaskin Semenov-Rudnev*, 30, 35–36, 42.

147. Ibid., 60, 61.

148. Ibid., 83–90; Aleksandrenko, "Proekt bogoslovskogo fakul'teta," 310–12.

149. Gorozhanskii, *Damaskin Semenov-Rudnev*, 87–88.

150. Ibid., 85.

151. This was noted by Clarke in his *Travels*, 1:197.

152. Barsov, "Samborskii," *RBS* 18:147–48.

153. Barsov, "Samborskii," *RBS* 18:148.

154. Barsov, "Samborskii," *RBS* 18:148–49, 151; see also Zhmakin, "Pis'ma protoiereia A. A. Samborskogo," 425–52.

155. Pelikan, *The Reformation of the Bible*; Stephens, *The Bible*. On the Tridentine revisions of the Bible, see Metzger, *The Early Versions*, 347–50.

156. Eleonskii, *Po povodu 150-letiia Elizavetinskoi Biblii*, 2, 5–12; "Po sinodal'nomu prigovoru o napechatanii novoispravlennoi Slavianskoi Biblii 10 noiabria 1752 goda," *ODDS* 3 (1723): no. 38, pp. 27–31.

157. See "Mnenie Feofana Prokopoviche o ispravlenii Biblii," ODDS 3 (1723): pril. 6 and 8; Arsenii [Matseevich], "Vozrazhenie na pashkvil' liuteranskii," ll. 100 ob.–101; Winter, *Ketzerschicksale*, 245–46. The Synodal collection of documents regarding the revision of the Bible is found in RGIA, f. 796, op. 4, d. 38. It is interesting that Feofan believed the Ostrog Bible to have been translated from an "Arian," i.e., Socinian edition.

158. "Mnenie Feofana Prokopoviche o ispravlenii Biblii," *ODDS* 3 (1723): pril. 8.

159. "Po sinodal'nomu prigovoru o napechatanii novoispravlennoi Slavianskoi Biblii 10 noiabria 1752 goda," *ODDS* 3 (1723): no. 38, p. 33.

160. Ibid., no. 38, pp. 34–44.

161. Ibid.; "O ostanovivshemsia novoispravlenoi Biblii pechatanii mnenie . . . 1740-go goda," and "Ee Imperatorskomu Velichestvu . . vsepoddanneishee donoshenie Sinoda," *ODDS* 3 (1723): pril. 12 and 13, respectively.

162. Valeriia Nichyk lists the teachers of Hebrew at the academy between 1751 (when Liashchevskii stopped teaching) and 1808 in her *Symon Todors'kyi i hebraistyka*, 39.

163. Nichyk, *Symon Todors'kyi i hebraistyka*, 40.

164. Eleonskii, *Po povodu 150-letiia Elizavetinskoi Biblii*, 16–18; see encyclopedic entries on "Reineccius," *ADB* (1889), 28:15–17; and "Breitinger," *ADB* (1876), 3:295; Lambrtus Bos's philological guide to the New Testament is *Exercitationes philologicae*.

165. "Po sinodal'nomu prigovoru o napechatanii novoispravlennoi Slavianskoi Biblii 10 noiabria 1752 goda," *ODDS* 3 (1723): no. 38, pp. 74–75.

166. Ibid., no. 38, pp. 89–91.

167. Ibid., no. 38, 93–94.

168. For comparison, one can consult the Danish Bible of 1612, *The Holy Bible*, or *Biblia, Det er den ganske Helige Skrift*. Similar images as well as a depiction of Stockholm are featured on the title page of the 1655 Swedish Bible *Biblia, thet ar all then Helga skrifft*. The depiction of Leiden is found in the first official Dutch Bible, *Biblia dat is de gantsche H. Schrifture*.

169. See a similar pictorial dedication to a monarch in 1728's *Biblia, thet ar all then Heliga Skrift*.

170. *Bibliia*, ll. 10–11, 12–12 ob.

171. Ivanov, "Reforming Orthodoxy," 282–90; see the table demonstrating northern humanist and Protestant influences in the structural composition of his sermons (rhetorical genus, exordium, thema, exempla, and so on) on page 422.

172. Ibid., 281–83; there was some interaction between northern humanism, French Catholicism, and Calvinism in homiletics, albeit not with southern European preaching trends. Edwards, *A History of Preaching*, 310.

173. Feofan [Prokopovich], *Veshchi i dela*, 2; Morozov, *Feofan Prokopovich kak pisatel'*, 109, 127; *DR*, 49 (on superstitions) and 51 (on Chrysostom).

174. *DR*, 51.

175. *DR*, 51; Prokopovich, "De Arte Rhetorica Libri X," in Lachmann, *Feofan Prokopovic*, 465. He approved of the movement of the face but in a very moderate manner. The voice should fluctuate according to occasion, while the eyebrows could lower when sad or rise when joyful.

176. *DR*, 49–51; and Feofan, *Veshchi i dela*, 2.

177. Edwards, *A History of Preaching*, 843, 413. Edwards notes on the popularity of this style: "it is hard for ordinary people of today to understand how it could have been so popular at the time." Ibid., 413.

178. "An Introduction to *Sinners in the Hands of an Angry God*."

179. *DR*, 66.

180. Ivanov, "Reforming Orthodoxy," 294–95.

181. *DR*, 67; Samarin, *Stefan Iavorskii*, 398. This last criticism mirrored Erasmus's invective against preachers who staggered left and right "as if preaching from a rowboat." Pevnitskii, "Gomiletika Erazma Rotterdamskogo," 56–57.

182. *DR*, 51.

183. Ivanov, "Reforming Orthodoxy," 284–85.

184. Ibid., 287–90.

185. Prokopovich, "Slovo o vlasti i chesti tsarskoi," in *Sochineniia*, 78–81.

186. Ivanov, "Reforming Orthodoxy," 304–6.

187. Zalesski, "Sil'vestr Kuliabka," 63.

188. *Istoriko-statisticheskie svedeniia o Sankt-Peterburgskoi eparkhii* 6:1–5; contemporaries described his sermons as being full of "strict morality and reasonableness." Zalesskii, "Sil'vestr Kuliabka," 253.

189. Zalesskii, "Sil'vestr Kuliabka," 200.

190. Ivanov, "Reforming Orthodoxy," 308.

191. Todorskii, "Ieromonakh Simon Todorskii," 1228.

192. Johanna-Elisabetha, "Izvestiia," 29, 54; the sermon was titled "Bozhie osoboe blagoslovenie" (God's special blessing) and was delivered on August 21, 1745, and printed in same year at the Academy of Sciences in St. Petersburg.

193. Todorskii, "Ieromonakh Simon Todorskii," 1226–27.

194. Todorskii, "Ieromonakh Simon Todorskii," 1513–14.

195. Ibid., 1518.

196. Ibid., 1517–18.

197. Ibid., 1518.

198. Todorskii, *Slovo . . . den' rozhdeniia . . . Petra Fedorovicha*. This observation has not been made before in the literature, but it was quite common for Todorskii to follow Francke in this pattern. For comparison, see the prayer in the *Sonntag Exaudi 1699* (May 21), a sermon printed in Francke, *Predigten*, 1:556–63. For further discussion, see Ivanov, "Reforming Orthodoxy," 311–12, n170.

199. Barsov, "Maloizvestnye russkie propovedniki," 269.

200. Ibid., 269, 577–78.

201. Ibid., 584.

202. Ibid., 27.

203. Ibid.

204. Ibid., 272.

205. Ibid., 272–73.

206. Ibid., 275.

CHAPTER 6. ENLIGHTENING THE CHURCH

1. "Kratkoe opisanie bolezni i konchiny Ee Velichestva Gosudaryni i Imperatritsy Elizavety Petrovny," in "Pribavlenie," *MV*, January 15, 1762.

2. Kurukin, *Epokha "dvorskikh bur'*," 370–402; Leonard, *Reform and Regicide*, 117–39; Rulhière, *Histoire*; Schwan, *Anecdotes russes*, 1:207.

3. He also praised the tsar's protection against some "slanderers unsatisfied by the judgments of the church." See Dmitrii Sechenov's sermon in "Smes'," *Otechestvennye Zapiski* 6 (1838): 1–4. It was published in 1762 in the German version, *Feyerliche Danck-Rede*, and in 1763 in Russian as *Rech' blagodarstvennaia*.

4. "Iz Moskvy," *SPV*, September 24, 1762.

5. "Pribavlenie 13," *MV*, February 12, 1762; Gavriil, *Slovo v vysokotorzhestvennyi den'* and *Slovo v torzhestvennyi den'*, 13–14.

6. "Catherine II à Voltaire," in *Voltaire-Catherine II*, 48.

7. See Catherine's introduction to her translation of *Bélisaire* in Marmontel', *Velizer*, 3–5; Znamenskii, "Chteniia iz istorii russkoi tserkvi," 110. Some of Gavriil's "enlightened" views appear in a small booklet he commissioned in 1770 for publication at the Synod, titled "Short Christian Moral Teachings." The work contained moralistic instructions for cultivating "virtues" and against superstitions. RGIA, f. 796, op. 51, d. 133, ll. 3–4.

8. Ternovskii, "Russkoe vol'nodumstvo," 414–15; for a concise survey of the impact of German, English, and French Enlightenment thought in Russia, see Raeff, "The Enlightenment in Russia," 25–47.

9. Sorkin, *The Religious Enlightenment*, 23–39, 70, 158–61, 167–69.

10. Ibid., 11, 20. Lehner, *The Catholic Enlightenment*, 4–12; Wallmann, *Kirchengeschichte Deutschlands*, 154–55. See also Beutel's book, *Aufklärung in Deutschland*.

11. Lehner, *The Catholic Enlightenment*, 30–32, 34–36, 38–39, 53–67.

12. Jones, *The Cambridge Platonists*, 39; "Latitudinarianism," in Cross and Livingstone, *The Oxford Dictionary of the Christian Church*.

13. Old, *Reading and Preaching*, 1–5; Edwards, *A History of Preaching*, 396. For identification of Tillotson with Latitudinarians and the Cambridge Platonists, see Force and Popkin's *Essays*, 122–24; Gascoigne, "Latitudinarianism, Rational Dissent and Radicalism," in Knud Haakonssen, *Enlightenment and Religion*, 238; Rivers, "Tillotson, John," in *Oxford Dictionary of National Biography*.

14. Fitzpatrick, "The Enlightenment," 64; the Newtonian "argument from design" became the cornerstone of Moderatist cosmology. Sorkin, *The Religious Enlightenment*, 28.

15. Beutel, *Aufklärung in Deutschland*, 226; Sorkin, *The Religious Enlightenment*, 59.

16. Beutel, *Aufklärung in Deutschland*, 226.

17. Sorkin, *The Religious Enlightenment*, 59–60.

18. Beutel, *Aufklärung in Deutschland*, 226.

19. This chronology is supported by such important scholars of German Enlightenment theology as Albrecht Beutel, Johannes Wallmann, and Karl Aner: Beutel, *Aufklärung in Deutschland*, 262 and 225–305; Wallmann, *Kirchengeschichte Deutschlands*, 154–65; Aner, *Die Theologie der Lessingzeit*, 3–32; in English, see a discussion of Aner by Allison, *Lessing and the Enlightenment*, 38–49; see also Gericke, *Theologie und Kirche*.

20. Beutel, *Aufklärung in Deutschland*, 232 and 243.

21. Ibid., 228; Sorkin, *The Religious Enlightenment*, 125–28, 135–36, 141, 158–59; see also Schloemann, *Siegmund Jacob Baumgarten*, 38, 224–29.

22. J. A. Fabricius (1668–1736) and his "Hamburg Circle" became the center of physicotheology in Germany. Beutel, *Aufklärung in Deutschland*, 226–27, 233; Wallmann, *Kirchengeschichte Deutschlands*, 155.

23. Wallmann, *Kirchengeschichte Deutschlands*, 156; Sorkin, *The Religious Enlightenment*, 115. For the role of Wolffianism, see Dorner, *History of Protestant Theology*, 2:266–79.

24. Beutel, *Aufklärung in Deutschland*, 251.

25. Ibid., 249.

26. Ibid., 250, 252–63.

27. Ibid., 265.

28. Ibid., 251.

29. Age information is from Evgenii [Bolkhovitinov], *Slovar' istoricheskii*; for Rusanov, see Rostislavov, "Zapiski D. I. Rostislavova,"94.

30. Evgenii [Bolkhovitinov], *Slovar' istoricheskii*, i–ii, 72–73. Seven years was more common, as in the case of Anastasii Bratanovskii and Amvrosii Podobedov. Ibid., 34–35, 37–38.

31. "Moisei Gumilevskii," 799–800; Stroev, *Spiski ierarkhov i nastoiatelei*, 1:491.

32. Evgenii [Bolkhovitinov], *Slovar' istoricheskii*, 64, 87; Kislova, "Slovo v den' iavleniia," 110.

33. Innokentii Nechaev was a serf of the Naryshkin estate and remained friends with the Naryshkins even after his education at the Moscow Academy. A. V. Naryshkin was Pskov's governor when Innokentii was the bishop there. The hierarch was buried next to the Naryshkins in the Aleksandr Nevskii Lavra. *RBS*, 8:118–19; Dmitriev, *Istoriia Korel'skoi (Keksgol'mskoi) eparkhii*. Simon Lagov, archbishop of Riazan, was born a monastery-owned serf but distinguished himself in Bishop Amvrosii Iushkevich's boys' choir in 1736, from where his career took off. *RBS*, 18:498–99.

34. Znamenskii, "Chteniia iz istorii russkoi tserkvi," 120. "The Hermitage Theater had a special secret lodge, called 'the archbishops' lodge,' where Platon was an especially frequent visitor [*osobenno chastyi zritel'*]." Mel'nikov, "Iz proshlogo," 501.

35. Shmurlo, *Mitropolit Evgenii kak uchenyi*, 176.

36. Znamenskii, "Chteniia iz istorii russkoi tserkvi," 106.

37. Znamenskii, "Chteniia iz istorii russkoi tserkvi," 17–18. Amvrosii's property included 42 paintings, 12,000 rubles in cash, velvet and silk cassocks, various furs, 252 shirts, 37 handkerchiefs, 3 clocks, and various women's dresses.

38. Ibid., 345. Metropolitan Gavriil, among others, disapproved of his beard-shaving.

39. Rostislavov, "Zapiski D. I. Rostislavova," 96. In addition to these bishops, Arsenii Vereshchagin also wore face powder. Titov, "Poslednii rostovskii arkhiepiskop," 393.

40. Smirnov, *Istoriia Troitskoi lavrskoi seminarii*, 8.

41. Ibid., 34; Evgenii [Bolkhovitinov], *Slovar' istoricheskii*, 269; Rostislavov, "Feofilakt Rusanov," 611.

42. Nevzorov, "Poslanie M.I. Nevzorova mitropolitu Serafimu," 766.

43. Ibid., 767.

44. Ibid., 767.

45. "Ob odezhde lits dukhovnogo sosloviia," 444.

46. Ibid., 443. See also Alexander I's "Ukaz o nebritii diakonami usov," 37. It must be noted that the initiative came from the tsar or concerned laity, not from the Holy Synod themselves, who liked their clothing.

47. Kislova, "Frantsuzskii iazyk," 16–34.

48. Ibid., 21; Kniazev, *Ocherk istorii Pskovskoi seminarii*, 27; Krinitskii, *Tverskie Arkhipastyri*, 27–30, 47; Filaret [Gumilevskii], *Obzor russkoi dukhovnoi literatury*, 399–400. French remained popular even after the official bans following the French Revolution—in 1797 Metropolitan Platon successfully petitioned Tsar Paul to restore the teaching of the language in Moscow that was banned in 1794. Kislova, "Frantsuzskii iazyk," 22.

49. Arsenii, "Dnevnik," 44 (1894) 699–700; 1 (1895): 15; 4 (1895): 62.

50. Kislova, "Frantsuzskii iazyk," 31.

51. Shmurlo, *Mitropolit Evgenii kak uchenyi*, 100–101, 106.

52. Rostislavov, "Feofilakt Rusanov," 608.

53. Bryner, *Der geistliche Stand*, 29–31.

54. Kharlampovich, *Malorossiiskoe vliianie*, 486.

55. Todorskii spoke to her in German, while Catherine "memorized the Russian text like a parrot," not knowing that the bishop's Russian was actually "Little Russian [i.e., Ukrainian]." Catherine II, *Zapiski*, 48–49.

56. Kharlampovich, *Malorosiiskoe vliianie*, 489. The commission proposed that the bishops should forward the candidates for approval with a disclosure "of what nation [*natsiia*] he is and where and what he studied." *PSZ*, 17, no. 12332.

57. Bryner, *Der geistliche stand*, 32.

58. Ibid., 50.

59. Theotikis studied in Leipzig while Voulgaris studied in Leipzig, Halle, and Göttingen. Bruess, *Religion, Identity, and Empire*, 4–14, 28–29, 56. For a wider discussion, see Kitromilides, *Enlightenment, Nationalism, Orthodoxy*.

60. Bruess, *Religion, Identity, and Empire*, 61–75, 94–115.

61. Semevskii, *Krest'iane*, 2:vii. Seventy percent of church institutions owned one hundred souls or more (only 16 percent of the gentry). Ibid., 195, 197.

62. The Stroganovs, for example, owned 19,000 serfs (ibid., 199), while Moscow's Resurrection Convent owned 15,582. Ibid., 196–97.

63. See, for example, Miliutin's *O nedvizhimykh imushchestvakh*; Zav'ialov's *Vopros o tserkovnykh imeniiakh*; Ivanovskii's *Russkoe zakonodatel'stvo*, and Komissarenko's *Russkii absoliutizm i dukhovenstvo*.

64. Cracraft, *Church Reform*, 101–16, 185; Kommisarenko, *Russkii absoliutizm i dukhovenstvo*, 14–39, 125; see also Burbee, "Catherine and the Convents."

65. Semevskii, *Krest'iane*, 207–9, 226.

66. Ibid., 208–10, 211–12, 218, 220–23.

67. Peasants rebelled because they believed their enserfment to the dioceses was a mistake in the first place, but the Senate rejected their petition. Ibid., 225.

68. Ibid., 248.

69. Ibid., 226–35.

70. Ibid., x.

71. *PSP*, 4 (1757): no. 1566.

72. Ibid.; Verkhovskoi, *Naselennye nedvizhimye*, 112–17.

73. *PSZ*, nos. 11396, 11441, 11486; Ikonnikov, "Arsenii Matseevich," 25, 582.

74. *PSP*, 4 (1762): no. 1758.

75. *PSP*, 4 (1762): no. 1755.

76. Kochetkova, "Teplov." The rumor is most likely baseless. Teplov was born in Pskov in 1716 or in 1717. Since Feofan does not arrive until St. Petersburg until October 1716 and then, becomes the bishop of Pskov in June 1718.

77. Ikonnikov, "Arsenii Matseevich," 600–608; Semevskii, *Krest'iane*, 245–46; *PSZ*, 16, no. 11. The impact of the revolts upon the commission's meetings was later noted by Catherine II in "Rasskazy imperatritsy Ekateriny II," 485.

78. Semevskii, *Krest'iane*, 250–51.

79. Kapterev, *Dubinshchina*, 18–22.

80. Ibid., 30–32.

81. Ibid., 22, 23–24, 33–36.

82. "Please, help me with advice!" she wrote to Bestuzhev-Riumin, being unsure whether to "set up the Commission without returning the lands or to return the lands, and then set up the Commission." "Delo ob Arsenii Matseeviche," document No. 16.

83. De Madariaga, *Russia in the Age of Catherine the Great*, 113–14. See also Smolitsch, *Geschichte der Russischen Kirche*, 349.

84. Popov, *Arsenii Matseevich*, 370.

85. Popov, *Arsenii Matseevich*, appendix, 23. The text of his 1742 report, "Doklad ee velichestvu o nezavisimosti tserkovnykh imenii ot Kollegii Ekonomii" is printed in ibid., appendix, 37–41.

86. Ibid., 11. He sent numerous letters with such threats to the Synod and to Catherine's father-confessor. Ikonnikov, "Arsenii Matseevich," 8–9; Kartashev, *Ocherki*, 2:121–24.

87. Ikonnikov, "Arsenii Matseevich," 12.

88. "Il abhorre la proposition de deux puissances." *Voltaire-Catherine II*, 48.

89. Grotsii, *Istinnoe blagochestie*, 3–4 in translator's dedication.

90. Ibid., 49. For a broader discussion of Matseevich's trial and exile, as well as his polemic, see Ivanov, "Reforming Orthodoxy," 184–95.

91. "Delo ob Arsenii Matseeviche," document no. 16; Popov, *Arsenii Matseevich*, 370.

92. *PSZ*, no. 12060.

93. Ibid.

94. Despite "secularization," the College of Economy had mixed jurisdiction: the Senate oversaw its functions in secular matters, while the Synod's authority extended to the use of the land for spiritual purposes. The clergy and Synod received their funding from the college's collection of the church land tax (and not from the general state budget), which at least theoretically implied the church's fiscal connection to the land. The lands generated an annual income of 1.3 million rubles, and according to the 1763 quotas, 149,585 rubles were designated for bishoprics, 207,750 for monasteries, and 115,000 for hospitals, with separate quotas for seminaries. "Neskol'ko tsifr," 182–200.

95. Ibid.

96. Kartashev, *Ocherki*, 2:123; Komissarenko, *Russkii absoliutizm*, 129.

97. Semevskii, *Krest'iane*, xlii–xliii, 274–86.

98. Znamenskii, "Chteniia iz istorii russkoi tserkvi," 140–41.

99. Semevskii, *Krest'iane*, 255, 265.

100. Ibid., 267; Radishchev, *Journey*.

101. Semevskii, *Krest'iane*, 284–86.

102. Ibid., 279–84.

103. Leskov, "Sviatitel'skie teni," 61–67.

104. Bogdanova, "Sekuliarizatsiia zemel'," 5–14.

105. Mokshina, "Rol' russkoi pravoslavnoi tserkvi," 170–76.

106. Makarii [Miroliubov], *Skazanie o zhizni i trudakh*, 8.

107. "Delo . . . o trebuemykh v tamoshniuiu apteku seminaristov," RGIA, f. 802, op. 1, d. 44, ll. 1–17; "O mediko-khirurgicheskoi akademii," RGIA, f. 802, op. 1, d. 14, ll. 1–18.

108. Freeze, "Handmaiden of the State?," 93–94.

109. See chapter 9.

110. *PU* (1780): 203; see also Miranda, *Puteshestvie po Rossiiskoi Imperii*, 200.

111. Karatsuba, "'Dobro samo po sebe est' obshchitel'no,'" 141.

112. On Calmet, see Schaff, *The New Schaff-Herzog Encyclopedia*, 2:352.

113. Chistovich, *Istoriia Sankt-Peterburgskoi Dukhovnoi Akademii*, 78. Winkler's *Institutiones philosophiae Wolfianae* was popular in Russian seminaries from the 1750s. Gabriel François Lejay's French Jesuit work (probably *Bibliotheca rhetorum* [1725]), was also used in the Moscow seminary alongside Protestant Joachim Lange's *Hodegus latini sermonis* (1724). Smirnov, *Istoriia Moskovskoi dukkhovnoi akademii*, 301–4.

114. He was Jonathan Edwards's favorite theologian, "demonstrably dependent upon the writings of . . . Turretin." Ramsey, *Ethical Writings*, 742.

115. Chistovich, *Istoriia Sankt-Peterburgskoi Dukhovnoi Akademii*, 188–89; Schaff, *The New Schaff-Herzog Encyclopedia*, 8:28; on Schubert, see the entry in *ADB*, 32: 635–37.

116. Chistovich, *Istoriia Sankt-Peterburgskoi Dukhovnoi Akademii*, 78.

117. Ibid., 189–90; Christoph Wolff, *Johann Sebastian Bach*, 324.

118. Chistovich, *Istoriia Sankt-Peterburgskoi Dukhovnoi Akademii*, 201–5; on Buffon's ties to Russia, see Kuliabko, "Nauchnye sviazi Zh.-L. Biuffona," 282–86.

119. Chistovich, *Istoriia Sankt-Peterburgskoi Dukhovnoi Akademii*, 191.

120. Platon recommended that students use Beveridge in order to understand apostolic canon law and interpret the *Kormchaia*. "The students," he said, "must know the acts of the councils, and the rules of the holy Fathers. To learn this, reading Beveridge is recommended." Smirnov, *Istoriia Moskovskoi dukhovnoi akademii*, 298.

121. Smirnov, *Istoriia Troitskoi lavrskoi seminarii*, 54–56. The seminary's library ordered a large number of patristic texts and Bible commentaries from Amsterdam and London, as well as many Western theological works, particularly those of Bingham, Gerhard, Quenstedt, Buddeus, Johann Osiander, and Edmond Purchot.

122. Ibid., 275–79, on eclecticism, 288.

123. Ibid., 285. For more literature on Whiston, see Farrell, *William Whiston*; William Whiston also believed that apocrypha formed the "cornerstones of true Christianity." Sheehan, *The Enlightenment Bible*, 42–44.

124. Smirnov, *Istoriia troitskoi seminarii*, 285; Hunt, *Religious Thought in England*, 3:117–18; Sorkin, *The Religious Enlightenment*, 60; Derham's work and his "school of physicotheology" was quite popular in North America as well, influencing much of

Jonathan Edwards's natural theology. Zakai, *Jonathan Edward's Philosophy of Nature*, 36–45.

125. Smirnov, *Istoriia Troitskoi lavrskoi seminarii*, 286. The 1784 title publication of his physicotheology in Russian was *Estestvennaia bogosloviia ili dokazatel'stvo bytiia i svoistv Bozhiikh.*

126. Mefodii [Smirnov], *Razsuzhdenie o Paskhe Iudeiiskoi*, 10–14.

127. Mefodii [Smirnov], *K Rimlianom Poslanie.*

128. Ibid., 157–58, 234–35.

129. Ibid., 126–29. Damaskin also taught German and held theological and philosophical disputes at the seminary in the same manner that they were held in Göttingen. Ibid., 129–39.

130. Ibid.,126–29; his sermon "O istinnom grazhdanine" mentioned the works of the Göttingen natural law scholar Samuel Hollmann. Ibid., 191–92.

131. Shmurlo, *Mitropolit Evgenii kak uchenyi*, 25–28.

132. Ibid., 109–10, 119.

133. He recommended Mosheim for Russian readers as an "honorable historian." Ibid., 111 and 303.

134. More precisely, he had Thomas Hobbes's *Elementa philosophica*. The complete book list is found in Shmurlo, *Metropolit Evgenii kak uchenyi*, pril. no. 2.

135. Sprunger, "Ames, William."

136. Ibid. On the casuistry of Puritan ethics and its influence in New England, also see Bremer, *Puritans and Puritanism*, 2:5–6.

137. Sprunger, "Ames, William."

138. Shmurlo, *Mitropolit Evgenii kak uchenyi*, pril. 4.

139. Evgenii [Bolkhovitinov], *Razsuzhdenie*, 4–7; this work was written by Ivan Stavrov with Evgenii's supervision.

140. *PSZ*, no. 15634.

141. Rostislavov, "Zapiski D. I. Rostislavova," 96,105.

142. The Russian titles for these works were the following: the translation of Jenyns, commissioned by Metropolitan Amvrosii was published as *Sozertsanie khristianstva* (1803), *Considérations* was translated as *O prevoskhodstve religii* (1804); while Feofilakt's translation of *Mélanges* remains in manuscript as "Esteticheskie rassuzhdeniia Ansilliona" and archived in RGIA, f. 802, Op. 1, d. 374. Rostislavov, "Feofilakt Rusanov," 613–14.

143. The titles for the two translations were *Istinnyi Messiia* and *Opyt o sovershenstve—iz Formeiia*. Bratanovskii was religion instructor to the Cadet Corps and a member of the Academy of Sciences. Filaret [Gumilevskii], *Obzor russkoi dukhovnoi literatury*, 396; Formey was a Berlin-born Huguenot theologian who collaborated with Diderot and d'Alembert on editions of the *Encyclopédie*. Paul Isaiah or Eliazar Isajah was a Jewish convert to Protestantism and a member of the Baptist congregation of London's Rev. Peter Chamberlain Katz, *Sabbath and Sectarianism*, 60–62.

144. Smirnov, *Istoriia Troitskoi lavrskoi seminarii*, 280–83.

145. Plimak, "Osnovnye etapy v razvitii russkogo Prosveshcheniia," 126–33.

146. Alekseev and Grotius, *Istinnoe blagochestie*. This work was popular in Russia with three editions in 1768, 1786, and 1801.

147. Ibid., 91.

148. Rostislavov, "Feofilakt Rusanov," 233.

149. Ibid., 241–43.

150. Feofilakt [Rusanov], *Pouchitel'nye slova*, 1:118–19.

151. Bychkov, *V pamiat' grafa Mikhaila Mikhailovicha Speranskogo*, 2:371.

152. Kislova, "Frantsuzskii iazyk," 26.

153. Shmurlo, *Mitropolit Evgenii kak uchenyi*, 100–101, 106.

154. Rukavitsyna-Hordziivska, *Kyivs'kyi mytropolyt Ievhenii*, 218; Shmurlo, *Mitropolit Evgenii kak uchenyi*, 60–64.

155. Evgenii [Bolkhovitinov], *Razsuzhdenie*, 4–7.

156. Shmurlo, *Mitropolit Evgenii kak uchenyi*, 53; Evgenii [Bolkhovitinov], *Parnasskaia istoriia*, i–iv, 4–6, 21–22.

157. In particular, he translated Coquelet's *L'éloge de rien*, Laugier de Tassy work on his travel in Algeria, and Mirabeau's piece about Cagliostro. Shmurlo, *Mitropolit Evgenii kak uchenyi*, 67–77, 121.

158. Evgenii [Bolkhovitinov], "Pis'mo mitropolita Evgeniia," 316.

159. Mushketov and Orlov, *Katalog zemletriasenii Rossiiskoi imperii*, no. 819.

160. Evgenii [Bolkhovitinov], "Letter No. 37, ot 15 Noiabria 1802 g., Sankt Peterburg," in "Vyderzhki iz druzhestvennykh pisem Evgeniia k Vasiliiu Ignat'evichu Makedontsu," *RA 8* (1871): 818–19; similarly, he did not see supernatural forces at work in such phenomena as ball lightning. Once a ball of lightning entered a room, and he asked the monks to remove their iron crosses and clothes with iron buttons and hide them. The ball of lightning went away. Shmurlo, *Mitropolit Evgenii kak uchenyi*, 379.

161. Shmurlo, *Mitropolit Evgenii*, 187–88. Evgenii Bolkhovitinov also supervised the translation of Alexander Pope's *Essay on Man*.

162. Here are a few examples from his *Istinna*: extracts from Diderot's *Encyclopédie* are found on pp. 24, 39, 41, 45, 62, 88, 210, 211, 213, 347; Voltaire's Candide on p. 303; Pope on pp. 105, 177, 252; Catherine-Joseph de Propiac on pp. 46–48, 57, 73, 88, 95, 111, 177, 222, 255, and Marmontel on pp. 36, 83, 186, 209, 231, 241, 244, 275, 302, 345.

163. Filaret [Gumilevskii], *Obzor russkoi dukhovnoi literatury*, 399–400.

164. Kandorskii, *Nauka o dushe*, 110–14.

165. Mackridge, *Language and National Identity in Greece*, 83–87; Evgenii [Bolkhovitinov], *Slovar' istoricheskii*.

166. Galanakis and Dimoliatis, "Early European Attitudes," S1(4).

167. Levshin, *Pis'mo*; for similar works, see Irinei [Klement'evskii], *Torzhestvo nashei very*; Bratanovskii, *Predokhranenie ot neveriia i nechestiia*.

168. Amvrosii [Zertis-Kamenskii], *Razsuzhdenie*, 116–17.

169. Nonot, *Vol'terovy zabluzhdeniia*; Shmurlo, *Mitropolit Evgenii kak uchenyi*, 134.

170. Rozanov, *Moskovskii mitropolit Platon*, i.

171. Ibid., ii.

172. Znamenskii, "Chteniia iz istorii russkoi tserkvi," 120.

173. Snegirev, *Zhizn' moskovskago mitropolita Platona*, 1–2.

174. Platon [Levshin], "Avtobiografiia," 16.

175. Ibid.

176. Snegirev, *Zhizn' moskovskago mitropolita Platona*, 28 and 34.

177. The 1758 letter to Levshin is printed in Snegirev, *Zhizn' moskovskago mitro-polita Platona*, pril. A.

178. Ibid., 29; Platon [Levshin], "Avtobiografiia," 31.

179. Platon [Levshin], "Avtobiografiia," 24, 31.

180. Ibid., 26.

181. Ligne, *Lettres*, lettre 9.

182. Platon [Levshin], "Avtobiografiia," 12.

183. Ibid., 23.

184. On food, see Platon [Levshin], "Avtobiografiia," 25; Heber, *Life of Reginald Heber, by His Widow*, 1:166.

185. Snegirev, *Zhizn' moskovskago mitropolita Platona*, 81–82.

186. Znamenskii, "Chteniia iz istorii russkoi tserkvi," 38–39; Snegirev, *Zhizn' moskovskago mitropolita Platona*, 81–82; Beliaev, *Mitropolit Platon*, 39.

187. Snegirev, *Zhizn' moskovskago mitropolita Platona*, 87–88, 92.

188. Platon [Levshin], "Avtobiografiia," 22.

189. Ibid.

190. Krinitskii, *Tverskie Arkhipastyri*, 29–36.

191. Shil'der, "Dve kharakteristiki," 377–78.

192. Snegirev, *Zhizn' moskovskago mitropolita Platona*, 29.

193. Smirnov, *Istoriia Moskovskoi dukhovnoi akademii*, 291–93; Smirnov, *Istoriia Troitskoi lavrskoi seminarii*, 275–77; Kniazev, *Ocherk istorii Pskovskoi seminarii*, 41.

194. It is likely that Platon used the version of the catechism in Latin. In Latin, the Westminster Larger Catechism was printed along with the Westminster Confession and was often known as such. See, for example, the 1670 *Confessio fidei conventu theologorum*.

195. Compare *LWC*, Qs 18–20 with *PU*, 1:8–9. On the two branches of Providence, see Beattie, *The Presbyterian Standards*; Ivanov, "Reforming Orthodoxy," 237–40.

196. Rozanov, *Moskovskii mitropolit Platon*, 60; Papmehl, *Metropolitan Platon of Moscow*, 94; according to Snegirev, Platon's theology was used in theology lectures in Glasgow and Oxford. Snegirev, *Zhizn' moskovskago mitropolita Platona*, 101.

197. Bacmeister, *Russische Bibliothek*, 1:120.

198. See, for example, Schwan's remarks on the catechism in his *Anecdotes*, 1:174–75.

199. Bacmeister, *Russische Bibliothek*, 1:125–29.

200. Ibid., 131.

201. "Even if I had all the kingdoms of the world, I would not give the hand of my daughter, unless I were sure that she would also be saved in this faith as a part of the Christian faith," she said (Snegirev, *Zhizn' moskovskago mitropolita Platona*, 37–38). Panzer, *Die Große Landgräfin Caroline*.

202. Rozanov, *Moskovskii mitropolit Platon*, 39–40.

203. Platon [Levshin], *Kratkaia rossiiskaia tserkovnaia istoriia*, 1:10–14, 2:97–98; Rozanov, *Moskovskii mitropolit Platon*, 66.

204. Platon, *Kratkaia rossiiskaia tserkovnaia istoriia*, 1:15, lamented that Old Rus' had "superfluous religiousity and immoderate monasticism." Ibid., 1:120. The first

Rus' princes did not have proper piety, since "the first shepherds of the Russian Church themselves did not understand what true religion was while the Greek bishops only cared about their profit." Rozanov, *Moskovskii mitropolit Platon*, 67.

205. Gorozhanskii, *Damaskin*, 173–208, 258–61. Regarding the issue of Iavorskii's *Kamen' very*, he acknowledged that in the 1720s, "this book had strong opponents among the Russian clergy." Ibid., 268.

206. Golovkin, *Dvor i tsarstvovanie Pavla*, 144, 151.

207. Beliaev, *Mitropolit Platon*, 37–38.

208. Skvortsov, *Arkhiv moskovskoi Sv. Sinoda Kontory*, 86; Clarke, *Travels*, 1:156.

209. "Po donosheniiu Moskovskoi Sv. Sinoda Kontory . . . o knige pravoslavnogo ispovedaniia very [January 2, 1770]," RGIA, f. 796, op. 51, d. 2, ll. 1–1 ob.

210. Ibid., l. 4 ob.

211. Ibid.

212. Ibid., ll. 13–15.

213. Tsapina, "K istorii," 63.

214. "Ob'iasneniia moskovskogo mitropolita Platona," OPI GIM, f. 33, ed. khr. 79, l. 6; punkty 12, 13.

215. Ibid., l. 6, punkt 15.

216. Ibid., l. 7, ll. 7 ob.–8. Although he did admit that "some venerate the icons more than necessary . . . a superstitious habit of the unenlightened."

217. Ibid., l. 7, punkt 19.

218. Ibid., l. 6.

219. *PU*, 2:4, compare with *LWC*: "The visible church is a society made up of all such as in all ages and places of the world do profess the true religion" (Q. 62).

220. Irinei [Fal'kovskii], *Christianae*, 2:165.

221. See chapter 9 for further discussion.

222. Michels, "From Persecuted Minority to Confessional Church," 322–37; Paert, *Old Believers*; Robson, *Old Believers in Modern Russia*.

223. Platon [Levshin], *Uveshchanie*.

224. *PSZ*, nos. 11720, 11725, 11738, 11989, 12067; Riazhev, *"Prosveshchennyi absoliutizm."*

225. Varadinov, *Istoriia Ministerstva vnutrennikh del*, 8:32.

226. Palkin, *Edinoverie*, 56–60.

227. Ibid., 60–62.

228. Ibid., 71–77.

229. Ibid., 80–88; Platon, "Punkty," 117–28.

230. Catherine II, "Chetyre pis'ma," 198–99; Dmitrii [Sechenov] and Gavriil [Petrov], "Doklad Sinoda," 712–13; it must be noted that much like the tolerant Neologists in Germany, the Russian bishops did not think that toleration of such minorities should come at the expense of the privileges of the ruling religion, including financial ones. Sorkin, *The Religious Enlightenment*, 156–57.

231. Lehner, *The Catholic Enlightenment*, 56–57, 62–63.

232. "Pastor Vigand," 551–52, 567.

233. Among the best works describing the settlement of marginal Protestant groups in Russia and their impact on the empire's landscape and native population

include Urry's *None but Saints*; Zhuk's, *Lost Reformation*; and Breyfolge's *Heretics and Colonizers*.

234. Andreev, "Pravoslavno-protestantskie otnosheniia," 87–88.

235. Ibid.

236. Ibid., 91.

237. Bessarabova, "Mirovozzrenie i deiatel'nost'," 143.

238. "Love toward the common good" (*obshchemu dobru*) was higher than "love toward oneself." *PU*, 168. The church was part of this social contract, promoting the "sacred union" as "the soul of society." Platon [Levshin], *Pouchitel'nye slova*, 1:79–80.

239. Miranda, *Fransisko de Miranda v Rossii*, 191.

240. Ibid., 200.

241. Ibid., 192.

242. Benz, *Die Abendländische Sendung*, 785–807.

243. Tsapina, "Tserkovnaia tsenzura," 254–61; Karpuk, "Dukhovnaia tsenzura," 42–51. See also Kotovich, *Dukhovnaia tsenzura v Rossii*, 26–31.

244. Clarke, *Travels*, 1:153.

245. Heber and Heber, *Life of Reginald Heber*, 1:171.

246. Ibid., 170–71.

247. Mel'nikova, *Armiia i pravoslavnaia tserkov*, 93–94.

248. Leonid [Tolmachev], "Mitropolit Platon v vospominaniiakh," 38.

249. Florovskii, *Puti russkogo bogosloviia*, 167.

Chapter 7. Light from the Pulpit

1. Wirtschafter, "Orthodoxy and Enlightenment," 43–63.

2. For a good description of the "classical" style in this "neoclassical" sermon, see Eijnatten, *Preacher, Sermon and Audience*.

3. Brilioth, *A Brief History of Preaching*, 112.

4. Old, *Reading and Preaching*, 5:1–5.

5. Edwards, *A History of Preaching*, 396.

6. Dargan, *A History of Preaching*, 207–12. This cannot be said of the Italian pulpit or the Austrian pulpit of the mid-eighteenth century, for example, where *conceptus* homilies still enjoyed popularity at court. Ibid., 189–97.

7. Ibid., 209, 221–26; for German preaching during this period, see also Niebergall, "Der Geschichte der Christlichen Predigt," 2:306–15; and Wehrle, *Orientierung am Hörer*.

8. Old, *Reading and Preaching*, 5:1–3; Edwards, *A History of Preaching*, 392–406. See, for example, Zollikofer, *Sermons on Education*.

9. Old, *Reading and Preaching*, 5:45, Walsham, *Providence in Early Modern England*.

10. Old, *Reading and Preaching*, 4:475.

11. Ibid., 4:475–77, 505–6.

12. Ibid., 5:39.

13. Edwards, *A History of Preaching*, 413.

14. Old, *Reading and Preaching*, 4:505; Willett, *Sermons of John-Baptist Massillon*, 374–410.

15. Saurin, *The Sermons of the Rev. James Saurin*, 2:3–58.

16. Zollikofer, *Sermons on the Dignity of Man*.

17. Old, *Reading and Preaching*, 5:87–88.

18. Lomonosov, *Polnoe sobranie sochinenii*, 7:821.

19. Sumarokov, "O rossiiskom dukhovnom krasnorechii," 6:295–302.

20. Amvrosii [Podobedov] and Damaskin [Semenov-Rudnev], "K blagosklonnomu Chitateliu," in Platon [Levshin], *Pouchitel'nye slova*, 1:x–xi.

21. Ibid.

22. Fonvizin, *Sobranie sochinenii*, 2:64. The popularity of these authors extended to the literate classes as well. A. T. Bolotov read Johann Friedrich Jerusalem and Mosheim in 1760–61. Vengerov, "Bolotov," 5:96.

23. Amvrosii [Podobedov] and Damaskin [Semenov-Rudnev], "K blagosklonnomu Chitateliu," ix–xii.

24. Gavriil marked the adapted sermon manuscripts with notations like "Soren [et] ego," or "Gesner [et] ego." Titlinov, *Gavriil Petrov*, 1154.

25. Nadezhin, "Platon Levshin," 112.

26. In 1795 Platon gave the library of Trinity-Sergius Monastery twelve volumes by Jacques Saurin and in 1803, he gave it the sermons of Durand, Fléchier, Sturm, Zollikopfer, Mosheim, and Stockhausen. Smirnov, *Istoriia Troitskoi lavrskoi seminarii*, 377–79.

27. Lebedev, "Khar'kovskii Kollegium," 62–63.

28. Shmurlo, *Mitropolit Evgenii kak uchenyi*, 109–10; see also Pevnitskii, "Propovednicheskie trudy," 21–55, 527–29.

29. Sukhomlinov, *Istoriia rossiiskoi akademii*, 1:112.

30. Among the Church Fathers, only Chrysostom made it into the collection. Ibid., 1:113–14, 394–95; see also Titlinov, *Gavriil Petrov*, 1153–54.

31. Titlinov, *Gavriil Petrov*, 1153–54. For Miniates and Enlightenment, see Bruess, *Religion, Identity and Empire*, 8, 44; see also Kitromilides, "The Enlightenment," 45–46.

32. Titlinov, *Gavriil Petrov*, 1153–54.

33. Eijnhatten, *Preaching, Sermon and Audience*, 73–74; Harnack, *History of Dogma*, 26–27.

34. Titlinov, *Gavriil Petrov*, 1153–54.

35. Ibid.

36. Georg Zollikofer's sermons were translated into Russian in 1780, 1781, 1798, and 1799; Jacques Saurin's sermons were translated and published in 1791 and 1799; Esprit Fléchier's funeral oration for Henri de Turenne was printed in 1763 and 1794. Ivan Kondakov, *Svodnyi katalog*, 3: nos. 8125–27, nos. 7369–70, and nos. 7803–4.

37. Bushkovitch, *Religion and Society*, 150.

38. Heber and Heber, *The Life of Reginald Heber*, 171.

39. Among the compendia of Antonii's sermons delivered in various provincial cities were *Slova pri nachale i okonchaniia otkrytiia Nizhegorodskogo namestnichestva* (Moscow, 1780); *Slova pri nachale i okonchaniia otkrytiia Simbirskogo namestnichestva* (St. Petersburg, 1781); and *Slova pri nachale i okonchaniia otkrytiia Kazanskogo namestnichestva* (Moscow, 1782).

40. See, for example, his *Vtoroe sobranie slov* (Moscow, 1781) and *Poucheniia skazyvannyia v gorode Kostrome v 1775 i 1776 godakh* (Moscow, 1776).

41. Anisov, "Mitropolit Platon," 29.

42. Golovkin, *Dvor i tsarstvovanie*, 325; Shil'der, "Dve kharakteristiki," 377–78.

43. Skvortsov, *Arkhiv moskovskoi Sv. Sinoda Kontory*, 113–14.

44. Clarke, *Travels*, 1:153.

45. Skvortsov, *Arkhiv*, 128–29.

46. Arsenii, "Dnevnik preosviashennogo Arseniia Vereshchagina," 43 (1894): 674–76; 44 (1894): 693–98; 45 (1894): 708–13; 46 (1894): 731–35; 47 (1894): 749–50; 48 (1894): 766–68.

47. Bolotov, *Zhizn' i prikliucheniia*, 3:489.

48. Ibid., 490.

49. Rostislavov, *Provincial Russia*, 174.

50. Platon [Levshin], "Avtobiografiia," 23.

51. Znamenskii, "Chteniia iz istorii russkoi tserkvi," 112–13.

52. Kudriavtseva, "Iz istorii pskovskikh arkhiereiskikh bibliotek," 154–59.

53. Evgenii [Bolkhovitinov], *Slovar' istoricheskii*, 62.

54. Znamenskii, "Chteniia iz istorii russkoi tserkvi," 113.

55. Snegirev, *Zhizn' moskovskago mitropolita Platona*, 13.

56. Platon [Levshin], "Avtobiografiia," 23.

57. Gedeon [Krinovskii], *Sobranie raznykh pouchitel'nykh slov*, 1:210. After going through the possible causes of happiness (wealth, fame, and so on), the author concluded that not even the pope himself was satisfied with his life and argued that the source of happiness was only found in God. Ibid., 1:211–19.

58. Ibid., 2:289–301.

59. Ibid., 2:290.

60. Ibid., 2:297.

61. Nadezhdin, "Platon Levshin," 19–20.

62. Platon [Levshin], "Avtobiografiia," 23–24.

63. Snegirev, *Zhizn' moskovskago mitropolita Platona*, 17–18; Platon's "Avtobiografiia" mentions this visit as happening in October 17, 1762, while stating that he saw her again in May 1763 when Catherine traveled to Rostov. Platon [Levshin], "Avtobiografiia," 26–27.

64. See this sermon in Platon [Levshin], *Pouchitel'nye slova*, 1:9–23.

65. Platon [Levshin], "Avtobiografiia," 28.

66. Cathcart, "Lord Cathcart," 351.

67. Timkovskii "Zapiski," 1434.

68. Poroshin, "Sto tri dnia," 53.

69. Ibid.; Nadezhdin, "Platon Levshin. . . . kak propovednik," 143.

70. Nadezhdin, "Platon Levshin," 143.

71. Snegirev, *Zhizn' moskovskago mitropolita Platona*, 23; see also Kazanskii, "Otnosheniia mitropolita Platona."

72. Platon [Levshin], *Pouchitel'nye slova*, 1:264–65.

73. Ibid., 1:266–67.

74. Ibid., 1:267.

75. Ibid., 1:269–80. Interestingly, he acknowledged the scientific debate over the health merits of meat consumption and the vegetarian diet. Nadezhin, "Platon Levshin," 112.

76. Platon [Levshin], *Pouchitel'nye slova*, 2:98–107.

77. Ibid., 2:203–16.

78. Ibid., 2:207–8.

79. Ibid., 2:207.

80. Ibid., 2:201–3.

81. Nadezhdin, "Platon Levshin," 127–29.

82. Evgenii [Bolkhovitinov], *Slovar' istoricheskii*, 32; Mel'nikov, "Iz proshlogo," 456; Martin, *Enlightened Metropolis*, 14–16. The eyewitness details of the Moscow events are supplied in Father Petr Alekseev's report, "Opisanie moskovskogo bunta."

83. Martin, *Enlightened Metropolis*, 15.

84. Amvrosii [Podobedov], *Sobranie pouchitel'nykh slov*, 322.

85. Ibid., 323.

86. Ibid., 325.

87. Ibid., 326.

88. Mel'nikov, "Iz proshlogo," 456–57.

89. Amvrosii [Podobedov], *Slovo skazyvannoe pri pogrebenii*.

90. Mel'nikov, "Iz proshlogo," 457.

91. Ibid., 456–57.

92. Amvrosii [Podobedov], *Sobranie pouchitel'nykh slov*, 254.

93. Ibid., 240.

94. Ibid., 248.

95. Ibid., 251.

96. Ibid., 254; Mel'nikov, "Iz proshlogo," 457.

97. Mel'nikov, "Iz proshlogo," 457.

98. Ibid. Catherine told Platon Levshin that she was traveling there specifically for the ceremony of Amvrosii's consecration.

Chapter 8. Spiritual Napoleons

1. Martin, *Romantics, Reformers, Reactionaries*, 5–7.

2. Pypin, *Obshchestvennoe dvizhenie*; Chistovich, *Rukovodiashchie deiateli dukhovnogo prosveshcheniia*; Chistovich, *Istoriia perevoda Biblii*; Beyreuther, *Die Erweckungsbewegung*; Rosa, *Settecento religioso*.

3. For a description of the ministries of the preachers of the Bavarian Awakening, see Beyreuther, *Die Erweckungsbewegung*, 32; Batalden, *Russian Bible Wars*, 78–80.

4. For the latest scholarly assessment of the debate on the Awakening's reaction against the Enlightenment, see Kloes, *The German Awakening*.

5. Weeks, *German Mysticism*, 196; Reid-Maroney, *Philadelphia's Enlightenment*, 1–24; Shantz, *A Companion*, 163–65; Kuhn, *Religion und neuzeitliche Gesellschaft*; *ADB*, 5:608–9.

6. Shantz, *A Companion*, 163–64, 457–58; Weeks, *German Mysticism*, 198.

7. Beyreuther, *Die Erweckungsbewegung*, 20.

8. Ibid.

9. Ibid., 4–16; Noll, *The Rise of Evangelicalism*; Noll, *America's God*; Owen, *History*.

10. Weigelt, *Erweckungsbewegung*.

11. Swedenborg, *The Earths in Our Solar System*.

12. Faivre, *Eckarthausen*.

13. Shantz, *A Companion*, 365–67, 386–89; Breul and Schnurr, *Geschichtsbewusstsein und Zukunftserwartung*, 281.

14. Vondung, *The Apocalypse in Germany*, 100–105, 126–28; Shantz, *A Companion*, 108–9.

15. Vondung, *The Apocalypse in Germany*, 126–28, Zimmermann, *Aufklärung und Erfahrungswandel*, 120.

16. Jung-Stilling, *Das Heimweh*.

17. Hatch, *The Democratization of American Christianity*.

18. Reid-Maroney, *Philadelphia's Enlightenment*, 36; Pypin, "Rossiiskoe bibleiskoe," 639.

19. Beyreuther, *Die Erweckungsbewegung*, 7.

20. Vondung, *The Apocalypse in Germany*, 133; Benz, *Schellings theologische Geistesahnen*.

21. Weeks, *German Mysticism*, 208–10, 228.

22. Martin, *Romantics, Reformers, Reactionaries*, 148.

23. Chistovich, *Rukovodiashchie deiateli dukhovnogo prosveshcheniia*, 202–3, Batalden, *Russian Bible Wars*, 77–78.

24. Chistovich, *Rukovodiashchie deiateli dukhovnogo prosveshcheniia*, 203; Batalden, *Russian Bible Wars*, 22.

25. Vigel', *Zapiski*, 253–54; Zacek, "The Russian Bible Society," 424.

26. Vigel', *Zapiski*, 253–54; Martin, *Romantics, Reformers, Reactionaries*, 190.

27. Vigel', *Zapiski*, 253–54.

28. Vigel', *Zapiski*, 253; a 1756 synodal decree classified the Khlysty as a "Quaker heresy." See Andreev, "Kvakery."

29. Koshelev was a famous Freemason who met and corresponded with Eckartshausen, Swedenborg, and Johann Kaspar Lavater. Sawatsky, "Prince Alexander N. Golitsyn," 162–64, 159–65; Martin, *Romantics, Reformers, Reactionaries*, 147.

30. Sawatsky, "Prince Alexander N. Golitsyn," 165.

31. Ibid., 193–95.

32. Batalden, *Russian Bible Wars*, 31.

33. Martin, *Romantics, Reformers, Reactionaries*, 148–49.

34. Grellet, *A Concise Memoir*; Empaytaz, *Notice sur Alexandre*, 17–18.

35. Sawatsky, "Prince Alexander N. Golitsyn," 192, 197–98.

36. Ley, *Alexandre Ier*, 88–89, 314; Martin, *Romantics, Reformers, Reactionaries*, 155.

37. *DRMID*, 7:63, 223, 238, 272, 293, 435, 460, 504, 563, 583, 592.

38. AT-OeStA/HHStA UR AUR 1815 IX 26, "Heilige Allianz," fol. 1; this spiritual fraternization within the anti-Napoleonic coalition was not unfashionable—in his October 6, 1815, letter to Francis I, King George referred to the addressee as "my brother glorious." "Lettre autographe . . . à S. M. Impériale d'Autriche," AT-OeStA/HHStA UR AUR 1815 IX 26, fols. 3–7.

39. Discussed at the end of this chapter.

40. Longinov, *Novikov i Moskovskie Martinisty*, 109–111; Tsapina, "Tserkovnaia tsenzura," 254; Novikov used to purchase atheistic or freethinking works just to burn them. Longinov, *Novikov i Moskovskie Martinisty*, 221.

41. For Platon's "good will" and his relations with Lopukhin, see Longinov, *Novikov i Moskovskie Martinisty*, 184 and 306.

42. Longinov, *Novikov i Moskovskie Martinisty*, 123–24, 129–30, 186–87; Pypin, *Russkoe masonstvo*, 235; Tsapina, "Tserkovnaia tsenzura," 254.

43. Heber and Heber, *The Life of Reginald Heber*, 1:172.

44. Tsapina, "Tserkovnaia tsenzura," 255n36.

45. His relationship with the Levshins remained very rocky throughout the 1770s and 1780s, when Platon and his brother Aleksandr were for some time (1782–95) the sole two members of Moscow's Synodal Bureau. Tsapina, "Tserkovnaia tsenzura," 253.

46. Solonin, "Dukhovenstvo," 128; Alekseev, "Iz bumag protoiereia," 62–90; Tsapina, "Tserkovnaia tsenzura," 255.

47. The report was titled "Primechaniia o sinodal'noi kontore," and dated September 27, 1789. Alekseev, "Iz bumag protoiereia," 76–77. He personally selected seminary students to study under the direction of Novikov and another Mason, Ivan Schwartz, "chief teacher of the Martinists and their pastor." Solonin, "Dukhovenstvo," 128–29.

48. Ibid., 301–3.

49. According to Tsapina, the reports had influenced the assessment of the situation by Ivan Pamfilov and Metropolitan Gavriil at the St. Petersburg court. Tsapina, "Tserkovnaia tsenzura," 255.

50. Longinov, *Novikov i Moskovskie Martinisty*, appendix, pp. 35–36.

51. OR RGB, f. 439, kart. 24, ed. khr. 5. This membership roll is printed in Serkov's *Russkoe Masonstvo*, 1107.

52. "Iz zapisok . . . Fotiia o skoptsakh, khlystakh i drugikh tainykh sektakh v Peterburge v 1819 godu," *RA* (1873): 1434.

53. Serkov, *Russkoe Masonstvo*, 361, 1106–8.

54. Ibid., 234, 451, 955, 1034.

55. Chicherin, *Vospominaniia*, 40; Tolstoi, *Khranilishche*, 125.

56. Sushkov, *Zapiski*, 11, 15–17.

57. Ibid., 17.

58. Serkov, *Russkoe Masonstvo*, 1034.

59. David, "The Influence of Jacob Boehme," 46–51; Filaret [Gumilevskii], *Obzor russkoi dukhovnoi literatury*, 360–69.

60. Bitovt, *Redkie russkie knigi*, 406, 454, 535.

61. See Arndt, *Ioanna Arndta* (1784 and 1800 editions).

62. See the bibliography for the full titles of Gerhard's *Sviashchennyia khristianskiia razmyshleniia*; *Myslennyi vertograd*; *Vertograd nasazhdennyi*.

63. The work was so commercially popular that it was printed again "at the expense of the bookseller Semen Nikiforov"; see the title page of Gerhard, *Glas Trubnyi*.

64. The work called Amvrosii "the fine Lover and Patron of the sciences" (dedication page, Gerhard, *Myslennyi vertograd*).

65. Gerhard, *Myslennyi vertograd*, 4. The work contained a typically Lutheran theological description of the consubstantive presence of Christ in the Eucharist, 81–87.

66. See the dedication section of Hervey, *Blagogoveinyi zritel' prirody*.

67. Hervey, *Meditations and Contemplations*, 1:i–ii, 7.

68. Hervey, *Blagogoveinyi zritel' prirody*, 113–19; Hervey, *Meditations and Contemplations*, 12–14.

69. Faggionato, *A Rosicrucian Utopia*, 476–77.

70. Fotii Spasskii, "Avtobiografiia," *RS* 81, no. 5 (1894): 93–94, 101; the same two mystics also "influenced" Metropolitan Anatolii of Minsk. Schmidt, *Kritische Geschichte*, 241.

71. Chicherin, *Vospominaniia*, 40; Tolstoi, *Khranilishche*, 125.

72. Sushkov, *Zapiski*, 15–17.

73. "Germogen," *RBS*, 5:78–80.

74. Dostoevsky, *Pis'ma*, 2:263–64; Smolitsch, *Russkoe monashestvo*, 257–79; see also his chapter 15 on Tikhon and *starchestvo*.

75. Ivanov, "The Saint of 'Russian Reformation,'" 81–106; Ivanov, "The Impact of Pietist and Anglican Spirituality," 40–72.

76. Ivanov, "The Impact of Pietist and Anglican Spirituality," 40–72.

77. Smirnova, *Knigi grazhdanskoi pechati*, 6–7.

78. In Ben'ian, *Liubopytnoe i dostopamiatnoe puteshestvie* and *Sochineniia Ioanna Biuniana*. It is interesting to note that during the searches of 1787, the 1782 edition of *Pilgrim's Progress* was not banned and confiscated, while the *Sochineniia* was. Longinov, *Novikov i Moskovskie Martinisty*, appendix, 52–55.

79. Printed in *The Works of Joseph Hall*, 11:191–229. The translated title was *Obraz zhitiia Enokhova ili rod i sposob khozhdeniia s Bogom*.

80. Smirnova, *Kniga grazhdanskoi pechati*, 6–7. Kirillo-Beloozero's monks had a few other unusual practices in the eighteenth century, for example, a communion cup made of coconut and gilded with Dutch inscriptions, used by the monks. Varlaam [Denisov], *Opisanie istoriko-arkheologicheskoe*, 77.

81. Ivanov, "Reforming Orthodoxy," 258–59; Podskalsky, *Griechische Theologie*, 372–99.

82. Podskalsky, *Griechische Theologie*, 372–99.

83. Florovskii, *Puti russkogo bogosloviia*, 167–69.

84. Filaret [Drozdov], *Sochineniia*, 1:176–84.

85. Ibid., 176, 185.

86. Ibid., 23–27, 185–86.

87. Chistovich, *Rukovodiashchie deiateli dukhovnogo prosveshcheniia*, 309.

88. Filaret [Drozdov], *Razgovory mezhdu ispytuiushchim i uverennym o pravsolavii Greko-Rossiiskoi tserkvi* (St. Petersburg, 1815). The second edition came out in 1833.

89. Ibid., 5–6.

90. Ibid., 9–11.

91. Ibid., 14–15.

92. Sushkov, *Zapiski*, 293.

93. Ibid., 281–83.

94. Filaret, *Razgovory mezhdu ispytuiushchim*, 71–72, 128–29.

95. Men', *Bibliogicheskii slovar'*, 3:320–21.

96. Orlov, "Lankasterskie shkoly v Rossii," 11–16.

97. Filaret [Drozdov], *Tablitsa chteniia*; Pypin, *Obshchestvennoe dvizhenie*, 411.

98. Orlov, "Lankasterskie shkoly v Rossii," 16–18.

99. "Proklamatsiia 1820-go goda," in Oksman, *Dekabristy*, 37–38; for a description of the revolutionary "soldiers' movement" of the period, see Fedorov, *Soldatskoe dvizhenie*.

100. Baten'kov's testimony is printed as "Pokazanie 22 marta 1826," in Nechkina and Pokrovskii, *Vosstanie dekabristov: Materialy*, 14:100.

101. Herzen, "Byloe i dumy," 70.

102. Ibid.

103. Batalden, *Russian Bible Wars*, 13.

104. Cherviakovskii, "Vvedenie v bogoslovie" (1877): 308–12; Rizhskii, *Istoriia perevodov*, 130.

105. Letter, August 10, 1736, *ODDS* 3 (1723): pril. 23–26.

106. Discussed in chapter 6; see also Gorozhanskii, *Damaskin Semenov-Rudnev*, 60–61.

107. Ibid., 61–62, 68–70.

108. Nichols, "Metropolitan Filaret," 111–12.

109. Mikhailov, "Metropolit Platon," 37–40.

110. Nichols, "Metropolitan Filaret," 30–31.

111. Mikhailov, "Metropolit Platon," 37–40.

112. Skinner, "Russia's Scriptural 'Reformation,'" 76.

113. Mikhailov, "Metropolit Platon," 37–40; see Amvrosii [Podobedov], *Kratkoe Rukovodstvo* (1779 Moscow edition). The work was published again in 1803, 1818, and 1826, and in Kiev in 1781. One of Hoffmann's works used for this guide was *Introductio in lectionem*.

114. See Feoktist [Mochul'skii], *Opyt germenevticheskogo ob'iasneniia*; Feoktist [Mochul'skii], *Drakhma*.

115. See Mikhail [Desnitskii], *Besedy o pokaianii*.

116. See Mefodii [Smirnov], *K rimlianam poslanie*.

117. While Platon Levshin supported the exposition of Scripture for Moscow's laity in the vernacular, he remained a strong supporter of the Latin language in the seminary curriculum. This was necessary, he argued, to "maintain our honor" in relation with foreign theologians (Florovskii, *Puti russkogo bogosloviia*, 113). The popularization of the Bible in the vernacular for the lower classes and the maintenance of Latin curricular high culture for seminarians were not mutually exclusive or contradictory goals.

118. Filaret [Drozdov], "Mneniia o raznosti."

119. Ibid., 20–31.

120. Martin, *Enlightened Metropolis*.

121. Faggionatto, *A Rosicrucian Utopia*, 459–63.

122. Ibid., 469.

123. Florovskii, *Puti russkogo bogosloviia*, 147–48; Zacek, "The Russian Bible Society," 418.

124. Pypin, "Rossiiskoe bibleiskoe," 668; Batalden, *Russian Bible Wars*, 61–70; Ilarion Chistovich, "Ispravlenie teksta Slavianskoi Biblii."

125. Batalden, *Russian Bible Wars*, 46–48.

126. Ibid., 66–68.

127. Ibid., 71–72.

128. British and Foreign Bible Society, *Thirteenth Report*, 65.

129. Batalden, *Russian Bible Wars*, 53.

130. Ibid., 54–55; Zacek, "The Russian Bible Society," 415–16.

131. British and Foreign Bible Society, *Thirteenth Report*, 60.

132. Ibid., 58.

133. Ibid., 64–65.

134. Batalden, *Russian Bible Wars*, 55.

135. "Podlinnye svidetel'stva o bednosti lits kotorym vydany besplatno," RGIA, f. 808, op. 1, d. 118, ll. 1–18; see also "Svidetel'stva o bednosti lits," RGIA, f. 808, op. 1, d. 133, ll. 1–27 ob.; Faggionato, *A Rosicrucian Utopia*, 480. A thorough discussion of the impact of Bible vernacularization on the lower classes in Russia is outside the scope of this study. One of the consequences of the increased availability of the Bible and Awakening ideas in peasant Russia was the rise of peasant sects, depicted in the works of Sergei Zhuk, Laura Engelstein, Nicholas Breyfolge, Robert Nichols, and Daniel Shubin, among others.

136. British and Foreign Bible Society, *Thirteenth Report*, 58, 63, 80.

137. Zacek, "The Russian Bible Society," 420.

138. British and Foreign Bible Society, *Thirteenth Report*, 57, 68–69, 73.

139. Taimasov and Denisov, "Kazanskii komitet," 92–95.

140. Makarov, "O perevodnom pamiatnike," 70–79.

141. "Shmidt, Iakov," *RBS*, 23:353–54.

142. Mikhail [Desnitskii], Filaret [Drozdov], and Serafim [Glagolevskii], "Vozglashenie ko khristoliubivym chitateliam," iii–vii.

143. Pinkerton's report, quoted by Batalden, *Russian Bible Wars*, 29.

144. Martin, *Romantics, Reformers, Reactionaries*, 3.

145. Titlinov, *Dukhovnaia shkola*, 58.

146. Uvarov, "Pis'mo Grafa Sergeia S. Uvarova," 129–31; on Uvarov, see Whittaker, *The Origins of Modern Russian Education*.

147. Uvarov, "Pis'mo Grafa Sergeia S. Uvarova," 131.

148. Martin, *Romantics, Reformers, Reactionaries*, 193.

149. Technically anonymous, the essay's most likely author was Count Shikhmatov, as per the introduction in Shirinskii-Shikhmatov, "Zapiski o kramolakh," 1333–34.

150. Ibid., 1335.

151. Ibid., 1336–46, 1378, 1384.

152. Ibid., 1381, 1383–85.

153. Ibid., 1383.

154. Martin, *Romantics, Reformers, Reactionaries*, 20.

155. Iurii Kondakov, *Dukhovno-religioznaia politika*, 99–100.

156. Ibid.; Shishkov, *Zapiski*, 2:184.

157. Iurii Kondakov, *Dukhovno-religioznaia politika*, 97.

158. Shishkov, *Zapiski*, 2:217.

159. Ibid., 2:183–84.

160. Ibid., 2:250, 2:170–230.

161. Ibid., 2:294.

162. Ibid.

163. Ibid., 2:297.

164. Ibid., 2:228.

165. Quoted in his December 16, 1824, letter to Metropolitan Evgenii Bolkhovitinov. Ibid., 2:236.

166. Chistovich, *Rukovodiashchie deiateli dukhovnogo prosveshcheniia*, 250.

167. Fotii Spasskii, "Zhitie Episkopa Penzenskogo i Saratovskogo Innokentiia (Smirnova)," in Ulybin, *Bor'ba za veru*, 106–9.

168. Ibid., 91, 99–101, 110.

169. Michelson, *Beyond the Monastery Walls*, 59–170; Kenworthy, *The Heart of Russia*, 1–110; Paert, *Spiritual Elders*, 71–140.

170. Fotii [Spasskii], "Avtobiografiia," *RS* 81, no. 5 (1894): 91.

171. Ibid., 102.

172. Ibid., *RS* 83, no. 2 (1895): 203.

173. Ibid., *RS* 81, no. 5 (1894): 94–101.

174. Ibid., *RS* 83, no. 2 (1895): 197.

175. Ibid., 180.

176. Ibid., *RS* 81, no. 5 (1894): 101.

177. Ibid., *RS* 81, no. 4 (1894): 119–23; *RS* 82, no. 7 (1894): 196, 207–11.

178. Ibid.; Ulybin, *Bor'ba za veru*, 71.

179. He drank tea at least twice daily and a cup of coffee, often with almond milk. Kozlov, "Cherty iz zhizni Mitropolita Filareta," 79.

180. Fotii [Spasskii], "Avtobiografiia," *RS* 82, no. 7 (1894): 218–19.

181. Foti [Spasskii], "Pis'ma k Praskov'e Mikhailovne Tolstoi," 129–31, 234.

182. Fotii [Spasskii], "Avtobiografiia," *RS* 82, no. 7 (1894): 218–19; *RS* 84, no. 7 (1895): 178; *RS* 83, no. 2 (1895): 191–93.

183. Nichols, "Metropolitan Filaret," 159.

184. Iurii Kondakov, *Liberal'noe i konservativnoe napravlenie*, 102.

185. Pushkin, *Alexander Pushkin*, 112; Ulybin, *Bor'ba za veru*, 21.

186. Iurii Kondakov, *Dukhovno-religioznaia politika*, 122.

187. Fotii [Spasskii], "Pis'ma k Praskov'e Mikhailovne Tolstoi," 233; Marchenko, "Zapiska stats-sekretaria," 63–64.

188. Spasskii, "Avtobiografiia," *RS* 84, no. 11 (1895): 208–14.

189. Nichols, "Metropolitan Filaret," 174–75; Shishkov, *Zapiski*, 2:205–8.

190. Fotii [Spasskii], "Avtobiografiia," *RS* 83, no. 2 (1895): 193, 199.

191. Nichols, "Metropolitan Filaret," 157; Fotii [Spasskii], "Avtobiografiia," *RS* 84, no. 8 (1895): 185–86, and no. 11 (1895): 219–24; Chistovich, *Rukovodiashchie deiateli dukhovnogo prosveshcheniia*, 214, 217–18, 225–26.

192. Chistovich, *Rukovodiashchie deiateli dukhovnogo prosveshcheniia*, 246.

193. Ibid., 254–55, 259.

194. Ibid., 253–54.

195. Florovskii, *Puti russkogo bogosloviia*, 159.

196. Iurii Kondakov, *Liberal'noe i konservativnoe napravlenie*, 284.

197. Ibid., 261; Beyreuther, *Die Erweckungsbewegung*, 32.

198. Johannes Gossner, *Zerkalo vnutrennego cheloveka* (St. Petersburg, 1819, also 1821 and 1822); Johannes Gossner, *Serdtse chelovecheskoe est ili khram bozhii ili zhilishche satany* (St. Petersburg, 1853).

199. Iurii Kondakov, *Liberal'noe i konservativnoe napravlenie*, 273–75.

200. Ibid., 276–79. Since the printing of the work was never completed and much of what was printed was burned, only a few partial copies of this commentary exist. One, in the Russian National Library, is titled *Dukh zhizni i ucheniia Iisusa Khrista: Evangelie ot Matfeia* (St. Petersburg, 1824); its text ends abruptly on page 856.

201. Printed in Ulybin, *Bor'ba za veru*, 364–66.

202. Fotii [Spasskii], "Avtobiografiia," *RS* 84, no. 8 (1895): 187; Ulybin, *Bor'ba za veru*, 365–66; Iurii Kondakov, *Dukhovno-religioznaia politika*, 191.

203. For the best summaries of the Gossner Affair, see Batalden, *Russian Bible Wars*, 77–81; and Kondakov, *Dukhovno-religioznaia politika*, 139–77.

204. The catechism sold out at three times the original price. "Pis'ma V. I. Shteingelia," in *Vosstanie Dekabristov: Dokumenty*, 14:188.

205. Sawatsky, "Prince Alexander N. Golitsyn," 22, 404–9.

206. Martin, *Romantics, Reformers, Reactionaries*, 199.

207. Liut'ko, "Mitropolit Platon," 240–45.

208. Evgenii [Bolkhovitinov], *Slovar' istoricheskii*, 34, 37, 59, 119, 223, 269.

209. Shishkov, *Zapiski*, 2:222–23.

210. Iurii Kondakov, *Dukhovno-religioznaia politika*, 139–77.

211. Shishkov, *Zapiski*, 2:192–97.

212. Pushkin, *Alexander Pushkin*, 31.

213. Shishkov, *Zapiski*, 2:205, 230.

214. Ibid., 2:205; 2:207–8.

215. In the Slavonic version of the Bible, the advice to the slaves seeking freedom appeared as "*bol'she poraboti sebe* [submit oneself to more enslavement]"; in Russian, the translation was "*luchshe vospol'zuisia* [take advantage (of freedom)]." Quoted in Magnitskii's letter to Shteingel, in Nichkina and Pokrovskii, *Vosstanie dekabristov: Materialy*, 14:187, 188–89.

216. Shirinskii-Shikhmatov, "Zapiski o kramolakh," 1383.

217. "Perepiska po povodu uvol'neniia ot krepostnoi zavisimosti," RGIA, f. 808, op. 1, d. 136, ll. 1–5.

218. A. Smith, *For the Common Good*, 27; Nikitenko, *Up from Serfdom*.

219. "O litseiskom dukhe, donos 1826 g.," *RS* 18, no. 4 (1877): 657–59.

220. "Perepiska po povodu oskorbitel'nogo pis'ma prislannogo Obshchestvu Magnitskim," RGIA, f. 808, op. 1, d. 221, ll. 1–14.

221. Iurii Kondakov, *Liberal'noe i konservativnoe napravlenie*, 271–72.

222. Martin, *Romantics, Reformers, Reactionaries*, 146.

223. Printed in Ulybin, *Bor'ba za veru*, 382–85.

224. Ibid., 382.

225. Ibid., 382–83.

226. Fotii [Spasskii], "Avtobiografiia," *RS* 84, no. 12 (1895): 196–97.

227. Ibid.; see also Ulybin, *Bor'ba za veru*, 379, 384–85.

228. Chistovich, *Istoriia perevoda Biblii*, 117–18. The Bible-burning ceremony was organized by Shishkov with Serafim's approval. Florovskii, *Puti russkogo bogosloviia*, 163.

229. Marchenko, "Zapiska stats-sekretaria," 62–66, 68, as well as M. A. Bestuzhev's notes in Oksman, *Dekabristy*, 306–7.

230. Marchenko, "Zapiska stats-sekretaria," 71; Sawatsky, "Prince Alexander N. Golitsyn," 444–46.

231. Oksman, *Dekabristy*, 350–51.

232. Pestel', *Russkaia pravda*, 153–55; Dovnar-Zapol'skii, *Idealy Dekabristov*, 395, 420–21.

233. Dovnar-Zapol'skii, *Idealy Dekabristov*, 304–6.

CONCLUSION

1. Stein, *Encyclopedia of Apocalypticism*, 3:115–16, 310.

2. Sawatsky, "Prince Alexander N. Golitsyn," 469.

3. The Holy Synod rejected Fotii's innovations and restored the monks' freedom of choice in wearing whatever they wanted under their cassocks. Chistovich, *Rukovodiashchie deiateli dukhovnogo prosveshcheniia*, 297–311.

4. Ibid., 315.

5. Palmer, *Notes of a Visit*, 65.

6. On the subject of transubstantiation, Protasov claimed that "the Greek Church agrees (that is, agrees unreservedly) with the Roman doctrine." Ibid., 117.

7. Titlinov, *Dukhovnye shkola*, 80.

8. Rostislavov, "Peterburgskaia dukhovnaia akademiia," *VE* 4 (1883): 137–39; 5 (1883): 230–37.

9. Ibid., *VE* 4 (1883): 140–47.

10. Ibid., 173.

11. Titlinov, *Dukhovnye shkola*, 74–75.

12. Ibid., 79. Archimandrite Nikodim Kazantsev's defense that "our philosophy is very humble, for it is guided by theology" was not persuasive. Chistovich, *Rukovodiashchie deiateli dukhovnogo prosveshcheniia*, 323.

13. Freeze, *The Parish Clergy*, 40.

14. Ibid., 17, 126–28; Titlinov, *Dukhovnye shkola*, 73–74.

15. Rostislavov, "Peterburgskaia dukhovnaia akademiia," *VE* 4 (1883): 129.

16. Kazantsev, "O Filarete," 38.

17. Palmer, *Notes of a Visit*, 119.

18. Ibid., 227.

19. Ibid., 119, 276.

20. Rostislavov, "Peterburgskaia dukhovnaia akademiia," *VE* 5 (1883): 235–37.

21. Chistovich, *Rukovodiashchie deiateli dukhovnogo prosveshcheniia*, 327.

22. Florovskii, *Puti russkogo bogosloviia*, 216.

23. The pretext was that "the Sovereign does not tolerate the very name, philosophy." Kazantsev, "O Filarete," 41.

24. Korsunskii, *Filaret, mitropolit moskovskii*, 96–103; Florovskii, *Puti russkogo bogosloviia*, 206, 536.

25. Tal'berg, *Istoriia russkoi tserkvi*, 796–97.

26. See chapter 1.

27. Florovskii, *Puti russkogo bogosloviia*, 216.

28. Chistovich, *Rukovodiashchie deiateli dukhovnogo prosveshcheniia*, 338–46; Florovskii, *Puti russkogo bogosloviia*, 208.

29. Florovskii, *Puti russkogo bogosloviia*, 218–26. Not all adaptations of Catholic theology from this era harkened back to Iavorskii's days, however. Innokentii Borisov (1800–1857), for example, organized his dogmatic theology in accordance with Marian Dobmayr's (1753–1805) *Conspectus* and *Systema Theologicae Catholicae*; his works represented a more enlightened trend among the Bavarian Benedictines. Ibid., 196, 539–40; Lehner, *Enlightened Monks*.

30. Rostislavov, "Peterburgskaia dukhovnaia akademiia," *VE* 5 (1883): 235–37.

31. Florovskii, *Puti russkogo bogosloviia*, 166; Chistovich, *Rukovodiashchie deiateli dukhovnogo prosveshcheniia*, 328.

32. Rostislavov, "Peterburgskaia dukhovnaia akademiia," *VE* 4 (1883): 147; Florovskii, *Puti russkogo bogosloviia*, 215.

33. Chistovich, *Rukovodiashchie deiateli dukhovnogo prosveshcheniia*, 253.

34. Ibid., 260–78.

35. Iurii Kondakov, *Dukhovno-religioznaia politika*, 187.

36. Filaret's 1823 catechism was written in reaction to Peter Mohyla. For example, he opposed Mohyla's explanation of "the commandments of the church" as "an imitation of Latin books" since he argued "the Church never approved of any particular commandments." Korsunksii, *Filaret, mitropolit moskovskii*, 21.

37. Chistovich, *Rukovodiashchie deiateli dukhovnogo prosveshcheniia*, 268–70, 280.

38. Golburt, *The First Epoch*, 3–4.

39. Rostislavov, "Peterburgskaia dukhovnaia akademiia," *VE* 5 (1883): 248.

40. Palmer, *Notes of a Visit*, 221.

41. Freeze, *The Parish Clergy*, 11.

42. Nikolskii, *Istoriia russkoi tserkvi*, 240.

43. For Prokopovich's rejection of subordination to state bureaucracy and his insistence on the equality of the Synod and the Senate, see chapter 3. The Petrine reforms "did not transform the church into an 'ordinary branch of state bureaucracy.'" Freeze, "Handmaiden of the State?," 85–86.

44. Ibid., 82–102.

45. Eliseev, "Iz dalekogo proshlogo," 282–312; Florovskii, *Puti russkogo bogosloviia*, 190.

46. By saying this here, Herzen likely admitted that he was not a theologian. Herzen, "Byloe i dumy," 70.

47. Freeze, *The Parish Clergy*, 394, 389–97.

48. Manchester, *Holy Fathers, Secular Sons*, 135–54.

49. Kotkin, *Stalin*, 1:46–47. The seminary reopened in 1912 in a new building.

50. Ibid., 470–74; Kravtsov, "Tserkovnyi antiklerikalizm," 190–98.

51. Kravtsov, "Tserkovnyi antiklerikalizm," 190–98.

52. Freeze, *The Parish Clergy*, 467; Manchester, *Holy Fathers, Secular Sons*, 216–17.

BIBLIOGRAPHY

Archives and Manuscript Collections

AFSt/HA   Archiv der Franckesche Stiftungen zu Halle. Hauptarchiv.
Archive of the Francke Foundation in Halle, Germany.

APCG   Archivio del Pontificio Collegio Greco. Archives of the Greek
Pontifical College. Rome, Italy.

AT-OeStA/HHStA   Österreichische Staatsarchiv: Hof-, Haus-, und Staatsarchiv
(Minoritenplatz). Austrian State Archives: Court, House of
Habsburg, and State Archives (on the Minoritenplatz). Vienna,
Austria.

BAV   Biblioteca Apostolica Vaticana. Vatican Apostolic Library, The
Holy See.

HA HAB   Handschriftenabteil, Herzog August Bibliothek. Manuscript
Unit of the Herzog August Library, Wolfenbüttel,
Germany.

NB RK   Natsional'naia Biblioteka Respubliki Kareliia. National Library
of the Republic of Karelia, Petrozavodsk, Russia.

NBU   Natsional'na Biblioteka Ukrainy im. V. I. Vernads'koho. V. I.
Vernads'kyi National Library, Kyiv, Ukraine.

NLA-W   Niedersächsischen Landesarchiv. Federal Land Archives of
Lower Saxony. Wolfenbüttel, Germany.

OPI GIM   Otdel Pis'mennykh Istochnikov, Gosudarstvennyi Istoricheskii
Muzei. Manuscript Sources Unit, State Historical Museum,
Moscow, Russia.

OR RGB   Otdel Rukopisei, Rossiiskaia Gosudarstvennaia Biblioteka.
Manuscript Unit, Russian State Library, Moscow, Russia.

RGADA   Rossiiskii Gosudarstvennyi Arkhiv Drevnikh Aktov. Russian
State Archive of Ancient Acts. Moscow, Russia.

RGIA   Rossiiskii Gosudarstvennyi Istoricheskii Arkhiv. Russian State
Historical Archive, St. Petersburg, Russia.

Periodicals, Reference, and
Published Primary Source Collections

Acta SCPF   *Acta Sacrae Congregationis de Propaganda Fide Ecclesiam
            Catholicam Ucrainae et Bielarusjae.* Rome, 1953–.

ADB   *Allgemeine Deutsche Biographie.* 56 volumes (1875–1912).
            Munich, 2003.

ADKA   *Akty i Dokumenty, otnosiashchiesia k istorii Kievskoi akademii.*
            2 vols. Kiev, 1904.

AE   *Acta Eruditorum Publicata Lipsiae* and *Nova Acta Eruditorum,*
            1682–1782.

ChIODR   *Chteniia v imperatorskom obshchestvie istorii i drevnostei
            rossiiskikh pri Moskovskom universitete,* 1846–1918.

CODOIN   *Colección de documentos inéditos para la historia de España.* 120
            vols. Madrid, 1842–95.

DR   *Dukhovnyi reglament, tshchaniiem i poveleniiem
            Vsepresvetleishogo, Derzhavneishogo Gosudaria Petra Pervogo.*
            St. Petersburg, 1779.

DRMID   *Vneshniaia politika Rossii XIX i nachala XX veka: Dokumenty
            Rossiiskogo ministerstva inostrannykh del.* 16 vols. Moscow,
            1957–.

KEV   *Kievskie eparkhial'nye vedomosti,* 1861–1917.

KFZh   *Kamer-fur'erskii tseremonial'nyi zhurnal,* 1695–1817. St.
            Petersburg, 1853–1916.

KhCh   *Khristianskoe chtenie,* 1821–1918; 1991–.

KS   *Kievskaia starina,* 1882–1907.

LW   *Luther Werke.* Weimar, 1883–2009.

LWC   *The Larger Catechism, Agreed upon by the Assembly of Divines at
            Westminster.* Edinburgh, 1648.

MV   *Moskovskie vedomosti,* 1756–1917.

NDB   *Neue Deutsche Biographie.* 26 vols. Berlin, 1953–2016.

ODDS   *Opisanie dokumentov i del khraniashchikhsia v arkhivakh
            Sviateishego pravitelstvuiushchego sinoda.* 50 vols. St. Petersburg,
            1868–1915.

OSBM   *Analecta Ordinis Sancti Basilii Magni,* 1949–.

PE   *Pravoslavnaia entsiklopediia.* Moscow, 2000–.

PO   *Pravoslavnoe obozrenie,* 1860–91.

PS   *Pravoslavnyi sobesednik,* 1855–1917.

PSP   *Polnoe sobranie postanovlenii po vedomstvu pravoslavnogo
            ispovedaniia Rossiiskoi Imperii.* 7 vols. St. Petersburg,
            1898–1912.

PSZ   *Polnoe sobranie zakonov Rossiiskoi Imperii, s 1649 goda.* St.
            Petersburg, 1830–1916.

PU   Platon [Levshin]. *Pravoslavnoe uchenie ili sokrashchennaia
            Khristianskaia bogosloviia.* Moscow, 1780.

PUO   Feofan Prokopovich. *Pervoe uchenie otrokom.* Moscow, 1790.
PVTS   *Protokoly, zhurnaly i ukazy Verkhovnogo Tainogo Soveta, 1726–*
               1730. Edited by N. F. Dubrovin. St. Petersburg, 1887.
RA   *Russkii arkhiv,* 1863–1908.
RBS   *Russkii biograficheskii slovar'.* 25 vols. St. Petersburg,
               1896–1918.
RS   *Russkaia starina,* 1825, 1870–1918.
SIRIO   *Sbornik Imperatorskogo Russkogo Istoricheskogo Obshchestva,*
               1867–1916.
SPV   *Sanktpeterburgskie vedomosti,* 1728–1917.
TKDA   *Trudy Kievskoi Dukhovnoi Akademii,* 1860–1917.
VE   *Vestnik Evropy,* 1866–1918.
VEV   *Viatskie eparkhial'nye vedomosti,* 1863–1917.
ZfOG   *Zeitschrift für Osteuropäische Geschichte,* 1911–35.
ZhMNP   *Zhurnal Ministerstva Narodnogo Prosveshcheniia,* 1834–1917.
ZSlPh   *Zeitschrift für slavische Philologie,* 1924–.

PUBLISHED PRIMARY SOURCES

"Akty otnosiashchiesia k istorii raskola v XVIII." *ChIODR* 2 (1889): 1–87.

Alekseev, Petr. "Iz bumag protoiereia Petra Alekseeva." *RA* 2 (1882): 68–96.

———. "Opisanie moskovskogo bunta 1771-go goda sentiabria 15-go dnia." *RA* 12 (1863): 910–16.

———. "Rasskaz Petra Velikogo o patriarkhe Nikone." *RA,* nos. 8–9 (1863): 697–707.

Alexander I. "Ukaz o nebritii diakonami usov." *Istoriko-statisticheskie svedeniia po S-Peterburgskoi eparkhii* 9 (1884): 37.

Amvrosii [Iushkevich]. "Slovo Amvrosiia, Episkopa Vologodskogo na brakosocheta-nie." *Vologodskie eparkhial'nye vedomosti: Pribavleniia* 14 (1870): 485–48.

Amvrosii [Podobedov]. *Kratkoe Rukovodstvo k chteniiu knig Vetkhogo i Novogo Zavetov.* Moscow, 1779.

———. *Slovo skazyvannoe pri pogrebenii preosviashchennogo Amvrosiia.* St. Petersburg, 1771.

———. *Sobranie pouchitel'nykh slov v raznye vremena propovedannykh.* Moscow, 1810.

Amvrosii [Podobedov] and Damaskin [Semenov-Rudnev]. "K blagosklonnomu Chi-tateliu." In *Pouchitel'nye slova,* by Platon [Levshin], 1:i–xiv. Moscow, 1780.

Amvrosii [Zertis-Kamenskii]. *Razsuzhdenie protiv ateistov i neutralistov.* Moscow, 1781.

Anastasii [Bratanovskii]. *Predokhranenie ot neveriia i nechestiia.* St. Petersburg, 1794.

Andreev, Aleksandr. "Pravoslavno-protestantskie otnosheniia v Rossii v XVIII v." *Vestnik Cheliabinskogo gosudarstvennogo universiteta* (2009): 83–93.

Arndt, Johann. *Chtiri knigi o istinnom Khristianstve.* Translated by Simon [Todorskii]. Halle, 1735.

———. *Ioanna Arndta o istinnom Khristianstve shest' knig.* Translated by Ivan Turgenev. Moscow, 1784.

———. *Ioanna Arndta o istinnom Khristianstve shest' knig.* Translated by Ivan Turgenev. Moscow, 1800.

Arsenii [Matseevich], "Vozrazhenie na pashkvil' liuteranskii Molotok na Kamen' Very." OR RGB, f. 173, op. 1, rukopis' 127.

Arsenii [Vereshchagin]. "Dnevnik preosviashennogo Arseniia Vereshchagina." *Iaro-slavskie eparkhial'nye vedomosti* 43 (1894): 673–77; 44 (1894): 692–700; 45 (1894): 708–13; 46 (1894): 730–35; 47 (1894): 749–50; 48 (1894): 766–68; 49 (1894): 780–83; 1 (1895): 8–16; 2 (1895): 25–32; 3 (1895): 40–47; 4 (1895): 56–64.

Bacmeister, Hartwig. *Russische Bibliothek.* Vol. 1. St. Petersburg, Riga, and Leipzig, 1772.

Bancks, John. *The Life of Peter the Great, Formerly Emperor of Russia.* Trenton, N.J., 1813.

Bassevitz, H.-F. "Zapiski grafa Bassevicha." Translated by I. O. Ammon. *RA* 1 (1865): 6–54; 2 (1865): 141–204; 5 (1865): 567–635.

Bayer, Theophil Siegfried. "Vita Theophanis Procopovitsch." In *Nordische Neben-studen*, Theil 1, edited by Johann Scherer, 249–70. Frankfurt, 1776.

Ben'ian, Dzhon [John Bunyan]. *Liubopytnoe i dostopamiatnoe puteshestvie Khristian-ina.* 2 vols. Moscow, 1782.

———. *Sochineniia Ioanna Biuniana.* 4 vols. Translated by D. I. Dmitrievskii. Moscow, 1786–87.

Bergholz, Friedrich Wilhelm von. "Tagebuch. II. Theil von 1722." *Magazin für die neue Historie und Geographie* 20:331–592.

———. "Tagebuch. III. Theil.1721–1723." *Magazin für die neue Historie und Geogra-phie* 21:178–360.

———. "Tagebuch. IV. Theil., 1724." *Magazin für die neue Historie und Geographie* 22:425–506.

Biblia dat is de gantsche H. Schrifture. Leiden, 1637.

Biblia, Det er den ganske Helige Skrift. Copenhagen, 1633.

Bibliia, sirech knigi sviashennago pisaniia Vetkhogo i Novogo Zaveta. Moscow, 1751.

Biblia, thet ar all then Heliga Skrift. Stockholm, 1655.

Biblia, thet ar all then Heliga Skrift. Stockholm, 1728.

Bilfinger, Georg. *Stephani Javorskii Discursum de poena haereticorum.* Tübingen, 1731.

Blackmore, R. *The Doctrine of the Russian Church: Being the Primer or Spelling Book, the Shorter and Longer Catechisms, and a Treatise on the Duty of Parish Priests.* Aberdeen, 1845.

Bolotov, Andrei. *Zhizn' i prikliucheniia Andreia Bolotova opisannye im samim.* Moscow, 1931. Reprint, Cambridge, 1973.

Bos, Lambertus. *Exercitationes philologicae in quibus Novi Foederis loca nonnulla ex auctoribus graecis illustrantur et exponuntur.* Franeker, 1700.

British and Foreign Bible Society. *Thirteenth Report of the British and Foreign Bible Society.* London, 1817.

Buddeus, Johann Franz. *Ecclesia Romana cum Ruthenica Irreconciliabilis.* Jena, 1719.

———. *Epistola Apologetica Pro Ecclesia Lutherana contra calumnias et obtrectationes Stephani Javorskii.* Jena, 1729.

Campredon. "Diplomaticheskaia perepiska [. . .] 1723–1725." *SIRIO* 52 (1886): 427–38.

———. "Doneseniia [. . .] za 1725." *SIRIO* 58 (1887): 11.

Canisius, Peter. *Petri Canisii Societatis Jesu theologi parvus catechismus Catholicorum Latine.* London, 1687.

Cathcart, Charles. "Lord Cathcart to the Right Honorable Lord Viscount Weymouth, August 12 (23) 1768." *SIRIO* 12 (1873): 351–52.

Catherine I. *Die Gewisse Nachricht von Ihro Russ. Kayserliche Majestät.* N.p., 1727.

Catherine II. "Chetyre pis'ma imperatritsy Ekateriny II k Dmitriiu." *RA* 2 (1869): 198–99.

———. "Rasskazy imperatritsy Ekateriny II-i o pervykh piati godakh ee tsarstvovaniia." *RA* 3 (1865): 485–88.

———. *Zapiski imperatritsy Ekateriny Vtoroi.* St. Petersburg, 1907.

Clarke, Edward. *Travels in Various Countries of Europe, Asia, and Africa.* Vol. 1. Hartford, Conn., 1817.

Consett, Thomas. *The Present State and Regulations of Church in Russia.* London, 1729.

Damaskin [Semenov-Rudnev]. "Vita Auctoris." In *Theophanis Procopowicz Archiepiscopi Novogrodensis Tractatus De Processione Spiritus Sancti,* 18–27. Gotha, 1772.

"Delo Feofana Prokopovicha." *ChIOIDR* 1 (1862): 1–92.

"Delo ob Arsenii Matseeviche." *ChIOIDR* 3 (1862): 134–94.

Dmitrii [Sechenov]. *Feyerliche Danck-Rede des hochwürdigen Ertz-Bischoffens von Gross-Novogrod.* Stuttgart, 1762.

———. *Rech' blagodarstvennaia.* Moscow, 1763.

———. "Smes'." *Otechestvennye Zapiski* 6 (1838): 1–5.

Dmitrii [Sechenov] and Gavriil [Petrov]. "Doklad Sinoda o dozvolenii gernguteram selit'sia v Rossii 22 dekabria 1763 goda." *RS* 23 (1878): 712–13.

Dostoevsky, Fedor. *Pis'ma 1867–1871.* Vol. 2. Edited by A. S. Dolinin. Moscow, 1930.

Empaytaz, Henri-Louis. *Notice sur Alexandre.* Geneva, 1828.

Erasmus, Desiderius. *Razgovory druzheskie [Colloquies].* Edited and translated by Gavriil [Buzhinskii]. St. Petersburg, 1716.

Evgenii [Bolkhovitinov]. *Parnasskaia istoriia zakliuchaiushchaiasia v dvukh knigakh.* Moscow, 1788.

———. "Pis'mo mitropolita Evgeniia k preosv. Arkhangelogorodskomu Parfeniiu [October 30, 1811]." *RA* 3 (1875): 315–16.

———. *Razsuzhdenie o neobkhodimosti grecheskogo iazyka dlia bogoslovii.* Voronezh, 1800.

———. *Slovar' istoricheskii o byvshikh v Rossii pisateliakh dukhovnogo china greko-rossiiskoi tserkvi.* 1827. Reprint, Moscow, 1995.

Feofan [Prokopovich]. *Chetyre sochineniia.* Moscow, 1773.

———. *Christianae Orthodoxae Theologiae in Academia Kiowiensi a Theophane Prokopovicz.* 5 vols. Leipzig, 1792–93.

———. *Filosofs'ki tvory.* 3 vols. Translated by V. I. Shynkaruk. Kyiv, 1981.

———. *Miscellanea Sacra.* Edited by David Nashchinskii. Breslau, 1744.

———. *Ob neudobenosimom ige.* Moscow: U Novikova, 1784.

———. *Pervoe uchenie otrokom.* St. Petersburg, 1720.

———. *Pervoe uchenie otrokom.* Serbian translation. Grábóc, Diocese of Buda, 1744.

———. "Pis'ma Feofana Prokopovicha." *TKDA* 1 (1865): 141–59; 2 (1865): 260–310, 595–637; 3 (1865): 538–64.

―――. *Rozysk istoricheskii, koikh radi vin i v"iakovom razume byli i naritsalisia imperatory rimstii* [. . .]. St. Petersburg, 1721.

―――. *Slova i rechi pouchitel'nye, pokhval'nye i pozdravitel'nyie sobrannye i nekotorye vtorym tisneniem, a drugiia vnov' napechatannyie.* 4 vols. St. Petersburg, 1760–74.

―――. *Sochineniia.* Edited by I. Eremin. Moscow, 1953.

―――. *Theophanis Procopowicz Archiepiscopi Novogrodensis Tractatus de processione Spiritus Sancti.* Gotha, 1772.

―――. *Veshchi i dela o kotorykh dukhovnyi uchitel' narodu khristianskomu propovedati dolzhen.* Moscow, 1784.

―――. "Zateika verkhovnikov: O vazhnykh proishestviiakh posle konchiny Imperatora Petra II vosposledovavshikh." In appendix to *Zapiski Diuka Liriiskogo i Bervikskogo vo vremia prebyvaniia ego pri imperatorskom rossiiskom dvore*, edited and translated by Dmitrii Iazykov, 186–217. St. Petersburg, 1845.

Feofilakt [Rusanov]. *Pouchitel'nye slova i rechi govorennye v raznye vremena.* Vol. 1. Moscow, 1809.

Feoktist [Mochul'skii]. *Drakhma ot sokrovishcha bozhestvennykh pisanii [. . .] sokrashchenie pravil pri chtenii Sviashchennogo Pisaniia potrebnykh.* Moscow, 1809.

―――. *Opyt germenevticheskogo ob'iasneniia.* Moscow, 1799.

Feuerlein, Jakob. *Dissertatio historico-ecclesiastica de religione Ruthenorum hodierna.* Göttingen, 1745.

Filaret [Drozdov]. "Mneniia o raznosti mezhdu vostochnoiu i zapadnoiu tserkov'iu, s istorieiu razdeleniia ikh predstavlennyia eia imperatorskomu velichestvu." *ChIOIDR* 1 (1870): 1–44.

――― *Razgovory mezhdu ispytuiushchim i uverennym o pravsolavii Greko-Rossiiskoi tserkvi.* St. Petersburg, 1815.

――― *Sochineniia: Slova i Rechi.* Vol. 1. Moscow, 1873.

Fonvizin, Denis. *Sobranie sochinenii.* Moscow, 1959.

Formei, Zhan Anri Samiuel' [Jean Henri Samuel Formey]. *Opyt o sovershenstve—iz Formeiia.* Translated by Anastasii [Bratanovskii]. St. Petersburg, 1805.

Fotii [Spasskii]. "Avtobiografiia." *RS* 81, no. 4 (1894): 99–123; *RS* 81, no. 5 (1894): 81–114; *RS* 82, no. 7 (1894): 195–230; *RS* 82, no. 10 (1894): 127–42; *RS* 83, no. 2 (1895): 174–216; *RS* 84, no. 11(1895): 207–36; *RS* 84, no. 12 (1895): 189–203.

―――. "Pis'ma k Praskov'e Mikhailovne Tolstoi." In *Bor'ba za veru*, edited by Viacheslav Ulybin, 122–234. Moscow, 2010.

Francke, August Hermann. *Predigten.* Vol. 1. Berlin, 1987.

Freyer, Hieronymus. *Programmata latino-germanica cum additamento miscellaneorum vario.* Halle, 1737.

Gavriil [Buzhinskii]. "Predislovie, presvetleishii i nepobedimyi avtokrator i imperator." In *Vvedenie v gistoriiu evropeiskuiu chrez Samuelia Pufendorfiia na nemetskom iazyke slozhennoe*, by Samuel Pufendorf, translated by Gavriil [Buzhinskii], 1–9. St. Petersburg, 1718.

Gavriil [Petrov]. *Slovo v torzhestvennyi den'.* St. Petersburg, 1770.

―――. *Slovo v vysokotorzhestvennyi den' koronovaniia.* Moscow, 1763.

Gerhard, Johann. *Glas trubnyi.* Translated by Iakov Romanovskii. Moscow, 1798.

———. *Myslennyi vertograd ili Khristianskoe uprazhnenie.* Translator unknown. Moscow, 1783.

———. *Sviashchennyia khristianskiia razmyshleniia.* Translated by Aleksei Lisitsyn. Moscow, 1783.

———. *Vertograd nasazhdennyi v pol'zu dushi greshnoi.* Translated by Ivan Kurbatov. Moscow, 1799.

Gerhard, Johann. [*Casimiriana*] *Ordnung Wie es in des Durchleuchtige[n] Hochgebornen Fürsten und Herrn Johann Casimiri Herzogen zu Sachsen.* Coburg, 1626.

Golikov, Ivan. *Deianiia Petra Velikogo, mudrogo preobrazovatelia Rossii.* 15 vols. Moscow, 1837–43.

Golovkin, Fedor. *Dvor i tsarstvovanie Pavla I: Portrety, Vospominaniia.* Moscow, 2003.

Grellet, Etienne. *A Concise Memoir.* Oxford, 1877.

Grotius, Hugo. *Istinnoe blagochestie khristianskoe dokazano protiv bezbozhnikov, iazychnikov, zhidov i makhometan.* Translated by Petr Alekseev. Moscow, 1768.

Haigold, Johann Joseph. *Beylagen zum neuveränderten Russland.* Band 1. Riga und Mietau, 1769–70.

Hall, Joseph. *The Works of Joseph Hall.* Vol. 11. Oxford, 1839.

———. *Obraz zhitiia Enokhova ili rod i sposob khozhdeniia s Bogom.* Moscow, 1784.

Haven, Peder von. *Reise in Russland.* Copenhagen, 1744.

Heber, Amelia, and Reginald Heber. *The Life of Reginald Heber, the Lord Bishop of Calcutta.* Vol. 1. New York, 1830.

Hempel, Christian. *Merckwürdiges Leben und Trauriger Fall des weltberufenen, russischen Staats-Ministers Andreä Grafen von Ostermann [. . .].* Bremen, 1743.

Hervey, James. *Blagogoveinyi zritel' prirody, ili Utrennie poludennye vechernie i noshchnye razmyshleniia slavnogo Gerveia.* Translated by Ivan Kandorskii. Moscow, 1800.

———. *Meditations and Contemplations by the Rev. James Hervey.* Vol. 1. New York, 1824.

Herzen, Aleksandr. *Byloe i dumy: Napechatano v Vol'noi russkoi tipografii v Londone.* Book 1. London, 1861.

Historische Nachricht von dem ehemahligen großen Russischen Staats-ministro Alexandro Danielowiz, Fürst von Menzikof. N.p., 1728.

Hoffmann, Karl Gottlob. *Introductio in lectionem Novi Testamenti.* Leipzig, 1737.

The Holy Bible. London, 1612.

Ioanikii [Galiatovskii or Haliatovs'kyi]. *Kliuch Rozuminnia.* Edited by Inna Chepiha. Kyiv, 1985.

Ioil' [Bykovskii]. *Istinna ili Vypiska o istinne.* Iaroslavl, 1787.

Irinei [Fal'kovskii]. *Christianae, orthodoxae, dogmatico-polemicae Theologiae compendium.* Vol. 2. Petropolis, 1827.

Irinei [Klement'evskii], ed and trans. *Torzhestvo nashei very nad neveruiushchimi i vol'nomyslishchimi.* Moscow, 1792.

Istinnyi Messiia. Translated by Anastasii [Bratanovskii]. Moscow, 1801.

Istoriko-statisticheskie svedeniia o S.-Peterburgskoi eparkhii. Vol. 6. St. Petersburg, 1878.

Jablonski, Johann. *Genius Stephani Jaworscii, Quondam Metropolitae Rezanensis et Muroniensis Ex Ejus Opere posthumo Theosophico Petra Fidei Dicto In Epistola Familiari develatus.* N.p., 1730.

Jenyns, Soame. *Sozertsanie khristianstva*. Translated by Feofilakt [Rusanov]. Moscow, 1803.

Johanna-Elisabeth of Anhalt-Zerbst. "Izvestiia pisannye kniagineiu Ioannoiu-Elisavetoiu Angal't-Tserbstkoiu." *SIRIO* 7 (1871): 29–54.

Jubé, Jacques. *La religion, les mœurs, et les usages des moscovites*. Edited by Michel Mervaud. Oxford, 1992.

Kandorskii, Ivan. *Nauka o dushe*. Moscow, 1796.

Kantemir, Antiokh. *Satiry i drugiia stikhotvorcheskiia sochineniia*. St. Petersburg, 1762.

———. *Sobranie Stikhotvorenii*. Edited by Z. I. Gershkovich. Leningrad, 1956.

Kazantsev, Nikodim. "O Filarete, mitropolite Moskovskom, moia pamiat'." *ChIOIDR* 2 (1877): 38–48.

King, John Glen. *Rites and Ceremonies of the Greek Church in Russia*. London, 1772.

Kohl, Johann Peter. *Ecclesia Graeca Lutheranizans*. Lübeck, 1723.

———. *Introductio in historiam et rem literariam Slavorum*. Altona, 1729.

Kowalyk, Volodimirus [Volodymyr Kowlyk]. *Ecclesiologia Theophanis Prokopovycz: Influxus Protestantismi*. Rome, 1947.

Kratter, Franz. *Das Mädchen von Marienburg: Ein fürstliches Familiengemälde in fünf Aufzügen*. Frankfurt, 1795.

Krinovskii, Gedeon. *Sobranie raznykh pouchitel'nykh slov*. St. Petersburg, 1755–59.

La Luzerne, César-Guillaume. *Pastyrskoe nastavlenie o prevoskhodstve religii*. Edited by Feofilakt [Rusanov]. Moscow, 1804.

Leskov, Nikolai. "Sviatitel'skie teni." *Istoricheskii vestnik* (May 1881): 53–69.

Levshin, Vasilii. *Pis'mo soderzhashchee nekotorye rassuzhdeniia o poeme Vol'tera "Na razrushenie Lissabona."* Moscow, 1788.

Ligne, Charles-Joseph. *Lettres du Prince de Ligne à la Marquise de Cigny*. Paris, 1886.

Liria, Jacobo Francisco Fitz James Stuart de Berwick y de. "Zapiski Diuka de Liria." *RA* 1, no.3 (1909): 337–453.

Luther, Martin. *The Babylonian Captivity of the Church: The Annotated Luther Study Edition*. Minneapolis, 2016.

———. *Luther's Large Catechism: Missouri Synod Official Edition*. Accessed July 18, 2019. http://www.lcms.org/Document.fdoc?src=lcm&id=950.

———. *Martin Luther: Selections from His Writings*. Edited by John Dillenberger. New York, 1962.

Magnitskii, Leontii. *Zapiska Leontiia Magnitskogo po delu Tveritinova*. St. Petersburg, 1882.

Maikov, L., ed. *Razskazy Nartova o Petre Velikom*. St. Petersburg, 1891.

Makarii [Miroliubov]. *Skazanie o zhizni i trudakh preosviashchenneishego Gavriila mitropolita Novgorodskogo i Sanktpeterburgskogo*. St. Petersburg, 1857.

Malvenda, Tomas. *De Antichristo Libri Undecim*. Rome, 1604.

Mardefeld, Gustav von. "Diplomaticheskie dokumenty [. . .] Relationen des Freiherrn Gustav von Mardefeld." *SIRIO* 15 (1875): 175–415.

Markell [Rodyshevskii]. *Slovo na den' rozhdestva . . . v pridvornoi tserkvi Imperatritsy Elizavety Petrovny*. St. Petersburg, 1741.

Marmontel', Zhan Fransua [Jean François Marmontel]. *Velizer*. Translated by Ekaterina II Imperatritsa. Moscow, 1768.

Martini, Christian. *Nachricht aus Russland.* Frankfurt, 1731.

Mazzuchelli, Giammaria. *Gli scrittori d'Italia cioé nitizie storiche.* Vol. 2. Brescia, 1763.

Mefodii [Smirnov]. *K rimlianom poslanie sv. Apostola Pavla.* Moscow, 1794.

———. *Razsuzhdenie o Paskhe Iudeiskoi i khristianskoi [. . .].* Moscow, 1793.

Mencken, Johann. "Stephanii Iavorscii. . . . Petra fidei." *AE* (May 1729): 226–29.

Menshikov, Aleksandr. *Povsednevnye zapiski delam kniazia A. D. Menshikova 1716–1720, 1726–1727.* Edited by T. A. Lapteva. Moscow, 2004.

Mikhail [Desnitskii]. *Besedy o pokaianii, ili iz'iasnenie piatidesiatogo psalma.* St. Petersburg, 1798.

Mikhail [Desnitskii], Filaret [Drozdov], and Serafim [Glagolevskii]. "Vozglashenie ko khristoliubivym chitateliam." In *Gospoda nashego Iisusa Khrista Sviatoe evangelie, ot Matfeia Marka, Luki i Ioanna, i Deianiia sviatykh apostolov,* iii–vii. St. Petersburg, 1820.

Miranda, Francisco de. *Fransisko de Miranda v Rossii.* Translated by Moisei Alperovich. Moscow, 1986.

———. *Puteshestvie po Rossiiskoi Imperii.* Translated by Moisei Alperovich. Moscow, 2001.

Mosheim, Johann Lorenz von. *De poenis haereticorum cum Stephano Javorskio disputatio.* Helmstädt, 1731.

Motraye, Aubry de la. *Voyages en anglois et en françois d'A. de la Motraye en diverses provinces et places.* The Hague, 1732.

Nechkina, Militsa, and Mikhail Pokrovskii, eds. *Vosstanie dekabristov: Materialy.* 23 vols. Moscow, 1925–2008.

Nevzorov, Maksim. "Poslanie M. I. Nevzorova mitropolitu Serafimu." *VE* 6 (1868): 758–68.

Nikitenko, Aleksandr. *Up from Serfdom: My Childhood and Youth in Russia, 1804–1824.* Translated by Helen Jacobson. New Haven, Conn., 2001.

Nonnotte, Claude François. *Vol'terovy zabluzhdeniia.* Edited and translated by Evgenii [Bolkhovitinov]. Moscow, 1793.

"Ob odezhde lits dukhovnogo sosloviia." *RS* 4 (1871): 443–45.

Owen, John. *History of the British and Foreign Bible Society.* London, 1820.

Palmer, William. *Notes of a Visit to the Russian Church.* Edited by John Henry Newman. London, 1882.

Pestel', Pavel. *Russkaia pravda.* Edited by M. V. Nechkina. Moscow, 1958.

Peter I. *Curieuse Nachricht von der itzigen Religion.* N.p., 1725.

———. *Pokhodnyi zhurnal 1711-go goda.* St. Petersburg, 1854.

Peter [Mohyla]. *Pravoslavnoe ispovedanie very sobornyia i apost ol'skiia.* Moscow, 1709.

Philipps, Jenkin, ed. and trans. *The Russian Catechism, Composed and Published by Order of the Czar.* London, 1723.

Pierling, Pierre. *La Sorbonne et la Russie (1717–1747).* Paris, 1882.

Pis'ma russkikh gosudarei i drugikh osob tsarskogo semeistva. Moscow, 1862.

Platon [Levshin]. "Avtobiografiia." In *"Iz Glubiny Vozzvakh k Tebe, Gospodi—": Avtobiografiia, izbrannye propovedi, pis'ma preosviashchennogo Platona Mitropolita Moskovskogo.* Edited by P. V. Kalitin. Moscow, 1996.

———. *Kratkaia rossiiskaia tserkovnaia istoriia.* Moscow, 1805.

———. *Pouchitel'nye slova i drugie sochineniia*. 15 vols. Moscow, 1780–92.

———. *Pravoslavnoe uchenie ili sokrashchennaia khristianskaia bogosloviia*. Moscow, 1765.

———. "Punkty Metropolita Platona." In *Otvet edinovertsa staroobriadtsu na ego voz-razheniia*, edited by Grigorii [Postnikov], 117–28. St. Petersburg, 1857.

———. *Uveshchanie vo utverzhdenie istiny*. St. Petersburg, 1766.

Polanus, Amandus. *Syntagma theologiae Christianae*. Geneva, 1617.

Poroshin, Semen. "Sto tri dnia iz detskoi zhizni imperatora Pavla Petrovicha (Neizdannaia tetrad' Zapisok S. A. Poroshina)." *RA* 7 (1869): 1–68.

Pufendorf, Samuel. *Vvedenie v gistoriiu evropeiskuiu chrez Samuelia Pufendorfiia na nemetskom iazyke slozhennoe*. Translated by Gavriil [Buzhinskii]. St. Petersburg, 1718.

Radishchev, Aleksandr. *A Journey from St. Petersburg to Moscow*. Translated by Leo Weiner. Cambridge, Mass., 1958.

Regole da osservarsi dal rettore, alunni, ministri, ed uffiziali del Collegio urbano de propaganda fide. Rome, 1831.

Reinkingk, Theodor von [Dieterich Reinkingk]. *Biblische Policey [. . .]*. Frankfurt, 1670.

———. *Tractatus de regimine seculari et ecclesiastico*. Frankfurt, 1651.

Ribera, Bernardo de. *Responsum ant-apologeticum ecclesiae Catholicae contra calumniosas blasphemias Joannis Francisci Buddei*. Vienna, 1731.

Rondeau, Claudius. "Doneseniia i drugie bumagi angliiskikh poslov 1728–1733. Doneseniia K. Rondo lordu Taunsendu. Doneseniia K. Rondo lordu Garringtonu." *SIRIO* 66 (1889): 21–136, 146–636.

Rostislavov, Dmitrii. "Feofilakt Rusanov, pervyi ekzarkh Gruzii." *VE* 6 (November–December 1873): 598–615.

———. "Peterburgskaia dukhovnaia akademiia pri grafe Pratasove." *VE* 4 (July–August 1883): 121–87, 547–81; 5 (September–October 1883): 200–257.

———. "Zapiski D. I. Rostislavova o Feofilakte, Arkhiepiskope Riazanskom." *RS* 83 (March 1895): 88–97.

Rostislavov, Dmitrii. *Provincial Russia in the Age of Enlightenment: The Memoir of a Priest's Son*. Edited and translated by Alexander Martin. DeKalb, Ill., 2002.

Rulhière, Claude Carloman de. *Histoire ou anecdotes sur la révolution de Russie en l'année 1762*. Paris, 1797.

Saurin, Jacques. *The Sermons of the Rev. James Saurin, Late Pastor of the French Church at the Hague*. New York, 1836.

Schmidt, Hermann Joseph. *Kritische Geschichte der neugriechischen und der russischen Kirche*. Mainz, 1854.

Schmidt-Phiseldek, Christoph von. *Materialien zu der Russischen Geschichte*. Vol. 2. Riga, 1784.

Schwan, Christian. *Anecdotes russes, ou lettres d'un officier allemande à un gentilhomme Livonien*. London, 1769.

Shil'der, Nikolai, ed. "Dve kharakteristiki—iz zapisok grafa F. G. Golovkina." *RS* 88 (1896): 367–79.

Shirinskii-Shikhmatov, Platon. "Zapiski o kramolakh vragov Rossii." *RA* 43 (1868): 1329–91.

Shishkin, Andrei. "Simon Todorskii." In *Slovar' russkikh pisatelei XVIII veka*, 3rd ed., edited by A. Panchenko, 247–48. St. Petersburg, 2010.

Shishkov, Aleksandr. *Zapiski, mneniia i perepiska admirala A. S. Shishkova*. Berlin, 1870.

Simon [Todorskii]. *Slovo v vysochaishee prisutstvie eia sviashchenneishago imperatorskago velichestva blagochestiveishiia samoderzhavneishiia velikiia gosudaryni nasheia Elizavety Petrovny imperatritsy vseia Rossii, v vysokotorzhestvenni den' rozhdeniia ego imperatorskogo vysochestva gosudaria naslednika blagovernago velikago kniazia Petra Fedorovicha*. St. Petersburg, 1743.

Skuminowicz, T. *Przyczyny porzuczenia dysunii*. Wilno, 1643.

Skvortsov, Nikolai. *Arkhiv moskovskoi Sv. Sinoda Kontory: Materialy po Moskve i Moskovskoi eparkhii za XVIII vek*. Moscow, 1914.

Stefan [Iavorskii]. "Apologiia ili slovesnaia oborona o voznoshenii iavstvennom i vospominanii v molitvakh tserkovnykh Sviateishikh Pravoslavnykh Patriarkhov." In *Iz tserkovnoi istorii vremen Petra Velikogo: Issledovaniia i materialy*, edited by Viktor Zhivov, 245–65. Moscow, 2004.

———. *Kamen' very: Pravoslavnym tserkve sviatyia synom na utverzhdenie i dukhovnoe sozidanie*. Moscow, 1728.

———. "Poslanie Stefana Iavorskogo Metropolita Riazanskogo . . . ob uchenii ieromonakha Feofana Prokopovicha." *ChIOIDR* 4 (1864): 5–8.

———. *Ritoricheskaia ruka, perevod s latinskago Feodora Polikarpova, 1721*. St. Petersburg, 1878.

———. "Slova." *TKDA* 1 (1875): 631–47; 10 (1875): 107–21.

———. *Tvoreniia preosviashchennogo Stefana Iavorskogo*. Edited by Petr Palamarchuk. Moscow, 1999.

———. "Znameniia prishestviia antikhristova i konchiny veka." In Stefan [Iavorskii], *Tvoreniia preosviashchennogo Stefana Iavorskogo*, 29–116. Moscow, 1999.

Steigen und Fall eines grossen Ministers in der vollständigen Lebens-Beschreibung des Fürstens von Menzikoff gezeiget. N.p., 1728.

Stephanus, Joachim. *Institutiones iuris canonici: In tres libros [. . .]*. Greifswald, 1604.

Strahlenberg, Philipp Johann von. *An Historico-geographical Description of the North and Eastern Parts of Europe and Asia*. London, 1738.

Strateman, Vil'gel'm [Wilhelm Stratemann]. *Featron ili pozor istoricheskii: Iz'iavliaiushchii povsiudnuiu istoriiu Sviashchennogo Pisaniia i grazhdanskuiu*. Edited by Gavriil [Buzhinskii]. St. Petersburg, 1724.

Sumarokov, Aleksandr. "O rossiiskom dukhovnom krasnorechii." In *Polnoe sobranie vsekh sochinenii v stikhakh i proze*, 6:295–302. Moscow, 1787.

Sushkov, Nikolai. *Zapiski o zhizni i vremeni sviatitelia Filareta, Mitropolita Moskovskago*. Moscow, 1868.

Swedenborg, Emanuel. *The Earths in Our Solar System [. . .] Their Inhabitants, and Also of the Spirits and Angels There, from What Has Been Seen and Heard*. New York, 1896.

Tatishchev, Vasilii. *Izbrannye proizvedeniia*. Leningrad, 1979.

Timkovskii, Il'ia. "Zapiski I. F. Timkovskogo." *RA* 12 (1874): 1377–1466.

Tolstoi, Mikhail. *Khranilishche moei pamiati*. 1891. Reprint, Moscow, 1995.

Uvarov, Sergei. "Pis'mo Grafa Sergeia S. Uvarova 18 November 1813." *RA* 9 (1871): 129–31.

Varlaam [Liashchevskii]. *Grecheskaia grammatika, v kotoroi sintaksis [. . .].* St. Petersburg, 1788.

Vierorth, Anton. "Lebenslauf der Bruders Albert Anton Vierorth, Bischofs der Brüder-Kirche, heimgegangen zu Herrnhut am 29 September 1761." *Nachrichten aus der Brüder-Gemeine* 1 (1845): 107–35.

Vigel', Filipp. *Zapiski.* Moscow, 2000.

Vockerodt, Johann. *Russland unter Peter dem Grossen.* Edited by Ernst Hermann. Leipzig, 1872.

Voltaire-Catherine II: Correspondance 1763–1778. Edited by Alexandre Stroev. Paris, 2006.

Weber, Friedrich. *Das veränderte Russland, in welchem die jetzige Verfassung des Geist- und Weltlichen Regiments [. . .].* Frankfurt, 1738.

Weller, Jacob. *Grammatica graeca nova.* Leipzig, 1636.

Wilhelm of Hesse. *Agenda, das ist: Kirchen-Ordnung, wie es im Fürstentum Hessen [. . .].* Kassel, 1657.

Zeltner, Gustav. *Breviarum Controversiarum cum Ecclesia Graeca.* Nuremberg, 1737.

Zollikofer, Georg. *Sermons on Education, on Reflection, on the Greatness of God in the Works of Nature and in the Government of the World, on Charity, and on Various Other Topics.* Vol. 2. Translated and edited by William Tooke. London, 1806.

———. *Sermons on the Dignity of Man: And the Value of the Objects Principally Relating to Human Happiness.* Vol. 1. Translated and edited by William Tooke. Worcester, Mass., 1807.

Secondary Literature

Akimov. "Feofil Krolik." *Bol'shaia Biograficheskaia Entsiklopediia.* Accessed September 4, 2019. http://dic.academic.ru/dic.nsf/enc_biography/28750.

Aleksandrenko, Vasilii. "Iz zhizni russkikh studentov v Oksforde v tsarstvovanie imperatritsy Ekateriny II." *ZhMNP* (January 1893): 1–15.

———. "Proekt bogoslovskogo fakul'teta pri Ekaterine II." *VE* (November 1873): 300–317.

———. *Russkie diplomaticheskie agenty v Londone v XVIII veke.* 2 vols. Warsaw, 1897.

Alekseev, Aleksei. "Varlaam." *PE* (2009) 6:600–601.

Allison, Henry. *Lessing and the Enlightenment: A Study of G. E. Lessing's Philosophy of Religion and Its Place within the Context of Eighteenth-Century Thought.* Ann Arbor, 1966.

Andreev, Aleksandr. "Kvakery na zapade i v Rossii." *Novaia i noveishaia istoriia* (April 2010): 165–77.

Androsov, Sergei. *Zhivopisets Ivan Nikitin.* St. Petersburg, 1998.

Aner, Karl. *Die Theologie der Lessingzeit.* Halle, 1929.

Anisimov, Evgenii. *Rossiia v seredine XVIII veka: Bor'ba za nasledie Petra.* Moscow, 1986.

———. *Vremia petrovskikh reform: XVIII vek 1-ia chetvert'.* Leningrad, 1989.

Anisov, Lev. "Mitropolit Platon i ekaterininskoe vremia." *Platonovskie chteniia* 4 (2007): 27–34.

Askochenskii, Viktor. *Kiev, s drevneishim ego uchilishchem akademieiu.* Vol. 2. Kiev, 1856.

Avgustin [Nikitin]. "Rossiia i Sorbonna." *KhCh* 34 (2010): 46–73.

Avtukhovich, Tatiana. "Prokopovich." In *Slovar' russkikh pisatelei XVIII veka*, 2nd ed., edited by Nataliia Kochetkova, 488–96. St. Petersburg, 1999.

Barsov, Nikolai. "Maloizvestnye russkie propovedniki XVIII stoletiia." *KhCh* 2 (1874): 247–86; 4 (1874): 575–623.

Bartenev, Petr, ed. "Podlinnoe delo arkhiepiskopa Novgorodskogo Feodosiia." *RA* 2 (1864): 168–207.

Batalden, Stephen. *Russian Bible Wars: Modern Scriptural Translation and Cultural Authority*. Cambridge, 2013.

Bautz, F. "Carl Heinrich von Bogatzky." *Biographisch-Bibliographisch Kirchen-Lexikon* 1 (1975): 669–71.

Beattie, Francis. *The Presbyterian Standards: An Exposition of the Westminster Confession of Faith and Catechisms*. Richmond, Va., 1896.

Beliaev, Andrei. *Mitropolit Platon v otnosheniiakh k Vifanskoi seminarii: K 100-letiiu so vremeni ee osnovaniia 1797–1 maia 1897 g.* Moscow, 1897.

Benz, Ernst. *Die Abendländische Sendung der östlich-orthodoxen Kirche: Die russische Kirche und das abendländische Christentum im Zeitalter der Heiligen Allianz*. Wiesbaden, 1950.

———. *Schellings theologische Geistesahnen*. Mainz, 1955.

Bessarabova, Nina. "Mirovozzrenie i deiatel'nost' mitropolita Platona (Levshina)." *Voprosy istorii* (January 2008): 141–47.

Beutel, Albrecht. *Aufklärung in Deutschland*. Göttingen, 2006.

———. *Kirchengeschichte im Zeitalter der Aufklärung*. Göttingen, 2009.

Beyreuther, Erich. *Die Erweckungsbewegung: Ein Handbuch*. Göttingen, 1977.

Bida, Konstantyn. *Ioanikii Galiatovs'kyi i ioho "Kliuch razumieniia."* Rome, 1975.

Bil'basov, Vasilii. *Istoriia Ekateriny Vtoroi*. Berlin, 1900.

Binnis, John. *An Introduction to the Christian Orthodox Churches*. Cambridge, 2002.

Bitovt, Iurii. *Redkie russkiia knigi i letuchiia izdaniia XVIII veka [. . .]*. Moscow, 1905.

Blažejovskyj, Dmytro. "Ukrainian and Bielorussian Students at the Pontifical Greek College of Rome (1576–1976)." *Analecta OSBM* 10 (1979): 133–69.

———. "Ukrainian and Bielorussian Students in the Pontificio Collegio Urbano De Propaganda Fide (1627–1846)." *Analecta OSBM* 9 (1974): 199–212.

Blom, Hans. "Grotius and Socinianism." In *Socinianism and Arminianism: Antitrinitarians, Calvinists, and Cultural Exchange in Seventeenth-Century Europe*, edited by Martin Mulsow and Jan Rohls, 121–47. Leiden, 2005.

Bödeker, Hans. *Strukturen der deutschen Frühaufklärung 1680–1720*. Göttingen, 2008.

Bogdanova, Aleksandra. "Sekuliarizatsiia zemel' solovetskogo monastyria v 1764 godu." *Vestnik Severnogo (Arkticheskogo) federal'nogo universiteta, Gumanitarnye i sotsial'nye nauki* 2 (2018): 5–14.

Bogoslovskii, Mikhail. *Issledovaniia po istorii mestnogo upravleniia pri Petre Velikom: Byt i nravy russkogo dvorianstva v pervoi polovine XVIII v.* Petrograd, 1918.

Bremer, Francis, ed. *Puritans and Puritanism in Europe and America: A Comprehensive Encyclopedia*. Santa Barbara, Calif., 2006.

Breul, Wolfgang, and Jan Schnurr. *Geschichtsbewusstsein und Zukunftserwartung in Pietismus und Erweckungsbewegung*. Göttingen, 2013.

Breyfogle, Nicholas. *Heretics and Colonizers: Forging Russia's Empire in the South Caucasus*. Ithaca, N.Y., 2005.

Brilioth, Yngve. *A Brief History of Preaching*. Translated by Karl Mattson. Philadelphia, 1965.

Briukhovets'kyi, Viacheslav, and Zoia Khyzhniak, eds. *Kyievo-Mohylians'ka akademiia v imenakh XVII–XVIII st.: Entsyklopedychne vydannia*. Kyiv, 2001.

Bruess, Gregory. *Religion, Identity, and Empire: A Greek Archbishop in the Russia of Catherine the Great*. New York, 1997.

Bryner, Erich. *Der geistliche Stand in Russland: Sozialgeschichtliche Untersuchungen [. . .]*. Göttingen, 1982.

Buevskii [Aleksandr Vereshchagin]. "Aleksei Titov." In *Pamiatnaia knizhka Viatskoi gubernii za 1901 god*, 397–400. Viatka, 1900.

———. "Epizody iz zhizni osnovatelia Viatskoi seminarii Lavrentiia Gorki." In *Pamiatnaia knizhka Viatskoi gubernii za 1899 god*, 1–103. Viatka, 1898.

Buevskii [Aleksandr Vereshchagin]. "Epizody iz zhizni osnovatelia Viatskoi seminarii Lavrentiia Gorki." In *Pamiatnaia knizhka Viatskoi gubernii za 1902 god*, 1–209. Viatka, 1901.

Burbee, Carolynn. "Catherine and the Convents: The 1754 Secularization of Church Lands and Its Effects on the Lives of Russian Nuns." PhD diss., University of Missouri, 2000.

Burstein, Miriam. *Victorian Reformations: Historical Fiction and Religious Controversy, 1820–1900*. Notre Dame, Ind., 2013.

Bushkovitch, Paul A. "The Clergy at the Russian Court, 1689–1796." In *Monarchy and Religion: The Transformation of Royal Culture in Eighteenth-Century Europe*, edited by Michael Schaich, 105–28. New York, 2007.

———. *Peter the Great: The Struggle for Power, 1671–1725*. Cambridge, 2001.

———. "Political Ideology in the Reign of Peter I: Feofan Prokopovich, Succession to the Throne and the West." *DHI Moskau: Vorträge zum 18. und 19. Jahrhundert* 11 (2012): 1–19.

———. *Religion and Society in Russia: The Sixteenth and Seventeenth Centuries*. New York, 1992.

Bychkov, Afanasii. *V pamiat' grafa Mikhaila Mikhailovicha Speranskogo, 1772–1872*. 2 vols. St. Petersburg, 1872.

Chepiha, Inna. "Kliuch Rozuminnia Ioanykiia Galiatovs'kogo." In *Kliuch Rozuminnia*, by Ioanikii [Galiatovskii], edited by Ivan Chepiha, 5–34. Kyiv, 1985.

Cherviakovskii, Platon. "Vvedenie v bogoslovie Feofana Prokopovicha." *KhCh* 2 (1876): 32–86; *KhCh* 3/4 (1877): 291–330.

Chicherin, Boris. *Vospominaniia*. Moscow, 2001.

Chistovich, Ilarion. *Feofan Prokopovich i ego vremia*. 1868. Reprint, Nendeln, Liechtenstein, 1966.

———. "Ispravlenie teksta Slavianskoi Biblii pered isdaniem 1751 goda." *PO* 1 (1860): 479–510; 2 (1860): 41–72.

———. *Istoriia perevoda Biblii na russkii iazyk*. St. Petersburg, 1899.

———. *Istoriia Sankt-Peterburgskoi Dukhovnoi Akademii*. St. Petersburg, 1857.

———. "Neizdannye propovedi Stefana Iavorskogo." *KhCh* 1 (1867): 830–32.

———. *Novogorodskii Mitropolit Iov: Zhizn' ego I perepiska s raznymi litsami.* St. Petersburg, 1861.

———. *Reshilovskoe delo: Feofan Prokopovich i Feofilakt Lopatinskii; Materialy dlia istorii pervoi poloviny XVIII stoletiia.* St. Petersburg, 1861.

———. *Rukovodiashchie deiateli dukhovnogo prosveshcheniia v Rossii v pervoi polovine tekushchego stoletiia.* St. Petersburg, 1894.

Chrissidis, Nikolaos. *An Academy at the Court of the Tsars: Greek Scholars and Jesuit Education in Early Modern Russia.* DeKalb, Ill., 2016.

———. "Creating the New Educated Elite: Learning and Faith in Moscow's Slavo-Greco-Latin Academy, 1685–1694." PhD diss., Yale University, 2000.

Coleman, Heather. *Russian Baptists and spiritual revolution, 1905–1929.* Bloomington, Ind., 2005.

———. "Tales of Violence Against Religious Dissidents in the Orthodox Village." In *Sacred Stories: Religion and Spirituality in Modern Russia,* edited by Heather Coleman and Mark Steinberg, 200–221. Bloomington, Ind., 2007.

Collis, Robert. *The Petrine Instauration: Religion, Esotericism and Science at the Court of Peter the Great, 1689–1725.* Leiden, 2012.

Cracraft, James. *The Church Reform of Peter the Great.* Stanford, Calif., 1971.

Craig, J. *History of the Protestant Church in Hungary: From the Beginning of the Reformation to 1850; With Special Reference to Transylvania.* New York, 1854.

Crews, Robert. "Empire and the Confessional State: Islam and Religious Politics in Nineteenth-Century Russia." *American Historical Review* 108, no. 1 (2003): 50–83.

Croce, Benedetto. *Storia dell'età Barocca in Italia: Pensiero, poesia e letteratura, vita morale.* Bari, 1929.

Cross, Anthony. "Russian Students in Eighteenth-Century Oxford (1766–65)." *Journal of European Studies* 5 (1975): 91–110.

Cross, Frank, and Elizabeth Livingstone, eds. *The Oxford Dictionary of the Christian Church.* Oxford, 2005.

Crummey, Robert. *Old Believers in a Changing World.* DeKalb, Ill., 2011.

Czok, Karl, and Siegfried Hoyer. *Leipzig und Sachsen: Beiträge zur Stadt- und Landesgeschichte vom 15.–20. Jahrhundert; Seigfried Hoyer zum 70. Geburtstag.* Beucha, 2000.

Dargan, Edwin. *A History of Preaching.* Grand Rapids, Mich., 1954–.

David, Zdenek V. "The Influence of Jacob Boehme on Russian Religious Thought." *Slavic Review* 21, no. 1 (March 1962): 46–51.

Davies, Norman. *Europe: A History.* Oxford, 1996.

De Madariaga, Isabel. *Russia in the Age of Catherine the Great.* New Haven, Conn., 1981.

Denisov, Leonid. *Pravoslavnye monastyri Rossiiskoi Imperii [. . .].* Moscow, 1908.

Dixon, C. Scott. *Contesting the Reformation.* Malden, Mass., 2012.

Dmitriev, Andrei. *Istoriia Korel'skoi (Keksgol'mskoi) eparkhii.* Priozersk, 2000.

Domanitskii, V. "Dva Ukaza Rafaila Zaborovskogo." *KS* 13 (1883): 307–9.

Dorner, Isaak. *History of Protestant Theology: Particularly in Germany, Viewed according to Its Fundamental Movement and in Connection with the Religious, Moral, and Intellectual Life.* Translated by George Robson and Sophia Taylor. New York, 1970.

Dovnar-Zapol'skii, Mitrofan. *Idealy Dekabristov.* Moscow, 1907.

Drummond, Andrew. *German Protestantism since Luther.* Eugene, Ore., 1951.

Durov, Valerii. *Ordena rossiiskoi imperii.* Moscow, 2017.

Dziuba, Olena. "Ukraiintsi v evropeis'kykh mistakh (XVIII st.)." *Sotsium* (2003): 55–63.

Edwards, Otis. *A History of Preaching.* Nashville, Tenn., 2004.

Eijnatten, Joris van, ed. *Liberty and Concord in the United Provinces: Religious Tolera-tion and the Public in the Eighteenth-Century Netherlands.* Leiden, 2003.

———. *Preacher, Sermon and Audience in the Long Eighteenth Century: From Bossuet to Schleiermacher (1680–1815).* Leiden, 2009.

Eleonskii, Fedor. *Po povodu 150-letiia Elizavetinskoi Biblii: O novom peresmotre slavian. per. Biblii.* St. Petersburg, 1902.

Elert, Werner. *Law and Gospel.* Philadelphia, 1967.

Eliav-Feldon, Miriam, and Tamar Herzig, eds. *Dissimulation and Deceit in Early Mod-ern Europe.* Basingstoke, UK, 2015.

Eliseev, G. "Iz dalekogo proshlogo." *VE* 26 (1891): 282–312.

Erren, Lorenz. "Der Russische Hof nach Peter dem Großen 1725–1730." Mainz, 2018.

Esipov, Grigorii. *Liudi starogo veka: rasskazy iz del Preobrazhenskogo prikaza i Tainoi kantseliarii.* St. Petersburg, 1880.

Estes, James. *Peace, Order and the Glory of God: Secular Authority and the Church in the Thought of Luther and Melanchthon, 1518–1559.* Leiden, 2005.

Faggionato, Raffaella. *A Rosicrucian Utopia in Eighteenth-Century Russia: The Masonic Circle of N. I. Novikov.* Dordrecht, 2005.

Faivre, Antoine. *Eckarthausen et la théosophie chrétienne.* Paris, 1969.

Farrell, Maureen. *William Whiston.* New York, 1981.

Fedorov, Vladimir. *Soldatskoe dvizhenie nakanune vostaniia dekabristov, 1816–1825 gg.* Moscow, 1963.

Fedyukin, Igor. "The 'German' Reign of Empress Anna: Russia's Disciplinary Moment?" *Kritika* 19, no. 2 (2018): 363–84.

Fedyukin, Igor, Robert Collis, and Ernest Zitser. "Drinking Diplomacy: The St. Petersburg 'Ordre des Antisobres' and Fraternal Culture among European Envoys in Early Imperial Russia." *International History Review* (2019). DOI:10.1080/07075 332.2018.1541421.

Felmy, Karl. *Die Deutung der Göttlichen Liturgie in der russischen Theologie: Wege und Wandlungen russischer Liturgie-Auslegung.* Berlin, 1984.

———. *Die Orthodoxe Theologie der Gegenwart: Eine Einführung.* Darmstadt, 1990.

Feofan [Prokopovich]. *Kratkaia povest o smerti Petra Velikogo, imperatora rossiiskogo.* St. Petersburg, 1819.

Filaret [Gumilevskii]. *Obzor russkoi dukhovnoi literatury, 1862–1863.* 2 vols. St. Peters-burg, 1884.

Fitzmaurice-Kelly, James. *A History of Spanish Literature.* New York, 1898.

Fitzpatrick, Martin. "The Enlightenment, Politics and Providence: Some Scottish and English Comparisons." In *Enlightenment and Religion,* edited by Knud Haakons-sen, 64–98. Cambridge, 1996.

Florovskii, Georgii. *Puti russkogo bogosloviia.* 1991. Reprint, Minsk, 2006.

Florovsky, Georges. *Bible, Church, Tradition: An Eastern Orthodox View.* Belmont, Mass., 1972.

Force, James, and Richard Popkin. *Essays on the Context, Nature, and Influence of Isaac Newton's Theology.* Dordrecht, 1990.

Frazee, Charles. *Catholics and Sultans: The Church and the Ottoman Empire, 1453–1923.* Cambridge, 1983.

Freeze, Gregory. "Handmaiden of the State? The Church in Imperial Russia Reconsidered." *Journal of Ecclesiastical History* 36, no. 1 (1985): 82–102.

———. *The Parish Clergy in Nineteenth-Century Russia: Crisis, Reform, Counter-reform.* Princeton, N.J., 1983.

———. "Recent Scholarship on Russian Orthodoxy: A Critique." *Kritika* 2, no. 2 (2001): 269–78.

———. "Subversive Piety: Religion and the Political Crisis in Late Imperial Russia." *Journal of Modern History* 68, no. 2 (1996): 308–50.

Frick, David. *Meletij Smotryc'kyj.* Cambridge, Mass., 1995.

Friedeburg, Robert von. *Luther's Legacy: The Thirty Years War and the Modern Notion of "State" in the Empire, 1530s to 1790s.* Cambridge, 2006.

Frumenkova, Tatiana. "Tsifirnye i arkhiereiskie shkoly pervoi treti XVIII veka." *Voprosy istorii* (July 2003): 136–39.

Fundaminski, Mikhail. "The Communications Network of Halle Pietists in Russia." In *Foreign Churches in St. Petersburg and Their Archives, 1703–1917*, edited by Pieter N. Holtrop, 115–27. Leiden, 2007.

Galanakis, Emm, and Ioannis Dimoliatis. "Early European Attitudes towards 'Good Death': Eugenios Voulgaris, *Treatise on Euthanasia*, St Petersburg, 1804." *Medical Humanities* 33, no. 1 (June 2007): 1–4.

Gascoigne, "Latitudinarianism, Rational Dissent and Radicalism." In *Enlightenment and Religion*, edited by Knud Haakonssen, 219–40. Cambridge, 1996.

Geertz, Clifford. *The Interpretation of Cultures: Selected Essays.* New York, 1973.

"Geheimer Rat." In *Meyers Großes Konversations-Lexikon*, edited by Hermann Julius Meyer, 7:461–62. Leipzig, 1907.

Geiger, Max. *Aufklärung und Erweckung: Beiträge zur Erforschung Johann Heinrich Jung-Stillings und der Erwackungstheologie.* Zurich, 1963.

Geraci, Robert, and Michael Khodorkovsky. *Of Religion and Empire: Missions, Conversion, and Tolerance in Tsarist Russia.* Ithaca, N.Y., 2001.

Gericke, Wolfgang. *Theologie und Kirche im Zeitalter der Aufklärung.* Berlin, 1989.

Golburt, Luba. *The First Epoch: The Eighteenth Century and the Russian Cultural Imagination.* Madison, Wis., 2014.

Gorozhanskii, Iakov. *Damaskin Semenov-Rudnev, episkop Nizhegorodskii, 1737–1795: Ego zhizn' i trudy.* Kiev, 1894.

Green, Vivian. *A New History of Christianity.* New York, 1996.

Greene, Robert. *Bodies Like Bright Stars: Saints and Relics in Orthodox Russia.* DeKalb, Ill., 2009.

Greene, Robert, and Valerie Kivelson, eds. *Orthodox Russia: Belief and Practice under the Tsars.* University Park, Pa., 2003.

Gregory, Brad. *An Unintended Reformation: How a Religious Revolution Secularized Society.* Cambridge, Mass., 2012.

Grigor'ev, Anton. "Sochinenie metropolita riazanskogo i muromskogo Stefana Iavor-skogo." *Vestnik PSTGU: Bogoslovie* 38 (2011): 101–14.

———. "Sochinenie metropolita riazanskogo i muromskogo Stefana Iavorskogo . . . Izveshchenie glagolemykh ot Stefana Iavorskogo." *Vestnik PTSGU: Bogoslovie* 39 (2012): 87–113.

Gritsch, Eric. *A History of Lutheranism.* Minneapolis, 2002.

Gurvich, Georgii. *"Pravda voli monarshei" Feofana Prokopovicha i eia zapadnoevro-peiskie istochniki.* Iur'ev, 1915.

Haakonssen, Knud, ed. *Enlightenment and Religion: Rational Dissent in Eighteenth Century Britain.* Cambridge, 1996.

Hagenbach, Karl. *A History of Christian Doctrines.* Translated by E. H. Plumptre. Edinburgh, 1881.

Halfin, Igal. *From Darkness to Light: Class, Consciousness, and Salvation in Revolution-ary Russia.* Pittsburgh, Pa., 2000.

Harnack, Adolf von. *History of Dogma.* London, 1899.

Hatch, Nathan. *The Democratization of American Christianity.* New Haven, Conn., 1989.

Hauptmann, Peter. *Katechismen der Russisch-orthodoxe Kirche: Entstehungsgeschichte und Lehrgehalt.* Göttingen, 1971.

Headley, John, ed. *Confessionalization in Europe, 1555–1700: Essays in Honor and Mem-ory of Bodo Nischan.* Aldershot, 2004.

Hellbeck, Jochen. *Revolution on My Mind: Writing a Diary under Stalin.* Cambridge, Mass., 2009.

Hillerbrand, Hans J. "Reformation." In *Encyclopedia of Religion*, edited by Lindsay Jones, 7656–65. Detroit, 2005.

Hjärne, Harald. "Ett svenskt vittnesbörd om holsteinska partistämplingar i Ryssland." In *Historiska studier: Festskrift tillägnad Carl Gustaf Malmström*, 1–34. Stockholm, 1897.

Honecker, Martin. *Cura religionis magistratus Christiani: Studien zum Kirchenrecht im Luthertum des 17. Jahrhunderts.* Munich, 1968.

Hsia, Ronnie Po-Chia. *Social Discipline in the Reformation: Central Europe, 1550–1750.* New York, 1989.

Hughes, Lindsey. *Russia in the Age of Peter the Great.* New Haven, Conn., 1998.

Hunt, John. *Religious Thought in England, from the Reformation to the End of Last Cen-tury.* London, 1873.

Iaremenko, Maksym. *Kyivs'ke chernetstvo XVIII st.* Kyiv, 2007.

Ikonnikov, Vladimir. "Arsenii Matseevich." *RS* 25 (1879): 577–608, 731–52; 26 (1880): 1–35, 177–98.

"An Introduction to *Sinners in the Hands of an Angry God.*" Yale University Jonathan Edwards Center. Accessed July 12, 2019. http://edwards.yale.edu/files/Sinners%20 -%20Introduction.doc.

Israel, Jonathan. *Radical Enlightenment: Philosophy and the Making of Modernity, 1650–1750.* Oxford, 2001.

Ivanov, Andrey. "Escape from Rome: Feofan Prokopovych and Ukrainian Orthodox Ties to the Eternal City, 1650–1750." *Harvard Ukrainian Studies* 37 (2020): forthcoming.

———. "The Impact of Pietist and Anglican Spirituality in Catherinian Russia: The Works of St. Tikhon of Zadonsk." *Vivliofika* 5 (2017): 40–72.

———. "Reformation and the Muscovite Czar: Anti-Protestant Polemic in the Writings of Ivan the Terrible." *Sixteenth Century Journal* 40, no. 4 (Winter 2009): 1109–29.

———. "Reforming Orthodoxy: Russian Bishops and Their Church, 1721–1801." PhD diss., Yale University, 2012.

———. "The Saint of 'Russian Reformation': St. Tikhon of Zadonsk and the Protestant Influences in the Eighteenth-Century Russian Orthodox Church." In *Religion and National Identity in Russia and the Soviet Union: A Festschrift for Paul Bushkovich*, edited by Cathy Potter, Jennifer Spock, Nikolaos Chrissidis, 81–106. Bloomington, Ind., 2011.

Ivanova, Maria, and Michelle Viise. "Dissimulation and Memory in Early Modern Poland-Lithuania: The Art of Forgetting." *Slavic Review* 76, no. 1 (2017): 98–121.

Ivanovskii, Vladimir. *Russkoe zakonodatel'stvo XVIII i XIX vv. v svoikh postanovleniiakh otnositel'no monashestvuiushchikh lits i monastyrei: Opyt istoriko-kanonicheskago izsledovaniia.* Kharkov, 1905.

Izmozik, Vladlen. *Zhandarmy Rossii: Politicheskii rozysk v Rossii XV–XX vv.* Moscow, 2002.

Izvekov, Dmitrii. "Odin iz maloizvestnykh literaturnykh protivnikov Feofana Prokopovicha." *Pamiatniki novoi Russkoi istorii* 1 (1871): 1–11.

Jabłonowski, Aleksander. *Akademia Kijowsko-Mohylańska: Zarys Historyczny.* Kraków, 1899–1900.

Jones, Tod, ed. *The Cambridge Platonists: A Brief Introduction.* Dallas, 2005.

Jung-Stilling, Johann. *Das Heimweh: Vollständige, ungekürzte Ausgabe nach der Erstausgabe von 1794–1796.* Dornach, 1994.

Kapterev, Leonid. *Dubinshchina: Ocherk po istorii vosstaniia Dalmatovskikh monastyrskikh krest'ian v XVIII veke.* Ekaterinburg, 1924.

Kapterev, Nikolai. *Snosheniia Ierusalimskogo Patriarkha Dosifeiia s russkim pravitel'stvom, 1669–1707 gg.* Moscow, 1891.

Karatsuba, Irina. "'Dobro samo po sebe est' obshchitel'no': Mitropolit moskovskij Platon (Levshin) v besedakh s inostrantsami." In *Vera, Dialog, Obshchenie: Problemy dialoga v tserkvi; Materialy mezhdunarodnoi nauchnoi bogoslovskoi konferentsii, Moskva 24–26 sentiabria 2003 g.*, edited by Larisa Musina, 131–57. Moscow, 2004.

Karpuk, Dmitrii. "Dukhovnaia tsenzura: Osnovnye vekhi iz istorii komitetov v sinodal'nyi period." *Pravoslavnoe knizhnoe obozrenie* 36 (January 2014): 42–51.

Kartashev, Anton. *Ocherki po istorii russkoi tserkvi.* 2 vols. Paris, 1959.

Kashuba, Mariia. *Pamiatniki eticheskoi mysli na Ukraine XVII–pervoi poloviny XVIII st.* Kyiv, 1987.

Kasper, Peter. *Das Reichsstift Quedlinburg (936–1810).* Göttingen, 2014.

Katz, David. *Sabbath and Sectarianism in Seventeenth-Century England.* Leiden, 1988.

Kazanskii, Petr. "Otnosheniia mitropolita Platona k imperatritse Ekaterine i Pavlu I." *ChOIDR* 4 (1875): 175–97.

"K biografii preosv. Amvrosiia Iushkevicha." *Vologodskie eparkhial'nye vedomosti: Pribavleniia* 10 (1866): 389–94.

Kempa, Tomasz. *Wobec kontrreformacji: Protestanci i prawosławni w obronie swobód wyznaniowych w Rzeczypospolitej w końcu XVI i w pierwszej połowie XVII wieku.* Toruń, 2007.

Kenworthy, Scott. *The Heart of Russia: Trinity-Sergius, Monasticism, and Society after 1825.* Washington, D.C., 2010.

Kharlampovich, Konstantin. *Malorossiiskoe vliianie na velikorusskuiu tserkovnuiu zhizn'.* Kazan, 1914.

Khyzhniak, Zoia. "Kyevo-Mohylians´ka akademiia ta ukraiins´ko-nimets´ki kul´turni zv'iazky." *Naukovi zapysky KMA* 18 (2000): 12–24.

———. "Liashchevs'kyi, Varlaam." In Briukhovets'kyi and Khyzhniak, *Kyievo-Mohylians'ka akademiia,* 338–41.

———. "Nashchyns'kyi, Danylo." In Briukhovets'kyi and Khyzhniak, *Kyievo-Mohylians'ka akademiia,* 386–87.

———. "Todors'kyi, Symon." In Briukhovets'kyi and Khyzhniak, *Kyievo-Mohylians'ka akademiia,* 535–36.

———. "Zaborovs'kyi, Rafaiil." In Briukhovets'kyi and Khyzhniak, *Kyievo-Mohylians'ka akademiia,* 213–14.

Kirchner, Walther. "Death of Catherine I." *AHR* 51, no. 2 (1946): 254–61.

Kislova, Ekaterina. "Frantsuzskii iazyk v russkikh seminariiakh XVIII veka." *Vestnik PSTGU: Filologiia* 44, no. 4 (2015): 16–34.

———. "Propoved' Simona Todorskogo 'Bozhie osoboe blagoslovenie . . .' i brakoso-chetanie Petra Fedorovicha i Ekateriny Alekseevny." *Literaturnaia kul'tura Rossii XVIII veka* (March 2009): 115–38.

———. "Slovo v den' iavleniia ikony Presv. Bogoroditsy Dmitriia Sechenova." *Literaturnaia kul'tura Rossii XVIII veka* (April 2011): 110–47.

Kitromilides, Paschalis. "The Enlightenment and the Greek Cultural Tradition." *History of European Ideas* 36, no. 1 (2010): 39–46.

———. *Enlightenment, Nationalism, Orthodoxy: Studies in the Culture and Political Thought of Southeastern Europe.* Aldershot, 1994.

Kizenko, Nadieszda. *A Prodigal Saint: Father John of Kronstadt and the Russian People.* University Park, Penn., 2000.

Kloes, Andrew. *The German Awakening: Protestant Renewal after the Enlightenment, 1815–1848.* Oxford, 2019.

Kniazev, Aleksandr. *Ocherk istorii Pskovskoi seminarii ot nachala do preobrazovaniia ee po proektu ustava 1814 goda.* Moscow, 1866.

Koch, Hans. *Die russische Orthodoxie im Petrinischen Zeitalter, im Beitrag zur Geschichte westlicher Einflüsse auf das ostslavische Denken.* Breslau, 1929.

Kochetkova, Nataliia. "Teplov." In *Slovar' russkikh pisatelei XVIII veka,* 3rd ed., edited by A. Panchenko, 229–34. St. Petersburg, 2010.

Kolb, Robert. *Lutheran Ecclesiastical Culture, 1550–1675.* Leiden, 2008.

Komissarenko, Arkadii. *Russkii Absoliutizm i dukhovenstvo v XVIII veke: Ocherki istorii sekuliarizatsionnoi reformy 1764 g.* Moscow, 1990.

Kondakov, Ivan. *Svodnyi katalog russkoi knigi grazhdanskoi pechati XVIII veka.* 5 vols. Moscow, 1962–65.

Kondakov, Iurii. *Dukhovno-relioznaia politika Aleksandra I i russkaia pravoslavnaia oppozitsiia, 1801–1825.* St. Petersburg, 1998.

———. *Liberal'noe i konservativnoe napravleniia v religioznykh dvizheniiakh v Rossii pervoi chetverti XIX veka.* St. Petersburg, 2005.

Korsakov, Dmitrii. *Votsarenie imperatritsy Anny Ioannovny.* Kazan, 1880.

Korsunskii, Ivan. *Filaret, mitropolit moskovskii v svoikh Katekhizisakh.* Moscow, 1883.

Korzo, Margarita. "Katekheticheskie sochineniia Feofana Prokopovicha." *Slavianskii al'manakh* (2013): 263–80.

———. "O protestantskikh vliianiiakh deistvitel'nykh i mnimykh: Pravoslavnye katekhizisy ot Stefana Zizaniia do Feofana Prokopovicha." *Vivliofika* 5 (2017): 5–17.

———. "Sintez kul'turnykh i religioznykh tradititsii v shkol'nykh katekhizisakh XVII–XVIII vv." *Filosofiia i ku'tura* 73 (January 2014): 99–107.

———. *Ukrainskaia i belorusskaia katekheticheskaia traditsiia kontsa XVI–XVIII vv.* Moscow, 2007.

Kotkin, Stephen. *Magnetic Mountain: Stalinism as a Civilization.* Berkeley, 1997.

———. *Stalin: The Paradoxes of Power, 1878–1928.* Vol. 1. New York, 2014.

Kotovich, Aleksei. *Dukhovnaia tsenzura v Rossii (1799–1855).* St. Petersburg, 1909.

Kozlov, Ivan. "Cherty iz zhizni Mitropolita Filareta." *Pushkinskaia epokha i khristianskaia kul'tura* 14, no. 6 (1995): 74–86.

Krashennikova, Olga. "Podmetnoe pis'mo 1732 goda—vydaiushchiisia pamiatnik russkoi publitsistiki XVIII v." *Vestnik slavianskikh kul'tur* 38 (December 2015): 81–97.

Kravtsov, Il'ia. "Tserkovnyi antiklerikalizm v pravoslavnoi Rossii kontsa XIX–XX vekov." *Vestnik Russkoi Khristianskoi Akademii* 15, no. 2 (2014): 190–98.

Krinitskii, Nikolai. *Tverskie Arkhipastyri, revniteli dukhovnogo prosveshcheniia v XVIII v.* Tver, 1887.

Krupnyts'kyi, Borys. "Teofan Prokopovych i shvedy." *Zapysky Chyna sv. Vasyliia Velykoho* 4 (1934): 295–310.

Kryzhanovskii, E. "Feofan Prokopovich i Varlaam Vanatovich." *TKDA* 3 (1861): 267–315.

Kudriavtseva, Olga. "Iz istorii pskovskikh arkhiereiskikh bibliotek XVIII v. (knizhnye sobraniia Gedeona Krinovskogo i Innokentiia Nechaeva)." In *Materialy Pervykh Pskovskikh arkhivnykh chtenii,* edited by O. V. Fedotov, 154–59. Pskov, 2007.

Kuhn, Thomas. *Religion und neuzeitliche Gesellschaft: Studien zum sozialen und diakonischen Handeln in Pietismus, Aufklärung und Erweckungsbewegung.* Tübingen, 2003.

Kuliabko, E. S. "Nauchnye sviazi Zh.-L. Biuffona s Peterburgskoi Akademiei Nauk." In *Frantsuzskii ezhegodnik: Stat'i i materialy po istorii Frantsii, 1971,* edited by A. Z. Manfred, 282–86. Moscow, 1973.

Kurukin, Igor. *Epokha "dvorskikh bur'": Ocherki politicheskoi istorii poslepetrovskoi Rossii, 1725–1762 gg.* Riazan, 2003.

Kutsenko, Nataliia. "Rossiiskie bogoslovy." *Istoriia filosofii* 6 (2000): 146–54.

Lachmann, Renate. *Feofan Prokopovic: De Arte Rhetorica Libri X Kijoviae 1706.* Cologne, 1982.

Lavrov, Aleksandr. *Koldovstvo i religiia v Rossii: 1700–1740.* Moscow, 2000.

Lebedev, Amfian. "Khar'kovskii Kollegium kak prosvetitel'nyi tsentr." *ChIOIDR* 4 (1885): 1–103.

LeDonne, John. *Absolutism and Ruling Class: The Formation of the Russian Political Order, 1700–1825.* New York, 1991.

Lehmann, Roland. *Die Transformation des Kirchenbegriffs in der Frühaufklärung.* Tübingen, 2013.

Lehner, Ulrich. *The Catholic Enlightenment: The Forgotten History of a Global Movement.* New York, 2016.

———. *Enlightened Monks: The German Benedictines, 1740–1803.* New York, 2011.

———, ed. *The Oxford Handbook of Early Modern Theology, 1600–1800.* New York, 2016.

Leonard, Carol. *Reform and Regicide: The Reign of Peter III in Russia.* Bloomington, Ind., 1993.

Leonid [Tolmachev]. "Mitropolit Platon v vospominaniiakh angliiskikh puteshestvennikov." *Platonovskie chteniia* (2013): 25–40.

Lexutt, Athina. *Die Reformation: Ein Ereignis macht Epoche.* Cologne, 2009.

Ley, Francis. *Alexandre Ier et sa Sainte-Alliance: 1811–1825, avec ses documents inédits.* Paris, 1975.

Liechtenhan, Francine-Dominique. *La Russie entre en Europe: Elisabeth 1re et la succession d'Autriche (1740–1750).* Paris, 1997.

Lindberg, Carter. *European Reformations.* Oxford, 1996.

Liubarskii, Platon. *Sbornik Drevnostei Kazanskoi eparkhii i drugikh prisnopamiatnykh obstoiatel'stv, staraniem i trudami Spasokazanskogo Preobrazhenskogo monastyria arkhimandrita Platona sostavlennyi, 1782 goda.* Kazan, 1868.

Liut'ko, Evgenii. "Mitropolit Platon i episkopat vtoroi poloviny Aleksandrovskogo tsarstvovaniia." In *Materialy VIII mezhdunarodnoi konferentsii,* 240–45. St. Petersburg, 2016.

Longinov, Mikhail. *Novikov i Moskovskie Martinisty.* Moscow, 1867.

Longworth, Philip. *The Three Empresses: Catherine I, Anne and Elizabeth of Russia.* New York, 1973.

Los'kyi, Ihor. "Ukraiintsi na studiiakh v Nimechchyni XVI–XVIII st." *Zapysky Naukovoho Tovarystva im. Shevchenka* 151 (1931): 99–100.

Louthan, Howard, and Graeme Murdoch, eds. *A Companion to the Reformation in Central Europe.* Leiden, 2015.

L'vov, Aleksandr. "Pervoe uchenie otrokom i genesis russkogo sektanstva." *Russkaia literatura* 1 (2008): 159–70.

Lytvynov, Volodymyr. *Ideii rann'oho prosvitnytstva u filosofs'kii dumtsi Ukrainy.* Kyiv, 1984.

Mackridge, Peter. *Language and National Identity in Greece, 1766-1976.* Oxford, 2010.

Mainberger, Gonsalv. *Die französische Gelehrtenrepublik zur Zeit der Frühaufklärung: Fromme Denker und radikale Reformer.* Würzburg, 2016.

Makarii [Miroliubov]. *Istoriia nizhegorodskoi ierarkhii soderzhashchaia v sebe skazanie o nizhegorodskikh ierarkhakh s 1672 do 1850 goda.* St. Petersburg, 1857.

———. "Izvlechenie iz sledstvennogo dela o Tverskom Arkhiepiskope Feofilakte Lopatinskom." *ChIOIDR* 4 (1863): 52–73.

Makarov, G. "O perevodnom pamiatnike karel'skogo iazyka." *Trudy Karel'skogo Filiala Akademii Nauk SSSR* 29 (1963): 70–79.

Malia, Martin. *Russia under Western Eyes: From the Bronze Horseman to the Lenin Mausoleum.* Cambridge, Mass., 1999.

Malvy, Antoine and Marcel Viller, eds. *La Confession Orthodoxe de Pierre Moghila métropolite de Kiev (1633–1646) approuvée par les Patriarches grecs du XVIIe siècle.* Rome, 1927.

Manchester, Laurie. *Holy Fathers, Secular Sons: Clergy, Intelligentsia and the Modern Self in Revolutionary Russia.* DeKalb, Ill., 2008.

Manning, David. "Reformation and the Wickedness of Port Royal, Jamaica 1655–1692." In *Puritans and Catholics in the Trans-Atlantic World 1600–1800*, edited by Crawford Gribben and Scott Spurlock, 131–63. New York, 2015.

Marchenko, Vasilii. "Zapiska stats-sekretaria tainogo sovetnika Marchenko." In *Istoricheskii sbornik vol'noi russkoi tipografii v Londone*, book 1, 61–79. London, 1861.

Marker, Gary. *Imperial Saint: The Cult of St. Catherine and the Dawn of Female Rule in Russia.* DeKalb, Ill., 2007.

Markovskii, Mikhail. *Antonii Radivilovskii: Iuzhno-russkii propovednik XVII v.* Kiev, 1894.

Marshall, Peter, ed. *Oxford Illustrated History of the Reformation.* Oxford, 2015.

Martin, Alexander. *Enlightened Metropolis: Constructing Imperial Moscow, 1762–1855.* Oxford, 2013.

———. *Romantics, Reformers, Reactionaries: Russian Conservative Thought and Politics in the Reign of Alexander I.* DeKalb, Ill., 1997.

Maslov, Sergei. *Biblioteka Stefana Iavorskogo.* Kiev, 1914.

Matseevich, Lev. "Polskii propovednik Foma Mlodzianovskii." *TKDA* 4 (1870): 108–53; 9 (1870): 457–566.

Matushek, Olena. *Propovidi Lazaria Baranovycha v dyskursi ukrains'koho Baroko.* Kharkiv, 2013.

Matviishyn [Matwiiszyn], Iaroslav. "Feofan Prokopovych i Astronomiia." In *Ukrains'ke nebo: Studii nad istorieu astronomii v Ukraini*, edited by Oleh Petruk, 534–605. L'viv, 2014.

———. "Idee Kopernika na Ukrainie." *Kwartalnik historii nauki i techniki* 19 (1974): 657–76.

McGinness, Frederick J. "Preaching Ideals and Practice in Counter-Reformation Rome." *Sixteenth Century Journal* 11, no. 2 (Summer 1980): 109–27.

McGrath, Alister. *Reformation Thought: An Introduction.* Oxford, 1999.

Mel'nikov, P. "Iz proshlogo." *RV* 74 (1868): 438–513.

Mel'nikova, Liubov. *Armiia i pravoslavnaia tserkov v epokhu napoleonovskikh voin.* Moscow, 2007.

Men', Aleksandr. *Bibliologicheskii slovar'.* Moscow, 2002.

Mervaud, Michel. "Introduction." In *La religion, les mœurs, et les usages des moscovites*, by Jacques Jubé, edited by Michel Mervaud, 1–78. Oxford, 1992.

Metzger, Bruce. *The Early Versions of the New Testament: Their Origin, Transmission, and Limitations.* Oxford, 1977.

Michels, Georg. "From Persecuted Minority to Confessional Church: Some Thoughts on the Near Extinction and Ultimate Survival of Old Belief (1650s–1730s)." *Canadian-American Slavic Studies* 49, nos. 2–3 (2015): 322–37.

Michelson, Patrick. *Beyond the Monastery Walls: The Ascetic Revolution in Russian Orthodox Thought, 1814–1914.* Madison, Wis., 2017.

Michelson, Patrick, and Judith Kornblatt, eds. *Thinking Orthodox in Modern Russia: Culture, History, Context.* Madison, Wis., 2014.

Mikhailov, Maksim. "Metropolit Platon (Levshin) i Sviashchennoe Pisanie." *Platonovskie chteniia* (2007): 37–40.

Miliutin, Vladimir. *O nedvizhimykh imushchetsvakh dukhovenstva v Rossii.* St. Petersburg, 1859.

Moiseeva, Galina. "Ioil' (Bykovskii)." In *Entsiklopediia "Slova o polku Igoreve,"* 2:302–4. St. Petersburg, 1995.

"Moisei Gumilevskii." *RS* (March 1888): 799–800.

Mokshina, Elena. "Rol' russkoi pravoslavnoi tserkvi v podgotovke i provedenii krest'ianskoi reformy 1861 g." *Sotsial'no-politicheskie nauki* (January 2011): 170–76.

Morev, Ivan. *"Kamen' very" mitropolita Stefana Iavorskago: Ego mesto sredi otechestvennykh protivoprotestantskikh sochinenii i kharakteristicheskiia osobennosti ego dogmaticheskikh vozzrenii.* St. Petersburg, 1904.

Morokhin, Aleksei. *Arkhiepiskop Nizhegorodskii i Alatyrskii Pitirim: Tserkovnyi deiatel' epokhi peremen.* Nizhnii Novgorod, 2009.

Moroshkin, Ivan. "Feodosii Ianovskii, arkhiep. Novgorodskii." *RS* 47 (1887): 275–86.

———. "Feofilakt Lopatinskii, Episkop Tverskoi." *RS* 46 (1886): 1–98, 265–92.

Morozov, Petr. *Feofan Prokopovich kak pisatel': Ocherk iz istorii russkoi literatury v epokhu preobrazovaniia.* St. Petersburg, 1880.

Mushketov, Ivan, and Andrei Orlov. *Katalog zemletriasenii Rossiiskoi imperii.* St. Petersburg, 1893.

Nadezhdin, Aleksandr. "Platon Levshin Metropolit Moskovskii kak Propovednik." *PS* 2 (1882–83): 2–54.

"Neskol'ko tsifr iz statistiki russkoi tserkvi." *TKDA* 2 (1867): 182–200.

Netzhammer, Raymund. *Das griechische Kolleg in Rom.* Salzburg, 1905.

Nevskaia, Nina. "Pervyi disput v zashchitu ucheniia Kopernika." In *Nikolai Kopernik 1473–1973,* edited by V. Kotel'nikov, 124–30. Moscow, 1973.

Nichols, Robert. "Metropolitan Filaret of Moscow and the Awakening of Orthodoxy." PhD diss., University of Washington, 1972.

———. "Orthodox Spirituality in Imperial Russia: St. Seraphim of Sarov and the Awakening of Orthodoxy." *Modern Greek Studies Yearbook* 16/17 (2000–2001): 19–42.

Nichyk, Valeriia. *Feofan Prokopovich.* Moscow, 1977.

———. "Filosofiia v Kyevomohylians'kii akademii—Stefan Kalynovs'kyi." *Filosofs'ka dumka* (March 1969): 78–91.

———. *Kyevo-Mohylians'ka akademiia i nimets'ka kul'tura.* Kyiv, 2001.

———. "Kyevo-Mohylians'ka akademiia ta ukraiins'ko-nimets'ki kul'turni zv'iazky." *Naukovi zapysky KMA* 18 (2000): 12–24.

———. *Symon Todors'kyi i hebraistyka v Kyevo-Mohylians'kii Akademii.* Kyiv, 2002.

Niebergall, Alfred. "Der Geschichte der Christlichen Predigt." In *Leiturgia: Handbuch des Evangelischen Gottesdienstes,* edited by Karl Ferdinand Mueller and Walter Blankenburg, 2:306–15. Kassel, 1955.

Niess, Hans. *Kirche in Russland zwischen Tradition und Glaube?: Eine Untersuchung der Kirillova kniga und der Kniga o vere aud der 1. Hälfte des 17. Jahrhunderts.* Göttingen, 1977.

Nikolskii, Nikolai. *Istoriia russkoi tserkvi.* Moscow, 1985.

Noll, Mark. *America's God: from Jonathan Edwards to Abraham Lincoln.* Oxford, 2002.

———. *The Rise of Evangelicalism: The Age of Edwards, Whitefield and the Wesleys.* Downers Grove, Ill., 2003.

Norman, Corrie. "The Social History of Preaching: Italy." In *Preachers and People in the Reformations and Early Modern Period,* edited by Larissa Taylor, 125–62. Leiden, 2001.

Obolevitch, Teresa. "Galileo in the Russian Orthodox Context: History, Philosophy, Theology and Science." *Journal of Religion and Science* 50, no. 4 (December 2015): 788–808.

Oksman, Iurii, ed. *Dekabristy: Neizdannye materialy i stat'i.* Moscow, 1925.

Old, Hugh Oliphant. *The Reading and Preaching of the Scriptures in the Worship of the Christian Church: Moderatism, Pietism and Awakening.* Vol. 5. Grand Rapids, Mich., 2004.

Olin, John. *The Catholic Reformation: From Savonarola to Ignatius Loyola.* New York, 1969.

O'Malley, John. *Trent and All That: Renaming Catholicism in the Early Modern Era.* Cambridge, Mass., 2002.

Oparina, Tatiana. *Ivan Nasedka i polemicheskoe bogoslovie kievskoi metropolii.* Novosibirsk, 1998.

Orlov, Aleksandr. "Lankasterskie shkoly v Rossii v nachale XIX v." *Vestnik MGGU* 2 (2013): 11–16.

Ospovat, Kirill. "Kazn' avtora: Delo A. P. Volynskogo 'absoliutizm' i problema politicheskoi slovesnosti v 1740 godu." *Novoe literaturnoe obozrenie* 151 (2018): 143–63.

Paert, Irina. *Old Believers, Religious Dissent, and Gender in Russia, 1760–1850.* Manchester, 2003.

———. *Spiritual Elders: Charisma and Tradition in Russian Orthodoxy.* DeKalb, Ill., 2010.

Palkin, Aleksandr. *Edinoverie v seredine XVIII–nachale XX veka: Obshcherossiiskii kontekst i regional'naia spetsifika.* Ekaterinburg, 2016.

Panchenko, Aleksandr. *Russkaia istoriia i kul'tura: Raboty raznykh let.* St. Petersburg, 1999.

Panzer, Marita. *Die Große Landgräfin Caroline von Hessen-Darmstadt.* Regensburg, 2005.

Papmehl, Karl. *Metropolitan Platon of Moscow (Petr Levshin, 1737–1812): The Enlightened Prelate, Scholar and Educator.* Newtonville, MA, 1983.

Parker, Charles, and Jerry Bentley. *Between the Middle Ages and Modernity: Individual and Community in the Early Modern World.* Lanham, Md., 2007.

"Pastor Vigand: Ego zhizn' i deiatel'nost' v Rossii, 1764–1808." *RS* 74 (1892): 551–52, 567.

Paz y Melia, Antonio, ed. *Conquista de Nápoles y Sicilia y Relación de Moscovia por el duque de Berwick.* Madrid, 1890.

Pelikan, Jaroslav. *The Reformation of the Bible: The Bible of the Reformation.* New Haven, Conn., 1996.

Pekarskii, P. P. *Istoriia Imperatorskoi akademii nauk v Peterburge.* 2 vols. St. Petersburg, 1870–73.

———. *Nauka i literatura v Rossii pri Petre Velikom.* 2 vols. St. Petersburg, 1862.

———. "Predstaviteli Kievskoi uchenosti v pervoi polovine XVII veka." *Otechestvennye zapiski* (February 1862): 570–90.

Pestana, Carla Gardina. *Protestant Empire: Religion and the Making of the British Atlantic World.* Philadelphia, 2009.

Petrov, Nikolai. "Iz istorii gomiletiki staroi Kievskoi akademii." *TKDA* 1 (1866): 86-124.

———. *Opisanie rukopisei tserkovno-arkheologicheskogo muzeia pri Kievskoi Dukhovnoi Akademii.* Kiev, 1875.

———. "Vyderzhki iz rukopisnoi retoriki F. Prokopovicha, soderzhashchie v sebe izobrazheniia papistov i iezuitov." *TKDA* 4 (1865): 614–37.

Petrov, Petr. *Istoriia Sankt-Peterburga s osnovaniia goroda.* St. Petersburg, 1885.

Petrukhintsev, Nikolai. *Tsarstvovanie Anny Ioannovny: Formirovanie vnutripoliticheskogo kursa i sud'by armii i flota 1730–1735 g.* St. Petersburg, 2001.

Pettegree, Andrew, ed. *The Reformation World.* London, 2000.

Pevnitskii, Vasilii. "Gomiletika Erazma Rotterdamskogo." *TKDA* 3 (1894): 317–42; 7 (1894): 426–48; 8 (1894): 491–525.

———. "Propovednicheskie trudy pokoinogo metropolita kievskogo Evgeniia." *TKDA* 3 (1867): 522–79; 4 (1867): 5–51.

Pirie, Valérie. *The Triple Crown: An Account of Papal Conclaves from the Fifteenth Century to the Present Day.* London, 1935.

Pirillo, Diego. *The Refugee-Diplomat: Venice, England, and the Reformation.* Ithaca, N.Y., 2018.

Plimak, Evgenii. "Osnovnye etapy v razvitii russkogo Prosveshcheniia." In *Problemy russkogo prosveshcheniia v literature XVIII v*, edited by Pavel Berkov, 126–33. Leningrad, 1961.

Podskalsky, Gerhard. *Griechische Theologie in der Zeit der Türkenherrschaft (1453–1821): Die Orthodoxie im Spannnungsfeld der nachreformatorischen Konfessionen des Westens.* Munich, 1988.

Pokrovskii, Nikolai. "Bor'ba s protestantskimi ideiami v petrovskoe vremia." *RV* (September 1872): 223–31.

———. "Feofilakt Lopatinskii." *PO* (December 1872): 684–710.

Popov, M. S. *Arsenii Matseevich i ego delo.* St. Petersburg, 1912.

Praz, Mario. *Studies in Seventeenth-Century Imagery.* Vol. 1. Rome, 1974.

Prokop'ev, Andrei. "Pogrebenie Petra Velikogo: Protestantskii standart v pravoslavnoi Rossii." In *Severnaia voina, Sankt-Peterburg i Evropa v pervoi chetverti XVIII v.,* edited by V. E. Vozgrin, 47–67. St. Petersburg, 2007.

Pushkin, Alexander. *Alexander Pushkin: Epigrams and Satirical Verse.* Edited by Cynthia H. Whittaker. Ann Arbor, Mich., 1984.

Pyliaev, Mikhail. *Zabytoe proshloe okrestnostei Peterburga.* St. Petersburg, 1889.

Pypin, Aleksandr. *Istoriia russkoi literatury.* 4 vols. St. Petersburg, 1907.

———— *Obshchestvennoe dvizhenie v Rossii pri Aleksandre I*. St. Petersburg, 1885.

————. "Rossiiskoe bibleiskoe obshchestvo: 1812–1826." *VE* 3, no. 8 (1868): 639–712.

————. *Russkoe masonstvo*. Petrograd, 1916.

Raeff, Marc. "The Enlightenment in Russia and Russian Thought in the Enlightenment." In *The Eighteenth Century in Russia*, edited by J. G. Garrard, 25–47. Oxford, 1973.

————. "The Well-Ordered Police State and the Development of Modernity in Seventeenth- and Eighteenth-Century Europe: An Attempt at a Comparative Approach." *American Historical Review* 80, no. 5 (1975): 1221–43.

————. *The Well-Ordered Police State: Social and Institutional Change through Law in the Germanies and Russia, 1600–1800*. New Haven, Conn., 1983.

Ramazanova, Dzhamilia. "Ekzempliary sochinenii ierusalimskogo patriarkha Khrisanfa Notara." In *Vivliofika: Istoriia knigi i izuchenie knizhnykh pamiatnikov*, edited by A. Iu. Samarin, 2:166–86. Moscow, 2011.

Ramsey, Paul, ed. *Ethical Writings*. Vol. 8 of *The Works of Jonathan Edwards*. New Haven, Conn., 1989.

Reid-Maroney, Nina. *Philadelphia's Enlightenment 1740–1800: Kingdom of Christ, Empire of Reason*. Westport, Conn., 2000.

Riazhev, Andrei. *"Prosveshchennyi absoliutizm" i staroobriadtsy: Vtoraia polovina XVIII– nachalo XIX v.* Tol'iatti, 2006.

Rivers, Isabel. "John Tillotson." In *Oxford Dictionary of National Biography*. Oxford, 2004. Accessed April 18, 2012. http://www.oxforddnb.com/view/article/27449.

Rizhskii, Mikhail (Moisei). *Istoriia perevodov Biblii v Rossii*. Novosibirsk, 1978.

Robson, Roy. *Old Believers in Modern Russia*. DeKalb, Ill., 1996.

Rolland, Peter. "'Nieskoro' prawi 'munsztuk do tych trąb otrzymacie': On Lazar Baranovych's *Truby sloves propovidnyx* and Their Non-publication in Moscow." *HUS* 17, nos. 1–2 (1992): 205–16.

Rosa, Mario. *Settecento religioso: Politica della ragione e religione del cuore*. Venice, 1999.

Rozanov, Nikolai. *Moskovskii mitropolit Platon, 1737–1812*. St. Petersburg, 1913.

Rudolph, Oliver-Pierre. *Christian Wolff und die europäische Aufklärung*. Hildesheim, 2007.

Rublack, Ulinka. *Reformation Europe*. Cambridge, 2005.

Rukavitsyna-Hordziivska, Ievheniia. *Kyivs'kyi mytropolyt Ievhenii*. Kyiv, 2010.

Runkevich, Stefan. *Arkhierei petrovskoi epokhi v ikh perepiske s Petrom Velikim*. St. Petersburg, 1906.

————. *Uchrezhdenie i pervonachal'noe ustroistvo Sviateishego Pravitel'stvuiushchego Sinoda (1721–1725)*. Vol. 1. St. Petersburg, 1900.

Ryndziunskii, Pavel. "Antitserkovnoe dvizhenie v Tambovskom kraie v 60-e gody XVIII v." *Voprosy istorii religii i ateizma* 2 (1954): 154–93.

Samarin, Iurii. *Stefan Iavorskii i Feofan Prokopovich kak propovedniki*. Moscow, 1844.

————. *Stefan Iavorskii i Feofan Prokopovich*. Moscow, 1880.

Savelov, Leonid. *Savelkovy i Savelovy XV–XX vv.: Rodoslovie*. Moscow, 1914.

Sawatsky, Walter. "Prince Alexander N. Golitsyn (1773–1844), Tsarist Minister of Piety." PhD diss., University of Minnesota, 1976.

Schaff, Philip. *The New Schaff-Herzog Encyclopedia of Religious Knowledge.* 13 vols. Grand Rapids, Mich., 1952–63.

———. *Theological Propaedeutic: A General Introduction to the Study of Theology, Exegetical, Historical, Systematic, and Practical.* New York, 1907.

Schloemann, Martin. *Siegmund Jacob Baumgarten: System und Geschichte in der Theologie des Übergangs zum Neuprotestantismus.* Göttingen, 1974.

Semevskii, Vasilii. *Krest'iane v tsartstvovanie Imperatritsy Ekateriny II.* Vol. 2. St. Petersburg, 1906.

Serkov, Andrei. *Russkoe Masonstvo, 1731–2000.* Moscow, 2001.

Shantz, Douglas. *A Companion to German Pietism, 1660–1800.* Boston, 2014.

Shchegolev, Nikolai. "Primechanie ot Izdatelia." Comment on "Slova Varlaama Liashchevskogo." *TKDA* 12 (1866): 380–81, 458, 463–64.

Shcherbatov, Mikhail. *O povrezhdenii nravov v Rossii.* Moscow, 1984.

Shchukin, Vasilii. "Simon (Todorskii): Arkhiepiskop Pskovskii i Narvskii." *Pskovskie eparkhial'nye vedomosti: Chast' neofitsial'naia* (February 1898): 53–57; (April 1898): 72–77.

Sheehan, Jonathan. *The Enlightenment Bible: Translation, Scholarship, Culture.* Princeton, N.J., 2005.

Sheremet'evskii, Vladimir. *Famil'nye prozvischa velikorusskogo dukhovenstva v XVIII i XIX st.* Moscow, 1908.

Shevelov, Iurii [George]. *Two Orthodox Ukrainian Churchmen: Teofan Prokopovych and Stefan Iavors'kyi.* Cambridge, Mass., 1985.

Shevzov, Vera. *Russian Orthodoxy on the Eve of the Revolution.* New York, 2004.

Shliapkin, Il'ia. "O polemike mezhdu moskovskimi i malorusskimi uchenymi." *ZhMNP* 212 (October 1885): 210–52.

Shmurlo, Evgenii. *Mitropolit Evgenii kak uchenyi: Rannie gody zhizni 1767–1804.* St. Petersburg, 1888.

Shpet, Gustav. *Ocherk razvitiia russkoi filosofii.* Petrograd, 1922.

Shubinskii, Sergei. "Graf Osterman." *Severnoe Siianie* 2 (1863): 400–475.

Silano, Francesca. "'In the Language of the Patriarch': Patriarch Tikhon, the Soviet State, and the Orthodox Church, 1865–1925." PhD diss., University of Toronto, 2017.

Skinner, Barbara. "Russia's Scriptural 'Reformation' in the Late Eighteenth and Early Nineteenth Centuries." *Vivliofika* 5 (2017): 73–102.

———. *The Western Front of the Eastern Church: Uniate and Orthodox Conflict in Eighteenth-Century Poland, Ukraine, Belarus, and Russia.* DeKalb, Ill., 2009.

Smirnov, Sergei. *Istoriia Moskovskoi dukhovnoi akademii do eia preobrazovaniia, 1814–1870.* Moscow, 1879.

———. *Istoriia Troitskoi lavrskoi seminarii.* Moscow, 1867.

Smirnova, A. *Knigi grazhdanskoi pechati v sobranii Kirillo-Belozerskogo muzeia-zapovednika.* Vologda, 2015. e-book. https://kirmuseum.org/sites/default/files/ebook/2018/1015_file.pdf.

Smith, Alison. *For the Common Good: Social Estates in Imperial Russia.* New York, 2014.

Smith, Hilary. *Preaching in the Spanish Golden Age: A Study of Some Preachers of the Reign of Philip III.* New York, 1978.

Smolitsch, Igor. *Geschichte der Russischen Kirche 1700–1917.* Leiden, 1964–91.

———. *Russkoe monashestvo 988–1917*. Moscow, 1997.

Snegirev, Ivan. *Zhizn' moskovskago mitropolita Platona*. Moscow, 1890–91.

Soldatov, Georgii. *Arsenii Matseevich, Mitropolit Rostovskii*. St. Paul, 1971.

Solonin, Iurii. "Dukhovenstvo v russkom prosveshchenii." *Veche: Al'manakh russkoi filosofii i kul'tury* 18 (2007): 46–129.

Solov'ev, Sergei. *Istoriia Rossii s drevneishikh vremen*. 29 vols. Moscow, 1959–66.

Sorkin, David. *The Religious Enlightenment: Protestants, Jews, and Catholics from London to Vienna*. Princeton, N.J., 2008.

Spitz, Lewis. "Luther's Ecclesiology and His Concept of the Prince as Notbischof." *Church History* 22, no. 2 (1953): 113–41.

Sprunger, Keith. "Ames, William (1576–1633)." *Oxford Dictionary of National Biography*. Oxford, 2004. Accessed 18 April 2012. http://www.oxforddnb.com/view/article/440.

Stein, Stephen. *The Encyclopedia of Apocalypticism*. Vol. 3, *Apocalypticism in the Modern Period and the Contemporary Age*. London, 1998.

Steinberg, Mark. "Workers on the Cross: Religious Imagination in the Writings of Russian Workers, 1910–1924." *Russian Review* 53, no. 2 (April 1994): 213–39.

Stephens, W. Peter, ed. *The Bible, the Reformation and the Church*. Sheffield, 1995.

Stratii, Iaroslava. "Hryhorii Shcherbats'kyi i Kartezianstvo v Kyevo-Mohilianskii akademii." In *Relihiino-filosofs'ka dumka v Kyevo-Mohylians'kii akademii: Evropeis'kyi kontekst*, edited by V. S. Hors'kyi, 152–74. Kyiv, 2002.

———. *Opisanie kursov filosofii i retoriki professorov Kievo-Mogilianskoi akademii*. Kyiv, 1982.

Stroev, Pavel. *Spiski ierarkhov i nastoiatelei monastyrei rossiiskoi tserkvi*. St. Petersburg, 1877.

Stupperich, Robert. "Feofan Prokopovič und Johann Franz Buddeus." *ZfOG* 9 (1935): 341–62.

———. "Feofan Prokopovič und seine akademische Wirksamkeit in Kiew." *ZSlPh*, no. 17 (1941): 70–102.

Sukhomlinov, Mikhail. *Istoriia rossiiskoi akademii*. St. Petersburg, 1874.

Sutorius, Konstantin. "Bogoslovie v Kievo-Mogilianskoi Akademii v 1751–1763 gg." In *Religioznoe obrazovanie v Rossii i Evrope v kontse XVIII–nachale XIX v.*, edited by M. Inglot and E. Tokareva, 133–65. St. Petersburg, 2009.

Taimasov, Leonid, and Petr Denisov. "Kazanskii komitet Rossiiskogo Bibleiskogo Obshchestva i perevody Sviashchennogo pisaniia na iazyki narodov Srednego Povolzh'ia." *Vestnik Chuvashskogo Universiteta* 2 (2012): 92–95.

Tal'berg, N. D. *Istoriia russkoi tserkvi*. Jordanville, N.Y., 1959.

Tamborra, Angelo. "Il Collegio greco di S. Atanasio e la sua rinascita nel sec. XIX (1798–1897)." *Archivio della Società Romana di Storia Patria* 55 (1979): 361–92.

Tarasov, Oleg. *Rama i obraz: Ritorika obramleniia v russkom isskustve*. Moscow, 2007.

Teigeler, Otto. *Die Herrnhuter in Russland: Ziel, Umfang und Ertrag ihrer Aktivitäten*. Göttingen, 2006.

Ternovskii, Filipp. "Ocherki iz istorii russkoi ierarkhii XVIII veka." *Rossiia drevniaia i novaia* 8 (August 1879): 305–26.

————. "Russkoe vol'nodumstvo pri imperatriste Ekaterine II i epokha reaktsii." *TKDA* 1 (1868): 109–46, 406–64.

————. "Stefan Iavorskii." *TKDA* 1 (1864): 36–70, 237–90.

Thomson, Francis. *The Reception of Byzantine Culture in Medieval Russia.* Aldershot, 1999.

Tikhonravov, Nikolai. "Moskovskie vol'nodumtsy nachala XVII veka i Stefan Iavorskii." In *Sochineniia*, 2:231–56. Moscow, 1898.

Titlinov, Boris. *Gavriil Petrov, metropolit novgorodskii i sanktpeterburgskii (1730–1801 gg.): Ego zhizn' i deiatel'nost', v sviazi s tserkovnymi delami togo vremeni.* St. Petersburg, 1916.

————. *Dukhovnaia shkola v Rossii v XIX stoletii.* Vilnius, 1908–9.

————. *Pravitel'stvo imperatritsy Anny Ioannovny v ego otnosheniiakh k delam pravoslavnoi tserkvi.* Vilna, 1905.

Titov, Andrei. "Poslednii rostovskii arkhiepiskop Arsenii Vereshchagin." *Istoricheskii vestnik* (February 1886): 385–97.

Titov, Fedor. *Russkaia pravoslavnaia tserkov' v Pol'sko-Litovskom gosudarstve v XVII–XVIII vv.* Vol. 2. Kiev, 1905.

Todorskii, P. P. "Ieromonakh Simon Todorskii (arkhiepiskop Pskovskii i Narvskii) i ego chetyre neizdannykh slova." *KhCh* (November 1909): 1513–18.

Tracy, James. *Europe's Reformations, 1450–1650: Doctrine, Politics, and Community.* Lanham, Md., 2006.

Treadgold, Donald W. *The West in Russia and China: Religious and Secular Thought in Modern Times.* Vol. 1, *Russia, 1472–1917.* Cambridge, 1973.

Trotsky, Leon. *History of the Russian Revolution.* Translated by Max Eastman. Chicago, 2008.

Tsapina, Olga. "K istorii novikovskogo izdaniia 'Sokrovishche Rossiiskikh drevnostei.'" In *Rukopisi, redkie izdaniia, arkhivy: iz fondov biblioteki MGU*, edited by Galina Kosmolinskaia, 49–65. Moscow, 1997.

————. "Tserkovnaia tsenzura i svetskie tipografii v Rossii vo vtoroi polovine 1770-kh nachale 1790-kh godov." In *Vek Prosveshcheniia*, 2nd ed., book 1, edited by S. Ia. Karp, 247–75. Moscow, 2006.

Zhivov, Viacheslav, ed. *Bor'ba za veru.* Moscow, 2010.

Urry, James. *None but Saints: The Transformation of Mennonite Life in Russia 1789–1889.* Winnipeg, 1989.

Uspenskii, Boris, and Fedor Uspenskii. *Inocheskie imena na Rusi.* Moscow, 2017.

Ustrialov, Nikolai. *Istoriia tsarstvovaniia Petra Velikogo.* Vols. 1–6. St. Petersburg, 1863.

Varadinov, Nikolai. *Istoriia Ministerstva vnutrennikh del.* Vol. 8, *Istoriia rasporiazhenii po raskolu.* St. Petersburg, 1863.

Varlaam [Denisov]. *Opisanie istoriko-arkheologicheskoe drevnostei i redkikh veshchei nahodiashchikhsia v Kirillo-Belozerskom monastyre.* Moscow, 1859.

Vengco, Sabino. *Juan de Cartagena, O.F.M. (1563–1618): The Mariology of His Homiliae catholicae and Its Baroque Scripturism.* St. Bonaventure, N.Y., 1978.

Vereshchagin, Aleksandr. "Sviatitel'skie teni gospodina Leskova." *VEV* (December 1882): 340–46.

Verkhovskoi, Pavel. *Naselennye nedvizhimye imeniia Sv. Sinoda, arkhiereiskikh domov i monastyrei pri blizhaishikh preemnikakh Petra Velikogo.* St. Petersburg, 1909.

———. *Uchrezhdenie Dukhovnoi Kollegii i Dukhovnyi Reglament: K Voprosu ob otnoshenii tserkvi i gosudarstva v Rossii.* Farnborough, 1972.

Vondung, Klaus. *The Apocalypse in Germany.* Columbia, Mo., 2000.

Vodarskii, Iakov. "Tserkovnye organizatsii." In *Istoricheskaia geografiia Rossii XII–nachala XX v.: Territoriia, naselenie, ekonomika ocherki.* Moscow, 1975.

Vollhardt, Friedrich, ed. *Christian Thomasius (1655–1728): Neue Forschungen im Kontext der Frühaufklärung.* Tübingen, 1997.

Vostokov, Aleksandr. *Opisanie russkikh i slovenskikh rukopisei Rumiantsevskogo Muzeuma.* St. Petersburg, 1842.

Vozdvizhenskii, Tikhon. *Istoricheskoe obozrenie Riazanskoi ierarkhii i vsekh tserkovnykh del seia eparkhii ot uchrezhdeniia eia do nyneshnikh vremen.* Moscow, 1820.

Vvedenskii, Sergei. "K biografii mitropolita Stefana Iavorskogo." *KhCh,* nos. 7–9 (1912): 892–919.

Vysotskii, Nikolai. "Feofan Prokopovich i ego sotrudniki." *RA* (August 1913): 255–71.

———. "Novye materialy iz ranneishei istorii dukhoborcheskoi sekty." *RA* (1914): 66–86, 235–61.

Wallace, Peter. *The Long European Reformation: Religion, Political Conflict, and the Search for Conformity, 1350–1750.* New York, 2004.

Wallmann, Johannes. *Kirchengeschichte Deutschlands seit der Reformation.* Tübingen, 2000.

Walsham, Alexandra. *Providence in Early Modern England.* New York, 1999.

Weeks, Andrew. *German Mysticism: From Hildegard of Bingen to Ludwig Wittgenstein; A Literary and Intellectual History.* Albany, N.Y., 1993.

Wehrle, Paul. *Orientierung am Hörer: Die Predigtlehre unter dem Einfluss des Aufklärungsprozesses.* Cologne, 1975.

Weigelt, Horst. *Erweckungsbewegung und konfessioneles Luthertum im 19. Jahrhundert.* Stuttgart, 1968.

Wengert, Timothy. *Law and Gospel: Philip Melanchton's Debate with John Agricola of Eisleben over "Poenitentia."* Grand Rapids, Mich., 1997.

Werth, Paul. "Lived Orthodoxy and Confessional Diversity: The Last Decade on Religion in Modern Russia." *Kritika* 12, no. 4 (2011): 849–65.

———. *The Tsar's Foreign Faiths: Toleration and the Fate of Religious Freedom in Imperial Russia.* Oxford, 2014.

Whittaker, Cynthia. *The Origins of Modern Russian Education: An Intellectual Biography of Count Sergei Uvarov, 1786–1855.* DeKalb, Ill., 1984.

———. *Russian Monarchy: Eighteenth-Century Rulers and Writers in Political Dialogue.* DeKalb, Ill., 2003.

Willett, William, ed. *Sermons by John-Baptist Massillon, Bishop of Clermont.* Boston, 1845.

Winter, Eduard. *Frühaufklärung: Der Kampf gegen den Konfessionalismus in Mittel- und Osteuropa und die deutsch-slawische Begegnung.* Berlin, 1966.

———. *Halle als Ausgangspunkt der deutschen Rußlandkunde im 18. Jahrhundert.* Berlin, 1953.

———. *Ketzerschicksale: Christliche Denker aus neun Jahrhunderten.* Berlin, 1979.

Wirtschafter, Elise. "Orthodoxy and Enlightenment in Catherinian Russia: The Tsarevich Dimitrii Sermons of Metropolitan Platon." In *Thinking Orthodox in Modern Russia,* edited by Patrick L. Michelson and Judith D. Kornblatt, 43–63. Madison, Wis., 2014.

———. *Religion and Enlightenment in Catherinian Russia. The Teachings of Metropolitan Platon.* DeKalb, Ill., 2013.

Witte, John. *Law and Protestantism: The Legal Teachings of the Lutheran Reformation.* Cambridge, 2002.

Wittram, Reinhard. *Peter I, Czar und Kaiser.* 2 vols. Gottingen, 1964.

Wolff, Christoph. *Johann Sebastian Bach: The Learned Musician.* Oxford, 2002.

Worobec, Christine. "Lived Orthodoxy in Imperial Russia." *Kritika* 7, no. 2 (2006): 329–50.

———. "The Long Road to Kiev: Nineteenth-Century Orthodox Pilgrimages." *Modern Greek Studies Yearbook* 30/31 (2014/15): 1–24.

———. "Miraculous Healings." In *Sacred Stories: Religion and Spirituality in Modern Russia,* edited by Heather Coleman and Mark Steinberg, 22–40. Bloomington, Ind., 2007.

Wotschke, Theodor. "Pietismus in Moskau." *Deutsche Zeitschrift für Polen* 18 (1930): 53–95.

Yannaras, Christos. *Orthodoxy and the West.* Translated by Peter Chamberas and Norman Russell. Brookline, Mass., 2006.

Yates, Frances. *The Art of Memory.* Chicago, Ill., 1966.

Zacek, Judith. "The Russian Bible Society and the Russian Orthodox Church." *Church History* 35, no. 4 (1966): 411–37.

Zakai, Avihu. *Jonathan Edward's Philosophy of Nature: The Re-enchantment of the World in the Age of Scientific Reason.* Princeton, N.J., 2013.

Zakrzhevskii, Aleksandr. "Arkhiereiskaia vlast' v sisteme tserkovno-gosudarstvennykh otnoshenii v pervoi polovine XVIII veka." PhD diss., St. Petersburg State University, 2000.

Zalesski, Petr. "Sil'vestr Kuliabka, Arkhiepiskop S.Peterburgskii kak dukhovnyi pisatel'." *TKDA* 1 (1884): 66–82.

Zav'ialov, Aleksei. *Vopros o tserkovnykh imeniiakh pri imperatritse Ekaterine II.* St. Petersburg, 1900.

Zhevakhov, Nikolai. *Sviatitel' Ioasaf Gorlenko, episkop belgorodskii i oboianskii: Materialy dlia biografii.* 2 vols. Kiev, 1907.

Zhivov, Viktor. *Iz tserkovnoi istorii vremen Petra Velikogo: Issledovaniia i materialy.* Moscow, 2004.

———. *Razyskaniia v oblasti istorii i predystorii russkoi kul'tury.* Moscow, 2002.

Zdravomyslov, K. *Ierarkhi novgorodskoi eparkhii ot drevneishikh vremen do nastoiashchego vremeni.* Novgorod, 1897.

Zhmakin, V. "Pis'ma protoiereia A. A. Samborskogo." *KhCh* (November–December 1894): 425–52.

Zhuk, Sergei. *Russia's Lost Reformation: Peasants, Millennialism, and Radical Sects in Southern Russia and Ukraine, 1830–1917.* Baltimore, 2004.

Zimmermann, Harro. *Aufklärung und Erfahrungswandel: Studien zur deutschen Literaturgeschichte des spaten 18. Jahrhunderts.* Göttingen, 1999.

Zitser, Ernest. *The Transfigured Kingdom: Sacred Parody and Charismatic Authority at the Court of Peter the Great.* Ithaca, N.Y., 2004.

Zlatar, Zdenko. *Our Kingdom Come: The Counter-Reformation, the Republic of Dubrovnik, and the Liberation of the Balkan Slavs.* Boulder, 1992.

Znamenskii, Petr. "Chteniia iz istorii russkoi tserkvi za vremia tsarstvovaniia Ekateriny II." *PS* 1 (1875): 19–406; 2 (1875): 2–361.

———. *Dukhovnye shkoly v Rossii do reformy 1808-go goda.* 1881. Reprint, St. Petersburg, 2001.

Zverinskii, Vasilii. *Monastyri v Rossiiskoi Imperii.* St. Petersburg, 1887.

INDEX